The CSSLP™ Prep Guide

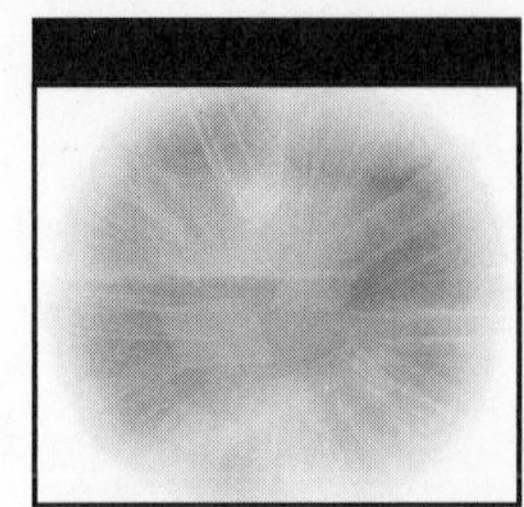

The CSSLP™ Prep Guide:

Mastering the Certified Secure Software Lifecycle Professional

Ronald L. Krutz
Ph.D., P.E., CISSP, ISSEP
Alexander J. Fry
CSSLP, CISSP, ISSAP, ISSEP, LPT

Wiley Publishing, Inc.

The CSSLP™ Prep Guide

Published by
Wiley Publishing, Inc.
10475 Crosspoint Boulevard
Indianapolis, IN 46256
www.wiley.com

Published by Wiley Publishing, Inc., Indianapolis, Indiana

Published simultaneously in Canada

ISBN: 978-0-470-46190-7

Manufactured in the United States of America

10 9 8 7 6 5 4 3 2 1

For general information on our other products and services please contact our Customer Care Department within the United States at (877) 762-2974, outside the United States at (317) 572-3993 or fax (317) 572-4002.

Wiley also publishes its books in a variety of electronic formats. Some content that appears in print may not be available in electronic books.

Library of Congress Control Number: 2009930065

To three Guys and a Doll . . .
Patrick, Ryan, Aaron, and Emma.
They've made me the proudest,
luckiest, happiest Grandpa in the world.

—RLK

In loving memory of my cousin and friend, Britt Sommerfield.

—AJF

About the Authors

RONALD L. KRUTZ, Ph.D., P.E., CISSP, ISSEP, is a senior information system security consultant. Prior to this position, Dr. Krutz was chief technical officer for Threatscape Solutions, Inc., and a senior information systems security researcher in the Advanced Technology Research Center of Lockheed Martin Information Technologies. He has over thirty years of experience in distributed computing systems, computer architectures, real-time systems, information assurance methodologies, and information security training. He has been a senior information security consultant at BAE Systems and REALTECH Systems Corporation, an associate director of the Carnegie Mellon Research Institute (CMRI), and a professor in the Carnegie Mellon University Department of Electrical and Computer Engineering. He was also a lead instructor for $(ISC)^2$ in their CISSP training seminars. Dr. Krutz founded the CMRI Cybersecurity Center and was founder and director of the CMRI Computer, Automation, and Robotics Group. Dr. Krutz conducted sponsored-applied research and development in the areas of computer security, artificial intelligence, networking, modeling and simulation, robotics, and real-time computer applications.

He co-authored *The CISSP Prep Guide* for John Wiley and Sons and is co-author of *The Wiley Advanced CISSP Prep Guide, The CISSP Prep Guide, Gold Edition, The Security + Certification Guide, The CISM Prep Guide, The CISSP Prep Guide, 2nd Edition: Mastering CISSP and ISSEP, The Network Security Bible, The CISSP and CAP Prep Guide, Platinum Edition: Mastering CISSP and CAP*, and *The Certified Ethical Hacker (CEH) Prep Guide.* He is also the author of *Securing SCADA Systems* and of three textbooks in the areas of microcomputer system design, computer interfacing, and computer architecture. Dr. Krutz has seven patents in the area of digital systems and has published more than forty technical papers.

Dr. Krutz also serves as consulting editor for John Wiley and Sons Information Security Certification Series, is a Distinguished Visiting Lecturer at the University of New Haven Henry C. Lee College of Criminal Justice and Forensic Sciences, and is an adjunct professor at Midway College, Kentucky.

Dr. Krutz holds B.S., M.S., and Ph.D. degrees in Electrical and Computer Engineering and is a Registered Professional Engineer in Pennsylvania.

Alexander J. Fry, CSSLP, CISSP, ISSAP, ISSEP, LPT, is the founder and principal security consultant at Strong Crypto LLC, a software security consultancy based in the Washington, D.C., metropolitan area. Prior to this position, Mr. Fry was application security lead at Northrop Grumman Mission Systems for the Defense Travel System, and chief technology officer for Systems Management Enterprises, Inc. He has over fifteen years of experience in the IT industry in the areas of software development, security engineering, security testing, networking, government contracting, start-up companies, project management, education, and regulatory compliance. He is active in the software assurance community and participates in defining open source software security standards and creating useful tools with the Open Web Application Security Project (OWASP). He was also a subject matter expert (SME) for $(ISC)^2$, involved in writing and reviewing exam questions for the CSSLP credential.

Mr. Fry is a Certified Secure Software Lifecycle Professional (CSSLP), a Certified Information Systems Security Professional (CISSP), an Information Systems Security Architecture Professional (ISSAP), an Information Systems Security Engineering Professional (ISSEP), a Licensed Penetration Tester (LPT) and holds other high-level certifications from Cisco, Microsoft, Red Hat, EC-Council, CompTIA, and Sun Microsystems.

Mr. Fry attended the United States Merchant Marine Academy (USMMA) in Kings Point, New York, and graduated with a B.S. degree in Marine Engineering Systems.

Credits

Executive Editor
Carol Long

Project Editor
Sydney Jones

Production Editor
Eric Charbonneau

Copy Editor
Lunaea Weatherstone

Editorial Director
Robyn B. Siesky

Editorial Manager
Mary Beth Wakefield

Production Manager
Tim Tate

Vice President and Executive Group Publisher
Richard Swadley

Vice President and Executive Publisher
Barry Pruett

Associate Publisher
Jim Minatel

Project Coordinator, Cover
Lynsey Stanford

Proofreader
Kyle Schlesinger, Word One

Indexer
Johnna VanHoose-Dinse

Cover Image
Michael E. Trent

Acknowledgments

Both authors would like to thank our peers and colleagues who work in the software assurance and software security fields, including the wider community of researchers who have shared their ideas and contributed to the collective body of knowledge that the CSSLP encompasses. We would also like to thank Carol Long, Kevin Kent, and Sydney Jones of Wiley for their enthusiasm and hard work on this book.

I would like to thank Hart Rossman, vice president, CTO cyber programs, and chief security technologist at SAIC, for his direct assistance on this book. He provided me with an insightful technical review of material in the chapters I authored.

This book would not be possible without the support and tolerance of my friends and family over the many nights, weekends, and holidays I spent writing instead of sharing our love and friendship. Thank you for understanding how important this book is to me. In particular, I would like to thank my immediate clan members Julie Fry, Enzo Barbato, Sylvia Angles, and Rudy Fry. You all became experts at prioritizing my activities and obligations so that I could focus on this project.

—Alexander J. Fry

I would like thank my wife, Hilda, for her patience, support, and encouragement for yet another ''last'' writing project.

—Ronald L. Krutz

Contents at a Glance

Contents

Introduction

The CSSLP™ Professional Certification is designed to establish an industry standard and credential that attests to the holder's knowledge and ability to apply best practices in delivering secure software. The certification is language neutral and focuses on professionals whose work is related to the software life cycle, including software architects, software engineers, developers, programmers, project managers, quality assurance testers, and analysts.

The impetus behind the CSSLP certification is the ever-increasing losses incurred by all types of organizations from both insider and outsider attacks because of software that is not secure. Also, because of the increased exploitation of software vulnerabilities, additional regulatory and compliance requirements are being imposed by governmental bodies.

Secure software controls should be an integral part of the software life cycle, from conception to disposal, and should address the fundamental security concepts of confidentiality, integrity, availability, authentication, authorization, and auditing.

CSSLP Domains

As defined by (ISC)^2, the domains comprising the CSSLP Common Body of Knowledge (CBK®) are:

- **Secure software concepts**—Security implications in software development
- **Secure software requirements**—Capturing security requirements in the requirements gathering phase
- **Secure software design**—Translating security requirements into application design elements
- **Secure software implementation/coding**—Testing for security functionality and resiliency to attack, and developing secure code and exploit mitigation

- **Secure software testing**—Testing for security functionality and resiliency to attack
- **Software acceptance**—Security implications in the software acceptance phase
- **Software deployment, operations, maintenance, and disposal**—Security issues around steady state operations and management of software

The seven CSSLP domains are explored in detail in this text and presented in a manner to convey the key concepts and principles embodied in the CSSLP CBK to the CSSLP candidate and other professionals. With this information and the hundreds of review questions provided for the seven domains, the CSSLP candidate will be well-positioned to take the certification examination and become a CSSLP.

Requirements

In order to become certified, the candidate must provide evidence of four years experience with the software development life cycle (SDLC) process or three years experience plus a bachelor's degree or regional equivalent in an IT discipline, subscribe to the $(ISC)^2$ code of ethics, pass the examination, and complete the endorsement process.

A CSSLP candidate who has passed the examination must obtain an endorsement from another $(ISC)^2$ certified professional in good standing, verifying that the candidate is in good standing in the information security arena and has the claimed professional experience and qualifications. Then the CSSLP credential can be awarded. Those candidates who have passed the exam but need to obtain the required experience are categorized as an Associate of $(ISC)^2$. In addition, randomly selected candidates who have passed the CSSLP exam will be audited by $(ISC)^2$ before certification is awarded.

The registration fee for the four-hour CSSLP examination is U.S. $549 (early registration) and U.S. $599 (standard registration).

The CSSLP is required to be recertified every three years by obtaining 90 continuing professional education (CPE) credits, with a minimum of 15 CPEs being earned each year of the three-year period. An annual maintenance fee of $100 must also be paid to maintain the certification.

$(ISC)^2$ offers five-day CSSLP review seminars to prepare candidates for the CSSLP exam. The registration fees for these seminars are U.S. $2,495 (early registration) and U.S. $2,695 (standard registration).

Additional information on the CSSLP certification can be found at the $(ISC)^2$ Web site, `www.ISC2.org`.

The Approach of this Book

In order to counter the increasing threats against software vulnerabilities, the field of secure software development is emerging as a vital element to protect sensitive data and critical computational resources. A fundamental approach to obtaining secure software is to ensure that security is included in all phases of the software development life cycle (SDLC).

A number of governmental and private organizations have conducted research to determine the best methodologies that can be used to effect secure software design, development, implementation, and maintenance. The authors have distilled the critical principles from these efforts as well as the guidelines promoted by the (ISC)^2 to develop a text that will impart the required knowledge to the reader in an understandable and efficient format.

This text will fill the need for a single, high-quality study source that the candidate can use to prepare for the Certified Secure Software Lifecycle Professional (CSSLP) examination as well as providing a reference for practicing professionals in the software engineering field. The CSSLP is a level 1 certification and is considered the 11th domain of the (ISC)^2 Common Body of Knowledge (CBK)®. It is a natural complement to the CISSP credential, which represents the first 10 domains of the CBK.

The information presented in the text is reinforced with hundreds of example test questions and answers that the reader can use to further increase his or her comprehension of the material. This text is also useful if the candidate is taking the (ISC)^2 CSSLP training seminars.

How this Book Is Organized

The text is organized into the following seven domains that make up the CSSLP CBK® and emphasizes incorporating security into the SDLC:

- Secure Software Concepts
- Secure Software Requirements
- Secure Software Design
- Secure Software Implementation/Coding
- Secure Software Testing
- Software Acceptance
- Software Deployment, Operations, Maintenance, and Disposal

CD-ROM

The CD-ROM included with this book offers a test engine designed to help you prepare for taking the CSSLP exam.

Who Should Read this Book

This book is aimed at candidates who are seeking the CSSLP certification and want the latest information presented in a concise, professional manner in an easy to understand format in order to pass the certification examination. The ideal reader for this book would be an information security manager, high-level technical professional, or government INFOSEC professional seeking to gain certification and recognition in his or her field.

Because this book provides a focused presentation of the CSSLP material, it is also extremely valuable to professionals seeking to advance their careers, level of competence, and recognition in the information system security and software assurance fields. The knowledge gained is applicable to commercial, industrial, military, and government organizations.

The primary audience includes:

- Professionals working in the software security field
- Chief information officers and their support personnel
- Chief information security officers
- Professionals working in the software industry, including programmers, evaluators and testers, project managers, acquisition personnel, and standards developers
- Professionals responsible for certifying and accrediting information systems
- Professionals developing or acquiring software for organizations subject to regulatory compliance, such as PCI and FISMA
- Information system security audit professionals
- Information system and information system security professionals working in the military establishment
- Professionals working at a variety of government agencies, including the State Department, FBI, Homeland Security, CIA, Defense Intelligence Agency, Naval Intelligence, Treasury, etc
- State and local law enforcement officers

The secondary audience comprises the following:

- Information security professionals with other INFOSEC certifications seeking to add to their professional stature. Other such certifications include CISSP, CAP, SSCP, CISA, and GIAC
- Programmers with certifications such as SCJP and GIAC Secure Programmer
- IT management personnel with certifications such as MCSE, CBCP, or CompTIA Security
- Students in university programs emphasizing computer science, software development, information security, information security management, information security architecture, business continuity planning, and risk management

CHAPTER 1

Secure Software Concepts

Designing secure software is based on the application of secure software design principles. These principles will be discussed in this chapter and form the fundamental basis for software assurance. Software assurance has been given many definitions, and it is important to understand the concept. The Software Security Assurance Report[1] defines *software assurance* as follows, "The basis for gaining justifiable confidence that software will consistently exhibit all properties required to ensure that the software, in operation, will continue to operate dependably despite the presence of sponsored (intentional) faults. In practical terms, such software must be able to resist most attacks, tolerate as many as possible of those attacks it cannot resist, and contain the damage and recover to a normal level of operation as soon as possible after any attacks it is unable to resist or tolerate."

The U.S. Department of Defense (DoD) Software Assurance Initiative[2] defines software assurance as "the level of confidence that software functions as intended and is free of vulnerabilities, either intentionally or unintentionally designed or inserted as part of the software."

The Data and Analysis Center for Software (DACS)[3] requires that software must exhibit the following three properties to be considered secure:

- **Dependability**—Software that executes predictably and operates correctly under a variety of conditions, including when under attack or running on a malicious host.

[1]Information Assurance Technology Analysis Center (IATAC), Data and Analysis Center for Software (DACS), *Software Security Assurance, State-of-the-Art Report (SOAR)*, July 31, 2007.
[2]Komaroff, M., and Baldwin, K., DoD Software Assurance Initiative, September 13, 2005 (`https://acc.dau.mil/CommunityBrowser.aspx?id=25749`).
[3]Goertzel, K., Winograd, T., et al., *Enhancing the Development Life Cycle to Produce Secure Software*, Draft Version 2.0. Rome, New York: United States Department of Defense Data and Analysis Center for Software, July 2008.

- **Trustworthiness**—Software that contains a minimum number or no vulnerabilities or weakness that could sabotage the software's dependability. It must also be resistant to malicious logic.
- **Survivability (Resilience)**—Software that is resistant or tolerant of attacks and has the ability to recover as quickly as possible with as little harm as possible.

Chapter 1 explores the fundamentals of software assurance through basic design principles, risk management, supporting software architectures, legal issues, standards, acquisition methods, and information security models.

Seven complementary principles that support information assurance are confidentiality, integrity, availability, authentication, authorization, auditing, and accountability. These concepts are summarized in the following sections.

Confidentiality, Integrity, and Availability

Confidentiality, integrity, and availability are sometimes known as the C-I-A triad of information system security.

Confidentiality

Confidentiality refers to the prevention of intentional or unintentional unauthorized disclosure of information. Confidentiality in information systems is related to the areas of intellectual property rights, covert channels, traffic analysis, encryption, and inference.

- **Intellectual property rights**—*Intellectual property* (IP) includes inventions, designs, and artistic, musical, and literary works. Rights to intellectual property are covered by copyright laws, which protect creations of the mind, and patents, which are granted for new inventions.
- **Covert channels**—A *covert channel* is an unauthorized and unintended communication path that provides for exchange of information. Covert channels can be accomplished through timing of messages or inappropriate use of storage mechanisms.
- **Traffic analysis**—*Traffic analysis* is a form of confidentiality breach that can be accomplished by analyzing the volume, rate, source, and destination of message traffic, even if it is encrypted. Increased message activity and high bursts of traffic can indicate a major event is occurring. Countermeasures to traffic analysis include maintaining a near constant rate of message traffic and disguising the source and destination locations of the traffic.
- **Encryption**—*Encryption* involves scrambling messages so that they cannot be read by an unauthorized entity, even if they are intercepted. The amount of effort (*work factor*) required to decrypt the message is a function of the strength of the encryption key and robustness and quality of the encryption algorithm.

- **Inference**—*Inference* is usually associated with database security. Inference is the ability of an entity to use and correlate information protected at one level of security to uncover information that is protected at a higher security level.

Integrity

The concept of *integrity* requires that the following three principles are met:

- Modifications are not made to data by unauthorized personnel or processes.
- Unauthorized modifications are not made to data by authorized personnel or processes.
- The data is internally and externally consistent—in other words, the internal information is consistent among all sub-entities and that the internal information is consistent with the real-world, external situation.

Availability

Availability ensures the reliable and timely access to data or computing resources by the appropriate personnel. Availability guarantees that the systems are functioning properly when needed. In addition, this concept guarantees that the security services of the system are in working order. A denial-of-service attack is an example of a threat against availability.

The reverse of confidentiality, integrity, and availability is disclosure, alteration, and destruction (D-A-D).

Authentication, Authorization, Auditing, and Accountability

There are additional factors that directly affect information system and software assurance. These factors include authentication, authorization, auditing, and accountability, as summarized in the following sections.

Authentication

Authentication is the testing or reconciliation of evidence of a user's identity. It establishes the user's identity and ensures that users are who they claim to be. For example, a user presents an identity (user ID) to a computer login screen and then has to provide a password. The computer system authenticates the user by verifying that the password corresponds to the individual presenting the ID.

Authorization

Authorization refers to rights and privileges granted to an individual or process that enable access to computer resources and information assets. Once a user's identity and authentication are established, authorization levels determine the extent of system rights a user can hold.

Auditing

To maintain operational assurance, organizations use two basic methods: system audits and monitoring.

- A *system audit* is a one-time or periodic event to evaluate security.
- *Monitoring* refers to an ongoing activity that examines either the system or the users, such as intrusion detection.

Information technology (IT) auditors are often divided into two types: internal and external. Internal auditors typically work for a given organization whereas external auditors do not. External auditors are often certified public accountants (CPAs) or other audit professionals who are hired to perform an independent audit of an organization's financial statements. Internal auditors, on the other hand, usually have a much broader mandate: checking for compliance and standards of due care, auditing operational cost efficiencies, and recommending the appropriate controls.

IT auditors typically audit the following functions:

- System and transaction controls
- Systems development standards
- Backup controls
- Data library procedures
- Data center security
- Contingency plans

In addition, IT auditors might recommend improvements to controls, and they often participate in a system's development process to help an organization avoid costly reengineering after the system's implementation.

An *audit trail* or *log* is a set of records that collectively provide documentary evidence of processing used to aid in tracing from original transactions forward to related records and reports, and/or backward from records and reports to their component source transactions. Audit trails may be limited to specific events, or they may encompass all of the activities on a system.

The audit logs should record the following:

- The transaction's date and time
- Who processed the transaction
- At which terminal the transaction was processed
- Various security events relating to the transaction

In addition, an auditor should examine the audit logs for the following:

- Amendments to production jobs
- Production job reruns

- Computer operator practices
- All commands directly initiated by the user
- All identification and authentication attempts
- Files and resources accessed

Accountability

Accountability is the ability to determine the actions and behaviors of a single individual within a system and to identify that particular individual. Audit trails and logs support accountability and can be used to conduct a postmortem study to analyze acts that previously occurred and the individuals or processes associated with those acts. Accountability is related to the concept of *nonrepudiation*, wherein an individual cannot successfully deny the performance of an action.

Security Design Principles

Historically, computer software was not written with security in mind. Because of the increasing frequency and sophistication of malicious attacks against information systems, modern software design methodologies include security as one of the primary objectives. With any system that seeks to meet multiple objectives such as cost, performance, reliability, maintainability, and security, trade-offs have to be made. A completely secure system will exhibit poor performance characteristics or might not function at all.

Technically competent hackers can usually find a way to break into a computer system, given enough time and resources. The goal is to have a system that is secure enough for everyday use while exhibiting reasonable performance and reliability characteristics.

In a 1974 paper[4], Saltzer and Schroeder of the University of Virginia addressed the protection of information stored in a computer system by focusing on hardware and software issues that are necessary to support information protection. The paper presented the following 11 security design principles:

- Least privilege
- Separation of duties
- Defense in depth
- Fail safe
- Economy of mechanism
- Complete mediation
- Open design
- Least common mechanism

[4]Saltzer, J. H., and Schroeder, M. D., "The Protection of Information in Computer Systems," Fourth ACM Symposium on Operating Systems Principles, October 1974.

- Psychological acceptability
- Weakest link
- Leveraging existing components

The fundamental characteristics of these principles are summarized below.

Least Privilege

The principle of *least privilege* maintains that an individual, process, or other type of entity should be given the minimum privileges and resources for the minimum period of time required to complete a task. This approach eliminates capabilities that are not needed for the assigned task and, thus, reduces the opportunity for unauthorized access to sensitive information.

Separation of Duties

Separation of duties requires that completion of a specified sensitive activity or access to sensitive objects is dependent on the satisfaction of multiple conditions. For example, an authorization would require signatures of more than one individual or the arming of a weapon system would require two individuals with different keys. Thus, separation of duties forces collusion among entities in order to compromise the system.

Defense in Depth

Defense in depth is the application of multiple layers of protection wherein a subsequent layer will provide protection if a previous layer is breached.

The Information Assurance Technical Framework Forum (IATFF), an organization sponsored by the National Security Agency (NSA), has produced a document entitled the "Information Assurance Technical Framework" (IATF) that provides excellent guidance on the defense-in-depth concepts.

The IATFF encourages and supports technical interchanges on the topic of information assurance among U.S. industry, U.S. academic institutions, and U.S. government agencies. Information on the IATFF document can be found at the Web site, `www.niap-ccevs.org/cc-scheme/IATF_3.1-Chapter_03-ISSEP.pdf`.

The IATF document 3.1[5] stresses the importance of the *people* involved, the *operations* required, and the *technology* needed to provide information assurance and to meet the organization's mission.

The defense-in-depth strategy as defined in IATF document 3.1 promotes application of the following information assurance principles:

- **Defense in multiple places**—Information protection mechanisms placed in a number of locations to protect against internal and external threats

[5]National Security Agency, "Information Assurance Technical Framework (IATF)," Release 3.1, September 2002.

- **Layered defenses**—A plurality of information protection and detection mechanisms employed so that an adversary or threat will have to negotiate multiple barriers to gain access to critical information
- **Security robustness**—An estimate of the robustness of information assurance elements based on the value of the information system component to be protected and the anticipated threats
- **Deploy KMI/PKI**—Use of robust key management infrastructures (KMI) and public key infrastructures (PKI)
- **Deploy intrusion detection systems**—Application of intrusion detection mechanisms to detect intrusions, evaluate information, examine results, and, if necessary, to take action

Fail Safe

Fail safe means that if a system fails it should fail to a state where the security of the system and its data are not compromised. One implementation of this philosophy would be to make a system default to a state where a user or process is denied access to the system. A complementary rule would be to ensure that when the system recovers it should recover to a secure state and not permit unauthorized access to sensitive information. This approach is based on using permissions instead of exclusions.

In the situation where system recovery is not done automatically, the failed system should permit access only by the system administrator and not by users, until security controls are reestablished.

Economy of Mechanism

Economy of mechanism promotes simple and comprehensible design and implementation of protection mechanisms, so that unintended access paths do not exist or can be readily identified and eliminated.

Complete Mediation

In *complete meditation*, every request by a subject to access an object in a computer system must undergo a valid and effective authorization procedure. This mediation must not be suspended or become capable of being bypassed, even when the information system is being initialized, undergoing shutdown, being restarted, or is in maintenance mode. Complete mediation entails the following:

1. Identification of the entity making the access request
2. Verification that the request has not changed since its initiation
3. Application of the appropriate authorization procedures
4. Reexamination of previously authorized requests by the same entity

Open Design

There has always been a continuing discussion on the merits and strength of security of designs that are kept secret versus designs that are open to scrutiny and evaluation by the community at large. A good example is an encryption system. Some feel that keeping the encryption algorithm secret makes it more difficult to break. The opposing philosophy believes that exposing the algorithm to review and study by experts at large while keeping the encryption key secret leads to a stronger algorithm because the experts have a higher probability of discovering weaknesses in the algorithm. In general, the latter approach has proven more effective, except in the case of organizations such as the National Security Agency (NSA), which employs some of the world's best cryptographers and mathematicians.

For most purposes, an open access control system design that has been evaluated and tested by a myriad of experts provides a more secure authentication method than one that has not been widely assessed. Security of such mechanisms depends on protecting passwords or keys.

Least Common Mechanism

This principle states that a minimum number of protection mechanisms should be common to multiple users, as shared access paths can be sources of unauthorized information exchange. Shared access paths that provide unintentional data transfers are known as *covert channels*. Thus, *least common mechanism* promotes the least possible sharing of common security mechanisms.

Psychological Acceptability

Psychological acceptability refers to the ease of use and intuitiveness of the user interface that controls and interacts with the access control mechanisms. The user must be able to understand the user interface and use it without having to interpret complex instructions.

Weakest Link

As in the old saying, "A chain is only as strong as its weakest link," the security of an information system is only as good as its weakest component. Thus, it is important to identify the weakest mechanisms in the security chain and layers of defense and improve them so that risks to the system are mitigated to an acceptable level.

Leveraging Existing Components

In many instances, the security mechanisms of an information system are not configured properly or used to their maximum capability. Reviewing the state and settings of the extant security mechanisms and ensuring that they are operating at their optimum design points will greatly improve the security posture of an information system.

Another approach that can be used to increase system security by leveraging existing components is to partition a system into defended subunits. Then, if a security mechanism is penetrated for one subunit, it will not affect the other subunits and damage to the computing resources will be minimized.

Risk Management

This section examines risk management for information system security and, after providing this base of knowledge, develops the concepts of software security risk management, which are more directly focused on application software risk and security.

Information System Risk Management

The U.S. National Institute of Standards and Technology (NIST) Special Publication (SP) 800-30 defines *risk management* as comprising three processes: risk assessment, risk mitigation, and evaluation. These three processes are summarized as follows:

- **Risk assessment**—Identification and evaluation of risks and risk impacts and recommendation of risk-reducing measures. It is the process that allows IT managers to balance the operational and economic costs of protective measures and obtain improvements in the security of a system.
- **Risk mitigation**—Prioritizing, implementing, and maintaining the appropriate risk-reducing measures recommended from the risk assessment process.
- **Evaluation**—A continuous appraisal process and application of key methods for implementing a successful risk management program. In this step, the system authorizing official is responsible for determining whether the remaining risk is at an acceptable level or whether additional security controls should be implemented to further reduce or minimize the residual risk.

The Risk Assessment Process

As defined in NIST SP 800-30, ''Risk is a function of the likelihood of a given threat-source's exercising a particular potential vulnerability, and the resulting impact of that adverse event on the organization.'' Risk assessment comprises the following steps:

1. System characterization
2. Threat identification
3. Vulnerability identification
4. Control analysis
5. Likelihood determination
6. Impact analysis

7. Risk determination
8. Control recommendations
9. Results documentation

Each of these steps is summarized in the following sections.

System Characterization

NIST SP 800-30 describes and defines the scope of the risk assessment process. During this step, information about the system has to be gathered. This information, taken from SP 800-30, includes:

- Software
- Hardware
- Data
- Information
- System interfaces
- IT system users
- IT system support personnel
- System mission
- Criticality of the system and data
- System and data sensitivity
- Functional system requirements
- System security policies
- System security architecture
- Network topology
- Information storage protection
- System information flow
- Technical security controls
- Physical security environment
- Environmental security

This information can be obtained using questionnaires, on-site interviews, review of documents, and automated scanning tools. The outputs from this step are:

- Characterization of the assessed IT system
- Comprehension of the IT system environment
- Delineation of the system boundary

Threat Identification

This step identifies potential threat-sources and compiles a statement of the threat-sources that relate to the IT system under evaluation. A *threat* is defined in NIST SP 800-30 as "the potential for a threat-source to exercise (accidentally trigger or intentionally exploit) a specific vulnerability." A *threat-source* is defined in the same document as "either (1) intent and method targeted at the intentional exploitation of a vulnerability or (2) a situation and method that may accidentally trigger a vulnerability." Common threat-sources include *natural threats* such as storms and floods, *human threats* such as malicious attacks and unintentional acts, and *environmental threats* such as power failure and liquid leakage. A *vulnerability* is defined as "a flaw or weakness in system security procedures, design, implementation, or internal controls that could be exercised (accidentally triggered or intentionally exploited) and result in a security breach or a violation of the system's security policy."

Sources of threat information include the Federal Computer Incident Response Center (FedCIRC), intelligence agencies, mass media, and Web-based resources. The output from this step is a statement that provides a list of threat-sources that could exploit the system's vulnerabilities.

Vulnerability Identification

This activity results in a list of system vulnerabilities that might be exploited by potential threat-sources. Vulnerabilities can be identified through vulnerability analyses, including information from previous information assessments, audit reports, the NIST vulnerability database (`http://icat.nist.gov/icat.cfm`), FedCIRC and DOE security bulletins, vendor data, commercial computer incident response teams, and system software security analyses. Testing of the IT system will also yield important results. This testing can be accomplished using penetration testing techniques, automated vulnerability scanning tools, and security test and evaluation (ST&E) procedures.

This phase also involves determining whether the security requirements identified during system characterization are being met. Usually, the security requirements are listed in a table with a corresponding statement about how the requirement is or is not being met. This *security requirements checklist* addresses management, operational, and technical information system security areas. Some useful references for this activity are:

- The Computer Security Act of 1987
- The Privacy Act of 1974
- The organization's security policies
- Industry best practices
- Federal Information Processing Standard (FIPS) 200/NIST Special Publication 800-53, *Recommended Security Controls for Federal Information Systems, Rev.2*, December 2007
- NIST Special Publication 800-53A, *Guide for Assessing the Security Controls in Federal Information Systems*, June 2008

NIST SP 800-53 and NIST SP 800-53A have superseded NIST SP 800-26, *Security Self-Assessment Guide for Information Technology Systems.*

The output from this step is a list of system vulnerabilities that could be exploited by the potential threat-sources.

Control Analysis

The control analysis step analyzes the controls that are in place or in the planning stage to minimize or eliminate the probability that a threat will exploit a vulnerability in the system.

Controls can be implemented through technical means such as computer hardware or software, encryption, intrusion detection mechanisms, and identification and authentication subsystems. Other controls such as security policies, administrative actions, and physical and environmental mechanisms are considered nontechnical controls. Both technical and nontechnical controls can further be classified as preventive or detective controls. As the names imply, *preventive* controls attempt to anticipate and stop attacks. Examples of preventive technical controls are encryption and authentication devices. *Detective* controls are used to discover attacks or events through such means as audit trails and intrusion detection systems.

Changes in the control mechanisms should be reflected in the security requirements checklist.

The output of this step is a list of current and planned control mechanisms for the IT system to reduce the likelihood that a vulnerability will be exercised and to reduce the impact of an attack or event.

Likelihood Determination

This activity develops a rating that provides an indication of the probability that a potential vulnerability might be exploited based on the defined threat environment. This rating takes into account the type of vulnerability, the capability and motivation of the threat-source, and the existence and effectiveness of information system security controls. The likelihood levels are given as high, medium, and low, as illustrated in Table 1-1.

Table 1-1: Likelihood Levels

LEVEL OF LIKELIHOOD	DEFINITION OF LIKELIHOOD
High	A highly motivated and capable threat-source and ineffective controls to prevent exploitation of the associated vulnerability
Medium	A highly motivated and capable threat-source and controls that might impede exploitation of the associated vulnerability
Low	Lack of motivation or capability in the threat-source or controls in place to prevent or significantly impede the exploitation of the associated vulnerability

Impact Analysis

If a threat does exploit a vulnerability in an IT system, it is critical to know the negative impact that would result to the system. Three important factors should be considered in calculating the negative impact:

- The mission of the system, including the processes implemented by the system
- The criticality of the system, determined by its value and the value of the data to the organization
- The sensitivity of the system and its data

The information necessary to conduct an impact analysis can be obtained from existing organizational documentation, including a *business impact analysis* (BIA), sometimes called a mission impact analysis report. This document uses either quantitative or qualitative means to determine the impacts caused by compromise or harm to the organization's information assets. An attack or adverse event can result in compromise or loss of information system confidentiality, integrity, and availability. As with the likelihood determination, the impact on the system can be qualitatively assessed as high, medium, or low, as shown in Table 1-2.

Table 1-2: Definitions of Likelihood

IMPACT MAGNITUDE	DEFINITION OF IMPACT
High	Possibility of costly loss of major tangible assets or resources; might cause significant harm or impedance to the mission of an organization; might cause significant harm to an organization's reputation or interest; might result in human death or injury
Medium	Possibility of costly loss of tangible assets or resources; might cause harm or impedance to the mission of an organization; might cause harm to an organization's reputation or interest; might result in human injury
Low	Possibility of loss of some tangible assets or resources; might noticeably affect an organization's mission; might noticeably affect an organization's reputation or interest

Qualitative analysis is more easily accomplished and provides identifiable areas for immediate improvement. However, it does not provide specific magnitudes of measures and thus makes a cost-benefit analysis difficult. *Quantitative analysis* does provide magnitudes of measurements but may take more time. It is sometimes very difficult or impossible to place quantitative values on abstract items such as reputation.

Other items that should be included in the impact analysis are the estimated frequency of the threat-source's exploitation of a vulnerability on an annual basis, the approximate cost of each of these occurrences, and a weight factor based on the relative impact of a specific threat exploiting a specific vulnerability.

The output of this step is the magnitude of impact: high, medium, or low.

Risk Determination

This step, the seventh step in the risk assessment process, determines the level of risk to the IT system. The risk is assigned for a threat/vulnerability pair and is a function of the following characteristics:

- The likelihood that a particular threat-source will exploit an existing IT system vulnerability
- The magnitude of the resulting impact of a threat-source successfully exploiting the IT system vulnerability
- The adequacy of the existing or planned information system security controls for eliminating or reducing the risk

Mission risk is calculated by multiplying the threat likelihood ratings (the probability that a threat will occur) by the impact of the threat realized. A useful tool for estimating risk in this manner is the risk-level matrix. An example risk-level matrix is shown in Table 1-3. In the table, a high likelihood that the threat will occur is given a value of 1.0; a medium likelihood is assigned a value of 0.5; and a low likelihood of occurrence is given a rating of 0.1. Similarly, a high impact level is assigned a value of 100, a medium impact level 50, and a low impact level 10.

Table 1-3: A Risk-Level Matrix Example

LIKELIHOOD OF THREAT	LOW IMPACT (10)	MEDIUM IMPACT (50)	HIGH IMPACT (100)
High (1.0)	Low 10 × 1.0 = 10	Medium 50 × 1.0 = 50	High 100 × 1.0 = 100
Medium (0.5)	Low 10 × 0.5 = 5	Medium 50 × 0.5 = 25	High 100 × 0.5 = 50
Low (0.1)	Low 10 × 0.1 = 1	Medium 50 × 0.1 = 5	High 100 × 0.1 = 10

Using the risk level as a basis, the next step is to determine the actions that senior management and other responsible individuals must take to mitigate estimated risk. General guidelines for each level of risk are:

- **High risk level**—At this level, there is a high level of concern and a strong need for a plan for corrective measures to be developed as soon as possible.
- **Medium risk level**—For medium risk, there is concern and a need for a plan for corrective measures to be developed within a reasonable period of time
- **Low risk level**—For low risk, the approving authority of the system must decide whether to accept the risk or implement corrective actions.

The output of the risk determination step is a risk level of high, medium, or low.

Control Recommendations

With the risks identified and general guidelines provided for risk mitigation in the previous step, this step specifies the controls to be applied for risk mitigation. In order to specify appropriate controls, issues such as cost-benefit, operational impact, and feasibility have to be considered. Other factors such as applicable legislative regulations, organizational policy, safety, reliability, and the overall effectiveness of the recommended controls should also be taken into account.

The output of this step is a recommendation of controls and any alternative solutions to mitigate risk.

Results Documentation

The last step in the risk assessment process is the development of a risk assessment report. This report is directed at management and should contain information to support appropriate decisions on budget, policies, procedures, management, and operational issues.

The output of this step is a risk assessment report that describes threats and vulnerabilities, risk measurements, and recommendations for implementation of controls.

Risk Mitigation

Risk mitigation prioritizes, evaluates, and implements the controls that are an output of the risk assessment process. Risk mitigation is the second component of the risk management process.

Because risk can never be completely eliminated and control implementation must make sense under a cost-benefit analysis, a least-cost approach with minimal adverse impact on the IT system is usually taken.

Risk Mitigation Options

Risk mitigation can be classified into the following options:

- **Risk assumption**—Accept the risk and keep operating
- **Risk avoidance**—Forgo some functions
- **Risk limitation**—Implement controls to minimize the adverse impact of threats realized
- **Risk planning**—Develop a risk mitigation plan to prioritize, implement, and maintain controls
- **Research and development**—Research control types and options
- **Risk transference**—Transfer risk to other sources, such as purchasing insurance

NIST SP 800-30 emphasizes the following guidance on implementing controls: Address the greatest risks and strive for sufficient risk mitigation at the lowest cost, with minimal impact on other mission capabilities.

The control implementation approach from the risk mitigation methodology recommended by NIST SP 800-30 is given in Figure 1-1.

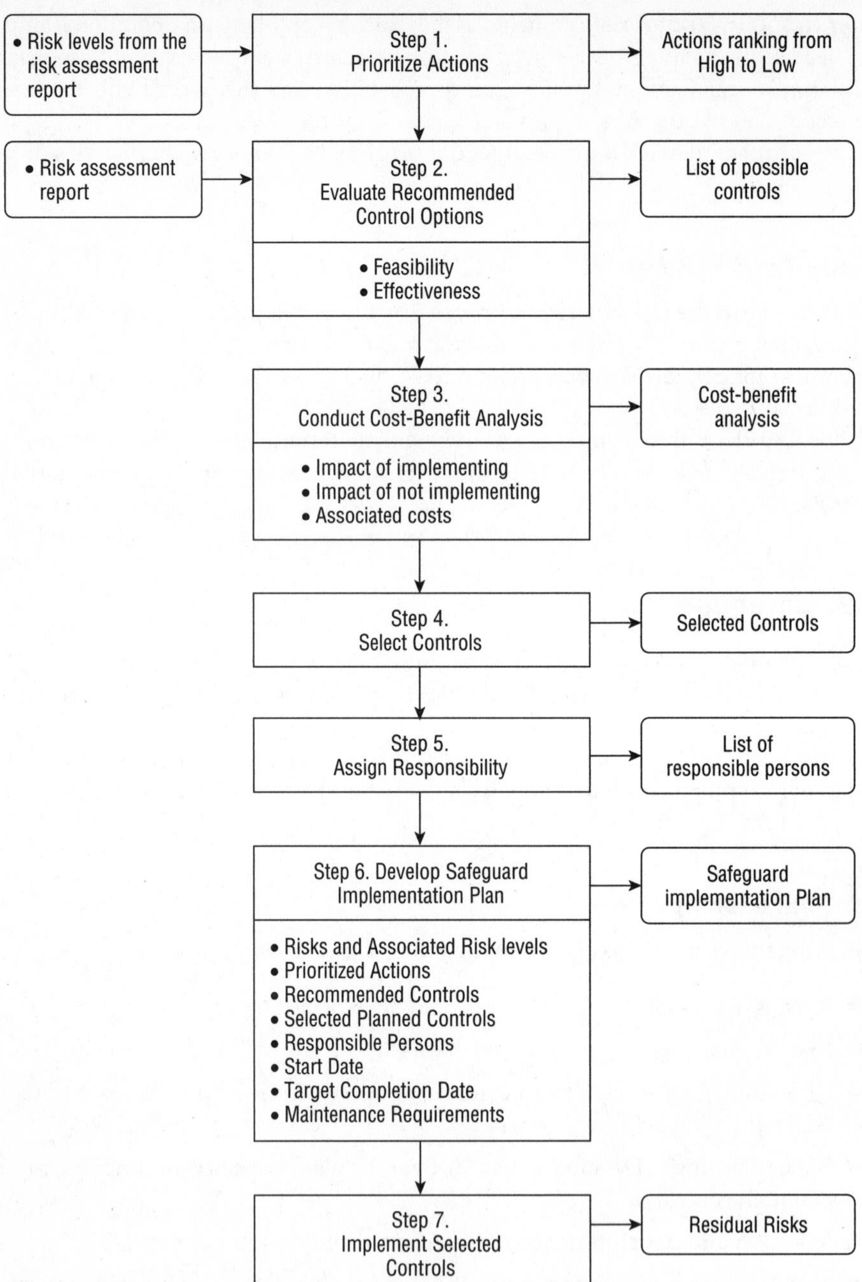

Figure 1-1: A control implementation approach

Figure source: from NIST SP 800-30

Categories of Controls

Controls to mitigate risks can be broken into the following categories:

- Technical
- Management
- Operational
- A combination of the above

Each of the categories of controls can be further decomposed into additional subcategories.

Technical controls can be subdivided into:

- **Supporting controls**—These controls implement identification, cryptographic key management, security administration, and system protections.
- **Preventive controls**—Preventive technical controls include authentication, authorization, access control enforcement, nonrepudiation, protected communications, and transaction privacy.
- **Detection and recovering controls**—These technical controls include audit, intrusion detection and containment, proof of wholeness (system integrity), restoration to a secure state, and virus detection and eradication.

Management controls comprise:

- **Preventive controls**—Preventive management controls include assigning responsibility for security, developing and maintaining security plans, personnel security controls, and security awareness and technical training.
- **Detection controls**—Detection controls involve background checks, personnel clearance, periodic review of security controls, periodic system audits, risk management, and authorization of IT systems to address and accept residual risk.
- **Recovery controls**—These controls provide continuity of support to develop, test, and maintain the continuity of the operations plan and establish an incident response capability.

Operational security controls are divided into preventive and detection types. Their functions are listed as follows:

- **Preventive controls**—These operational controls comprise control of media access and disposal, limiting external data distribution, control of software viruses, securing wiring closets, providing backup capability, protecting laptops and personal computers, protecting IT assets from fire damage, providing an emergency power source, and control of humidity and temperature.
- **Detection controls**—Detection operational controls include providing physical security through the use of items such as cameras and motion detectors and ensuring environmental security by using smoke detectors, sensors, and alarms.

Determination of Residual Risk

The risk that remains after the implementation of controls is called the *residual risk*. All systems will have residual risk because it is virtually impossible to completely eliminate risk to an IT system. An organization's senior management or the designated approving authority is responsible for authorizing/accrediting the IT system to begin or continue to operate. The authorization/accreditation must take place every three years in federal agencies or whenever major changes are made to the system. The approving authority signs a statement accepting the residual risk when accrediting the IT system for operation. If the approving authority determines that the residual risk is at an unacceptable level, the risk management cycle must be redone with the objective of lowering the residual risk to an acceptable level.

Figure 1-2 shows the relationship between residual risk and the implementation of controls.

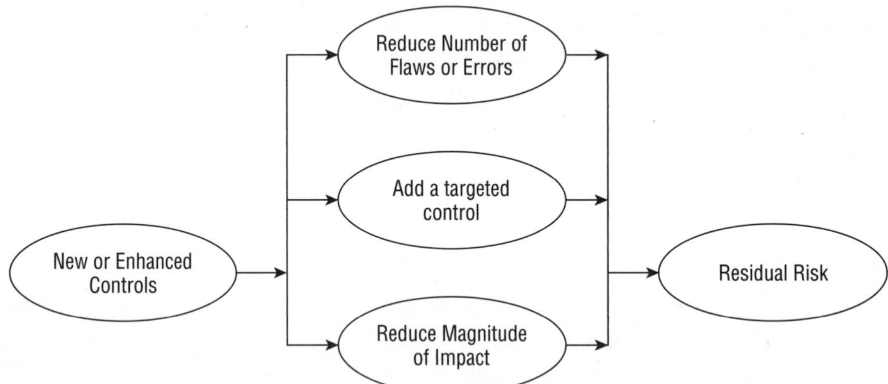

Figure 1-2: The relationship between residual risk and implementation of controls
Figure source: from NIST SP 800-30

Personnel Involved in the Risk Management Process

As with any enterprise endeavor, risk management must have the support of senior managers and the commitment of appropriate and qualified personnel. These personnel and their functions as outlined in NIST SP 800-30 are:

- **Senior management**—Provides the required resources and meets responsibilities under the principle of due care
- **Chief information officer (CIO)**—Considers risk management in IT planning, budgeting, and meeting system performance requirements
- **System and information owners**—Ensure that controls and services are implemented to address information system confidentiality, integrity, and availability
- **Business and functional managers**—Make trade-off decisions regarding business operations and IT procurement that affect information security

- **Information system security officer (ISSO)**—Participates in applying methodologies to identify, evaluate, and reduce risks to the mission-critical IT systems
- **IT security practitioners**—Ensure the correct implementation of IT system information system security requirements
- **Security awareness trainers**—Incorporate risk assessment in training programs for the organization's personnel

Software Security Risk Management Concepts

A number of risk management concepts for the security of software have evolved from the IT approach to risk management. These methodologies include the Microsoft Security Risk Management Discipline (SRMD),[6] vulnerability-oriented risk management proposed by Charles LeGrand,[7] Morana[8] risk management activities, and Cigital risk management[9] methods. These approaches are summarized in the following sections.

Microsoft Security Risk Management Discipline (SRMD)

The SRMD comprises the following steps:

1. **Assessment**
   a. **Asset assessment and valuation**—The value placed on an information asset and the cost to maintain or recover an asset value or the value of the asset to another entity
   b. **Identifying security risks**—Acquisition of data on vulnerabilities, threats, and countermeasures and discovery of possible risks to security
   c. **Analyzing and prioritizing security risks**—Identification of risks, determining the impact of potential threats, and making technical and economic decisions on the cost of countermeasures versus the impact of threats materialized
   d. **Security risk tracking, planning, and scheduling**—Application of information derived from security risk analysis to plan and schedule mitigation approaches

[6]Microsoft Corporation, "Understanding the Security Risk Management Discipline," revised May 31, 2006, Chapter 3 in *Securing Windows 2000 Server* (Redmond, WA: Microsoft Corporation, November 17, 2004). Available from: `www.microsoft.com/technet/security/prodtech/windows2000/secwin2k/swin2k03.mspx`.
[7]LeGrand, Charles H. (CHL Global Associates), "Managing Software Risk: an Executive Call to Action" (Waltham, MA: Ounce Labs, September 21, 2005).
[8]Morana, Marco M. (Foundstone Professional Services), "Building Security into the Software Life Cycle: A Business Case," paper presented at BlackHat USA, Las Vegas, NV, August 2–3, 2006.
[9]Viega, John and McGraw, Gary, *Building Secure Software: How to Avoid Security Problems the Right Way* (Boston: Addison-Wesley, 2001).

2. **Development and implementation**
   a. **Security remediation development**—Creation of policies and procedures addressing strategies for patch management, configuration management, auditing, monitoring, and operations using the results of the risk assessment phase
   b. **Security remediation testing**—Determination of the means to deploy the remediation strategies into an operational environment and evaluation of the countermeasures' ability to mitigate risk as planned
   c. **Capturing security knowledge**—Continuous determination of the methods used to acquire knowledge concerning the securing of information assets and to document known vulnerabilities and exploits
3. **Operating**
   a. **Reassessing new and changed assets and security risks**—Application of change management and security configuration management to modified and new assets and potential new risks
   b. **Stabilizing and deploying new or changed countermeasures**—The assessment of modified and new assets and the deployment of corresponding countermeasures on a day-to-day operational basis

LeGrand Vulnerability-Oriented Risk Management

Charles LeGrand has proposed a risk management method based on vulnerability analysis. The four principal steps in this approach are:

1. **Risk assessment**—Identification of vulnerabilities, estimation of possible losses caused by threats materialized, cost-benefit examination of countermeasures, and assessment of attacks
2. **Vulnerability management**—Identification, measurement, and remediation of specific vulnerabilities
3. **Adherence to security standards and policies for development and deployment**—Formal implementation methods to minimize or, possibly, eliminate the introduction of vulnerabilities
4. **Assessment, monitoring, and assurance**—Determination of required compliance provided by risk management practices and evaluation of risk levels to ensure they are within desired limits

Morana Risk Management Activities

Marco Morana postulates the following risk management procedure that maps onto the software development life cycle.

NOTE System and software development life cycles are covered in detail later in this chapter.

1. **Requirements**—Conducting security requirements engineering, incorporating appropriate standards, ensuring compliance requirements are met, performing vulnerability and threat analyses, determining technical security needs, and evaluating extant system security
2. **Architecture and design**—Performing security architecture and design reviews, modeling threat patterns, preparing security tests, and conducting measurements of security posture
3. **Development**—Analyzing code and eliminating/reducing coding errors, testing code units for security, revising threat models based on new information, and evaluating system security posture
4. **Testing**—Use of attack patterns, application of automated testing (including black box and white box testing)
   - *Black box* testing is also known as "zero knowledge" testing, where the testing team is provided no knowledge of the resources to be tested and has to acquire information on its own.
   - In *white box* or "full knowledge" testing, the testing team has as much knowledge as possible about the network and computing resources to be evaluated.

   Additional testing such as regression testing is also performed along with developing new threat models and conducting additional evaluations of the systems' security posture.

Cigital Risk Management Method

Gary McGraw of Cigital and John Viega of Stonewall Software proposed the following software security risk management steps:

1. Security requirements derivation/elicitation and specification
2. Security risk assessment
3. Secure architecture and design
4. Secure implementation
5. Security testing
6. Security assurance

Risk Management and Assurance Activities in the SDLC

The term *SDLC* is used to refer to a number of different development life cycles. In developing systems, SDLC refers to the system development life cycle. When you are focusing on the software development portion of a system, SDLC represents the software development life cycle. However, in the context of developing secure software, SDLC or SDL stands for the security development life cycle.

SOFTWARE LIFE CYCLE (SLC) AND SYSTEM LIFE CYCLE

In the context of the CSSLP certification, the software life cycle (SLC) is also used. The SLC processes are defined in ISO/IEC Standard 12207, "Software Life Cycle Processes," as a grouping of the following three classes:

- **Primary processes—Principal elements of the SLC, which are acquisition, supply, development, operation, and maintenance.**
- **Supporting processes—Complementary items such as documentation, configuration management, quality assurance, joint review, audit, verification, validation, and problem resolution, which support other processes. A supporting process supports another process in performing a specialized function.**
- **Organizational processes—Components including management, infrastructure, process improvement, and training.**

ISO/IEC 12207 defines the system life cycle as covering "the phases of needs determination and demonstration, development, production, use, and disposal or retirement." The system life cycle is sometimes used interchangeably with the system development life cycle.

As discussed in this chapter, risk management provides the means to reduce the negative impact of threats on an information system. To be effective, risk management must not be an "add-on" process, but must be integrated into the system development life cycle. Because the concepts of the system development life cycle are applicable to software and form a basis for software security, this section addresses risk management in the system development life cycle. The software security development life cycle is covered later in this chapter.

System Development Life Cycle

The five phases of the SDLC as described in IATF document 3.1 are:

1. **Initiation**—Documentation of the need for the system and its mission. A sensitivity assessment, which evaluates the sensitivity of the IT system and the information to be processed, is included in this phase.
2. **Development/acquisition**—Comprises the system acquisition and development cycles. In this phase, the system is designed, developed, programmed, and acquired.
3. **Implementation**—Installation, testing, security testing, and accreditation are conducted.

4. **Operation/maintenance**—In this phase, the system performs its designed functions. Administration, security operations, modification/addition of hardware and/or software, operational assurance, monitoring, and audits are also conducted in this phase.
5. **Disposal**—This final phase involves the disposition of system components and products, such as hardware, software, and information; disk sanitization; archiving files; and moving equipment.

Incorporating Risk Management into the SDLC

The risk management processes of risk assessment, risk mitigation, and evaluation should be conducted in each phase of the SDLC. Table 1-4, from NIST SP 800-30, details the risk management activities that should be performed for each SDLC phase.

Incorporating Assurance in the SDLC

The Data and Analysis Center for Software[10] defines 13 key elements of a secure SDLC process, summarized as follows:

1. Incorporation of security criteria in each SDLC phase checkpoint at the exit of the phase
2. Application of secure software principles and practices
3. Employment of adequate requirements
4. Use of secure coding
5. Integration of secure software
6. Performance of secure testing
7. Practicing secure distribution and deployment
8. Practicing secure sustainment and maintenance
9. Deployment of supportive development tools
10. Practicing secure configuration management
11. Employment of security-knowledgeable developers
12. Practicing secure project management and obtaining upper management commitment
13. Robust design and architecture

[10]Goertzel, K., Winograd, T. et al., "Enhancing the Development Life Cycle to Produce Secure Software," Draft Version 2.0. (Rome, New York: United States Department of Defense Data and Analysis Center for Software, July 2008).

Table 1-4: Risk Management in the SDLC

SDLC PHASE	DESCRIPTION	RISK MANAGEMENT ACTIVITIES
Phase 1—Initiation	The need for an IT system is expressed and the purpose and scope of the IT system is documented.	Identified risks are used to support the development of the system requirements, including security requirements, and a security concept of operations (strategy).
Phase 2—Development or acquisition	The IT system is designed, purchased, programmed, developed, or otherwise constructed.	The risks identified during this phase can be used to support the security analyses of the IT system that may lead to architecture and design trade-offs during system development.
Phase 3—Implementation	The system security features should be configured, enabled, tested, and verified.	The risk management process supports the assessment of the system implementation against its requirements and within its modeled operational environment. Decisions regarding risks identified must be made prior to system operation.
Phase 4—Operation or maintenance	The system performs its functions. Typically the system is being modified on an ongoing basis through the addition of hardware and software and by changes to organizational processes, policies, and procedures.	Risk management activities are performed for periodic system reauthorization (or reaccreditation) or whenever major changes are made to an IT system in its operational, production environment (for example, new system interfaces).
Phase 5—Disposal	This phase may involve the disposition of information, hardware, and software. Activities may include moving, archiving, discarding, or destroying information and sanitizing the hardware and software.	Risk management activities are performed for system components that will be disposed of or replaced to ensure that the hardware and software are properly disposed of, that residual data is appropriately handled, and that system migration is conducted in a secure and systematic manner.

NIST SP 800-30, "Risk Management Guide for Information Technology Systems," July 2002.

The following list, taken from NIST SP 800-64, summarizes the information system security steps to be applied to the SDLC. An organization will use the general SDLC described in SP 800-64 document or will have developed a tailored SDLC that meets its specific needs. In either case, NIST recommends that organizations incorporate the associated IT security steps of this general SDLC into their development process:

- **Initiation phase:**
  - **Security categorization**—Defines three levels (low, moderate, or high) of potential impact on organizations or individuals should there be a breach of security (a loss of confidentiality, integrity, or availability). Security categorization standards assist organizations in making the appropriate selection of security controls for their information systems.
  - **Preliminary risk assessment**—Results in an initial description of the basic security needs of the system. A preliminary risk assessment should define the threat environment in which the system will operate.
- **Acquisition/development phase:**
  - **Risk assessment**—Analysis that identifies the protection requirements for the system through a formal risk assessment process. This analysis builds on the initial risk assessment performed during the Initiation phase, but will be more in depth and specific.
  - **Security functional requirements analysis**—Analysis of requirements that may include the following components: (1) system security environment (that is, enterprise information security policy and enterprise security architecture) and (2) security functional requirements.
  - **Assurance requirements analysis security**—Analysis of requirements that address the developmental activities required and assurance evidence needed to produce the desired level of confidence that the information security will work correctly and effectively. The analysis, based on legal and functional security requirements, will be used as the basis for determining how much and what kinds of assurance are required.
  - **Cost considerations and reporting**—Determine how much of the development cost can be attributed to information security over the life cycle of the system. These costs include hardware, software, personnel, and training.
  - **Security planning**—Ensures that agreed-upon security controls, planned or in place, are fully documented. The security plan also provides a complete characterization or description of the information system as well as attachments or references to key documents supporting the agency's information security program (for example, configuration management plan, contingency plan, incident response plan, security awareness and training plan, rules of behavior, risk assessment, security test and evaluation results, system interconnection agreements, security authorizations/accreditations, and plan of action and milestones).
  - **Security control development**—Ensures that security controls described in the respective security plans are designed, developed, and implemented. For

information systems currently in operation, the security plans for those systems may call for the development of additional security controls to supplement the controls already in place or the modification of selected controls that are deemed to be less than effective.

- **Developmental security test and evaluation**—Ensure that security controls developed for a new information system are working properly and are effective. Some types of security controls (primarily those controls of a nontechnical nature) cannot be tested and evaluated until the information system is deployed—these controls are typically management and operational controls.
- **Other planning components**—Ensure that all necessary components of the development process are considered when incorporating security into the life cycle. These components include selection of the appropriate contract type, participation by all necessary functional groups within an organization, participation by the certifier and accreditor, and development and execution of necessary contracting plans and processes.

- **Implementation phase:**
  - **Inspection and acceptance**—Ensure that the organization validates and verifies that the functionality described in the specification is included in the deliverables.
  - **Security control integration**—Ensures that security controls are integrated at the operational site where the information system is to be deployed for operation. Security control settings and switches are enabled in accordance with vendor instructions and available security implementation guidance.
  - **Security certification**—Ensures that the controls are effectively implemented through established verification techniques and procedures. Gives organization officials confidence that the appropriate safeguards and countermeasures are in place to protect the organization's information system. Security certification also uncovers and describes the known vulnerabilities in the information system.
  - **Security accreditation**—Provides the necessary security authorization of an information system to process, store, or transmit information that is required. This authorization is granted by a senior organization official and is based on the verified effectiveness of security controls to some agreed-upon level of assurance and an identified residual risk to agency assets or operations.
- **Operations/maintenance phase:**
  - **Configuration management and control**—Ensure adequate consideration of the potential security impacts due to specific changes to an information system or its surrounding environment. Configuration management and configuration control procedures are critical to establishing an initial baseline of hardware, software, and firmware components for the information system and subsequently controlling and maintaining an accurate inventory of any changes to the system.

- **Continuous monitoring**—Ensures that controls continue to be effective in their application through periodic testing and evaluation. Security control monitoring (that is, verifying the continued effectiveness of those controls over time) and reporting the security status of the information system to appropriate agency officials are essential activities in a comprehensive information security program.

- **Disposition phase:**
  - **Information preservation**—Ensures that information is retained, as necessary, to conform to current legal requirements and to accommodate future technology changes that may render the retrieval method obsolete.
  - **Media sanitization**—Ensures that data is deleted, erased, and written over as necessary.
  - **Hardware and software disposal**—Ensures that hardware and software are disposed of as directed by the information system security officer.

After discussing these phases and the information security steps in detail, the guide provides specifications, tasks, and clauses that can be used in a request for proposal (RFP) to acquire information security features, procedures, and assurances.

The CSSLP candidate should also understand the relationship between the SDLC phases and the acquisition process for the corresponding information system. This relationship is illustrated in Table 1-5, also taken from NIST SP 800-64.

Table 1-5: Relationship Between Information Systems Acquisition Cycle Phases and the SDLC

	ACQUISITION	CYCLE	PHASES	
Mission and Business Planning	Acquisition Planning	Acquisition	Contract Performance	Disposal and Contract Close-Out
Initiation	Acquisition/ Development	Implementation	Operation/ Maintenance	Disposition
		SDLC	**Phases**	

NIST SP 800-64, "Security Considerations in the System Development Life Cycle," October 2008.

NIST SP 800-64 also defines the following acquisition-related terms:

- **Acquisition**—Includes all stages of the process of acquiring property or services, beginning with the process for determining the need for the property or services and ending with contract completion and closeout.
- **Acquisition initiator**—The key person who represents the program office in formulating information technology requirements and managing presolicitation activities.
- **Acquisition technical evaluation**—A component of the selection process, defined as the examination of proposals to determine technical acceptability and merit.

ACQUISITION SPIRAL MODEL

An additional, valuable tool in the acquisition process is the *spiral model of the acquisition management process*. This approach is known as an evolutionary acquisition strategy. This model depicts the acquisition management process as a set of phases and decision points in a circular representation. The model illustrates the concept that a mission need is defined and translated into a solution that undergoes a continuous circle of improvement and evolution until it is no longer required.

NIST SP 800-64 also lists the key personnel associated with system acquisition and development as follows:

- **Chief information officer (CIO)**—The CIO is responsible for the organization's information system planning, budgeting, investment, performance, and acquisition. As such, the CIO provides advice and assistance to senior organization personnel in acquiring the most efficient and effective information system to fit the organization's enterprise architecture.
- **Contracting officer**—The contracting officer is the person who has the authority to enter into, administer, or terminate contracts and make related determinations and findings.
- **Contracting officer's technical representative (COTR)**—The COTR is a qualified employee appointed by the contracting officer to act as his or her technical representative in managing the technical aspects of a particular contract.
- **Information technology investment board (or equivalent)**—The information technology (IT) investment board, or its equivalent, is responsible for managing the capital planning and investment control process defined by the Clinger-Cohen Act of 1996 (Section 5).
- **Information security program manager**—The information security program manager is responsible for developing enterprise standards for information security. This individual plays a leading role in introducing an appropriate, structured methodology to help identify, evaluate, and minimize information security risks to the organization. Information security program managers coordinate and perform system risk analyses, analyze risk mitigation alternatives, and build the business case for the acquisition of appropriate security solutions that help ensure mission accomplishment in the face of real-world threats. They also support senior management in ensuring that security management activities are conducted as required to meet the organization's needs.
- **Information system security officer**—The information system security officer is responsible for ensuring the security of an information system throughout its life cycle.
- **Program manager (owner of data)/acquisition initiator/program official**—This person represents programmatic interests during the acquisition process. The program manager, who has been involved in strategic planning initiatives of

the acquisition, plays an essential role in security and is, ideally, intimately aware of functional system requirements.

- **Privacy officer**—The privacy officer is responsible for ensuring that the services or system being procured meet existing privacy policies regarding protection, dissemination (information sharing and exchange), and information disclosure.
- **Legal advisor/contract attorney**—This individual is responsible for advising the team on legal issues during the acquisition process.

CSSLP candidates who are interested in additional information contained in NIST SP 800-64 can obtain the document from the NIST Web site: `http://csrc.nist.gov/publications/nistpubs/`.

Regulations, Privacy, and Compliance

In addition to focusing on assurance in software applications, organizations are required to comply with regulations and laws designed to provide protections in the consumer and financial arenas. Some of the important compliance requirements and acts are:

- The U.S. Federal Information Security Management Act (FISMA) has data security management requirements for United States federal government organizations.
- Privacy laws
- Sarbanes-Oxley (SOX) is the U.S. mandate that requires adequate controls to be in place to protect sensitive data and assets for publicly-traded companies.
- The Gramm-Leach-Bliley Act (GLB) Act includes provisions to protect consumers' financial information is mandatory for financial institutions.
- The Health Insurance Portability and Accountability Act (HIPAA) requires protection of personal health information.
- The Payment Card Industry Data Security Standard (PCI DSS) encompasses credit card transaction protection.

FISMA

In order to increase the security of federal information systems, the Federal Information Security Management Act (FISMA), which is Title III of the E-Government Act of December 2002 (Public Law 107-347), was passed. FISMA was enacted to:

- Provide a comprehensive framework for ensuring the effectiveness of information security controls over information resources that support federal operations and assets
- Recognize the highly networked nature of the current federal computing environment and provide effective government-wide management and oversight of the related information security risks, including coordination of information

security efforts throughout the civilian, national security, and law enforcement communities

- Provide for development and maintenance of minimum controls required to protect federal information and information systems
- Provide a mechanism for improved oversight of federal agency information security programs

FISMA; the Paperwork Reduction Act (PRA) of 1980, as amended by the Paperwork Reduction Act of 1995 (44 U.S.C., Chapter 35); and the Clinger-Cohen Act (also known as ''Information Technology Management Reform Act of 1996'') (Pub. L. 104-106, Division E) promote a risk-based policy for cost effective security. The Clinger-Cohen Act supplements the information resources management policies contained in the PRA by establishing a comprehensive approach for executive agencies to improve the acquisition and management of their information resources. FISMA also specifies that national security classified information should be handled in accordance with the appropriate national security directives as provided by DoD and NSA.

FISMA charges the director of the Office of Management and Budget (OMB) with the responsibility of overseeing the security policies and practices of all agencies of the executive branch of the federal government, including ''coordinating the development of standards and guidelines between NIST and the NSA and other agencies with responsibility for national security systems.'' Agencies of the executive branch of the U.S. government are defined as:

- An executive department specified in 5 U.S.C., Section 101
- Within the executive office of the president, only OMB and the Office of Administration
- A military department specified in 5 U.S.C., Section 102
- An independent establishment as defined in 5 U.S.C., Section 104(1)
- A wholly owned government corporation fully subject to the provisions of 31 U.S.C., Chapter 91

OMB Circular A-130, Appendix III, ''Security of Federal Automated Information Resources,'' specifies that federal government agencies perform the following functions:

- Plan for security
- Ensure that appropriate officials are assigned security responsibility
- Review the security controls in their information systems
- Authorize system processing prior to operations and periodically thereafter

OMB Circular A-130, Appendix III, also requires that each agency perform security accreditation, which is considered ''a form of quality control and challenges managers and technical staffs at all levels to implement the most effective security controls possible in an information system, given mission requirements, technical constraints, operational constraints, and cost/schedule constraints. By accrediting an information system, an agency official accepts responsibility for the security of the system and is fully accountable for any adverse impacts to the agency if a breach of security occurs.''

FISMA Performance Requirements

The actions that FISMA requires each government agency to perform in developing and implementing an agency-wide information security program are specified in NIST Special Publication 800-37, ''Guide for the Security Certification and Accreditation of Federal Information Systems,'' May 2004. FISMA specifies that the program must include:

- Periodic assessments of risk, including the magnitude of harm that could result from the unauthorized access, use, disclosure, disruption, modification, or destruction of information and information systems that support the operations and assets of the agency
- Policies and procedures that are based on risk assessments, cost-effectively reduce information security risks to an acceptable level, and ensure that information security is addressed throughout the life cycle of each agency information system
- Subordinate plans for providing adequate information security for networks, facilities, information systems, or groups of information systems, as appropriate
- Security awareness training to inform personnel (including contractors and other users of information systems that support the operations and assets of the agency) of the information security risks associated with their activities and their responsibilities in complying with agency policies and procedures designed to reduce these risks
- Periodic testing and evaluation of the effectiveness of information security policies, procedures, practices, and security controls to be performed with a frequency depending on risk, but no less than annually
- A process for planning, implementing, evaluating, and documenting remedial action to address any deficiencies in the information security policies, procedures, and practices, of the agency
- Procedures for detecting, reporting, and responding to security incidents
- Plans and procedures to ensure continuity of operations for information systems that support the operations and assets of the agency

Identification of Information Types

FISMA assigned to NIST the responsibility for developing the following information system-related standards and guidelines:

1. Standards to be used by all federal agencies to categorize all information and information systems collected or maintained by or on behalf of each agency based on the objectives of providing appropriate levels of information security according to a range of risk levels

2. Guidelines recommending the types of information and information systems to be included in each category
3. Minimum information security requirements (that is, management, operational, and technical controls)

In order to satisfy item 1, NIST developed FIPS Publication 199, "Standards for Security Categorization of Federal Information and Information Systems." FIPS 199 and the recently developed FIPS 200 standard, entitled "Minimum Security Requirements for Federal Information and Information Systems," are two mandatory standards specified in the FISMA legislation.

FIPS 199 is used to identify and categorize information and information systems and, as cited in the standard, should be used "[t]o provide a common framework and understanding for expressing security that, for the Federal government promotes: (i) effective management and oversight of information security programs, including the coordination of information security efforts throughout the civilian, national security, emergency preparedness, homeland security, and law enforcement communities; and (ii) consistent reporting to the Office of Management and Budget (OMB) and Congress on the adequacy and effectiveness of information security policies, procedures, and practices."

Information Privacy and Privacy Laws

Privacy is the right of an individual to protection from unauthorized disclosure of the individual's personally identifiable information (PII). For example, the Health Insurance Portability and Accountability Act (HIPAA) lists the following 16 items as a person's individual identifiers:

- Names
- Postal address information, other than town or city, state, and zip code
- Telephone numbers
- Fax numbers
- Electronic mail addresses
- Social security numbers
- Medical record numbers
- Health plan beneficiary numbers
- Account numbers
- Certificate/license numbers
- Vehicle identifiers and serial numbers, including license plate numbers
- Device identifiers and serial numbers
- Web Universal Resource Locators (URLs)

- Internet Protocol (IP) address numbers
- Biometric identifiers, including finger- and voiceprints
- Full face photographic images and any comparable images

FUNDAMENTAL PRINCIPLES OF PRIVACY

An individual's right to privacy is embodied in the following fundamental principles of privacy:

- **Notice—Regarding collection, use and disclosure of PII**
- **Choice—To opt out or opt in regarding disclosure of PII to third parties**
- **Access—By consumers to their PII to permit review and correction of information**
- **Security—To protect PII from unauthorized disclosure**
- **Enforcement—Of applicable privacy policies and obligations**

Privacy Policy

Organizations develop and publish privacy policies that describe their approach to handling PII. Web sites of organizations usually have their privacy policies available to read online and these policies usually cover the following areas:

- Statement of the organization's commitment to privacy
- The type of information collected, such as names, addresses, credit card numbers, phone numbers, and so on
- Retaining and using email correspondence
- Information gathered through cookies and Web server logs and how that information is used
- How information is shared with affiliates and strategic partners
- Mechanisms to secure information transmissions, such as encryption and digital signatures
- Mechanisms to protect PII stored by the organization
- Procedures for review of the organization's compliance with the privacy policy
- Evaluation of information protection practices
- Means for the user to access and correct PII held by the organization
- Rules for disclosing PII to outside parties
- Providing PII that is legally required

Privacy-Related Legislation and Guidelines

The following list summarizes some important legislation and recommended guidelines for privacy:

- The Cable Communications Policy Act provides for discretionary use of PII by cable operators internally but imposes restrictions on disclosures to third parties.
- The Children's Online Privacy Protection Act (COPPA) is aimed at providing protection to children under the age of 13.
- Customer Proprietary Network Information rules apply to telephone companies and restrict their use of customer information both internally and to third parties.
- The Financial Services Modernization Act (Gramm-Leach-Bliley) requires financial institutions to provide customers with clear descriptions of the institution's policies and procedures for protecting the PII of customers.
- The Telephone Consumer Protection Act restricts communications between companies and consumers, such as in telemarketing.
- The 1973 U.S. Code of Fair Information Practices states that:
  1. There must not be personal data recordkeeping systems whose very existence is secret.
  2. There must be a way for a person to find out what information about them is in a record and how it is used.
  3. There must be a way for a person to prevent information about them, which was obtained for one purpose, from being used or made available for another purpose without their consent.
  4. Any organization creating, maintaining, using, or disseminating records of identifiable personal data must ensure the reliability of the data for their intended use and must take precautions to prevent misuses of that data.
- The Health Insurance Portability and Accountability Act (HIPAA), Administrative Simplification Title, includes Privacy and Security Rules and standards for electronic transactions and code sets.

Sarbanes-Oxley

The Sarbanes-Oxley Act was enacted in July of 2002 to regulate corporate financial practices and reporting. The act has 11 titles and includes deadlines for compliance. The titles include sections, where Sections 302, 401, 404, 409, 802, and 906 are considered the most important relative to compliance. The 11 titles are:

1. Establishment of the Public Company Accounting Oversight Board (PCAOB)
2. Standards for External Auditor Independence
3. Corporate Responsibility by Senior Executives for Accuracy and Completeness of Corporate Financial Reports

4. Enhanced Financial Disclosures and Reporting
5. Code of Conduct for Securities Analysts and Disclosure of Analyst Conflicts of Interest
6. Commission Resources and Authority that Defines Practices for Securities Analysts and the Authority to Censure Securities Professionals.
7. Studies and Reports for Conducting Research Relevant to Enforcement of Violations by the Securities and Exchange Commission (SEC) Registered Companies
8. Corporate and Criminal Fraud Accountability, which Describes Criminal Penalties for Fraud
9. White Collar Crime Penalty Enhancement, which Recommends Stronger Sentencing Guidelines for White Collar Crimes
10. Corporate Tax Returns Specifies that the Corporate CEO Sign the Company Tax Return.
11. Corporate Fraud Accountability Established Tampering with Records and Committing Fraud as Criminal Offenses.

Gramm-Leach-Bliley

The Gramm-Leach-Bliley Act, "Financial Services Modernization Act," Public Law 106-102, was passed in 1999. It comprises seven titles as follows:

1. **Facilitating Affiliation among Banks, Securities Firms, and Insurance Companies**—Permits banks to affiliate with securities firms and to have financial subsidiaries
2. **Functional Regulation**—Modifies federal securities laws to include functional regulation of bank securities activities
3. **Insurance**—Includes functional regulation of insurance activities of banks and bank subsidiaries
4. **Unitary Savings and Loan Holding Companies**—Unitary thrift holding companies may be sold only to financial organizations
5. **Privacy**—All financial organizations must provide clear disclosure of their privacy policies regarding sharing of PII
6. **Federal Home Loan Bank System Modernization**—Establishes rules of operation for federal home loan banks
7. **Other Provisions**—Covers a number of other items including ATM fees, foreign banks establishing units in the United States, and the administration of Community Reinvestment Act (CRA) loan agreements

HIPAA

The Health Insurance Portability and Accountability Act (HIPAA) addresses the security and privacy of protected health information (PHI). Covered entities under

HIPAA include health plans, health care providers, health care clearinghouses, and any employer that stores, manages, or communicates protected health information. HIPAA addresses the protection of health information through two specific rules: the Final Security Rule and the Final Privacy Rule.

HIPAA Final Security Rule

The HIPAA Final Security Rule was adopted in February 2003 and specified compliance by April 21, 2005, and April 21, 2006 for small health plans. The Final Security Rule was designed to be compatible with the HIPAA Final Privacy Rule and is structured into four overlapping categories:

- Protection for transmitted data
- Protection for data at rest
- Physical protection
- Administrative procedures

The standards in the Final Security Rule fall into the categories of administrative, technical, and physical safeguards. The Final Security Rule requires the covered entity to:

- Protect against any reasonably anticipated threats or hazards to the security of protected health information (PHI)
- Protect the confidentiality, integrity, and availability of all electronic PHI that is created, transmitted, received, or maintained by the covered entity
- Protect against any reasonably anticipated uses or disclosures of (PHI) that are not permitted under HIPAA
- Ensure that the employees of the covered entity are trained in and comply with the Final Security Rule

The Final Security Rule also requires covered entities to enter into agreements with business associates with whom they exchange electronic information. In these agreements, the business associates must be willing and able to safeguard the PHI.

HIPAA Final Privacy Rule

Under the Final Privacy Rule, a covered entity may use or disclose protected health information for its own treatment, payment, or health care operations. Additional provisions of the Final Privacy Rule are:

- A covered entity must obtain an individual's prior written authorization to use his or her protected health information for marketing purposes except for a face-to-face encounter or a communication involving a promotional gift of nominal value.
- A covered entity is prohibited from selling lists of patients and enrollees to third parties or from disclosing protected health information to a third party for the marketing activities of the third party, without the individual's authorization.

- Covered entities must provide patients with notice of the patient's privacy rights and the privacy practices of the covered entity.
- Direct treatment providers must make a good faith effort to obtain patient's written acknowledgement of the notice of privacy rights and practices. (The rule does not prescribe a form of written acknowledgement; the patient may sign a separate sheet or initial a cover sheet of the notice.)
- Covered entities may disclose protected health information, without authorization, to a person subject to the jurisdiction of the FDA for public health purposes related to the quality, safety, or effectiveness of FDA-regulated products or activities (collecting or reporting adverse events, dangerous products, and defects or problems with FDA-regulated products.)
- State law, or other applicable law, governs in the area of parents and minors.
- A covered entity is permitted to disclose PHI to a business associate who performs a function or activity on behalf of the covered entity that involves the creation, use, or disclosure of PHI, provided that the covered entity enters in a contractual relationship with the business associate detailing specific safeguards.
- A researchers' use of a single combined form to obtain informed consent for research and authorization to use or disclose protected health information for such research is permitted.
- The creation and dissemination of a limited data set (that does not include directly identifiable information) for research, public health, and health care operations is permitted.

PCI Data Security Standard

The Payment Card Industry (PCI) group was formed in 2004 to address the security of credit card transactions and to apply to all cardholder associations, such as MasterCard and Visa. The results are documented in the most recent PCI Data Security Standard (DSS) document, Version 1.2, released October 1, 2008. The DSS document can be found at the PCI Council Web site at `www.pcisecuritystandards.org/`.

The standard addresses card and cardholder authentication and is organized as 12 requirements under 6 logically consistent control objectives. Compliance requires that all 12 requirements are met, with noncompliance penalties up to a maximum of $500,000 per incident. Merchants and member banks were required to meet the DSS starting on June 30, 2005.

The 6 control objectives of the DSS and their corresponding 12 requirement areas as listed in "Payment Card Industry (PCI) Data Security Standard Requirements and Security Assessment Procedures," version 1.2, October 2008, are summarized as follows:

1. **Build and maintain a secure network**
   - **Requirement 1**—Install and maintain a firewall configuration to protect cardholder data

- **Requirement 2**—Do not use vendor-supplied defaults for system passwords and other security parameters

2. **Protect cardholder data**
   - **Requirement 3**—Protect stored cardholder data
   - **Requirement 4**—Encrypt transmission of cardholder data across open, public networks
3. **Maintain a vulnerability management program**
   - **Requirement 5**—Use and regularly update antivirus software or programs
   - **Requirement 6**—Develop and maintain secure systems and applications
4. **Implement strong access control measures**
   - **Requirement 7**—Restrict access to cardholder data by business need-to-know
   - **Requirement 8**—Assign a unique ID to each person with computer access
   - **Requirement 9**—Restrict physical access to cardholder data
5. **Regularly monitor and test networks**
   - **Requirement 10**—Track and monitor all access to network resources and cardholder data
   - **Requirement 11**—Regularly test security systems and processes
6. **Maintain an information security policy**
   - **Requirement 12**—Maintain a policy that addresses information security for employees and contractors

Software Architecture

In general, a *software architecture* is a high-level design structure comprising abstract-level components of the required software system functionality and descriptions of their interactions. It is a design plan that assigns and portrays roles and behavior among all IT assets.

Software Architecture Definitions

Some additional definitions of software architecture are as follows:

- Software architecture is concerned with global organization as a composition of components, global control structures, communication protocols, and physical locations.[11]

[11] Dijkstra, E. W., "Notes on Structured Programming," *Structured Programming* (London: Academic Press, 1972).

- Software architecture is a level of design that involves the description of elements from which systems are built, interactions among those elements, patterns that guide their composition, and constraints on those patterns.[12]
- The software architecture of a program or computing system is the structure or structures of the system, which comprise software components, the externally visible properties of those components, and the relationships among them.[13]

A software architecture can be considered a composition system comprising the following elements:

- Components (modules with interfaces)
- Connectors (abstraction of communication)
- Operators that create systems from subsystems

The software architecture employs *abstraction*, which is the neglect of unnecessary details.

Software architecture systems are represented by a *component model* that incorporates the following concepts:

- Connector; components attached to ports
- Binding point or port; abstract interface points that specify transfers to and from components
- Glue code generated from connectors
- Separation of application and communication
- Use of a composition language such as an architecture description language (ADL)
- Components and connectors bound together to form a configuration

These concepts are illustrated in Figure 1-3 and Figure 1-4.

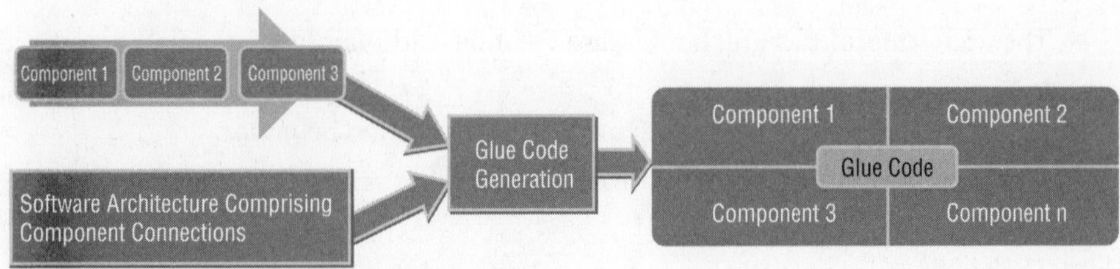

Figure 1-3: Software architecture overview

[12]Shaw, M., and Garlan, D., *Software Architecture: Perspectives on an Emerging Discipline* (Upper Saddle River, NJ: Prentice Hall, 1996).

[13]Bass, L., Clements, P., and Kazman, R., *Software Architecture in Practice* (Reading, MA: Addison-Wesley, 1998).

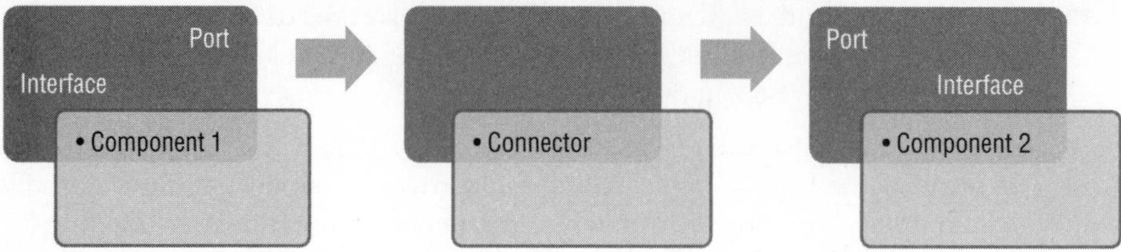

Figure 1-4: Configuration example

Software Architecture Styles

An *architecture style* defines a vocabulary of components and connector types, and a set of constraints on how they can be combined. For many styles there may also exist one or more semantic models that specify how to determine a system's overall properties from the properties of its parts.[14] Some typical architecture styles include:

- **Pipes and filters**—A component receives inputs from connectors (pipes) and produces a transformed (filtered) set of outputs.
- **Layered**—Multiple layers exist in which a layer acts as a client to the layer below and a server to the layer above.
- **N-tiered**—This type enforces a strict separation of concerns that is not demanded in the layered architecture style. Each tier is responsible for a specific functional area.
- **Heterogeneous**—These systems use a number of architecture styles.

Software Architecture Assurance

The Software Assurance Common Body of Knowledge (CBK) developed by the U.S. Department of Homeland Security Software Initiative lists a number of important architectural design assurance objectives. These objectives, summarized from the DHS CBK document, are listed as follows:[15]

- The architectural design should ease creation and maintenance of an assurance case.
- The architecture should provide predictable execution behavior.
- The architectural design should ease traceability, verification, validation, and evaluation.
- The architecture should eliminate possibilities for violations.
- The architectural design should help ensure certification and accreditation of the operational system.

[14]Shaw, M., and Garlan, D., *Software Architecture: Perspectives on an Emerging Discipline*, Prentice Hall, Upper Saddle River, NJ, 1996.
[15]DHS, "Secure Software Assurance, A Guide to the Common Body of Knowledge to Produce, Acquire, and Sustain Secure Software," Draft Version 0.9, January 9, 2006.

- The design should avoid and work around any security-endangering weaknesses in the environment or development tools.
- The number of components to be trusted should be minimized.
- The system should be designed to do only what the specification calls for and nothing else.
- The system should be designed to tolerate security violations.
- The designer should make weak assumptions.
- The system should not cause security problems for other systems in the environment.

Software Development Methodologies

A number of software development life cycles (SDLCs) have been developed over the years to define the software development process and the life cycle of the resultant software. A typical SDLC comprises the following phases:

1. Requirements
2. Design
3. Implementation
4. Testing
5. Deployment
6. Operations/maintenance
7. Decommissioning

A number of the popular and effective software development methodologies are presented in the following sections.

Software Development Life Cycle Characteristics

One characterization of the software development life cycle process is by the "weight" of the process. A *heavyweight* process employs extensive reviews, evidence, and formal methods. Some elements of a heavyweight process that include software assurance are:

- Security policy
- Test specifications
- Formal specifications
- Formal design
- Coding
- Proof of formal design
- Proof of functional properties

- Static analysis
- Proof of consistency

A *lightweight* process is less restrictive and builds on elements of an extant software development process. The Trustworthy Security Development Life Cycle conceived by Microsoft is a good example of a lightweight process that will be discussed in following section. Examples of software development processes are:

- **Waterfall or linear sequential**—Assumes software development progresses in a linear sequence from one step to another without any backtracking or iteration.
- **Iterative and incremental**—Assumes software development is nonlinear and development might have to recycle to the previous step, if required.
- **Evolutionary or rapid prototyping**—Operates by developing prototypes that are tested and evaluated and then go back to continue the development process incorporating feedback obtained during the prototyping phase.
- **Spiral**—Depicts the software development process as a set of phases and decision points in a circular representation. The model illustrates the concept that software development undergoes a continuous circle of improvement and evolution until the improvement and evolution is no longer required.
- **Concurrent release or cascade model**—Performs iterative development cycles (sprints) and ensures schedules, objectives, quality, and competition issues are met.
- **Unified process**—Comprehensive processes that include items such as maintain business rules, find business actors and use cases, find business workers and entities, and define automation requirement (Rational Unified Process).
- **Agile**—Characterized by early and frequent delivery of workable and usable software, customer involvement in the development process, iterative development, acceptance of late requirements changes, employment of self-managing teams with appropriate expertise, and delivery of multiple releases.

Microsoft Trustworthy Security Development Life Cycle

In 2002, Microsoft developed the Trustworthy Security Development Life Cycle paradigm to increase the security of the resultant software. The objective of the process was to reduce the impact severity of problems in the code as well as minimizing the security-related design and coding "bugs" in the software.

An organization that employs the Microsoft SDL is expected to have a central security entity or team that performs the following functions:

- Develop security best practices
- Serve as a source of security expertise to the organization
- Conduct a final review of the completed software prior to its release
- Consult as needed with the software development organization as a whole

Microsoft Software Development Baseline Process

The basic software development process at Microsoft is a spiral approach in that the software requirements and design are reviewed and updated, if necessary, during the implementation phase. The phases of the Microsoft software development process are summarized as follows:

1. Requirements
   a. Schedules
   b. Quality guidelines
   c. Feature lists
   d. Architecture documentation
2. Design
   a. Functional specifications
   b. Design specifications
3. Implementation
   a. Development of new code
   b. Testing and verification
4. Verification
   a. Testing and verification
   b. Bug fixes
5. Release
   a. Code signing and signoff
   b. Release
6. Support and servicing
   a. Product support
   b. Service packs
   c. Quick Fix Engineering (QFE)
   d. Security updates

Microsoft Trustworthy Security Development Life Cycle (SDL) Principles and Model

The Microsoft SDL for software is based on the following set of principles expounded in the 2005 Microsoft document, "The Trustworthy Computing Security Development Lifecycle," by Lipner and Howard. The following summarizes the principles presented in the paper:

- **Secure by design**—The product should be specified, designed, and developed to safeguard against attacks.

- **Secure by default**—Recognizing that there will always be vulnerabilities in real-world software, software should be designed to default to a secure state when problems occur, such as reducing privileges or disabling infrequently used features. Secure by default attempts to minimize the software vulnerability exposure or *attack surface*, as it is sometimes called.
- **Secure in deployment**—Recommendations and guidance should be provided with software in the field to assist system administrators and users in deploying the software in the most secure fashion.
- **Communications**—Software developers should be cognizant of vulnerabilities discovered in the software and should readily communicate this information to users and system administrators along with appropriate patches and updates.

These principles are known as SD^3 + C.

Incorporating SD^3 + C into the basic software development life cycle yields the following spiral model as presented in the "The Trustworthy Computing Security Development Lifecycle":

1. Requirements
   a. Security kickoff and coordinate with central security team
   b. Consideration of security feature requirements
2. Design
   a. Review security design best practices
   b. Security architecture and attack surface review
   c. Threat modeling
3. Implementation
   a. Application of security development tools
   b. Application of security best development practices
   c. Application of security best test practices
   d. Creation of security documentation and product tools
   e. Application of static analysis tools
   f. Conduct of code reviews
4. Verification
   a. Preparation of security response plan
   b. Security push (additional security code reviews beyond those performed in the implementation phase)
   c. Penetration testing
5. Release
   a. Final security review (FSR)
   b. Release

6. Support and servicing
   a. Security servicing
   b. Evaluation of vulnerability reports
   c. Response execution

CLASP

The Comprehensive, Lightweight Application Security Process (CLASP) is an open source application of the Open Web Application Security Project (OWASP) that can be referenced at `www.owasp.org`.

> **CLASP ORIGINS**
>
> **CLASP was developed originally by Secure Software, Inc., with major contributions by John Viega and Pravir Chandra. Additional input was provided by Jerry Epstein and IBM. Secure Software was acquired by Fortify Software, Inc., in 2007, and in the transaction, Fortify Software obtained the rights to CLASP. Fortify Software then donated CLASP to the Open Web Application Security Project (OWASP). One of the valuable features of CLASP is that it defines roles that can affect the security of a software system and assigns activities to those roles.**

CLASP is designed to support the incorporation of information security processes into each phase of the software development life cycle. OWASP members include educational institutions, corporations, and security-conscious individuals. Its mission is to develop methodologies, technologies, and publications focusing on application security.

CLASP is based on the following seven key best practices for application security listed on the OWASP Web site:

- Institute awareness programs
- Perform application assessments
- Capture security requirements
- Implement secure development practices
- Build vulnerability remediation procedures
- Define and monitor metrics
- Publish operational security guidelines

In addition, CLASP defines 30 security activities, which are organized as discrete process components, and linked to one or more specific project roles. The CLASP security activities as listed on the OWASP Web site are presented as follows:

1. Institute security awareness program
2. Monitor security metrics integrator

3. Manage certification process
4. Specify operational environment
5. Identify global security policy
6. Identify user roles and requirements
7. Detail misuse cases
8. Perform security analysis of requirements
9. Document security design assumptions
10. Specify resource-based security properties
11. Apply security principles to design
12. Research and assess security solutions
13. Build information labeling scheme
14. Design UI for security functionality
15. Annotate class designs with security properties
16. Perform security functionality usability testing
17. Manage system security authorization agreement
18. Specify database security configuration
19. Perform security analysis of system design
20. Integrate security analysis into build process
21. Implement and elaborate resource policies
22. Implement interface contracts
23. Perform software security fault injection testing
24. Address reported security issues
25. Perform source-level security review
26. Identify and implement security tests
27. Verify security attributes of resources
28. Perform code signing
29. Build operational security guide
30. Manage security issue disclosure process

CLASP also provides a means to assist developers in avoiding specific design and code errors that might create vulnerabilities. This mechanism is the CLASP *Vulnerability Lexicon*, which provides a classification structure that enables development teams to find Lexicon vulnerability information acquired from different historical views and sources of data.

To provide guidelines for employing information assurance processes into the SDL, CLASP is structured into *views*, *resources*, and *vulnerability use cases*.

CLASP Views

This component of the CLASP methodology is organized in a hierarchical fashion with a view being the top level, activities being the second level, and process components being the third level. There are five CLASP views as presented on the OWASP Web site:

I. **Concepts view**—Develop understanding of the interaction among CLASP process components and the application of following views II through V.

II. **Role-based view**—Develop rules needed by the security-related project and apply these rules in views III through V.

III. **Activity-assessment view**—Evaluate 24 security-related CLASP activities for possible application in view IV.

IV. **Activity-implementation view**—Conduct subset of 24 security-related CLASP activities chosen in view III.

V. **Vulnerability view**—Incorporate solutions to problem types into activities III and IV.

CLASP Resources

CLASP resources, which are provided as part of the CLASP package and labeled alphabetically, provide references to objects that support automation tools for CLASP process elements. Table 1-6 identifies the resources, their alphabetical location reference, and the views they are designed to support.

Table 1-6: CLASP Resources and Supported Views

CLASP RESOURCES	LOCATION
Basic Principles in Application Security (all views)	Resource A
Example of Basic Principle: Input Validation (all views)	Resource B
Example of Basic-Principle Violation: Penetrate-and-Patch Model (all views)	Resource C
Core Security Services (all views, especially III)	Resource D
Sample Coding Guideline Worksheets (views II, III, and IV) * System Assessment Worksheets (views III and IV) *	Resource F
Sample Road Map: Legacy Projects (view III)	Resource G1
Sample Road Map: New-Start Projects (view III)	Resource G2
Creating the Process Engineering Plan (view III)	Resource H
Forming the Process Engineering Team (view III)	Resource I
Glossary of Security Terms (all views)	Resource J

From OWASP Web site, `www.owasp.org/index.php/CLASP_Concepts`

Vulnerability Use Cases

CLASP vulnerability use cases serve as a connection between the CLASP concepts view and the CLASP Vulnerability Lexicon of the vulnerability view. The vulnerability use cases provide examples of situations where security services such as those designed to protect confidentiality, availability, and integrity and to provide authorization and authentication are subject to exploitation because of vulnerabilities. The role of CLASP use cases in the overall CLASP SDL is shown in Figure 1-5.

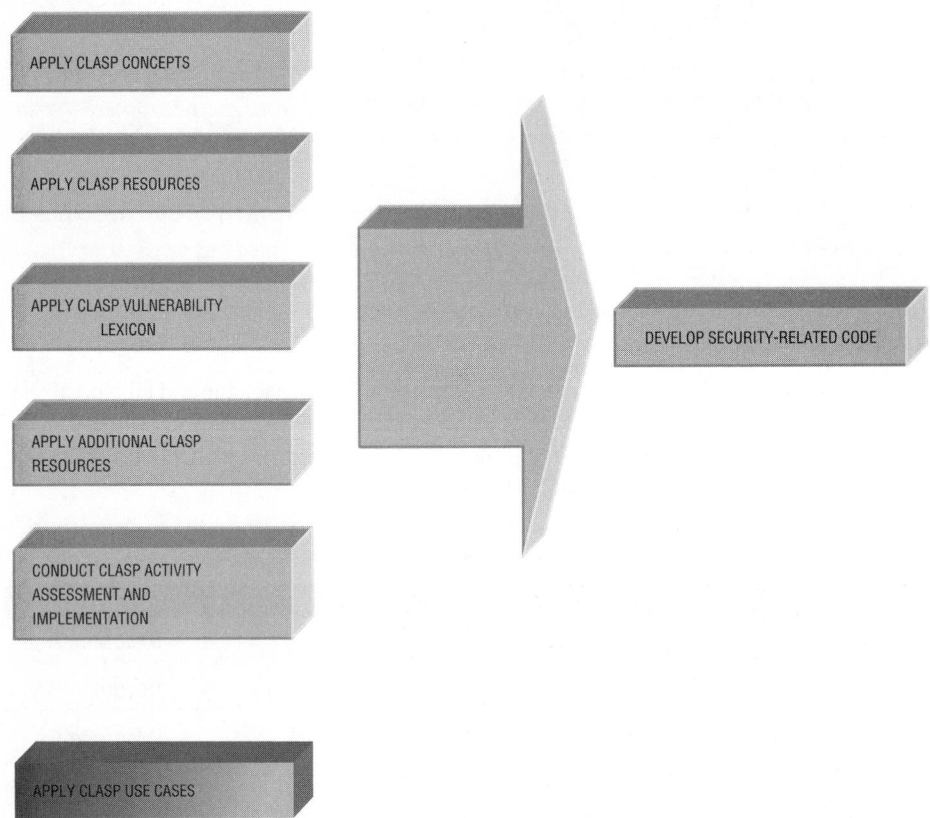

Figure 1-5: Use cases in the CLASP SDL
From OWASP Web site, `www.owasp.org/index.php/CLASP_Concepts`

Seven Touchpoints for Software Security

In addition to the 30 security activities defined in CLASP, Gary McGraw of Cigital developed seven additional security activities, which he called touchpoints.[16] These touchpoints are summarized in the following list:

1. Employ static analysis of source code

[16]McGraw, Gary, "The 7 Touchpoints of Secure Software," *Software Development*, September 2005.

2. Conduct risk analysis of architecture and design
3. Perform penetration testing
4. Perform security functionality testing and risk-based security testing
5. Categorize abuse cases by analyzing system behavior when the system is under attack
6. Specify security requirements for functional security and emergent security characteristics
7. Monitor post deployment security operational behavior

McGraw has since identified an additional touchpoint of having independent outside analysts conduct a review of the security of the software design and implementation.

TSP-Secure

The Carnegie Mellon University Software Engineering Institute (SEI) and CERT Coordination Center (CERT/CC) have developed a method designed to estimate the probability of vulnerabilities in production software and to minimize or eliminate software vulnerabilities. The approach is based on the SEI Team Software Process (TSP) and is called TSP-Secure. TSP-Secure purposely directs engineers through the development process and requires engineers and managers to institute and support a teamwork environment.

TSP-Secure provides the means to incorporate security practices in the SDLC through the following processes:

- Establishment of operational procedures, organizational policies, management oversight, resource allocation, training, and project planning and tracking, all in support of secure software production
- Vulnerability analysis by defect type
- Establishment of security-related predictive process metrics, checkpoints, and measurement
- Risk management and feedback, including asset identification, development of abuse/misuse cases, and threat modeling
- Secure design process that includes conformance to security design principles, use of design patterns for avoiding common vulnerabilities, and design security reviews
- Quality management for secure programming, including use of secure language subsets and coding standards, and code reviews using static and dynamic analysis tools
- Security review, inspection, and verification processes that include development of security test plans, white and black box testing, and test defect reviews/vulnerability analyses by defect type
- Removal of vulnerabilities from legacy software.

Intellectual Property and Privacy Legal Issues

Intellectual property is one of the most valuable assets of an organization. It is what distinguishes the organization from others in the field and provides a competitive advantage in the marketplace. As such, intellectual property must be protected from compromise. The means to protect intellectual property are varied and depend on the type of information that is to be safeguarded. The types of intellectual property law are summarized in the following section.

Intellectual Property Law

The following categories fall under intellectual property law:

Patent

A patent provides the owner of the patent with a legally enforceable *right to exclude* others from practicing the invention covered by the patent for a specified period of time. It is of interest to note that a patent does not necessarily grant the owner the right to make, use, or sell the invention. A patent obtained by an individual might build on other patents, and thus, the individual must obtain permission from the owner(s) of the earlier patent(s) to exploit the new patent.

There are four criteria that an invention must meet in order to be patentable. These criteria are:

- The invention must fall into one of the following five classes:
  - Processes
  - Machines
  - Manufactures (objects made by humans or machines)
  - Compositions of matter
  - New uses of any of the above
- The invention must be *useful*. One aspect of this test for utility is that the invention cannot be only a theoretical phenomenon.
- The invention must be *novel*; it must be something that no one has developed before.
- The invention must be *obvious* to "a person having ordinary skill in the art to which said subject matter pertains."

Patent law protects inventions and processes (utility patents), ornamental designs (design patents), and new varieties of plants (plant patents). In the United States, as of June 8, 1995, utility patents are granted for a period of 20 years from the date the application was filed. For patents in force prior to June 8, 1995, and patents granted on applications pending before that date, the patent term is the greater of 17 years from the date of issue (the term under prior law) or 20 years from the date of filing. Design patents are granted for a period of 14 years and a plant patent has a term of 17 years.

Once the patent on an invention or design has expired, anyone is free to make, use, or sell the invention or design.

Copyright

A copyright protects "original works of authorship" and protects the right of the author to control the reproduction, adaptation, public distribution, and performance of these original works. Copyrights can also be applied to software and databases. The copyright law has two provisions that address uses of copyrighted material by educators, researchers, and librarians. These provisions:

- Codify the doctrine of fair use, under which limited copying of copyrighted works without the permission of the owner is allowed for certain teaching and research purposes
- Establish special limitations and exemptions for the reproduction of copyrighted works by libraries and archives

The Sonny Bono Copyright Term Extension Act, signed into law on October 27, 1998, amends the provisions concerning duration of copyright protection. The act states that the terms of copyright are generally extended for an additional 20 years. Two specific example provisions of the Sonny Bono Copyright Term Extension Act are as follows:

- Works originally created on or after January 1, 1978, are protected from the time of their creation and are usually given a term of the author's life plus an additional 70 years after the author's death.
- Works originally created before January 1, 1978, but not published or registered by that date are covered by the statute, also with a duration of the author's life plus an additional 70 years after the author's death. In addition, the statute provides that in no case will the term of copyright for these types of works expire before December 31, 2002. For works published on or before December 31, 2002, the term of copyright will not expire before December 31, 2047.

Materials might fall into other copyright categories depending on the age of the work, if the copyright was renewed, if it was developed as work for hire, and so on. Detailed information can be found in the following publications of the U.S. Copyright Office:

- Circular 15, "Renewal of Copyright"
- Circular 15a, "Duration of Copyright"
- Circular 15t, "Extension of Copyright Terms"

Trade Secret

A trade secret secures and maintains the confidentiality of proprietary technical or business-related information that is adequately protected from disclosure by the owner. Corollaries to this definition are that the owner has invested resources to develop this information, it is valuable to the business of the owner, it would be valuable to a competitor, and it is not obvious.

Trademark

A trademark establishes a word, name, symbol, color, sound, product shape, device, or combination of these that will be used to identify goods and to distinguish them from those made or sold by others.

Warranty

A warranty is a contract that commits an organization to stand behind its product. There are two types of warranties, implied and express. An *implied* warranty is an unspoken, unwritten promise created by state law that goes from a manufacturer or merchant to the customer. Under implied warranties, there are two categories—the implied warranty of fitness for a particular purpose and the implied warranty of merchantability. The implied warranty of *fitness for a particular purpose* is a commitment made by the seller when the consumer relies on the advice of the seller that the product is suited for a specific purpose. The implied *warranty of merchantability* is the seller's or manufacturer's promise that the product sold to the consumer is fit to be sold and will perform the functions that it is intended to perform. An *express* warranty is a warranty that is explicitly offered by the manufacturer or seller to the customer at the time of the sales transaction. This type of warranty contains voluntary commitments to remedy defects and malfunctions that some customers may encounter in using the product. An express warranty can be made orally or in writing. If it is in writing, it falls under the Magnuson-Moss Warranty Act.

The Magnuson-Moss Warranty Act is the 1975 U.S. federal law that governs warranties on consumer products. The Act requires manufacturers and sellers of consumer products to provide consumers with detailed information concerning warranty coverage. In addition, the FTC adopted three rules under the Act. These rules are the *Rule on Disclosure of Written Consumer Product Warranty Terms and Conditions* (the *Disclosure Rule*), the *Rule on Pre-Sale Availability of Written Warranty Terms* (the *Pre-Sale Availability Rule*), and the *Rule on Informal Dispute Settlement Procedures* (the *Dispute Resolution Rule*.) These rules and the act detail three basic requirements that apply to a warrantor or seller. These requirements are:

1. A warrantor must designate, or title, the written warranty as either *full* or *limited*.
2. A warrantor must state certain specified information about the coverage of the warranty in a single, clear, and easy-to-read document.
3. The warrantor or seller must ensure that warranties are available at the site of sale of the warranted consumer products so that consumers can read them before purchasing a product.

Regarding used products, an implied warranty can be disclaimed if a written warranty is not provided. This disclaimer must be made in a conspicuous manner, preferably in writing, so that the consumer is aware that there is no warranty on the product. Terms such as "this product is being sold with all faults" or "as is" should be used. Some states do not permit disclaiming of the implied warranty."

Information Privacy Principles

Privacy is the right of an individual to protection from unauthorized disclosure of the individual's personally identifiable information (PII).

As stated earlier in this chapter, an individual's right to privacy is embodied in the following fundamental principles of privacy:

- **Notice**—Regarding collection, use and disclosure of PII
- **Choice**—To opt out or opt in regarding disclosure of PII to third parties
- **Access**—By consumers to their PII to permit review and correction of information
- **Security**—To protect PII from unauthorized disclosure
- **Enforcement**—Of applicable privacy policies and obligations

The European Union has established privacy principles that serve as guidelines for a number of privacy policies. These principles are reviewed in the next section.

European Union (EU) Principles

The protection of information on private individuals from intentional or unintentional disclosure or misuse is the goal of the information privacy laws. The intent and scope of these laws vary widely from country to country. The European Union (EU) has defined privacy principles that in general are more protective of individual privacy than those applied in the United States. Therefore, the transfer of personal information from the EU to the United States, when equivalent personal protections are not in place in the United States, is prohibited. The EU principles include the following:

- Data should be collected in accordance with the law.
- Information collected about an individual cannot be disclosed to other organizations or individuals unless authorized by law or by consent of the individual.
- Records kept on an individual should be accurate and up to date.
- Individuals have the right to correct errors contained in their personal data.
- Data should be used only for the purposes for which it was collected, and it should be used only for a reasonable period of time.
- Individuals are entitled to receive a report on the information that is held about them.
- Transmission of personal information to locations where equivalent personal data protection cannot be assured is prohibited.

Health Care–Related Privacy Issues

An excellent example of the requirements and application of individual privacy principles is in the area of health care. The protection from disclosure and misuse of a private individual's medical information is a prime example of a privacy law. Some of the common health care security issues are as follows:

- Access controls of most health care information systems do not provide sufficient granularity to implement the principle of least privilege among users.
- Most off-the-shelf applications do not incorporate adequate information security controls.
- Systems must be accessible to outside partners, members, and some vendors.
- Providing users with the necessary access to the Internet creates the potential for enabling violations of the privacy and integrity of information.
- Criminal and civil penalties can be imposed for the improper disclosure of medical information.
- A large organization's misuse of medical information can cause the public to change its perception of the organization.
- Health care organizations should adhere to the following information privacy principles (based on European Union principles):
    - An individual should have the means to monitor the database of stored information about him or her and should have the ability to change or correct that information.
    - Information obtained for one purpose should not be used for another purpose.
    - Organizations collecting information about individuals should ensure that the information is provided only for its intended use and should provide safeguards against the misuse of this information.
    - The existence of databases containing personal information should not be kept secret.

Platform for Privacy Preferences (P3P)

The Platform for Privacy Preferences was developed by the World Wide Web Consortium (W3C) to implement privacy practices on Web sites. The W3C P3P specification states, "P3P enables Web sites to express their privacy practices in a standard format that can be retrieved automatically and interpreted easily by user agents. P3P user agents will allow users to be informed of site practices (in both machine- and human-readable formats) and to automate decision-making based on these practices when appropriate. Thus users need not read the privacy policies at every site they visit."

The W3C P3P document can be found at `www.w3.org/TR/P3P/`. With P3P, an organization can post its privacy policy in machine-readable form (XML) on its Web site. This policy statement should include:

- Who has access to collected information
- The type of information collected

- How the information is used
- The legal entity making the privacy statement

The P3P specification contains the following items:

- A standard vocabulary for describing a Web site's data practices
- A set of data elements that Web sites can refer to in their P3P privacy policies
- A standard schema for data a Web site may wish to collect, known as the ''P3P base data schema''
- A standard set of uses, recipients, data categories, and other privacy disclosures
- An XML format for expressing a privacy policy
- A means of associating privacy policies with Web pages or sites and cookies
- A mechanism for transporting P3P policies over HTTP

A useful consequence of implementing P3P on a Web site is that Web site owners are required to answer multiple-choice questions about their privacy practices. This activity will cause the organization sponsoring the Web site to think about and evaluate their privacy policy and practices in the event that they have not already done so. After answering the necessary P3P privacy questions, an organization can then proceed to develop their policy. A number of sources provide free policy editors and assistance in writing privacy policies. Some of these resources can be found at `www.w3.org/P3P/` and `http://p3ptoolbox.org/`.

P3P also supports user agents that allow a user to configure a P3P-enabled Web browser with the user's privacy preferences. Then, when the user attempts to access a Web site, the user agent compares the user's stated preferences with the privacy policy in machine-readable form at the Web site. Access will be granted if the preferences match the policy. Otherwise, either access to the Web site will be blocked or a pop-up window will appear notifying the user that he or she must change the privacy preferences.

Standards and Guidelines

Two of the most popular standards and guidelines for information and software assurance are the International Organization for Standardization (ISO) 27000 series and the Open Web Application Security Project (OWASP) guidelines outlining the ''top ten'' Web application security vulnerabilities.

ISO 27000 Series

The ISO series 27000 (2700X) standards are dedicated to the field of information system security. The relevant standards are ISO 27001, 27002, 27003, 27004, 27005, and 27006, which are summarized in the following sections.

ISO 27001

The British Standards Institution (BSI) 7799-2 standard was the predecessor and basis for ISO 27001, which is the specification for an information security management system (ISMS). According to ISO, the standard is designed to "provide a model for establishing, implementing, operating, monitoring, reviewing, maintaining, and improving an Information Security Management System."

ISO 27001 comprises the following topics:

- Management responsibility
- Internal audits
- ISMS improvement
- Annex A—Control objectives and controls
- Annex B—Organization for Economic Cooperation and Development (OECD) principles and this international standard
- Annex C—Correspondence between ISO 9001, ISO 14001, and this standard

ISO 27001 emphasizes developing an ISMS through an iterative plan-do-check-act (PDCA) cycle. The activities in each cycle component are summarized from the 27001 document as follows:

1. Plan
   - Establish scope
   - Develop a comprehensive ISMS policy
   - Conduct risk assessment
   - Develop a risk treatment plan
   - Determine control objectives and controls
   - Develop a statement of applicability describing and justifying why the specific controls were selected and others not selected
2. Do
   - Operate selected controls
   - Detect and respond to incidents properly
   - Conduct security awareness training
   - Manage resources required to accomplish security tasks
3. Check
   - Intrusion detection operations
   - Incident handling operations
   - Conduct internal ISMS audit
   - Conduct a management review

4. Act
   - Implement improvements to the ISMS in response to items identified in Check phase
   - Take corrective actions in response to items identified in Check phase
   - Take preventive actions in response to items identified in Check phase

ISO 27002

ISO 27002, the "Code of Practice for Information Security Management," is a repackaged version of (ISO) 17779:2005. It is designed to serve as a single source for best practices in the field of information security and presents a range of controls applicable to most situations. It provides high level, voluntary guidance for information security management.

ISO 27002 presents requirements for building, maintaining, and documenting ISMSs. As such, it lists recommendations for establishing an efficient information security management framework. ISO 27002 is also used as the basis of a certification assessment of an organization. It lists a variety of control measures that can be implemented according to practices outlined in ISO 27001. The areas covered in ISO 27002 are:

- Structure
- Risk assessment and treatment
- Security policy
- Organization of information security
- Asset management
- Human resources security
- Physical security
- Communications and operations management
- Access control
- Information systems acquisition, development, maintenance
- Information security incident management
- Business continuity
- Compliance

ISO 27003

ISO 27003, "Information Technology – Security Techniques – Information Security Management System Implementation Guidance," is in draft form as of this writing and uses the PDCA paradigm to provide recommendations and guidance in developing an ISMS.

The draft table of contents is as follows:

1. Introduction
2. Scope
3. Terms and Definitions
4. CSFs (Critical Success Factors)
5. Guidance on Process Approach
6. Guidance on Using PDCA
7. Guidance on Plan Processes
8. Guidance on Do Processes
9. Guidance on Check Processes
10. Guidance on Act Processes
11. Inter-Organization Co-operation

ISO 27004

ISO 27004, ''Information Technology – Security Techniques – Information Security Management – Measurement,'' is in second final committee draft form as of this writing. According to ISO, the standard ''provides guidance on the specification and use of measurement techniques for providing assurance as regards the effectiveness of information security management systems. It is intended to be applicable to a wide range of organizations with a correspondingly wide range of information security management systems.''

ISO 27005

ISO 27005:2008, ''Information Technology – Security Techniques – Information Security Risk Management,'' provides guidelines for information security risk management (ISRM) according to the requirements outlined in ISO 27001.

The main headings of ISO 27005 are:

- Terms and Definitions
- Structure
- Background
- Overview of the ISRM Process
- Context Establishment
- Information Security Risk Assessment (ISRA)

- Information Security Risk Treatment
- Information security Risk Acceptance

ISO 27006

ISO 27006, ''Information Technology – Security Techniques –Requirements for Bodies Providing Audit and Certification of Information Security Management Systems,'' provides guidelines for the accreditation of organizations that are concerned with certification and registration relating to ISMSs.

The main elements covered in the standard document are:

- Scope
- References
- Terms
- Principles
- General requirements
- Structural requirements
- Resource requirements
- Information requirements
- Process requirements
- Management system requirements
- Information security risk communication
- Information security risk monitoring and review
- Annex A: Defining the scope of the process
- Annex B: Asset valuation and impact assessment
- Annex C: Examples of typical threats
- Annex D: Vulnerabilities and vulnerability assessment methods
- Annex E: Information security risk assessment (ISRA) approaches

OWASP Top Ten Project

The Open Web Application Security Project (OWASP) Top Ten Project provides a minimum standard for Web application security. It summarizes the top ten Web application security vulnerabilities based on input from a variety of information system security experts. The results provide guidance to standards that can be used to address these security weaknesses. The Top Ten vulnerabilities are summarized in Table 1-7.

Table 1-7: Summary of OWASP Top Ten Web Application Vulnerabilities

A1—Cross Site Scripting (XSS)
A2—Injection Flaws
A3—Malicious File Execution
A4—Insecure Direct Object Reference
A5—Cross Site Request Forgery (CSRF)
A6—Information Leakage and Improper Error Handling
A7—Broken Authentication and Session Management
A8—Insecure Cryptographic Storage
A9—Insecure Communications
A10—Failure to Restrict URL Access

From OWASP Top Ten 2007 Web site, `www.owasp.org/index.php/Top_10_2007`

OWASP Development Guide

Another document that addresses application security is the OWASP Development Guide, version 3.0, which focuses on Web application security. The guide describes how to make Web applications self-defending. The chapters in the guide are organized into the following three sections:

- **Best practices**—Key features that should be included in applications
- **Secure patterns**—Optional security patterns that can be used as guides
- **Anti-patterns**—Patterns in code that increase vulnerability

Some of the topics addressed by the guide include:

- Secure coding principles
- Threat risk modeling
- Phishing
- Ajax and other "rich" interface technologies
- Session management
- Data validation
- Error handling, auditing, and logging
- Distributed computing
- Buffer overflows

- Cryptography
- Software quality assurance

OWASP Code Review Guide

The OWASP Code Review Guide defines secure code review as "the process of auditing code for an application on a line by line basis for its security quality. Code review is a way of ensuring that the application is developed in an appropriate fashion so as to be self defending in its given environment (`www.owasp.org/index.php/Category:OWASP_Code_Review_Project`)." Review code for security is usually a manual effort, although some tools have been developed to assist in the process.

Secure code review comprises the following phases, according to the OWASP Code Review Guide:

- Discovery
- Transactional analysis
- Post-transaction analysis
- Procedure peer review
- Reporting and presentation
- Laying the groundwork

In secure code review, the important items that have to be considered are:

- **Code**—The language and associated features used
- **Context**—Knowledge of the application
- **Audience**—The users of the application
- **Importance**—Criticality of the availability of the application

The OWASP Code Review Guide has also identified the following "top nine" source code flaw categories:

- Input validation
- Source code design
- Information leakage and improper error handling
- Direct object reference
- Resource usage
- API usage
- Best practices violation
- Weak session management
- Using `HTTP GET` query strings

NIST SP 800-95

NIST Special Publication 800-95, "Guide to Secure Web Services," provides guidance on security Web services. It address the following issues:

- **Functional integrity of Web services during transactions**
- **Confidentiality and integrity of data transmitted during Web services protocols**
- **Availability in the event of attacks, such as denial of service**

The security techniques covered in NIST SP 800-35 are:

- **Confidentiality of Web services messages using XML Encryption**
- **Integrity of Web services messages using XML Signature**
- **Web service authentication and authorization using XML Signature**
- **Web Services (WS) Security**
- **Security for Universal Description, Discovery, and Integration (UDDI)**

NIST SP 800-95 recommends that organizations consider the following security actions where applicable:

- **Replicate data and services to improve availability**
- **Use logging of transactions to improve nonrepudiation and accountability**
- **Use threat modeling and secure software design techniques to protect from attacks**
- **Use performance analysis and simulation techniques for end-to-end quality of service and quality of protection**
- **Digitally sign UDDI entries to verify the author of registered entries**
- **Enhance existing security mechanisms and infrastructure**

OWASP Testing Guide

The OWASP Testing Guide 2008, V3.0 (`www.owasp.org/index.php/Category:OWASP_Testing_Project`) defines testing as "a process of comparing the state of a system/application against a set of criteria." The testing techniques described in the guide are:

- Manual inspections and reviews
- Threat modeling
- Code review
- Penetration testing

Testing is used to determine if security controls are functioning as desired, validate security requirements, and determine threats and the root causes of vulnerabilities.

Common security tests that should be performed to evaluate security controls include:

- Authentication and access control
- Input validation and encoding
- Encryption
- User and session management
- Error and exception handling
- Auditing and logging

Information Security Models

Models are used in information security to formalize security policies. These models might be abstract or intuitive and will provide a framework for the understanding of fundamental concepts. In this section, three types of models are described: access control models, integrity models, and information flow models.

Access Control Models

Access control philosophies can be organized into models that define the major and different approaches to this issue. These models are the access matrix, the Take-Grant model, the Bell-LaPadula confidentiality model, and the state machine model.

Access Matrix

The *access matrix* or *access control matrix* is a straightforward approach that provides access rights to subjects for objects.

- *Access rights* are of the type read, write, and execute
- A *subject* is an active entity that is seeking rights to a resource or object. A subject can be a person, a program, or a process.
- An *object* is a passive entity, such as a file or a storage resource.

In some cases, an item can be a subject in one context and an object in another. A typical access control matrix is shown in Figure 1-6.

The columns of the access matrix are called *access control lists* (ACLs), and the rows are called *capability lists*. The access matrix model supports discretionary access control because the entries in the matrix are at the discretion of the individual(s) who have the authorization authority over the matrix. In the access control matrix, a subject's capability can be defined by the *triple* (object, rights, and random #). Thus, the triple defines the rights that a subject has to an object along with a random number used to prevent a replay or spoofing of the triple's source.

Subject \ Object	File Object	File Salaries	Process Deductions	Print Server A
Joe	Read	Read/Write	Execute	Write
Jane	Read/Write	Read	None	Write
Process Check	Read	Read	Execute	None
Process Tax	Read/Write	Read/Write	Call	Write

Figure 1-6: Access control matrix

Take-Grant Model

The Take-Grant model uses a directed graph to specify the rights that a subject can transfer to an object or that a subject can take from another subject. For example, assume that Subject A has a set of rights (S) that includes Grant rights to Object B. This capability is represented in Figure 1-7a. Then assume that Subject A can transfer Grant rights to Subject C and that Subject A has another set of rights (Y) to Object D. In some cases, Object D acts as an object, and in other cases, it acts as a subject. Then, as shown by the heavy arrow in Figure 1-7b, Subject C can grant a subset of the Y rights to Subject/Object D because Subject A passed the Grant rights to Subject C.

The Take capability operates in an identical fashion as the Grant illustration.

Bell-LaPadula Model

The Bell-LaPadula model was developed to formalize the U.S. Department of Defense (DoD) multi-level security policy. The DoD labels materials at various levels of security classification. These levels are Unclassified, Confidential, Secret, and Top Secret—ordered from least sensitive to most sensitive. An individual who receives a clearance of Confidential, Secret, or Top Secret can access materials at that level of classification or below. An additional stipulation, however, is that the individual must have a need-to-know for that material. Thus, an individual cleared for Secret can access only the Secret-labeled documents that are necessary for that individual to perform an assigned job function. The Bell-LaPadula model deals *only with the confidentiality* of classified material. It does not address integrity or availability.

The Bell-LaPadula model is built on the *state machine* concept. This concept defines a set of allowable states (A_i) in a system. The transition from one state to another upon receipt of input(s) (X_j) is defined by transition functions (f_k). The objective of this model is to ensure that the initial state is secure and that the transitions always result in a secure state. The transitions between two states are illustrated in Figure 1-8.

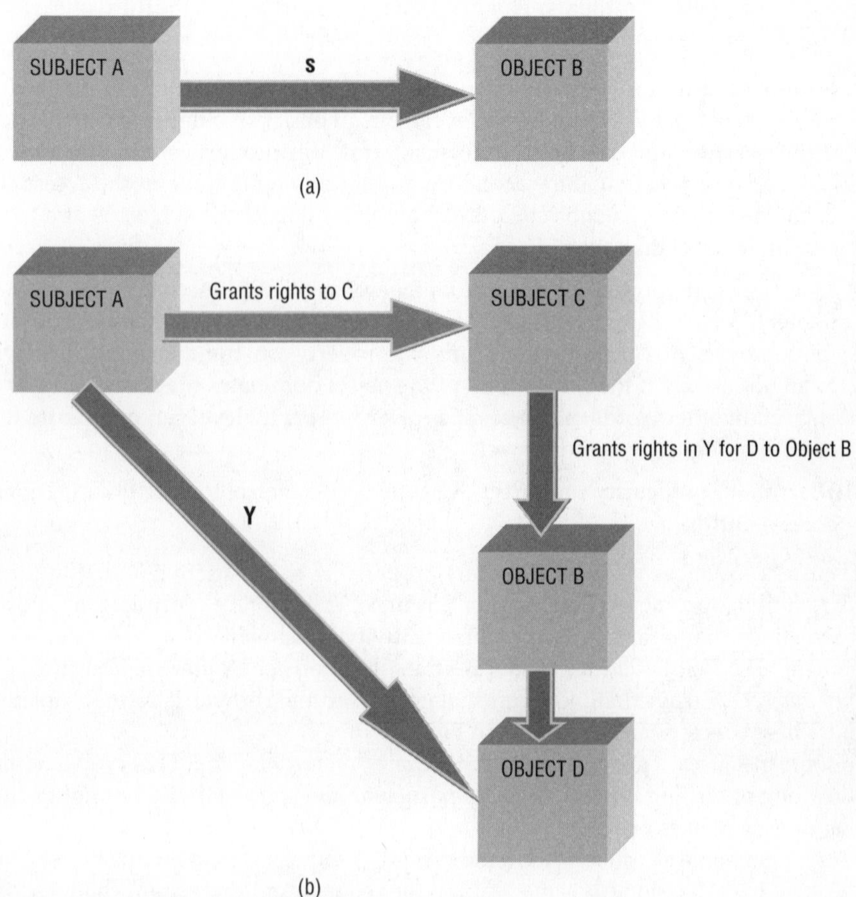

Figure 1-7: Take-Grant model illustration

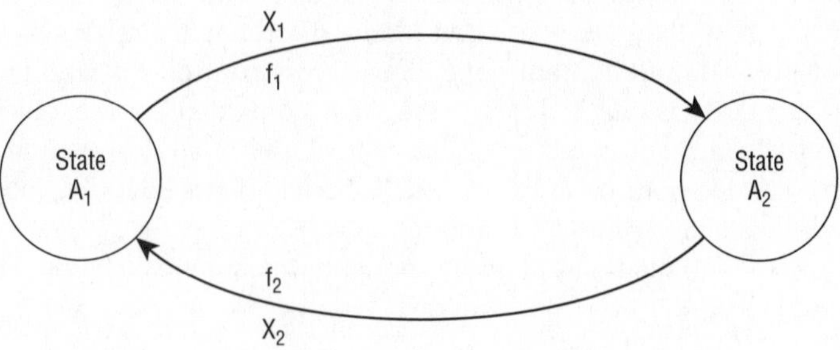

Figure 1-8: State transitions defined by the function f with an input X

The Bell-LaPadula model defines a *secure state* through three multi-level properties. The first two properties implement mandatory access control, and the third one permits discretionary access control. These properties are defined as follows:

- **Simple security property (ss property)**—States that the reading of information by a subject at a lower sensitivity level from an object at a higher sensitivity level is not permitted (no read-up). In formal terms, this property states that a subject can read an object only if the access class of the subject dominates the access class of the object. Thus, a subject can read an object only if the subject is at a higher sensitivity level than the object.
- *** (star) security property**—States that the writing of information by a subject at a higher level of sensitivity to an object at a lower level of sensitivity is not permitted (no write-down). Formally stated, under * property constraints, a subject can write to an object only if the access class of the object dominates the access class of the subject. In other words, a subject at a lower sensitivity level can only write to an object at a higher sensitivity level.
- **Discretionary security property**—Uses an access matrix to specify discretionary access control

There are instances where the * (star) property is too restrictive and it interferes with required document changes. For instance, it might be desirable to move a low-sensitivity paragraph in a higher-sensitivity document to a lower-sensitivity document. The Bell-LaPadula model permits this transfer of information through a *trusted subject*. A trusted subject can violate the * property, yet it cannot violate its intent. These concepts are illustrated in Figure 1-9.

In some instances, a property called the *strong * property* is cited. This property states that reading or writing is permitted at a particular level of sensitivity but not to either higher or lower levels of sensitivity.

This model defines requests (R) to the system. A request is made while the system is in the state v1; a decision (d) is made upon the request, and the system changes to the state v2. (R, d, v1, v2) represents this tuple in the model. Again, the intent of this model is to ensure that there is a transition from one secure state to another secure state.

The discretionary portion of the Bell-LaPadula model is based on the access matrix. The system security policy defines who is authorized to have certain privileges to the system resources. *Authorization* is concerned with how access rights are defined and how they are evaluated. Some discretionary approaches are based on context-dependent and content-dependent access control. *Content-dependent* control makes access decisions based on the data contained in the object, whereas *context-dependent* control uses subject or object attributes or environmental characteristics to make these decisions. Examples of such characteristics include a job role, earlier accesses, and file creation dates and times.

As with any model, the Bell-LaPadula model has some weaknesses. These are the major ones:

- The model considers normal channels of the information exchange and does not address covert channels.

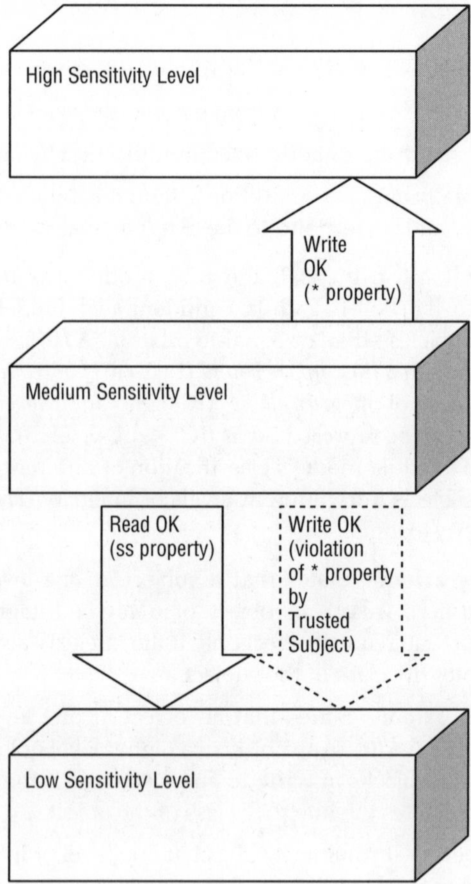

Figure 1-9: The Bell-LaPadula simple security and * properties

- The model does not deal with modern systems that use file sharing and servers.
- The model does not explicitly define what it means by a secure state transition.
- The model is based on a multi-level security policy and does not address other policy types that might be used by an organization.

Integrity Models

In many organizations, both governmental and commercial, the integrity of the data is as important or more important than confidentiality for certain applications. Thus, formal integrity models evolved. Initially, the integrity model was developed as an analog to the Bell-LaPadula confidentiality model and then became more sophisticated to address additional integrity requirements.

Biba Integrity Model

Integrity is usually characterized by the three following goals:

- The data is protected from modification by unauthorized users.
- The data is protected from unauthorized modification by authorized users.
- The data is internally and externally consistent; the data held in a database must balance internally and correspond to the external, real-world situation.

To address the first integrity goal, the Biba model was developed in 1977 as an integrity analog to the Bell-LaPadula confidentiality model. The Biba model is lattice-based and uses the less-than or equal-to relation. A *lattice structure* is defined as a partially ordered set with a *least upper bound* (LUB) and a *greatest lower bound* (GLB). The lattice represents a set of *integrity classes* (ICs) and an ordered relationship among those classes. A lattice can be represented as (IC, ≤, LUB, GUB).

Similar to the Bell-LaPadula model's classification of different sensitivity levels, the Biba model classifies objects into different levels of integrity. The model specifies the three following integrity axioms:

- **Simple integrity axiom**—States that a subject at one level of integrity is not permitted to observe (read) an object of a lower integrity (no read-down). Formally, a subject can read an object only if the integrity access class of the object dominates the integrity class of the subject.
- *** (star) integrity axiom**—States that an object at one level of integrity is not permitted to modify (write to) an object of a higher level of integrity (no write-up). In formal terms, a subject can write to an object only if the integrity access class of the subject dominates the integrity class of the object.
- **Invocation property**—Prohibits a subject at one level of integrity from invoking a subject at a higher level of integrity. This property prevents a subject at one level of integrity from invoking a utility such as a piece of software that is at a higher level of integrity. If this invocation were possible, the software at the higher level of integrity could be used to access data at that higher level.

These axioms and their relationships are illustrated in Figure 1-10.

Clark-Wilson Model

The approach of the Clark-Wilson model (1987) was to develop a framework for use in the real-world, commercial environment. This model addresses the three integrity goals and defines the following terms:

- **Constrained data item (CDI)**—A data item whose integrity is to be preserved
- **Integrity verification procedure (IVP)**—Confirms that all CDIs are in valid states of integrity
- **Transformation procedure (TP)**—Manipulates the CDIs through *a well-formed transaction*, which transforms a CDI from one valid integrity state to another valid integrity state

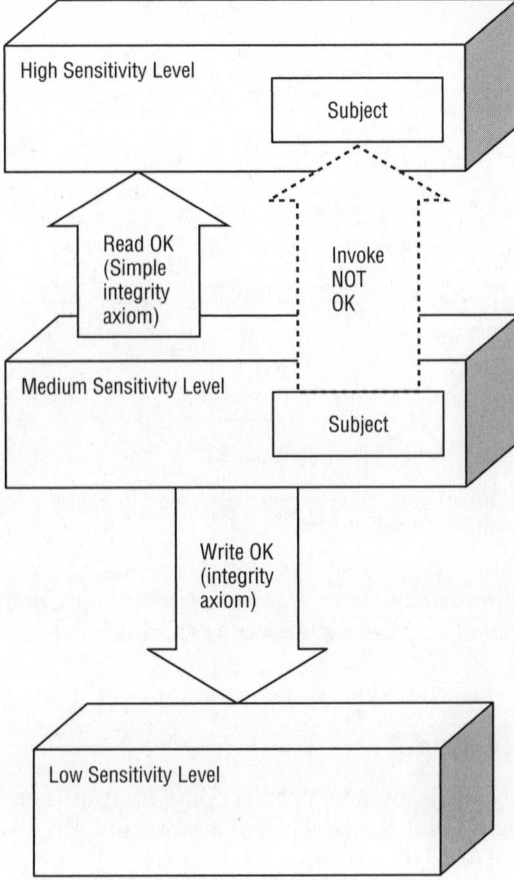

Figure 1-10: The Biba integrity model

- **Unconstrained data item**—Data items outside the control area of the modeled environment, such as input information

The Clark-Wilson model requires integrity labels to determine the integrity level of a data item and to verify that this integrity was maintained after an application of a TP. This model incorporates mechanisms to enforce internal and external consistency, a separation of duty, and a mandatory integrity policy.

Information Flow Models

An information flow model is based on a state machine, and it consists of objects, state transitions, and lattice (flow policy) states. In this context, objects can also represent users. Each object is assigned a security class and value, and information is constrained to flow in the directions that are permitted by the security policy. An example is shown in Figure 1-11.

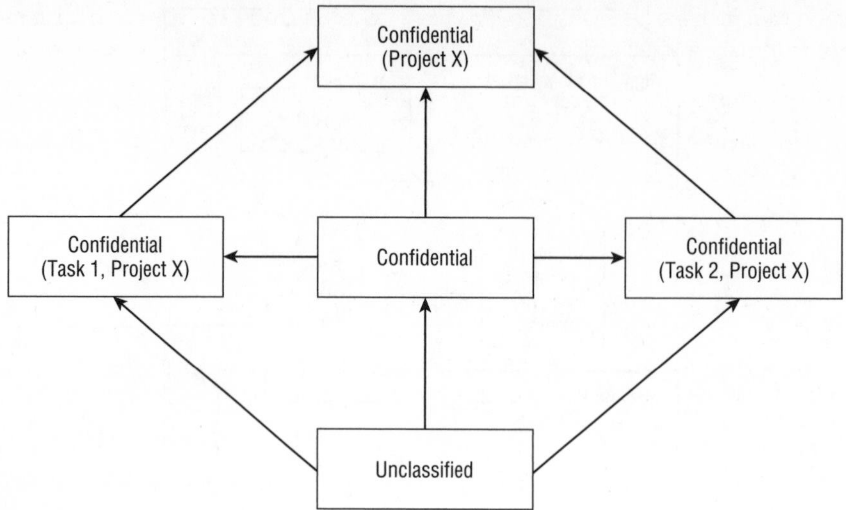

Figure 1-11: An information flow model

In Figure 1-11, information flows from Unclassified to Confidential in tasks in Project X and to the combined tasks in Project X. This information can flow in only one direction.

Non-interference Model

This model is related to the information flow model with restrictions on the information flow. The basic principle of this model is that a group of users (A) who are using the commands (C) do not interfere with the user group (B) who are using commands (D). This concept is written as A, C:| B, D. Restating this rule, the actions of Group A who are using commands C are not seen by users in Group B using commands D.

Chinese Wall Model

The Chinese Wall model, developed by Brewer and Nash, is designed to prevent information flow that might result in a conflict of interest in an organization representing competing clients. For example, in a consulting organization, analyst Joe might be performing work for the Ajax corporation involving sensitive Ajax data while analyst Bill is consulting for a competitor, the Beta corporation. The principle of the Chinese Wall is to prevent compromise of the sensitive data of either or both firms because of weak access controls in the consulting organization.

Composition Theories

In most applications, systems are built by combining smaller systems. An interesting situation to consider is whether the security properties of component systems are maintained when they are combined to form a larger entity.

John McClean studied this issue in 1994.[17] He defined two compositional constructions: external and internal. The following are the types of external constructs:

- **Cascading**—One system's input is obtained from the output of another system.
- **Feedback**—One system provides the input to a second system, which in turn feeds back to the input of the first system.
- **Hookup**—One system communicates with another system as well as with external entities.

The internal composition constructs are intersection, union, and difference.

The general conclusion of this study was that the security properties of the small systems were maintained under composition (in most instances) in the cascading construct, yet are also subject to other system variables for the other constructs.

Systems Security Engineering Capability Maturity Model (SSE-CMM)

The Systems Security Engineering Capability Maturity Model (SSE-CMM[18]; copyright © 1999 by the Systems Security Engineering Capability Maturity Model [SSE-CMM] Project) is based on the premise that if you can guarantee the quality of the processes that are used by an organization, then you can guarantee the quality of the products and services generated by those processes. It was developed by a consortium of government and industry experts and is now under the auspices of the International Systems Security Engineering Association (ISSEA) at `www.issea.org`. The SSE-CMM has the following salient points:

- Describes those characteristics of security engineering processes essential to ensure good security engineering
- Captures the industry's best practices
- Presents an accepted way of defining practices and improving capability
- Provides measures of growth in capability of applying processes

The SSE-CMM addresses the following areas of security:

- Operations security
- Information security
- Network security
- Physical security
- Personnel security
- Administrative security

[17]McLean, J. "A General Theory of Composition for Trace Sets Closed Under Selective Interleaving Functions," *Proceedings of 1994 IEEE Symposium on Research in Security and Privacy*, IEEE Press, 1994.

[18]"The Systems Security Engineering Capability Maturity Model v3.0," 2003.

- Communications security
- Emanations security
- Computer security

The SSE-CMM methodology and metrics provide a reference for comparing existing systems' security engineering best practices against the essential systems security engineering elements described in the model. It defines two dimensions that are used to measure the capability of an organization to perform specific activities. These dimensions are domain and capability.

- The domain dimension consists of all the practices that collectively define security engineering. These practices are called base practices (BPs). Related BPs are grouped into process areas (PAs).
- The capability dimension represents practices that indicate process management and institutionalization capability. These practices are called generic practices (GPs) because they apply across a wide range of domains. The GPs represent activities that should be performed as part of performing BPs.

For the domain dimension, the SSE-CMM specifies 11 security engineering PAs and 11 organizational and project-related PAs, each consisting of BPs. BPs are mandatory characteristics that must exist within an implemented security engineering process before an organization can claim satisfaction in a given PA. The 22 PAs and their corresponding BPs incorporate the best practices of systems security engineering. The PAs are as follows:

- Security Engineering
  - PA01—Administer Security Controls
  - PA02—Assess Impact
  - PA03—Assess Security Risk
  - PA04—Assess Threat
  - PA05—Assess Vulnerability
  - PA06—Build Assurance Argument
  - PA07—Coordinate Security
  - PA08—Monitor Security Posture
  - PA09—Provide Security Input
  - PA10—Specify Security Needs
  - PA11—Verify and Validate Security
- Project and Organizational Practices
  - PA12—Ensure Quality
  - PA13—Manage Configuration
  - PA14—Manage Project Risk
  - PA15—Monitor and Control Technical Effort
  - PA16—Plan Technical Effort

- PA17—Define Organization's Systems Engineering Process
- PA18—Improve Organization's Systems Engineering Process
- PA19—Manage Product Line Evolution
- PA20—Manage Systems Engineering Support Environment
- PA21—Provide Ongoing Skills and Knowledge
- PA22—Coordinate with Suppliers

The GPs are ordered in degrees of maturity and are grouped to form and distinguish among five levels of security engineering maturity. The attributes of these five levels as given in the SSE-CMM model document are as follows:

- Level 1

  1.1 BPs Are Performed
- Level 2

  2.1 Planning Performance

  2.2 Disciplined Performance

  2.3 Verifying Performance

  2.4 Tracking Performance
- Level 3

  3.1 Defining a Standard Process

  3.2 Perform the Defined Process

  3.3 Coordinate the Process
- Level 4

  4.1 Establishing Measurable Quality Goals

  4.2 Objectively Managing Performance
- Level 5

  5.1 Improving Organizational Capability

  5.2 Improving Process Effectiveness

The corresponding descriptions of the five levels are given as follows:

- Level 1, "Performed Informally," focuses on whether an organization or project performs a process that incorporates the BPs. A statement characterizing this level would be, "You have to do it before you can manage it."
- Level 2, "Planned and Tracked," focuses on project-level definition, planning, and performance issues. A statement characterizing this level would be, "Understand what's happening on the project before defining organization-wide processes."
- Level 3, "Well Defined," focuses on disciplined tailoring from defined processes at the organization level. A statement characterizing this level would be, "Use the best of what you've learned from your projects to create organization-wide processes."

- Level 4, "Quantitatively Controlled," focuses on measurements being tied to the business goals of the organization. Although it is essential to begin collecting and using basic project measures early, measurement and use of data is not expected organization-wide until the higher levels have been achieved. Statements characterizing this level would be, "You can't measure it until you know what 'it' is" and "Managing with measurement is only meaningful when you're measuring the right things."
- Level 5, "Continuously Improving," gains leverage from all the management practice improvements seen in the earlier levels and then emphasizes the cultural shifts that will sustain the gains made. A statement characterizing this level would be, "A culture of continuous improvement requires a foundation of sound management practice, defined processes, and measurable goals."

A SOFTWARE SECURITY FRAMEWORK

In 2008, Gary McGraw and Brian Chess introduced a software security framework (SSF) that incorporates a maturity model. The model, summarized at `www.informit.com/articles/article.aspx?p=127138`, defines and provides means to measure software security initiatives.

The SSF comprises 4 domains that encompass 12 practices. These domains are:

- **Governance—Managing, measuring, and organizing the software security project**
- **Intelligence—Collecting corporate knowledge and modeling threats**
- **SDL touchpoints—Analyzing software development processes**
- **Deployment—Interfacing with network security and software maintenance organizations**

Table 1-8 summarizes the 12 practices of the framework. As of this writing, maturity models are being developed for each practice, including a Software Assurance Maturity Model called OpenSAMM (`www.opensamm.org`).

Table 1-8 summarizes the 12 practices of the framework.

Table 1-8: Practices of the Software Security Framework

GOVERNANCE	INTELLIGENCE	SDL TOUCHPOINTS	DEPLOYMENT
Strategy and metrics	Attack models	Architecture analysis	Penetration testing
Compliance and policy	Security features and design	Code review	Software environment
Training	Standards and requirements	Security testing	Configuration management and vulnerability management

Additional related efforts include the Building Security In Maturity Model (BSIMM) (`http://www.bsi-mm.com/`) and the Software Assurance Maturity Model (OpenSAMM) (`http://www.opensamm.org`). The BSIMM comprises 110 activities that are based on the SSF framework. It is designed to assist an organization in developing a software security program. In general, there are a number of activities for each of the twelve practices, with each activity divided into levels of maturity for that particular practice. The Software Assurance Maturity Model provides guidance for developing a software security approach customized to the identified risks to the organization. It is an open model and is available at no cost to users.

Trusted Computing

The threats to computers and networks are becoming increasingly sophisticated and adaptable. In many instances, software alone is not robust enough to protect information systems from attack. In order to counter malicious attacks, a not-for-profit organization comprising a variety of industrial members from around the globe was formed in 2003. This entity is the Trusted Computing Group (TCG), and its mission is to develop and promote vendor-independent, open specifications addressing the security of computing platforms, including hardware and software. These specifications are designed to provide the following capabilities:

- Authentication using two or more factors
- Secure file storage and privacy protections
- Access control to networks based on an organization's security policy
- Access to operating system–provided security capabilities

TCG Elements

Key elements of the TCG are:

- The Trusted Platform Module (TPM), an embedded hardware-based protection mechanism designed to protect the security and privacy of individual computer users. It refers to both a specification and a hardware device.
- The TCG Software Stack (TSS), which developers can use as a foundation for various applications.
- The Trusted Network Connect (TNC) specifications for network security implementations.

Trusted Platform Modules

TPMs are usually mounted on PC motherboards and are designed to protect cryptographic keys and authentication processes. The TPM is an element that can securely generate, store, and manage cryptographic keys. Encrypted data cannot be decrypted unless the key is provided by the secure TPM after appropriate authentication. Each TPM chip contains a secret and unique RSA key built into the chip during its production and can be used to verify the authenticity of other systems with TPM chips.

TCG Software Stack

The TSS is a specification for the software interface to the TPM and provides support for developers in creating interfaces to a number of cryptographic application programming interfaces (APIs). These APIs allow developers to gain access to TPM functions.

Trusted Network Connect

The TNC specification provides the means for network managers to employ network security policies, monitor end point devices, and provide authorized network access based on the security policy.

Trusted Computing Base (TCB)

Another fundamental component of trusted computing is the *trusted computing base* (TCB). The TCB is the total combination of protection mechanisms within a computer system, which includes the hardware, software, and firmware that are trusted to enforce a security policy. The TCB components are responsible for enforcing the security policy of a computing system and, therefore, these components must be protected from malicious and untrusted processes. The TCB must also provide for memory protection and ensure that the processes from one domain do not access memory locations of another domain.

The *security perimeter* is the boundary that separates the TCB from the remainder of the system. A *trusted path* must also exist so that a user can access the TCB without being compromised by other processes or users. A *trusted computer system* is one that employs the necessary hardware and software assurance measures to enable its use in processing multiple levels of classified or sensitive information. This system meets the specified requirements for reliability and security.

Acquisition Assurance Issues

A large amount of the software produced historically did not take into account assurance issues. The resultant vulnerabilities in the software expose their computing platforms to malicious and dangerous attacks. This situation is of particular concern in software that is used in the nation's critical infrastructure systems. Software assurance is aimed at reducing the risks to these sensitive computer systems.

In addition to suppliers, the responsibility for software assurance must also be assumed by acquirers and included in the acquisition process. According to NIST Special Publication 800-64, "Security Considerations in the System Development Life Cycle," acquisition is defined as "all stages of the process of acquiring property or services, beginning with the process for determining the need for the property or services and ending with contract completion and closeout." In many instances, the acquiring elements are not trained to ensure that software assurance is delivered by contractors, particularly in the U.S. defense establishment. To meet this need, the U.S. Department of Defense and the U.S. Department of Homeland Security (DHS) joined in an effort to address software assurance issues in the acquisition process.

A part of the joint DoD and DHS project was the Acquisition and Outsourcing Working Group, which produced a document "that provides information on how to incorporate software assurance (SwA) considerations in key decisions and how to exercise due diligence throughout the acquisition process relative to potential risk exposures that could be introduced by the supply chain." This document is a prepublication version as of this writing and is entitled "Software Assurance in Acquisition: Mitigating Risks to the Enterprise, A Reference Guide for Security-Enhanced Software Acquisition and Outsourcing: Building Security in Software Assurance."

The Working Group recognized that software procurement can take a multitude of paths and all the pertinent elements of the supply chain have to be considered. Figure 1-12, taken from the prepublication document, illustrates these paths.

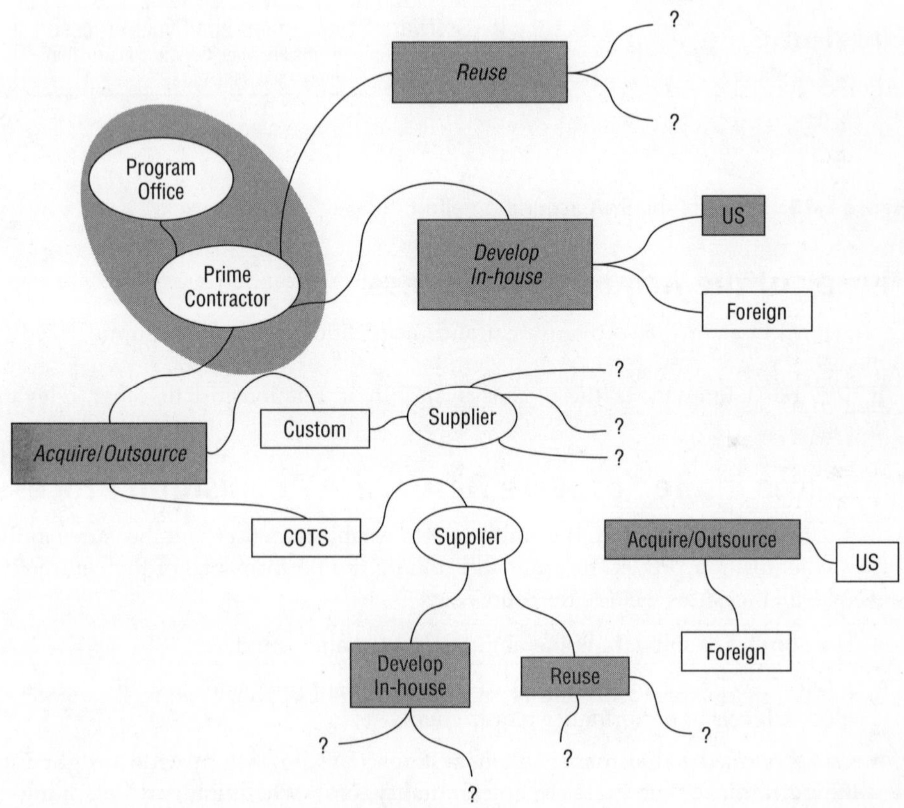

Figure 1-12: Potential software acquisition paths

From "Software Assurance in Acquisition: Mitigating Risks to the Enterprise, A Reference Guide for Security-Enhanced Software Acquisition and Outsourcing: Building Security in Software Assurance," October 22, 2008.

Some of the issues addressed in the Working Group document are:

- Example contract provisions
- An outline of a general acquisition process and associated acquisition phases
- Recommended purchasing practices for SwA in acquisition

- Support of risk mitigation efforts by providing due diligence questionnaires to obtain information concerning the software supply chain
- Language samples to include in statements of work

The scope of the Working Group effort, as presented in the document, is given in Figure 1-13.

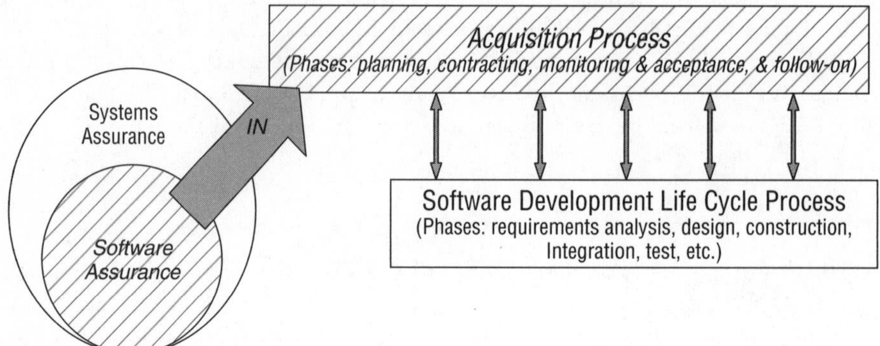

Figure 1-13: Scope of the SwA acquisition effort

Phases of the Acquisition Process

The major phases of the software assurance acquisition process are summarized in Table 1-9.

Figure 1-14 summarizes these phases and their relationship to other relevant processes.

Measures in the Software Assurance Acquisition Process

As with any acquisition effort, it is important to establish metrics and measures in the software acquisition process in order to evaluate the performance of the contractor. Some typical measures include the following:

- The number of software vulnerabilities created and found.
- Service level agreements (SLA) in which the supplier contractually agrees to specific levels of performance requirements.
- Use of earned value management systems (EVMS) that provide insight into the performance, progress, technical quality, cost, scheduling, and planning of suppliers. EVMS are defined in ANSI/EIA 748-1998.

Additional Software Acquisition Assurance Issues

In the development/acquisition phase of the system development life cycle (SDLC) described earlier in this chapter, the following security considerations should be addressed:

- Performance of a risk assessment
- Security requirements analysis

- Conduct of functional testing
- Conduct of security testing
- Development of security architecture
- Preparation of first draft documents for system certification and accreditation
- Determination if the proposed system is capable of performing in a manner expected by the acquiring agency
- Supply chain assurance goals of predictable execution, trustworthiness, and conformance to requirements and standards

The following acquisition planning considerations for software assurance during the development/acquisition phase of the SDLC are excerpted from Appendix F of NIST Special Publication 800-64.

- **Type of contract**—The type of contract (e.g., firm fixed price, time and materials, cost plus fixed fee) can have significant security implications. The information security technical representative developing the specifications and the contracting officer should work together to select the contract type that will be most advantageous to the organization.

<table>
<tr><th></th><th colspan="2">Planning</th><th colspan="2">Contracting</th><th colspan="3">Monitoring
& Acceptance</th><th>Follow-on</th></tr>
<tr><td>IEEE 1082
1888</td><td colspan="2">Planning</td><td colspan="2">Contracting</td><td colspan="2">Product
Implementation</td><td>Product
Acceptance</td><td>Follow-on</td></tr>
<tr><td>PMBOK
3.0</td><td colspan="4">Initiating</td><td colspan="2">1.
Planning
2.
Exeoulting
3.
Monitoring
&
controlling</td><td>Closing</td><td></td></tr>
<tr><td>NIST SP
800-84
Rev. 1
2004</td><td>Mission &
Business
Planning</td><td>Acquisition
Planning</td><td colspan="2">Acquisition</td><td colspan="2">Contract
Performance</td><td>Contract
Closeout</td><td>Follow-on
Contracts
&
Disposal</td></tr>
<tr><td>DoD
Instruction
5000.2
2003</td><td colspan="2">Pre-Systems
Aequicition</td><td colspan="5">Systems Acquisition</td><td>Sustainment</td></tr>
<tr><td>ISO/IEC
12207
2008 (E)</td><td colspan="2">Acquisition
Preparation</td><td>Acquisition
Advertisement</td><td>Supplier
Selection
& Contract
Agreement</td><td>Agreement
Monitoring</td><td colspan="2">Acquirer
Acceptance
& Closure</td><td></td></tr>
</table>

Figure 1-14: Software assurance acquisition phases

Figure source: "Mitigating Risks to the Enterprise, Software Assurance in Acquisition," October 22, 2008.

Table 1-9: Phases in the Software Assurance Acquisition Process

PHASE	ACTIVITY
Planning	Software product or service needs determination: identification of associated risks; developing software requirements; creating acquisition strategy; developing evaluation criteria and evaluation plan; development and use of SwA due diligence questionnaires.
Contracting	Creating and issuing the solicitation with a work statement, instructions to offerers, terms and conditions, and certifications; evaluating supplier proposals submitted in response to the solicitation; finalizing contract negotiation to include changes in terms and conditions; awarding the contract. (Software risks are addressed and mitigated through terms and conditions, certifications, evaluation factors for award, and risk mitigation requirements in the work statement.)
Monitoring and Acceptance	Establishing and consenting to the contract work schedule; implementing change (or configuration) control procedures; evaluating risk management and assurance case deliverables to determine compliance in accepted risk mitigation strategies as stated in the requirements; reviewing and accepting software deliverables.
Follow-on	Sustainment (maintenance) of the software, including risk management, assurance case management, and change management; (risks must be managed through continued analysis of the assurance case and should be adjusted to mitigate changing risks); disposal or decommissioning.

From "Mitigating Risks to the Enterprise, Software Assurance in Acquisition," October 22, 2008.

- **Review by other functional groups**—Depending on the size and scope of the system, a review of the system by participants from various functional groups (e.g., legal, human resources, physical security, records management) may be useful. These functional groups should have insight into the confidentiality, integrity, and availability requirements. Involving these groups early in the planning process is important because it may result in reduced life-cycle costs, and it is easier to change requirements in the early stages.
- **Review by certification agent and authorizing official**—OMB Circular A-130, Appendix III, requires that systems be approved, or authorized, to process data in specific environments. Management, operational, and technical controls must be employed to adequately protect the information system. Management and operational security controls can sometimes be outside the scope of the contract,

as the developer, in most cases, cannot be responsible for the organization's implementation of these security controls. The technical security control functional and assurance specifications must be contained in the contract with the developer. These security controls should be factored into the development of the technical specifications. The authorizing official (AO) can take these assumptions into account when deciding on the adequacy of the total set of security controls for reducing the residual risks to an acceptable level.

- **Cyclical nature of the process**—Security steps in the development/acquisition phase may need to be addressed cyclically. These security steps interrelate and build on each other. Depending on the size and complexity of the system, these steps may be performed often as ideas are refined.
- **Evaluation and acceptance**—The system evaluation plan and appropriate acceptance criteria are developed in the development/acquisition phase. The solicitation should be designed for evaluation, which should include testing and analysis. Specifications should be written in a way to make it easy to clearly determine if the implemented system complies with the specification. In general, two separate activities require security testing—contract acceptance and certification and accreditation (C&A).
- **Request for proposal (RFP) development**—An RFP enables an organization to make a best-value decision based on an offeror's proposal. One strength of the RFP process is the flexibility it provides the government and the offeror to negotiate a contract that best meets the government's needs. The organization can identify needed information security features, procedures, and assurances in many ways. An RFP can be a flexible document. Guidance on acquisition alternatives should be obtained from the organization's acquisition office or the contracting officer.
- **Security specifications and statement of work development**—Security specifications and the statement of work (SOW) are based on the requirements analysis. The specifications provide details of what the system is supposed to do. Specifications should also be written independently of the implementation mechanisms, strategy, and design. In other words, the specifications should state what the system is to do, not how. The developer's implementation of the system in conformance with the specifications can and should be tested. This implies that well-written specifications are those that can be tested. The SOW details what the developer must do in the performance of the contract. Documentation developed under the contract, for example, is specified in the SOW. Security assurance requirements, which detail many aspects of the processes the developer follows and what evidence must be provided to assure the organization that the processes have been conducted correctly and completely, may also be specified in the SOW.

Summary

Chapter 1 defined the basic assurance terms and developed the security design principles for software assurance. Risk management was defined and the basics of risk management were reviewed based on NIST SP 800-30. With this foundation, the system and software development life cycles were reviewed and a number of the prominent software assurance development life cycle methodologies were presented. The chapter concluded with a review of relevant assurance standards, legal issues, security models, and acquisition guidelines for software assurance projects.

Assessment Questions

1. The level of confidence that software functions as intended and is free of vulnerabilities, either intentionally or unintentionally designed or inserted as part of the software, is the definition of:
   A. Software risk
   B. Software impact
   C. Software assurance
   D. Software accountability
2. Seven complementary elements that support information assurance are confidentiality, integrity, availability, authentication, authorization, accountability, and:
   A. Repudiation
   B. Auditing
   C. Operations
   D. Acquisition
3. A form of confidentiality breach that is accomplished by studying the volume, rate, source, and destination of transmitted messages is:
   A. Inference analysis
   B. Covert channel analysis
   C. Messaging analysis
   D. Traffic analysis
4. An unauthorized and unintended communication path that provides for exchange of information is a:
   A. Secret link
   B. Covert channel
   C. Covert encryption
   D. Communication pipe
5. The ability of an entity to use and correlate information protected at one level of security to uncover information that is protected at a higher security level is called:
   A. Inference
   B. Knowledge acquisition
   C. Covert channeling
   D. Cryptanalysis

6. Confidentiality, integrity, and availability are the principal components of information system security. The reverse of these concepts is:
   A. Disclosure, authentication, and destruction
   B. Disclosure, alteration, and destruction
   C. Encryption, alteration, and destruction
   D. Disclosure, alteration, and disposal
7. The testing or reconciliation of evidence of a user's identity is:
   A. Authorization
   B. Accountability
   C. Auditing
   D. Authentication
8. An ongoing activity that examines either the system or the users, such as intrusion detection, is:
   A. Auditing
   B. Monitoring
   C. Accounting
   D. Eavesdropping
9. A set of records that collectively provides documentary evidence of processing used to aid in tracing from original transactions forward to related records and reports, and/or backward from records and reports to their component source transactions, is called:
   A. Data library
   B. Data dictionary
   C. Audit trail
   D. Monitor data
10. The ability to determine the actions and behaviors of a single individual within a system and to identify that particular individual is:
    A. Authentication
    B. Accountability
    C. Authorization
    D. Nonrepudiation
11. Economy of mechanism, separation of duties, fail-safe, open design, and psychological acceptability are 5 of the 11:
    A. Security design principles
    B. Security bible principles
    C. Defense-in-depth principles
    D. Security trade-off principles

12. What principle maintains that an individual, process, or other type of entity should be given the minimum privileges and resources for the minimum period of time required to complete a task?
    A. Separation of duties
    B. Complete mediation
    C. Least privilege
    D. Limited access
13. The principle that requires that completion of a specified sensitive activity or access to sensitive objects is dependent on the satisfaction of multiple conditions is:
    A. Defense-in-depth
    B. Fail-safe
    C. Economy of mechanism
    D. Separation of duties
14. The application of multiple layers of protection wherein a subsequent layer will provide protection if a previous layer is breached is:
    A. Defense-in-depth
    B. Weakest link
    C. Fail-safe
    D. Control analysis
15. The condition that every request by a subject to access an object in a computer system must undergo a valid and effective authorization procedure, and must not be suspended or become capable of being bypassed, is known as:
    A. Fail-safe
    B. Complete mediation
    C. Economy of mechanism
    D. Accountability
16. According to the National Institute for Standards and Technology (NIST) Special Publication (SP) 800-30, the three major components of risk management are:
    A. Risk assessment, risk analysis, and evaluation
    B. Risk assessment, risk mitigation, and risk reduction
    C. Risk assessment, risk determination, and evaluation
    D. Risk assessment, risk mitigation, and evaluation
17. Which of the following steps are components of the NIST SP 800-30 risk assessment process?
    A. System characterization, threat elimination, vulnerability identification, and control analysis
    B. System characterization, threat identification, vulnerability identification, and control implementation

C. System characterization, threat identification, vulnerability identification, and control analysis

D. System characterization, threat identification, vulnerability reduction, and control analysis

18. In the NIST SP 800-30 risk assessment process, which one of the following is the likelihood rating in which a highly motivated and capable threat-source will exploit an existing vulnerability? In addition, there are also ineffective controls to prevent exploitation of the associated vulnerability.

A. Medium

B. High

C. Low

D. Intermediate

19. In the NIST SP 800-30 risk assessment process, the type of analysis that is more easily accomplished and provides identifiable areas for immediate improvement, but does not provide specific magnitudes of measures, is called:

A. Qualitative analysis

B. Measurable analysis

C. Quantitative analysis

D. Qualified analysis

20. NIST SP 800-30 risk mitigation options include which one of the following groups?

A. Risk assumption, risk avoidance, risk planning, and research and development

B. Risk assumption, risk avoidance, risk planning, and risk elimination

C. Risk assumption, risk avoidance, risk deterrence, and research and development

D. Risk calculation, risk avoidance, risk planning, and research and development

21. The categories of controls to mitigate risks are:

A. Administrative, management, operational, and a combination of these

B. Technical, logical, operational, and a combination of these

C. Technical, management, qualitative, and a combination of these

D. Technical, management, operational, and a combination of these

22. The Microsoft Security Risk Management Discipline (SRMD) comprises which one of the following groups of steps?

A. Aggregation, development and implementation, operating

B. Assessment, development and implementation, operating

C. Assessment, evaluation, operating

D. Assessment, development and implementation, maintenance

23. The LeGrand Vulnerability-Oriented Risk Management method includes which one of the following groups of steps?

A. Risk mitigation, vulnerability management, adherence to security standards and policies

B. Risk assessment, vulnerability management, adherence to operational standards and policies

C. Risk assessment, vulnerability elimination, adherence to security standards and policies

D. Risk assessment, vulnerability management, adherence to security standards and policies

24. The Morana Risk Management Activities include which one of the following groups of steps that map onto the software development life cycle?

    A. Requirements, architecture and design, development, and testing

    B. Assessment, architecture and design, development, and testing

    C. Requirements, vulnerability management, development, and testing

    D. Requirements, architecture and design, vulnerability management, and testing

25. In black box testing of information systems:

    A. The testing team is provided full knowledge of the resources to be tested.

    B. The testing team is provided partial knowledge of the resources to be tested and has to acquire some information on its own.

    C. The testing team is provided no knowledge of the resources to be tested and has to acquire information on its own.

    D. The testing team is not permitted direct access to the resources to be tested.

26. The Information Assurance Technical Framework (IATF) document 3.1 defines the five phases of the system development life cycle (SDLC) as:

    A. Initiation, development/acquisition, implementation, operation/maintenance, upgrade

    B. Initiation, evaluation, implementation, operation/maintenance, disposal

    C. Initiation, development/acquisition, assessment, operation/maintenance, disposal

    D. Initiation, development/acquisition, implementation, operation/maintenance, disposal

27. The IATF document 3.1 stresses the importance of which one of the following groups to provide information assurance?

    A. People, operations, and technology

    B. Assessment, operations, and technology

    C. People, security, and technology

    D. People, operations, and management

28. In NIST SP 800-64, the process for determining the need for property or services and ending with contract completion and closeout is defined as:

    A. Initiation

B. Acquisition

C. Subcontracting

D. Development

29. The U.S. federal act that was passed to "provide a comprehensive framework for ensuring the effectiveness of information security controls over information resources that support Federal operations and assets" and "to provide for development and maintenance of minimum controls required to protect Federal information and information systems" is known as the:

A. Gramm-Leach-Bliley Act (GLB) Act

B. Sarbanes-Oxley (SOX) Act

C. Federal Information Security Management Act (FISMA)

D. Health Insurance Portability and Accountability Act (HIPAA)

30. Which one of the following specifies that U.S. federal government agencies plan for security, ensure that appropriate officials are assigned security responsibility, review the security controls in their information systems, and authorize system processing prior to operations and periodically thereafter?

A. Sarbanes-Oxley (SOX)

B. U.S. Office of Management and Budget (OMB) Circular A-130

C. Health Insurance Portability and Accountability Act (HIPAA) Final Security Rule

D. Gramm-Leach-Bliley

31. Which NIST publication is used to identify and categorize U.S. federal information and information systems?

A. Federal Information Processing Standard (FIPS) 200

B. Federal Information Processing Standard (FIPS) 300

C. Federal Information Processing Standard (FIPS) 199

D. Federal Information Processing Standard (FIPS) 198

32. The right of an individual to protection from unauthorized disclosure of personally identifiable information (PII) is the definition of:

A. Security

B. Confidentiality

C. Authorization

D. Privacy

33. Notice, choice, access, security, and enforcement are fundamental principles of:

A. Privacy

B. Assurance

C. Access

D. Authorization

34. The U.S. act that was passed to regulate corporate financial practices and reporting is:
    A. Sarbanes-Oxley (SOX)
    B. U.S. Office of Management and Budget (OMB) Circular A-130
    C. Health Insurance Portability and Accountability Act (HIPAA)
    D. Gramm-Leach-Bliley
35. The U.S. Financial Services Modernization Act, Public Law 106-102, is also known as:
    A. Sarbanes-Oxley (SOX)
    B. U.S. Office of Management and Budget (OMB) Circular A-130
    C. FISMA
    D. Gramm-Leach-Bliley
36. Which U.S. health care–related law addresses protection for transmitted data, protection for data at rest, physical protection, and administrative procedures?
    A. Health Insurance Portability and Accountability Act (HIPAA) Final Privacy Rule
    B. Health Insurance Portability and Accountability Act (HIPAA) Final Security Rule
    C. Health Insurance Portability and Accountability Act (HIPAA) Transactions and Code Sets Rule
    D. Health Insurance Portability and Accountability Act (HIPAA) Final Authorization Rule
37. Which standard addresses credit card and cardholder authentication and is organized as 12 requirements under 6 logically consistent control objectives?
    A. Payment Card Industry (PCI) Data Privacy Standard (DPS)
    B. Payment Card Industry (PCI) Data Confidentiality Standard (DCS)
    C. Payment Card Industry (PCI) Data Security Standard (DSS)
    D. Payment Card Industry (PCI) Data Authorization Standard (DAS)
38. A high-level design structure comprising abstract-level components of the required software system functionality and descriptions of their interactions is the definition of:
    A. Software specification
    B. Software assurance
    C. Software requirements
    D. Software architecture

39. A software architecture can be considered a composition system comprising the following elements:
    A. Components, connectors, operators
    B. Components, requirements, operators
    C. Specifications, connectors, operators
    D. Components, connectors, links
40. Software architecture systems can also be represented by a component model that includes the following concepts:
    A. Binding point, operators, glue code, separation of application and communication
    B. Binding point, connector, glue code, separation of application and communication
    C. Binding point, connector, authorization, separation of application and communication
    D. Binding point, connector, glue code, requirements
41. Some typical software architecture styles include:
    A. Pipes and filters, layered, P-level, heterogeneous
    B. Matrix, layered, N-tiered, homogeneous
    C. Pipes and filters, layered, N-tiered, heterogeneous
    D. Matrix, layered, N-tiered, heterogeneous
42. The document that lists a number of important architectural design assurance objectives—including: the architecture should provide predictable execution behavior; the architectural design should ease traceability, verification, validation, and evaluation; and the architecture should eliminate possibilities for violations—is entitled:
    A. The Software Assurance Common Body of Knowledge (CBK), developed by the U.S. Department of Homeland Security Software
    B. The Microsoft Trustworthy Security Development Life Cycle Paradigm
    C. The Microsoft Software Development Baseline Process
    D. The Comprehensive, Lightweight Application Security Process (CLASP)
43. Which type of software development life cycle process employs extensive reviews, evidence, and formal methods?
    A. Lightweight
    B. Agile
    C. Spiral
    D. Heavyweight

44. Which software development process is characterized by early and frequent delivery of workable and usable software, customer involvement in the development process, iterative development, acceptance of late requirements changes, employment of self-managing teams with appropriate expertise, and delivery of multiple releases?
    A. Agile
    B. Evolutionary
    C. Waterfall
    D. Unified
45. Which software development process operates by first developing prototypes that are tested and evaluated and then going back to continue the development process and incorporating feedback obtained during the prototyping phase?
    A. Waterfall
    B. Spiral
    C. Evolutionary
    D. Concurrent release
46. The basic Microsoft Software Development Baseline Process is a spiral approach in that the software requirements and design are reviewed and updated, if necessary, during the implementation phase. The phases of this process are:
    A. Requirements, review, implementation, verification, release, support and servicing
    B. Requirements, design, implementation, verification, release, support and servicing
    C. Evaluation, design, implementation, verification, release, support and servicing
    D. Requirements, design, implementation, verification, release, disposal
47. The Microsoft Security Development Life Cycle (SDL) is based on which one of the following sets of principles?
    A. Secure in requirements, secure by default, secure in deployment, communications
    B. Secure by design, secure by evaluation, secure in deployment, communications
    C. Secure by design, secure by default, secure in deployment, verification
    D. Secure by design, secure by default, secure in deployment, communications
48. The Microsoft Security Development Life Cycle (SDL) set of principles is known as:
    A. SD^3+C
    B. SD^3+V
    C. SD^2+E+C
    D. SD^2+R+C

49. Which security process includes 7 key best practices for application security and 30 security activities?
    A. Microsoft Security Development Life Cycle (SDL)
    B. The Comprehensive, Lightweight Application Security Process (CLASP)
    C. Touchpoints for Software Security
    D. Team Software Process (TSP)-Secure
50. What mechanism in the Comprehensive, Lightweight Application Security Process (CLASP) provides a classification structure that enables development teams to find vulnerability information acquired from different historical views and sources of data?
    A. Vulnerability View
    B. Vulnerability Resource
    C. Vulnerability Module
    D. Vulnerability Lexicon
51. To provide guidelines for employing information assurance processes into the security development life cycle (SDL), CLASP is structured into:
    A. Views, resources, and vulnerability use cases
    B. Views, principles, and vulnerability use cases
    C. Views, resources, and security use cases
    D. Views, activities, and vulnerability use cases
52. The five CLASP views are:
    A. Concepts view, resource-based view, activity-assessment view, activity-implementation view, vulnerability view
    B. Concepts view, role-based view, resource-assessment view, activity-implementation view, vulnerability view
    C. Concepts view, role-based view, activity-assessment view, activity-implementation view, vulnerability view
    D. Requirements view, role-based view, activity-assessment view, activity-implementation view, vulnerability view
53. When a system is under attack, one of the following includes these activities: Employ static analysis of source code; conduct risk analysis of architecture and design; perform penetration testing; and categorize abuse cases by analyzing system behavior. Which one?
    A. Comprehensive, Lightweight Application Security Process (CLASP)
    B. Microsoft Security Development Life Cycle
    C. Team Software Process (TSP)-Secure
    D. Seven Touchpoints for Software Security

54. The Carnegie Mellon University Software Engineering Institute (SEI) and CERT Coordination Center (CERT/CC) have developed a method designed to estimate the probability of vulnerabilities in production software and to minimize or eliminate software vulnerabilities. This method is called:

    A. Team Software Process (TSP)-Secure

    B. Digital Design Process

    C. Design Capability Maturity Model (CMM)

    D. Seven Touchpoints for Software Security

55. Which one of the following provides the owner with a legally enforceable right to exclude others from practicing a covered invention for a specified period of time?

    A. Copyright

    B. Patent

    C. Warranty

    D. Trade Secret

56. In the U.S., patent law protects which one of the following groups of items?

    A. Original works of authorship, ornamental designs, and new varieties of plants

    B. Inventions and processes; words, names, or symbols; and new varieties of plants

    C. Inventions and processes, ornamental designs, and words, names, or symbols

    D. Inventions and processes, ornamental designs, and new varieties of plants

57. Which one of the following ''secures and maintains the confidentiality of proprietary technical or business-related information that is adequately protected from disclosure by the owner''?

    A. Trade secret

    B. Trademark

    C. Warranty

    D. Patent

58. The International Organization for Standardization (ISO) series 27000 (2700X) standards are dedicated to the field of information system security. Which one of the ISO 27000 series is designed to ''provide a model for establishing, implementing, operating, monitoring, reviewing, maintaining, and improving an Information Security Management System (ISMS)''?

    A. 27002

    B. 27004

    C. 27001

    D. 27006

59. The ISO 27000 series emphasizes the PDCA cycle. PDCA stands for:

    A. Plan-Do-Check-Act

    B. Prepare-Do-Check-Act

C. Plan-Develop-Check-Act

D. Plan-Do-Certify-Act

60. The Code of Practice for Information Security Management is a repackaged version of (ISO) 17779:2005. It is designed to serve as a single source for best practices in the field of information security and presents a range of controls applicable to most situations. It is:

A. ISO 27001

B. ISO 27002

C. ISO 27003

D. ISO 27006

61. What provides a minimum standard for Web application security and summarizes the primary Web application security vulnerabilities based on input from a variety of information system security experts?

A. The British Standards Institute (BSI) 7799

B. ISO 27002

C. The Open Web Application Security Project (OWASP) Top Ten Project

D. TSP-Secure

62. In an access matrix, an active entity that is seeking rights to a resource is called:

A. Object

B. Subject

C. Capability

D. Grantor

63. The columns of the access matrix are called:

A. Access control lists (ACLs)

B. Capability lists

C. Triples

D. Properties

64. What model uses a directed graph to specify the rights that a subject can transfer to an object or that a subject can acquire from another subject?

A. Access matrix

B. Information flow

C. Take-Grant

D. Bell-LaPadula

65. What model was developed to formalize the U.S. Department of Defense (DoD) multi-level security policy?

A. Biba

B. Take-Grant

C. Clark-Wilson

D. Bell-LaPadula

66. What model was developed to address the first integrity goal of protecting data from modification by unauthorized users?

 A. Bell-LaPadula

 B. Biba

 C. Clark-Wilson

 D. Information flow

67. What model is built on the state machine concept and addresses only the confidentiality of classified material?

 A. Bell-LaPadula

 B. Biba

 C. Clark-Wilson

 D. Information flow

68. The * (star) property of which one of the following models states that writing of information by a subject at a higher level of sensitivity to an object at a lower level of sensitivity is not permitted (no write-down)?

 A. Take-Grant

 B. Biba

 C. Clark-Wilson

 D. Bell-LaPadula

69. Which one of the following is the * (star) integrity axiom of the Biba model?

 A. A subject at one level of integrity is not permitted to observe (read) an object of a lower integrity (no read-down).

 B. An object at one level of integrity is not permitted to modify (write to) an object of a higher level of integrity (no write-up).

 C. A subject at one level of integrity is prohibited from invoking a subject at a higher level of integrity.

 D. Integrity labels are required to verify the integrity of an object.

70. In the Clark-Wilson model, an activity that confirms that all constrained data items are in valid states of integrity is:

 A. Invocation procedure

 B. Unconstrained data item procedure

 C. Transformation procedure

 D. Integrity verification procedure

71. What model describes those characteristics of security engineering processes essential to ensure good security engineering?

 A. Systems Security Engineering Capability Maturity Model (SSE-CMM)

B. Capability Maturity Model Integration (CMMi)

C. Bell-LaPadula model

D. Systems Engineering Capability Maturity Model (SE-CMM)

72. The Trusted Platform Module (TPM), the Software Stack (TSS), and the Trusted Network Connect (TNC) specifications are key elements of the:

A. Trusted Computing Base (TCB)

B. Trusted Computing Group (TCG)

C. Security Boundary

D. Security Perimeter

73. The total combination of protection mechanisms within a computer system, which includes the hardware, software, and firmware that are trusted to enforce a security policy, defines the:

A. Trusted platform module (TPM)

B. Security perimeter

C. Trusted path

D. Trusted computing base (TCB)

74. According to the U.S. Department of Defense (DoD) and Department of Homeland Security (DHS) Acquisition and Outsourcing Working Group, the major phases of the software assurance acquisition project are:

A. Planning, contracting, monitoring and acceptance, and follow-on

B. Requirements, contracting, monitoring and acceptance, and follow-on

C. Planning, contracting, implementation, and follow-on

D. Planning, contracting, monitoring and acceptance, and auditing

75. According to NIST Special Publication 800-64, ''Security Considerations in the System Development Life Cycle,'' ''all stages of the process of acquiring property or services, beginning with the process for determining the need for the property or services and ending with contract completion and closeout'' is the definition of:

A. Contracting

B. Acquisition

C. Planning

D. Purchasing

CHAPTER

2

Secure Software Requirements

The requirements for secure software are concerned with nonfunctional issues such as minimizing or eliminating vulnerabilities and ensuring that the software will perform as required, even under attack. This goal is distinct from security functionality in software, which addresses areas that derive from the information security policy, such as identification, authentication, and authorization.

Software requirements engineering is the process of determining customer software expectations and needs and is conducted before the software design phase. The requirements have to be unambiguous, correct, quantifiable, and detailed.

Karen Goertzel, Theodore Winograd, and their contributors in "Enhancing the Development Life Cycle to Produce Secure Software"[1] from the United States Department of Defense Data and Analysis Center for Software (DACS) state that all software shares the following three security needs:

- It must be dependable under anticipated operating conditions, and remain dependable under hostile operating conditions.
- It must be trustworthy in its own behavior, and in its inability to be compromised by an attacker through exploitation of vulnerabilities or insertion of malicious code.
- It must be resilient enough to recover quickly to full operational capability with a minimum of damage to itself, the resources and data it handles, and the external components with which it interacts.

In this chapter, the considerations for software being secure functionally and software having secure properties are explored in the context of software requirements

[1]Goertzel, K., Winograd, T. et al., "Enhancing the Development Life Cycle to Produce Secure Software," Draft Version 2.0. Rome, New York: United States Department of Defense Data and Analysis Center for Software, July 2008.

engineering. Secure requirements for security-related software functions generally define what the software has to accomplish to perform a task securely.

Approaches to Software Requirements Engineering

Software requirements engineering demands extensive interaction with the user, and the product of the process includes both nonfunctional and functional software performance characteristics. Figure 2-1 illustrates the major elements of the software requirements engineering process.

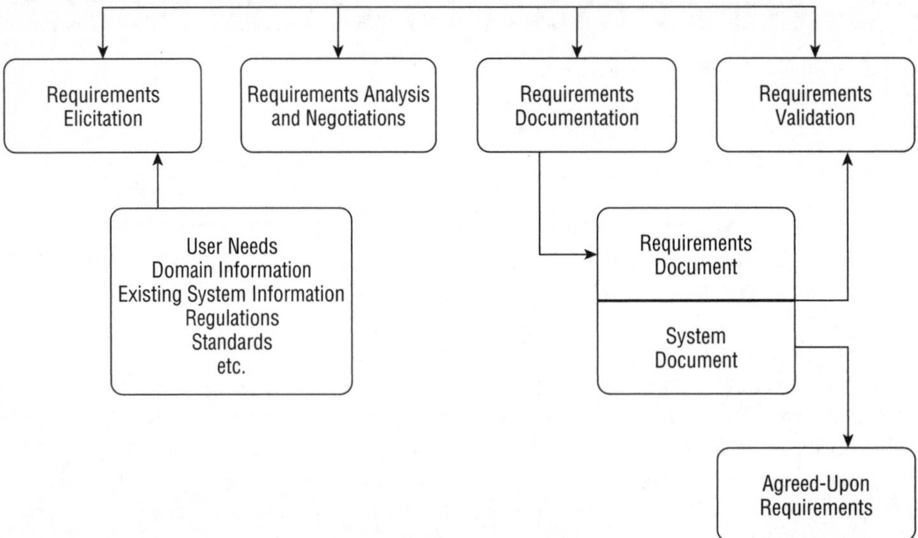

Figure 2-1: Software requirements engineering components

Source: Information Assurance Technology Analysis Center (IATC), Data and Analysis Center for Software (DACS), "State-of-the-Art Report," July 31, 2007)

Figure 2-2 illustrates additional elements that can be used to augment traditional software requirements engineering to increase software security.

Approaching software security requirements derivation from a resource perspective provides an effective method for addressing software security requirements. In their April 1995 paper, "SMART Requirements," (`www.win.tue.nl/~wstomv/edu/2ip30/references/smart-requirements.pdf`) Mike Mannion and Barry Keepence of Napier University, Edinburgh, U.K., take this approach by defining the following SMART basic properties that requirements should possess:

- **Specific**—The requirement should be unambiguous and direct. Mannion and Keepence define this characteristic as being clear, consistent, and simple.
- **Measurable**—The requirement should be able to be measured to ensure that it has been met.

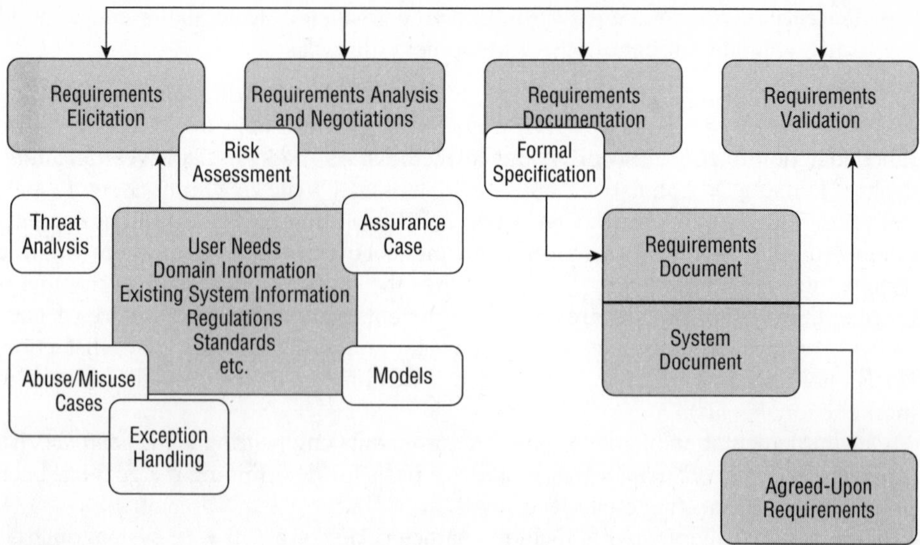

Figure 2-2: Additions to the software requirements engineering process to promote secure software

Source: Information Assurance Technology Analysis Center (IATC), Data and Analysis Center for Software (DACS), "State-of-the-Art Report," July 31, 2007)

- **Attainable**—The system must be able to exhibit the requirement under the specified conditions.
- **Realizable**—The requirement must be achievable under the system and project development constraints.
- **Traceable**—The requirement should be able to be traced both forward and backward throughout the development life cycle from conception through design, implementation, and test.

OWASP has modified the SMART acronym (`www.owasp.org/index.php/Document_security-relevant_requirements`) to be SMART+ requirements. These requirements, taken from the OWASP Web site, are given as follows:

- **Specific**—Requirements should be as detailed as necessary so there are no ambiguities.
- **Measurable**—It should be possible to determine whether the requirement has been met, through analysis, testing, or both.
- **Appropriate**—Requirements should be validated, thereby ensuring that they not only derive from a real need or demand but also that different requirements would not be more appropriate.
- **Reasonable**—While the mechanism or mechanisms for implementing a requirement need not be solidified, one should conduct some validation to determine whether meeting the requirement is physically possible, and possible given other likely project constraints.

- **Traceable**—Requirements should also be isolated to make them easy to track/validate throughout the development life cycle.

Another complementary method for software security requirements engineering is a *goal-oriented* paradigm in which a goal is a software objective. Goal types are functional, nonfunctional, security, and correctness. As Axel van Lamsweerde, Simon Brohez, Renaud De Landtsheer, and David Janssens write in "From System Goals to Intruder Anti-Goals: Attack Generation and Resolution for Security Requirements Engineering,"[2] "A goal is a prescriptive statement of intent about some system (existing or to-be) whose satisfaction in general requires the cooperation of some of the agents forming that system. Agents are active components such as humans, devices, legacy software or software-to-be components that play some role towards goal satisfaction. Goals may refer to services to be provided (functional goals) or to quality of service (nonfunctional goals)."

One implementation of goal-oriented requirements engineering is the *nonfunctional requirements framework (NFR)*[3] that provides a basis for determining if a goal has been satisfied through meeting lower level goals.

Nonfunctional requirements include characteristics of a software system such as reliability, performance, security, accuracy, costs, reliability, and maintainability. According to Goertzel and Winograd et al., these requirements should specify the following:[4]

1. Properties the software must exhibit (e.g., its behavior must be correct and predictable; it must remain resilient in the face of attacks)
2. Required level of assurance or risk-avoidance of individual security functions and constraints
3. Controls and rules governing the processes by which the software will be built, deployed, and operated (e.g., it must be designed to operate within a virtual machine, its source code must not contain certain function calls)

Goertzel and Winograd et al. also provide an example of a negative nonfunctional requirement as the following: "The software must validate all input to ensure it does not exceed the size specified for that type of input."

A related goal-oriented requirements engineering approach is the MILOS[5] project methodology for goal-oriented security requirements engineering.

The MILOS security model uses generic specification patterns that map to the information system's properties of confidentiality, integrity, availability, privacy, authentication, authorization, and nonrepudiation. The security patterns are transformed into goals that are used to develop a correlated "anti-model" that comprises a

[2]van Lamsweerde A., Brohez, S., De Landtsheer, R., and Janssens, D., "From System Goals to Intruder Anti-Goals: Attack Generation and Resolution for Security Requirements Engineering," in *Proceedings of the Requirements for High Assurance Workshop*, Monterey Bay, CA, September 8, 2003, pp. 49–56.

[3]Chung, L., "Representing and Using Nonfunctional Requirements," Ph.D. Thesis, Dept. of Computer Science, University of Toronto, 1993.

[4]Goertzel, Winograd, et al., "Enhancing the Development Life Cycle to Produce Secure Software."

[5]van Lamsweerde, Brohez, De Landtsheer, and Janssens, "From System Goals to Intruder Anti-Goals: Attack Generation and Resolution for Security Requirements Engineering."

pattern of "anti-goals" an attacker would use to prevent meeting the specified system security goals.

NOTE It is important to note that software security requirements address necessary attributes for software behavior and limitations on software functionality, whereas software requirements are concerned with necessary software functionality and performance specifications.

Security Policy Decomposition

Software security requirements are a function of policies such as system security policies, software policies, and information system policies. Requirements also have to satisfy regulations and directives such as FISMA, Gramm-Leach-Bliley, Sarbanes-Oxley, and HIPAA (see Chapter 1). For proper secure software implementation, these issues have to be accounted for during the software development life cycle and through an effective software security policy.

Important areas addressed by a software system's security policy include:

- Access controls
- Data protection
- Confidentiality
- Integrity
- Identification and authentication
- Communication security
- Accountability

In the context of secure software, a requirement should follow from the general policy statements. Goertzel and Winograd et al.,[6] provide the following example:

- Derive the detailed functional requirements, e.g., "The server should return public-access Web pages to any browser that requests those pages."
- Identify the related constraint requirements, e.g., "The server should return restricted Web pages only to browsers that are acting as proxies for users with authorized privileges sufficient to access those Web pages."
- Derive the functional security requirements, e.g., "The server must authenticate every browser that requests access to a restricted Web page."
- Identify the related negative requirements, e.g., "The server must not return a restricted Web page to any browser that it cannot authenticate."

The security requirements in a software security policy can also be specified in terms of functionality properties, such as restrictions on system states and information flows.

[6]Goertzel, Winograd, et al., "Enhancing the Development Life Cycle to Produce Secure Software."

Goertzel and Winograd et al. list the common sources of security requirements as:

- Stakeholders' expressed security concerns
- Security implications of the functional specification
- Requirements for security functions
- Compliance and conformance mandates
- Secure development and deployment standards, guidelines, and best practices
- Attack models and environment risk analysis
- Known and likely vulnerabilities in the technologies and COTS and OSS components that, due to preexisting commitments, must be used

Considerations in the SDLC

As presented in Chapter 1, the phases of the SDLC according to NIST SP 800-14[7] are:

1. **Initiation phase**—During the initiation phase, the need for a system is expressed and the purpose of the system is documented.
2. **Development/acquisition phase**—During this phase, the system is designed, purchased, programmed, developed, or otherwise constructed.
3. **Implementation phase**—During implementation, the system is tested and installed or fielded.
4. **Operation/maintenance phase**—During this phase, the system performs its work. The system is almost always being continuously modified by the addition of hardware and software and by numerous other events.
5. **Disposal phase**—The disposal phase of the IT system life cycle involves the disposition of information, hardware, and software.

Integrating security into the SDLC, based on the NIST SDLC Bulletin,[8] yields the process illustrated in Figure 2-3.

Another approach to defining elements of an information security policy is to correlate the system engineering process and the secure software engineering process. This can be accomplished through a derivation of the "Vee" model,[9] which illustrates the relationship between secure systems engineering and secure software engineering.

The secure system engineering "Vee" model is illustrated in Figure 2-4. In this model, the left side, called the *decomposition and definition sequence*, contains the major technical phases involved in transforming systems requirements into an operational software system. The right side, the *integration and verification sequence*, contains the

[7]NIST SP 800-14, "Generally Accepted Principles and Practices for Securing Information Technology Systems," National Institute of Standards and Technology, September 1996.
[8]NIST ITL Bulletin, "Information Security in the Systems Development Life Cycle," September 2004.
[9]Forsberg, K., and Mooz, H., "The Relationship of System Engineering to the Project Cycle," *Proceedings of the First Annual Symposium of National Council on System Engineering*, October 1991: 57–65.

testing, integration, and validation phases associated with the corresponding phase on the left side of the model. The horizontal arrows depict the introduction of the system security requirements analyses and system security design analyses into the testing processes of the integration and verification phases.

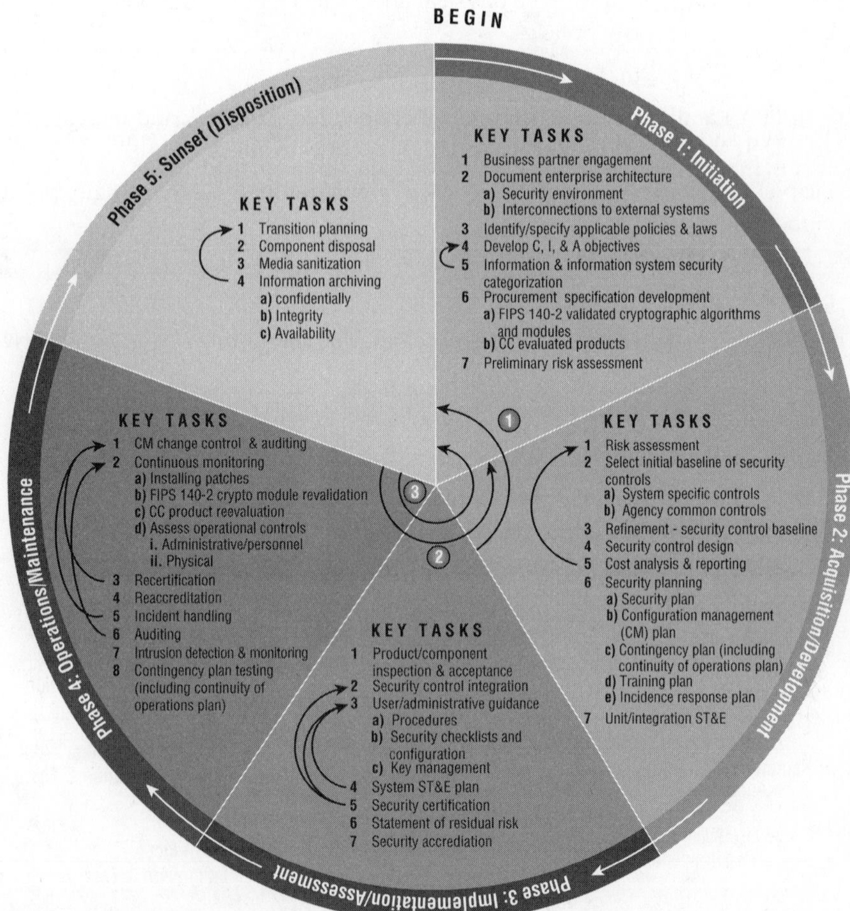

Figure 2-3: Integrating security into the SDLC
Source: NIST SDLC Bulletin

NIST 33 Security Principles

In June 2001, the National Institute of Standards and Technology's Information Technology Laboratory (ITL) published NIST Special Publication 800-27, "Engineering Principles for Information Technology Security (EP-ITS)," to assist in the secure design, development, deployment, and life cycle of information systems. The document was revised (Revision A) in 2004. It presents 33 security principles that start at the design phase of the information system or application and continue until the system's retirement and secure disposal. Some of the 33 principles that are most applicable to security policies and management are:

Principle 1. Establish a sound security policy as the "foundation" for design.

Principle 2. Treat security as an integral part of the overall system design.

Principle 3. Clearly delineate the physical and logical security boundaries governed by associated security policies.

Principle 6. Assume that external systems are insecure.

Principle 7. Identify potential trade-offs between reducing risk and increased costs and decreases in other aspects of operational effectiveness.

Principle 16. Implement layered security; ensure there is no single point of vulnerability.

Principle 20. Isolate public access systems from mission critical resources (e.g., data, processes, etc.).

Principle 21. Use boundary mechanisms to separate computing systems and network infrastructures.

Principle 25. Minimize the system elements to be trusted.

Principle 26. Implement least privilege.

Principle 32. Authenticate users and processes to ensure appropriate access control decisions both within and across domains.

Principle 33. Use unique identities to ensure accountability.

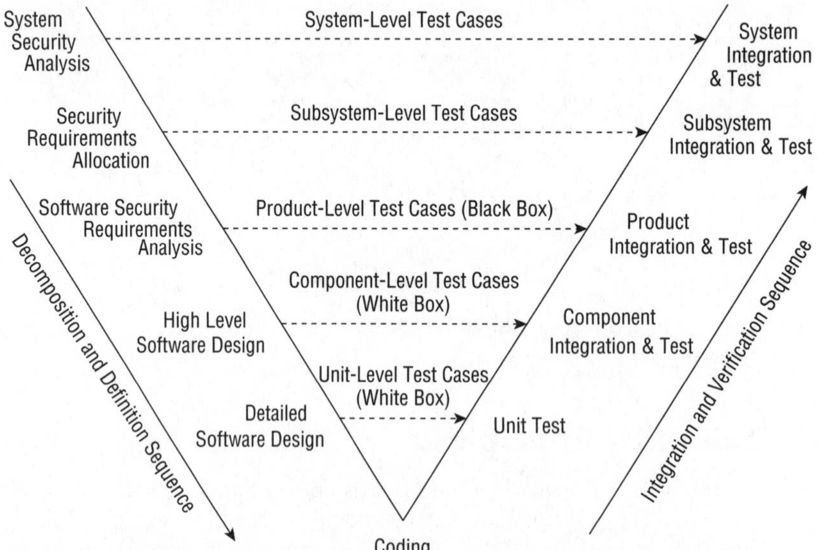

Figure 2-4: "Vee" process model for secure system engineering

Source: Information Assurance Technology Analysis Center (IATAC), Data and Analysis Center for Software (DACS), "State-of-the-Art Report," July 31, 2007)

Information Security Policy Implementation and Decomposition

Components of secure software requirements can flow directly from policies, regulations, and legislation. The policies and legal mandates normally reference secure software issues at a general and high level, and these statements have to be interpreted to generate the necessary software requirements. For example, NIST FIPS Publication 200[10] specifies the following items, which can be used to provide inputs to secure software policies:

System and Services Acquisition—"Organizations must ... (ii) employ system development life cycle processes that incorporate information security considerations; (iii) employ software usage and installation restrictions; and (iv) ensure that third-party providers employ adequate security measures to protect information, applications, and/or services outsourced from the organization."

System and Communications Protection—"Organizations must ... (ii) employ architectural designs, software development techniques, and systems engineering principles that promote effective information security within organizational information systems."

System and Information Integrity—"Organizations must: (i) identify, report, and correct information and information system flaws in a timely manner; (ii) provide protection from malicious code at appropriate locations within organizational information systems."

Security policies are the foundation of a sound security implementation. Often organizations will implement technical security solutions without first creating this foundation of policies, standards, guidelines, and procedures, unintentionally creating unfocused and ineffective security controls.

According to the Data and Analysis Center for Software (DACS), "Information security policy is concerned, in large part, with defining the set of rules by which system subjects are allowed to change the states of data objects in the system. In practical terms, this means defining for every system subject whether, and if so how, it may store, transmit, create, modify, or delete a given data object (or type of data object)."[11]

The same document also lists three main objectives common to all system security policies and the mechanisms and countermeasures used to enforce those policies:

1. They must allow authorized access and connections to the system while preventing unauthorized access or connections, especially by unknown or suspicious actors.
2. They must enable allowable reading, modification, destruction, and deletion of data while preventing unauthorized reading (data leakage), modification (data tampering), destruction (denial of service), or deletion (denial of service).

[10]NIST FIPS Publication 200, "Minimum Security Requirements for Federal Information and Information Systems," March 2006.

[11]Goertzel, Winograd, et al., "Enhancing the Development Life Cycle to Produce Secure Software."

3. They must block the entry of content (user input, executable code, system commands, etc.) suspected of containing attack patterns or malicious logic that could threaten the system's ability to operate according to its security policy and its ability to protect the information.

Policies, Standards, Guidelines, and Procedures

Policy is one of those terms that can mean several things. For example, there are security policies on firewalls, which refer to the access control and routing list information. Standards, procedures, and guidelines are also referred to as policies in the larger sense of a global information security policy.

A good, well-written policy is more than an exercise created on paper—it is an essential and fundamental element of sound security practice. A policy can literally be a lifesaver during a disaster, or it might be a requirement of a governmental or regulatory function. A policy can also provide protection from liability due to an employee's actions, or it can control the access to trade secrets.

NIST categorizes computer system security policies into three basic types:

- **Program policies**—Used to create an organization's computer security program
- **Issue-specific policies**—Used to address specific issues of concern to the organization
- **System-specific policies**—Technical directives taken by management to protect a particular system

Program policies and issue-specific policies both address policy from a broad level, usually encompassing the entire organization. A program policy is traditionally more general and strategic; for example, the organization's overall computer security program may be defined in a program policy. This high-level policy defines the purpose of the program and its scope within the organization, addresses compliance requirements, and assigns responsibilities for program implementation.

An issue-specific policy is a nontechnical policy addressing a single or specific issue of concern to the organization, such as the procedural guidelines for checking disks brought to work or email privacy concerns. Issue-specific policies are similar to program policies, in that they are not technically focused. A program policy is at such a high level that it usually does not require much modification over time, whereas issue-specific policies are likely to require more frequent modifications as changes in technology and other organizational factors occur.

However, program policies and issue-specific policies do not provide sufficient information or direction, for example, to be used in establishing an access control list or in training users on what actions are permitted. A system-specific policy is technically focused and addresses only one computer system or device type. It also includes security objectives and operational security rules.

Table 2-1 illustrates the differences among these three types of NIST security policies.

Fundamentally important to any security program's success is senior management's high-level statement of commitment to the information security policy process and their understanding of how important security controls and protections are to the enterprise's continuity. Senior management must be aware of the importance of security implementation to preserve the organization's viability (and for their own due care protection) and must publicly support that process throughout the enterprise.

Table 2-1: Types of Security Policies

POLICY TYPE	DESCRIPTION	EXAMPLE
Program policy	High-level program policy	Senior-level management statement
Issue-specific policy	Addresses single issue	Email privacy policy
System-specific policy	Single system directives	Router access control lists

National Institute of Standards and Technology, "An Introduction to Computer Security: The NIST Handbook, Special Publication 800-12," October 1995.

The formal issuance of a security policy should be given high visibility. Including security as a regular topic at staff meetings at all levels of the organization can also be helpful. Providing visibility through such avenues as management presentations, panel discussions, guest speakers, question/answer forums, and newsletters can be extremely beneficial.

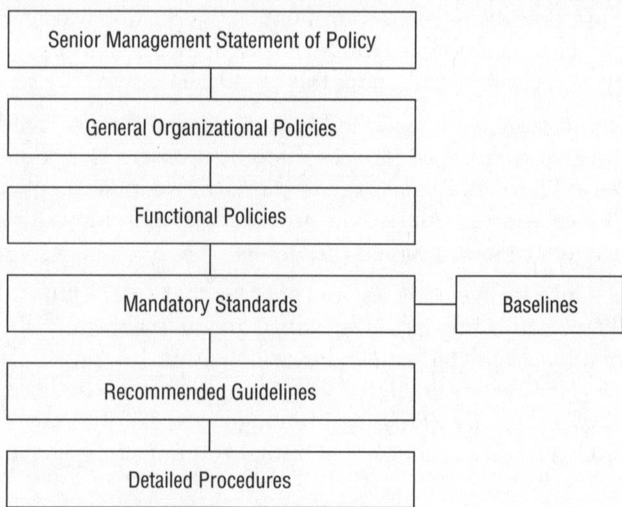

Figure 2-5: Policy hierarchy

In general, policies fall into a hierarchy as shown in Figure 2-5. The higher-level policies, which are the more general policies and statements, should be created first in the process for strategic reasons, and then the elements of standards, procedures, guidelines, and baselines can follow.

Four important types of higher-level policies are summarized as follows:

Senior management statement of policy—The first policy of any policy creation process is the senior management statement of policy. This is a general, high-level statement of a policy that contains the following elements:

- An acknowledgment of the importance of the computing resources to the business model
- A statement of support for information security throughout the enterprise
- A commitment to authorize and manage the definition of the lower-level standards, procedures, and guidelines

Regulatory—Regulatory policies are security policies that an organization must implement due to compliance, regulation, or other legal requirements. These companies might be financial institutions, public utilities, or some other type of organization that operates in the public interest. These policies are usually very detailed and are specific to the industry in which the organization operates. Regulatory policies commonly have two main purposes:

1. To ensure that an organization is following the standard procedures or base practices of operation in its specific industry
2. To give an organization the confidence that it is following the standard and accepted industry policy

Advisory—Advisory policies are security policies that are not mandated to be followed but are strongly suggested, perhaps with serious consequences defined for failure to follow them (such as termination, a job action warning, and so forth). A company with such policies wants most employees to consider these policies mandatory. Most policies fall under this broad category.

Advisory policies can have many exclusions or application levels. Thus, these policies can control some employees more than others, according to their roles and responsibilities within that organization. For example, a policy that requires a certain procedure for transaction processing might allow for an alternative procedure under certain specified conditions.

Informative—Informative policies are policies that exist simply to inform the reader. There are no implied or specified requirements, and the audience for this information could be certain internal (within the organization) or external parties. This does not mean that the policies are authorized for public consumption, but that they are general enough to be distributed to external parties (vendors accessing an extranet, for example) without a loss of confidentiality.

Standards, Guidelines, Procedures, and Baselines

The next level down from policies comprises the three elements of policy implementation: standards, guidelines, and procedures. These three elements contain the actual details of the policy, such as how it should be implemented and what standards and procedures should be used. They are published throughout the organization via manuals, the intranet, handbooks, or awareness classes.

It is important to know that standards, guidelines, and procedures are separate yet linked documents from the general policies (especially the senior-level statement). Unfortunately, companies will often create one document that satisfies the needs of all of these elements. This situation is not good. There are a few good reasons why they should be kept separate:

- Each of these elements serves a different function and focuses on a different audience. Also, physical distribution of the policies is easier.
- Security controls for confidentiality are different for each policy type. For example, a high-level security statement might need to be available to investors, but the procedures for changing passwords should not be available to anyone who is not authorized to perform the task.
- Updating and maintaining the policy is much more difficult when all the policies are combined into one voluminous document. Mergers, routine maintenance, and infrastructure changes all require that the policies be routinely updated. A modular approach to a policy document will keep the revision time and costs down.

Standards, guidelines, procedures, and baselines are summarized as follows:

Standards—Standards specify the use of particular technologies in a uniform way. This standardization of operating procedures can be a benefit to an organization by specifying the uniform methodologies to be used for the security controls. Standards are usually compulsory and are implemented throughout an organization for uniformity.

Guidelines—Guidelines are similar to standards; they refer to the methodologies of securing systems, but they are recommended actions only and are not compulsory. Guidelines are more flexible than standards and take into consideration the varying nature of the information systems. Guidelines can be used to specify the way standards should be developed, for example, or to guarantee the adherence to general security principles.

Procedures—Procedures embody the detailed steps that are followed to perform a specific task. They are considered the lowest level in the policy chain. Their purpose is to provide steps for implementing the policies, standards, and guidelines previously created. *Practices* is also a term that is frequently used in reference to procedures.

Baselines—Baselines are standards and represent a level of implementation of security controls that provides protection that is equivalent to the protection available to other similar reference entities. The baseline controls should be applied consistently across an organization and provide a basis for development of the computer and network security architectures.

Baselines take into consideration the differences between various operating systems, for example, to ensure that the security is being uniformly implemented throughout the enterprise.

Roles and Responsibilities

Although members of an organization frequently wear multiple hats, defined roles and responsibilities are important in the security administration process. Also, roles and responsibilities are central to the "separation of duties" concept—the concept that security is enhanced through the division of responsibilities in the production cycle. Therefore, it is important that individual roles and responsibilities are clearly communicated and understood as follows:

Senior management—Executive or senior-level management is assigned the overall responsibility for the security of information. Senior management might delegate the function of security, but they are viewed as the end of the food chain when liability is concerned.

Information systems security professionals—Information systems security professionals are delegated the responsibility for implementing and maintaining security by the senior-level management. Their duties include the design, implementation, management, and review of the organization's security policy, standards, guidelines, and procedures.

Data owners—Data owners are primarily responsible for determining the data's sensitivity or classification levels. They can also be responsible for maintaining the information's accuracy and integrity.

Users—Users are responsible for following the procedures set out in the organization's security policy during the course of their normal daily tasks.

Information systems auditors—Information systems auditors are responsible for providing reports to the senior management on the effectiveness of the security controls by conducting regular, independent audits. They also examine whether the security policies, standards, guidelines, and procedures effectively comply with the company's stated security objectives.

Decomposing Confidentiality, Integrity, Availability, Identification, Authentication, Authorization, and Auditing into Secure Software Requirements

Before you consider the decomposition of these issues in relation to secure software requirements, a review of the definitions of confidentiality, integrity, availability, authentication, authorization, and auditing is in order:

- **Confidentiality** refers to the prevention of intentional or unintentional unauthorized disclosure of information.

- The concept of **integrity** requires that the following three principles are met:
  - Modifications are not made to data by unauthorized personnel or processes.
  - Unauthorized modifications are not made to data by authorized personnel or processes.
  - The data is internally and externally consistent; in other words, the internal information is consistent among all sub-entities and the internal information is consistent with the real-world, external situation.
- **Availability** ensures the reliable and timely access to data or computing resources by the appropriate personnel. Availability guarantees that the systems are functioning properly when needed.
- **Identification** is the means by which users claim their identities on a system.
- **Authentication** is the testing or reconciliation of evidence of a user's identity.
- **Authorization** refers to rights and privileges granted to an individual or process that enable access to computer resources and information assets. Once a user's identity and authentication are established, authorization levels determine the extent of system rights that a user can hold.
- **Auditing**—A *system audit* is a one-time or periodic event to evaluate security; *monitoring* refers to an ongoing activity that examines either the system or the users, such as intrusion detection.

An information system security policy addresses these critical issues and decomposes their elements into the following secure software requirements.

Confidentiality

Confidentiality in a policy is concerned with protecting data during transfers between entities. A policy defines the requirements for ensuring the confidentiality of data by preventing unauthorized disclosure of information being sent between two end points. The policy will address the decisions concerning who can exchange information and what type of data can be exchanged. Related issues include intellectual property rights, access control, encryption, inference, anonymity, and covert channels. These policy statements should translate into requirements that address the following:

- Mechanisms that should be applied to enforce authorization
- What form of information is provided to the user and what the user can view
- The means of identify establishment
- What other types of confidentiality utilities should be used

Integrity

A policy has to provide the requirements for ensuring the integrity of data both in transit and in storage. It should also specify means to recover from detectable errors, such as deletions, insertions, and modifications. The means to protect the integrity of information include access control policies and decisions on who can transmit and receive data and which information can be exchanged. Derived requirements for integrity should address:

- Validation of the data origin
- Detection of alteration of data
- Determination if the data origin has changed

The policy should also provide for the integrity of data stored on media through monitoring for errors. Consideration should be given to determining the attributes and means that will be used as the basis for the monitoring and the actions that need to be taken in the event of a discovery of an integrity error. One type of integrity can also be described as maintaining a software system in a predefined ''legitimate'' state.

Availability

Policy requirements for availability are concerned with denying illegitimate access to computing resources and preventing external attacks such as denial-of-service attacks. Additional issues that have to be addressed include attempts by malicious entities to control, destroy, or damage computing resources and deny legitimate access to systems. While availability is being preserved, confidentiality and integrity have to be maintained. Requirements for this category should address the means to ensure that the computing resources are available to authorized users when needed.

Authentication and Identification

A policy should specify the means of authenticating a user when the user is requesting service on a computer resource and presenting his or her identity. The authentication must be performed in a secure manner. Strong authentication using a public key certificate should be employed to bind a user to an identity. Exchanged information should not be able to be altered. This safeguard can be accomplished using a certificate-based digital signature. Some corresponding requirements include:

- Mechanisms for determining identity
- Binding of a resource to an identity
- Need for identification of communication origins
- Management of out-of-band authentication means
- Reaffirmations of identities

Authorization

After authentication, the policy must address authorization to allow access to resources, including the following areas:

- A user requesting that specified services not be applied to his or her message traffic
- Bases for negative or positive responses
- Reponses to requests for services specified in a simple and clear manner

- Authorization to access services include the type of service and the identity of the user
- Identification of entities that have the authority to set authorization rules between users and services
- Means for the provider of services to identify the user and associated traffic
- Means for the user to acquire information concerning the service profile kept by the service provider on the user

These policy issues should generate requirements addressing:

- Specific mechanisms to provide for access control
- Privileges assigned to subjects during the system life
- Management of access control subsystems

Auditing

The auditing of information systems has characteristics similar to auditing in the SDLC in that the auditing plan must address the following:

- Determination of the scope of the audit
- Determination of the objectives of the audit
- Validation of the audit plan
- Identification of necessary resources
- Conduct of the audit
- Documentation of the audit
- Validation of the audit results
- Report of final results

The Information Systems Audit and Control Association (ISACA) has developed information systems (IS) audit standards, guidelines, and a code of ethics for auditors. This information can be found at the ISACA Web site at `www.isaca.org`. The information system security policy should decompose the audit requirements to risk-based elements that consider the following three types of audit-related risks:

- **Inherent risk**—Concerns the susceptibility of a process to perform erroneously, assuming that no internal controls exist
- **Detection risk**—Associated with the probability that an auditor's methods will not detect a material error
- **Control risk**—Involves the probability that extant controls will not prevent or detect errors in a timely fashion

The information system security policy decomposition for audit should also consider organizational characteristics such as supervisory issues, institutional ethics, compensation policies, organizational history, and the business environment. In particular, the following elements of the information system organizational structure and management should be taken into account:

- Organizational roles and responsibilities
- Separation of duties
- IS management
- IS training
- Qualifications of IS staff
- Database administration
- Third party–provided services
- Managing of contracts
- Service level agreements (SLAs)
- Quality management and assurance standards
- Change management
- Problem management
- Project management
- Performance management and indicators
- Capacity management
- Economic performance
  - Application of SOP 98-1,[12] which is an accounting statement of position that defines how information technology software development or acquisition costs are to be expended or capitalized
  - Expense management and monitoring
- Information system security management
- Business continuity management

The policy decomposition for the audit component is recursive in that the audit has to address the IS security policy, standards, guidelines, and procedures.

The audit policy decomposition should delineate the three basic types of controls, which are preventive, detective, and corrective. It should provide the basis for the qualitative audit risk assessment guidelines of:

- Identification of all relevant assets
- Valuation of the assets
- Identification of threats
- Identification of regulatory requirements

[12]American Institute of Certified Public Accountants (AICPA), ''Accounting for the Costs of Computer Software Developed or Obtained for Internal Use,'' AICPA Statement of Position (SOP) No. 98-1, March 1998, www.aicpa.org/.

- Identification of organizational risk requirements
- Identification of the likelihood of threat occurrence
- Definition of organizational entities or subgroupings
- Review of previous audits
- Determination of audit budget constraints

The policy should ensure that auditing should be able to pass a test of *due care*, which is defined by the ISACA as "the level of diligence that a prudent and competent person would exercise under a given set of circumstances."[13]

In order to conduct forensic investigations, the confidentiality and integrity of audit information must be protected at the highest level of security.

A valuable audit planning and execution tool that was introduced by ISACA in 1996 is the "Control Objectives for Information and related Technology (CobiT)" document. As of this writing, CobiT is now in version 4.1. It is divided into 4 domains comprising 34 high-level control objectives. These 34 control objectives are further divided into 318 specific control objectives. CobiT defines a *control objective* as a goal that some set of risks does not occur. The four CobiT domains are:

- Planning and organization
- Acquisition and implementation
- Delivery and support

Monitoring Internal and External Requirements

The requirements of the information system security policy relative to software assurance should be analyzed to ensure their consistency and correctness. Two of types of secure software requirements analysis should be performed:

- **Internal**—Necessary in order to ascertain that the requirements are complete, correct, and consistent with the related specification requirements. The analysis should address:
  - Security constraints
  - The software's nonfunctional properties
  - The software's positive functional requirements
- **External**—Necessary to determine if:
  - The software assurance requirements address the legal regulatory and required policy issues
  - The nonfunctional security requirements represent a proper decomposition of the system security goals
  - Software assurance requirements conflict with system security goals
  - The software is resilient

[13]ISACA, "IS Auditing Guideline on Due Professional Care," Information Systems Audit and Control Association, March 1, 2008, `www.isaca.org`.

Also, in the context of internal and external access to information systems, the issues in Table 2-2 should be considered:

Table 2-2: Internal and External Security Requirements

INTERNAL	EXTERNAL
Maintain identity of active users	External connections must incorporate adequate controls to safeguard IT resources
Implement internal access controls	At a minimum, all external connections must incorporate a firewall
Use secure gateways to allow internal users to connect to external networks	If the user access originates from outside the protected network, user must be identified and authenticated at the gateway
Hide internal Domain Name Systems (DNSs)	Use external authentication databases, such as RADIUS
Dial-up modems should not be connected to computers that are connected to the internal network	Employ content filtering to permit or deny services to specific external hosts
Email messages flowing through the information systems should be monitored for internal policy compliance	Accredit external connections prior to use
	External connections should be periodically reviewed by an independent organization

National Institute of Standards and Technology, "An Introduction to Computer Security: The NIST Handbook, Special Publication 800-12," October 1995.

Identification of Data and Gathering of Threat Information

User identity and the corresponding account information have to be managed according to the information system security policy. Data about the individual or process requesting authentication and authorization has to be gathered and evaluated. Identity information can be obtained by conventional means such as an entity claiming an identity, but it can also be acquired from inference, some type of recognition mechanism, or from metadata. Identity management involves such items as the entities' personal information, security clearance, biometric data, encrypted passwords, and role. Strong verification of a claimed identity is critical to the preservation of confidentiality and integrity. Authentication of a user or process identity provides the means to:

- Support nonrepudiation
- Enable authorization
- Enforce accountability
- Support access control decisions
- Deny access to unauthorized users

Gathering and preserving data are critical to the identification process. The following sections categorize the types of data in an information system and typical cases of data use and abuse.

Data Classification

For the purposes of information system security and the related software assurance, data can be considered to be a passive object that exists in one of the following four states:

- In storage or "at rest"
- Being created
- In motion from one location to another
- Being modified or overwritten

Data can also be categorized according to its value or its frequency of access. Important and frequently accessed data should be stored on the fastest storage media. According to the DACS, this data can be classified as the following:[14]

- **Input data**—Data read into a system and stored in an internal representation
- **Output data**—Data written to an output destination following processing
- **Internal data**—Data initialized by the application, read into an internal representation, or computed within the application
- **Security-critical data**—A subset of internal data of high value to an attacker
- **Hidden data**—Concealing data to protect it from unauthorized disclosure using obfuscation techniques

Other data classifications include file size, date of creation or last use, and entities that accessed the information. According to Stephen Bigelow, "The practice of data classification seeks to align information with business needs, categorizing the data based on these needs and then using the resulting classifications as a roadmap for retaining and storing information."[15]

Data classification is also driven by compliance requirements with such laws as HIPAA and Sarbanes-Oxley.

Use Cases

A described in the DACS State-of-the-Art Report (SOAR), a "*use case* in software engineering and systems engineering is a description of a system's behavior as it responds to a request that originates from outside of that system. The use case technique is used to capture the functional requirements of a system."[16]

[14]Goertzel, Winograd, et al., "Enhancing the Development Life Cycle to Produce Secure Software."

[15]Bigelow, Stephen J., "Data Classification: An Overview," SearchStorage.com, November 2005.

[16]Information Assurance Technology Analysis Center (IATAC), Data and Analysis Center for Software (DACS), State-of-the-Art Report (SOAR), July 2007.

Use case modeling was introduced by Ivar Jacobson[17] and has been augmented by other researchers in the field.

A use case is concerned with an external *actor* that interacts with a system in order to achieve a desired outcome and should not include any implementation-specific language. An actor can be another system or user, and the use case is viewed from the perspective of the actor.

Use cases can be represented graphically by a use case diagram through the application of the Unified Modeling Language (UML).[18] A use case diagram depicts actors and a system's use cases. An actor is drawn as a stick figure with an associated name. A use case is drawn as an oval with a corresponding use case label. In the UML use case diagram, *associations* between actors and uses cases are depicted by solid lines. Optional *system boundary* boxes can be drawn around use cases to show the system borders. A UML *package* can be used to group use cases when the diagrams become large and complex. A *trigger* in a use case is an internal, external, or time-based occurrence that initiates the use case. The trigger depends on use case *preconditions* that specify which circumstances must exist for the trigger to initiate the use case, if the system is in the appropriate state. A use case *summary* should be written to give the reader a short description of the particular use case.

A simple use case diagram example illustrating banking transactions is given in Figure 2-6.

BUSINESS AND SYSTEM USE CASES

Use cases can be categorized as business (essential) use cases or system use cases. A *business use case* is presented at a high level with minimal technical language and represents processes that provide services to the business actor. A *system use case* gives more detail and describes the functions and results provided to the actor. Use cases that include details of interaction protocols are also known as *real* or *implementation* use cases.

Abuse Cases

With use cases as a basis, another approach to developing software security requirements is to consider the system behavior under attack and from the perspective of the attacker. This method is known as using *abuse cases,* which define how a software system should not respond to a malicious or unintentional attack. In "Using Abuse Case Models for Security Requirements Analysis," John McDermott and Chris Fox define an abuse case as "a specification of a type of complete interaction between a

[17]Jacobson, I., *Object-Oriented Software Engineering* (Upper Saddle River, NJ: Addison-Wesley Professional, 1992).

[18]Rumbaugh, J., Jacobson, I., and Booch, G., *The Unified Modeling Language Reference Manual* (Upper Saddle River, NJ: Addison-Wesley, 1999).

system and one or more actors, where the results of the interaction are harmful to the system, one of the actors, or one of the stakeholders in the system.''[19]

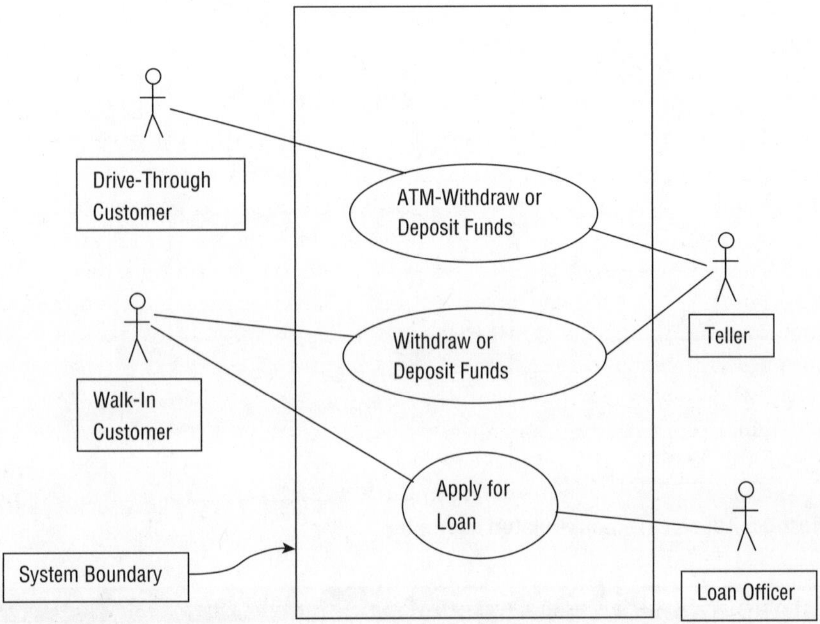

Figure 2-6: Banking use case

Abuse cases are sometimes categorized as misuse or hostile use cases. A *misuse case* involves either unintentional or intentional non-malicious threats, while a *hostile use case* relates to an intentional, malicious threat to a use case.

Abuse cases identify probable attack targets, evaluate threats to be addressed, determine software security objectives, and define software security countermeasures. An abuse case is concerned with an attacker's potential actions and the response of the software to these actions. In order to accomplish this end, each abuse case is associated with a particular software requirement and software test condition. An abuse case should also identify the abuse of privilege used to complete the abuse case.

Abuse case models are not identical to use case models in that the actors in the abuse case are usually malicious and labeled as such. Actors might be internal unauthorized users or outsiders. In an abuse case, an actor is usually defined by its *objectives, skills, and resources*. Also, because it is not possible to define which vulnerabilities might be exploited by a malicious actor, an abuse case describes a family of possible harmful interactions and transactions instead of a single interaction as conducted in a use case. Thus, an abuse case, by necessity, will describe a number of possible damage descriptions caused by a range of security privileges that might be compromised.

A simple abuse case bank example is shown in Figure 2-7.

[19]McDermott, J., and Fox, C., ''Using Abuse Case Models for Security Requirements Analysis,'' Department of Computer Science, James Madison University, Harrisonburg, VA, 1999.

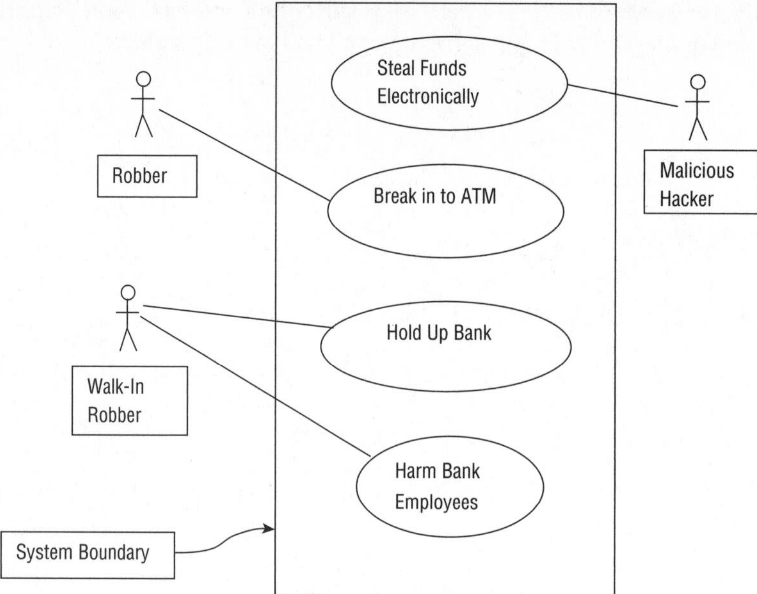

Figure 2-7: Abuse case bank-related example

> **ATTACK GRAPHS**
>
> **Tools such as *attack graphs* and *attack trees* are useful in determining an attacker's possible approaches, and *attack response graphs* can be applied to model the software's responses to different types of attacks. Then, the abuse cases can be used to develop corresponding security cases to deal with each of the possible threats.**

A summary of the process of developing an abuse case against a use case is as follows:

1. Determine the ways that harmful agents would try to interfere with or corrupt the interactions in a use case description
2. List each of these attack scenarios as a potential abuse case
3. Ascertain the security threats against the use case processes, functions, and transactions from possible risks
4. Identify possible unintentional activities that could cause harm and the results of these activities

Abuse cases are useful in providing insights on the security features of a software product. Some of the advantages of using abuse cases in requirements specification include:

- They are simple and easy to understand.
- They illustrate what can and cannot be protected.

- They are useful in discovering security requirements.
- They prioritize threats that have to be addressed.
- They identify trade-offs between functionality and security.
- They support the evaluation of design alternatives in the development cycle.

Summary

Secure software requirements are driven by an organization's information system security policy. In turn, guidelines, standards, procedures, and baselines derive from senior management intent incorporated in the security policy. These documents address confidentiality, integrity, availability, identification, authentication, authorization, and auditing requirements for software systems.

Classifying data by its use and location also provides an important input to software security requirements. Additional important tools that give a different perspective to software security requirements specification are use cases and abuse cases, which describe interactions among users and systems and model potential attacks and threats from the viewpoint of the attacker.

Assessment Questions

1. Risk assessment, abuse/misuse cases, threat analysis, and models are additional elements that can be used to augment traditional software requirements engineering in order to accomplish which one of the following?

   A. Increase software security

   B. Develop a use case diagram

   C. Develop an abuse/case diagram

   D. Support requirements traceability

2. In goal-oriented software requirements engineering, active components such as humans, devices, and legacy software that play some role toward goal satisfaction are called:

   A. Actors

   B. Agents

   C. Users

   D. Objects

3. One implementation of goal-oriented requirements engineering that provides a basis for determining if a goal has been satisfied through meeting lower-level goals such as reliability, performance, security, and reliability is known as:

   A. Noncritical requirements (NFR) framework

   B. Noninterference requirements (NFR) framework

C. Misuse case

D. Nonfunctional requirements (NFR) framework

4. One goal-oriented requirements engineering approach uses generic specification patterns that map to the information system's properties of confidentiality, integrity, availability, privacy, authentication, authorization, and nonrepudiation. The security patterns are then transformed into goals that are used to develop a correlated "anti-model." This approach is known as the:

   A. Nonfunctional requirements (NFR) framework

   B. MILOS security model

   C. Noninterference requirements (NFR) framework

   D. MODE security model

5. The phases of the SDLC according to NIST SP 800-14 are:

   A. Initiation, development/acquisition, implementation, operation/maintenance, disposal

   B. Initiation, design, implementation, operation/maintenance, disposal

   C. Initiation, development/acquisition, implementation, operation/maintenance, re-initiation

   D. Initiation, development/acquisition, implementation, testing, disposal

6. One approach to defining elements of an information security policy is to correlate the system engineering process and the secure software engineering process. This correlation can be accomplished through which one of the following models?

   A. Secure model

   B. Zee model

   C. Verify model

   D. Vee model

7. The left side of the model that correlates the system engineering process and the secure software engineering process and contains the major technical phases involved in transforming systems requirements into an operational software system is known as the:

   A. Integration and verification sequence

   B. Decomposition and verification sequence

   C. Decomposition and definition sequence

   D. Integration and definition sequence

8. The right side of the model that correlates the system engineering process and the secure software engineering process and contains the major technical phases involved in transforming systems requirements into an operational software system is known as the:

   A. Integration and verification sequence

   B. Decomposition and verification sequence

C. Decomposition and definition sequence

D. Integration and definition

9. Which NIST Special Publication presents 33 security principles that start at the design phase of the information system or application and continue until the system's retirement and secure disposal?

A. NIST Special Publication 800-64

B. NIST Special Publication 800-30

C. NIST Special Publication 800-27

D. NIST Special Publication 800-20

10. The NIST FIPS Publication "Minimum Security Requirements for Federal Information and Information Systems" specifies items that can be used to provide inputs to secure software policies. This NIST publication is:

A. FIPS 300

B. FIPS 200

C. FIPS 220

D. FIPS 210

11. NIST categorizes computer system security policies into which one of the following three basic types?

A. Project, issue-specific, system-specific

B. Program, issue-specific, implementation-specific

C. Program, security-specific, system-specific

D. Program, issue-specific, system-specific

12. Which one of the following is a nontechnical policy addressing a single or specific item of concern to an organization?

A. System specific

B. Issue specific

C. Security specific

D. Project specific

13. Which policy is technically focused and addresses only one computer system or device type and includes security objectives and operational security rules?

A. Security specific

B. Program specific

C. Issue specific

D. System specific

14. Security policies that an organization must implement due to compliance or other legal requirements are called:

A. Guidelines

B. Advisory policies

C. Regulatory policies

D. Organizational policies

15. Which one of the following specifies the use of particular technologies in a uniform way and is usually compulsory?

A. Standards

B. Guidelines

C. Procedures

D. Baselines

16. Which one of the following refers to the methodologies of securing systems, but are recommended actions only and are not compulsory.

A. Standards

B. Guidelines

C. Procedures

D. Baselines

17. Which one of the following embodies the detailed steps that are followed to perform a specific task?

A. Standards

B. Guidelines

C. Procedures

D. Baselines

18. Who is assigned the overall responsibility for the security of information?

A. Senior-level management

B. Data owners

C. Users

D. Information systems auditors

19. Which one of the following refers to rights and privileges granted to an individual or process that enable access to computer resources and information assets?

A. Authentication

B. Authorization

C. Auditing

D. Identification

20. According to the Data and Analysis Center for Software (DACS), which one of the following "is concerned, in large part, with defining the set of rules by which system subjects are allowed to change the states of data objects in the system"?

A. Risk analysis

B. Regulatory policy

C. Guidelines

D. Information security policy

21. Which one of the following policy requirements is concerned with denying illegitimate access to computing resources and prevention of external attacks such as denial-of-service attacks?

    A. Confidentiality

    B. Availability

    C. Integrity

    D. Authentication

22. The information system security policy should decompose the audit requirements to risk-based elements that consider which one of the following three types of audit-related risks?

    A. Aggregation risk, development risk, implementation risk

    B. Inherent risk, detection risk, control risk

    C. Assessment risk, evaluation risk, operating risk

    D. Inherent risk, development risk, control risk

23. Which one of the following is an accounting statement of position that defines how information technology software development or acquisition costs are to be expended or capitalized?

    A. SOP 90-1

    B. SOP 98-1

    C. SOP 98-3

    D. SOP 95-1

24. Which one of the following tests is defined as "the level of diligence that a prudent and competent person would exercise under a given set of circumstances"?

    A. Due care

    B. Separation of duties

    C. Exigent circumstances

    D. Authorization

25. The confidentiality and integrity of audit information must be protected at which one of the following levels of security?

    A. Moderate

    B. Lowest

    C. Highest

    D. Not at all

26. Which one of the following is a valuable audit planning and execution tool that was introduced by the Information Systems Audit and Control Association (ISACA)?

    A. CobiT

    B. SATAN

    C. AuditSecure

    D. ATEST

27. Which one of the following represents the two of types of secure software requirements analysis that should be performed pursuant to an information system security policy?
    A. Internal and external
    B. Detailed and specific
    C. Qualitative and quantitative
    D. Development and operational
28. Which one of the following groups of states describes the best complete set of states in which data can exist for the purposes of software assurance?
    A. In storage or "at rest," being created, in motion from one location to another, being modified or overwritten
    B. In storage or "at rest," being created, in motion from one location to another
    C. In storage or "at rest," in motion from one location to another, being modified or overwritten
    D. Being created, in motion from one location to another, being modified or overwritten
29. Data can be categorized according to its value or its frequency of access. Important and frequently accessed data should be stored on the fastest storage media. This data can be classified as which one of the following?
    A. Input data, output data, external data, security-critical data, hidden data
    B. Input data, output data, internal data, security-critical data, hidden data
    C. Input data, output data, internal data, security-critical data, visible data
    D. Input data, output data, internal data, pseudo- data, hidden data
30. In software engineering and systems engineering, what is a description of a system's behavior as it responds to a request that originates from outside of that system?
    A. Misuse case
    B. Use case
    C. Abuse case
    D. External case
31. What is a specification of a type of complete interaction between a system and one or more actors, where the results of the interaction are harmful?
    A. Abuse case
    B. Use case
    C. Internal case
    D. Malicious case
32. Use cases can be represented graphically by a use case diagram through the application of which one of the following?
    A. Uniform Method Language (UML)

B. Unified Case Language (UCL)
C. Unified Simulation Language (USL)
D. Unified Modeling Language (UML)

33. In a use case diagram, associations between actors and use cases are depicted by which one of the following?
A. Solid lines
B. Dotted lines
C. Oval shapes
D. Flags

34. In a use case, an internal, external, or time-based occurrence that initiates the use case is called a:
A. Threshold
B. Boundary
C. Trigger
D. Starter

35. A use case that is presented at a high level with minimal technical language and represents processes that provide services to the actor is known as which one of the following?
A. System use case
B. Real use case
C. Implementation use case
D. Business use case

36. Actors in an abuse case usually have which one of the following characteristics?
A. Do not intend harm to the system
B. Are not normally malicious
C. Are authorized users
D. Are malicious and labeled as such

37. In an abuse case, an actor is usually defined by its:
A. Type, skills, and resources
B. Objectives, persistence, and resources
C. Objectives, skills, and resources
D. Type, persistence, and resilience

38. In most situations, an abuse case describes which one of the following?
A. A family of possible harmful interactions
B. A single interaction
C. An interaction as conducted in a use case
D. A benign interaction

39. Advantages such as simplicity, ease of understanding, illustrating what can and cannot be protected, and prioritizing of threats refer to which one of the following?

    A. Using abuse cases in requirements specification

    B. Using use cases in requirements specification

    C. Using component cases in requirements specification

    D. Using trade-off cases in requirements specification

CHAPTER 3

Secure Software Design

Secure software should not contain design flaws with security implications.

Design flaws may or may not be encountered during normal use of a software application, and may not lead to a security failure. However, if a flaw with security implications is discovered by an attacker, an attacker could induce a failure by setting up specific conditions to exploit the flaw.

Therefore, the design process should include activities for decreasing the likelihood that the design will contain flaws, so that the software will perform as required, even under attack.

The design process should include a design specification that is easily comprehensible and traceable. For example, the Data and Analysis Center for Software (DACS)[1] writes that:

> *Comprehensibility will make the design specification easier to analyze to reveal possible vulnerabilities and weaknesses. A specification that is fully traceable will make it easy to determine whether the design satisfies all of its requirements, including its security-relevant requirements. This traceability should be backward and forward, i.e., it should be possible to trace forward from a requirement to its manifestation in the design, and backward from a point in the design to derive the requirement(s) satisfied at that point. It should also be possible to trace forward from any point in the design to its manifestation in the implemented code, and backward from the code to the part of the design realized by that code.*

This chapter explores the fundamentals of secure software design through design processes, design considerations, architecture, technologies, and technical review.

[1]Goertzel, K., Winograd, T., et al., "Enhancing the Development Life Cycle to Produce Secure Software," Version 2.0. Rome, New York: United States Department of Defense Data and Analysis Center for Software, October 2008.

Design Processes

The first stage of secure software design is concerned with identifying potential threats to an information system's applications and finding ways to minimize the risk of those threats. These objectives may be accomplished by conducting activities that approach the design from an adversary's perspective, which includes identifying the pathways that could be used to conduct an attack. A formal threat modeling process is then followed to enumerate potential threats and map each threat to a corresponding mitigation. The models and documentation created to support the threat modeling process are subsequently revised as the requirements are developed into ever more detailed specifications. The first activity in secure software design is attack surface evaluation, which helps identify the pathways that could be used to conduct attacks against the application.

Attack Surface Evaluation

The entry points and exit points of an application that are accessible to users and attackers are commonly referred to as the application's *attack surface*. Attack surface evaluation is concerned with analyzing and reducing the attack surface of a software application.

The term *application* refers to software in its operating environment or a grouping of software components for a common purpose, such as an operating system. Entry points are the inputs to the application through interfaces, services, protocols, and code. Exit points are the outputs from the application, including error messages produced by the application in response to user interaction. The entry and exit points should be accessible only to users who possess the required level of trust.

The term, *relative attack surface,* is an informal notion of the relative security between similar versions of a software product. It was first introduced by Michael Howard of Microsoft in an article entitled "Fending Off Future Attacks By Reducing Attack Surface."[2] In this article, Howard surmised that it may be possible to calculate the "attackability" of a product or its exposure to attack, but not necessarily its vulnerability. In other words, a product has certain features that are likely opportunities of attack, but the features may or may not contain flaws that could be triggered to induce a security failure. Howard states that "relative attack surface can be thought of as the *cyclomatic complexity* of security." Cyclomatic complexity is a widely used software metric introduced by Thomas McCabe in 1976. The Carnegie Mellon Software Engineering Institute Software Technology Roadmap defines cyclomatic complexity as "a broad measure of soundness and confidence for a program."[3] Cyclomatic complexity is often referred to as just program complexity, or as McCabe's complexity.

To demonstrate how the relative attack surface is calculated for a specific product, Howard first identified 17 features that are likely opportunities of attack (attack vectors) for the Windows operating system, such as open sockets, services running as SYSTEM, and Guest account enabled. Each instance of an attack vector is assigned a

[2] `http://msdn.microsoft.com/en-us/library/ms972812.aspx`
[3] `www.sei.cmu.edu/str/str.pdf`

weight or bias based on its likelihood of being attacked and the severity of the damage that would result from a successful compromise. For example, a service that runs by default under the SYSTEM account and opens a world accessible socket is a visible and attractive target for attack. Even if the underlying code is secure, because it is running by default, with elevated privileges, and is capable of being probed remotely, it has a greater likelihood of being attacked. And if the code is vulnerable, a successful attack could result in severe damage such as a system compromise. Therefore, the instances of the attack vectors involved in this attack scenario would be assigned high weights. In comparison, a weak Registry ACL that is locally accessible would be assigned a low weight.

Based on the 17 attack vectors, he then computed a measure of the attack surface, which he calls the Relative Attack Surface Quotient (RASQ), for seven running versions of the Windows operating system. A comparison of the RASQ scores confirm perceived beliefs about the relative security of Windows versions by showing that either Windows NT4 or Windows 2000 has a greater relative attack surface than Windows 2003.

The RASQ model quantifies the relative ''attackability'' provided by each version of Windows. In summary, it can be calculated as follows:

- Identify the attack vectors—these are the features often used on attacks in Windows, e.g., the 17 attack vectors for Windows identified by Michael Howard.
- Assign weights to the attack vectors—a weight should be assigned to each instance of an attack vector based on its contribution to the attack surface. All features are not equally likely to be used in attacks on Windows. For example, a service running as SYSTEM is more likely to be attacked than a service running as an ordinary user. Therefore, that instance of the attack vector would be assigned greater weight.
- Estimate the total attack surface—for each instance of an attack vector, the attack vector's weight is added to the total attack surface.

In March 2003, Microsoft contracted the Ernst & Young LLP Advanced Security Center to validate the RASQ model. The methodology used for validating the model, analysis, and test results are described in the customer paper entitled, ''Using Attack Surface Area And Relative Attack Surface Quotient To Identify Attackability.''[4] In this paper, the authors write that the RASQ model can meet its stated objective of quantifying the ''attackability'' of an operating system, but specify certain caveats for its use:

- The RASQ model's objective should not be misinterpreted to measure a system's vulnerability to attacks, and/or more importantly, its security risk.
- Test results based on this model are only meaningful for products of a similar nature. This is an especially important condition because the root attack vectors used by the model are very dependent on specific technologies and features.
- Since the model uses parameters that are only valid within the Microsoft domain of operating systems, its applicability at this stage should be restricted to Microsoft platforms.

[4] `www.microsoft.com/windowsserver2003/docs/AdvSec.pdf`

- The RASQ scores alone may not signify that a platform with a lower RASQ score is more secure than a platform with a higher RASQ score.

Subsequent research has focused on creating a formal model to measure attack surface. In one of the first papers published on this subject, "Measuring Relative Attack Surfaces,"[5] the researchers (Howard, Wing, and Pincus) propose a general metric for determining whether one version of a system is more secure than another with respect to a fixed set of dimensions: targets and enablers, channels and protocols, and access rights:

- Targets and enablers—resources that an attacker can use or take over. There are two kinds of resources: processes and data. A target in one attack may be an enabler for another attack. Examples of process targets/enablers are browsers, mailers, and database servers. Examples of data targets/enablers are files, directories, registries, and access rights.
- Channels and protocols—a channel is a means of communicating information from sender to receiver. There are two kinds of channels: message passing, e.g., sockets, RPC connections, named pipes; and shared memory, e.g., files, directories, registries. The end point of a channel is the process. A protocol is associated with each channel. Example protocols for message passing channels include ftp, RPC, and http.
- Access Rights—permissions such as read, write, and execute that are associated with resources such as files, directories, channels, and channel end points.

The researchers mapped Howard's original 17 attack vectors for Windows to the formal terminology of targets and enablers, channels and protocols, and access rights. They also noted that the original attack vectors did not take scripting engines into account. Thus, they added three scripting engines as process enablers, bringing the total count to 20. The mapping of the 20 RASQ attack vectors to the formal terminology is shown in Table 3-1.

The researchers then calculated RASQ scores for Windows versions using the 20 attack vectors and improved weight functions. This yielded similar results to Howard's initial calculations. The researchers write that the RASQ scores are consistent with anecdotal evidence for the relative security of the Windows operating systems. The default version of a running Windows Server 2003 system is more secure than the default version of a running Windows 2000 system, and a running Windows Server 2003 with IIS installed is only slightly less secure than a running Windows Server 2003 without IIS installed.

Carnegie Mellon University student Pratyusa K. Manadhata and Professor Jeannette M. Wing have a large repository of additional research on attack surface measurement, including research on Linux, at `www.cs.cmu.edu/~pratyus/as.html`.

[5]Howard, M., Pincus, J., and Wing, J., "Measuring Relative Attack Surfaces," Proceedings of Workshop on Advanced Developments in Software and Systems Security, Taipei, December 2003.

Table 3-1: Mapping of 20 RASQ Attack Vectors to Formal Terminology

20 RASQ ATTACK VECTORS	FORMAL TERMINOLOGY
Open sockets	Channels
Open RPC end points	Channels
Open named pipes	Channels
Services	Process targets
Services running by default	Process targets, constrained by access rights
Services running as SYSTEM	Process targets, constrained by access rights
Active Web handlers (e.g., HTR files)	Process targets
Active ISAPI Filters	Process targets
Dynamic Web pages (e.g., ASP)	Process targets
Executable virtual directories	Data targets
Enabled accounts	Data targets
Enabled accounts in admin group	Data targets, constrained by access rights
Null sessions to pipes and shares	Channels
Guest account enabled	Data targets, constrained by access rights
Weak ACLs in file system	Data targets, constrained by access rights
Weak ACLs in Registry	Data targets, constrained by access rights
Weak ACLs on shares	Data targets, constrained by access rights
VBScript enabled	Process enabler
Jscript enabled	Process enabler
ActiveX enabled	Process enabler

Howard, M., Pincus, J., and Wing, J., "Measuring Relative Attack Surfaces," Proceedings of Workshop on Advanced Developments in Software and Systems Security, Taipei, December 2003.

Organizations involved in software development have traditionally focused on improving code quality for improving software security and quality. The software quality effort focuses on reducing the number of design and coding errors in software. The results of this practice have typically been positive. For example, Ross Anderson writes in Security Engineering that "It has been shown that investment in software quality will reduce the incidence of computer security problems, regardless of whether security was a target of the quality program or not."[6]

[6]Anderson, R., *Security Engineering: A Guide to Building Dependable Distributed Systems*, 1st ed. (New York, NY: John Wiley and Sons, Inc., 2001).

However, building large and complex software systems devoid of errors, including those that may lead to security vulnerabilities, remains a very difficult task. The reality is that software contains both known and unknown errors, such that the security of the highest quality code is just a snapshot in time. Because the vulnerability research landscape is constantly evolving, it is highly likely that security researchers or attackers will discover new security vulnerabilities. A smaller attack surface makes the exploitation of the vulnerabilities more difficult and reduces the damage due to exploitation. Therefore, if security vulnerabilities will eventually be discovered, reducing the attack surface also reduces the severity of those vulnerabilities once found.

Microsoft refers to analyzing the attack surface as Attack Surface Analysis (ASA) and minimizing the attack surface as Attack Surface Reduction (ASR). ASA focuses on reducing the amount of code available to untrusted users. This reduction comes from understanding the application's entry and exit points and the trust levels required to access them.

The "core tenet of ASR is that all code has a nonzero likelihood of containing one or more vulnerabilities. The exploitation of some of these vulnerabilities will result in a customer compromise. Since the only way to prevent compromise is to reduce code use to zero, the only practical choice is to minimize the code exposed to untrusted users. Therefore, the goals of ASR are to reduce the amount of code executing by default, reduce the volume of code that is accessible to untrusted users by default, and to limit the damage if the code is exploited."[7]

Ultimately, reducing the attack surface is a risk mitigation strategy for lowering the probability of compromise. Since attack surface is a function of the level of trust and the type of access, the first way to realize this strategy is to minimize the amount of code available to untrusted or remote users. Each entry point in the application should be analyzed to determine who needs access by default—for example, unauthenticated (anonymous) user, authenticated user, administrator—and how they need access, such as remote, local subnet, local, or loopback.

If possible, each user should be authenticated, especially at network end points, before being granted access. An example of how this best practice could prevent an exploit is illustrated through the spread of the blaster worm. The blaster worm exploited a distributed component object model (DCOM) remote procedure call (RPC) buffer overrun vulnerability in Windows XP computers that were exposed to the public Internet. One reason the blaster worm was able to spread so quickly is that the RPC end points were remotely accessible and did not require authenticated access. In Windows XP Service Pack 2, Microsoft reduced the attack surface by limiting access to RPC end points to valid Windows users, and made it easier to configure the built-in Windows firewall to block outside sources from connecting to the computer by default.

Another example comes from Internet-based Web applications. Since these applications are remotely accessible by default, some applications reduce attack surface by limiting anonymous access to the login screen only, requiring all users to sign up and authenticate to do business.

Requiring authentication and limiting access to entry points and exit points in the application significantly reduces the attack surface. For example, an entry point that is

[7] http://msdn.microsoft.com/en-us/magazine/cc163882.aspx.

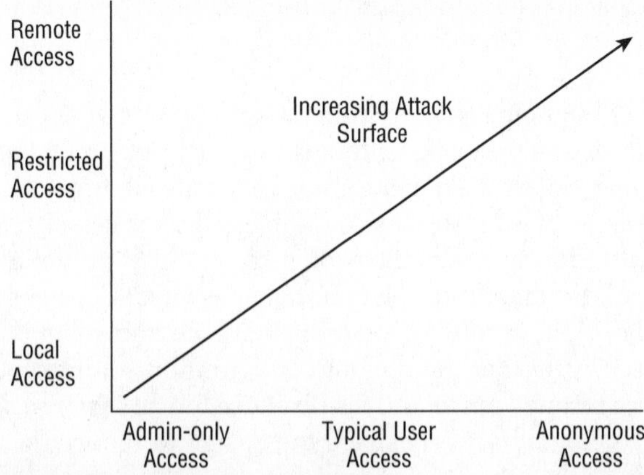

Figure 3-1: Accessibility increases attack surface

Howard, M., and Lipner, S., "The Security Development Lifecycle, SDL: A Process for Developing Demonstrably More Secure Software, 2006."

restricted to local access by an administrator has a smaller attack surface than an entry point exposed to remote access by an anonymous user, as shown in Figure 3-1.

To evaluate fully the attack surface of an application under design, it is helpful to picture a running application from the perspective of an adversary. The typical application user may see entry points and exit points only as the functionality exposed through the user interface, whereas an attacker will view the application in the context of its operating environment.

For example, a typical user will interact with a Web application through a Web browser. The designer of the application may have counted on the Web browser to enforce security policy for the application. Therefore, the Web browser may restrict the interaction between the user and the Web application by interpreting client-side code that validates user input. On the other hand, an attacker will interact with the Web application through a proxy tool that intercepts all HTTP requests and responses to and from the Web application. The intercepting proxy tool allows the attacker to observe and modify client-side code, including "hidden" variables, enumerate the application's content and functionality, and bypass client-side security controls. This unrestricted interaction with the Web application may also reveal additional entry and exit points such as an administrative interface or undocumented screens. The attacker also explores the Web application server software through the TCP port on which the application server is listening. This entry point may allow the attacker to detect the presence of other Web applications running on the same application server or provide clues concerning the security posture of the underlying operating system.

Likewise, in a local application, if the attacker controls the operating environment, the attacker may use commonly available operating system tools to enumerate local resource dependencies and determine access permissions of shared or persistent resources.

An understanding of the attacker's perspective can help inform design decisions. For example, knowing that the attacker can bypass client-side security controls, the designer may choose to validate input on the client-side only to promote usability while also validating input on the server-side to prevent abuse. This is a secure design decision.

The principle of designing software from the ground up to be secure is called *secure by design*. However, even if the designer follows security best practices, and implements layered security defenses, the designer cannot anticipate all future security challenges. Therefore, the designer should strive to implement only necessary functionality with the overall goal of reducing the number of entry and exit points in the application. The designer must also take into consideration the threats present in the operating environment of the application. To protect against both known and unknown threats, the designer must ensure that the default configuration settings for the application are the most secure settings possible. This is referred to as *secure by default*. These two principles taken together effectively shape the design to reduce the attack surface of the application.[8]

Secure by design and secure by default are based on the founding secure design principles of *economy of mechanism* and *least privilege*, defined in Chapter 1 and explained in depth later in this chapter. The principle of *economy of mechanism* means to keep the design as simple and small as possible. When complexity is introduced in the software, it makes the design and its security implications difficult to understand, increasing the likelihood of errors in the code. When the design is simple and small, less can go wrong. Applying economy of mechanism to secure design involves determining the minimum amount of functionality required by the application to perform its tasks, and providing only the features that implement that functionality. If the software must provide a number of features to a large and diverse set of users, it should be possible for the user to turn off those features or disable them if they are not necessary.

An example of economy of mechanism in practice is using a custom build and configuration process to secure an Apache Web server. When compiling the Apache Web server from the source code, specific features can be enabled through command-line flags to the build tools. After Apache is compiled, other functionality provided through the Apache `httpd` executable or modules can be removed by modifying the configuration files. Following this process to tailor the software provides the needed usability while reducing the attack surface.

Another principle that aids in reducing the attack surface is the principle of least privilege. This principle requires the designer to think about the actual privilege necessary by a subject to perform a specific task, rather than assigning a general set of privileges for all tasks performed. The designer should make a list of resources each subject must access and the specific tasks it must perform, to identify the appropriate privilege level. Each subject may also temporarily elevate privileges to perform a specific task, but must immediately relinquish privileges when the task is completed. The level of privilege should be enforced at the lowest level in the software stack and at the finest granularity.

In practice, this means the most restrictive set of operating system permissions or access control list (ACL) entries should be applied to all application files, including executables and configuration files. The application should also run as a low privilege

[8]Terms from `http://msdn.microsoft.com/en-us/library/ms995349.aspx`.

user account, with the smallest amount of privileges necessary to accomplish the application tasks. If the application is compromised, it should not have access to the resources of the entire operating environment.

A common example of least privilege in operation is the Apache Web server running on a *nix operating system such as Linux. When Apache first starts up, the *parent* `httpd` process runs as the highest privileged account on the system, known as root or superuser. The parent process then spawns a number of *child* processes to handle incoming connections. The child processes run as a lower privileged account, usually "apache" or "nobody." The role of the parent process is to perform administrative tasks such as stopping and starting the server, opening the HTTP ports, and managing the child processes. All untrusted user requests are handled by the lower privileged account. This deployment strategy serves to improve the security of the design by limiting the potential damage if Apache is compromised. For example, if a security weakness is discovered in Apache and an attacker exploits the weakness by inserting malicious code in an exposed child process, the malicious code will run with the same privileges as the compromised child process rather than the parent process.

Even though this restricts the compromise to a lower privileged account, the attacker has gained a foothold in the operating system. This foothold may enable an attacker to conduct an *elevation of privilege* attack against a process with higher privileges running on the operating system or the parent process of Apache itself. This particular attack should be considered in the security context of the operating environment of the application. For example, to further secure the operating environment, the designer can choose to employ a *defense-in-depth* strategy, which involves providing layers of security controls in case one or more of the other defenses are defeated. An additional security layer could be added by confining all of the running Apache processes to as small a protection domain as possible, which helps reduce the attack surface. In the *nix operating system, this involves employing a security mechanism known as a chroot jail. A *chroot* is an operation that changes the apparent disk root directory of the parent and child processes of an application. The re-rooted processes do not have access to files outside of that directory or "jail." However, if the attacker has somehow managed to gain root privileges within the jail, he is not prevented from making system calls, tracing processes outside the jail, or obtaining access to block devices. In recent years, virtualization and mandatory access control have supplanted the chroot jail as more effective ways to reduce the size of the protection domain and contain the damage of a compromise.

There are a number of other network, software, and environmental elements that contribute to creating a larger or smaller attack surface. These attack surface elements are specific to the type of application, technology, or operating system. For example, applications built with *managed code* technology, such as Java EE and Microsoft .NET, have a smaller attack surface than applications built with an *unmanaged code* technology. For example, consider an untrusted ActiveX control that runs in Internet Explorer. After the user authorizes the ActiveX control to run, it may have unrestricted access to the client computer. Conversely, .NET code that targets the common language runtime executes in a secure sandbox and runs with fine-grained permissions monitored by a central policy-enforcement mechanism. Chapter 4 discusses the security benefits of .NET managed code.

The choice of protocols also contributes to the size of the attack surface. UDP has a larger attack surface than TCP does because the source IP address is easy to spoof. UDP is a connectionless protocol that can send a datagram to a destination recipient without prior arrangement. TCP is a connection-oriented protocol that first arranges delivery with the destination recipient through a setup sequence known as the three-way handshake. Since UDP does not have to maintain an initial conversation with the destination recipient, it is possible to "fire and forget" the UDP datagram with a spoofed source IP address. The nature of UDP has been exploited in the past by malicious code. For example, the Slammer worm generated random source IP addresses, which made it difficult to block with IP-based filtering mechanisms. The payload delivered by the Slammer worm also fit in one UDP datagram, contributing to its rapid spread. Many applications that listen for TCP traffic also listen for UDP by default. Therefore, support for UDP should be removed if not needed.

CROSS-REFERENCE A good explanation of the rapid spread of the Slammer worm can be found at `www.caida.org/publications/papers/2003/sapphire/sapphire.html`.

In summary, the larger the size of the attack surface, the more exposed the software is to attack. The attack surface can be quantified using a software metric such as RASQ, or characterized by enumerating all possible attack vectors.

To effectively evaluate the attack surface, it is necessary to accurately identify the application's entry and exit points and the trust levels required to access them. Entry points, exit points, and trust levels are also key components of threat modeling, introduced in the next section. Threat modeling is a means of analyzing threats to a software application. In the process of threat modeling, data is traced from entry point to exit point, across trust boundaries, ultimately revealing security weaknesses in the application.

Threat Modeling

The Data and Analysis Center for Software (DACS)[9] defines a threat to a software-intensive system as "any actor, agent, circumstance, or event that has the potential to cause harm to that system or to the data or resources to which the system has or enables access." A threat can be categorized based on its intentionality. For example, a threat can be unintentional, intentional but non-malicious, or malicious; a malicious threat is assumed to be intentional. Although threats in all three categories have the potential to compromise the security of software, only malicious threats are realized by attacks. The DACS states that "the majority of attacks against software take advantage of, or exploit, some vulnerability or weakness in that software."

Modeling software is a way to envision the interactions of the proposed software within its intended environment. The better the model reflects the intended environment, the more useful the modeling approach becomes. Therefore, secure software

[9]Source: Goertzel, K., Winograd, T., et al., "Enhancing the Development Life Cycle to Produce Secure Software."

design and development benefits from modeling that explicitly incorporates security threats. As described in the DACS State-of-the-Art Report (SOAR), the primary issues in modeling are[10]:

- Doing it well
- Doing it thoroughly enough
- Knowing what to do with the results, e.g., how to transform the analysis into a metric and/or otherwise usable decision point

CROSS-REFERENCE **See `https://buildsecurityin.us-cert.gov/daisy/bsi/articles/tools/modeling/697-BSI.html` for a document that introduces general modeling concepts that provide a background for understanding modeling tools for software security.**

Combining the concepts of threats and modeling, the DACS State-of-the-Art Report (SOAR) defines threat modeling as:

> *. . . a methodical process for assessing and documenting the weaknesses or security risks associated with an application. It allows a development team to identify the highest risk components by approaching security from the perspective of an adversary who has specific goals in attacking an application.*[11]

NOTE **The term "threat modeling" is used in The Microsoft Trustworthy Security Development Lifecycle (SDL). Another secure software development methodology, Cigital's Seven Touchpoints for Software Security, refers to a similar activity and calls it "architectural risk analysis."**

There are a number of methodologies and tools designed to support software and/or system attack modeling and security risk analysis. These tools are listed in Table 3-2 along with additional resources.

Using an application tool for threat analysis and modeling has a number of advantages over using manual processes:

- Manual threat analysis and modeling tends to be time-consuming and error-prone when used to analyze and model large software projects.
- It is possible to automatically generate new threats after making a change to application context.
- The tool may assist in producing useful visualizations such as threat trees and attack surface that are difficult and time-consuming to create and update by hand.
- All of the secure software requirements are captured centrally in the tool's data store.

Of the methodologies and tools designed to support software and/or system attack modeling and security risk analysis, Microsoft Threat Modeling is one of the more popular. It has also evolved significantly since first being introduced as part of the

[10]IATAC/DACS, "Software Security Assurance State-of-the-Art Report (SOAR)," July 31, 2007.
[11]IATAC/DACS, "Software Security Assurance State-of-the-Art Report (SOAR)." July 31, 2007.

Microsoft software security initiative. An overview of this specific methodology as it evolved should provide insight into the most useful threat modeling activities in general and how they contribute to the larger software security strategy.

Table 3-2: Threat Modeling Tools

TOOL	RESOURCE(S)
Application Consulting and Engineering Threat Analysis and Modeling	Microsoft Security Developer Center Application Threat Modeling Web site: `http://msdn.microsoft.com/en-us/security/aa570413.aspx`
Calculative Threat Modeling Methodology	Practical Threat Analysis Web site: `www.ptatechnologies.com`
Trike	Octotrike.org Tools Web site: `www.octotrike.org`
Consultative Object Risk Analysis System (CORAS)	The CORAS Project Web site: `http://coras.sourceforge.net`
Threat Modeling based on Attacking Path (T-MAP)	University of Southern California Center for Systems and Software Engineering, "Security Economics and Threat Modeling for Information Technology (IT) Systems – A Stakeholder Value Driven Approach" project Web site: `http://sunset.usc.edu/csse/research/COTS_Security/` (Note: The T-MAP tool cannot be downloaded from this page; those interested in use of T-MAP should send email or call the point of contact listed on the Web site.) Yue Chen, "Software Security Economics and Threat Modeling Based on Attack Path Analysis: A Stakeholder Value Driven Approach," University of Southern California Doctoral Dissertation, December 2007: `http://sunset.usc.edu/csse/TECHRPTS/PhD_Dissertations/files/ChenY_Dissertation.pdf`

The first version of Microsoft Threat Modeling used STRIDE to help the user envision potential threat scenarios from the perspective of an adversary. The Microsoft Developer Network (MSDN) defines STRIDE as:

- **Spoofing**—attempting to gain access to a system by using a false identity. This can be accomplished using stolen user credentials or a false IP address. After the attacker successfully gains access as a legitimate user or host, elevation of privileges or abuse using authorization can begin.
- **Tampering**—unauthorized modification of data, for example as it flows over a network between two computers.
- **Repudiation**—ability of users (legitimate or otherwise) to deny that they performed specific actions or transactions. Without adequate auditing, repudiation attacks are difficult to prove.

- **Information disclosure**—unwanted exposure of private data. For example, a user views the contents of a table or file he or she is not authorized to open, or monitors data passed in plaintext over a network. Some examples of information disclosure vulnerabilities include the use of hidden form fields, comments embedded in Web pages that contain database connection strings and connection details, and weak exception handling that can lead to internal system-level details being revealed to the client. Any of this information can be very useful to the attacker.
- **Denial of service**—process of making a system or application unavailable. For example, a denial-of-service attack might be accomplished by bombarding a server with requests to consume all available system resources or by passing it malformed input data that can crash an application process.
- **Elevation of privilege**—occurs when a user with limited privileges assumes the identity of a privileged user to gain privileged access to an application. For example, an attacker with limited privileges might elevate his or her privilege level to compromise and take control of a highly privileged and trusted process or account.[12]

To complement STRIDE, a risk calculation methodology known as DREAD was created. The Microsoft Developer Network (MSDN) defines DREAD as:

- **Damage potential**—How great is the damage if the vulnerability is exploited?
- **Reproducibility**—How easy is it to reproduce the attack?
- **Exploitability**—How easy is it to launch an attack?
- **Affected users**—As a rough percentage, how many users are affected?
- **Discoverability**—How easy is it to find the vulnerability?

STRIDE and DREAD are useful techniques for employing the Microsoft Threat Modeling methodology. However, they have some drawbacks:

- They are subjective, requiring security subject matter expertise to employ effectively
- They are focused on attacks rather than threats

The second version of Microsoft Threat Modeling evolved to become an easier, more streamlined, and coherent process. The "Software Security Assurance State-of-the-Art Report (SOAR)" characterizes the revision of the Microsoft Threat Modeling methodology, now named Microsoft Threat Analysis and Modeling, released by Microsoft in March 2006, and its two key features:

- A new threat modeling methodology and process intended to be more user-friendly for software developers, architects, and other stakeholders who are not security experts to understand and execute
- A revised threat modeling application tool

[12] http://msdn.microsoft.com/en-us/library/aa302418.aspx.

To make threat modeling more user-friendly, Microsoft eliminated the STRIDE and DREAD features from Threat Modeling version 1 and shifted the perspective from the attacker to the defender. The user identifies closely with threats, rather than attacks, reflecting Microsoft's beliefs that the defender can better understand threats to the system than the attacker.[13]

NOTE Although STRIDE and DREAD were eliminated from Microsoft Threat Modeling, STRIDE is still a useful guide for classifying the threat type and related mitigation techniques. DREAD requires more security expertise to use with any degree of certainty, but it can help rank the risks of the threats relative to each other.

As with Threat Modeling version 1, Microsoft Threat Analysis and Modeling version 2 is an iterative process for modeling the design, adding layers of detail to an initial high-level threat model as the design progresses into subsequent phases of the life cycle. However, it prioritizes the business security requirements by more strictly defining a threat as an event that results in negative business or mission impact. The new threat model attempts to clarify the distinctions between threats, attacks, and vulnerabilities. The modeling process is facilitated through the use of a threat modeling tool that does not require security subject matter expertise to utilize.

NOTE The latest version of the Microsoft Threat Analysis and Modeling methodology and tool is version 2.1.2. The focus of this tool is the Line of Business (LOB) applications, with business objectives clearly defined, deployment patterns well understood, and a good understanding of the data assets managed by the application. Examples of applications include managing expenses or managing HR data. The methodology uses an asset-focused approach to try to understand the business risk in the application and help identify controls to manage that risk. For more information and to download the tool see `(http://msdn.microsoft.com/en-us/security/aa570413.aspx)`

Microsoft also released the Microsoft SDL Threat Modeling Tool version 3.0 in December 2008. The focus of this tool is products where the final deployment pattern is not known, such as Windows and SQL Server. For example, it is not known if the software is going to manage an e-commerce application on the public Internet, or a message board on a private Intranet. The focus of the methodology and the tool is on the software to try to ensure security of the underlying code. For more information and to download the tool see `http://msdn.microsoft.com/en-us/security/dd206731.aspx`

The Microsoft Threat Analysis and Modeling tool enables robust and contextualized threat analysis for evaluating the application security posture. The user of this tool can

[13]IATAC/DACS, "Software Security Assurance State-of-the-Art Report (SOAR)."

either employ a wizard to provide the tool with the data necessary to create the threat model or follow a manual process with five high-level steps:

1. Define the application requirements
2. Define application architecture
3. Model
4. Measure
5. Assimilate the model

To better illustrate the threat modeling capabilities of the tool and threat modeling principles in general, an example consumer loan Web application will be modeled with the tool. The first step in the process is to define the application requirements.

First, describe the business objectives or concept of operations for the consumer loan Web application:

- Provide customers with loan quotes
- Provide marketing information to entice potential customers
- Exchange information with banks and the three principal credit bureaus
- Store and protect customer account details and credit history
- Ensure application availability at five nines, i.e., 99.999% uptime
- Enforce authorization for specific user roles

Next, group all the users that interact with the application in user roles:

- Remote Anonymous User
- Remote User
- Consumer Loan Agent
- Web Site Administrator
- Database Administrator
- Network Administrator
- Application Administrator
- Application Server Process Identity
- Secure Web Server Process Identity

Then define the data types maintained or processed by the application. Set access control for each of the data types defined. The input to the Microsoft Threat Analysis and Modeling tool can be shown as a matrix of data type, role, and permissions, as in Table 3-3.

NOTE This access control information should be available from the secure software requirements phase.

Table 3-3: Data Types and Access Control

DATA TYPE	ROLE	PERMISSIONS
User ID	Remote Anonymous User	Create
User ID	Remote User	Update, Delete
User ID	Web Site Administrator	Create, Read, Update, Delete
User ID	Consumer Loan Agent	Delete
User password	Remote User	Update
User password	Web Site Administrator	Update
User password	Remote Anonymous User	Create (along with User ID)
Agent ID	Web Site Administrator	Create, Read, Update, Delete
Agent ID	Consumer Loan Agent	Update, Delete
Agent password	Web Site Administrator	Update
Agent password	Consumer Loan Agent	Create, Update
Personal data	Remote User	Create, Read, Update, Delete
Personal data	Consumer Loan Agent	Create, Read, Update, Delete
Personal data	Database Administrator	Delete
Loan request data	Remote User	Create, Read, Update, Delete
Loan request data	Consumer Loan Agent	Read, Update, Delete
Loan request data	Database Administrator	Delete
Loan response data	Remote User	Read
Loan response data	Consumer Loan Agent	Create, Read, Update, Delete
Loan response data	Database Administrator	Delete
Credit report	Consumer Loan Agent	Read, Delete
Credit report	Database Administrator	Delete
Unsecured Web pages	Remote Anonymous User	Read
Unsecured Web pages	Remote User	Read
Unsecured Web pages	Consumer Loan Agent	Read
Unsecured Web pages	Web Site Administrator	Create, Read, Update, Delete
Secured Web pages	Web Site Administrator	Create, Read, Update, Delete

Finally, define use cases based on access control for each of the data types:

- Any user reads welcome page.
- Application Administrator updates the application server.
- Application Server Process Identity exchanges information with the database.
- Application Server Process Identity exchanges information with banks.
- Application Server Process Identity exchanges information with credit bureau.
- Consumer Loan Agent creates agent password.
- Consumer Loan Agent deletes user ID.
- Consumer Loan Agent updates loan response data.
- Consumer Loan Agent or Database Administrator deletes loan response data.
- Network Administrator updates firewall.
- Remote Anonymous User or Web Site Administrator creates user ID.
- Remote User creates loan request data.
- Remote User updates loan request data.
- Remote User or Database Administrator deletes loan request data.
- Remote User or Consumer Loan Agent creates personal data.
- Remote User or Consumer Loan Agent reads loan request data.
- Remote User or Consumer Loan Agent reads loan response data.
- Remote User or Consumer Loan Agent reads personal data.
- Remote User or Consumer Loan Agent updates personal data.
- Remote User or Consumer Loan Agent or Database Administrator deletes personal data.
- Remote User or Web Site Administrator deletes user ID.
- Remote User or Web Site Administrator updates user password.
- Remote User or Web Site Administrator updates user ID.
- Web Site Administrator creates agent ID.
- Web Site Administrator creates Web pages.
- Web Site Administrator deletes Web pages.
- Web Site Administrator reads agent ID.
- Web Site Administrator updates Web pages.
- Web Site Administrator or Consumer Loan Agent deletes agent ID.
- Web Site Administrator or Consumer Loan Agent updates agent ID.
- Web Site Administrator or Consumer Loan Agent updates agent password.
- Web Site Administrator reads user ID.

The second high-level step in the threat modeling process is to define application architecture. First, define the high-level *components* of the application, such as the Web site or database. Next, define the access controls on each component by choosing all the roles through which each component is accessible. Import a predefined attack library into the threat model, which includes a list of *relevancies*. Then select the relevancies that are applicable to the component such as "Component utilizes HTTP" or "Component performs arithmetic operations." The input to the Microsoft Threat Analysis and Modeling tool can be shown as a matrix of component, roles, and relevancies, as in Table 3-4.

Table 3-4: Component Access Control

COMPONENT	ROLES	RELEVANCIES
Secure Web server	Remote User Consumer Loan Agent Web Site Administrator	Component performs file input/output (I/O) Component exposes a Web browser interface Component utilizes cryptography Component utilizes a network protocol Component utilizes HTTP Component constructs LDAP queries Component utilizes forms authentication Component constructs SQL queries
Database server	Remote User Consumer Loan Agent Database Administrator Secure Web Server Process Identity Application Server Process Identity	Component performs file input/output (I/O) Component utilizes cryptography Component utilizes a network protocol Component performs arithmetic operations
Application server	Consumer Loan Agent Application Administrator	Component utilizes C/C++ code Component performs file input/output (I/O) Component utilizes cryptography Component utilizes a network protocol Component performs arithmetic operations Component constructs SQL queries
Firewall	Network Administrator	Component utilizes a network protocol

COMPONENT	ROLES	RELEVANCIES
Credit bureau gateway	Consumer Loan Agent Application Server Process Identity	Component performs file input/output (I/O) Component utilizes cryptography Component utilizes a network protocol Component exposes a Web browser interface
Bank gateway	Consumer Loan Agent Application Server Process Identity	Component performs file input/output (I/O) Component utilizes cryptography Component utilizes a network protocol Component exposes a Web browser interface
Web server	Remote Anonymous User Remote User Consumer Loan Agent Web Site Administrator Database Administrator Network Administrator Application Administrator	Component utilizes a network protocol Component exposes a Web browser interface Component utilizes HTTP

Next, enter the *service roles* for the application that represent the context in which the components operate. The service role has an authentication mechanism such as Windows Integrated or Passport and an approximate number of *identities*. The identities can be used by components as default impersonation identities, such as NETWORK_SERVICE or SYSTEM:

- Web Server, Windows Integrated, NETWORK_SERVICE
- Application Server, Windows Integrated, NETWORK_SERVICE
- Database Server, Windows Integrated, NETWORK_SERVICE

Then define *external dependencies*, which are the network and architectural components that the application interacts with but does not control. They include the following:

- Security of the network between Web server and database server
- Security of the network between application server and database server
- Security of the network between the application server and banks
- Security of the network between the application server and credit bureaus
- Web site
- Database server

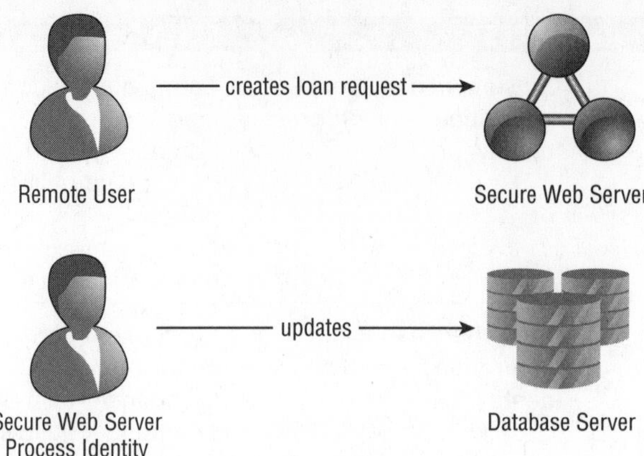

Figure 3-2: Remote User creates loan request data

- Web server session management
- Operating system, e.g., remote procedure call (RPC), loadable kernel modules (LKM), Distributed Component Object Model (DCOM)

Finally, for each defined use case, define the sequence of *calls* that fulfill the use case. The sequence of calls can be verified by viewing the *call graph* of the use case. An example use case is "Remote user with login credentials creates loan request data." The sequence of calls is "Remote user creates loan request data" and "Secure web server process identity updates database server." The call graph is represented in Figure 3-2.

Now that the Microsoft Threat Analysis and Modeling tool possesses all the information necessary to define the application context, the Model step can be performed. This consists of using the threat analysis and modeling tool to generate threats automatically. The tool identifies contextualized threats and countermeasures based on known attacks captured in a customizable and extensible attack library. Using this library, the tool will automatically determine potential attacks that can be used to realize given threats, and then propose effective countermeasures. Threats are generated by systematically corrupting the allowable actions of the application as defined in the calls, and then classified under the categories Confidentiality, Integrity, and Availability.

After the threats have been generated, select the primary *threat factor* for each threat. These threat factors help refine the context to aid in the process of analyzing the threats. An example threat factor is "Confidentiality – Unauthorized disclosure of <reads webpages> using <Web Server> by <Remote Anonymous User>."

The two possible threat factors for this threat are "Unauthorized disclosure of the identity" and "Unauthorized disclosure of the data." For this particular threat, "Unauthorized disclosure of the data" could be considered the primary threat factor.

The fourth high-level step, Measure, is concerned with quantifying the level of risk associated with each threat in order to prioritize the threat and its related countermeasures. First, assign a probability and impact value to each threat. The probabilities and impact choices are low, medium, and high. The risk rating associated with each threat, values from 1 (low/low) to 9 (high/high), are automatically calculated based on these selections.

Then select a response as a planned mitigation to those identified risks. The choices are to reduce, accept, avoid, or transfer the risk. Make a choice and provide a justification for each choice. For example, choose to reduce the threat "Confidentiality – Unauthorized disclosure of <reads webpages> using <Web Server> by <Remote Anonymous User>," and note that you get a result that says "the unauthorized access to protected web pages is not allowed." After selecting responses for all the threats, prioritize the threats from highest to lowest.

The final step in the use of the Microsoft Threat Analysis and Modeling tool is Assimilate the Model. It is concerned with providing different perspectives for modeling the data including analytics, visualizations, and reports.

Analytics provide structured views of component attributes, trust levels, and relationships in the form of matrices to facilitate the analysis of threats to the application. The analytical views consist of a data access control matrix, component access control matrix, subject/object matrix, and component profile.

The data access control matrix outlines the permissions on the data, as shown in Figure 3-3.

The component access control matrix outlines the permissions on the component. A subset of this matrix is shown for the secure Web server in Figure 3-4. In this figure, the Consumer Loan Agent, Remote User, and Web Site Administrator roles are allowed access on the secure Web server.

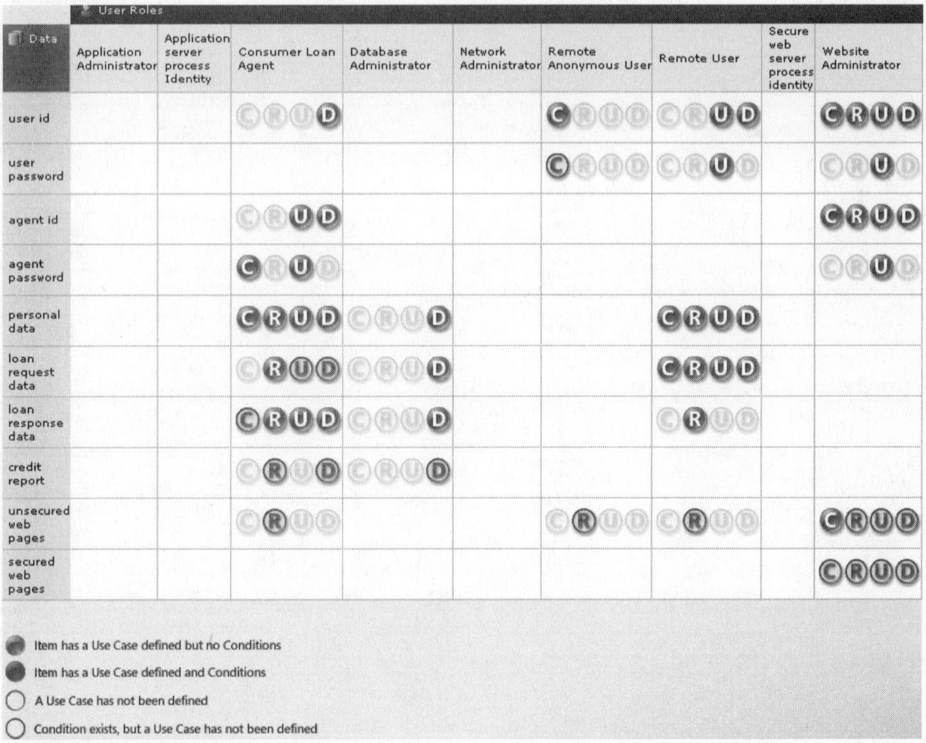

	User Roles								
Data	Application Administrator	Application server process Identity	Consumer Loan Agent	Database Administrator	Network Administrator	Remote Anonymous User	Remote User	Secure web server process identity	Website Administrator
user id			CRUD			CRUD	CRUD		CRUD
user password						CRUD	CRUD		CRUD
agent id			CRUD						CRUD
agent password			CRUD						CRUD
personal data			CRUD	CRUD			CRUD		
loan request data			CRUD	CRUD			CRUD		
loan response data			CRUD	CRUD			CRUD		
credit report			CRUD	CRUD					
unsecured web pages			CRUD			CRUD	CRUD		CRUD
secured web pages									CRUD

Item has a Use Case defined but no Conditions

Item has a Use Case defined and Conditions

A Use Case has not been defined

Condition exists, but a Use Case has not been defined

Figure 3-3: Data access control matrix

	Service Roles			User Roles								
Components	Application Server	Database Server	Secure Web Server	Application Administrator	Application server process Identity	Consumer Loan Agent	Database Administrator	Network Administrator	Remote Anonymous User	Remote User	Secure web server process identity	Website Administrator
Secure Web Server						[1] user id C R U D agent id C R U D agent password C R U D personal data C R U D loan request data C R U D loan response data C R U D				[2] user id C R U D user password C R U D personal data C R U D loan request data C R U D loan response data C R U D		[3] user id C R U D user password C R U D agent id C R U D agent password C R U D

Figure 3-4: Component access control matrix

The subject/object matrix outlines the relationships between the roles and the components. A subset of this matrix is shown for the secure Web server in Figure 3-5. In this figure, the Consumer Loan Agent, Remote User, and Web Site Administrator roles are allowed access and the Remote Anonymous User is denied access.

	User Roles								
Components	Application Administrator	Application server process Identity	Consumer Loan Agent	Database Administrator	Network Administrator	Remote Anonymous User	Remote User	Secure web server process identity	Website Administrator
Secure Web Server			1. creates password 2. delete user id 3. update loan response data 4. delete loan response data 5. create personal data 6. Read loan request data 7. Read loan request data 8. read personal data 9. update personal data 10. deletes personal data 11. deletes agent ID 12. updates agent ID 13. updates agent password			1. Creates user ID and Password	1. creates loan request 2. updates loan request 3. delete loan request data 4. create personal data 5. Read loan request data 6. Read loan response data 7. read personal data 8. update personal data 9. deletes personal data 10. deletes user id 11. update password 12. updates user id		1. creates a User ID or Agent ID 2. deletes user id 3. updates user id 4. creates Agent ID 5. creates webpages 6. deletes webpages 7. reads agent ID's 8. updates webpages 9. deletes agent ID 10. updates agent ID 11. updates agent password 12. reads user id's

Figure 3-5: Subject/object matrix

Component Name:	Secure Web Server
Description:	Hosts the loan broker website and has access to the database
ACL:	1. Remote User 2. Consumer Loan Agent 3. Website Administrator

Calling Roles

	Data Received	Data Sent
Consumer Loan Agent	1. agent id 2. agent password 3. user id 4. loan response data 5. personal data	1. secured web pages 2. loan request data 3. loan response data 4. personal data
Remote Anonymous User	1. user id 2. user password	1. secured web pages
Website Administrator	1. user id 2. agent id 3. user password 4. secured web pages 5. agent password	1. secured web pages 2. user id 3. agent id
Remote User	1. loan request data 2. user id 3. personal data 4. user password	1. secured web pages 2. loan request data 3. loan response data 4. personal data 5. user id

Figure 3-6: Component profile

The component profile provides a detailed view of a given component in the context of the defined application context. The component profile is shown for the secure Web server in Figure 3-6.

Visualizations provide diagrams representing the state of data, code execution, and trust at different points in the application. Microsoft also provides a visual representation of the attack surface, which is useful for attack surface evaluation, and a threat tree for understanding the hierarchy of threats, attacks, and vulnerabilities in the application.

A call flow depicting the sequence of calls for the use case ''Remote user with login credentials, create loan request data,'' is shown in Figure 3-7.

Of all the visualizations provided by the Microsoft Threat Analysis and Modeling Tool, the data flow diagram (DFD) is one of the most widely used in other threat modeling practices. The DFD provides a visual representation of how data is processed as it flows through the system. This allows the system to be modeled by focusing on transformations and processes applied to data and requests an adversary might supply. One advantage of the DFD is that it can provide low-level detail and thus a greater understanding of specific use cases, especially security relevant use cases. A data flow shown in Figure 3-8 illustrates the movement of data through a use case, ''Remote user with login credentials, create loan request data.''

A trust flow shows how the trust level changes throughout a use case, ''Remote user with login credentials, create loan request data,'' as shown in Figure 3-9.

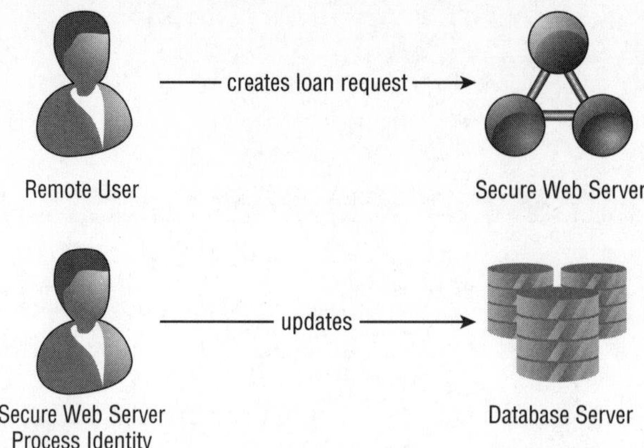

Figure 3-7: Call flow

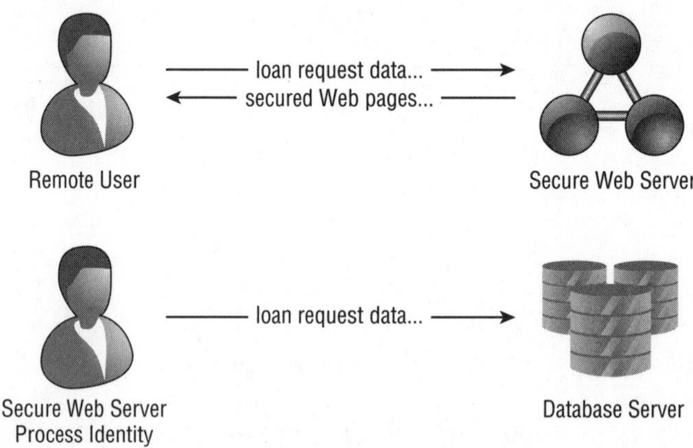

Figure 3-8: Data flow

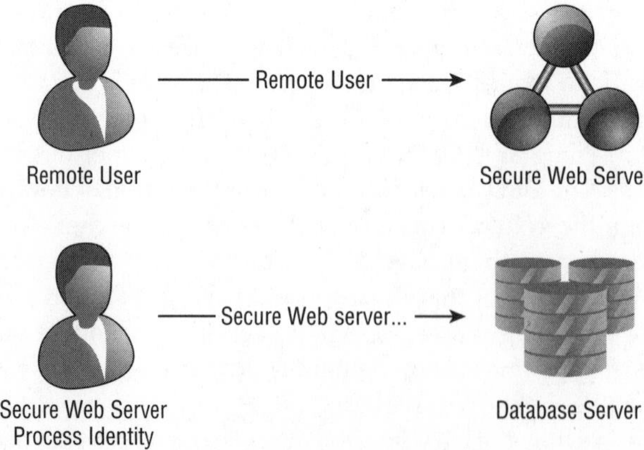

Figure 3-9: Trust flow

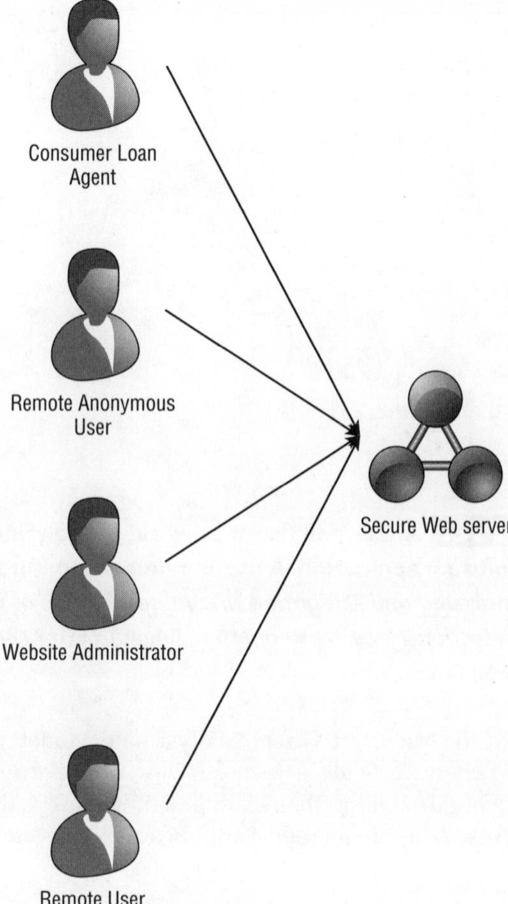

Figure 3-10: Attack surface for secure Web server

An attack surface for given data represents all the paths throughout the application by which you can reach the data store that persists that given data. The attack surface is shown for the secure Web server in Figure 3-10.

A threat tree is a visual representation that defines an instance of the threat, attack, vulnerability, and countermeasure. A partial threat tree is shown for the threat "Confidentiality – Unauthorized disclosure of <reads webpages> using <Web Server> by <Remote Anonymous User>," in Figure 3-11.

The threat tree illustrates one or more countermeasures for each of the attacks and vulnerabilities. These countermeasures are also listed in the tool itself, under each threat pane. For example, "Every object needs to have an authorization control" is the countermeasure for the threat "Confidentiality – Unauthorized disclosure of <reads webpages> using <Web Server> by <Remote Anonymous User>," the attack "Forceful browsing: Every object needs to have an authorization control," and the vulnerability "Poor authorization control."

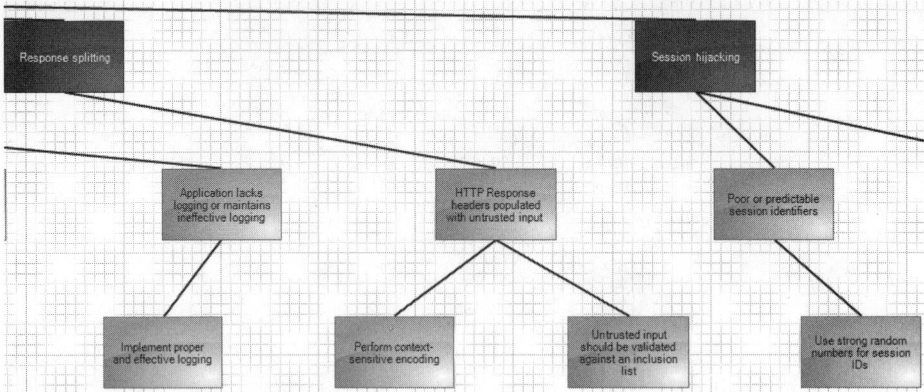

Figure 3-11: Partial threat tree

CROSS-REFERENCE **Attack and threat trees aid in analyzing and mitigating the threats to a software application. A useful reference for further study is *A Framework for Analyzing and Mitigating the Vulnerabilities of Complex Systems via Attack and Protection Trees*, by Kenneth S. Edge: `http://handle.dtic.mil/100.2/ADA472310`.**

Another feature of the Microsoft Threat Analysis and Modeling tool is the report generation facility. Reports provide a focused view of the threat model from the perspective of different roles within the development team. The threat modeling tool provides a facility to create a custom report and the following canned report types:

- Risk Owners Report
- Design Team Report
- Development Team Report
- Operations Team Report
- Test Team Report
- Comprehensive Report

These reports are part of the documentation set created during the process of threat modeling. Maintaining documentation is discussed later in this chapter.

Control Identification

The identification of a countermeasure for each vulnerability illustrated in the threat tree is known as control identification. The Microsoft Threat Analysis and Modeling tool described in the previous section automatically generates possible countermeasures for each of the attacks and vulnerabilities specific to a given threat. When threat modeling an application without the benefit of a tool, it is helpful to use a guideline such as

STRIDE to identify mitigation techniques and technologies based on a threat type. The following are STRIDE threat types/mitigation techniques:

- Spoofing/authentication
- Tampering/integrity
- Repudiation/nonrepudiation services
- Information disclosure/confidentiality
- Denial of service/availability
- Elevation of privilege/authorization

The identification of one or more mitigation technologies for each threat type also depends on the type and technology of the application. For example, Windows Vista Mandatory Integrity Control is a good mitigation technology for the tampering threat type, but it works only for applications that run on Windows Vista. SELinux Mandatory Access Control is a good mitigation technology for the elevation of privilege threat type, but it works only for applications that run on the Linux operating system. On the other hand, both Windows and Linux support the use of Kerberos authentication to counter a spoofing threat type. No matter what mitigation technologies are selected, the choice of the technologies should follow security best practices.

Control Prioritization

The Microsoft Threat Analysis and Modeling tool was able to quantify the level of risk associated with each threat in order to prioritize the threat and its related countermeasures. Prioritizing the countermeasures in this way is known as control prioritization and is done by first assigning a probability and impact value to each threat of low, medium, or high. The risk rating associated with each threat, values from 1 (low/low) to 9 (high/high) are automatically calculated based on these selections.

A number of different risk analysis techniques can be used to determine risk. The first version of Microsoft Threat Modeling used the DREAD model. DREAD consisted of numeric ratings for damage potential, reproducibility, exploitability, affected users, and discoverability. Unfortunately, the DREAD model is subjective. In fact, numeric ratings like those used by DREAD and the Microsoft Threat Analysis and Modeling tool vary so much because it is difficult to assign a value relative to chance of attack. However, in place of numeric calculations, it is still possible to rank risks based on the type of application and the characteristics of threats. For example, Microsoft has created a *bug bar* that maps the characteristics of a threat to the level of risk. Using the bug bar, you could evaluate an elevation of privilege threat, where the attacker gains the ability to either execute arbitrary code or obtain greater privileges than intended. If this threat is realized by a remote anonymous user, it is assigned a higher level of risk than if it is realized by a local administrative user. The Microsoft bug bar assigns risk from level 1 to level 4, highest to lowest. The bug bar was derived in part from security bulletins published in the Microsoft Security Response Center (MSRC).

CROSS-REFERENCE **You can access the Microsoft bug bar at `http://msdn.microsoft.com/en-us/library/cc307404.aspx`.**

The National Institute of Standards and Technology publishes a Risk Management Guide that describes a detailed risk analysis and management process for information systems. A detailed treatment of risk management was presented in Chapter 1.

CROSS-REFERENCE **You can find NIST SP 800-30 *Risk Management Guide for Information Technology* at `http://csrc.nist.gov/publications/nistpubs/800-30/sp800-30.pdf`.**

After the threats have been ranked based on risk, appropriate mitigations should be planned. The highest risk threats should be addressed first. To reduce the risk of a threat to zero, the threat must be eliminated by removing the feature or functionality from the application. If the goal is to reduce the risk of a threat, but not remove the feature from the application, then perhaps the feature can be turned off by default. If it is a high-risk feature, and the user chooses to turn the feature back on, this is not an appropriate mitigation. For risks that require an extra degree of configuration to be properly mitigated, a user warning may be appropriate. However, some users may not be technically proficient in heeding the warning, and many users make poor trust decisions concerning application security posture. The most common risk mitigation is to counter the threat with technology. This involves selecting one or more mitigation technologies. If a host-based firewall is selected as one of the mitigation technologies, it should not be solely relied upon to mitigate the risk, but can be part of a defense-in-depth strategy. Finally, if the threat presents a low risk, the designer may choose to accept the risk.

The implementation of security controls should be prioritized from highest to lowest according to the risk ranking of the threats. All risks and mitigations should be documented as part of the threat modeling process or in a separate risk assessment of the application.

Throughout the software life cycle, the threat model should be revised, taking into account new code, attacks, and security controls.

Documentation

In addition to the diagrams and reports produced in the threat modeling process, it is important to create detailed security configuration instructions for the end users of the software, including the roles of installer and administrator. After the product has been shipped, the end users must make informed decisions on how to securely deploy a product. These decisions involve understanding all required security constraints of the software and the available security features.

All the documentation produced in these activities should be placed under secure version control. Version control is part of the overall configuration management process discussed throughout this book.

Design Considerations

As the software design is decomposed from detailed requirements into components, it is useful to follow accepted security design patterns and security design principles to achieve software assurance goals. The design decisions should also take into consideration the operational environment of the software, including interconnectivity with external systems, and management of identities and administrative interfaces.

The first design principles to address are six complementary principles that support software assurance: confidentiality, integrity, availability, authentication, authorization, and auditing.

Confidentiality, Integrity, and Availability

It is necessary to consider the core principles (the C-I-A triad) of confidentiality, integrity, and availability when designing software assurance mechanisms.[14] NIST FIPS Publication 200 *Minimum Security Requirements for Federal Information Systems,* March 2006, identifies core security properties for information systems. These same properties can also be interpreted as applying to software assurance as discussed in the following sections.

Confidentiality

Confidentiality refers to the prevention of intentional or unintentional unauthorized disclosure of information. In the case of software, the information consists of the details that pertain to the nature of the software in its operational environment. This includes configuration settings, logic, and interfaces, and in some cases, its very existence must not be disclosed to entities who aren't explicitly authorized to know those details. In practical terms, this means the software must be protected from both reconnaissance attacks and reverse engineering. In addition, all software artifacts (specification, source code, binary code, test plans, reports, etc.) must be protected from unauthorized disclosure.

Encryption is commonly used to preserve confidentiality in software (and encapsulated data) as the software changes states and requires access to resources. The following are examples of the use of encryption:

- Software may need access to a database. A possible scheme for protecting the database user password is by encrypting the password and storing it in a protected file. The decryption key should be supplied to the software via a command line or protected file, and the salt should be embedded in the code itself. In this way, the software requires the decryption key, salt, algorithm, and encrypted password to gain access to the database.

[14]Goertzel, K., Winograd, T., et al., "Enhancing the Development Life Cycle to Produce Secure Software."

- Software needs to generate a random number for cryptographic or security purposes. A secure random number should comply with the statistical random number generator tests specified in FIPS 140-2 *Security Requirements for Cryptographic Modules*, Section 4.1, and must produce nondeterministic output.

To help preserve the confidentiality of the software source code, such as from disclosure of sensitive data or intellectual property through reverse engineering, a code obfuscation technology may be used as a countermeasure. Since managed code is compiled into an intermediate state, such as Java bytecode, it is potentially easier to reverse engineer than unmanaged code that is compiled into machine language.

CROSS-REFERENCE **ProGuard (`http://proguard.sourceforge.net/`) is a free Java class file shrinker, optimizer, obfuscator, and preverifier.**

The configuration data and include files for a Web application should be placed outside the Web application root directory that is served by the Web server. This will prevent the Web server from serving these files as Web pages. The documentation for the Web and/or application server should be consulted to allow or disallow access to files outside the document root.

CROSS-REFERENCE **For the article "Mapping URLs to Filesystem Locations for Apache 2.2," see `http://httpd.apache.org/docs/2.2/urlmapping.html`.**

Also see "Configure a Web Server to Serve Content for IIS 7.0," at `http://technet.microsoft.com/en-us/library/cc754437.aspx`.

Integrity

Integrity refers to the prevention of unauthorized modification (corrupting, tampering, overwriting, inserting unintended logic, destroying, or deleting) by valid entities (persons or processes) and of all modifications by invalid, unauthorized entities.

Integrity should be ensured by checking that the software's data has not been tampered with and has remained the same since it was created or introduced. The data must be checked as it crosses trust boundaries in the software, especially from a trusted to a less-trusted boundary. Integrity should also be ensured for the software source code, compiled code, and supporting files.

Using a cryptographic hash function is a common way of ensuring the integrity of data and software components. A cryptographic hash function takes an arbitrary block of data as input and returns a fixed-size string or hash value such that an accidental or intentional change to the data will almost certainly change the hash value. The ideal hash function has four main properties:

- It is easy to compute the hash for any given data.
- It is difficult to construct a text that has a given hash.
- It is difficult to modify a given text without changing its hash.
- It is unlikely that two different messages will have the same hash.

FIPS 180-2 *Secure Hash Standard* specifies algorithms for computing five cryptographic hash functions: SHA-1, SHA-224, SHA-256, SHA-384, and SHA-512.

NOTE In recent years, several of the non-NIST approved cryptographic hash functions have been successfully attacked, and serious attacks have been published against SHA-1. Therefore, NIST held a competition for a new Secure Hash Standard, to be called SHA-3. The competition was closed on October 31, 2008, and NIST is currently in the process of evaluating the entries.

Availability

Availability means the software must be operational and accessible to its intended, authorized users (humans and processes) whenever they need it to be. Software under attack must be survivable or resilient. Survivable software is resilient enough to resist (i.e., protect itself against) or tolerate (i.e., continue operating dependably in spite of) most known attacks plus as many novel attacks as possible. It must also recover as quickly as possible, and with as little damage as possible, from those attacks it can neither resist nor tolerate.[15]

Software must have awareness of or be alerted to an operational error or anomaly in order to recover properly. All expected and unexpected errors should be properly caught and handled. If software fails or is made unavailable to its intended users (denial of service), it should recover to a known state, even if that state is to be shut down. High-availability or life-critical systems must be especially fault tolerant.

Fault-tolerant software should have the following properties:

- No single point of failure
- No single point of repair
- Fault isolation to the failing component
- Fault containment to prevent propagation of the failure
- Availability of fallback or reversion modes

To ensure availability, the software should know what sort of attacks to protect itself against.

Software that is susceptible to an Internet denial-of-service (DoS) attack can respond through containment, graceful degradation, or automatic fail-over. In a containment response, software with more than a single connectivity point may disconnect the affected connectivity point. Through graceful degradation, the software may vary its response times to subsequent requests, resulting in a lower quality of service, but preserving a degree of availability. Software receiving a large number of requests may even fail-over to a higher-availability service.

Software should be built with redundancy in mind to reduce the possibility of failure. This may be a deployment consideration, such as through the use of redundant

[15]Goertzel, K., Winograd, T., et al., "Enhancing the Development Life Cycle to Produce Secure Software."

arrays of inexpensive disks (RAID), or deploying the software in a distributed fashion, such as a cluster of machines running the software. Software should be backed up regularly so it can be restored if it is corrupted or destroyed.

Redundancy is discussed in more detail in the section "Distributed Computing" later in this chapter.

Authentication, Authorization, and Auditing

Authentication, authorization, and auditing are components for managing trust in software.

Authentication

Authentication is when a user proves to the software that he knows or possesses some secret information. When designing or selecting an authentication component for software, it should meet a minimum assurance level. For example, NIST SP 800-63-1 *Electronic Authentication Guideline* of December 2008 (based on OMB M-04-04 *E-Authentication Guidance for Federal Agencies*) defines four levels of authentication. These levels are defined in terms of the consequences of the authentication errors and misuse of credentials. Level 1 is the lowest assurance and Level 4 is the highest. OMB guidance defines the required level authentication assurance in terms of the likely consequences of an authentication error. As the consequences of the authentication error become more serious, the required level of assurance increases. The OMB guidance provides agencies with the criteria for determining the level of E-authentication assurance required for specific applications and transactions, based on the risks and their likelihood of occurrence in each application or transaction. OMB guidance outlines a five-step process by which agencies can meet the assurance requirements:

1. Conduct a risk assessment of the government system
2. Map identified risks to the appropriate assurance level
3. Select technology based on E-authentication technical guidance
4. Validate that the implemented system has met the required assurance level
5. Periodically reassess the information system to determine technology refresh requirements

The assurance level determines what kind of technology should be used for the authentication component. The assurance levels are summarized below:

- **Level 1**—There is no identity proofing requirement at this level, but there must be a minimum level of assurance. Plaintext usernames and passwords are not transmitted across a network, but challenge-response protocols are allowed. Passwords are vulnerable to offline dictionary attacks by eavesdroppers on the communication. Token methods of Levels 2, 3, and 4 may be used through a secure protocol.
- **Level 2**—Provides single-factor remote network authentication. Proofing requirements are introduced requiring presentation of identifying materials

or information. A wide variety of single-factor technologies can be employed, including memorized secret tokens, registered knowledge tokens, look-up secret tokens, out-of-band tokens, and single factor one-time password devices. Token methods of Levels 3 or 4 may be used through a secure protocol. Online guessing, replay, session hijacking, and eavesdropping attacks are prevented. Protocols are weakly resistant to man-in-the-middle attacks. In addition to Level 1 requirements, assertions must be resistant to disclosure, redirection, capture, and substitution attacks. Approved cryptographic techniques are required for all assertion protocols used at Level 2 and above.

- **Level 3**—Provides multi-factor remote network authentication requiring at least two authentication factors. Identity proofing procedures require verification of identifying materials and information. Multi-factor software cryptographic tokens are allowed at Level 3 along with any of the token methods of Level 4. Level 3 authentication requires cryptographic strength mechanisms that protect the primary authentication token against compromise by the protocol threats for all threats at Level 2 as well as verifier impersonation attacks. The claimant must prove possession of the allowed types of tokens through a cryptographic protocol. The claimant must first unlock the token with a password or biometric, or must use a secure multi-token authentication protocol to establish two-factor authentication (through proof of possession of a physical or software token in combination with some memorized secret knowledge). In addition to Level 2 requirements, assertions are protected against repudiation by the verifier.
- **Level 4**—Provides the highest practical remote network authentication assurance. Level 4 authentication is based on proof of possession of a key through a cryptographic protocol. Identity proofing is done in person. Level 4 is similar to Level 3 except that only "hard" cryptographic tokens are allowed, FIPS 140-2 cryptographic module validation requirements are strengthened, and subsequent critical data transfers must be authenticated via a key bound to the authentication process. The token is a hardware cryptographic module validated at FIPS 140-2 Level 2 or higher overall with at least FIPS 140-2 Level 3 physical security. The PIV card authentication key meets Level 4 token requirements. Level 4 requires strong cryptographic authentication of all parties and all sensitive data transfers between the parties using either public key or symmetric key technology. All protocol threats at Level 3 are prevented at Level 4. Protocols are also strongly resistant to man-in-the-middle attacks.

It is important to design authentication components correctly. The U.S. Department of Homeland Security "Build Security In" Web site describes the following as frequent authentication design defects that lead to vulnerability[16]:

- Using no authentication when it is required
- Failing to understand the limitations of the authentication scheme or mechanism. For example, HTTP basic authentication authenticates the user, not the server

[16] https://buildsecurityin.us-cert.gov/daisy/bsi/articles/knowledge/guidelines/321-BSI.html

- Failing to separate authentication and authorization
- Designing passwords that are inherently weak and disallowing passwords that are strong. For example, a system that supports only eight-character passwords composed of alphanumeric characters is a poor design (something that many Web sites do)
- Using weak authentication based on untrustworthy attributes, such as network address information
- Disabling a subsystem's built-in access controls through identity sharing. This is a common practice in Web sites that use back-end databases
- Failing to propagate authentication across a multi-tier application
- Designing a secure container for secrets and then exposing the secrets outside the container. This has occurred in several implementations of smart cards

A number of design patterns related to authentication in Web applications are explored in the section "Security Design Patterns" later in this chapter.

Design of a secure authentication component is a difficult task. It involves an understanding of protocols, applied cryptography, and other disciplines from security engineering. Unless there is no component available that meets the requirements of the software, it may be a better choice to select a secure and proven authentication component rather than design one from scratch. Indeed, Ross Anderson writes in Security Engineering that:

> *It is difficult to design effective security protocols. They suffer from a number of potential problems, including middleperson attacks, modification attacks, reflection attacks, and replay attacks. These threats can interact with implementation vulnerabilities such as poor and random number generators. Using mathematical techniques to verify the correctness of protocols can help, but it won't catch all the bugs. Some of the most pernicious failures are caused by creeping changes in the environment for which a protocol was designed, so that the protection it gives is no longer adequate.*[17]

Authorization

Authorization refers to checking the privileges of a software actor before granting it access to a restricted service or protected resource. Authorization takes place after the actor has been successfully authenticated to the software. The authentication component establishes the identity of the actor, and the authorization component checks the identity based on a security policy represented by specific rules. The policy may be based on the matching of required access privileges with the privileges associated with the actor's:

> *... identity (as in discretionary access control), the user's role (as in role-based access control), the user's clearance (as in mandatory access control), the perceived level of risk the access poses to the system (as in risk-adaptive access control), or some other attribute or combination of attributes (as in attribute-based access control).*[18]

[17] Anderson, R., *Security Engineering: A Guide to Building Dependable Distributed Systems*, 2nd ed. (Indianapolis, IN: Wiley Publishing, Inc., 2008).

[18] IATAC/DACS, "Software Security Assurance State-of-the-Art Report (SOAR)." July 31, 2007.

The authorization component should enforce the security design principle of *complete mediation*, discussed later in this chapter—that is, not be bypassable.

It is important to design authorization components correctly. The U.S. Department of Homeland Security ''Build Security In'' Web site describes the following as frequent authorization design defects that lead to vulnerability[19]:

- Trying to interpret access control rules for lower-level subsystems instead of using the subsystems to interpret their rules. This is a common error in `setuid` programs in Unix
- Designing authorization systems with an insufficiently rich privilege menu that encourages privilege overloading. An example of this is the Unix superuser
- Using *unauthenticated* authorization systems that appear to control access, but without proper authentication don't control anything
- Employing ambiguity of authentication. Many authorization systems use ambiguous symbols (i.e., principal names) to identify principals, allowing circumvention of authorization by using a different, though equivalent, principal name. For example, there are many implementations for restricting remote host access to local services that may allow many proper, but apparently different, names for unique hosts (e.g., fully qualified domain names, shortened names, CNAMEs, IPv4 addresses, IPv6 addresses)

Auditing

The traditional means of enforcing accountability in software has been a combination of auditing and nonrepudiation measures. Auditing amounts to security-focused event logging to record all security-relevant actions performed by actors while interacting with the system. What distinguishes auditing from standard event logging is (1) the type of information captured in the audit record; (2) the level of integrity protection applied to the audit records to prevent them from being intentionally or inadvertently deleted, corrupted, or tampered with.

Additional factors that contribute to the accuracy, level of detail, and type of information that should be captured in the audit trail include compliance requirements (such as Sarbanes-Oxley) and law enforcement requirements (such as forensic investigation). The following design considerations and best practices for auditing in a Web application are summarized from the Open Web Application Security Project (OWASP):

- Ensure that the software records the correct time (timestamp); for example, synchronize with atomic clock time source.
- Secure the communications channel with encryption, for example, SSL between the logging host and the destination.
- Use an HMAC or similar tamper-proofing mechanism to prevent changes from the time of the logging activity to when it is reviewed.

[19]https://buildsecurityin.us-cert.gov/daisy/bsi/articles/knowledge/guidelines/322-BSI.html

- Ensure that relevant logs can be easily extracted in a legally sound fashion to assist with prosecution.
- Audit only truly important events; debug and informational messages may not be security-relevant.
- Log centrally as appropriate and ensure that primary audit trails are not kept on vulnerable systems, particularly front-end Web servers.
- Review only copies of the logs, not the actual logs themselves
- Ensure that audit logs are sent to trusted systems.
- For highly protected systems, use write-once media or similar to provide trustworthy long-term log repositories.
- For highly protected systems, ensure there is end-to-end trust in the logging mechanism. World-writeable logs, logging agents without credentials (such as SNMP traps, syslog, etc.) are legally vulnerable to being excluded from prosecution.[20]

NOTE "The Apache Logging Services project creates and maintains open-source software related to the logging of application behavior and released at no charge to the public." See `http://logging.apache.org`.

In ''Enhancing the Development Life Cycle to Produce Secure Software,'' Goertzel and Winograd et al. state that ''nonrepudiation measures are applied to any data objects created or manipulated as a result of an actor's interaction with the system. Such data objects can range from electronic documents to email messages to database or form field entries to interprocess communications (e.g., SOAP messages between Web services). The nonrepudiation measure, most often a digital signature, binds proof of identity of the actor responsible either for the creation or manipulation (modification, transmission, receipt) of the data object, so that the actor cannot later deny responsibility for that act.

A prerequisite for auditing and nonrepudiation is the ability to bind the authenticated identity of the actor to the act/event of the data object for which it is to be held accountable. This presumes that strong authentication of the actor will occur and that some mechanism, such as a digital identity certificate, will be irrevocably associated with that actor as a result of the authentication of its identity.

In a software-intensive system, auditing and nonrepudiation measures need to extend beyond the human users to include semi- and fully autonomous software entities, such as agents, and Web and grid services that operate without human intervention, and in some cases without human knowledge. The accurate attribution of all software actors is the only way to establish a ''paper trail'' by which responsibility for security violations or compromises can be traced back to whatever human agent is responsible for the software entity (or entities) that caused the violation/compromise.''[21]

[20]www.owasp.org/index.php/Error_Handling,_Auditing_and_Logging

[21]Goertzel, K., Winograd, T., et al., ''Enhancing the Development Life Cycle to Produce Secure Software.''

Security Design Principles

Designing secure software is based on the application of security design principles. A number of security design principles were defined by Saltzer and Schroeder in the famous paper, "The Protection of Information in Computer Systems," published in 1974. The Software Security Assurance State-of-the-Art Report (SOAR) analyzed the following subset of Saltzer and Schroeder's design principles and found them to be directly relevant to software assurance[22]:

- **Least privilege**—Least privilege is a principle whereby each principal (user, process, or device) is granted the most restrictive set of privileges needed for the performance of each of its authorized tasks. A more recent corollary is least authorization, which is less transactional.
- **Complete mediation**—Before granting access to a resource or execution of a process, the user or process requesting that access or execution should be checked for proper authorization, and the request should be rejected if the requestor is not appropriately authorized.
- **Fail-safe defaults**—This principle calls for defaulting, in security-relevant decision making, toward denial rather than permission. Thus, the default situation is to deny all requests that do not explicitly conform to the conditions under which such requests are permitted.
- **Separation of privilege**—A high-assurance or otherwise high-consequence function should require two keys to unlock it, i.e., to cause its execution. By requiring two keys, no single accident, deception, or breach of trust will be sufficient to compromise the trusted function. In practical application, code signatures provide this type of separation: code cannot be executed by one entity unless it has been signed using a certificate from a valid certificate authority, and moreover, that signature can be validated by a second entity, i.e., a certificate validation service.
- **Open design**—Security should not depend on security-through-obscurity—that is, the ignorance of potential attackers—but rather on assurance of dependability and/or the possession by users of specific, easily protected, authorization credentials. This permits the software to be examined by a number of reviewers without concern that the review may itself compromise the software's security. The practice of openly exposing one's design to scrutiny is not universally accepted. The notion that security should not depend on attacker ignorance is generally accepted, but some would argue that obfuscation and hiding of both design and implementation have advantages: they raise the cost to the attacker of compromising the system.
- **Recording of compromises**—If the software behaves suspiciously or is compromised, trails of evidence can aid in determining whether the behavior or compromise resulted from an intentional attack, and if so, in understanding the attack patterns so as to better resist or tolerate it. After compromises, evidence

[22]IATAC/DACS, "Software Security Assurance State-of-the-Art Report (SOAR)." July 31, 2007.

trails also aid resilience—recovery, diagnosis and repair, forensics, and accountability. Records of legitimate behaviors also have value, because they provide a "normal" baseline against which anomalous behavior can be compared.

- **Defense-in-depth**—Defense-in-depth is a strategy in which the human, technological, and operational capabilities that comprise a system are integrated to establish variable protective barriers across multiple layers and dimensions of that system. This principle ensures that an attacker must penetrate more than one element of the overall system to compromise successfully that system. Diversity of mechanisms can make the attacker's efforts even more difficult. The increased cost of an attack may dissuade an attacker from continuing the attack. Note that composition of multiple less expensive but weak mechanisms is subject to the same composability issues as other software: combining them is unlikely to create a barrier that is stronger than the least secure of its individual parts, let alone the sum of its parts.
- **Work factor**—The cost of a countermeasure or mitigation for a vulnerability or weakness (or of an overall increase in the level of security, which should eliminate a number of vulnerabilities and weaknesses) should be commensurate with the cost of the loss that would result were an attack to exploit that vulnerability or weakness.
- **Economy of mechanism**—"Keep the design as simple and small as possible" applies to any aspect of a system, but it deserves emphasis for trusted software. This principle minimizes the likelihood of errors in the code and directly aids its analyzability.
- **Analyzability**—Systems whose behavior is analyzable from their engineering descriptions such as design specifications and code have a greater chance of performing correctly because relevant aspects of their behavior can be predicted in advance.

The SOAR report also introduces new principles in addition to those selected from Saltzer and Schroeder:

- **Security-aware error and exception handling**—Software needs to handle exceptions correctly so that active faults triggered by attack patterns will not result in a software crash (denial of service). The software needs to validate all user input to ensure it does not exceed the memory buffer allocated to receive it and does not contain segments of executable code.
- **Mutual suspicion**—Components should not trust other components except when explicitly intended. Each component in an interacting pair should always be prepared to protect itself against an attack from the other.
- **Isolation and constraint of untrusted processes**—Sandboxing, virtual machines, trusted processor modules, and access control configurations can be used to isolate untrusted processes so that their misbehavior does not affect trusted processes or grant access to restricted memory areas to malicious code or human attackers.
- **Isolation of trusted/high-consequence processes**—In high-risk environments especially, it may be sensible to isolate trusted and other high-consequence

processes, to protect their integrity and availability from potential threats posed by untrusted processes and external entities. Trusted platform modules (TPM) were expressly conceived for this purpose—that is, for hosting trusted processes (such as cryptographic functions) in a physically separate execution environment with only tightly controlled interfaces to the rest of the software application or system.

The Data and Analysis Center for Software (DACS) also introduces three new general principles for software assurance. The general principles serve as a framework for categorizing a number of secure design principles, some of which are based on the work of Saltzer and Schroeder and others:

- **General Principle 1**—Minimize the number of high-consequence targets
  - Principle of least privilege
  - Principle of separation of privileges, duties, and roles
  - Principle of separation of domains
- **General Principle 2**—Don't expose vulnerable or high-consequence components
  - Keep program data, executables, and program control/configuration data separated
  - Segregate trusted entities from untrusted entities
  - Minimize the number of entry and exit points into and out of any entity
  - Assume environment data is not trustworthy
  - Use only safe interfaces to environment resources
- **General Principle 3**—Deny attackers the means to compromise
  - Simplify the design
  - Hold all actors accountable, not just human users
  - Avoid timing, synchronization, and sequencing issues
  - Make secure states easy to enter and vulnerable states difficult to enter
  - Design for controllability
  - Design for secure failure
  - Design for survivability
  - Server functions should never rely on clients to perform high-consequence functions or trust client-originated data

The secure design principles and general principles they support are summarized in the following sections.

General Principle 1: Minimize the Number of High-Consequence Targets

The following principles and practices contribute to the design's ability to conform to this general principle.

Principle of Least Privilege

Least privilege supports General Principle 1 by minimizing the number of actors in the system granted high levels of privilege and the amount of time any actor holds on to its privileges.

Least privilege is easier to enforce in a design that minimizes the number of "sensitive" and trusted (i.e., highly privileged) functions. In a software system in which multiple functions will require different privileges, the functions should be designed and implemented as multiple discrete, small, simple (ideally single-purpose) executables that call each other, and not as a single, large, complex multifunction executable that requires a variety of privileges. Modularizing functions into separate simple executables minimizes the number of privilege changes that must occur during the software's execution. It should be possible to decompose complex functions that on first glance appear to require a high level of privilege into multiple, simpler functions (or tasks), most of which will not require high-level privileges. For example, a cross-domain solution that is used to review, reclassify, and release documents from a classified network to an unclassified network can be decomposed into a series of tasks that will collectively accomplish the file downgrade and release. When parsing the text content of the file:

1. Determine whether parsed text is unclassified or classified
2. Change the sensitivity label on the file if unclassified
3. Route the downgraded file to its intended destination/recipient on the unclassified network

Only one of these tasks actually needs a high level of privilege that will enable it to violate the mandatory access control policy of the file system in which the file to be downgraded resides: the label-changing function. While it is crucial to protect the integrity of the other functions to ensure their trustworthiness, these functions do not require high levels of privilege.

Software that is comprised of small, simple functions (implemented by small, simple executables) will be easier to analyze and troubleshoot, and its security will be much easier to assure.

Least privilege alone will not guarantee secure software. Other principles of secure design must also be followed, including avoiding single points of failure and not presenting high-value targets to attackers. For this reason, highly privileged functions should never be centralized in a single component or module.

Principle of Separation of Privileges, Duties, and Roles

No single entity (human or software) should possess all the privileges required to cause destruction of the software system as a whole or all of the components that make up the system. Separation of privileges and duties/roles supports General Principle 1 by helping minimize the number of different privileges required by any single actor in the system.

Instead of granting all entities access to all components in the software or allowing them to perform all tasks, entities should be assigned roles or duties that require them to perform only a subset of the overall functions provided by the software.

In practice, this relates to simplicity of design. For example, instead of designing a complex monolithic entity requiring "superuser" privileges to operate, the system should specify a number of modular, single-function entities that require only the privileges needed to accomplish their function.

An example of this type of design is the Postfix software that is used to route mail on the Internet and typically runs on the Linux operating system. Postfix uses a modular architecture that is the basis for its strong security posture. Each Postfix process runs with the minimum privileges necessary to complete its particular task. Postfix processes that are not required can be disabled, and interprocess communication is minimized among all running processes.

Principle of Separation of Domains

Separation of domains is a principle that supports General Principle 1 by making separation of roles and privileges easier to implement. It also supports General Principle 2 by reducing the exposure of different actors and objects in the system to each other, which minimizes the likelihood that non-malicious actors will interact with malicious actors, or that a malicious actor will be able to easily gain access to any memory locations or data objects on the system. Together, these two controls ensure that users and processes are able to perform only tasks that are absolutely required, and to perform them on only the data, in only memory space, and using only the functions that they absolutely must access to accomplish those tasks. In practical terms, this is achieved through compartmentalization of users, processes, and data. This compartmentalization also helps contain the impact of faults and failures.

General Principle 2: Don't Expose Vulnerable or High-Consequence Components

The following principles and practices contribute to the design's ability to conform to this general principle.

Keep Program Data, Executables, and Program Control/Configuration Data Separated

This practice supports General Principle 2 by reducing the likelihood that an attacker who gains access to program data will easily locate and gain access to program executables and/or control/configuration data.

For example, when deploying the software, data files, configuration files, and executables should be placed in separate file system directories. An executable or script should be installed and not be writable by anyone except the system administrator. The deployed executable should not be readable by anyone, and the application users should be granted only execute privileges.

Segregate Trusted Entities from Untrusted Entities

This practice supports General Principle 2 by reducing the exposure of the software's high-consequence functions from its high-risk (vulnerable and untrustworthy) functions, which are susceptible to delivery of malicious code or corruption by attackers so that their execution threatens the dependable, trustworthy operation of the software as a whole.

NOTE **High-consequence functions are those whose failure would have a high negative impact on the ability of the software's users to accomplish their objectives.**

High-risk functions should be isolated to limit the propagation of the impact and to minimize the damage that results from the execution of any malicious logic embedded in the code.

Minimize the Number of Entry and Exit Points into and out of Any Entity

Each software entity—function, process, module, component—should have one entry point and one or very few exit points. This principle supports General Principle 2 by reducing the attack surface of the software. It also makes the resulting software easier to analyze, and when implemented at the component level, it makes substitution and replacement of components easier.

Assume Environment Data Is Not Trustworthy

The designer should assume that all components of the execution environment are neither dependable nor trustworthy unless and until this assumption is proved wrong. This principle supports General Principle 2 by reducing the exposure of the software to potentially malicious execution environment components or attacker-intercepted and modified environment data.

NOTE **This principle is not limited to environment components. The designer should assume that all entities external to the software are untrustworthy, and should accordingly validate all data received from those entities.**

Use Only Safe Interfaces to Environment Resources

This practice supports General Principle 2 by reducing the exposure of the data passed between the software and its environment.

While system commands may seem like the most efficient way to implement an interface to the underlying operating system, a secure application will never issue a direct call to the underlying operating system, or to system-level network programs, such as sendmail, *unless* controls are imposed that are adequate to prevent any user, attacker, or malicious program from gaining control of the calling program and exploiting its direct calling mechanism(s). Not only does each application call to a system-level function create a potential target for attack, whenever the software issues a system call, the homogeneity of the system's design is reduced and its reliability diminishes.

Application-level programs should call only other application-layer programs, middleware, or explicit APIs to system resources. Applications should not use APIs intended for human users rather than software nor rely on a system-level tool (versus an application-level tool) to filter/modify their own output.

General Principle 3: Deny Attackers the Means to Compromise

The following principles and practices contribute to the design's ability to conform to this general principle.

Simplify the Design

By keeping the design as simple as possible, the designer will be less likely to include weaknesses and vulnerabilities, especially hard to detect weaknesses/vulnerabilities, or to introduce complexities that make the design and its security implications difficult to analyze and understand. This principle supports General Principle 3 by minimizing the number of attacker-exploitable vulnerabilities and weaknesses in the system. This principle will also make the design, and the implemented software, easier to analyze and test.

Hold All Actors Accountable, Not Just Human Users

This practice supports General Principle 3 by ensuring that all attacker actions are observed and recorded, contributing to the ability to recognize and isolate/block the source of attack patterns and thereby prevent attacks from succeeding.

Accountability is typically enforced through auditing and nonrepudiation. Auditing involves recording all security-relevant actions performed by actors when interacting with the system. Nonrepudiation includes measures such as digital signatures to prevent actors from later denying responsibility for an action taken.

Avoid Timing, Synchronization, and Sequencing Issues

This practice supports General Principle 3 by reducing the likelihood of race conditions, order dependencies, synchronization problems, and deadlocks. The developer should be careful to understand and apply effective techniques and measures to avoid such issues and to ensure asynchronous consistency within any multitasked and multithreaded programs.

Many timing and sequencing issues are caused by the sharing of state information (particularly real-time and sequence-order information) across disjoint program abstractions such as unrelated or conflicting classes in object-oriented programs.

NOTE An example of a disjoint abstraction is a class called `CustomerTable` in an object-oriented database application. The class is disjoint because the objects `customer` and `table` have nothing in common; by contrast, `circle` and `ellipse` are related abstractions; both are geometric shapes defined by continuous curved lines; therefore, the class `CircleEllipse` in an object-oriented drawing program would not be disjoint.

Make Secure States Easy to Enter and Vulnerable States Difficult to Enter

This practice supports General Principle 3 by reducing the likelihood that the software will be allowed to inadvertently enter a vulnerable (exploitable) state.

Software should always begin and end its execution in a secure state. State changes should always be deliberate and never inadvertent; this is particularly important for changes from secure to vulnerable states.

If multiple secure states are possible, as a result of different processing conditions, the software should include a decision-making capability that enables it to choose the most appropriate secure state to enter.

Design for Controllability

Include logic for the control of the software's execution to increase the resilience of the software. This principle supports General Principle 3 by making it easier to detect attack paths and disengage the software from its interactions with attackers. Some specific design features that will increase the software's controllability include:

- The ability to self-monitor and limit resource usage.
- Feedback that enables all assumptions and models upon which the program makes decisions to be validated before those decisions are taken. This feedback should include intermediate states and partial results of processing events.
- Exception, error, and anomaly handling and recovery that:
  - Place critical flags and conditions as close as possible to the code they protect.
  - Interpret the absence of a protected condition as indicating the software process is not protected.
  - Use interlocks (batons, critical sections, synchronization mechanisms) to enforce sequences of actions or events so that no event can occur inadvertently or when an undesirable condition exists or out of sequence. For example, lockouts can be used to block access to a vulnerable process, or to preserve secure state and protect the software against using invalid data or valid data received in the wrong order or at an unexpected time or speed.

Design for Secure Failure

This practice supports General Principle 3 by reducing the likelihood that a failure in the software will leave it vulnerable to attack.

Implement watchdog timers that check for "I'm alive" signals from processes. Each watchdog timer should be set by software other than that which it is responsible for observing.

The exception handling logic should always attempt to take corrective action before a failure can occur, and to allow thresholds to be set to indicate "points of no return" beyond which recovery from a fault, vulnerable state, or encroaching failure is recognized to be unlikely or infeasible. Upon reaching this threshold, the exception handler should allow the software to enter a secure failure state (i.e., a failure state in which none of the software's program and control data and no other sensitive data or resources controlled by the software are suddenly exposed, and in which damage resulting from the failure is minimized).

Design for Survivability

This practice supports General Principle 3 by minimizing the amount of time a faulty or failed software component remains unable to protect itself from attack.

The software design should enable the software to take advantage of any redundancy and rapid recovery features at the system level. For example, if the system will support automatic backups and hot sparing of high-consequence components with automatic swap-over, the software system's design should be modularized in such a way that its high-consequence components can be decoupled and replicated on the "hot spare" platforms.

The software's own error, anomaly, and exception handling and recovery should support both backward and forward recovery. Backward recovery enables the software to detect every anomaly and error before it is able to create an exploitable vulnerability or escalate to a failure.

If a failure does occur, the exception handler should return that software to a known good state that is more secure than the failure state. The biggest challenge will be detecting and recognizing anomalous and erroneous states in the first place.

Forward recovery measures include the use of robust data structures, the dynamic alteration of flow controls, and the tolerance (i.e., ignoring) of errors that do not persist beyond one cycle.

Error handling in the software should recognize and tolerate errors likely to originate with human mistakes, such as input mistakes. The designer needs to:

- Allow enough fault tolerance in the software to enable it to continue operating dependably in the presence of a fairly large number of user input mistakes
- Determine just how much information to provide in error messages by weighing the benefit of helping human users correct their own mistakes against the threat of reconnaissance attackers being able to leverage the knowledge they gain from overly verbose error messages

Do Not Trust Client-Originated Data

This principle supports General Principle 1 by reducing the consequence of the client (and thus eliminating a high-consequence target) and General Principle 3 by eliminating an attack path frequently used by attackers to target server applications. Browsers and other clients should never be trusted to perform security-critical or other high-consequence functions. Reliance on client-originated data makes a server application vulnerable to attacks in which client-side data is altered before or in transit from client to server to compromise server-side security properties or functions, for example, to subvert authentication checking or to gain access to confidential server-side data.

The designer should always assume that clients will run in the most hostile execution environments possible. Server applications, portals, and proxy agents that interact with clients should be designed to protect themselves against attacks originating from clients that have been subverted, hijacked, or spoofed. *Server-side software should always validate all data originating from a client, even if the client validated that data first.* While client-side input validation may be useful as a filtering mechanism to eliminate some unacceptable data before it can be sent to the server, the server should never count on the client to filter out bad data. It should always perform its own input validation.

Security Design Patterns

Security design patterns are reusable building blocks defining commonly needed and well-understood design features. A security design pattern that achieves software assurance objectives upholds secure design principles and practices. For example, a security design pattern may prescribe a centralized input validation solution to address the secure design principle "do not trust client-originated data."

IBM has developed a set of design patterns for WebSphere-based Web service applications (`www.ibm.com/developerworks/patterns/edge/at1-runtime.html`), including a set of "Non-Functional Requirements: High Availability: Runtime" patterns that correspond to software availability, survivability, and general resilience secure design principles: single load balancer, load balancer hot standby, mutual high availability, wide area load balancing, caching proxies with security plug-in.

A number of security patterns were developed for Web applications by Kienzle, Elder, Tyree, and Edwards-Hewitt under a DARPA contract.[23] Some of these patterns are applicable to aspects of authentication in Web applications, including:

- **Account lockout**—Account lockout protects customer accounts from automated password-guessing attacks by implementing a limit on incorrect password attempts before further attempts are disallowed.
- **Authenticated session**—An authenticated session allows a Web user to access multiple access-restricted pages on a Web site without having to re-authenticate on every page request. Most Web application development environments provide basic session mechanisms. This pattern incorporates user authentication into the basic session model.
- **Password authentication**—Protects against weak passwords, automated password-guessing attacks, and mishandling of passwords.
- **Password Propagation**—Provides an alternative by requiring that an individual user's authentication credentials be verified by the database before access is provided to that user's data.

A number of these patterns are applicable to software assurance in general, including:

- **Hidden implementation**—This pattern limits an attacker's ability to discern the internal workings of an application, which would provide information that could be used to carry out a successful attack or reverse engineer the application.
- **Partitioned application**—This pattern splits a large, complex application into two or more simpler components. Any dangerous privilege is restricted to a single, small component, enforcing least privilege.

[23] `www.scrypt.net/~celer/securitypatterns/`

- **Secure assertion**—This pattern disseminates application-specific sanity checks throughout the system. The assertions reveal attempts to abuse or attack the system.
- **Server sandbox**—This pattern builds a wall around the Web server in order to contain the damage that could result from an undetected fault in the server or an exploited vulnerability.

The DARPA paper also defines a number of procedural patterns for carrying out secure system development practices:

- **Build the server from the ground up**—This pattern advocates building the server from the ground up, understanding the default installation of the operating system and applications, following hardening procedures to remove unnecessary services, and identifying any vulnerable services for ongoing risk management.
- **Choose the right stuff**—This pattern provides security guidance in selecting appropriate commercial off-the-shelf (COTS) components and in deciding whether to use or build custom components.
- **Document the server configuration**—This pattern advocates creating an initial configuration baseline and keeping track of all modifications to servers and application configurations going forward.
- **Patch proactively**—This pattern advocates applying patches when they become available rather than waiting until the system or related systems are compromised.
- **Red team the design**—This pattern advocates an independent security evaluation from the perspective of an attacker in the quality assurance or testing stage, so that any security issues can be addressed before production.

Interconnectivity

In the paper "Software Component Interconnection Should Be Treated as a Distinct Design Problem," Chrysanthos Dellarocas writes that "Modern software systems consist of sets of heterogeneous pieces. The pieces interact across trust boundaries and share interconnection dependencies. As the size and complexity of software systems grows, the identification and proper management of interconnections among the pieces of the system becomes a central concern."[24]

The security properties of the software system can also be difficult to determine. The Software Assurance Common Body of Knowledge (CBK) states that "Composing pieces and reasoning about the composition's security properties from those of its parts and their interconnections can be quite difficult once any element of complexity is involved."[25]

[24]Dellarocas, C. "Software Component Interconnection Should Be Treated as a Distinct Design Problem," Proceedings of the 8th Annual Workshop on Software Reuse, 1997.

[25]Redwine, S. T., Jr. (Editor), "Software Assurance: A Guide to the Common Body of Knowledge to Produce, Acquire, and Sustain Secure Software," Version 1.1., U.S. Department of Homeland Security, 2006.

To gain a full understanding of the composition's security properties, it is necessary to provide clear distinctions between software components and their interconnection dependencies. Two such principles that can assist with this goal are:

- Explicitly represent software dependencies
  - Production activities—Activities directly related to the stated goals of the system, such as the SQL engine of a database system
  - Coordination activities—Activities that do not directly relate to the stated goals of a process, but are necessary in order to manage interdependencies among production activities, such as algorithms that control concurrent access in multi-user databases
- Build design handbooks of dependencies and coordination protocols
  - Flow dependencies—Relationships between producers and consumers of resources, such as synchronization
  - Sharing dependencies—Encode relationships among consumers who use the same resource or producers who produce for the same consumers, such as dividing a resource among competing users
  - Timing dependencies—Express constraints on the relative flow of control among a set of dependencies, such as mutual exclusion dependencies

Component frameworks such as OLE, CORBA, and OpenDoc enable the interoperation of independently developed components by defining the interfaces between components and providing a standardized way of managing components.

A common notation can also facilitate a greater understanding of component interdependencies. For example, in the paper ''A Notation for Component-Based Design of Java Applications,'' Catalin Amza and Gianna Reggio write that the ''Java Targeted Notation 2 (JTN2) defines a component model based on the fundamental object-oriented principles: abstraction, encapsulation, modularization, and typing. It is an extension of JTN, an object-oriented, formal, visual notation for designing concurrent Java applications. The JTN2 component model addresses component definition, component interconnection, and component implementation in Java. It allows a component to be described, understood, and analyzed independently from other components. Pre-designed components are interconnected to form complete systems.''[26]

Security Management Interfaces

Security management interfaces provide control over the trust features in a software application, such as add/remove users, set/reset passwords, and assignment of roles/privileges to users. These are high-consequence functions and should therefore be segregated from high-risk functions in the software according to the ''Segregate trusted entities from untrusted entities'' principle.

The Microsoft Developer Network (MSDN) refers to security management interfaces as COM interfaces that must be implemented by snap-in extensions. For example, the

[26] www.springerlink.com/content/rr70gmd9baypkbrg/

ISceSvcAttachmentData interface "retrieves configuration and analysis data about a specified security service from the Security Configuration snap-ins.[27] This interface is then called by attachment snap-ins to query configuration or analysis information."

Identity Management

Identity management is concerned with efficiently creating, maintaining, and managing digital identities and surrounding processes. Identities should always use strong authentication and may even require multi-stage authentication depending on the threat environment and asset value. Identities should be used to[28]:

- Maintain accountability and traceability of a user
- Assign specific rights to an individual user or process
- Provide for nonrepudiation
- Enforce access control decisions
- Establish the identity of a peer in a secure communications path
- Prevent unauthorized users from masquerading as an authorized user

Architecture

As the requirements are further decomposed into components of the software architecture, a number of security challenges are encountered. It is helpful to explore other software architectures where the order and interaction of the components vary, to understand how to address security challenges and meet software assurance goals. In this section, security challenges are examined in distributed computing, service-oriented architecture, rich Internet applications, pervasive computing, cloud computing, software-as-a-service, and integration with existing architectures.

Distributed Computing

In distributed computing, software is split up into processes that run simultaneously on multiple computers communicating over a network. Distributed computing is a form of parallel computing, but the term *parallel computing* is most commonly used to describe software processes running simultaneously on multiple processors, and on cores of multi-core processors, on the same computer. Both types of processing require dividing software into processes that can run simultaneously, but distributed programs often must deal with heterogeneous environments, network links of varying latencies, and unpredictable failures in the network of the computers. The key issues in securing distributed systems are concurrency, timing, and failure recovery.

[27] `http://msdn.microsoft.com/en-us/library/ms721852(VS.85).aspx`
[28] Redwine, S. T., Jr. (Editor), "Software Assurance."

Controlling the concurrency of processes (whereby two or more processes execute simultaneously) presents a security issue in the form of potential for denial of service by an attacker who intentionally exploits the system's concurrency problems to interfere with or lock up processes that run on behalf of other principals. Concurrency design issues may exist at any level of the system, from hardware to application. The SOAR report, created by the Information Assurance Technology Analysis Center (IATAC) Data and Analysis Center for Software (DACS), enumerates some examples of and best practices for dealing with specific concurrency problems including:

- **Processes using old data (e.g., out-of-date credentials, cookies)**—Propagating security state changes is a way to address this problem.
- **Conflicting resource updates**—Locking to prevent inconsistent updates (resulting from two programs simultaneously updating the same resource) is a way to address this.
- **Order of update in transaction-oriented systems and databases**—Order of arrival and update needs to be considered in transaction-oriented system designs.
- **System deadlock**—This occurs when concurrent processes or systems are waiting for each other to act (often one process is waiting for another to release resources). This is a complex issue, especially in dealing with lock hierarchies across multiple systems. There are four necessary conditions, known as the Coffman conditions (first identified by E. G. Coffman in 1971) that must be present for a deadlock to occur: mutual exclusion, hold and wait, no preemption, and circular wait.
- **Non-convergence in transaction-oriented systems**—Transaction-based systems rely on the ACID (atomic, consistent, isolated, and durable) properties of transactions (e.g., the accounting books must balance). Convergence is a state in transaction systems; when the volume of transactions subsides, there will be a consistent state in the system. In practice, when nonconvergence is observed, recovery from failures must be addressed by the systems' design.
- **Inconsistent or inaccurate time across the system**—Clock synchronization protocols, such as the Network Time Protocol or Lamport's logical locks, can be run to address this issue.

System failures may result because of physical disasters or from security failures. The system should be resilient through failure recovery and fault tolerance. Dealing with faults involves:

- **Error detection**—Detects that something in the system has failed.
- **Damage confinement**—Isolates the failure.
- **Error recovery**—Removes the effects of the error by restoring the system to a valid state.
- **Fault treatment**—Involves identifying and removing the root cause of the defect.

Failure models of the types of attacks that can be anticipated need to be created. Resilience can then be achieved through fail-stop processors and redundancy to protect the integrity of the data on a system and constrain the failure rates.

A fail-stop processor automatically halts in response to any internal failure and before the effects of that failure become visible. A combination of the following can help achieve redundancy at multiple levels:

- **Hardware redundancy**—Multiple processors, mirrored disks, multiple server farms, or redundant arrays of independent disks (RAID) can be installed.
- **Process redundancy**—Allows software to be run simultaneously on multiple geographically distributed locations, with voting on results. It can prevent attacks where the attacker gets physical control of a machine, inserts unauthorized software, or alters data.
- **Data redundancy**—Systems back up to unalterable media at regular intervals. For transaction-based systems, transaction journaling can also be performed.
- **Application redundancy**—The fallback system is typically a less capable system that can be used if the main system is compromised or unavailable.

While redundancy can improve the speed of recovery from a security incident, none of the redundancy techniques can provide protection against attack or malicious code insertion.[29]

Service-Oriented Architecture

NIST SP 800-95 *Guide to Secure Web Services*, August 2007, states that organizations are adopting Service-Oriented Architecture (SOA) to support their mission-critical applications. SOA is a computing paradigm emphasizing dynamic service discovery, composition, and interoperability. Web services are a technology that can be used to implement SOA and are increasingly becoming the SOA implementation of choice. For an SOA to truly meet its goals, applications must be secure and reliable. A large number of security standards have been proposed for Web services by a number of different organizations.

Ensuring the security of Web services involves augmenting traditional security mechanisms with security frameworks based on use of authentication, authorization, confidentiality, and integrity mechanisms. The following is a summary of security techniques for Web services:

- **Confidentiality of Web service messages using XML Encryption**—This is a specification from the World Wide Web Consortium (W3C) and it provides a mechanism to encrypt XML documents.
- **Integrity of Web service messages using XML Signature**—This is a specification produced jointly by the W3C and the Internet Engineering Task Force (IETF). The power of XML Signature is to selectively sign XML data.
- **Web service authentication and authorization using XML Signature**—Security Assertion Markup Language (SAML) and eXtensible Access Control Markup Language (XACML) as proposed by the Organization for Advancement of Structured Information Standards (OASIS) group. SAML and XACML provide mechanisms for authentication and authorization in a Web services environment.

[29]IATAC/DACS, "Software Security Assurance State-of-the-Art Report (SOAR)." July 31, 2007.

- **Web Services (WS) Security**—This specification, produced by OASIS, defines a set of SOAP header extensions for end-to-end SOAP messaging security. It supports message integrity and confidentiality by allowing communicating partners to exchange signed encrypted messages in a Web services environment.
- **Security for Universal Description, Discovery, and Integration (UDDI)**—Produced by OASIS, UDDI allows Web services to be easily located and subsequently invoked. Security for UDDI enables publishers, inquirers, and subscribers to authenticate themselves and authorize the information published in the directory.

Many of the Web services challenges have been met with existing standards, but there are a number of challenges that have yet to be addressed. Some examples of those challenges are:

- Repudiation of transactions
- Secure issuance of credentials
- Exploitation of covert channels
- Compromised services
- Spread of malware, such as viruses and Trojan horses via SOAP messages
- Denial-of-service attacks
- Incorrect service implementations

The following are possible actions that should be considered to address these challenges:

- **Replicate data and services to improve availability**—Since Web services are susceptible to DoS attacks, it is important to replicate data and applications in a robust manner. Replication and redundancy can ensure access to critical data in the event of a fault. They will also enable the system to react in a coordinated way to deal with disruptions.
- **Use logging of transactions to improve nonrepudiation and accountability**—Nonrepudiation and accountability require logging mechanisms involved in the entire Web service transaction. As of early 2007, there are few implemented logging standards that can be used across an entire SOA. In particular, the level of logging provided by various UDDI registries, identity providers, and individual Web services varies greatly. Where the provided information is not sufficient to maintain accountability and nonrepudiation, it may be necessary to introduce additional software or services into the SOA to support these security requirements.
- **Use threat modeling and secure software design techniques to protect from attacks**—The objective of secure software design techniques is to ensure that the design and implementation of Web services software does not contain defects that can be exploited. Threat modeling and risk analysis techniques should be used to protect the Web services application from attacks. Used effectively, threat modeling can find security strengths and weaknesses, discover vulnerabilities

and provide feedback into the security life cycle of the application. Software security testing should include security-oriented code reviews and penetration testing. By using threat modeling and secure software design techniques, Web services can be implemented to withstand a variety of attacks.

- **Use performance analysis and simulation techniques for end-to-end quality of service and quality of protection**—Queuing networks and simulation techniques have long played critical roles in designing, developing, and managing complex information systems. Similar techniques can be used for quality assured and highly available Web services. In addition to QoS of a single service, end-to-end QoS is critical for most composite services. For example, enterprise systems with several business partners must complete business processes in a timely manner to meet real-time market conditions. The dynamic and compositional nature of Web services makes end-to-end QoS management a major challenge for service-oriented distributed systems.
- **Digitally sign UDDI entries to verify the author of registered entries**—UDDI registries openly provide details about the purpose of a Web service as well as how to access it. Web services use UDDI registries to discover and dynamically bind to Web services at runtime. Should an attacker compromise a UDDI entry, it would be possible for requesters to bind to a malicious provider. Therefore, it is important to digitally sign UDDI entries so as to verify the publisher of these entries.
- **Enhance existing security mechanisms and infrastructure**—Web services rely on many existing Internet protocols and often coexist with other network applications on an organization's network. As such, many Web service security standards, tools, and techniques require that traditional security mechanisms, such as firewalls, intrusion detection systems (IDS), and secured operating systems, are in effect before implementation or deployment of Web services applications.

Rich Internet Applications

Rich Internet applications (RIA) are a class of online user-facing software with the interface richness of a desktop application, but the omnipresence of a Web page. Some of the most powerful RIA applications, such as those built with Adobe AIR or smartphone platforms, run outside the browser and most do not require permanent installation on the operating system. However, most do require a foundation layer of software to be present, such as a runtime library or virtual machine.

The major RIA frameworks include Adobe AIR, Microsoft Silverlight, Google Gears, Yahoo BrowserPlus, Mozilla Prism, JavaFX, and HTML 5.

There is ongoing debate as to what exactly constitutes a rich Internet application. However, in general, RIA frameworks may possess some of the following characteristics:[30]

- **Accessibility**—access to the content and functionality of the Web site by people with disabilities may be impaired.
- **Advanced communications**—supporting servers may be used to improve the user experience, for example by using optimized network protocols, asynchronous

[30] http://en.wikipedia.org/wiki/Rich_Internet_application

I/O and pre-fetching data. However, reliable and high performance broadband connections are often required to take advantage of these features.

- **Complexity**—a RIA may be more difficult to design, develop, debug, deploy, and maintain than traditional Web applications.
- **Consistency**—the appearance of the user interface and experience can be controlled across operating systems. However, performance monitoring and fault diagnosis can be difficult.
- **Installation and Maintenance**—use of a RIA may require plug-ins, sandboxes, or virtual machines to be installed on the end user's computer. Installation is typically faster than that of application software but slower than traditional Web applications. Automation of installation may not be possible.
- **Offline**—use of a RIA offline may be supported by retaining state locally on the client machine, but developments in formal standards and specifications by the World Wide Web Consortium (`www.w3.org`), and other standards bodies, have also enabled this feature for standard Web applications.
- **Performance**—some applications can avoid the latency of round-trips to the server by processing locally on the client. Offloading work to the clients can also improve server performance. Conversely, the resource requirements can be prohibitive for small, embedded, and mobile devices.
- **Richness**—enhanced media and content features are provided through proprietary extensions instead of natively by the Web browser, e.g., video capture.

RIAs have two key security protections:

- **Same origin policy**—If two sites share the same protocol (http), domain (`www.example.com`), and port (80), they are said to be from the same origin. The intention of this policy is to restrict RIA access to its origin.
- **Sandbox**—This is often referred to as a ''jail'' or secure environment. The sandbox is a policy to prevent access by a RIA to any operating system resource to which it has not been granted explicit authorization.

NOTE One of the most common reasons Web sites are prone to cross-site scripting (XSS) attacks is that developers must, by definition of the application's mission, violate the somewhat weak standards of same origin; that is how they inject context sensitive ads, fancy widgets, and so on, which are required of e-commerce applications.

Rich Internet applications face some of the same security challenges as typical Web applications and introduce new challenges at the operating system level and among the RIAs themselves. Some design considerations for addressing these security challenges include:

- Provide automatic updates for the RIA software
- Prevent predictably named data stores and use a per-user GUID embedded in dynamically generated page

- Use parameterized SQL queries
- Restrict a RIA to a specific domain
- Validate or disallow arguments; do not use arguments in JavaScript or to fetch URL resources
- Do not violate sandbox security models
- Use Flex or Flash if all the capabilities of Adobe Air are not required[31]

Pervasive Computing

The home page of the NIST Information Technology Laboratory (ITL) Pervasive Computing Program (`www.itl.nist.gov/pervasivecomputing.html`) describes pervasive computing as:

> *. . . a term that signifies several new elements of computing. One element involves pervasive computation-computers and sensors 'everywhere' in devices, appliances, equipment, in homes, workplaces and factories, and in clothing. Another element involves pervasive communication-a high degree of communication among devices and sensors through a ubiquitous and secure network infrastructure with a wired core and wireless adjuncts that communicate with the core. Because computation will become so integrated into our lives and activities, natural forms of human-computer interaction, such as spoken dialogue with computers, will become more important.*

Pervasive computing networks are by nature decentralized and flexible. Entities will be required to operate while being disconnected from the network, thus outside of any security context in which to determine their identities. Therefore, a key security challenge is how to manage trust among all the entities.

The properties of trust management frameworks should[32]:

- Be distributed
- Protect user anonymity, while providing accountability
- Be lightweight in terms of both required storage and scalability
- Minimize bandwidth demand
- Be robust to common attacks
- Evolve (social) trust as humans do (reputation)
- Support both types of recommendations (good and bad)
- Incorporate the three classical dimensions of computational trust: context, subjectivity, time
- Be integrated with a decision module
- Have a trust metric that is expressive, yet tractable

[31] `www.slideshare.net/astamos/ria-and-ajax-security-workshop-part-2-presentation`

[32] Quercia, D., Hailes, S., and Capra, L., "B-trust: Bayesian Trust Framework for Pervasive Computing," Proceedings of the International Conference on Trust Management. (May. 2006), pp. 298–312. `www.cs.ucl.ac.uk/staff/d.quercia/publications/querciaB-trust06.pdf`

A number of trust management schemes have been proposed to satisfy some of these properties, including:

- **Bayesian trust framework**—Evolves trust based on a Bayesian formalization whose trust metric is expressive, yet tractable. It is lightweight, protects user anonymity while being resistant to "Sybil attacks" (attacks resulting from users who maliciously use multiple identities), and enhances detection of two collusion attacks; and integrates risk-aware decision modules.
- **Reputation-based trust system**—Can track the behavior of nodes and reward well-behaved nodes while punishing misbehaving or malicious nodes. This involves developing a trust model, assigning credentials to nodes, updating private keys, managing the trust value of each node, and making appropriate decisions about nodes access rights.[33]

The paper "A Trust Analysis Methodology for Pervasive Computing Systems" introduces a trust analysis methodology for finding trust issues within pervasive computing systems. The methodology is "based on a systematic analysis of scenarios that describe the typical use of the pervasive system by using a Trust Analysis Grid. The Trust Analysis Grid is composed of eleven Trust Issue Categories that cover the various aspects of the concept of trust in pervasive computing systems. The Trust Analysis Grid is then used to guide the design of the pervasive computing system."[34]

Cloud Computing

NIST is developing a special publication that will cover cloud architectures, security, and deployment strategies for the federal government. As of June 2009, the NIST ITL Cloud Research Team (`http://csrc.nist.gov/groups/SNS/cloud-computing/index.html`) has provided a draft working definition of cloud computing that will serve as the foundation for this publication. The following information comes from this draft definition.

NIST states that cloud computing is still an evolving paradigm. Its definitions, use cases, underlying technologies, issues, risks, and benefits will be refined in a spirited debate by the public and private sectors. These definitions, attributes, and characteristics will evolve and change over time. The cloud computing industry represents a large ecosystem of many models, vendors, and market niches. This definition attempts to encompass all of the various cloud approaches.

NIST defines cloud computing as a model for enabling convenient, on-demand network access to a shared pool of configurable computing resources (e.g., networks, servers, storage, applications, and services) that can be rapidly provisioned and released with minimal management effort or service provider interaction. This cloud

[33]Boukerche, A., and Ren, Y., "A Trust-Based Security System for Ubiquitous and Pervasive Computing Environments," Computer Communications Volume 31, Issue 18 (December 2008), pp. 4343–4351.

[34]Lo Presti, S., Butler, M., Leuschel, M., and Booth, C., "A Trust Analysis Methodology for Pervasive Computing Systems," in *Trusting Agents for Trusting Electronic Societies*, LNCS Vol. 3577, 2005, Springer. `http://eprints.ecs.soton.ac.uk/10782/`

model promotes availability and is composed of five essential characteristics, three delivery models, and four deployment models.

Clouds have the following five essential characteristics:

- **On-demand self-service**—A consumer can unilaterally provision computing capabilities, such as server time and network storage, as needed automatically without requiring human interaction with each service's provider.
- **Ubiquitous network access**—Capabilities are available over the network and accessed through standard mechanisms that promote use by heterogeneous thin or thick client platforms (e.g., mobile phones, laptops, and PDAs).
- **Location independent resource pooling**—The provider's computing resources are pooled to serve all consumers using a multi-tenant model, with different physical and virtual resources dynamically assigned and reassigned according to consumer demand. The customer generally has no control or knowledge over the exact location of the provided resources but may be able to specify location at a higher level of abstraction (e.g., country, state, or datacenter). Examples of resources include storage, processing, memory, network bandwidth, and virtual machines.
- **Rapid elasticity**—Capabilities can be rapidly and elastically provisioned to quickly scale up and rapidly released to quickly scale down. To the consumer, the capabilities available for provisioning often appear to be infinite and can be purchased in any quantity at any time.
- **Measured Service**—Cloud systems automatically control and optimize resource use by leveraging a metering capability at some level of abstraction appropriate to the type of service (e.g., storage, processing, bandwidth, and active user accounts). Resource usage can be monitored, controlled, and reported providing transparency for both the provider and consumer of the utilized service.

Clouds have the following three delivery models:

- **Cloud Software as a Service (SaaS)**—The capability provided to the consumer is to use the provider's applications running on a cloud infrastructure and accessible from various client devices through a thin client interface such as a Web browser (e.g., Web-based email). The consumer does not manage or control the underlying cloud infrastructure, network, servers, operating systems, storage, or even individual application capabilities, with the possible exception of limited user-specific application configuration settings.
- **Cloud Platform as a Service (PaaS)**—The capability provided to the consumer is to deploy onto the cloud infrastructure consumer-created applications using programming languages and tools supported by the provider (e.g., java, python, .Net). The consumer does not manage or control the underlying cloud infrastructure, network, servers, operating systems, or storage, but the consumer has control over the deployed applications and possibly application hosting environment configurations.
- **Cloud Infrastructure as a Service (IaaS)**—The capability provided to the consumer is to provision processing, storage, networks, and other fundamental

computing resources where the consumer is able to deploy and run arbitrary software, which can include operating systems and applications. The consumer does not manage or control the underlying cloud infrastructure but has control over operating systems, storage, deployed applications, and possibly select networking components (e.g., firewalls, load balancers).

Clouds have the following four deployment models:

- **Private cloud**—The cloud infrastructure is operated solely for an organization. It may be managed by the organization or a third party and may exist on premise or off premise.
- **Community cloud**—The cloud infrastructure is shared by several organizations and supports a specific community that has shared concerns (e.g., mission, security requirements, policy, and compliance considerations). It may be managed by the organizations or a third party and may exist on premise or off premise.
- **Public cloud**—The cloud infrastructure is made available to the general public or a large industry group and is owned by an organization selling cloud services.
- **Hybrid cloud**—The cloud infrastructure is a composition of two or more clouds (private, community, or public) that remain unique entities but are bound together by standardized or proprietary technology that enables data and application portability (e.g., cloud bursting).

The NIST ITL Cloud Research Team presentation, "Effectively and Securely Using the Cloud Computing Paradigm"[35], lists the following primary and secondary technologies as foundational elements of cloud computing:

Primary technologies include:

- Virtualization
- Grid technology
- Service Oriented Architecture
- Distributed Computing
- Broadband Networks
- Browser as a platform
- Free and Open Source Software

Secondary technologies include:

- Autonomic Systems
- Web 2.0
- Web application frameworks
- Service Level Agreements

[35] `http://csrc.nist.gov/groups/SNS/cloud-computing/cloud-computing-v20.ppt`

The presentation also cites an IDC Enterprise Panel survey from August 2008 that shows security as the major issue in cloud computing and lists the following security advantages and challenges for cloud computing.

Security advantages include:

- Data fragmentation and dispersal
- Dedicated security team
- Greater investment in security infrastructure
- Fault tolerance and reliability
- Greater resiliency
- Hypervisor protection against network attacks
- Possible reduction of Certification and Accreditation activities, e.g., access to pre-accredited clouds
- Simplification of compliance analysis
- Data held by unbiased party (cloud vendor assertion)
- Low-cost disaster recovery and data storage solutions
- On-demand security controls
- Real-time detection of system tampering
- Rapid re-constitution of services
- Advanced honeypot capabilities

Security challenges include:

- Data dispersal and international privacy laws
  - European Union Data Protection Directive and United States Safe Harbor program
  - Exposure of data to foreign government and data subpoenas
  - Data retention issues
- Need for isolation management
- Multi-tenancy
- Logging challenges
- Data ownership issues
- Quality of service guarantees
- Dependence on secure hypervisors
- Attraction to hackers (high-value target)
- Security of virtual OS in the cloud
- Possibility for massive outages
- Encryption needs for cloud computing
  - Encrypting access to the cloud resource control interface

- Encrypting administrative access to OS instances
- Encrypting access to applications
- Encrypting application data at rest

- Public cloud versus internal cloud security
- Lack of public SaaS version control

Software-as-a-Service

Software-as-a-service (SaaS) is a business model of software delivery where a software application is available as a service hosted on the Internet. The end user of the service does not own the software, but rather pays a subscription or pay-as-you-go fee for the solution delivered by the software. SaaS applications are similar to normal Web applications that house external data, with the key difference that they employ a type of *multi-tenant* architecture. This refers to a principle in software architecture where a single instance of the software serves multiple client organizations (tenants). One key security requirement in multi-tenant architectures is data safety, the proper partitioning of data and configuration information for each client organization. In an online article entitled "Multi-Tenant Data Architecture"[36] Frederick Chong, Gianpaolo Carraro, and Roger Woler of Microsoft describe security patterns based on techniques such as filtering, permissions, and encryption to integrate security into multi-tenant architectures. The following is a summary of those patterns:

- **Trusted database connections**—A database account is created for each tenant. Access control lists (ACL) are used to grant each of the tenant accounts access to specific database objects. When an end user performs an action that directly or indirectly requires a call to a database, the application connects to the database using the tenant account credentials rather than the credentials of the end user.
- **Secure database tables**—Secure the database on the table level by using the `GRANT` command to grant a tenant user account access to a table or other database object.
- **Tenant view filter**—Uses SQL views to allow individual tenants access to some of the rows in a given table, while denying access to other rows.
- **Tenant data encryption**—Encrypts tenant data within the database so it will remain secure even if the data is compromised.

Well-designed SaaS applications also share common attributes. In an online article entitled "Architecture Strategies for Catching the Long Tail"[37] Frederick Chong and Gianpaolo Carraro of Microsoft describe three attributes that separate a well-designed SaaS application from a poorly designed one. These attributes are:

- **Scalable**—a scalable architecture should maximize concurrency by handling growing amounts of work in a graceful manner

[36] `http://msdn.microsoft.com/en-us/library/aa479086.aspx`
[37] `http://msdn.microsoft.com/en-us/library/aa479069.aspx`

- **Multi-tenant**—since one application may be serving multiple customers, the architecture should maximize the sharing of resources across tenants, but should still able to differentiate data belonging to different customers.
- **Configurable**—customizing the application for one customer could affect all other customers. Instead, each customer should use metadata to configure the way the application appears and behaves for its users. The task of configuring the applications should be intuitive for the customers, without incurring extra development or operation costs.

Integration with Existing Architectures

When integrating components into an existing architecture, the greatest problems involve the properties and interaction of the components. An individual component may meet security requirements, but a system composed of those components may not be secure. For example, a reused component may be exposed to inputs that were not previously tested. Thus, it may introduce vulnerabilities into the new system.

The paper "Trustworthy Composition: The System Is Not Always the Sum of Its Parts"[38] discusses software composition from the perspective of four software artifacts. The chosen artifacts provide a way to discuss the impact of distributed information systems on the required software assurance analysis:

- **Specific interface**—An interface controls access to a service. Interfaces that fail to validate the input are frequent members of published vulnerability lists.
- **Component-specific integration**—Assembly problems often arise because of conflicts in the design assumptions for the components. Project constraints may require using components, commercial off-the-shelf (COTS) software, or legacy systems that were not designed for the operating environment, which raises the likelihood of mismatches. The increasing importance of business integration requirements compounds the component integration problems and is the motivation for designs based on SOA.
- **Architecture integration mechanisms**—Commercial software tool vendors often provide the capability for purchasers to integrate the tool into their systems and tailor its functionality for their specific needs. However, the capability to reconfigure a system rapidly is matched by the increased probability of component inconsistencies generated by the more frequently changing component base, as well as the increased risk that the dynamic integration mechanisms could be misused or exploited. These mechanisms represent another interface that must be properly constrained.
- **System behavior, component interactions**—The behavior of a system is not the simple sum of the behavior of the individual components. System behavior is strongly influenced by the interactions of its components. Components may individually meet all specifications, but when they are composed into a system

[38] `https://buildsecurityin.us-cert.gov/daisy/bsi/articles/best-practices/assembly/50-BSI.html`

the unanticipated feedback among components can lead to unacceptable system behavior. Security and safety are system rather than component requirements. You can build a reliable system out of unreliable components by appropriately using redundancy. Components that are not secure as standalone components in an operating environment may be secure when used within the constraints maintained by a system.

The following two software assurance activities address some of the problems encountered when integrating components into existing architectures:

- **Model security properties**—How does the component address the required security properties such as confidentiality, integrity, and availability?
- **Use security design patterns**—Use proven patterns for addressing common vulnerabilities, such as validating input and escaping output

Technologies

In the process of designing software, technologies are selected that help meet software assurance goals. This section explores benefits and security concerns associated with some of those technologies.

Authentication and Identity Management

Each user's identity must be authenticated before the user is allowed to access a system or resource. This authentication is based on the presentation by the user of a unique identifier plus one or more credentials, such as a password, a digital certificate, or a biometric, to the authentication component of the trust management system.

Identity management is a means of managing user identity and account information that will be used as the basis for identifying, authenticating, and authorizing the user's access to a system or resource. Information managed by the identity management component of a trust management system includes the user's personal information, encrypted passwords, biometric data, financial information, security clearance, organizational roles, history of access/usage, and so on.[39]

Multi-factor Authentication

There are many different techniques (or factors) for performing authentication. The OWASP Comprehensive, Lightweight Application Security Process (CLASP)[40] refers to authentication factors are either strong or weak. The term *strong authentication factor* usually implies reasonable cryptographic security levels, although the terms are often used imprecisely.

[39] IATAC/DACS, "Software Security Assurance State-of-the-Art Report (SOAR)." July 31, 2007.
[40] www.owasp.org/index.php/Category:OWASP_CLASP_Project

Authentication factors are summarized in the following categories:

- **Something you know**—Passwords, personal identification numbers (PINs), passphrases, or other knowledge-based tokens. These tokens may be vulnerable to offline attacks by an attacker who eavesdropped on the network communication, malicious software such as a keylogger, or in the case of a shared secret, attacks against a verifier of that secret. Knowledge-based tokens may be considered a strong factor if implemented with a secure protocol such as Secure Remote Password (SRP) and a large randomly generated secret.
- **Something you have**—A debit/credit card or a hard token, such as RSA SecurID. Cards and tokens are vulnerable to theft and duplication. A token does not always have to be present, for example, with credit cards this is called a *card-not-present* transaction.
- **Something you are**—Biometrics such as fingerprints, hand geometry, facial recognition, retinal scan, DNA, or voice. Biometrics are vulnerable to circumvention and deception, and depend on the correct human characteristic being chosen for the correct security context

CROSS-REFERENCE **The Secure Remote Password (SRP) protocol has a number of desirable properties:**

- **It allows a user to authenticate to a server.**
- **It is resistant to dictionary attacks mounted by an eavesdropper.**
- **It does not require a trusted third party.**

http://en.wikipedia.org/wiki/Secure_remote_password_protocol

Software applications that require greater assurance use multi-factor authentication such as two-factor authentication. Two-factor authentication requires the user to present two factors in conjunction, such as something that the user knows (a password) with something the user has (a hardware or software token), thereby providing greater certainty that the user is indeed the user.

NOTE **NIST SP 800-63-1 *Electronic Authentication Guideline*, December 2008, provides additional information on factors and tokens.**

Two-factor authentication has the following benefits and weaknesses:

- **Benefits**
  - **Work factor**—The attacker must work harder to compromise the user because they must obtain both tokens for successful authentication. This can help reduce the incidence of identity theft and fraud within the group of two-factor authentication users in the short term while the attackers are occupied with more vulnerable users.

  - **Local access**—If two-factor authentication is used for access to known and verified—for example, with a valid Transport Layer Security (TLS) certificate—sites on the corporate intranet and the user's computer is not running any malicious software, use of two-factor authentication may provide greater assurance.
- **Weaknesses**
  - **Trojan horse**—Attackers trick the user into installing a *Trojan horse* (a program that is a "backdoor" to the user's computer), allowing the attacker to "piggy-back" on the user's access to a Web site. This attack is most common on the Internet.
  - **Man-in-the-middle**—The attacker tricks the user into logging into a fake Web site and redirects the credentials to the real Web site, giving the attacker full access. This attack is most common on the Internet.

In a joint paper by IBM and UBS entitled, "Secure Internet Banking Authentication,"[41] the authors suggest that to address these weaknesses in part, *transaction signing* should be added to the two-factor authentication process. In transaction signing, when the user first makes a transaction request, the transaction server returns a confirmation response to the user, and the user digitally signs the transaction by entering their password on the confirmation page.

Federated Identity Management

The two major enterprise identity management technologies are directory services and user provisioning systems.[42]

Directory services provide a centralized repository of user data in an enterprise. Common directory services include Microsoft Active Directory and LDAP. Directory services maintain the user data as a set of objects with similar attributes organized in a logical and hierarchical manner. Enterprise applications that call upon the directory must agree on objects such as common user identifier, attribute names, and meanings. There are difficulties involved in implementing a single directory system in the enterprise:

- **Lack of a single, coherent source of information**—There are usually several sources of information for a single user.
- **Need for a local user database**—Some systems must store the copies of user records in local databases to operate efficiently.
- **Stateful services**—Some services need to keep state for each user to operate.
- **Inconsistent policies**—Role names and access control attributes may not have the same meaning in all systems.

These difficulties show that a more complex mechanism is needed to manage user information in heterogeneous environments. User provisioning systems are good at

[41] `www.zurich.ibm.com/pdf/csc/SecureInternetBankingAuthentication.pdf`

[42] `http://storm.alert.sk/work/papers/files/2006-infosecon-contribution-final.pdf`

handling and automating complex user management tasks. However, they exhibit problems as well:

- **Slow operation**—The execution of a workflow process itself can take a considerable amount of time.
- **Risk of inconsistency**—The provisioning systems synchronize several data stores, can fail to detect an inconsistency, and become permanently out of sync.

Combining these two systems adds increased complexity to identity management. Instead, to address the requirements of interoperable, cross-domain identity management, it is necessary to create a new model that is standards-based and loosely coupled. Federated identity management was created to meet those requirements. Federated identity management is a combination of standards and technologies that allow the portability of identity information across domains. The basic principle of federated identity management is an exchange of identity claims (assertions) between interested parties.

"Use of identity federation standards can reduce cost by eliminating the need to scale one-off or proprietary solutions. It can increase security and lower risk by enabling an organization to identify and authenticate a user once, and then use that identity information across multiple systems, including external partner Web sites. It can improve privacy compliance by allowing the user to control what information is shared, or by limiting the amount of information shared. And lastly, it can drastically improve the end-user experience by eliminating the need for new account registration through automatic 'federated provisioning' or the need to redundantly log in through cross-domain single sign-on."[43]

Credential Management

In information security, *credential* normally refers to a cryptographic store of identity such as a digital certificate. The criterion for issuing a cryptographic credential is the unambiguous association of the credential with a specific, real individual or other entity. An X.509 digital certificate is an example of a cryptographic credential.

X.509 is an international standard. X.509 certificates often have the following characteristics:

- **Issued by a certificate authority (CA)**—The CA is the issuing authority that vets the identity of the individual or entity before issuing the certificate.
- **Expiration**—The certificate is normally valid only for a specific period of time, after which it expires
- **Revocation**—The certificate can be revoked by the issuing authority at any time. Certificate status checks can be automated using a technology such as Online Certificate Status Protocol (OCSP)

[43] http://en.wikipedia.org/wiki/Federated_identity

CROSS-REFERENCE **"The Online Certificate Status Protocol (OCSP) is an Internet protocol used for obtaining the revocation status of an X.509 digital certificate. It was created as an alternative to certificate revocation lists."** `http://en.wikipedia.org/wiki/Online_Certificate_Status_Protocol`

X.509 is normally one of the credentials used in single sign-on (SSO). SSO enables a user to log in once and gain access to the resources of multiple software systems without being prompted to log in again. *Single sign-off* is the reverse process whereby a single action of signing out terminates access to multiple software systems.

SSO may need to provide access to various applications and resources that implement different authentication mechanisms. To support these resources, SSO must translate internally and store (or retrieve from an external credential source) different credentials compared to those used for initial authentication.[44]

Some benefits of SSO include:

- Reducing password fatigue from different username and password combinations
- Reducing time spent re-entering passwords for the same identity
- Supporting conventional authentication such as Windows Credentials (i.e., username/password)
- Reducing IT costs due to lower number of IT help desk calls about passwords
- Providing security on all levels of entry/exit/access to systems without the inconvenience of re-prompting users
- Providing centralized reporting for policy compliance

SSO uses centralized authentication servers that all other applications and systems utilize for authentication purposes, and combines this with techniques to ensure that users do not actively have to enter their credentials more than once.

The primary security concern with SSO is that it provides access to many resources after the user is initially authenticated and thus increases the negative impact if the credentials are compromised. Therefore, SSO requires an increased focus on the protection of the user credentials, and should ideally be combined with strong authentication methods, such as personal identity verification (PIV) cards and X.509 digital certificates, instead of usernames and passwords.

Flow Control

Controlling the flow of data in an information system is related to the reference monitor concept in operating system security. A reference monitor is a conceptual device that mediates all access to objects by subjects in an operating system. An object is an entity that contains the data, and a subject is an entity that desires access to the object. In a system that implements a reference monitor, all access must first go through the reference monitor to ensure that the access conforms to the security policy.

[44] `http://en.wikipedia.org/wiki/Single_sign-on`

A reference monitor is typically implemented as the security kernel, the component with the highest privileges, in a trusted computing base (TCB). The TCB is the set of all the trusted hardware, firmware, and software components of a system and resides in the lowest level computing area of an operating system, known as computing Ring 0. The boundary between the trusted processes in Ring 0 and all processes outside the boundary is known as the security perimeter.

An example of a reference monitor implementation is the security kernel in computing Ring 0 of the Windows XP operating system. The security kernel guards the trusted processes of the operating system (system peripherals, memory, etc.) and mediates all access attempts by user programs outside the security perimeter to trusted processes within the security perimeter.

The reference monitor attempts to protect the operating system data, but it is difficult to determine which software to trust and which software to distrust. For example, a user could intentionally install prohibited software in violation of the organization's security policy or may inadvertently install malware when browsing a Web site on the Internet. Furthermore, if the user is logged on to the operating system with administrative privileges, it could allow untrusted software to change security properties of the system itself. Therefore, the reference monitor can't trust the user to make appropriate decisions regarding which applications are safe to run.

Since the reference monitor can't be solely counted upon to enforce an organization's security policy, other technologies have been created to assist. For example, Bit9 (`www.bit9.com`) provides an enterprise application whitelisting and control technology. The goal of this technology is to ensure that only trusted applications are authorized to run on Windows computers, eliminating the risk caused by malicious, illegal, and unauthorized software. The technology consists of a suite of tools that make trust decisions about software based on data maintained in the Bit9 Global Software Registry. The registry is a database that contains more than 6 billion raw software files and metadata, growing at the rate of 20 million files each day. The data is supplied by various sources and cross-checked against third-party vulnerability databases and anti-malware tools. Bit9 offers application whitelisting and control solutions that look up files in the registry using a unique hash of the file through a secure Web services interface.

The reference monitor concept can be extended into the network as well. In traditional information security, the information flowing into and out of a system may be protected at the network layer using a variety of security mechanisms, including firewalls and proxy filters. For example, a firewall on the perimeter of the network allows and disallows traffic by restricting information flow to certain ports. In the case of a Web application running on a server on the internal network, the firewall may refuse all external traffic addressed to the Web application server that is not destined to ports 80 (HTTP) and 443 (HTTPS). However, because the firewall is not content-aware, it allows both legitimate and attack traffic through to the Web application.

To improve the perimeter defense that the security infrastructure provides, application firewalls attempt to use application-specific knowledge to guard the entry and exit points to the Web application.

The OWASP describes a Web application firewall (WAF) as an appliance, server plugin, or filter that applies a set of rules to an HTTP conversation. A WAF, also referred to simply as an ''application firewall,'' typically intercepts all user data entering or leaving the Web application server. The intercepted data is compared against various (often customizable) rules to determine whether the data is bad or good. For example, form data can be examined to determine if it contains malicious logic, such as system commands that could lead to a server compromise. When attack strings are detected, the application firewall may actively defend the application by invalidating the application session or shunting the session to a ''honeypot'' system that is specially instrumented to gather details of attack methodologies. Running the application firewall in a separate process and memory space from the application further protects the applications, business logic, and data.

An application firewall typically needs to learn about the application in order to make reasonable judgments about the application data. Some application firewalls accomplish this by way of a database of known attacks, via signatures of actual attack data, behavioral patterns, or some hybrid of both. Other application firewalls observe the normal behavior of the application(s) they are to protect, preferably in a controlled environment, and then attempt to ensure that all live data conforms to similar content, size, and structure.

Web application firewalls have the following benefits and drawbacks, summarized from the article ''Application Firewalls and Proxies - Concept of Operations'' by Howard Lipson and Ken van Wyk of the Carnegie Mellon Software Engineering Institute[45]:

Benefits include:

- **Adds a security layer**—An application firewall provides an additional layer of protection between a Web application and its end users.
- **Utilizes security knowledge**—Since designing an application firewall requires specific security knowledge of Web applications, it is possible that more specialized application-specific security knowledge goes into the design of application firewalls than goes into most Web applications.
- **Utilizes application knowledge**—Specialized knowledge can provide generic security services that are independent of the application services being protected.
- **Provides flexible policy enforcement**—An application firewall provides centralized policy enforcement of acceptable application behavior.
- **Detects some attacks**—Since application firewalls are designed to detect suspected attacks as they occur, they can alert operational staff and act as intrusion detection and prevention mechanisms.
- **Facilitates application data logging**—Event logging of data to and from the application integrates into the enterprise-level auditing framework.
- **Augments third-party and legacy applications**—In production environments this provides immediate protection to legacy applications and provides security services that may be lacking in third-party applications, such as event logging.

[45] https://buildsecurityin.us-cert.gov/daisy/bsi/articles/best-practices/assembly/30-BSI.html

Drawbacks include:

- **Increases the configuration effort**—Many application firewalls require a controlled test bed to learn the application's normal behavior.
- **Decreases redundancy**—Depending on the design of the software system, the application firewall may be a single point of failure.
- **Reduces performance**—Since an application firewall sits in series with the application it protects, it may add overhead such as increased latency.
- **Increases complexity**—Maintaining a Web application plus multiple devices, such as a Web application firewall and a separate XML firewall, increases the complexity of a system, and the opportunity for misconfiguration, conflicts, and other problems that could limit functionality and availability or weaken security.
- **Fails to solve the real problem**—Some argue that deploying an application firewall effectively "passes the buck" of application security to another device. Further, since application firewalls require a good amount of time and effort to properly learn the normal behavior of an application, the argument could be made that application developers should be focusing their efforts on better software development techniques to improve quality and security instead of relying on an application firewall to do the work of developers.
- **Fails to block all attacks**—Some application firewall products function by identifying "known bad" sorts of behavior, as opposed to only allowing "known good" behavior. As such, they inherently implement a blacklist methodology that will eventually fail at identifying new attacks.
- **Creates additional work**—An application firewall that supports a "default deny" policy allows only "known good" behavior as defined in its rule set. This provides a much higher level of security but also presents an extremely difficult challenge for those configuring and maintaining the application firewall rule set.
- **Introduces incompatibility**—Application firewall rule sets and policies could be bypassed by a variety of attacks where the input appears legitimate to the application firewall but is problematic to the application the firewall was meant to protect.

Audit

Applications based on the Syslog protocol allow for the centralized logging of messages with the accuracy, level of detail, and type of information required in an audit trail. NIST SP 800-92 *Guide to Computer Security Log Management* states that Syslog provides a simple framework for log entry generation, storage, and transfer that any OS, security software, or application could use if designed to do so. Syslog assigns a priority to each message based on the importance of the following two attributes:

- **Message type, know as a *facility***—Examples of facilities include kernel messages, mail system messages, authorization messages, printer messages, and audit messages.

- **Severity**—Each log message has a severity value assigned, from most severe: 0 (emergency), to least severe: 7 (debug).

Syslog uses message priorities to determine which messages should be handled more quickly, forwarding higher-priority messages more quickly than lower-priority ones. However, the priority does not affect which actions are performed on each message. Syslog can be configured to handle log entries differently based on each message's facility and severity. For example, it could forward severity 0 kernel messages to a centralized server for further review, and simply record all severity 7 messages without forwarding them. Syslog does not offer any more granularity than that in message handling; it cannot make decisions based on the source or content of a message.

Syslog is intended to be very simple, and each Syslog message has only three parts. The first part specifies the facility and severity as numerical values. The second part of the message contains a timestamp and the hostname or IP address of the source of the log. The third part is the actual log message content. No standard fields are defined within the message content; it is intended to be human-readable and not easily machine-parseable.

This provides high flexibility for log generators, which can place whatever information they deem important within the content field, but it makes automated analysis of the log data very challenging. To address this problem, some organizations design the Syslog infrastructure so that similar messages are grouped together and assigned similar codes, which can facilitate log analysis, especially when log messages are coming from many sources.

Syslog was developed at a time when the security of logs was not a major consideration. Accordingly, it did not support the use of basic security controls that would preserve the confidentiality, integrity, and availability of logs.

As the security of logs has become a greater concern, several implementations of Syslog have been created that place a greater emphasis on security. Most have been based on a proposed standard, RFC 3195, which was designed specifically to improve the security of Syslog. Implementations based on RFC 3195 can support log confidentiality, integrity, and availability through several features, including the following:

- **Reliable log delivery**—Using Transmission Control Protocol (TCP) and/or log caching servers to ensure the reliable delivery of messages across networks
- **Transmission confidentiality protection**—Using Transport Layer Security (TLS) or Secure Shell (SSH) to protect the confidentiality of transmitted Syslog messages
- **Transmission integrity protection and authentication**—Using a secure hash algorithm, such as SHA, to create and verify message digests

Some Syslog implementations offer additional features based on RFC 1395. The most common additional features are:

- **Robust filtering**—Handling messages differently based on the host or program that generated the message, using regular expression matching of content in the body of the message, applying multiple filters to a single message

- **Log analysis**—Built-in log analysis capabilities, including correlation of multiple log entries
- **Event response**—Initiating actions when certain events are detected such as sending Simple Network Management Protocol (SNMP) traps, alerting administrators through pages or email, launching separate programs or scripts, creating a new Syslog message indicating the detection of a certain event
- **Alternative message formats**—Accepting data in non-Syslog format, such as SNMP traps, which is helpful for aggregating data from hosts that do not support Syslog
- **Log file encryption**—Encrypting rotated log files automatically to protect their confidentiality; can also be performed through third-party or OS mechanisms
- **Database storage for logs**—Enabling the storage of log entries in both traditional Syslog files and a database
- **Rate limiting**—Limiting the number of Syslog messages or TCP connections from a particular source during a certain period of time, useful for preventing a denial of service for the Syslog server and the loss of Syslog messages from other sources

Security information and event management (SIEM) software also allows for the centralized logging of messages with the accuracy, level of detail, and type of information required in an audit trail. SIEM products have one or more log servers that perform log analysis, and one or more database servers that store and collect logs from log generators. Most SIEM products support two ways of collecting logs from log generators:

- **Agentless**—The SIEM server receives data from the hosts without needing to have any special software (agents) installed on those hosts. Some servers pull logs from the hosts by having the server authenticate to each host and retrieve its logs regularly. Alternately, hosts push the logs to the servers, having each host authenticate to the server and transfer its logs regularly. The server then performs event filtering and aggregation and log normalization and analysis on the collected logs.
- **Agent-based**—An agent program is installed on the hosts to perform event filtering, aggregation, and log normalization for a particular type of log, good for transmitting the normalized log data to a SIEM server, on a real-time or near-real-time basis for analysis and storage. It may be necessary to install multiple agents for multiple logs of interest or for generic formats such as Syslog and SNMP.

The advantages to the agentless approach are that agents do not need to be installed, configured, and maintained on each logging host. The primary disadvantage is lack of filtering and aggregation at the individual host level, which can cause significantly larger amounts of data to be transferred over networks and increase the amount of time it takes to filter and analyze data. Another disadvantage is that the SIEM server may need credentials for authenticating to each logging host.

SIEM products usually include support for several dozen types of log sources, such as OSs, security software, application servers (e.g., Web servers, email servers), and even physical security control devices such as badge readers. For each supported log source type, except for generic formats such as Syslog, the SIEM products typically know how to categorize the most important logged fields (e.g., the value in field 12 of application XYZ's logs signifies the source IP address). This significantly improves the normalization, analysis, and correlation of log data over that performed by software with a less granular understanding of specific log sources and formats.

SIEM software can also perform event reduction by disregarding those data fields that are not significant to computer security, potentially reducing the SIEM software's network bandwidth and data storage.

The SIEM server analyzes the data from all the different log sources, correlates events among the log entries, identifies and prioritizes significant events, and initiates responses to events if desired. SIEM products usually include several features to help log monitoring staff, such as the following:

- **Graphical user interface (GUI)**—Specifically designed to assist analysis in identifying potential problems and reviewing all available data related to each problem
- **Security knowledge base**—Customizable knowledge base containing information on known vulnerabilities, a meaning based on context for certain log messages, and other technical data
- **Incident tracking and reporting**—Capabilities to track and report incidents sometimes with robust workflow features
- **Asset information storage and correlation**—For example, giving higher priority to an attack that targets a vulnerable OS or a more important host

SIEM products usually offer capabilities to protect the confidentiality, integrity, and availability of log data. For example, network communications between agents and the SIEM servers typically occur over the reliable TCP protocol and are encrypted. Also, agents and SIEM servers may need to provide credentials to each other and be authenticated successfully before they can transfer data (e.g., agent sending logs to server, server reconfiguring agent).

A host-based IDS is a mechanism to audit logs. It monitors the characteristics of a single host and the events occurring within the host for suspicious activity. Many host-based IDS products monitor hosts' OS, security software, and application logs. Some host-based IDS products use logs as only one of several sources of data in detecting suspicious activity, while other host-based IDS products monitor only logs. Generally, a host-based IDS that uses log data has signatures for known malicious activity that it matches against log entries to identify events of interest. However, such products often focus on the OS logs and the most common security software and applications, and offer little or no support for less common software.[46]

[46]NIST SP 800-92 *Guide to Computer Security Log Management*, September 2006.

Data Protection

Data protection technologies are concerned with protecting data in motion, at rest, and in use at the end points.

Data Loss Prevention

Data Loss Prevention (DLP) technology is designed to reduce the risk of data loss, whether the data is in motion on a network, at rest in storage, or in use at an end point.

- **In motion**—Data analysis using real-time passive network monitoring with full-packet capture, session reconstruction, and content analysis capabilities. Identifies content being sent across specific communication channels, including instant messages, email, and Web traffic. DLP technology integrates with a mail transfer agent (MTA) to block, quarantine, or encrypt email. Some DLP technology uses a proxy to buffer or queue traffic so that it can perform an in-depth analysis before passing the traffic along. Data analysis can identify structured data such as employee, patient, or customer records in a tab- or comma-delimited format, and unstructured data such as sensitive business plans or financial documents.
- **At rest**—Using content policy agents to connect to network shares to scan files for content violations. Some DLP technology uses local agents (for example, on file servers) to scan results locally with results sent securely to a central management server.
- **In use**—Using a content policy agent to analyze content at the network end points. The policy is enforced within the network stack and the file system at the end point. The DLP technology can enforce a number of policies, such as restricting the copying of sensitive data to unencrypted USB devices. As with data at rest, the agent can send results securely to a central management server.

For data in any state, if the agent detects a policy violation, such as a sensitive document or data left unencrypted, it can create an alert, notify an administrator of a violation, quarantine the file to a secure location, encrypt the file in place, or block the content from being transmitted.

Database Security

In modern society, databases store information of great significance such as medical records, bank accounts, pension benefits, credit history, real estate activity, phone records, retail inventory, and school grades.

Users typically interact with a database through client software applications such as Web applications over the Internet. As databases have become network-accessible and moved closer to the network perimeter, they have become an increasingly valuable target.

Database systems are also increasingly complex. Database vendors have introduced features so that a database can be easily integrated into any operating environment. These features include distributed replication, operating system services, service-oriented architecture, application server integration, and XML support.

Many databases in use today still support legacy features for backward compatibility. Some of these features were designed for the isolated operating environment in the back office of an organization. Now that databases are interconnected with other software systems and accessible over the network, those previously isolated mechanisms are exposed to attack. To reduce this threat, the use of legacy or insecure network protocols and authentication mechanisms should be avoided whenever possible. Legacy components can be replaced with secure equivalents such as Secure Shell (SSH) or Transport Layer Security (TLS).

The database can be further protected by controlling access to the database at all boundaries and network end points. For example, access to the database should only be granted to other software components, users, or hosts that possess the required level of trust. And access can be restricted by using multiple layers of security mechanisms, e.g., a database-specific configuration file, the TCP wrappers mechanism on *nix operating systems, and a host-based firewall.

A database is typically part of a larger software system that serves a business function such as e-commerce. Database administrators (DBAs), network administrators, and other database management personnel are often the only users provided direct access to the database. Other users interact indirectly with the database through a software application, such as a Web application, which is then provided direct access to the database. The trusted access by the Web application is frequently abused on the Internet through attacks such as SQL injection.

The OWASP writes that "a SQL injection attack consists of insertion of a SQL query via the input data from the client to the Web application."[47] A successful SQL injection can read sensitive data from the database and modify database data through commands such as Insert, Update, or Delete. A SQL injection can also execute administrative operations on the database, e.g., shutdown of the database management system (DBMS), recover the content of a given file present on the DBMS file system, and potentially issue commands to the operating system.

The Web application code and the database itself share responsibility for defending against SQL injection attacks. Some of the methods that can be used to mitigate these attacks include:

- Creating parameterized queries using bound, typed parameters
- Creating parameterized stored procedures
- Using a single encapsulated library for accessing databases
- Minimizing database permissions

The Defense Information Systems Agency (DISA) publishes additional guidance for securing database systems such as the *Database Security Technical Implementation Guide* at `http://iase.disa.mil/stigs/stig/index.html`.

Computing Environment

There are security concerns and benefits associated with the technologies that make up the computing environment, for example, programming languages on which the

[47] `www.owasp.org/index.php/Guide_to_SQL_Injection`

software is built, deployment technologies such as virtualization, and the operating systems on which the software runs.

Programming Languages

Programming languages are typically categorized as either *managed code* or *unmanaged code* technologies. Secure programming with either a managed or unmanaged code technology requires attention to specific security aspects of that technology.

Managed Code

Managed code is computer program code that is compiled into an intermediate code format, sometimes referred to as byte code, and executes under management of a runtime environment. Examples of managed code technologies are Java EE and Microsoft .NET. Specific security aspects of the Java language are summarized below from the paper "Enhancing the Development Life Cycle to Produce Secure Software."

- **Input handling**—The skills and mechanisms necessary to deal with malicious input
- **Authentication and session management**—The skills and mechanisms necessary to provide authentication and session management in Java
- **Access control**—The skills and mechanisms available for access control in Java, specifically Java EE controls and Java Authentication and Authorization Service (JAAS) API
- **Java types and JVM management**—Covers the security implications of Java types and garbage collection
- **Application faults and logging**—The skills and mechanisms available for securely handling application faults and logging output
- **Encryption services**—The skills and mechanisms necessary to take full advantage of the Java Cryptographic Extensions (JCE) API
- **Concurrency and threading**—The skills and mechanisms necessary to properly structure multi-threaded Java applications
- **Connection patterns**—The skills and mechanisms necessary to securely interface with other applications
- **Miscellaneous**—Covers language-specific security mechanisms, such as access modifiers, Java Archive (JAR) protections, and Java EE filters

Unmanaged Code

Unmanaged code is compiled into machine code and executed directly by the computer's central processing unit (CPU). Unmanaged code technologies include C and C++. C is one of the most popular programming languages in the world. Specific security aspects of the C language are summarized below from "Enhancing the Development Life Cycle to Produce Secure Software."

- **Environment and input**—The skills and mechanisms necessary to securely interface with the environment and external input to the application
- **Dynamic allocated resources**—The skills and mechanisms necessary to securely use dynamic resources in the C stack and heap memory spaces
- **Input, output, and files**—The skills and mechanisms necessary to securely interact with output functions such as `printf` and reading and writing to the file system
- **Security mechanisms**—Covers identification, authentication, authorization, privacy, encryption, and secure designs
- **Concurrency**—The skills and mechanisms necessary to securely implement multi-threaded applications
- **C types**—The skills and mechanisms necessary to securely interact with built-in C types (e.g., null-terminated strings, pointers, and arrays)
- **Error conditions**—The skills and mechanisms necessary to securely identify and handle error conditions in applications
- **Coding correctness and style**—The skills and mechanisms necessary to write simple, readable, and correct code to minimize the introduction of vulnerabilities (e.g., avoid dangerous functions and do not mix assignment and comparison operators)[48]

Virtualization

Virtualization is a general term that refers to the running of a *virtual machine* (VM), which is a simulated computer environment. The degree of isolation is the aspect of virtual machines that is most frequently cited as improving the reliability and security of software running within those VMs.[49] Isolation means that the software within the VM obtains the specific resources (memory, hard drive space, virtual network interface) it needs to operate. The hypervisor provides isolation (and therefore mediates access) to the host's resources.

In platform-based virtualization, a VM has its own copy of the operating system, and therefore does not share the usage of the operating system mechanisms. In other words, a single instance is not common across the users of the virtual machines.[50]

The NIST Information Security and Privacy Advisory Board (ISPAB) paper "Perspectives on Cloud Computing and Standards" lists potential security advantages and disadvantages of virtualization.[51]

[48]Goertzel, K., Winograd, T., et al., "Enhancing the Development Life Cycle to Produce Secure Software."
[49]Goertzel, K., Winograd, T., et al., "Enhancing the Development Life Cycle to Produce Secure Software."
[50]Redwine, S. T., Jr. (Editor), "Software Assurance."
[51]Mell, P., and Grance, T., "Perspectives on Cloud Computing and Standards."

Potential security advantages of virtualization include:

- Adds a layer of security for defense-in-depth
- Provides strong encapsulation of errors or attacks within a VM
- Increases intrusion detection via introspection
- Lowers exposure of buggy/weak software
- Increases flexibility for the discovery/eviction of kernel root kits
- Increases capabilities for fault/intrusion-tolerant computing using "snapshot" and "rollback" features

Potential security disadvantages of virtualization include:

- Increases configuration effort due to the complexity of the virtualization layer and composite system
- Introduces the problem of how to prevent overlap when mapping VM storage onto host files
- Introduces the problem of virtualizing the Trusted Platform Module (TPM)
- Creates the possibility that remote attestation may not work
- Introduces the problem of detecting VM covert channels
- Requires new protection mechanisms to prevent VM escape, VM detection, VM-VM interference
- Introduces the possibility of virtual networking configuration errors
- Introduces the risk that malicious software will target the VM environment
- Increases overall security risk due to shared resources: networks, clipboards, clocks, printers, desktop management, folders

Operating Systems

Since a majority of software is deployed on COTS operating systems—such as Microsoft Windows, Unix, Linux—the OS itself becomes an extension of the executing software and a critical part of the overall computing environment. Therefore, it is important to implement the guidance offered throughout this book on securing the OS. Special attention should also be paid to the following security constraints and recommendations for the protection of executing software:

- **Access controls**—On Unix or Linux, the chroot jail feature can be used to isolate running software, a Java Virtual Machine (JVM) can be used to isolate running Java software, and the .NET Common Language Runtime (CLR) can be used to provide a secure execution environment for .NET applications.
- **Trusted versions**—A trusted operating system implements mandatory access control. There are secure versions of common operating systems, including Security Enhanced Linux and Trusted Solaris.

- **Security enhancement**—Add-on security features or third-party solutions are available, such as mobile code signature validation, input/output filtering, disk encryption, and mandatory access control with reference monitor.
- **Hardening**—A minimal and highly restricted configuration of the operating system. The operating system is configured with the most restrictive access control possible, and only the necessary services and software are installed and running.

Digital Rights Management

Digital rights management (DRM) is an access control mechanism used by copyright holders, content providers, and manufacturers to limit usage of digital media or devices. The ''digital rights'' part of DRM refers to the rights of a subject (entity or end user) to perform an action with respect to the object (content). The content includes digital media such as songs, movies, and documents. ''Management'' refers to the implementation of the access control policy. DRM technology consists of:

- **Compliance rules**—Specifies the required behaviors of the DRM implementation and any applications accessing the implementation, including:
  - Definition of specific license rights
  - Device requirements
  - Revocation of license rights or penalties if the implementation is not robust enough or noncompliant
- **Robustness rules**—All DRM initiatives are standardizing on robustness rules similar to those developed by 4C Entity. 4C Entity (`www.4centity.com`) is the industry organization founded by IBM, Intel, Panasonic, and Toshiba that is leading the development, adoption and promotion of interoperable technology solutions for the authorized sharing of premium content.
  - Specifies the assets and different levels of robustness required to secure each asset
  - Includes assets such as device keys, content keys, algorithms, and profiling data
  - Defines minimum techniques to secure each asset, such as code signing, code encryption, obfuscation component, self-verification

The level of robustness is based on the types of tools and attacks to which they must be resistant or immune. The following are the types of tools:

- **Widely available tools**—Available to everyone and easy to use, such as screwdrivers and file editors
- **Specialized tools**—Available at a reasonable price, but requiring skill, such as debuggers, memory scanners, decompilers
- **Professional tools**—Expensive, not widely available, and require great skill, such as logic analyzers, chip disassembly systems, circuit emulators

The following are different levels of robustness and example assets, from most critical (Level 1) to least critical (Level 3)[52]:

- **Level 1**—Should be immune to widely available tools and specialized tools and resistant to professional tools; could result in a "break once, break everywhere" exploit; examples include device secrets, security functions
- **Level 2**—Should be immune to widely available tools and resistant to specialized tools such as memory scanners, debuggers, decompilers; could result in a "break once, break once exploit"; examples include serial numbers, content keys
- **Level 3**—Should be resistant to widely available tools such as file editors; could result in a leak of confidential information; an example would be profiling data

Security challenges for DRM include:

- **Key hiding**—Secret keys used for encryption, authentication, and node-locking; secure key hiding helps to prevent tampering attacks that target keys
- **Device fingerprinting**—Summary of hardware and software characteristics to uniquely identify a device; helps to prevent fraud and enable secure authentication
- **Over-the-air (OTA) provisioning**—Need to use end-to-end encryption or other secure means for delivery of copyrighted software to mobile devices, such as use of shared secrets to initiate or reestablish trust

Integrity

The OWASP writes that "code signing provides the stakeholder with a means of validating the origin and integrity of the software."[53] Code is signed to establish that it comes from a trustworthy vendor when it is being distributed over an untrusted medium such as the Internet. The signature must be validated using a trusted third party in order to establish identity. Code signing is performed in the following three steps:

1. **Obtain code-signing credentials**—A prerequisite for code signing is credentials that establish your identity to a third party. Most public key infrastructure (PKI) vendors (also known as certificate authorities, or CAs), such as Thawte and Verisign, offer software publishing certificates (i.e., code-signing credentials). The process for obtaining the credentials differs, depending on the CA.
2. **Identify signing targets**—Signatures are generally performed on a unit that contains all parts of an application, such as a single archive file (JAR, WAR, or CAB). Generally, the unit is an installable package. Any other granularity requires multiple signature checks per application install, which is inconvenient for the end user.
3. **Sign identified targets**—Running the code-signing tools usually will add a signature to the packaging unit, which can then be distributed directly.

[52] `http://wmlicense.smdisp.net/wmdrmcompliance/`

[53] `www.owasp.org/index.php/Category:OWASP_CLASP_Project`

Developers that utilize signed-code libraries should always validate signed code before integrating it in a software system.

Design and Architecture Technical Review

The Carnegie Mellon University Software Engineering Institute[54] states that "Designs need to be open and amenable to verification, validation, and evaluation, including certification and accreditation."

The Curriculum Guide to the Common Body of Knowledge[55] adds that "Design reviews should be performed by multiple persons covering each area of relevant expertise and legitimate stakeholder interests. Formal techniques that exist for reviews include a scenario-based one created for architecture reviews."

Reviews, including security-focused reviews, are essential at all levels of design. If possible, the design should be reviewed by an independent third party that has no stake in the success or failure of the project. Design-related portions of the assurance case should be reviewed as well. Since the best results occur when one develops much of the design assurance case along with the design, these parts may be best reviewed together. Using checklists can help make the design review a consistent and thorough process.

Properly performed design reviews also allow you to gain:

- Added assurance that the system does what the specification calls for and nothing else
- Added certainty that the assurance case and design map correctly to each other
- Improved likelihood of cost-effective and timely certification of the software system

Summary

Chapter 3 explored activities for decreasing the likelihood that the software design will contain flaws, so that the software will perform as required, even under attack. The chapter concluded with an overview of benefits and security concerns for technologies and guidelines for technical review.

[54]Bass, L., Klein, M., and Moreno, G., "Applicability of General Scenarios to the Architecture Tradeoff Analysis Method," CMU/SEI-2001-TR-014, ADA396098, Pittsburgh, PA: Software Engineering Institute, Carnegie Mellon University, 2001. Available at: `www.sei.cmu.edu/publications/documents/01.reports/01tr014.html`.

[55]Redwine, S. T., Jr. (Editor), "Software Assurance."

Assessment Questions

1. Entry points in a software application include interfaces, protocols, code and:
   A. Error messages
   B. Services
   C. Packaging
   D. Response codes
2. Using a custom build process to enable specific features in the Apache Web server is an example of what design principle?
   A. Least privilege
   B. Leveraging existing components
   C. Economy of mechanism
   D. Fail safe
3. Applying the most restrictive set of operating system permissions to all application files is an example of what design principle?
   A. Least common mechanism
   B. Least privilege
   C. Separation of duties
   D. Weakest link
4. Mitigating the risk of one security control being compromised by providing multiple layers of security controls is an example of what specific security strategy?
   A. Secure-by-default
   B. Secure-by-design
   C. Defense-in-depth
   D. Defense-by-design
5. Which of the following is a security advantage of managed code over unmanaged code?
   A. Size of the attack surface
   B. Number of roles
   C. Number of lines of code
   D. Size of the chroot jail
6. UDP has a larger attack surface than TCP because:
   A. It allows the spread of worms.
   B. It is a connection-oriented protocol.
   C. It is a "fire and forget" protocol.
   D. The IP address is easily spoofed.
7. Which of the following is a process for assessing and documenting the weaknesses or security risks associated with an application?

A. Control identification

B. Threat modeling

C. Control prioritization

D. Attack surface evaluation

8. Which of the following is attempting to gain access to a system by using a false identity?

A. Repudiation

B. Eavesdropping

C. Spoofing

D. Hijacking

9. Which of the following is the ability of users to deny that they performed specific actions or transactions?

A. Repudiation

B. Eavesdropping

C. Spoofing

D. Hijacking

10. An advantage of using a threat modeling tool over a manual process is:

A. It is faster for analyzing small software projects.

B. It can provide useful visualizations.

C. It defines the application context for you.

D. It can only be used by a security expert.

11. A risk calculation methodology created by Microsoft is known as:

A. STRIDE

B. DREAD

C. Monte Carlo

D. MSRCM

12. What is the best method for prioritizing a threat and its related countermeasures?

A. Measuring the relative attack surface

B. Quantifying the level of risk

C. Enumerating the entry points and exit points

D. Identifying the type of accessibility required

13. What type of aid provides low-level detail and thus greater understanding of specific use cases, especially security relevant use cases?

A. Subject object matrix

B. Component access control matrix

C. Data flow diagram

D. Attack surface

14. Which mitigation technique is the best match for the elevation of privilege threat type?
    A. Authentication
    B. Authorization
    C. Auditing
    D. Confidentiality
15. Which mitigation technique is the best match for the tampering threat type?
    A. Integrity
    B. Availability
    C. Auditing
    D. Confidentiality
16. Why should a host-based firewall not be relied upon solely to mitigate a risk?
    A. It does not block incoming traffic.
    B. It does not block outgoing traffic.
    C. It can be turned off.
    D. It can't be turned off.
17. The choice of mitigation technologies should:
    A. Follow security best practices
    B. Depend on the number of sources researched
    C. Not depend on the technology of the application
    D. Address as few threat types as possible
18. A normal user assuming the identity of an administrator is what kind of attack?
    A. Elevation of privilege
    B. Denial of service
    C. Spoofing
    D. Repudiation
19. A hardened operating system (OS):
    A. Has a smaller attack surface than an unhardened OS
    B. Implements mandatory access control
    C. Is less secure than an unhardened OS
    D. Has more entry and exit points than an unhardened OS system
20. It is important to create detailed security configuration instructions for end users because:
    A. All configuration information should be documented.
    B. The end users are not normally a part of the process.
    C. Configuration decisions have security implications.
    D. Documentation should be placed under secure version control.

21. Ranking risks based on the type of application and the characteristics of threats is:
    A. More objective than using numeric ratings
    B. The DREAD method
    C. More subjective than using numeric ratings
    D. The STRIDE method
22. Which of the following is a reverse engineering countermeasure?
    A. Encrypted password
    B. Code obfuscation technology
    C. Embed a salt in the code
    D. Secure random number generator
23. Which of the following is used to preserve confidentiality in software?
    A. Encryption
    B. Hashing
    C. Recovery
    D. Redundancy
24. Which of the following is used to preserve integrity in software?
    A. Encryption
    B. Hashing
    C. Recovery
    D. Redundancy
25. Which of the following is used to ensure availability in software?
    A. Encryption
    B. Hashing
    C. Recovery
    D. Redundancy
26. Which of the following is a property of an ideal hash function?
    A. Likely that two different messages will have the same hash
    B. Easy to compute the hash for any given data
    C. Easy to construct a text that has a given hash
    D. Easy to modify a given text without changing its hash
27. Which of the following is a property of fault-tolerant software?
    A. A single point of failure
    B. A single point of repair
    C. Fault propagation to the failing component
    D. Availability of "fallback" or reversion modes
28. How does software exhibit graceful degradation in response to a denial-of-service (DoS) attack?

A. Fail-over to a higher-availability service
B. Vary its response times to subsequent requests
C. Disconnect the affected connectivity point
D. Fail-over to a hot standby

29. Which of the following provides redundancy in a software system?
A. The use of redundant arrays of inexpensive disks (RAID)
B. Deploying the software to a single location
C. A variable backup schedule
D. An uninterruptible power supply

30. What is the basis of NIST SP 800-63-1 Electronic Authentication Guideline assurance levels?
A. Single-factor remote network authentication
B. Cryptographic authentication of all parties
C. The likely consequences of an authentication error
D. The verification of identifying materials and information

31. Which of the following is an authentication design defect?
A. Using authentication based on trustworthy attributes
B. Unifying authentication and authorization
C. Using authentication when it is required
D. Propagating authentication across a multi-tier platform

32. Checking privileges before granting access to a restricted service is known as:
A. Authentication
B. Authorization
C. Auditing
D. Accountability

33. What distinguishes auditing from standard event logging?
A. The type of information captured in the audit record
B. The level of confidentiality applied to the audit records
C. The addition of debug information to the audit record
D. The level of availability applied to the audit records

34. Which security design principle espouses the practice "Security should not depend on security-through-obscurity"?
A. Defense-in-depth
B. Open design
C. Complete mediation
D. Analyzability

35. Which principle can be categorized under "Minimize the number of high-consequence targets"?
    A. Design for controllability
    B. Traceability from requirements to design
    C. Segregate trusted entities from untrusted entities
    D. Least privilege
36. Which principle can be categorized under "Don't expose vulnerable or high-consequence components"?
    A. Design for controllability
    B. Traceability from requirements to design
    C. Segregate trusted entities from untrusted entities
    D. Least privilege
37. Which principle can be categorized under "Deny attackers the means to compromise"?
    A. Design for controllability
    B. Traceability from requirements to design
    C. Segregate trusted entities from untrusted entities
    D. Least privilege
38. What does it mean to "Hold all actors accountable, not just human actors"?
    A. Attacker actions are observed and recorded.
    B. Keep the design as simple as possible.
    C. Components are neither dependable nor trustworthy.
    D. Software execution ends in a secure state.
39. What software feature follows the principle "Design for controllability"?
    A. Ability to enter a secure state
    B. State changes should always be deliberate
    C. Ability to self-monitor and limit resource usage
    D. Ability to choose most appropriate secure state
40. Implementing a watchdog timer is part of what secure design principle?
    A. Design for survivability
    B. Design for secure failure
    C. Design for controllability
    D. Design for redundancy
41. Taking advantage of rapid recovery features at the system level is part of what secure design principle?
    A. Design for survivability
    B. Design for secure failure

C. Design for controllability
D. Design for redundancy

42. Security design patterns:
A. Uphold secure design principles
B. Define poorly understood design features
C. Are not reusable
D. Are not applicable to software assurance

43. Flow, sharing, and timing dependencies refer to what aspect of software?
A. Reusability
B. Survivability
C. Interconnectivity
D. Availability

44. Which of the following provides control over the trust features in a software application?
A. Security management interfaces
B. Secure configuration management
C. Application container
D. Security manager

45. Identity management provides for the following:
A. Integrity
B. Deniability
C. Confidentiality
D. Nonrepudiation

46. What describes software processes running simultaneously on multiple processors on the same computer?
A. Distributed computing
B. Parallel computing
C. Pervasive computing
D. Ubiquitous computing

47. What is a technique for dealing with processes that use old data in distributed systems?
A. Propagate security state changes
B. Implement network links of varying latencies
C. Include additional processes that run simultaneously
D. Run the data in a heterogeneous environment

48. What is a technique for dealing with conflicting resource updates?
A. Propagate security state changes

B. Locking to prevent inconsistent updates

C. Running a clock synchronization protocol

D. Recovery from failures must be addressed by systems design

49. Identifying and removing the root cause of the defect is known as:

A. Error detection

B. Damage confinement

C. Error recovery

D. Fault treatment

50. Which type of redundancy allows software to be run simultaneously on multiple geographically distributed locations?

A. Hardware

B. Process

C. Data

D. Application

51. What does Web Services (WS)-Security accomplish?

A. Supports message integrity and confidentiality

B. Enables the authorization of the information published

C. Provides mechanisms for authentication and authorization

D. Enables the selective signing of XML data

52. What is the best mechanism to address nonrepudiation in Web services?

A. Performance techniques

B. Threat modeling

C. Logging

D. Data replication

53. One of the key security protections of rich Internet applications is:

A. Offline operation

B. Loose coupling with the Web browser

C. Ability to store data locally

D. Same origin policy

54. Which type of computing involves a high degree of communication among devices?

A. Distributed computing

B. Parallel computing

C. Pervasive computing

D. Standard computing

55. Which kind of trust management scheme tracks the behavior of nodes?

A. Bayesian trust framework

B. Reputation-based trust system

C. Trust analysis methodology

D. Trust analysis grid

56. A type of system where the end user does not own the software is:

A. Ubiquitous computing

B. Software-as-a-service

C. Hosted software

D. Subscription-based software

57. Something you know and something you have are authentication:

A. Passwords

B. Factors

C. Credentials

D. Identities

58. Biometrics are an example of:

A. Something you know

B. Something you have

C. Something you are

D. Something you need

59. A centralized repository of user data is characteristic of what type of identity management system?

A. Directory services

B. Federated identity management

C. User provisioning system

D. Directory provisioning system

60. Which of the following has properties such as revocation and expiration?

A. Transaction signing

B. Secure Remote Password (SRP) protocol

C. X.509 digital certificate

D. Two-factor authentication

61. Problems exhibited by user provisioning systems include:

A. Slow execution of workflow processes

B. Lack of a single source of coherent information

C. Need for a local user database

D. Some services need to keep state

62. Reducing password fatigue from different username and password combinations is a characteristic of:

A. Two-factor authentication

B. Transaction signing

C. X.509 digital certificate

D. Single sign-on (SSO)

63. A Web application firewall may actively defend a Web application by:

A. Invalidating the application session

B. Intercepting data flowing to and from a Web application

C. Running in a separate process and memory space

D. Learning about the application behavior

64. Drawbacks of Web application firewall technology include:

A. Detection of some attacks

B. Configuration and performance

C. Flexible policy enforcement

D. Specialized security knowledge

65. Which logging technology provides agent-oriented and agent-less operation?

A. Syslog protocol

B. Web application firewall

C. Security information and event management (SIEM)

D. Simple Network Management Protocol (SNMP)

66. Reliable log delivery is an enhancement to which logging technology?

A. Syslog protocol

B. Web application firewall

C. Security information and event management (SIEM)

D. Simple Network Management Protocol (SNMP)

67. Security information and event management (SIEM) products include which of the following features?

A. Security knowledge base

B. Rate limiting

C. Limited log format support

D. Transmission over User Datagram Protocol (UDP)

68. Data loss prevention (DLP) technology may take the following action when it detects a policy violation:

A. Hash the data

B. Encrypt the data

C. Reconstruct the session

D. Analyze the content

69. Dynamic allocated resources are a security concern of which programming language?

A. C

B. Java
C. .NET
D. Managed Code

70. Authentication and session management are security concerns of which programming language?
A. C
B. Java
C. .NET
D. Managed Code

71. Potential security disadvantages of virtualization include:
A. VM layer configuration is security relevant
B. More intrusive intrusion detection via introspection
C. An extra layer for defense-in-depth
D. More flexible discovery/eviction of kernel root kits

72. Which of the following defines minimum techniques to secure each asset in digital rights management (DRM)?
A. Compliance rules
B. Licensing
C. Robustness rules
D. Requirements

73. Which of the following specifies the required behaviors in digital rights management (DRM)?
A. Compliance rules
B. Licensing
C. Robustness rules
D. Requirements

74. Specialized, professional, and what other type of tool is used to attack digital rights management (DRM):
A. Power
B. Hand
C. Widely available
D. Software

75. At the highest level of robustness in digital rights management (DRM), security functions should be:
A. Immune to professional tools
B. Resistant to professional tools
C. Resistant to specialized tools
D. Immune to all tools

76. An example of over-the-air (OTA) provisioning in digital rights management (DRM) is:
    A. Use of software and hardware to achieve deployment goals
    B. Use of concealment to evade tampering attacks
    C. Use of device properties for unique identification
    D. Use of shared secrets to initiate or reestablish trust
77. A means of validating the origin and integrity of software is:
    A. Code signing
    B. Digital rights management
    C. Robustness rules
    D. Compliance rules

CHAPTER

4

Secure Software Implementation/Coding

Secure coding includes both coding and integration of software components. Secure coding should follow secure coding practices and adhere to secure coding standards. This chapter explores these fundamentals and describes additional assurance concepts and activities that contribute to secure software implementation.

Declarative versus Programmatic Security

Declarative security enforces the security policy of the software application in its runtime environment. In declarative security, the application makes security decisions based on explicit statements that constrain security behavior. Declarative security may be implemented in a layer outside of the software code or may use attributes that are placed into the code itself. Declarative security is often used to set the permissions required by the application for access to local resources, and to provide role-based access control to individual software components and the application itself. The authorization decisions are normally coarse-grained in nature from an operational or external security perspective.

In programmatic security, the security behavior is controlled by the code of the software application. Authorization decisions are based on business logic, for example, the role of the user or the task the user is performing in a particular application context. Programmatic security enforces the internal security policy of the application independently of the runtime environment in which it is deployed.

Declarative Security

Declarative security can be used to control access to resources based on parameters defined in a configuration file external to an application.

For example, a Java Web application that is deployed in a Java Servlet Specification v2.4[1] compliant container, such as Apache Tomcat v5.5,[2] can be configured to control access to resources via the deployment descriptor (web.xml). The deployment descriptor is a structured representation of the security policy that is specific to the runtime environment. It describes the application's logical security requirements, including security roles, access control, and authentication. In the context of this example, declarative security has the following characteristics:

- **Programming is not required**—Security constraints are declared in the configuration file, not coded.
- **Container-managed security**—The process for enforcing the security constraints is managed by the application server, not the application itself.
- **Runtime environment**—The deployment descriptor represents the security policy of the runtime environment, it can be easily modified to support different environments—development, testing, production—without any changes to the code.

The deployment descriptor uses security constraints as a declarative way of defining the protection of Web content. A security constraint associates authorization and/or user data constraints with HTTP operations on Web resources. A security constraint, which is represented by *security-constraint* in web.xml, consists of the following elements summarized from the Java Servlet Specification v2.4:

- **Web resource collection** (*web-resource-collection*)—The HTTP operations and Web resources to which a security constraint applies, i.e., the constrained requests. The Web resource collection consists of the following elements:
  - URL patterns (*url-pattern*)
  - HTTP methods (*http-method*)
- **Authorization constraint** (*auth-constraint*)—Establishes a requirement for authentication and names the authorization roles permitted to perform the constrained requests. A user must be a member of at least one of the named roles to be permitted to perform the constrained requests. The special role "*" refers to all role names defined in the deployment descriptor. An authorization constraint that names no roles indicates that access to the constrained request must be denied. An authorization constraint consists of the following element:
  - Role name (*role-name*)
- User data constraint (*user-data-constraint*)—Establishes a requirement that the constrained requests be received over a protected transport layer connection, e.g., Transport Layer Security (TLS). The strength of the required protection is defined by the value of the transport guarantee. A transport guarantee of CONFIDENTIAL is used to establish a requirement for confidentiality. The transport guarantee of NONE indicates that the container must accept the constrained requests when

[1] `http://java.sun.com/products/servlet/download.html`
[2] `http://tomcat.apache.org`

received on any connection, including an unprotected one. A user data constraint consists of the following element:

- Transport guarantee (*transport-guarantee*)

If no authorization constraint applies to a request, the container must accept the request without requesting user authentication. If no user data constraint applies to a request, the container must accept the request when received over any connection, including an unprotected one.

When a *url-pattern* and *http-method* pair occurs in multiple security constraints, the constraints (on the pattern and method) are defined by combining the individual constraints. The rules for combining constraints in which the same pattern and method occur are as follows:

- A combination of authorization constraints that name roles or that imply roles via the name "*" will yield the union of the role names in the individual constraints as permitted roles.
- A security constraint that does not contain an authorization constraint will combine with authorization constraints that name or imply roles to allow unauthenticated access.
- An authorization constraint that names no roles will combine with any other constraints to override the other constraints and deny access.
- The combination of *user-data-constraints* that apply to a common *url-pattern* and *http-method* will yield the union of connection types accepted by the individual constraints as acceptable connection types.
- A security constraint that does not contain a *user-data-constraint* will combine with other *user-data-constraints* to cause the unprotected connection type to be an accepted connection type.

The following example from the Java Servlet Specification v2.4 illustrates the combinations of security constraints in a hypothetical deployment descriptor:

```
<security-constraint>
<web-resource-collection>
<web-resource-name>restricted methods</web-resource-name>
<url-pattern>/*</url-pattern>
<url-pattern>/acme/wholesale/*</url-pattern>
<url-pattern>/acme/retail/*</url-pattern>
<http-method>DELETE</http-method>
<http-method>PUT</http-method>
</web-resource-collection>
<auth-constraint/>
</security-constraint>

<security-constraint>
<web-resource-collection>
<web-resource-name>wholesale</web-resource-name>
<url-pattern>/acme/wholesale/*</url-pattern>
```

```
<http-method>GET</http-method>
<http-method>PUT</http-method>
</web-resource-collection>
<auth-constraint>
<role-name>SALESCLERK</role-name>
</auth-constraint>
</security-constraint>

<security-constraint>
<web-resource-collection>
<web-resource-name>wholesale</web-resource-name>
<url-pattern>/acme/wholesale/*</url-pattern>
<http-method>GET</http-method>
<http-method>POST</http-method>
</web-resource-collection>
<auth-constraint>
<role-name>CONTRACTOR</role-name>
</auth-constraint>
<user-data-constraint>
<transport-guarantee>CONFIDENTIAL</transport-guarantee>
</user-data-constraint>
</security-constraint>

<security-constraint>
<web-resource-collection>
<web-resource-name>retail</web-resource-name>
<url-pattern>/acme/retail/*</url-pattern>
<http-method>GET</http-method>
<http-method>POST</http-method>
</web-resource-collection>
<auth-constraint>
<role-name>CONTRACTOR</role-name>
<role-name>HOMEOWNER</role-name>
</auth-constraint>
</security-constraint>
```

Table 4-1 is a translation of the hypothetical deployment descriptor to a matrix of security constraints.

Programmatic Security

In programmatic security, business logic decisions can be based on the role of the user in a specific security context.

For example, the Java Servlet Specification v2.4 defines three methods in the `HTTPServletRequest` interface that control programmatic security:

- `getRemoteUser()`—This method returns the username the client used for authentication.
- `isUserInRole()`—This method determines whether a remote user is in a specified security role.

- getUserPrincipal()—This method determines the principal name of the current user and returns a java.security.Principal object.

Table 4-1: Security Constraints

URL-PATTERN	HTTP-METHOD	PERMITTED ROLES	SUPPORTED CONNECTION TYPES
/*	DELETE	Access precluded	Not constrained
/*	PUT	Access precluded	Not constrained
/acme/wholesale/*	DELETE	Access precluded	Not constrained
/acme/wholesale/*	GET	CONTRACTOR SALESCLERK	Not constrained
/acme/wholesale/*	POST	CONTRACTOR	CONFIDENTIAL
/acme/wholesale/*	PUT	Access precluded	Not constrained
/acme/retail/*	DELETE	Access precluded	Not constrained
/acme/retail/*	GET	CONTRACTOR HOMEOWNER	Not constrained
/acme/retail/*	POST	CONTRACTOR HOMEOWNER	Not constrained
/acme/retail/*	PUT	Access precluded	Not constrained

If no user has been authenticated, the getRemoteUser() method returns null, the isUserInRole() method always returns false, and the getUserPrincipal() method returns null.

Code Access Security

Code Access Security (CAS) is a mechanism in the Microsoft .NET framework that utilizes both declarative and imperative (programmatic) security to limit code access to protected resources and operations. It is intended to help protect computer systems from malicious code, to allow code from unknown sources to execute with protection, and to help prevent trusted code from intentionally or inadvertently compromising security. The overall goal of CAS is to allow code originating from one computer system to execute with protection on another system, even when there is no trusting relationship between the systems. CAS provides this protection by performing the following functions, summarized from the Microsoft Developer Network (MSDN)[3]:

- Defines permissions and permission sets that represent the right to access various system resources

[3]http://msdn.microsoft.com/en-us/library/930b76w0.aspx

- Enables administrators to configure security policy by associating sets of permissions with groups of code (code groups)
- Enables code to request the permissions it requires in order to run, as well as the permissions that may be necessary to provide additional functionality, and specifies which permissions the code should not possess
- Grants permissions to each assembly that is loaded, based on permissions requested by the code and on the operations permitted by security policy
- Enables code to demand that its callers have specific permissions
- Enables code to demand that its callers possess a digital signature, thus allowing only callers from a particular organization or site to call the protected code
- Enforces restrictions on code at runtime by comparing the granted permissions of every caller on the call stack to the permissions that callers must possess

CAS can be leveraged by programmers to increase the security of applications that target the .NET language runtime. The following practices should be followed to effectively utilize CAS:

- **Use imperative and declarative security**—Interaction with the runtime system is performed using imperative and declarative security calls. Declarative calls use attributes, and imperative calls are performed using new instances of classes within the code. Imperative and declarative calls are explained later in this section and illustrated with code samples.
- **Request permissions for your code**—*Requests* are applied to the assembly scope, where the code informs the runtime about permissions that it either needs to run or specifically does not want.
- **Use secure class libraries**—Class libraries use security *demands* and *overrides*. Demands are applied on the class and method level to protect resources from callers by specifying the permissions the callers must possess in order to access the code. Overrides limit the access of callers who have already been granted certain permissions. They are applied on the class and method scope as a way to overrule certain security decisions made by the runtime.

Declarative security syntax uses keyword-like descriptive declarations called *attributes* to annotate programming elements such as types, fields, methods, and properties. These attributes are added to the code as additional information called *metadata*. Attributes can be placed at the assembly, class, or member level, to indicate the type of request, demand, or override desired. For example, the following C# code fragment shows declarative syntax for requesting that the code's callers have a custom permission called NeedToKnow. The declarative call is placed directly before the class definition, specifying that the permission be applied to the class level. The attribute is passed a `SecurityAction.Demand` structure to specify that callers must have this permission in order to run:

```
 [NeedToKnow(SecurityAction.Demand, Unrestricted = True)]
public class Example1
{
```

```
    public Example1()
    {
    //This constructor is protected by the class-level security
     declaration.
    }

    public void ExampleMethod()
    {
    //This method is protected by the class-level security declaration.
    }
}
```

Imperative security syntax issues a security call by creating a new instance of the permission object that is required to perform an action. Imperative syntax is used to perform demands and overrides, but not requests. In order to make a security call, it is necessary to initialize the state data of the permission object so that it represents the correct form of the permission. It is also possible to initialize a group of permissions called a *permission set*. Imperative syntax can be used instead of declarative syntax to perform a demand when information that is required to initialize the permission state becomes known only at runtime—for example, if a caller wants access to a certain file, but the name of the file is not known until runtime. An imperative call may also be used to make an access decision based on an evaluation that can only be performed at runtime. The following C# code fragment shows imperative syntax for requesting a custom permission called RightToAccess. A new instance of RightToAccess is created in MyMethod, so that only this method is guarded with the security call.

```
public class Example2
{
    public Example2()
    {
    //This constructor is not protected.
    }

    public void MyMethod()
    {
    //RightToAccess is demanded using imperative syntax.
    RightToAccess rta = new RightToAccess();
    rta.Demand();
    //This method is protected by the security call.
    }

    public void OtherMethod()
    {
    //This method is not protected.
    }
}
```

Common Software Vulnerabilities and Countermeasures

NIST SP 800-27, *Engineering Principles for Information Technology Security*, June 2001, defines a vulnerability as "A weakness in system security requirements, design, implementation, or operation, that could be accidentally triggered or intentionally exploited and result in a violation of the system's security policy."

In software, a vulnerability is a weakness in some aspect or feature of the software that makes an exploit possible. A vulnerability caused by a problem with the syntax of the code is commonly called a bug, whereas a vulnerability caused by a non-syntactic problem is called a flaw, such as a business logic flaw. Vulnerabilities take on meaning in the context of attacks. For example, an attack is an action taken that exploits a vulnerability to realize a threat. A threat is a negative effect or undesired event, malicious or benign, that could damage or compromise an asset. Since the software itself or something that it protects is the asset (the goal of an attacker), the attacker attempts to attain that goal by exploiting the vulnerability, and in the process, compromising the software. A countermeasure addresses a vulnerability to reduce the probability of attack or the impact of a threat.

Common attacks on software include the following:

- **Reconnaissance attacks**—Enable the attacker to gather information on the software and its operating environment, so other attacks can be crafted to be more effective. Information obtained includes release and version information about the software and environment's COTS and OSS components. Such information can reveal whether the environment contains components with known vulnerabilities that can be exploited. A specific concern is the zero-day vulnerability. A "zero day" occurs when a vulnerability in a specific software version is discovered and exploited before the software's vendor is able to issue a patch, or in the delay that often occurs between when a vulnerability is discovered and a patch is issued. The less information that is readily available to zero-day attackers about the type of software being run, the less easily attacks can be crafted.
- **Enabling attacks**—These attacks make it easier to deliver other attacks. Examples of enabling attacks are buffer overflow exploits for delivering malicious code, and privilege escalation attacks.
- **Disclosure attacks**—These attacks reveal data that should not be disclosed to the attacker (compromise of confidentiality).
- **Subversion attacks**—These attacks tamper with and corrupt the software to change the way it operates (compromise of integrity).
- **Sabotage attacks**—These attacks cause the software to fail, or prevent it from being accessed by its intended users; also known as a denial of service (compromise of availability).
- **Malicious code attacks**—These attacks insert malicious logic into the software, trigger the execution of malicious code already embedded in the software, or deliver/execute malicious code in the software's execution environment.

NOTE **Appendix A of the National Institute of Standards and Technology (NIST) Special Publication 800-95, *Guide to Secure Web Services*, (`www.csrc.nist.gov/publications/nistpubs/800-95/SP800-95.pdf`) provides informative descriptions of common attacks within these categories that target Web applications and Web services.**

Vulnerability Categories

A technique for classifying the types of vulnerabilities is by dividing them into a hierarchy of categories and subcategories by common attributes. A number of worldwide organizations are involved in maintaining categories of common software vulnerabilities.

The Common Weakness Enumeration (CWE) (`http://cwe.mitre.org`) is a community-developed formal list of common software weaknesses that:

- Serves as a common language for describing software security weaknesses in architecture, design, or code
- Serves as a standard measuring stick for software security tools targeting these weaknesses
- Provides a common baseline standard for weakness identification, mitigation, and prevention efforts

The CWE was initiated by MITRE and leverages the diverse thinking on software weaknesses from academia, the commercial sector, and government. It encompasses a large portion of the Common Vulnerability and Exposures (CVE) List's 15,000 CVE names, and draws from other industry and academic sources including the CLASP methodology and *Seven Touchpoints for Secure Software*, both of which were reviewed in Chapter 1.

CROSS-REFERENCE **The Common Vulnerabilities and Exposures (CVE) (`http://cve.mitre.org`) is a dictionary of standardized identifiers for common computer vulnerabilities and exposures. CVE's common identifiers enable data exchange between security products and provide a baseline index point for evaluating coverage of tools and services.**

The CWE list is offered in three forms:

- **Dictionary**—A high-level view of its enumerated weaknesses
- **Classification tree**—A view that provides access to individual weaknesses with more simplicity to various potential users through classification layering
- **Graphical**—A view of the classification tree that allows a user to better understand individual weaknesses through their broader context and relationships

The CWE list contains over 600 weaknesses. Figure 4-1 is an example dictionary view of a buffer over-read weakness.

Buffer Over-read

Weakness ID: 126 *(Weakness Variant)* **Status:** Draft

Description

Summary

The software reads data past the end of the intended buffer.

Time of Introduction

- Implementation

Applicable Platforms

Languages

C

C++

Weakness Ordinalities

Primary *(where the weakness exists independent of other weaknesses)*

Relationships

Nature	Type	ID	Name	V
ChildOf	W	125	Out-of-bounds Read	**699** **1000**
CanFollow	W	170	Improper Null Termination	1000

Causal Nature

Explicit *(an explicit weakness resulting from behavior of the developer)*

Taxonomy Mappings

Mapped Taxonomy Name	Mapped Node Name
PLOVER	Buffer over-read

Content History

Submissions

PLOVER. *(Externally Mined)*

Modifications

CWE Content Team. MITRE. 2008-09-08. *(Internal)*

updated Applicable_Platforms, Relationships, Taxonomy_Mappings, Weakness_Ordinalities

Figure 4-1: Buffer over-read

CWE/SANS Top 25

The 2009 CWE/SANS Top 25 Most Dangerous Programming Errors (`http://cwe.mitre.org/top25/`) is a list of the most significant programming errors that can lead to serious software vulnerabilities. The criteria of a serious vulnerability is one that occurs frequently, is often easy to find, and easy to exploit. These vulnerabilities are dangerous because they will frequently allow attackers to completely take over the software, steal data, or prevent the software from functioning at all.

The Top 25 is the result of collaboration between the SANS Institute, MITRE, and many top software security experts in the United States and Europe.

The Top 25 list educates programmers on how to eliminate common mistakes in software and is also:

- A tool for education and awareness
- A source of information for consumer advocacy
- A measuring stick of progress for software managers and CIOs

The following are examples of the Top 25 Most Dangerous Programming Errors. The errors are grouped by a high-level category and describe the consequences of the error as well as a suggested mitigation:

- Insecure Interaction between Components
  - **Improper Input Validation**—Occurs when input is not compared against valid specifications, e.g., alphabetical input should not contain numbers or disallowed characters. This may lead to malicious code execution, data loss, or denial of service. The application should assume that all input is malicious and use a standard input mechanism to validate all input for length, type, syntax, and business rules. If the application combines data from multiple sources it should perform validation on that data after it is combined.
  - **Improper Encoding or Escaping of Output**—Occurs when control information and metadata are not separated from the actual data. This may lead to malicious code execution or data loss. The application should use stored procedures or other structured and strongly typed mechanisms. When exchanging data between components, both components should use the same character encoding and it should be explicitly set.
  - **Failure to Preserve SQL Query Structure (SQL Injection)**—Occurs when the logic of a SQL query is altered by an attacker. This may lead to data loss or a bypass of security. The application should use proper encoding or escaping of inputs.
  - **Failure to Preserve Web Page Structure (Cross-Site Scripting)**—Occurs when browser-executable content is inserted in a Web page that the application generates. This may lead to malicious code execution or a bypass of security. The application should use and specify a strong character encoding such as ISO-8859-1 or UTF-8.
  - **Failure to Preserve OS Command Structure (OS Command Injection)**—Occurs when the application allows untrusted input to be fed into the command string for executing a program on the operating system. This may lead to malicious code execution. The application should properly quote arguments and escape any special characters within those arguments.
  - **Cleartext Transmission of Sensitive Information**—Occurs when the application sends sensitive data across the network and fails to adequately protect it from eavesdropping. A Web application should use Transmission Layer Security (TLS) for the entire session, from login to logout, not just the login page.
  - **Cross-Site Request Forgery (CSRF)**—Occurs when an attacker tricks a user into activating a request to perform some unauthorized action. This could lead to data loss or malicious code execution. The application should be free of XSS issues.

- **Race Condition**—Occurs when access to a shared resource occurs at almost the same time by different processes, possibly revealing sensitive information or causing reliability problems. This may lead to denial of service, malicious code execution, or data loss. A multi-threaded application should only use thread-safe functions on shared variables.
- **Error Message Information Leak**—Occurs when error messages reveal sensitive information, e.g., personally identifiable information (PII), credentials, or server configuration. The application should handle exceptions internally and not display error messages containing sensitive data to the user.

- Risky Resource Management
  - **Failure to Constrain Operations within the Bounds of a Memory Buffer**—Occurs in applications written in or dependent on languages that manage their own memory allocation, e.g., C, C++, when the application attempts to put more data in a buffer than has been allocated, resulting in an overflow. This may lead to malicious code execution, data loss, or denial of service. The developer should double-check that the buffer is a large as specified.
  - **External Control of Critical State Data**—Occurs when critical state data is stored in a location that can be modified by an attacker. This may lead to a bypass of security, data loss, or malicious code execution. The application should use a proven container or framework for managing state as opposed to a proprietary implementation.
  - **External Control of File Name or Path**—Occurs when the application uses untrusted input to construct the name of a file or path to a file that it intends to retrieve, and retrieves another file in its place. This may lead to malicious code execution or data loss. The application should use a built-in path canonicalization function, e.g., `realpath()` in C.
  - **Untrusted Search Path**—Occurs when the software depends on a search path to find code libraries or configuration files and due to lack of protection, the attacker can control the search path to retrieve files. This may result in malicious code execution. The application should use fully qualified path names when invoking other programs.
  - **Failure to Control Generation of Code (Code Injection)**—Occurs when the application dynamically generates code and an attacker can provide inputs to determine which code gets executed. The application should use a mix of whitelist and blacklist evaluation to filter non-relevant code syntax from all input that should not contain code.
  - **Download of Code without Integrity Check**—Occurs when code is downloaded that may be potentially malicious. The application should use encrypted channels that perform integrity checking to transfer the code from the host server.
  - **Improper Resource Shutdown or Release**—Occurs when resources have reached an end-of-life but have not been disposed of properly, potentially

allowing an attacker to reuse or discover a resource. This may lead to denial of service or malicious code execution. The application should properly dispose of all the member components of a complex object or structure, not just the object itself.

- **Improper Initialization**—Occurs when data or variables are not properly initialized or reset, potentially allowing an attacker to read or reuse values from a previous session. This may lead to malicious code execution or data loss. The application should explicitly initialize all variables and all data stores, either during declaration or just before first usage.
- **Incorrect Calculation**—Occurs when values used in a calculation can be controlled by malicious user input. This may lead to denial of service, data loss, or malicious code execution. The application should perform input validation on any numeric inputs by ensuring that they are within the expected range.

- Porous Defenses
  - **Improper Access Control (Authorization)**—Occurs when an application does not properly check for authorization before allowing an action to be performed. This may lead to a bypass of security. The application should implement a proven authorization framework, e.g., JAAS Authorization Framework or ESAPI API.
  - **Use of a Broken or Risky Cryptographic Algorithm**—Occurs when a cryptographic algorithm is improperly implemented or poorly designed and therefore does not adequately provide protection. This may lead to data loss or bypass of security. The developer should not design a proprietary algorithm, but instead use a proven encryption algorithm, and follow best practices in implementation.
  - **Hard-Coded Password**—Occurs when a password is hard-coded in the application; if the password is discovered by an attacker, and it exists in multiple copies of the software, all instances may be vulnerable. This may lead to a bypass of security. Passwords should be stored outside of the code in a strongly protected, encrypted configuration file or database.
  - **Insecure Permission Assignment for Critical Resource**—Occurs when incorrect permissions are set on critical resources, e.g., configuration files, allowing an attacker to read or write to the file. This may lead to data loss or malicious code execution. When the application starts, it should explicitly set default permissions or `umask` to a restricted setting.
  - **Use of Insufficiently Random Values**—Occurs when an application function depends on a random number to protect a resource but the number turns out to be predictable. This may lead to a bypass of security or data loss. The application should use a proven, cryptographically strong, random number generator for any security-critical function.
  - **Execution with Unnecessary Privileges**—Occurs when an application function executes with privileges greater than necessary to perform a task. If the application function can be compromised, an attacker can employ the higher

privileges. This may lead to malicious code execution. The application should run code with the least privileges necessary to accomplish a given task and drop privileges as soon as possible after the task is completed.

- **Client-Side Enforcement of Server-Side Security**—Occurs when client-side code performs security checks that are not replicated on the server; client-side code can be modified and/or bypassed by an attacker. The application should not rely on the client to enforce security checks. Security checks should be enforced on the server side.

OWASP Top Ten

The Open Web Application Security Project (OWASP) is a worldwide free and open community focused on improving the security of Web application software. OWASP publishes the OWASP Top Ten (`www.owasp.org`), which is a list of the ten most common Web application security vulnerabilities.

The Top Ten for 2007 was created by analyzing the MITRE Vulnerability Trends for 2006[4] and ranking the top ten Web application security issues.

The Top Ten also describes basic countermeasures for protecting against these vulnerabilities. The following is a summary of the OWASP Top Ten vulnerabilities and countermeasures ranked from most prevalent to least prevalent:

- **Cross-Site Scripting (XSS)**—Occurs when an application takes data that originated from a user and sends it to a Web browser without first validating or encoding that content. XSS allows attackers to execute script, e.g., JavaScript, in the victim's browser, which can hijack sessions, deface Web sites, etc. Protections include input validation, strong output encoding, preventing canonicalization errors.
- **Injection Flaws**—Occurs when data originated from a user is sent to an interpreter as part of a command or query. Injection flaws may allow attackers to create, read, update, or delete any arbitrary data available to the application. There are many types of injection flaws, including SQL, LDAP, XPath, XSLT, HTML, XML, and OS command injection. Protections include input validation, using strongly typed parameterized query APIs, enforcing least privilege, avoiding detailed error messages.
- **Malicious File Execution**—Occurs when the application directly uses or concatenates potentially hostile input with file or stream functions, or improperly trusts input files. This may lead to arbitrary remote and hostile content being included, processed, or invoked by the Web server, e.g., remote root kit installation and system compromise. Protections include using an indirect object reference map, explicit taint checking mechanisms, input validation.
- **Insecure Direct Object Reference**—Occurs when a developer exposes a reference to an internal implementation object, such as a file, directory, database record, or key, as a URL or form parameter. Attackers may manipulate those references

[4] `http://cwe.mitre.org/documents/vuln-trends/`

to access other objects without authorization. Protections include avoiding the exposure of private object references to users, validating private object references, verifying authorization to all referenced objects.

- **Cross-Site Request Forgery (CSRF)**—Occurs when an attacker forces a logged-on victim's browser to send a request to a vulnerable Web application, which then performs the chosen action on behalf of the victim; the malicious code is often not located on the attacked site; this is why it is called cross-site. Protections include all the protections from XSS, inserting custom random tokens into every form and URL, using transaction signing.
- **Information Leakage and Improper Error Handling**—Applications may unintentionally leak information about their configuration or internal workings, or cause a privacy violation by leaking user data. Applications may also leak internal state with the length of time they take to process certain operations or by the difference in responses to varying input, e.g., displaying the same error text with different error numbers. Protections include consistent exception handling for the entire application, disabling error handling or limiting detailed error messages, ensuring that secure paths that have multiple outcomes return similar or identical error messages.
- **Broken Authentication and Session Management**—Occurs when session tokens and credentials are not properly protected throughout their life cycle. Attacks may result in hijacking user or administrative accounts, undermining authentication and authorization controls, and violating privacy. Protections include using the container or framework session management mechanism, not using custom cookies for authentication or session management, using a single authentication mechanism.
- **Insecure Cryptographic Storage**—Occurs when applications fail to encrypt or poorly encrypt sensitive data. Attacks may lead to disclosure of sensitive data or compliance violations. Protections include using tested and proven cryptographic algorithms, using strong cryptographic algorithms, generating keys offline, and storing keys with extreme care.
- **Insecure Communications**—Occurs when applications fail to encrypt network traffic when it is necessary to ensure secure communications. Protections include using Transmission Layer Security (TLS) for all connections that are authenticated or transmitting sensitive or valuable data such as credentials, credit card details, health, and other private information.
- **Failure to Restrict URL Access**—Occurs when an application protects sensitive functionality only by preventing the display of links or URLs to unauthorized users. Attackers may use this weakness to perform unauthorized operations through direct access to those URLs. Protections include ensuring that all URLs and business functions are protected by an effective access control.

In addition to the Top Ten, OWASP maintains over 200 articles on types of Web application security vulnerabilities.[5] The articles are organized in alphabetical order

[5] `www.owasp.org/index.php/Category:Vulnerability`

and provide information including a description, risk factors, examples, related attacks, related vulnerabilities, related controls, related technical impacts, and additional references.

Virtualization

An important concept in virtualization is the hypervisor, also called the virtual machine monitor (VMM). The hypervisor is platform virtualization software for computer hardware that allows multiple guest operating systems to run on a host computer concurrently. The hypervisor is a privileged component and is therefore the target of attack. For example, one still theoretical attack against the hypervisor, hyperjacking, is focused on taking over control of the hypervisor in order to take over the host computer. Potential vectors for this attack include physical access to the virtualization hardware or by injecting malicious code from the virtual machine (VM) into the hypervisor. Since the hypervisor and VM share trust boundaries, data flow needs to be controlled or isolated in order to prevent abuse.

Isolation is the aspect of a hypervisor that provides a measure of security to the software processes running within the VMs. If the integrity of the isolation is violated, damage or security bypass may result. For example, in a study of fault injection in virtualized systems,[6] fault injection was performed from the hypervisor with the potential to harm the guest operating system. In this type of fault injection, called memory injection, if a hypervisor-based injector randomly modifies any page that is part of the memory of the VM, it may modify a page table entry, thus allowing the VM to later access memory that belongs to other virtual machines or to the hypervisor itself. This could be the case in a paravirtualized system, where the page tables used by the VM are readable but not writable by the VM. To prevent this fault from becoming a vulnerability, a "random bit flip" may have to be virtualized by making sure that any possible error is properly mapped to affect only the behavior of the VM under test.

As virtualization software has gained adoption, it has come under increased scrutiny from both security researchers and attackers. This has led to serious vulnerabilities being discovered in some of the more common virtualization platforms, such as VMware. Vulnerabilities that are publicly known and reported are assigned Common Vulnerabilities and Exposures (CVE) numbers and are published to the CVE (`http://cve.mitre.org`) and the National Vulnerability Database (NVD) (`http://nvd.nist.gov`). An example VMware vulnerability is CVE-2008-4916, released in April 2009, which describes a vulnerability in a guest virtual device driver that allows guest OS users to cause a denial of service (host OS crash) via unknown attack vectors. CVE-2009-1244, also released in April 2009, could allow a local guest OS user to execute arbitrary code on the host OS, caused by an error in the virtual machine display function. Both of these vulnerabilities affect almost all VMware products from Workstation through ESX. Fortunately, VMware published security bulletins and patch releases for the affected products that appear to have been timed

[6] Le, M., Gallagher, A., and Tamir, Y., "Challenges and Opportunities with Fault Injection in Virtualized Systems," First International Workshop on Virtualization Performance: Analysis, Characterization, and Tools, Austin, TX (April 2008).

with the CVE notifications. However, there is no guarantee that the software is free of unreported or yet undiscovered vulnerabilities.

Virtualization hardware also presents security challenges. For example, the x86 architecture used in most PC systems is difficult to virtualize, and full virtualization on x86 has significant costs in hypervisor complexity and runtime performance.[7] Thus, to allow a hypervisor to run an unmodified guest operating system without incurring significant performance costs, both Intel and AMD have independently developed virtualization extensions to the x86 architecture. A prototype of malware, code-named the Blue Pill, targeted the Microsoft Windows Vista Operating System using the AMD SVM (Pacifica) extensions.[8] The malware could hypothetically exploit the AMD SVM extensions (or the Intel VT-x extensions) in order to trap a running instance of the operating system into a virtual machine, with complete control given to the thin Blue Pill hypervisor. Since this exploit first required a kernel level compromise before it could leverage virtualization features, it was mostly significant because it was claimed to be difficult to detect and could be installed "on the fly," without the need to restart the operating system. An argument for this claim is that hardware-virtualization-based malware like Blue Pill is more difficult to detect than malware based on software-virtualization such as SubVirt, using detection code like Red Pill.[9]

CROSS-REFERENCE **Microsoft Research created the proof-of-concept SubVirt rootkit. It exploits known security flaws and installs a hypervisor under a Windows or Linux operating system.** `www.eweek.com/c/a/Security/VM-Rootkits-The-Next-Big-Threat/` **(March 2006). The Red Pill is code for detecting a software-based hypervisor in almost only one CPU instruction:** `http://invisiblethings.org/papers/redpill.html` **(November 2004).**

Possible countermeasures to these attacks include: disabling the hardware virtualization extensions in the computer BIOS if they are not in use or until a patch can be developed by the vendor, following security best practices for deploying the virtualization technology, and providing proper malware detection and prevention on the host and guest operating systems.

Side-Channel

Cryptographic algorithms are implemented in software or hardware on physical devices that interact with and are influenced by their environments. These physical interactions can be instigated and monitored by adversaries, and may result in information useful to cryptanalysis. This type of information is called side-channel information and the attacks exploiting side-channel information are called side-channel attacks.[10]

[7] `http://en.wikipedia.org/wiki/Hypervisor`

[8] `http://en.wikipedia.org/wiki/Blue_Pill_(malware)`

[9] `http://securitywatch.eweek.com/rootkits/faceoff_amd_vs_joanna_rutkowsk.html`

[10] Y. Zhou, and Feng, D., "Side-Channel Attacks: Ten Years After Its Publication and the Impacts on Cryptographic Module Security Testing," Cryptology ePrint Archive, Report 2005/388.

Side-channel attacks are possible because there is a correlation between the physical measurements taken during computations (e.g., power consumption, computing time, temperature, radiation, etc.) and the internal state of the processing device, which is itself related to the secret key. It is the correlation between the side-channel information and the operation related to the secret key that the side-channel attack tries to discover. In their paper "Side-Channel Attacks: Ten Years After Its Publication and the Impacts on Cryptographic Module Security Testing," Zhou and Feng classify the most common types of side-channel attacks and evaluate potential countermeasures. These attacks and countermeasures are summarized in the following paragraphs.

Side-channel attacks are typically classified in the following ways:

- **Depending on the control over the computation process**—The intrusiveness of the physical implementation of the attack
  - **Passive attacks**—Information is gained about the system without interfering with its operation.
  - **Active attacks**—Some influence is exerted on the behavior of the system such that an observer would notice a difference in the operation.
- **The way of accessing the module**—When accessing the security of a cryptographic hardware module, it is useful to perform a review of the attack surface, i.e., physical, electrical, and logical interfaces that are accessible to the adversary.
  - **Invasive attack**—Involves de-packaging to get direct access to the internal components of cryptographic modules or devices, e.g., opening a hole in the passivation layer of a module and placing a probing needle on a data bus to see the data transfer. Tamper-resistant or tamper-responsive mechanisms are usually implemented in hardware to counter invasive attacks, e.g., some cryptographic modules of a higher security level will zeroize the memory when tampering is detected.
  - **Semi-invasive attack**—Involves access to the device, but without damaging the passivation layer or making electrical contact other than with the authorized surface, e.g., in a fault-induced attack, a laser beam may be used to ionize a device to change some of its memory and thus change the output of the device.
  - **Non-invasive attack**—Involves close observation or manipulation of the device's operation. This attack exploits only externally available information that is often unintentionally leaked. An important characteristic of this attack is that it is undetectable, e.g., there is no way for a smart card to know that its running time is being measured.
- **The method used in the analysis process**—How the sampled data is analyzed
  - **Simple side-channel attack (SSCA)**—Exploits the side-channel output depending on the performed operations. A single trace is used in an SSCA analysis, and therefore the secret key can be directly read from the side-channel trace. The side-channel information related to the attacked instructions (the signal) needs to be larger than the side-channel information related to the unrelated instructions (noise). SSCA exploits the relationship between the executed instructions and the side-channel output.

- **Differential side-channel attack (DSCA)**—When SSCA is not feasible, DSCA is attempted. DSCA exploits the correlation between the data and the instantaneous side-channel leakage of the cryptographic device. As this correlation is very small, statistical methods must be used to exploit it efficiently. In this type of attack, a hypothetical model of the device under attack is used to predict the side-channel output of the device. The output may consist of several values, e.g., values describing one type of information leakage for several time slots or values predicting the leakage of different side-channels. When only one side channel is used for an attack, the attack is called a *first-order attack*. If two or more output values for the same side-channel are used in an attack, the attack is called *second-order* and *higher-order*.

The following summarizes several known side-channel attacks:

- **Timing attack**—Due to performance optimizations, implementations of cryptographic algorithms often perform computations in non-constant time. If such operations involve secret parameters, these timing variations can leak some information, and provided enough is known about the implementation, a careful statistical analysis could lead to the total recovery of the parameters. A timing attack can be summed up as a way of obtaining some user's private information by carefully measuring the time it takes to carry out cryptographic operations, i.e., exploit the timing variance in the operation. A simple countermeasure to a timing attack is to make the operational parameters independent of the input data. For example, in the RSA algorithm for public-key cryptography, random data can be used to conduct a blinding transformation (noise injection) on the parameters before the operation, and then a reverse unblinding transformation afterwards. However, this depends on feeding the noise injection with a good source of randomness.
- **Fault attack**—Hardware faults and errors occurring during the operation of a cryptographic module have been demonstrated to seriously affect the security. Faulty behaviors or outputs may also become important side channels, and may increase a cipher's vulnerability to cryptanalysis. Fault attacks are practical and effective against cryptographic devices such as smart cards. The feasibility of a fault attack depends on the capabilities of the attacker and the type of faults that can be induced. Generally, a fault model should specify the following aspects:
  - The precision an attacker can reach in choosing the time and location on which the fault occurs during the execution of a cryptographic module
  - The length of the data affected by a fault, e.g., only one bit or one byte
  - The persistence of the fault, e.g., transient or permanent
  - The type of fault, e.g., flip one bit; flip one bit but only in one direction; byte changed to a random value

  There are two major kinds of fault side-channels:

  - **Inducing computational faults**—Random or intentional faults, e.g., caused by a precise voltage manipulation. This kind of attack can be used on almost every kind of cryptographic mechanism and is regarded as one of the most effective side-channel attacks.

- **Sending corrupted input data**—Creating a non-standard situation that the cryptographic module must handle gracefully. Usually the module has an error message to inform the user that the computation has stopped due to some reason.

  A successful attack on cryptographic modules or devices requires two steps:

- **Fault injection**—Inject the fault at the appropriate time in the process, which is dependent on the device's hardware. Faults can be induced in different smart cards by acting on the environment, e.g., abruptly high or low voltage, lock, temperature, radiations, light, etc.
- **Fault exploitation**—Take advantage of an erroneous result or unexpected behavior, which is dependent on design and implementation. In the case of an algorithm, it will depend on its specification since the fault exploitation will be combined with cryptanalysis.

Possible countermeasures to protect public key algorithms from some specific fault attacks include checksums, execution randomization, ratification counters and baits, and repeated refreshments.

- **Power analysis attack**—Power analysis attacks can be divided into two types of attacks:
  - **Simple power analysis (SPA)**—In SPA attacks, the aim is to guess from the power trace which particular instruction is being executed at a certain time and what are the values of input and output; this requires knowledge of the exact implementation.
  - **Differential power analysis (DPA)**—A DPA attack does not require knowledge of the implementation details; it exploits statistical methods in the analysis process.

Hardware-based countermeasures include using an internal power source, randomizing the order in which instructions are executed, randomized register renaming, and using two capacitors, one of which is charged by an external power supply and other supplies power to the device.

- **EM attack**—The components of a computer generated electromagnetic radiation in normal operation. These emanations can be observed and measured to understand their relationship to the underlying computation and data. EM attacks can be divided into the following types similar to power analysis:
  - **Simple electromagnetic analysis attacks (SEMA)**—In SEMA attacks, the aim is to guess from the emanations which particular instruction is being executed at a certain time and what are the values of input and output; this requires knowledge of the exact implementation.
  - **Differential electromagnetic analysis attacks (DEMA)**—A DEMA attack does not require knowledge of the implementation details; it exploits statistical methods in the analysis process.

Countermeasures against EM attacks fall into two broad categories:

- **Signal strength reduction**—Techniques include circuit redesign to reduce unintentional emanations and the use of shielding and physically secured zones to reduce the strength of compromising signals available to an adversary relative to ambient thermal noise.
- **Signal information reduction**—Techniques include the use of randomization and/or frequent key refreshing within the computation to substantially reduce the effectiveness of statistical attacks using the available signals.

- **Visible light attack**—The average luminosity of a cathode ray tube (CRT) diffuse reflection off a wall can be sufficient to reconstruct a signal displayed on the CRT, so shielding the CRT to protect against leakage may not be a sufficient countermeasure and physical access is not required. For example, even without line of sight, an attacker may be able to read signals emitted from a trusted computing platform's optical output. Optical radiation emitted from computer light-emitting diode (LED) status indicators can also be analyzed to infer the data being processed by a device.
- **Error message attack**—In many standards, e.g., Secure Sockets Layer (SSL)/ Transport Layer Security(TLS), Internet Protocol Security (IPSec), messages are first preformatted, then encrypted in cipher-block chaining (CBC) mode with a block cipher. Decryption needs to check whether the format is valid. Validity of the format can be leaked from communication protocols in a chosen ciphertext attack since the receiver usually sends an acknowledgement or error message.
- **Cache-based attack**—Most modern computers employ a *CPU cache* between the CPU and the main memory, to speed program runtime. If, however, a CPU accesses data not stored in the cache, i.e., if a cache miss occurs, a delay will be generated, as the target data must be loaded from main memory into the cache. The measurement of this delay may enable attackers to determine the occurrence and frequency of cache misses. For example, this attacking method can be used for cryptanalysis of cryptographic primitives that employ data-dependent table lookups, and requires knowledge of neither the specific plaintexts nor ciphertexts, and works merely by monitoring the cryptographic process. Countermeasures against these attacks include: removing the cache or cached S-box access; disabling cache flushing; performing time and miss skewing; using application-specific algorithm masking; using operating system support mechanisms; and adopting partitioned cache hardware architecture.
- **Cold boot attack**—In the research paper "Lest We Remember: Cold Boot Attacks on Encryption Keys,"[11] researchers took advantage of an unexpected property of dynamic random access memory (DRAM). Ordinary DRAM loses its contents gradually over a period of seconds. This is an effect known as DRAM remanence. Even at standard operating temperatures, and even if the chips are removed from the motherboard, the data will persist for minutes or even hours if the

[11]Halderman, J. A., Schoen, S. D., Heninger, N., Clarkson, W., Paul, W., Calandrino, J. A., Feldman, A. J., Appelbaum, J., and Felten, E. W., "Lest We Remember: Cold Boot Attacks on Encryption Keys," Center for Information Technology Policy, Princeton University, 2008.

chips are kept at low temperatures. Cold boot attacks pose a particular threat to laptop users who rely on disk encryption products. For example, if an adversary steals a laptop while an encrypted disk is mounted, a cold boot attack could be used to access the contents, even if the laptop is screen-locked or suspended. According to the researchers, successful attacks have been conducted against popular disk encryption products such as BitLocker, TrueCrypt, dm-crypt, and FileVault. These products no longer have a safe place to store cryptographic keys. Even the BitLocker encryption system was defeated despite its use of a TPM to store the encryption keys.

Although there are some countermeasures to defend against memory imaging attacks, there is no way to eliminate them. Since cryptographic keys in active use need to be stored somewhere, they are an available and attractive target for attack. To counter these attacks, the researchers describe the following countermeasures and their limitations, which focus on discarding or obscuring encryption keys before an adversary might gain physical access, preventing memory-dumping software from being executed on the machine, physically protecting DRAM chips, and making the contents of memory decay at a faster rate:

- **Scrubbing memory**—Software should overwrite keys when they are no longer needed, and it should attempt to prevent keys from being paged to disk. Runtime libraries and operating systems should clear memory proactively and at boot time, e.g., via a destructive power-on-self-test (POST) before loading the operating system. If the attacker cannot bypass the POST, they cannot image the PCs memory with local-executing software, but may still physically move the memory chips to another computer with a more permissive BIOS.
- **Limiting booting from network or removable media**—If an administrative password to boot from alternate devices is required, an attacker could still swap out the primary hard drive or reset the non-volatile random access memory (NVRAM) to re-enable booting from an alternate device.
- **Suspending a system safely**—Screen-locking, suspending a laptop's state (''sleeping''), and suspending a system to disk (''hibernating'') do not protect the system's memory. Suspending can be made safe by requiring a password or other form of authentication, for example, a biometric such as a fingerprint reader, in order to reawaken the machines, and encrypting the contents of the memory using a key derived from a strong password.
- **Avoiding precomputation**—Using precomputation to speed cryptographic operations can make keys more vulnerable since it tends to lead to redundant storage of key information, helping an attacker reconstruct keys in the presence of bit errors. Avoiding precomputation will affect performance, but a compromise could involve caching precomputed values for a predetermined period of time, to be discarded if not reused.
- **Key expansion**—This involves applying a transform to the key as it is stored in memory in order to make it more difficult to reconstruct in the case of errors.
- **Physically protecting the memory**—DRAM chips could be locked in place inside the machine, or encased in an epoxy material to discourage attempts at removal.

Or, the system could respond to low temperatures or the opening of the computer case by attempting to overwrite or zeroize the memory contents. This is similar to tamper-resistant hardware used in cryptographic modules.

- **Architectural changes**—Changes to the machine's architecture can be made, such as adding key-store hardware that is guaranteed to erase its state on power-up, reset, and shutdown; or routine encryption of memory contents. These solutions may prevent the attacks as long as the encryption keys were destroyed on reset or power loss.
- **Encrypting in the disk controller**—Encrypting the data in the hard disk controller hardware, as in Full Disk Encryption (FDE) systems such as Seagate's Drive Trust technology[12] is an approach that uses a write-only *key register* in the disk controller that can hold the software key. To be secure, the system must ensure that the key register is erased whenever a new operating system is booted on the computer.
- **Trusted computing**—Trusted computing hardware in the form of Trusted Platform Modules (TPM) is now installed in some PCs. TPMs don't prevent the storage of the key in RAM in all cases. Therefore, once the key is stored in RAM, it is subject to cold boot attacks.

Some strategies for combating side-channel attacks are:

- De-correlate the output traces on individual runs (e.g., by introducing random timing shifts and wait states, inserting dummy instructions, randomization of the execution of operations, etc.)
- Replace critical assembler instructions with ones whose "consumption signature" is hard to analyze, or re-engineer the critical circuitry that performs arithmetic operations or memory transfers
- Make algorithmic changes to the cryptographic primitives so that attacks are provably inefficient on the obtained implementation, e.g., masking data and key with random mask generated at each run

Among all the countermeasures, algorithmic techniques may be the most powerful and cheapest to put in place. Software-based countermeasures include introducing dummy instructions, randomization of the instruction execution sequence, balancing Hamming weights of the internal data, and bit splitting. On the hardware level, countermeasures usually include clock randomization, power consumption randomization or compensation, and randomization of instruction set execution and/or register usage. Countermeasures are summarized in the following list:

- **Randomization**—The most general method to counter side-channel attacks is to randomize data that may leak through various side-channels, such as power consumption, electromagnetic radiation, or execution time. The problem is to guarantee that an attacker may obtain only random information, and thus cannot gain any useful knowledge about the actual initial and/or intermediate data involved in computations.

[12] `www.seagate.com/docs/pdf/whitepaper/TP564_DriveTrust_Oct06.pdf`

- **Blinding**—This was originally a concept in cryptography that allows a client to have a provider compute a mathematical function $y= f(x)$, where the client provides an input x and retrieves the corresponding output y, but the provider would neither learn x nor y. This concept is useful if the client cannot compute the mathematical function f because the provider uses an additional private input in order to compute f efficiently. Blinding techniques are effective countermeasures against remote timing analysis of Web servers and against power analysis or timing analysis of hardware security modules.
- **Masking**—This is the most widely used countermeasure against power analysis and timing attacks at the software level. Masking an algorithm means masking the intermediate values, which are processed in the computation of the algorithm operation. Data masking is also one of the most powerful software countermeasures against side-channel attacks. For example, the message and the key are masked with some random masks at the beginning of computations. Then the value of the mask at the end of some fixed step (e.g., the end of the round at the end of a linear part of computations) must be known to reestablish the expected data value at the end of this execution; this is called *mask correction*.

Embedded Systems

An embedded system is a special-purpose computer system designed to perform a few dedicated functions, often with real-time operating requirements.

Embedded systems have the following characteristics:

- They are designed to do some specific task, rather than be a general-purpose computer for multiple tasks. Some also have real-time performance constraints that must be met, for reasons such as safety and usability; others may have low or no performance requirements, allowing the system hardware to be simplified to reduce costs.
- They are not always standalone devices. Many embedded systems consist of small, computerized parts, within a larger device that serves a more general purpose. For example, the Gibson Robot Guitar features an embedded system for tuning the strings, but the overall purpose of the Robot Guitar is to play music.
- The program instructions written for embedded systems are referred to as firmware, and are stored in read-only memory or flash memory chips. They run with limited computer hardware resources, e.g., little memory, small or nonexistent keyboard and/or screen.[13]

Examples of embedded systems range from small portable devices such as mobile phones, digital media players, and GPS receivers to industrial devices such as motor controllers and automotive safety systems.

Embedded systems have a much higher reliability expectation that most other software systems. They must continue to operate in spite of security threats—for example, it could be disastrous if an airplane's inertial guidance system were to fail.

[13] `http://en.wikipedia.org/wiki/Embedded_system`

Some embedded systems face a greater number of threats because the attacker may be in physical possession of the device. For example, a portable device that is in the hands of an attacker may be subject to physical attacks such as the side-channel attacks described in the previous section. These attacks include the use of sensitive test equipment to steal, disassemble, and probe small devices; to remove memory elements from the system and extract their contents; to use debugging ports and software to read sensitive data or force unintended operation; and to measure electromagnetic radiation or power consumption to gain information about hidden functions and concealed information such as secret keys. An attacker can also expose anomalous and vulnerable behaviors by forcing the system to operate outside its design parameters, such as through introduction of extreme temperatures, voltage excursions, or clock variations.[14]

One of the most publicized attacks on an embedded system was the 2002 attack on the flash memory of the Microsoft Xbox game cube in order to access the algorithm used by the game cube's cryptosystem to decrypt and verify its bootloader.[15]

An embedded system, including its software components, may also be subject to reverse engineering. Once the system is understood, the attacker may be able to devise countermeasures to the system's security protections or to the system itself, as in the case of a supervisory control and data acquisition (SCADA) or weapons system. There is also the possibility that the attacker will use information gained through reverse engineering to design a new version of the system to employ against the copied system or its originator.

The majority of software-intensive embedded systems in existence were conceived as non-networked, standalone systems, while most software-intensive control systems were, if networked at all, connected only to private dial-up links. However, an increasing number of these systems are being connected to and remotely administered over Internet links or other public networks. Even embedded controllers in automobiles are being monitored via wireless network-based systems such as OnStar. Besides monitoring or information update and reporting functions, it is possible that networked systems will be used to reset embedded processors, reconfigure embedded software, and download new software and firmware versions.

Given all the present and emerging threats to embedded systems, it is important that they are designed with proper safeguards. In addition to the traditional criteria for evaluating embedded systems—efficiency of code, smallness of circuitry, and long mean times between failures—embedded systems must be designed for dependability, trustworthiness, and resilience during normal operation and while under attack. The following software security design principles are particularly relevant to embedded systems:

- The design should separate low-consequence and high-consequence functions and public and private data. User access should be denied to high-consequence functions and private data.

[14]Goertzel, K. M., Winograd, T., et al., "Enhancing the Development Life Cycle to Produce Secure Software," Version 2.0., Rome, New York, United States Department of Defense Data and Analysis Center for Software, October 2008.

[15]IATAC/DACS, "Software Security Assurance State-of-the-Art Report (SOAR)," July 31, 2007.

- The design must provide protection during the embedded system's normal operation, during attack through a network connection, and during electronic probing (e.g., in the laboratory).

Most embedded operating system security specifications focus on implementing security protections defined in the Common Criteria. For example, an embedded operating system from LynuxWorks was designed according to the Multiple Independent Layers of Security (MILS) standard and is intended to achieve certified assurance at the highest level of the Common Criteria, Evaluation Assurance Level (EAL) 7. The MILS standard requires a partitioned real-time operating system (RTOS) that can be certified as secure through a set of rigorous tests. The MILS systems provide memory protection and guaranteed resource availability, enabling the user to securely host both trusted and untrusted data on the same processor. By adhering to the MILS standard, developers can create formally verified, always-invoked, tamperproof application code with non-bypassable security features. Green Hills Software, LynuxWorks, and Wind River Software are among vendors working on MILS-compliant RTOSs.

Physical packaging can also be strengthened to protect embedded software. This can be accomplished by using trusted platform modules (TPMs), such as those defined by the Trusted Computing Platform Alliance to secure platforms for embedded programs. An embedded TPM monitors the boot process to create hash values or checksums for important elements, such as BIOS, device drivers, and operating system loaders. The TPM stores these values and compares them with the reference values that define the trustworthy status of the platform. The TPM also provides public/private-key RSA-based encryption and decryption along with a tamperproof on-chip memory for storing keys and passwords.

Secure embedded design using hardware-software co-design techniques is also being used by researchers at Virginia Tech to strengthen protections in embedded systems. The objective of secure embedded system design is to protect the root-of-trust from being compromised. This protection is achieved by obtaining a systematic deployment of countermeasures that will protect the root-of-trust at different levels of abstraction. Specific techniques the researchers are applying include:

- Partitioning of systems into secure and non-secure parts
- Developing secure interfaces to integrate those partitions into a single system

Another major challenge in secure embedded system design being addressed in the Virginia Tech research is the implementation of end-point-security—that is, the creation of trusted channels that reach out into the peripherals and off-chip, off-board interface. Hardware-software code sign techniques are being used to build trusted channels to securely cross the hardware-software interface.

Defensive Coding Practices

Defensive coding should produce more secure and robust software. Karen Goertzel, Theodore Winograd, and their contributors in "Enhancing the Development Life Cycle to Produce Secure Software"[16] write that defensive coding "requires the software's behaviors to fall within the bounds of its design specification, regardless of the nature of its execution environment or the type of input it receives." The authors then define two characteristics of defensively coded software and introduce secure coding principles and practices that will contribute to defensive coding. Those characteristics and principles are summarized in the following paragraphs.

Defensively coded software:

- Does not rely on any parameters that are not self-generated
- Assumes that attempts will be made to subvert its behavior directly, indirectly, or through manipulation of the software to violate a security policy

The following secure coding principles and practices contribute to defensive coding:

- **Keep code simple and small**—It is easier to verify the security of the software if the code base is small and simple. A number of coding practices help simplify code:
  - Programmers should implement functions, especially high-consequence functions, in the smallest number of lines of code possible, while maintaining proper coding standards.
  - Software should not implement unnecessary functions and should implement only functions defined in the software specification.
  - Software should avoid ambiguities and hidden assumptions, and avoid recursions and GoTo statements that confuse the flow of control.
  - Complex functions should be divided into multiple small and simple functions that can be implemented by small and simple software modules.
  - All processes should have only one entry point and as few exit points as possible.
  - Interdependencies should be kept to a minimum so that any process module or component can be disabled when not needed, or replaced if found to be insecure or a better alternative is identified, without affecting the operation of the software.
  - Object-oriented techniques such as object inheritance, encapsulation, and polymorphism can be used to keep the code simple and small.

[16]Goertzel, K. M., Winograd, T., et al.

- **Use a consistent coding style**—The coding style defines the appearance of the code listing, e.g., indentation and spacing, so that the code can be easily comprehended by code reviewers and maintainers who were not involved in writing the code.
  - All programmers on the same team or project should follow the same coding style guidelines.
  - Coding style should also be considered as an evaluation criterion for open source software, especially software that will be used to implement high-consequence functions, and may make it easier to perform a security analysis of the code.
- **Follow secure coding standards and/or guidelines**—These describe secure coding best practices, common coding flaws, and functions that may have security implications, as well as secure alternatives to unsafe functions:
  - Standards and guidelines should cover both good and bad practices for coding in all languages used on a project.
  - Standards and guidelines may be written in-house based on project experience complemented with advice from commercial software vendors, and/or externally sourced from government or the open source community, e.g., CMU Software Engineering Institute (SEI), National Institute of Standards and Technology (NIST), Open Web Application Security Project (OWASP).
- **Make code forward and backward traceable**—Traceability is essential for validating requirements, preventing defects, and finding and solving inconsistencies among all artifacts generated in each phase of the software life cycle.
  - It should be possible to easily trace each requirement from the specification through detailed design to its manifestation in the code.
  - It should be possible to derive each requirement and design element from its manifestation in the code.
- **Code for reuse and maintainability**—Code features that make code elegant and secure, e.g., simplicity, comprehensibility, traceability, also contribute to its reliability and maintainability.
  - The code specification should be clear, understandable, and comprehensive enough to guide programmers in writing the specified code.
  - Code should be commented and documented to include the results of reviews and tests to help other programmers and maintainers gain a complete and accurate understanding of the code in case it needs to be modified or reused.
- **Allocate memory and other resources carefully**—Minimize the computer resources available to each process, e.g.:
  - If the software will run on a *nix-based operating system, use `ulimit()`, `getrlimit()`, `setrlimit()`, `getrusage()`, `sysconf()`, `quota()`, `quotactl()`, `quotaon()`, and `pam_limits` for pluggable extension module processes, to limit the potential damage that results when a particular process

fails or is compromised and to help prevent denial-of-service (DoS) attacks on the software.

- If the software is a Web server application or Web service, set up a separate process to handle each session, and limit the amount of central processing unit (CPU) time that each session in each process is allowed to use in order to prevent any attacker request that consumes a large amount of memory or CPU cycles from interfering with tasks beyond its own session. Designing all sessions to be atomic and resource-limited will make it difficult to create a DoS, e.g., by spawning multiple sessions.
- Memory locations for cache buffers should not be contiguous with the executable stack or heap space, and if possible, the stack should be set to be non-executable.

- **Minimize retention of state information**—The software should retain only necessary state information, and should frequently purge data written in cache memory and temporary files on disk. This will decrease the likelihood of unintentional disclosure of sensitive information, including information about the software itself, which could be leveraged by attackers, in the event of a software failure.
- **Leverage security through obscurity only as an additional defense measure**—Security through obscurity (using secrecy to provide security) techniques, including code obfuscation and hidden files, provide a weak deterrent against reconnaissance attacks and reverse engineering. Such techniques should be used only in addition to a robust set of true security measures, to provide enough of an inconvenience factor to possibly deter unsophisticated and casual attackers.
- **Avoid unauthorized privilege escalation**—The programmer should not write logic that enables users or processes to perform unexpected or unintended privilege escalations.
  - Higher privileged processes should not be visible or accessible to lower privileged processes. This prevents an attacker who is in control of a lower privileged process from exploiting a higher level process, e.g., through use of a race condition.
- **Use consistent naming**—Incorrect use of aliases, pointers, links, caches, and dynamic changes without relinking are common causes of security flaws in software.
  - Treat aliases symmetrically. Every alias should be unique, and should point to only one resource.
  - Be cautious when using dynamic linking. Dynamic linking can cause unpredictable behaviors that result from runtime introduction of components, e.g., Java-extensible Web browsers rely on static type systems with link checks to enforce a wide class of important safety properties that could be compromised through dynamic linking.

- Minimize use of global variables. Use a variable with local scope instead. If a global variable must be used, give it a globally unique name.
- Clear caches frequently to promote proper memory management.
- Limit variables to the smallest scope possible. If a variable is used only within a single function or block, that variable should be declared, allocated, and de-allocated only within that function or block.
- De-allocate objects as soon as they are no longer needed. If the object will be used later, reallocate the object. Use language idioms, e.g., Resource Acquisition Is Initialization (RAII) in C++, to automatically enforce this practice.

- **Use encapsulation cautiously**—Incorrect encapsulation can expose the internals of software procedures and processes by leaking sensitive information or externally inducing interference. Correct encapsulation can be achieved through a combination of effective system architecture, effective programming language design, effective software engineering, static checking, dynamic checking, and effective error handling.
  - Error messages sent to the user should be generic (uninformative), while error messages with enough detail to analyze the cause of the problem without disclosing sensitive information should be logged.
- **Leverage attack patterns**—Attack patterns should be used to identify vulnerabilities targeted by relevant attacks, and ensure that these flaws do not occur in the software. The following is an approach to leverage attack patterns:
  1. Determine which attack patterns are applicable, i.e., which subset of available attack patterns is relevant given the software's architecture and execution environment, and the technologies used to implement the software. For example, the *Buffer Overflow* attack pattern is relevant for a C or C++ program running on a *nix operating system, but not for a C# program running on .NET.
  2. Determine what constructs should not appear in the code, based on what attack patterns need to be avoided.
- **Use proper input encoding and validation**—Input from users and untrusted processes should be considered untrusted until properly validated. Proper validation includes ensuring that input contains no characteristics, or malicious code, that could corrupt the system or trigger a security exploit or compromise. Validation of both unintentionally or malicious malformed input is the most effective way to prevent buffer overflows.
  - Input should be validated for correct length, range, format, and data type. For example, the length of every input element should be checked, e.g., bounds checking, and the input should be constrained to the minimum acceptable length.
  - Any constructs that are not explicitly allowed or expected should be disallowed, e.g., query strings, cookies, file paths, and URL paths.

- Each component should do its own input validation unless the design ensures that trustworthy validation of the input has been successfully achieved before the component receives that input.
- The application framework or integrated development environment (IDE) may provide reusable code samples for input validation, e.g., ASP.NET Validator Controls and JavaScript filtering.
- Input should be validated against a positive specification of what is allowed (whitelist). Whitelisting verifies that input conforms to defined acceptable parameters, and rejects all input that does not conform.
- Bad input should be rejected rather than sanitized. However, there will be times when sanitization is necessary. In this case, the data should be sanitized and resubmitted for whitelist validation to ensure that the sanitization was effective.

- **Use proper output filtering and sanitization**—Output from processes to external entities should be validated to ensure that it contains allowable content. The same types of checks used for validating input are applied to output before the output is released to its intended recipient.
- **Avoid security conflicts arising between native and non-native, passive and dynamic code**—If an application relies on native code that is written in another programming language, that code may contain a security vulnerability, such as a buffer overflow. For example, a Java application may rely on vulnerable C code to interface with peripheral hardware, such as a personal identity verification (PIV) card reader.
  - Native and dynamic code should be treated as potentially untrusted entities.
  - Validation should be performed on data going to untrusted code and well as data received from untrusted code.
- **Review code during and after coding**—Code should be analyzed to identify coding flaws in modules before the code is checked into the version control system, and between interfaces before the code is submitted for compilation and linking. Code analysis techniques include manual review, automated source code analysis, and various forms of testing. Code analysis is covered later in this chapter.

NOTE The CERT Coordination Center (CERT/CC) Web site (`www.cert.org/certcc.html`) provides additional information on vulnerability remediation, secure coding, and malware analysis.

Exception Handling

An exception is an event that occurs during the execution of a software application that disrupts the normal flow of instructions. Exception handling mechanisms are designed to handle the occurrence of these events. A handler is the portion of the code that handles or performs the specific task of managing the exceptional event.

To understand exception handling, it is helpful to review how it is implemented in a common programming language. The Java programming language makes use of three kinds of exceptions[17]:

- **Checked exceptions**—These are exceptions that a properly coded application should anticipate and know how to handle. For example, an application prompts a user for an input filename, then opens the file by passing the name to the constructor of `java.io.FileReader`. If the file exists and is readable, the construction of the `FileReader` object succeeds and execution of the application proceeds normally. If the file does not exist, the code may throw a `java.io.FileNotFoundException`. A properly coded application will catch this exception and notify the user of the mistake, possibly prompting for a corrected filename.
- **Errors**—These are events that are external to the application. The application cannot usually anticipate them or recover from them. For example, an application successfully opens a file for input, but is unable to read the file because of a system malfunction, causing the application to throw a `java.io.IOError`. The application may choose to catch this exception, in order to notify the user of the problem, or print a stack trace and exit.
- **Runtime exceptions**—These are events that are internal to the application. The application cannot usually anticipate them or recover from them. This type of exception may be caused by coding flaws, such as logic errors or improper use of an API. For example, an application prompts a user for a filename as input to the `java.io.FileReader`. If a logic error causes a `null` to be passed as an argument to the constructor, the constructor will throw a `java.io.NullPointerException`. The application may catch the exception, but it may make more sense to print a stack trace and exit in order to identify and fix the coding flaw that caused the exception.

In Java, the three exception handler components are `try`, `catch`, and `finally`. The following code snippet shows how these components might be used to open a filename for reading using another example with the `FileReader`:

```
import java.io.*;                        // include Java IO library

...                                      // main method

FileReader fileReader = null;            // fileReader declaration

try {
        ...                              // read fileName from
                                            command line
```

[17]http://java.sun.com/docs/books/tutorial/essential/exceptions/catchOrDeclare.html

```
      fileReader = new FileReader(fileName);  // may throw a
 FileNotFoundException
      int x;                                  // declare int for read()
      while ( (x = fileReader.read()) != -1) {  // may throw an IOException

        ...                                   // do something

     }

       fileReader.close();                     // may throw an IOException

  }
  catch (FileNotFoundException fnf) {
        System.err.println("Can't find input file: " + fileName);
  }
  catch (IOException io) {
        System.err.println("Caught IOException: " + io.getMessage());
  }
  finally {
        if (fileReader != null) {
             try {
                   fileReader.close();    // close fileReader
             }
             catch (IOException io){
                   System.err.println("Caught IOException in
                     finally: " + io.getMessage());
             }
        }                                     // end if
  }                                           // end try - catch - finally
```

In this code snippet, the `try` block encloses the part of the code that may throw an exception. The name of the file is being passed to the `FileReader` constructor in `fileReader = new FileReader(filename)`. If the file cannot be opened, the file may throw a `FileNotFoundException`. The exception will be caught in the `catch` block that defines the `FileNotFoundException` and an error message will be printed out to standard error.

When the `while` loop, `while ( (x = fileReader.read()) != -1)`, reaches the end of the stream, it should close the `fileReader` and exit. If it encounters an error, it will throw an `IOException`. The exception will be caught in the `catch` block that defines the `IOException` and an error message will be printed out to standard error.

The `finally` block always executes when the `try` block exits. This ensures that the `finally` block is executed even if an unexpected exception occurs. The `finally` block is useful to address any unexpected exceptions and can help prevent resource leaks. For example, if an exception occurs and the `try` block exits, the `fileReader` may still be open. Checking if the `fileReader` is still open and if so, closing it, `fileReader.close()`, ensures that the resource is recovered.

The following best practices relate to how exception handling should be coded in Java:

- **`catch` blocks should never be empty**—Even if the exceptional condition might be rare, the `catch` block should still include a logger to record when and why an exception was thrown.
  - If the exception was caused by an attack on the application, not recording the exception may prevent the attack from coming to the attention of the application administrators.
  - If the exception was caused by an error, not recording the exception could make it difficult to identify and fix the error.
- **`catch` blocks should not catch `NullPointerException`**—If the program contains a null pointer dereference, it should be fixed, not caught.
- **`finally` blocks should not contain a `return` statement**—Returning from inside a `finally` block will cause an exception that might be thrown in the try block to be discarded.
- **`catch` blocks should address specific exceptions**—If the `catch` block handles a broad range of exceptions, it may trap dissimilar issues or problems that should be dealt with earlier in program execution.
- **Methods should throw specific exceptions**—When the method declares what exceptions it throws, it should specify individual exceptions, not just the `Exception` class, which is the parent of all checked exceptions. This makes it easier for callers of the method to perform correct error handling and recovery.

A number of software weaknesses related to exception handling can be found in the resources described in the ''Vulnerabilities and Countermeasures'' section of this chapter.

In the context of secure implementation, exception handling relates closely to the survivability of software. Error and exception handling can be considered to aid in survivability when the goal of all error and exception handling routines is to ensure that faults are handled in a way that prevents the software from entering an insecure state.

Software should include security-aware error and event handling mechanisms and should perform validation on all input it receives, including from the local execution environment. Input validation could help to prevent denial-of-service (DoS) attacks, such as a DoS resulting from a buffer overflow in software interacting with components written in C++.

In the event of an attack (for example, DoS), software should be designed to continue operating in a degraded manner (with reduction in performance or acceptance of fewer inputs) until a limit is reached. When the limit is reached, it should trigger a secure termination of the software's execution. The software should never throw exceptions that allow it to crash, dump core memory, or expose transient data such as caches and temporary files.

For example, the following are common software errors and security-aware error and event handling measures:

- **Called functions return results that contain errors**—Anticipate all likely errors and exceptions. Implement error and event handling to explicitly address those errors and exceptions.
- **Software contains unmitigated or undetected vulnerabilities**—Reduce exposure of untrusted and vulnerable components to external attack vectors (reduce attack surface), e.g., using wrappers, input filters, etc.

If errors within the software do not cause memory leaks, corrupted data, or invalid output, the code is said to be *exception-safe*. There are several levels of exception safety, from highest to lowest[18]:

- **Failure transparency (also known as the no-throw guarantee)**—Operations are guaranteed to succeed and satisfy all requirements even in the presence of exceptional situations. If an exception occurs, it will not throw the exception again to be caught further up the stack.
- **Commit or rollback semantics (also known as strong exception safety or no-charge guarantee)**—Operations can fail, but failed operations are guaranteed to have no side effects, so all data retains original values.
- **Basic exception safety**—Partial execution of failed operations can cause side effects, but invariants on the state are preserved. Any stored data will contain valid values even if data values from before the exception are different from the values after the exception.
- **Minimal exception safety** also known as no-leak guarantee—Partial execution of failed operations may store invalid data but will not cause a crash, and no resources get leaked.
- **No exception safety**—No guarantees are made.

Exception handling can be effectively implemented by following best practices such as these summarized from "Enhancing the Development Life Cycle to Produce Secure Software"[19]:

- **Anomaly awareness**—To detect anomalous behavior among software components, a baseline must be obtained for normal behavior. Subsequent behavior can be compared to this baseline to detect anything abnormal. For example, in most distributed systems, components maintain a high level of interaction with each other. Inaction, manifested by a lack of response in a particular component for an extended period of time or receipt from that component of improperly formatted messages, should indicate anomalous behavior. In order for the components to detect this behavior, they need to be designed with this capability, or in the case of acquired or legacy components, they need to be retrofitted with the capability, e.g., by adding anomaly detection wrappers to monitor the component's behavior and to report detected anomalies.

[18] `http://en.wikipedia.org/wiki/Exception_handling`
[19] Goertzel, K. M., Winograd, T., et al.

- **Event monitors**—An anomaly or error should be detected as close as possible to the actual time it occurs. This will enable the affected component to be isolated and diagnosed before erroneous data is able to propagate to other components. At a minimum, the software should self-check all security-critical states. Monitor checks should also be non-intrusive, i.e., not affecting the process or data being monitored, and implemented in such a way as not to introduce new vulnerabilities in the software. The effectiveness of event monitors for error or anomaly detection also depends on correct assumptions about:
  - The structure of the program being monitored
  - The anomalies and errors that are considered possible and likely, and those that are considered unlikely
- **Security error and failure handling**—Languages that provide robust security handling procedures at the code level include C++ and Java. These languages provide convenient and extensible exception handling support that includes "catching" exceptions and errors. Exceptions are considered faults that are not necessarily caused by flaws from external inputs or violations of software-level constraints. Errors are considered faults that are caused by external inputs or constraint violations; errors may or may not trigger exceptions.
- **Exception handling**—Exception handling should be proactively designed through the careful examination of constraints in the design and implementation phases of the software life cycle. One approach is to list all predictable faults, both exceptions and errors, that could occur during software execution, and define how the software will handle each of them. It should also be determined how the software will behave when confronted with an unanticipated error or fault.
- **Core dump prevention**—Applications should only be allowed to generate a core dump in test environments. The ability to generate core dumps should be turned off in production environments. Instead of dumping the core when the program fails, the exception handler should log the problem before the application exits. If possible, the size of the core file should be configured to be zero bytes, e.g., using `setrlimit` or `ulimit` in *nix operating systems, to further prevent the creation of core files.

Configuration Management

In software projects, configuration management (CM) is a process to control changes to software in order to maintain software integrity and traceability throughout the software development life cycle (SDLC). From a secure software development perspective, CM should also protect all artifacts created during the SDLC—documentation, software code, developer notes, test tools, test results—from subversive activities such as tampering, insertion of malicious code, and theft.[20] The following ways to increase the security of configuration management are summarized from "Enhancing the Development Life Cycle to Produce Secure Software":

- **Provide strong authentication and authorization of developers, testers, and other participants in the SDLC**—Strong authentication can be combined with granular access control to prevent unauthorized access.
  - Role-based access control (RBAC) can be combined with separation of duties to prevent personnel from modifying test results, e.g., to erase evidence of test failures.
  - Access to an artifact can further be controlled depending on the phase of the SDLC. For example, when the final version of an artifact is submitted, the permissions on the artifact can be changed from read-write to read-only to prevent changes to the artifact while under review or testing.
- **Provide a secure check-in/check-out process for artifacts**—An artifact is digitally signed and time stamped when it is first checked in. The checked-in version is baselined, for example, by storing critical metadata or creating a message digest of the artifact, so that each subsequent version can be compared against the original for changes. The comparison ensures that as each artifact is modified after review or test, the new version can be compared against the previous baseline to verify that the only changes to the new version correct noted deficiencies. If any changes do not directly address deficiencies, they can be flagged and analyzed. This minimizes the opportunity for malicious developers to tamper with development artifacts, e.g., by inserting malicious logic or intentional vulnerabilities.
- **Increase accountability for and traceability of modifications to SDLC artifacts**—All change artifacts are documented programmatically, allowing for easy comparison and monitoring of changes as the artifact moves through the various phases of the SDLC.
- **Support clear identification and security impact analysis of changes from one version to the next of each SDLC artifact**—The validity and security impact of the changes can be audited at appropriate intervals depending on the SDLC phase and type of artifact, e.g., each software release, as the artifact changes owners, at the completion of a phase.
- **Minimize the likelihood that undesirable changes will "slip in" to the artifact that would ultimately increase the vulnerability of the software**—Use secure configuration management tools that incorporate strong authentication and authorization, access control, time stamping, accountability, and other security features.

[20]Goertzel, K. M., Winograd, T., et al.

Build Environment

Since not all developers will have a good understanding of the security implications of coding choices, it is important that the build environment includes tools expressly intended to produce secure software. Tools that actively encourage secure specification, design, and implementation will assist with[21]:

- Reducing the number of exploitable flaws and weaknesses
- Reducing the attack surface, i.e., the accessibility to any residual exploitable flaws and weaknesses
- Implementing software security constraints, protections, and services
- Minimizing and constraining the propagation, extent, and damage caused by insecure software behavior

The following is a list of tools and best practices that aid in producing secure software. It is summarized from "Enhancing the Development Life Cycle to Produce Secure Software," except where noted:

- **Compiler security checking and enforcement**—The compiler should enforce correct language rules, and detect and warn (or eliminate in some cases) faults and dangerous constructs in the source code. The following are best practices for compiler security checking and enforcement:
  - **Use GCC compiler flags**—The GNU C Compiler (GCC) and g++ compilers include an `-ftrapv` compiler option that generates traps for signed overflow on addition, subtraction, and multiplication operations—that is, the compiler generates calls to existing library functions rather than generating assembler instructions to perform these arithmetic operations on signed integers.
  - **Enable Visual C++ warnings**—The Visual C++ .NET 2003 compiler generates a compiler warning (C4244) when an integer is assigned to a smaller integer type.[22] At warning level 1, a warning will be issued if a value of type `__int64` is assigned to a variable of type `unsigned int`. At compiler warning level 3 and 4, a "possible loss of data" error message is issued if an integer type is converted to a smaller integer type. In the following example, the assignment is flagged at warning level 4:

```
int b=0, c=0;
short a = b + c; // C4244
```

  - **Increase the level of type checking and related program analysis**—The level of type checking can be increased by turning on all available compilation flags when debugging code, and then revising the source code to compile cleanly with those flags. The strict use of American National Standards Institute (ANSI) prototypes in separate header files will also ensure that function calls use the correct types.

[21] Goertzel, K. M., Winograd, T., et al.

[22] http://msdn.microsoft.com/en-us/library/th7a07tz(VS.80).aspx

- **Turn off debug options when compiling and linking the production binary executable**—Critical vulnerabilities have been found in popular operating systems that enable an attacker to exploit the operating system's documented debug interface. The debug interface allows the developer to control program flow during testing. When this interface remains accessible in production systems, it can be exploited by an attacker to gain control of applications over the network to elevate privileges to that of the debugger.
- **Use more robust type-checking compilers for non-typed languages**—These types of compilers can flag and eliminate code constructs and flaws associated with insecure typing, e.g., pointer and array access semantics that could generate memory access errors. They also perform bounds checking on memory references to detect and prevent buffer overflow vulnerabilities. Two open source compilers that are intended to compile C programs in ways that eliminate buffer overflows are Memory Safe C (`www.seclab.cs.sunysb.edu/mscc/`) and Fail-Safe C (`www.rcis.aist.go.jp/project/FailSafeC-en.html`).
- **Use compilers that can detect a modified stack or data area**—For example, a value, called a canary, can be inserted in front of the return address on the stack by the subroutine entry code, and verified by the subroutine exit code. If the value is found to be modified (if the buffer overflow overwrites the return address), the exit code terminates the application. This technology was first introduced in StackGuard,[23] an extension to the standard GNU C compiler. IBM later built a stack protection system based on the ideas of StackGuard called IBM ProPolice (`www.trl.ibm.com/projects/security/ssp/`), which is also a GNU C extension to prevent "stack-smashing" attacks.
- **Many C/C++ compilers can detect inaccurate format strings**—The GNU C and C++ compilers support a C extension that can be used to mark functions that may contain inaccurate format strings, and the /GS compiler switch in Microsoft's Visual C++ .NET can be used to detect some buffer overruns that overwrite the return address, by injecting security checks into the compiled code.
- **Taint analysis tools can detect more complex vulnerabilities**—These tools are compile-time tools that flag data as "tainted" (invalid) and ensure that all such data are validated before allowing them to be used in vulnerable functions. An example is Flayer, an open source taint analysis logic and wrapper.
- **Full program verification**—Some C and C++ compilers include more extensive logic to perform full program verification to prove complex security properties based on formal specifications generated prior to compilation. These compilers are used to detect flaws and "dangerous" constructs in C and C++ applications and libraries. For example, Flayer (`http://code.google.com/p/flayer/`) can also detect constructs that leave the application vulnerable to format string attacks and buffer overflows.

[23]Cowan, C., Pu, C., Maier, D., Hinton, H., Walpole, J., Bakke, P., Beattie, S., Grier, A., Wagle, P., and Zhang, Q., "Stackguard: Automatic Adaptive Detection and Prevention of Buffer-Overflow Attacks," *Proceedings of the Seventh USENIX Security Symposium*. San Antonio, TX, January 26–29, 1998. Berkeley, CA: USENIX Association, 1998, pp. 63–77.

- **Address space layout randomization (ASLR)**—ASLR is compiler randomization of the location of the variables, code positions and, loaded libraries. For example, ASLR increases the difficulty of performing a `return-to-libc` buffer overflow attack by loading the shared system libraries, e.g., `libc`, into a random base address. In this attack, the return address on the stack is replaced by the address of another function, e.g., `system()`, and an additional portion of the stack is overwritten to provide arguments to this function. The success of this attack relies on the attacker being able to call the preexisting `libc` function. Since the memory location of the function is random, it makes this attack unlikely to succeed. ASLR depends on sufficient entropy for randomization and is more effective on 64-bit systems where the search space is much greater.[24] ASLR has been implemented in various ways in standard operating systems. For example, Microsoft Windows Vista and Windows Server 2008 have ASLR enabled for executables and specific dynamic link libraries; Linux has had a weak form on ASLR implemented since kernel 2.6.12, but a more complete implementation can be enabled with patches to the kernel, e.g., grsecurity, PaX, and ExecShield.

- **Safe software libraries**—As with the safe compilers, most safe libraries are for C or C++ and focus on replacing library routines that are prone to buffer overflow. Safe software libraries detect the presence at link time of calls by the software to unsafe runtime library functions, e.g., `strcpy()`, `strcat()`, known to be vulnerable to buffer overflow attacks, and replace them with calls to bounded replacements, e.g., `strcpy_s()`, `strcat_s()`. The latter functions take an extra argument of type `rsize_t` that specifies the maximum length of the destination buffer. Two open source examples of "safe" libraries are the Safe C String Library (`http://zork.org/safestr/safestr.html`) and Libsafe (`http://directory.fsf.org/project/libsafe/`).
- **Runtime error checking and safety enforcement**—Runtime protections are applied to prevent buffer overflows in binaries executed under a particular operating system, or to perform dynamic runtime security analyses of compiled binaries. For example, security wrappers and content validation filters can be applied to open source code and binary executables to minimize the exposure of any discovered vulnerabilities. Security wrappers and filters are used to add input and output filtering logic to software that does not have this capability built in. The wrappers intercept and analyze input to or output from the "wrapper" component. If the wrapper detects content that is suspected of being malicious or corrupt, it can remove, isolate, or sanitize the content. Examples of malicious content include code that contains unsafe constructs such as long data strings (associated with buffer overflows), and command strings associated with injection attacks and escalation of privilege. Security wrappers and content validation filters often have to be custom-coded.
- **Tools to detect memory violations**—Runtime analysis tools that can detect memory violations help to eliminate memory-related flaws that can lead to heap-based vulnerabilities. For example, the debug memory allocation library (`dmalloc`)

[24] `http://en.wikipedia.org/wiki/Address_space_layout_randomization`

library is a drop-in replacement for the system's `stdlib` memory functions, e.g., `malloc()`, `calloc()` (to reserve space), `realloc()` (to move a reserved block of memory), `free()` (to release space back to C), and other memory functions. It provides debugging facilities that are configurable at runtime including memory-leak tracing, fence-post write detection, file/line number reporting, and general logging of statistics.[25]

- **Code obfuscation**—This is used to protect products and technologies in which the implementation logic is accessible to the user, e.g., intermediate code such as Java byte code, and runtime-interpreted scripting source code such as Perl, PHP, Python, JavaScript, AJAX, etc. Code obfuscation transforms the byte code or script to a confused or opaque form, increasing the difficulty of decompilation, disassembly, and reverse engineering. For example, Java byte code can easily be decompiled into the original source code using tools such as Jad (`www.kpdus.com/jad.html`) and Jode (`http://jode.sourceforge.net`). There are legitimate reasons for decompiling byte code, such as to recover source code that was accidentally lost or troubleshoot a third-party application that was not properly documented. However, code can also be decompiled with the objective of violating the copyright protection or reverse engineering the software for profit. Available obfuscators for Java include commercial tools such as Zelix KlassMaster (`www.zelix.com/klassmaster`) and open source tools such as ProGuard (`http://proguard.sourceforge.net`). The level of protection varies with each obfuscator, but the following are common transformations performed by Java obfuscators:
  - **Removing debug information and modifying names**—Removes debug information from the byte code such as source filenames, line numbers, field names, method names, argument names, and variable names, and replaces the names with meaningless strings. This is the primary transformation performed by obfuscators, but it still leaves the control flow intact.
  - **Encrypting strings**—Encrypts string literals in the constant pools of the class files and adds code constructs to the classes so they are decrypted at runtime. This helps prevent an attacker from performing simple string searches on the decompiled source code.
  - **Changing control flow**—Makes changes to the byte code to obscure the control flow without changing the runtime behavior of the software. This is typically accomplished by changing selection (if/else) and looping (while/for) constructs so they no longer have a direct Java equivalent. When an attacker attempts to decompile the classes into the source code, the decompiler is forced to insert a series of labels and illegal GoTo statements into the source code, and may also produce errors due to the unexpected constructs encountered in the process.
  - **Shrinking**—Byte code is more compact than source code, but may still contain a significant portion of unused code, especially if it includes program libraries. Shrinking is eliminating unused code, e.g., unused classes, fields, methods.

[25]`https://buildsecurityin.us-cert.gov/daisy/bsi/articles/knowledge/coding/311-BSI.html`

This reduces the application size, especially useful for code that is downloaded over the Internet (for example, applets), or over-the-air (OTA) applications downloaded to wireless phones or PDAs, such as Midlets.

Code/Peer Review

The first time developers encounter formal code review is typically through a quality assurance process or a programming practice that emphasizes peer review of code. For example, peer review manifests itself in pair programming, which is a standard programming practice in extreme programming and other agile programming methods. In pair programming, one developer sits with another at the same workstation to continuously review the second developer's code as it is being written.

Code review is also a part of the Software Engineering Capability Maturity Model (SE-CMM), which was initially a tool for the U.S. military to use as an objective evaluation of software subcontractors. The SE-CMM defines five levels of process maturity for an organization—for example, level 1 is the initial starting point for the process when software development may be characterized as ad hoc or chaotic. At level 5, the organization manages all processes well, and is occupied with optimizing existing processes. Starting with levels 2 and 3, repeatable and defined processes are introduced, such as creation of software requirements, use of version control, and peer review of code with metrics. Peer review allows the developer to "walk through" the implementation, and to suggest improvements or changes. Peer review is an exit checkpoint, requiring a formal sign-off, in order to move on to the next stage of the software life cycle.

NOTE **Chapters 1 and 5 discuss the SE-CMM in more detail.**

From a secure software development perspective, code review is the review of code to discover security flaws and to identify potential fixes. The code review should provide enough detailed information about possible security weaknesses to enable a classification and prioritization of potential vulnerabilities based on the level of risk they pose to the system. If code review is already a part of the software life cycle, security considerations should be integrated into the existing process to increase the overall level of software assurance. For example, pair programming can be extended to consider the security implications of coding decisions and to search for and eliminate security weaknesses in the software being developed.

NOTE **Code review is also referred to as static analysis since it examines the software without executing it. Static analysis can be wholly manual, semi-automated, or automated. Manual code review is often a slow and tedious process. Automation can make the code review process significantly more efficient. Automated tools are discussed in the next section on code analysis.**

Code reviews can also be conducted according to peer review checklists that contain guidelines to assess whether the necessary nonfunctional and constraint requirements have been met. The peer review checklist also promotes consistency, enables sign-off by reviewers and managers, and serves as documented proof that the review was completed. For example, in addition to findings related to completeness, scope, data usage, standards of compliance, and performance, a Web application checklist can include guidance for security. Sample security checks for a Web application may include some of the following:

NOTE These checks are based on the OWASP Top Ten 2004. However, this is only a starting point. Other considerations should include the types of errors discovered in previous code reviews, the output from code analysis tools, and other common errors in the type of software being reviewed.

- Unvalidated input:
  - Is input validated against a "positive" specification of what is "allowed," as opposed to what is "denied"?
  - Is input checked for null values and empty strings?
  - If the input cannot be validated against a "positive" specification, are known bad inputs such as malformed parameters, strings of excessive length, and dynamic query strings rejected?
- Broken access controls:
  - Are user actions checked against a "positive" specification of what is "allowed," as opposed to what is "denied"?
  - Are users prevented from taking actions for which they are not authorized?
- Broken authentication:
  - Are users authenticated before given access to restricted information and functionality?
  - Are users denied access to all of the application's protected functionality after log out or session expiration?
- Broken session management:
  - If cookies are used, do they store only a session ID, with other state characteristics managed server-side?
  - If cookies are set via HTTPS, do they have the SECURE parameter set to prevent them from being sent in the clear via HTTP?
  - If session identifiers are used, are they opaque, unpredictable, and unique?
  - If server-side sessions are used, do they expire?
- Cross-site scripting flaws:
  - If data is received from user input or an external system, is it encoded before sending it back as output, storing it in a database, or writing it to a log?
- Command injection flaws:
  - Are Web application API calls being used instead of native code system calls wherever possible?

- If a native code system call is being used with user-supplied input, is the input being validated?
- SQL injection flaws:
  - Are stored procedures and prepared statements used in place of dynamic database queries wherever possible?
  - Are the results from database queries being matched against the expected results?
- Improper error handling:
  - Are all error conditions handled properly?
  - When error conditions are handled, does the server return a concise error message to the client, and otherwise write specific details securely to a log?
- Non-secure use of cryptography:
  - If a cryptographic system/capability was specified for this module, was it approved by the security staff to verify its compliance with legal, regulatory, and certification standards? (Cryptographic system/capability would include encryption, SSL certificates, public/private certificates, message digests, key exchange, and random functions.)

The OWASP Code Review Guide states that "security code review is the process of auditing the source code for an application to verify that the proper security controls are present, that they work as intended, and that they have been invoked in all the right places. Code review is a way of ensuring that the application has been developed so as to be 'self-defending' in its given environment."

"Security code review is a method of assuring secure application developers are following secure development techniques. A general rule of thumb is that a penetration test should not discover any additional application vulnerabilities relating to the developed code after the application has undergone a proper security code review."[26]

For a security code review to be effective, the reviewer should have an understanding of common security vulnerabilities in the programming language, technology, and type of application being reviewed. This understanding comes from both education and experience, but there is no substitute for experience. At Microsoft, senior code reviewers are often paired with apprentices to help pass on code review wisdom.[27]

After matching the reviewer(s) to the project, the next step is to prioritize the code that should be reviewed and criteria that should be used to review it. In "A Process for Performing Security Code Reviews," Microsoft software security expert Michael Howard specifies the following heuristics to determine code review priority:

- **Old code**—Newer code may have fewer security vulnerabilities because it often reflects a better understanding of software security. Older code, especially legacy code, should be reviewed in depth.

[26]OWASP Code Review Guide V1.1 2008, `www.owasp.org`.
[27]Howard, M., "A Process for Performing Security Code Reviews," *IEEE Security & Privacy*, Vol. 4, No. 4, July/August 2006, pp. 74–79.

- **Code that runs by default**—Code that runs by default is often the target of attack so it should be higher quality, and reviewed earlier and in greater depth than code that doesn't execute by default. Code running by default also increases the application's attack surface.
- **Code that runs in elevated context**—Code that runs with elevated privileges, e.g., Local System in Windows or root in *nix, should be higher quality, and reviewed earlier and in greater depth. Code that runs with elevated privileges also increases the application's attack surface.
- **Anonymously accessible code**—Code that anonymous users can access should be reviewed in greater depth than code that only valid users and administrators can access. Code that is anonymously accessible increases the application's attack surface.
- **Code listening on a globally accessible network interface**—Code that listens by default on the network, especially the Internet, is higher risk, and must be reviewed in depth for security vulnerabilities. Code that listens on the network increases the application's attack surface.
- **Code written in C/C++/assembly language**—Since these languages manage memory directly, they are prone to security vulnerabilities such as buffer overruns.
- **Code with a history of security vulnerabilities**—Code in which previous vulnerabilities were discovered may have additional vulnerabilities unless a concerted effort was made to eliminate them.
- **Code that handles sensitive data**—Code that handles personally identifiable information, financial, or other confidential data should be examined in depth to ensure that data is protected from unintentional disclosure.
- **Complex code**—By virtue of being more difficult to analyze manually and programmatically, complex code may contain undiscovered flaws, some of which may be security vulnerabilities.
- **Code that changes frequently**—Code that changes frequently often contains more security vulnerabilities than code that does not change frequently.

Another prioritization technique is to estimate the code's bug density. One way to estimate this value is the capture/recapture method.[28] The following example of the capture/recapture method and subsequent code review steps are summarized from "A Process for Performing Security Code Reviews":

1. A first team (Team A) of two or three people reviews some code for security vulnerabilities (Bugs A).
2. A second team (Team B) of two or three people reviews the same code, also looking for security vulnerabilities (Bugs B).
3. Note the number of security vulnerabilities found by both teams (the intersection in set theory) (Bugs AB).

[28]Amstrup S. C., et al., eds., *Handbook of Capture-Recapture Analysis* (Princeton, NJ: Princeton University Press, 2006).

4. Estimate the number of security vulnerabilities in the code using the formula: Bugs A / Estimate = Bugs AB / Bugs B

For example, if Team A finds 10 bugs and Team B finds 15 bugs, and there are 5 bugs in common, the estimate is 30 vulnerabilities in the code. This means that there are many more bugs to find. Although this is a useful metric for the overall quality of the code, Microsoft did not find a correlation between general bug quantity and security bug quantity.

The next step is to review the code, typically involving three steps:

- **Choose the method(s) of review**—Typically, the method of review is either a wholly manual code review, or a review guided by the results of an automated code analysis tool. A line-by-line manual code review of the entire code base is highly labor-intensive, but if the code base is simple and small, a manual code review can produce complete and accurate results. However, when there are many lines of code to review, the reviewer may begin by meticulously checking every line of code. But as fatigue sets in, the reviewer may skip over larger portions of code, so that by the end of the review, the inconsistent and decreasing amount of "code coverage" is inadequate to determine the true nature of the software. Instead of performing a wholly manual review, it may be preferable to use an automated code analysis tool and then manually examine code surrounding specific issues discovered by the tool and critical/high risk areas of the code.

NOTE Code coverage is the degree to which the source code of the program has been inspected.

- **Detect common vulnerability patterns**—The categories of vulnerabilities depend on the application type (such as Web application versus Windows device driver) and programming language (such as Java versus C/C++). Security vulnerabilities often appear identical with other benign software flaws and defects. The characteristics that distinguish them as security vulnerabilities are:
  - They can be exploited in a way that prevents (temporarily or permanently) the software's dependable and trustworthy operation.
  - They are externally accessible to an attacker.
- To search for these types of security vulnerabilities, it is first necessary to know what the attacker controls. For example, if the attacker controls nothing, no security vulnerability is possible. However, if the attacker controls the data, the potential for a security vulnerability increases. Searching for a security vulnerability can be illustrated by a decision graph. For example, Figure 4-2 shows a decision graph for reviewing for buffer overrun vulnerabilities. Good code analysis tools can find some classes of buffer overruns, but not all of them, so manual review is still important because many tools focus on dangerous functions rather than data origin. The first step is to identify all code that copies buffers. Instead of focusing on the function, look for `while()` or `for(;;)` loops or "safe" functions such as `memcpy`, typically used to copy buffers.

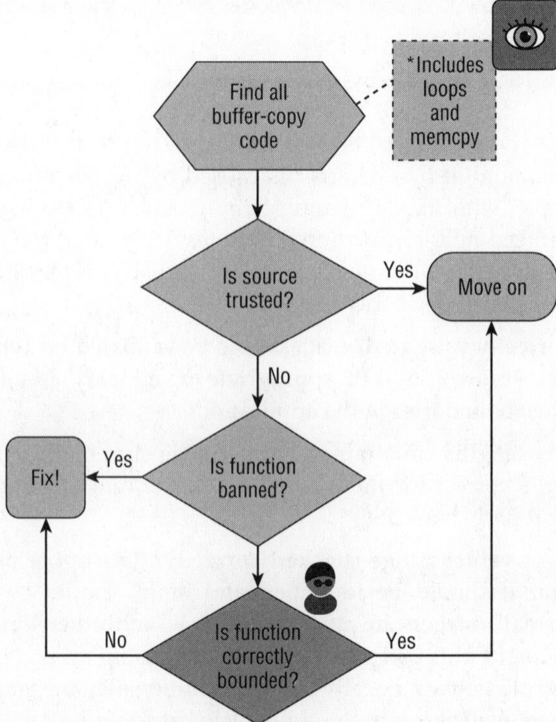

Figure 4-2: Code review for buffer overflows

The last block in Figure 4-2 asks "Is function correctly bounded?" Even if a function that is typically the source of buffer overflows (such as `strcpy`) is replaced by a bounded function (such as `strncpy`), the buffer size can still be set incorrectly. Therefore, even bounded functions should be examined for buffer overflows.

- **Identify high-risk code**—The previous steps, especially with the assistance of automated tools, can find all the "low hanging fruit," i.e., the security vulnerabilities that are easiest to discover. However, high-risk code deserves greater attention. Code that increases the application's attack surface is high-risk code, especially code that is accessible to anonymous users over an untrusted network connection. High-risk code can also be identified through the threat modeling process or through the code prioritization heuristics described earlier. Additionally, if the code analysis tool discovers a number of issues grouped in an area of the code or specific component, the code or component may be higher risk and should be examined in greater depth.

  For each high-risk component under review, determine where data enters, e.g., via `recv()` or `recvfrom()` in C/C++, or `HttpServletRequest` in a Java Web Application, then trace the data from that point forward, questioning the nature of the data and how it is used in the code. For example, the following questions could be considered for C/C++ applications:

- **Are there logic or "off-by-one" errors?** This can happen in a loop when a sequence starts at zero instead of one, or in a comparison mistake when "less than or equal" (<=) is used instead of the correct operator "less than" (<). A common off-by-one error is caused by misuse of bounded functions. For example, with `strncpy` and `strncat`, a common misconception is that the guaranteed null termination will not write beyond the maximum length, when in reality, it will write a terminating null character one byte beyond the maximum length specified.
- **Is data correctly validated?** Data should be validated for type, length, syntax, and business rules. It may be appropriate to validate data more than once as it crosses trust boundaries in the application.
- **Are buffer lengths constrained correctly?** Ensure that the maximum size of the buffer is correct for the operation and the function that operates on the buffer is properly bounded.
- **Are integer values range-checked correctly?** The upper and lower bounds of data input should be identified and limits should be enforced on too large or small integers to prevent overflow and other kinds of errors. The integers should also use strong typing, e.g., using an `unsigned int`, if the integer should not be a negative value. Additionally, integer conversions, both implicit and explicit (cast), should not truncate data.
- **Are pointers validated?** The code should check that the pointer is not NULL before dereferencing the pointer, and check that the pointer refers to an object before reading or writing to the pointer.
- **Can the code become inefficient?** Binary trees and hash tables can degenerate to relatively inefficient linked lists with malformed input from an attacker. Modern hashing techniques can perform just as well as commonplace hash functions while preventing these attacks.[29]
- **Are errors handled correctly?** Ensure that proper exception handling is implemented, e.g., C++ applications, or return and reason codes in C.

Code Analysis

Code analysis typically falls under two categories: static and dynamic. Terminology surrounding code analysis can be confusing, so the following descriptions of code analysis are intended to clarify ambiguities in common terms.

[29] Crosby, S. A., and Wallach, D. S., "Denial of Service via Algorithmic Complexity Attacks," Usenix Security Symposium - Volume 12, August 2003; `www.cs.rice.edu/~scrosby/hash/`.

Static Code Analysis

Static code analysis is the analysis of computer software that is performed without executing the software code. Static code analysis can be wholly manual, semi-automated, or automated:

- **Wholly manual**—When source code is examined manually line by line it is also technically "static analysis" because software code is not executed. However, the technique is typically called manual code review or simply code review.
- **Semi-automated**—An automated tool is run on portions or all of the code, with manual code reviews being conducted on critical subsets of the source code. The tool is used to locate portions of the code that contain known problem patterns as a jumping-off point for the reviewer's further analysis. In this way, the reviewer is guided toward problem areas in the code, but does not rely on the tool alone to locate any additional defects.[30] This approach may also be necessary if the tool does not check for certain types of software weaknesses, is unable to examine particularly complex code, or a greater level of scrutiny is required.
- **Automated**—The tool performs the entire code inspection, providing full coverage of the code base. The reviewer's job consists of interpreting the results of the automated code analysis tool. All automated static analysis tools are generally called static analysis tools. In most cases, static analysis tools inspect the source code. However, some static analysis tools inspect byte code or compiled code. The following terminology is based on the National Institute of Standards and Technology (NIST) Software Assurance Metrics and Tool Evaluation (SAMATE) (`http://samate.nist.gov`) project:
    - **Source code**—Static analysis is performed on the source code of the software. Tools that perform static analysis on source code are also called source code security analyzers.
    - **Byte code**—Static analysis is performed on the byte code (the intermediate code, e.g., Java, .NET). These tools are used like source code security analyzers but are called byte code scanners.
    - **Compiled code**—Static analysis is performed on the binary executable. Tools that perform static analysis on binaries (binary analysis) are called binary code scanners. Binary code scanners can use a combination of techniques to perform static analysis, including decompilation and disassembly.

Whether manual, semi-automated, or fully automated, a simple static analysis entails searching for strings, identifying user input vectors, tracing the flow of data through the application, mapping execution paths, and so on.

A more thorough analysis examines the structure of the source code to reveal the software's intended behaviors, data flows, function calls, and loops-and-branches.

The most resource-intensive form of static analysis is direct code analysis, which focuses on verifying the software's satisfaction of required security-related properties, such as non-interference, non-inference, separability, forward-correctability,

[30]Goertzel, K. M., Winograd, T., et al.

non-deducibility of outputs, and so on. Because of the time and resources required for direct code analysis, it is only practical for examining relatively small portions of code, and will probably be limited to code that implements high-consequence functions and external interfaces.

Dynamic Code Analysis

Dynamic code analysis examines the code as it executes in a running application, with the tester tracing the external interfaces in the source code to the corresponding interactions in the executing code, so that any vulnerabilities or anomalies that arise in the executing interfaces are simultaneously located in the source code, where they can then be fixed.

Unlike static analysis, dynamic analysis enables the tester to exercise the software in ways that expose vulnerabilities introduced by interactions with users and changes in the configuration or behavior of environment components. Because the software isn't fully linked and deployed in its actual target environment, these interactions and their associated inputs and environment conditions are essentially simulated by the testing tool.

Dynamic code analysis tools are also commonly called dynamic analysis tools.

SAMATE

The NIST SAMATE project is dedicated to improving software assurance by developing methods to enable software tool evaluations, measuring the effectiveness of tools and techniques, and identifying gaps in tools and methods. This project supports the U.S. Department of Homeland Security's Software Assurance Tools and R&D Requirements Identification Program, in particular, Part 3, Technology (Tools and Requirements), the identification, enhancement and development of software assurance tools. The scope of the SAMATE project is broad, ranging from operating systems to firewalls, SCADA to Web applications, source code security analyzers to correct-by-construction methods.

Support Tool Evaluation

One of the goals of SAMATE is to establish a methodology for evaluating software assurance tools. This is done by developing tool specifications, test plans, and test sets. The results provide information for tool developers to improve tools, for users to make informed choices about acquiring and using software tools, and for interested parties to understand tool capabilities. The efforts include:

- **Source code security analyzers**—This class of software tools examines source code files for security weaknesses and potential vulnerabilities. A specification is published as NIST Special Publication 500-268, *Source Code Security Analysis Tool Functional Specification*, which identifies a definitive set of requirements against which source code analysis tools can be measured. A draft test plan for source code security analyzers is published as NIST Special Publication 500-270, *Source Code Security Analysis Tool Test Plan*, which provides insight into using the SAMATE Reference Dataset (SRD).

- **Web application vulnerability scanners**—These tools crawl a Web application's pages and search the application for vulnerabilities by simulating attacks on it. A specification is published as NIST Special Publication 500-269, *Software Assurance Tools: Web Application Security Scanner Functional Specification*. A test framework for Web application scanners appeared in a paper entitled "Building a Test Suite for Web Application Scanners," published at the 41st Hawaii International Conference on System Sciences (HICSS), January 2008.
- **Binary code scanners**—Similar to source code security analyzers, this class of tool analyzes a compiled binary application, including libraries, and provides a report of code weakness over the entire application.
- **SAMATE Reference Dataset (SRD)**—A community repository of example code and other artifacts to help end users evaluate tools and developers test their methods. Currently, the SRD consists of over 1,800 test cases that encompass a wide variety of flaws, languages, platforms, and compilers.

Code analysis through the use of static and dynamic analysis tools can make the code review process more efficient, especially when tackling a large code base.

Static Analysis Tools

The majority of static analysis tools fall into one of these three categories according to the NIST SAMATE project:

- Source code security analyzers
- Byte code scanners
- Binary code scanners

Source Code Security Analyzers

Source code security analyzers examine source code to detect and report software weaknesses that can lead to security vulnerabilities. The principal advantage that source code security analyzers have over the other types of static analysis tools is the availability of the source code. The source code contains more information than code that must be reverse engineered from the byte code or binary. Therefore, it is easier to discover software weaknesses that can lead to security vulnerabilities. Additionally, if the source code is available in its original form, it will be easier to fix those security vulnerabilities once found.

Source code security analyzers can detect some anomalies more efficiently than a human reviewer can. For example, the first generation of tools were able to rapidly scan through a large code base for strings such as keywords or unsafe functions—for example, To Do, Fix Me, or `strcpy()`—and bring them to the attention of a developer to correct before the code is checked in to the version control system. Of course, many integrated development environments (IDEs), such as Eclipse or Visual Studio, and command-line utilities, such as `grep`, perform the same function. However, a source code security analyzer often possesses more advanced capabilities such as the following list of capabilities summarized from the Build Security In portal[31]:

- **Examining calls to potentially insecure library functions**—These were first-generation security analyzers that searched for calls to banned or unsafe library functions. A related capability is to examine arguments to library functions since some functions are only dangerous when called with certain types of arguments. There may be several components to this capability:
  - **A database of vulnerable library calls**—Maintenance of a database that contains the latest vulnerable library calls and is updated on a regular basis
  - **The ability to preprocess source code**—So that a C/C++ analyzer can see the same code as the compiler
  - **Lexical analysis**—Breaks a program into tokens prior to parsing, necessary to distinguish variables from functions and to identify function arguments
- **Detecting bounds-checking errors and scalar type confusion**—A number of vulnerabilities occur where scalar assignments transparently change the value being assigned. Examples include:
  - **Integer overflow**—An integer variable overflows and becomes negative.
  - **Integer truncation**—An integer value is truncated while being cast to a data type with fewer digits.
  - **Unsigned underflow**—An unsigned integer value underflows and becomes large.
- **Detecting type confusion among references or pointers**—C and C++ do not automatically provide runtime protection for type confusion with references or pointers.
- **Detecting memory allocation errors**—Vulnerabilities involving heap corruption can arise if an attacker is able to overwrite information used to maintain the heap. This can happen in a number of circumstances:
  - A buffer overflow in an allocated chunk of memory
  - A double free, where a chunk of memory is freed twice
  - A write to freed memory
- **Control-flow analysis**—Potential vulnerabilities are introduced when sequences are carried out in the incorrect order, e.g., the mask governing permissions of newly created files must be set explicitly if a new file is created, and integer ranges may have to be checked before being used without any modification taking place between time of check and time of use.
- **Data-flow analysis**—Used primarily to reduce false positives and negatives, e.g., a common example is that many buffer overflows are not exploitable because the attacker cannot control the data that overflows the buffer. *Taint analysis* is

[31]`https://buildsecurityin.us-cert.gov/daisy/bsi/articles/tools/code.html`

a common type of data-flow analysis—a piece of data is "tainted" if it can be influenced by a potential attacker.

- **Pointer-aliasing analysis**—This occurs when two pointers point to the same data. The data that would be found by dereferencing one of the pointers can change even though the source code contains no mention of that pointer.
- **Customizable detection capabilities**—The ability for an end user to write custom detection rules, e.g., custom data flow analyses by specifying new types of taint and source of taint, together with specific rules for how that taint propagates.

CROSS-REFERENCE **An in-depth discussion of the internals and capabilities of static analysis tools is outside the scope of this book. However, a good reference for this topic is *Secure Programming with Static Analysis*, by Brian Chess and Jacob West, published by Addison-Wesley in 2007, ISBN: 9780321424778.**

One of the primary concerns with source code security analyzers and static analysis tools in general is their accuracy. Accuracy is usually measured by the number of false positives (false alarms) and false negatives (vulnerabilities missed). A false positive is a problem detected in the software when no problem actually exists. A large number of false positives can increase the difficulty of finding the real security vulnerabilities in the software. However, for source code security analyzers, designed to detect security flaws more than code quality issues, the security cost of a false negative could be high. For that reason, it is much better to flag false positives than false negatives. In any case, the results of the source code security analyzer can often be tailored to eliminate known false positives.

Often, when relying on these tools to generate evidence to support an assurance case, the reviewer must provide strong evidence that the tool was used correctly and in a way that ensured that the number of false negatives and false positives were minimized, and the maximum number of *true* results was discovered. In particular, it is difficult for testers to rely solely on the information provided by vendors. Since vendors have a financial incentive to ensure that their respective tools have the lowest false positive and false negative rates, it is very difficult for an independent observer to truly judge a tool's false negative rate. Standards and specifications for source code security analysis tools can aid in this regard.

NIST Special Publication (SP) 500-268, *Source Code Security Analysis Tool Functional Specification v1.0,* May 2007, identifies a definitive set of requirements against which source code analysis tools can be measured. NIST SP 500-268 specifies that to meet a minimum capability, a source code security analysis tool or set of tools must be able to accomplish the following tasks[32]:

- Identify all security weaknesses from a base set of weaknesses
- Textually report any weakness that it identifies
- For any identified weakness from the base set of weaknesses, report the class using a semantically equivalent name

[32] www.itl.nist.gov/lab/specpubs/sp500.htm

- Report the location of any weaknesses by providing the directory path, filename, and line number
- Identify weaknesses despite the presence of coding complexities
- Have an acceptably low false positive rate

Optionally the tool should include the following features:

- Produce an XML-formatted report
- Not report a weakness instance that has been suppressed
- Use the Common Weakness Enumeration (CWE) name of the weakness class it reports

NIST SP 500-268 specifies that criteria for selection of the base set of weaknesses include:

- **Found in existing code today**—The weaknesses are found in existing software applications.
- **Recognized by tools today**—Tools today are able to identify these weaknesses in source code and identify their associated filenames and line numbers.
- **Likelihood of exploit is medium to high**—The weakness is fairly easy for a malicious user to recognize and exploit.

Table 4-2 contains the first listed weakness from each of the vulnerability categories of the base set of weaknesses defined in NIST SP 500-268. Version 1.0 of NIST SP 500-268 only addresses weaknesses in Java and C/C++:

To locate and identify the source code weaknesses identified in Table 4-2, a source code security analysis tool must be able to find those weaknesses within the complex coding structure relevant to that weakness. A general list of those structures is provided in Table 4.3. Some of the complexities are language-specific, such as the use of pointers in C/C++. However, most exist in C/C++ and Java.

Byte Code Scanners

Byte code scanners are used just like source code security analyzers, but they detect vulnerabilities in the byte code. For example, the Java language is compiled into a platform-independent byte code format that is executed in the runtime environment (Java Virtual Machine). Much of the information contained in the original Java source code is preserved in the compiled byte code, thus making decompilation possible.

Byte code scanners can be used in cases where the source code is not available for the software, for example, to evaluate the impact a third-party software component will have on the security posture of an application.

Table 4-2: Weaknesses Defined in NIST SP 500-268

VULNERABILITY CATEGORY	NAME	CWE ID	DESCRIPTION	LANGUAGE (S)	RELEVANT COMPLEXITIES
Input Validation	Basic XSS	80	Unfiltered input is passed to a Web application that in turn passes that data back to another client in the form of a malicious script.	C, C++, Java	Taint, scope, address alias level, container, local control flow, loop structure, buffer address type
Range Errors	Stack overflow	121	Input is used in an argument to the creation or copying of blocks of data beyond the fixed memory boundary of a buffer on the stack.	C, C++	All
API Abuse	Heap inspection	244	Using `realloc()` to resize buffers that store sensitive information can leave the sensitive information exposed to attack because it is not removed from memory.	C, C++	Taint, scope, address alias level, container, local control flow, loop structure, buffer address type
Security Features	Hard-coded password	259	Hard-coded data is passed as an argument to a login function.	C, C++, Java	Scope, address alias level, container, local control flow, loop structure, buffer address type

Table 4-2: *(continued)*

VULNERABILITY CATEGORY	NAME	CWE ID	DESCRIPTION	LANGUAGE (S)	RELEVANT COMPLEXITIES
Time and State	Time-of-check Time-of-use race condition	367	Between the time in which a given resource (or its reference) is checked, and the time that resource is used, a change occurs in the resource to invalidate the results of the check.	C, C++, Java	Asynchronous
Code Quality	Memory leak	401	Memory is allocated, but is not released after it has been used.	C, C++	Scope, address alias level, container, local control flow, loop structure
Encapsulation	Leftover debug code	489	Debug code can create unintended entry points in an application.	C, C++, Java	None

Binary Code Scanners

Binary code scanners analyze machine code to model a language-neutral representation of the program's behaviors, control and data flows, call trees, and external function calls. Such a model may then be traversed by an automated vulnerability scanner in order to locate vulnerabilities caused by common coding errors and simple back doors. A source code emitter can use the model to generate a human-readable source code representation of the program's behavior, enabling manual code review for design-level security weaknesses and subtle back doors that cannot be found by automated scanners.

NOTE Veracode (`www.veracode.com`) uses binary code scanning in on-demand application security testing.

Disassembly and decompilation can also be used to search for software weaknesses in code that result in security vulnerabilities.

Table 4-3: Coding Structures

COMPLEXITY	DESCRIPTION	ENUMERATION
Address alias level	Level of "indirection" of buffer alias using variable(s) containing the address	1 or 2
Array address complexity	Level of complexity of the address value of an array buffer	Constant, variable, linear expression, nonlinear expression, function return value, array content value
Array index complexity	Level of complexity of the index value of an array buffer using variable assignment	Constant, variable, linear expression, nonlinear expression, function return value, array content value
Array length/limit complexity	Level of complexity of the index of an array buffer's length or limit value	Constant, variable, linear expression, nonlinear expression, function return value, array content value
Asynchronous	Asynchronous coding construct	Threads, forked process, signal handler
Buffer address type	Method used to address buffer	Pointer, array index
Container	Containing data structure	Array, struct, union, array of structs, array of unions
Data type	Type of data read or written	Character, integer, floating point, wide character, pointer, unsigned character, unsigned integer
Index alias level	Level of buffer index alias indirection	1 or 2
Local control flow	Type of control flow around weakness	If, switch, cond, goto/label, setjmp, longjmp, function pointer, recursion
Loop complexity	Component of loop that is complex	Initialization, test, increment
Loop iteration	Type of loop iteration/termination	Fixed, indefinite
Loop structure	Type of loop construct in which weakness is embedded	Standard for, standard do while, standard while, non standard for, non standard do while, non standard while

Table 4-3: *(continued)*

COMPLEXITY	DESCRIPTION	ENUMERATION
Memory access	Type of memory access related to weakness	Read, write
Memory location	Type of memory location related to weakness	Heap, stack, data region, BSS, shared memory
Scope	Scope of control flow related to weakness	Local, within-file/inter-procedural, within-file/global, inter-file/inter-procedural, inter-file/global, inter-class
Taint	Type of tainting to input data	Argc/argv, environment variables, file or stdin, socket, process environment

Disassemblers

In disassembly, the binary code is reverse engineered to assembler code. The disadvantage of disassembly is that the resulting assembler code can only be meaningfully analyzed by an expert who thoroughly understands that particular assembler language and is skilled in detecting security-relevant constructs within assembler code.

Decompilers

In decompilation, the binary code is reverse engineered all the way back to source code, which can then be subjected to the same security code review techniques as original source code. However, decompilation is technically problematic because the quality of the source code generated through decompilation is often very poor. Such code is rarely as navigable or comprehensible as the original source code, and may not accurately reflect the original source code. This is particularly true when the binary has been obfuscated or an optimizing compiler has been used to produce the binary. Such measures, in fact, may make it impossible to generate meaningful source code. In any case, the analysis of decompiled source code will always be significantly more difficult and time consuming than review of original source code.

For this reason, decompilation for security analysis makes sense only for the most critical of high-consequence components.

Reverse engineering may also be legally prohibited. For example, vendor license agreements typically prohibit reverse engineering to source code and assembler form, and software vendors have repeatedly cited the Digital Millennium Copyright Act (DMCA) of 1999 to reinforce such prohibitions. Vendors take this measure even though the DMCA explicitly exempts reverse engineering as well as encryption research (which involves intentional breaking of encryption applied to the software being reverse engineered) from its prohibitions against copy-protection circumvention.[33]

NOTE **The IDA Pro disassembler and debugger (`www.hex-rays.com/idapro`) is an advanced tool for code analysis, vulnerability research, and software reverse engineering.**

Dynamic Analysis Tools

Dynamic analysis tools analyze a running application for potential security vulnerabilities and can be used to complement static analysis tools in the software life cycle. They operate by generating runtime vulnerability scenarios through the following functions summarized from NIST SAMATE[34]:

- Perform file corruption
- Resource fault injection
- Network fault injection
- System fault injection
- User interface fault injection
- Design attacks
- Implementation attacks

Dynamic analysis tools typically analyze the software application from the inside or from the outside.

An example of a tool that analyzes code externally is a Web application vulnerability scanner. A Web application vulnerability scanner is designed to automatically scan Web applications for potential vulnerabilities.[35]

Web application scanning tools actively attack an application, usually over HTTP or HTTPS, based on numerous known vulnerabilities and attack patterns in a very short period of time. They are very effective against COTS applications where the vulnerabilities are known in advance and "canned" tests can be written to check for the vulnerability. They also have the capability to perform Web application–specific checks, such as field manipulation, SQL injection, and cookie poisoning, which allows a reviewer to discover new vulnerabilities that are not based on a vulnerability signature. A number of these tools are also interactive and customizable, allowing the operator to tailor the attacks, for example, modify data in requests and responses, repeat specific attacks, and create scripting language macros to automate actions.

An example of a tool that analyzes code inside an application is a dynamic program analysis tool. These tools are typically used for performance analysis in unmanaged languages (for example, C), such as memory debugging, memory leak detection, profiling, and tracing.

[33] Goertzel, K. M., Winograd, T., et al.

[34] `http://samate.nist.gov/index.php/Dynamic_Analysis_Tools.html`

[35] `http://samate.nist.gov/index.php/Web_Application_Vulnerability_Scanners.html`

They typically function by executing programs built from that software system on a real or virtual processor. For dynamic program analysis to be effective, the target program must be executed with sufficient test inputs to produce interesting behavior. Software testing techniques such as code coverage are also employed to ensure that all paths of execution in the program have been exercised.[36]

Other dynamic analysis tools are security-focused. For example, the Program Trace Analyzer (PTA) by Fortify Software (`www.fortify.com`) integrates into .NET and JEE application builds to detect software weaknesses while software testing, such as security testing or functional testing in QA, is being conducted. PTA does not inject faults into an application; instead it uses attack path tracing to transparently observe an application during manual or automated testing and identify security vulnerabilities. It watches how data flows from entry point to exit point, providing root cause information on the issues, such as cross-site scripting and SQL injection. PTA also reports code-level details about runtime security issues and tracks API categories such as Web inputs, database calls, and environment variables. It also detects runtime issues that may not be seen through the application's Web interface. A significant benefit of PTA is that it reports each issue by filename, code line, and event details. This information can be correlated with a similar issue found in an analysis of the source code to verify that the issue exists in the running application and is not a false positive.

NOTE **Software security testing, including functional testing, is covered in Chapter 5.**

Code Analysis in the SDL

Code analysis tools may be used in different phases of the software life cycle. For example, developers can run a source code security analysis tool before checking code into the version control system at the end of the day. This approach can prevent vulnerabilities from being introduced into the software long before the software enters production.

Code analysis tools such as dynamic analysis tools can be used in quality assurance (QA) to correlate source code analysis results and discover any vulnerability that may have escaped earlier detection.

Code analysis tools can also be run by a software security specialist to aid the development and testing groups in discovering vulnerabilities. This person can act like an independent auditor to ensure that security is ''checked-off'' before moving on to the next phase in the software life cycle. For example, when the development group prepares a Web application for release, the source code must first be reviewed and approved by the security specialist using a tool such as a source code security analyzer. Then when the software is released to QA, the security specialist can test the running application using a dynamic analysis tool. Next, when the tool is deployed to staging (a replica of the production environment), the security analyst can test the security

[36] `http://en.wikipedia.org/wiki/Dynamic_program_analysis`

posture again with a Web application vulnerability scanner. Finally, the application can be released to production.

NOTE **Protection mechanisms for a production application are discussed in Chapter 7.**

Anti-tampering Techniques

One of the security requirements common to all software is to provide a measure of tamper resistance. Software code—source, runtime-interpretable, executable—should be protected from unauthorized execution, tampering, corruption, destruction, and deletion.[37]

Dr. Mikhail J. Atallah, Eric D. Bryant, and Dr. Martin R. Stytz write in ''A Survey of Anti-Tamper Technologies'' in the Journal of Defense Software Engineering that ''The primary objective of anti-tamper (AT) techniques is to protect critical program information by preventing unauthorized modification and use of software.''[38]

The authors proceed to describe the goals of an attacker in conducting unauthorized modification and misuse of software, and what anti-tampering techniques could be implemented to defend against those attacks. This information is summarized in the following paragraphs.

The goals of an attacker vary but typically include one of the following:

- **Gaining unauthorized access**—The attacker's goal is to disable software features that enforce security policy in areas such as access, usage, and dissemination. This is often referred to as *software cracking*. The intent of the software cracker who wants to conduct software piracy is to make and distribute illegal copies whose copy protection or usage control mechanisms have been disabled. A concern specific to classified environments is the protection of classified data. If the cracked software provides access to classified data, then the attacker's real goal may not be the software itself, but the data that is accessible through the software. The attacker can aim at modifying or unlocking specific functionality in the software. A demo, trial, or export version of software is often ''crippled''—that is, deliberately degraded by disabling features to prevent the distribution of fully functional software. An attacker seeks to make the software fully functional by re-enabling the missing features.
- **Reverse engineering**—The attacker's goal is to understand enough about the software to steal key routines, to gain access to proprietary intellectual property, or to carry out *code-lifting*, which consists of reusing a critical part of the code (without necessarily understanding how the internals of the code works) in some other software. Good programming practices, e.g., well-documented code, facilitate software engineering but can simultaneously make it easier to reverse engineer the software. Reverse engineering can allow a competitor (or adversary) to

[37]Goertzel, K. M., Winograd, T., et al.

[38]`www.stsc.hill.af.mil/crosstalk/2004/11/0411Atallah.html`

diminish the competitive advantage held by the original developer by narrowing the technology gap through insights gleaned from examining the software.

- **Violating code integrity**—The attacker's goal is to inject malicious code (*malware*) into the software; inject code that is not malicious but enhances functionality or creates unintended functionality; or otherwise subvert the software so that it performs new, hidden, and unauthorized functions. AT technology is similar to antivirus protection in that it impedes malware infection of an AT-protected executable. However, AT technology differs from virus protection in that the AT technology's goal is not only to protect the client's software from unauthorized modification by malevolent outsiders (infection by malware written by others), but also to protect the software from modification by an authorized client. In many situations, it is important that only authorized applications execute (e.g., in a taximeter or odometer), using only authorized functionality, and that only valid data is used.

AT technology should enforce the policy of the software publisher about the proper use of the software, even as the software is running in a potentially hostile environment where the user owns the processor and is intent on violating those policies.

AT techniques include hardware- and software-based protections.

Hardware-Based Protection

One type of hardware-based protection is trusted platform modules (TPMs). Similar in intent to virtual machines (VMs) and sandboxes, TPMs use hardware to enforce VM-like isolation of processes, in terms of their interactions with other processes and their access to data and resources. TPMs can provide public/private-key Rivest-Shamir-Adleman (RSA) based encryption and decryption along with a tamperproof on-chip memory for storing keys and passwords. In addition to the commercial TPMs available, the U.S. DoD Anti-Tamper/Software Protection Initiative is working to produce trustworthy, tamperproof hardware modules for hosting high-consequence software.

The most common hardware-based protection is a trusted, tamper-resistant processor. Tamper-resistant processors provide software license enforcement and intellectual property protection by deterring reverse engineering and illegal copying of software hosted on those processors. Tamper-resistant processors also deter unauthorized modification of that software, and thus provide a lower-assurance alternative to TPMs for protecting the integrity of trusted software.

During normal operation, the trusted processor checks and verifies every piece of hardware and software that requests to be run on a computer during the boot-up process. The processor is designed to guarantee integrity by checking every entity when the machine boots up, and every entity that will be run or used on that machine after it boots up. The hardware can store all of the keys necessary to verify digital signatures, decrypt licenses, decrypt software before running it, and encrypt messages for any online protocols it may need to run—for example, for updates with another trusted remote entity, such as the software publisher.

If software is downloaded onto the computer, it is stored encrypted on the hard drive and is decrypted and executed by the hardware, which also encrypts and decrypts data it sends and receives to random access memory. The same software or media could be encrypted in a different way for each trusted processor that would execute it because each processor has a unique decryption key. This aids in preventing piracy because the disseminated software is tied to the processor itself.

Another hardware-based protection involves the use of a smart card, physically secure token, or hardware dongle. Typically, the token needs to be present for the software to run, to have certain functionality, for access to a media file, and so on. Defeating this type of protection usually means circumventing the requirement for the hardware rather than duplicating the hardware. The difficulty of the circumvention depends on the role that the hardware-based protection plays in the protection. A device that outputs a serial number is vulnerable to a *replay attack*, where the serial number is replayed to the software, without the presence of the hardware device. On the other hand, a smart card that uses a challenge-response protocol (authenticating with different information every use) prevents the replay attack but is still vulnerable, for example, to modification of the software interacting with the smart card. A device that can be more difficult to defeat is a hardware device such as a dongle that plugs into the computer through the USB port, and decrypts content or provides some essential feature of the application or media file.

Software-Based Protection

Software-based protections include:

- Encryption wrappers
- Code obfuscation
- Software watermarking and fingerprinting
- Guarding

Encryption Wrappers

Encryption wrappers dynamically encrypt and decrypt critical portions (or all) of the software code at runtime. This approach has many advantages:

- It hinders an attacker's ability to statically analyze the software because the software is encrypted at rest.
- The attacker is then forced to perform more sophisticated types of dynamic attacks, which can significantly increase the amount of time needed to defeat the protection.
- At no time during execution is the entire software image in the clear; code decrypts just before it executes, leaving other parts of the application encrypted. Therefore, no single snapshot of memory can expose the whole decrypted application.
- It uses lightweight encryption to minimize the computational cost of executing the protected software. The encryption can be combined with compression (by compressing before encryption), resulting in a smaller footprint for the software (less storage space). The addition of compression also makes the encryption more difficult to defeat by cryptanalysis.

Disadvantages include:

- The attacker can expose the software by taking many snapshots of the decrypted application (e.g., through memory dumps), compare them, and piece them together to create the unencrypted image of the software.
- The attacker can attempt to discover the various decryption keys that are present in the software. To delay the attacker, defensive mechanisms can be implemented in the software to deprive the attacker of using runtime attack tools, such as an anti-debugger or anti-memory dump. The defensive mechanisms can make it more difficult for the attacker to run and analyze the program in a synthetic (virtual machine) environment. However, a determined attacker can typically defeat these protections through the use of virtual machines that perform faithful emulation of the PC, including rarely used instructions, cache behavior, etc.
- The software does not perform as well due to the performance penalty caused by the decryption overhead.

Code Obfuscation

Code obfuscation consists of transforming code so it becomes less intelligible to a human, thus making it harder to reverse engineer (as described in the ''Build Environment'' section in this chapter) and resistant to tampering. For example, byte code obfuscation is designed to help protect Java byte code from decompilation. Preventing byte code decompilation is a countermeasure against both disclosure and tampering (i.e., confidentiality and integrity issues).

In software that has specific areas where policy checks are made, these areas will be harder to identify and disable after the software has been obfuscated. Code obfuscation should:

- Not alter the software's functionality
- Only have a small impact on code performance (some obfuscation tools actually increase the performance of the code)
- Only have a small impact on the storage space used at rest and at runtime
- Be resilient to attack

The obfuscating transformations need to be resilient against tools designed to reverse the transformations, such as obfuscation-aware decompilers, and should be resilient to statistical analysis of the decompiled code.

Some general types of obfuscation transformations include:

- **Layout obfuscation**—Modifies the physical appearance of the code, e.g., replacing important variables with random strings, removing all formatting, etc.
- **Data obfuscation**—Obscures the data structures used within the application, e.g., the representation and the methods of using that data, independent data merging, splitting up data that is dependent.

- **Control obfuscation**—Manipulates the control flow of the application, making it difficult to trace the code execution. This is usually accomplished through merging or splitting various fragments of code, reordering expressions, loops, or blocks, etc. It is similar to creating a spurious application that is entangled with the original application to obscure important control features.
- **Preventive transformations**—Increase the difficulty for a de-obfuscation tool to extract the true application from the obfuscated version. These transformations can be implemented with *opaque predicates*, such as a conditional statement that always evaluates as true, but in a manner that is difficult to measure.

Obfuscation can be done at the source-code level (source-to-source translation) or at the assembly level. Although most obfuscators are source-code level, assembly-level obfuscation most effectively hides the operation of the binary. If the source-code level transformations hide information by creating inefficient code structures, the compiler may optimize them out. If, however, the transformations are left unoptimized by the compiler, it can decrease the performance of the code. Assembly-level obfuscation does not prevent the compiler from optimizing, but if the obfuscation is performed incorrectly, the resulting code may be so different than the normal code produced by the compiler that it inadvertently flags the areas of the code where the transformations were applied.

Obfuscation transformations are classified according to several criteria:

- **Potency**—Measures how much more difficult the obfuscated code is to understand for a human being than the original code, i.e., how much obscurity is added to the software.
- **Resilience**—Measures the resistance to attack, e.g., by an automatic de-obfuscator. Resilience takes two factors into account:
  - Programmer/attacker effort required to construct the de-obfuscator
  - Execution time and space required by the de-obfuscator to reduce the potency of the transformation
- **Cost**—How much computational overhead is added to the obfuscated application.

The best obfuscation is achieved by a combination of potency, resilience, and cost. However, like all software-based protections, obfuscation can only delay, not prevent, a determined attacker intent on reverse engineering or tampering with the software.

Software Watermarking and Fingerprinting

The goal of watermarking is to embed information into software in a manner that makes it difficult for an attacker to remove without measurably altering the software's functionality. The information embedded could be purchaser information, an integrity check to detect modification, caption-type information, and so on. Most watermarks are hidden, but visible watermarks also have a purpose as a deterrent, such as preventing piracy. However, in *steganography* (the art of hiding information or a message within a larger message), the existence of the watermark is required to be undetectable.

The watermark is typically required to be robust or resilient (difficult to remove) and is said to be *tamper-resistant*. However, if the watermark is required to show evidence of tampering, through slight alteration or by being destroyed, it is said to be *tamper-evident*. Software watermarks should be static (readable without running the software) or appear only at runtime, but be scarcely perceptible. In either case, reading the watermark should require a secret key, without which the watermark remains invisible.

A specific type of watermarking is *fingerprinting*, which embeds a unique message in each instance of the software for traitor tracing. This impacts the adversary's ability to attack the watermark. Two differently marked copies often make possible a *diff* attack that compares the two differently marked copies and can enable the adversary to create a usable copy that has neither one of the two watermarks. Therefore, in a fingerprinting scheme, it is critical to use techniques that are resilient against this type of comparison attack.

Watermarks can also be used for proof of software authorship or ownership. This type of watermark contains information about the copyright owner as well as the entity that is licensed to use the software, allowing the item to be traced back to the entity if the item were to be illegally disseminated to others. It is especially important that these watermarks be resilient to attack since violating the security of the watermark can enable the attacker to frame an innocent victim. Other uses of watermarks include fingerprinting for identifying the source of illegal information/software dissemination, proof of authenticity, tamper-resistant copyright protection, and captioning to provide information about the software.

Watermarks can demonstrate authorized possession and prove that software has been pirated, but they don't prevent reverse engineering or unauthorized execution. Therefore, a combination of software-based techniques is recommended to provide adequate anti-tampering protection.

Guarding

A guard is code that is injected into an application as an anti-tampering technique. The guard does not affect the basic functionality of the running application unless tampering is detected. Tampering with the application triggers a guard to take action that deviates from normal application behavior.

Guards perform tasks such as comparing a checksum of a code fragment to its expected value and repairing code that may have been maliciously damaged.

The preferred use of the guarding approach consists of injecting a large number of guards into the code to be protected, so that they mutually protect each other as well as the injected application. Guards can also be used in combination with hardware-based anti-tampering techniques to restrict the execution of the application to an authorized environment.

Some of the parameters that affect the strength of the resulting guard protection are:

- Number, type, and stealth of guards
- The protection topology (who protects whom)

- Where the guards are injected in the original code
- How the guards interact with the code

Guards must be installed every time the software is updated, so the mechanism for installing the guards is automated using high-level scripts that specify the protection guidelines and parameters. The installation of guards can be thought of as a compiler flag option for anti-tampering that results in code that is guarded and tamper-resistant.

A multitude of guards cooperatively enforce the code's integrity as well as protect each other against tampering. This is robust self-protection because the defense does not rely on a single point of attack that can be located or compromised.

The guard's response when it detects tampering is flexible and can range from a mild response to the disruption of execution through injection of runtime errors (crashes or even subtle errors in the answers computed). The reaction chosen depends on the software publisher's business model, security policy, and threat environment. Generally, it is better for a guard's reaction to be delayed rather than to occur immediately upon detection; this delay increases the difficulty (and therefore the time) for an attacker to trace the software's defense mechanism back to its guarded protection.

Interface Coding

Interfaces are a software abstraction for separating the methods of external communication between entities from the internal operation of the entities.

The following benefits of software interfaces are summarized from "Enhancing the Development Life Cycle to Produce Secure Software"[39].

Software Interfaces:

- Provide a programmatic means of communication between components that are written in different programming languages
- Prevent direct communication between components by requiring the components to indirectly communicate from interface to interface
- Allow the implementation of a component to be modified without affecting the specification of the interface
- Hide the implementation details of the component
- Control access to a component or a service

Examples of software interfaces include remote procedure calls, internal application programming interfaces (APIs), and external APIs. Internal interfaces exist between the software system's own components, modules, and processes. External interfaces exist between software and external entities including those in the execution environment, peer software that provides services to or receives services from the software system, and human and software-agent users.

One key principle of interface design is to prohibit access to all resources by default, restrict access to well-defined and documented entry points, and require

[39]Goertzel, K. M., Winograd, T., et al.

proper authentication for access. This principle translates into best practices for secure software integration, where software components are integrated with the following considerations in mind:

- Ensuring that all programmatic interfaces and procedure calls are inherently secure or that security mechanisms are added to secure them
- Minimizing the exposure to external access of high-risk and known-vulnerable components

Software components can also interface with other components or services whose security properties are uncertain or questionable. Third-party interfaces should be examined, taking into consideration trust relationships, and implementing additional protection mechanisms when necessary. For example, the JavaScript implementation in Firefox 2.0.0.6 allowed calling applications to read all variables set by existing plug-ins. Firefox enumerated all variables and registered objects that were present inside JavaScript files and allowed the calling of certain functions. This could lead to a disclosure of sensitive information, such as browsing history and passwords, depending on the plug-ins installed or a denial-of-service attack depending on which functions were called.

In this case, the JavaScript developers didn't think to have a separate sandbox for each visited Web site. In his book *Security Engineering*, Ross Anderson states that "the most common API failure mode is transactions that are secure in isolation become insecure in combination, whether because of application syntax, feature interaction, slow information leakage, or concurrency problems."[40]

NOTE The Java Open Review Project (`https://opensource.fortify.com`) identifies and reports bugs and security vulnerabilities in widely used Java open source software (third-party APIs).

Techniques such as *programming by contract* can assist with the proper coding of an interface. It prescribes that software designers should define formal, precise, and verifiable interface specifications for software components based upon the theory of abstract data types and the metaphor of a business contract. At the coding level, the contract for each method will contain the following pieces of information, as summarized from Wikipedia[41]:

- Acceptable and unacceptable input values or types, and their meanings
- Return values or types, and their meanings
- Error and exception conditions values or types, that can occur, and their meanings
- Side effects
- Preconditions, which subclasses may weaken (but not strengthen)
- Postconditions, which subclasses may strengthen (but not weaken)

[40] Anderson, R., *Security Engineering: A Guide to Building Dependable Distributed Systems*, 2nd ed. (Indianapolis, IN: Wiley Publishing, Inc., 2008).
[41] `http://en.wikipedia.org/wiki/Design_by_contract`

The contract conditions should never be violated in code execution.

When developing an application, it is often better to use a trusted API rather than build one from scratch. For example, the OWASP Enterprise Security API (ESAPI) (`www.owasp.org/index.php/ESAPI`) is a collection of classes that encapsulate the key security operations most applications need, and is designed to retrofit into existing applications or provide a foundation for new development.

Summary

The overall goal of secure software coding and implementation is to build software with a higher level of security and quality assurance. This chapter explored software assurance activities that must be followed in order to attain this goal. These activities include understanding common software weaknesses that lead to security vulnerabilities, following secure coding standards and practices, and performing code review.

Assessment Questions

1. Programmatic security controls access by:
   A. Calling functions to determine authorizations
   B. Delegating security decisions to the Web application container
   C. Defining the security constraints in the deployment descriptor
   D. Reading parameters defined in an external configuration file
2. Which of the following serves as a common language for describing software security weaknesses in architecture, design, or code?
   A. OWASP Top 10
   B. CWE/SANS Top 25
   C. OWASP
   D. CWE
3. Which of the following is a list that educates programmers on how to eliminate the most common mistakes in all types of software?
   A. OWASP Top 10
   B. CWE/SANS Top 25
   C. OWASP
   D. CWE
4. Which of the following is a list of the most common Web application security vulnerabilities?
   A. OWASP Top 10
   B. CWE/SANS Top 25

C. OWASP

D. CWE

5. Which of the following is an organization that promotes Web application security?

   A. OWASP Top 10

   B. CWE/SANS Top 25

   C. OWASP

   D. CWE

6. Which kind of vulnerability may result when data originates from a user and is sent to an interpreter as part of a command or query?

   A. Malicious file execution

   B. Injection flaw

   C. Insecure direct object reference

   D. Cross-site request forgery

7. Which kind of vulnerability occurs when an attacker forces a logged-on victim's browser to send a request to a vulnerable Web application?

   A. Malicious file execution

   B. Injection flaw

   C. Insecure direct object reference

   D. Cross-site request forgery

8. Which kind of vulnerability occurs when an application directly uses or concatenates potentially hostile input with file or stream functions?

   A. Malicious file execution

   B. Injection flaw

   C. Insecure direct object reference

   D. Cross-site request forgery

9. Which kind of vulnerability may occur when a developer refers to an internal implementation construct?

   A. Malicious file execution

   B. Injection flaw

   C. Insecure direct object reference

   D. Cross-site request forgery

10. Which kind of vulnerability may occur when an application takes data that originated from a user and sends it to a Web browser without first validating that content?

    A. Cross-site scripting

    B. Information leakage

    C. Failure to restrict URL access

    D. Insecure cryptographic storage

11. Which kind of vulnerability occurs when applications fail to encrypt sensitive data?
    A. Cross-site scripting
    B. Information leakage
    C. Failure to restrict URL access
    D. Insecure cryptographic storage
12. Which kind of vulnerability may occur when an application only protects sensitive functionality by preventing the display of links to unauthorized users?
    A. Cross-site scripting
    B. Information leakage
    C. Failure to restrict URL access
    D. Insecure cryptographic storage
13. Which kind of vulnerability occurs if an application unintentionally discloses information about its configuration?
    A. Cross-site scripting
    B. Information leakage
    C. Failure to restrict URL access
    D. Insecure cryptographic storage
14. Which type of attack involves taking over control of the virtual machine monitor (VMM) in order to take over the host computer?
    A. Virtualization
    B. Hyperjacking
    C. Hijacking
    D. Man-in-the-middle
15. Which type of attack exploits CPU virtualization extensions?
    A. Memory injection
    B. Blue Pill
    C. Red Pill
    D. SubVirt
16. Which of the following detects software-based hypervisors?
    A. Memory injection
    B. Blue Pill
    C. Red Pill
    D. SubVirt
17. Which of the following is an attack that exploits known security flaws to install a hypervisor in Windows or Linux?
    A. Memory injection
    B. Blue Pill

C. Red Pill

D. SubVirt

18. Which type of attack involves monitoring the physical interaction between a system and its environment?

    A. Passive

    B. Active

    C. Side-channel

    D. Cryptanalysis

19. Which type of side-channel attack exerts behavior on a system such that an observer would notice a difference in the operation?

    A. Passive

    B. Active

    C. Side-channel

    D. Cryptanalysis

20. In which type of side-channel attack is information gained about the system without interfering with its operation?

    A. Passive

    B. Active

    C. Side-channel

    D. Cryptanalysis

21. Invasive attack of a cryptographic security module involves:

    A. Decompiling to understand the implementation

    B. De-packaging to get access to the internal components

    C. Access to the device but no damage to the passivation layer

    D. Close observation or manipulation of the device's operation

22. Non-invasive attack of a cryptographic security module involves:

    A. Decompiling to understand the implementation

    B. De-packaging to get access to the internal components

    C. Access to the device but no damage to the passivation layer

    D. Close observation or manipulation of the device's operation

23. Semi-invasive attack of a cryptographic security module involves:

    A. Decompiling to understand the implementation

    B. De-packaging to get access to the internal components

    C. Access to the device but no damage to the passivation layer

    D. Close observation or manipulation of the device's operation

24. A countermeasure to a timing attack involves:

    A. Carefully measuring the time it takes to carry out cryptographic operations

B. Making the operational parameters independent of the input data

C. Protecting public-key algorithms by using checksums and execution randomizations

D. Using an internal power source and randomized register renaming

25. A countermeasure to a fault attack involves:

A. Carefully measuring the time it takes to carry out cryptographic operations

B. Making the operational parameters independent of the input data

C. Protecting public-key algorithms by using checksums and execution randomizations

D. Using an internal power source and randomized register renaming

26. A countermeasure to a power analysis attack involves:

A. Carefully measuring the time it takes to carry out cryptographic operations

B. Making the operational parameters independent of the input data

C. Protecting public-key algorithms by using checksums and execution randomizations

D. Using an internal power source and randomized register renaming

27. A countermeasure to an electromagnetic attack involves:

A. Reducing signal strength and signal information

B. Shielding the CRT to protect against leakage

C. Using application-specific algorithm masking

D. Physically protecting the memory

Answer: A

The correct option is A.

28. A countermeasure to a visible light attack involves:

A. Reducing signal strength and signal information

B. Shielding the CRT to protect against leakage

C. Using application-specific algorithm masking

D. Physically protecting the memory

29. A countermeasure to a cache-based attack involves:

A. Reducing signal strength and signal information

B. Shielding the CRT to protect against leakage

C. Using application-specific algorithm masking

D. Physically protecting the memory

30. A countermeasure to a cold boot attack involves:

A. Reducing signal strength and signal information

B. Shielding the CRT to protect against leakage

C. Using application-specific algorithm masking

D. Physically protecting the memory

31. A countermeasure to protect an embedded system is:

    A. Reducing signal strength and signal information

    B. Shielding the CRT to protect against leakage

    C. Using application-specific algorithm masking

    D. Strengthening the physical packaging

32. Software that avoids ambiguities and hidden assumptions relates best to what secure design principle?

    A. Keep code simple and small

    B. Use a consistent coding style

    C. Use encapsulation cautiously

    D. Allocate memory and other resources carefully

33. Proper indentation and spacing contribute to what secure design principle?

    A. Keep code simple and small

    B. Use a consistent coding style

    C. Use encapsulation cautiously

    D. Allocate memory and other resources carefully

34. Preventing the leakage of security information contributes to what secure design principle?

    A. Keep code simple and small

    B. Use a consistent coding style

    C. Use encapsulation cautiously

    D. Allocate memory and other resources carefully

35. The type of mechanism that manages events that interrupt the normal flow of software is:

    A. Flow control

    B. Event handling

    C. Interrupt handling

    D. Exception handling

36. The best or highest level of exception-safe software is:

    A. Basic exception safety

    B. Strong exception safety

    C. Failure transparency

    D. No-leak guarantee

37. The worst or lowest level of exception-safe software is:

    A. No guarantee

    B. Strong exception safety

C. Failure transparency

D. No-leak guarantee

38. An effective exception handling practice for detecting abnormal behavior is:

A. Event monitors

B. Anomaly awareness

C. Core dump prevention

D. Security error and failure handling

39. Which of the following does "secure" configuration management provide?

A. Strong authentication of SDLC participants

B. Version control for SDLC artifacts

C. Change management for SDLC artifacts

D. Capability to roll back changes

40. Which of the following categories of tools addresses taint analysis?

A. Compiler security checking and enforcement

B. Safe software libraries

C. Runtime error checking and safety enforcement

D. Code obfuscation

41. Which of the following categories of tools addresses security wrappers?

A. Compiler security checking and enforcement

B. Safe software libraries

C. Runtime error checking and safety enforcement

D. Code obfuscation

42. Which of the following categories of tools addresses functions that bound the buffer?

A. Compiler security checking and enforcement

B. Safe software libraries

C. Runtime error checking and safety enforcement

D. Code obfuscation

43. Which of the following categories of tools addresses changes to the control flow?

A. Compiler security checking and enforcement

B. Safe software libraries

C. Runtime error checking and safety enforcement

D. Code obfuscation

44. Which type of code is highest priority in a code review?

A. Code written in managed programming languages

B. Code written in unmanaged programming languages

C. Old code

D. Code that increases the attack surface

45. A wholly manual code review can produce good results if:
    A. The code base is small and simple.
    B. The code base is large and complex.
    C. The code does not contain high-consequence functions.
    D. The code does not handle sensitive data.
46. An automated code review is more efficient if:
    A. The code base is small.
    B. The code base is large.
    C. The code contains high-consequence functions.
    D. The code handles sensitive data.
47. The degree to which the source code of the program has been inspected is:
    A. Code definition
    B. Code specification
    C. Code complexity
    D. Code coverage
48. Software flaws can be considered vulnerabilities if they can be exploited in a way that can prevent the software's reliable information and:
    A. They are outside the control of an attacker.
    B. They are externally accessible to an attacker.
    C. They are extensible by an attacker.
    D. They are part of the attack surface.
49. No security vulnerability is possible if:
    A. The data is outside the control of an attacker.
    B. The data is externally accessible to an attacker.
    C. The data is extensible by an attacker.
    D. The data is part of the attack surface.
50. An off-by-one error is caused by:
    A. An increase in bug density
    B. Improper error handling
    C. Improper data validation
    D. Misuse of bounded functions
51. Examining software code without executing it is:
    A. Tracing
    B. Static analysis
    C. Dynamic analysis
    D. Profiling

52. Examining software code as it executes in a running application is:
    A. Tracing
    B. Static analysis
    C. Dynamic analysis
    D. Profiling
53. A type of static analysis performed on intermediate code is:
    A. Binary analysis
    B. Byte code scanning
    C. Source code analysis
    D. Manual code review
54. A type of static analysis performed on compiled C code is:
    A. Binary analysis
    B. Byte code scanning
    C. Source code analysis
    D. Manual code review
55. A false positive in code analysis refers to a:
    A. False alarm
    B. Vulnerability missed
    C. Code flaw
    D. Software weakness
56. A false negative in code analysis refers to a:
    A. False alarm
    B. Vulnerability missed
    C. Code flaw
    D. Software weakness
57. What can increase the difficulty of finding the real security vulnerabilities in the software?
    A. A large number of false positives
    B. A large number of false negatives
    C. A small number of false positives
    D. A small number of false negatives
58. The primary advantage of a byte code scanner over a source code security analyzer for a managed code programming language is:
    A. It has a lower false positive rate.
    B. It does not require the source code.
    C. It has a lower false negative rate.
    D. It analyzes the software in its execution environment.

59. A dynamic program analysis tool:
    A. Has a lower false positive rate than a static analysis tool
    B. Analyzes the source code of the program
    C. Has a lower false negative rate than a static analysis tool
    D. Analyzes the software in its execution environment
60. Attack path tracing:
    A. Is a static code analysis technique
    B. Is used to transparently observe an application during testing
    C. Has a lower false negative rate that a static analysis tool
    D. Analyzes the source code of the software
61. Code analysis tools are used in the development phase of the software life cycle (SDL) to:
    A. Performance test the application
    B. Transparently observe an application during testing
    C. Quality assurance test the application
    D. Analyze the source code of the software
62. Preventing unauthorized modification of software is known as:
    A. Anti-corruption
    B. Anti-tampering
    C. Anti-modification
    D. Un-deletion
63. The most common hardware-based anti-tampering protection is:
    A. Hardware dongles
    B. Trusted processors
    C. Trusted platform modules (TPMs)
    D. Key fobs
64. Which type of anti-tampering device checks and verifies every piece of hardware and software that requests to be run on a computer during the boot-up process?
    A. Hardware dongles
    B. Trusted processors
    C. Trusted platform modules (TPMs)
    D. Key fobs
65. Which type of anti-tampering device dynamically encrypts and decrypts critical portions (or all) of the software code at runtime?
    A. Encryption wrappers
    B. Code obfuscation
    C. Software watermarking and fingerprinting

D. Guarding

66. Which type of anti-tampering devices embeds information into software?
    A. Encryption wrappers
    B. Code obfuscation
    C. Software watermarking and fingerprinting
    D. Guarding
67. Which type of anti-tampering transforms code so it is more difficult to reverse engineer?
    A. Encryption wrappers
    B. Code obfuscation
    C. Software watermarking and fingerprinting
    D. Guarding
68. Which type of anti-tampering technique injects cooperating protection components into code?
    A. Encryption wrappers
    B. Code obfuscation
    C. Software watermarking and fingerprinting
    D. Guarding
69. A device designed to show that tampering occurred is:
    A. Tamper evident
    B. Tamper resistant
    C. Tamper proof
    D. Steganography
70. A device designed to be resilient to tampering is:
    A. Tamper evident
    B. Tamper resistant
    C. Tamper proof
    D. Steganography
71. Preventing direct communication between components is a characteristic of:
    A. Interfaces
    B. Guards
    C. Watermarking
    D. Encryption wrappers

CHAPTER

5

Secure Software Testing

Chapter 5 explores different types of secure software testing activities. Each activity is based on a formal standard or methodology and adds unique value to the overall secure software testing process. An organization typically selects testing activities based on a number of factors, including secure software requirements and available resources.

Analyses of test results form the basis for assessing risk and means of remediation. Standards and methodologies such as ISO 9126, the SSE-CMM, and the OSSTMM provide additional guidance for secure software evaluation and mitigation. After software has been modified, regression testing provides assurance that the original software system functionality and security characteristics are not negatively affected by the respective changes.

Testing for Security Quality Assurance

Secure software testing has considerations in common with quality assurance testing. For example, the correct version of the software should always be tested. However, secure software testing must also address the measure of the quality of the security properties of the software. For example, software should be tested to ensure that it meets its functional specifications, and does nothing else. Testing that software does nothing else—that is, does not contain any unintended functionality—is a measure of security quality.

There is a lack of commonly agreed-upon definitions for software quality. But it is possible to refer to software quality by its common attributes. One well-known characterization of software quality is the International Organization for Standardization (ISO) 9126 standard. The ISO 9126 standard characterizes software quality with six main attributes and 21 subcharacteristics as shown in Table 5-1.

Table 5-1: The ISO 9126 Software Quality Standards

ATTRIBUTES	SUBCHARACTERISTICS	DEFINITION
Functionality	Suitability	Attributes of software that bear on the presence and appropriateness of a set of functions for specified tasks
	Accurateness	Attributes of software that bear on the provision of right or agreed upon results or effects
	Interoperability	Attributes of software that bear on its ability to interact with specified systems
	Compliance	Attributes of software that make the software adhere to application-related standards or conventions or regulations in laws and similar prescriptions
	Security	Attributes of software that bear on its ability to prevent unauthorized access, whether accidental or deliberate, to programs or data
Reliability	Maturity	Attributes of software that bear on the frequency of failure by faults in the software
	Fault tolerance	Attributes of software that bear on its ability to maintain a specified level of performance in case of software faults or of infringement of its specified interface
	Recoverability	Attributes of software that bear on the capability to re-establish its level of performance and recover the data directly affected in case of a failure and on the time and effort needed for it
Usability	Understandability	Attributes of software that bear on the users' effort for recognizing the logical concept and its applicability
	Learnability	Attributes of software that bear on the users' effort for learning its application
	Operability	Attributes of software that bear on the users' effort for operation and operation control

Table 5-1: *(continued)*

ATTRIBUTES	SUBCHARACTERISTICS	DEFINITION
Efficiency	Time behavior	Attributes of software that bear on response and processing times and on throughput rates in performing its function
	Resource behavior	Attributes of software that bear on the amount of resources used and the duration of such use in performing its function
Maintainability	Analyzability	Attributes of software that bear on the effort needed for diagnosis of deficiencies or causes of failures or for identification of parts to be modified
	Changeability	Attributes of software that bear on the effort needed for modification, fault removal, or environmental change
	Stability	Attributes of software that bear on the risk of unexpected effect of modifications
	Testability	Attributes of software that bear on the effort needed for validating the modified software
Portability	Adaptability	Attributes of software that bear on the opportunity for its adaptation to different specified environments without applying other actions or means than those provided for this purpose for the software considered
	Installability	Attributes of software that bear on the effort needed to install the software in a specified environment
	Conformance	Attributes of software that make the software adhere to standards or conventions relating to portability
	Replaceability	Attributes of software that bear on opportunity and effort using it in the place of specified other software in the environment of that software

Conformance Testing

The National Institute of Standards and Technology (NIST) states that "conformance testing activities assess whether a software product meets the requirements of a particular specification or standard."[1] These standards are typically well-regarded and widely accepted such as those from the International Organization for Standardization (ISO), the Institute of Electrical and Electronics Engineers, Inc. (IEEE), or the American National Standards Institute (ANSI). They reflect a commonly accepted "reference system," whose standards recommendations are sufficiently defined and tested by certifiable test methods. They are used to evaluate whether the software product implements each of the specific requirements of the standard or specification.

An example of a conformance standard is the Common Criteria, ISO 15408. The Common Criteria is a multi-part standard used as the basis for evaluation of security properties of IT products and systems. It establishes a consistent criteria base so that the results of an IT security evaluation can be more meaningful to a wider audience and enables comparability between different products. The latest version of the Common Criteria is Version 3.1, Revision 1, published in September 2006.

The Common Criteria define a Protection Profile (PP), which is an implementation-independent specification of the security requirements and protections of a product that could be built. The Common Criteria terminology for the degree of examination of the product to be tested is the Evaluation Assurance Level (EAL). EALs range from EA1 (functional testing) to EA7 (detailed testing and formal design verification). The Common Criteria Target of Evaluation (TOE) refers to the product to be tested. A Security Target (ST) is a listing of the security claims for a particular IT security product. Also, the Common Criteria describe an intermediate grouping of security requirement components as a package. Functionality in the Common Criteria refers to standard and well-understood functional security requirements for IT systems. These functional requirements are organized around Trusted Computing Base (TCB) entities that include physical and logical controls, startup and recovery, reference mediation, and privileged states.

In the US, product vendors typically use an independent licensed laboratory to conduct the Common Criteria evaluation. Then validation is conducted by a government entity. Typically, validation of EAL levels 1-4 is conducted by the National Information Assurance Partnership (NIAP) and validation of EAL levels 5-7 is conducted by the National Security Agency (NSA).

Common Criteria-certified products can be used as part of an information system that needs to be certified and accredited to lower the residual risk perceived by the organization's Designating Approving Authority (DAA), who is the person that authorizes a system to operate. Chapter 6 discusses the Certification and Accreditation (C&A) process in greater detail.

Conformance testing methodologies have been developed for operating system interfaces, computer graphics, documented interchange formats, computer networks, and programming language processors. Most testing methodologies use test case

[1]Tassey, G., "The Economic Impacts of Inadequate Infrastructure for Software Testing," National Institute of Standards and Technology, Technical Report, 2002.

scenarios (e.g., abstract test suites, test assertions, test cases), which themselves must be tested.

Standardization is an important component of conformance testing. It usually includes developing the functional description and language specification, creating the testing methodology, and "testing" the test case scenarios.

A major benefit of conformance testing is that it facilitates interoperability between various software products by confirming that each software product meets an agreed-upon standard or specification.

One type of conformance testing, protocol-based testing, uses an application's communication protocol as a direct basis for testing the application. This method is useful for Web-based and Internet-based applications. Protocol-based testing is especially important for security testing in Web-based applications, since the easiest way for remote attackers to access such applications is through Web protocols.[2]

Functional Testing

In functional testing, a software application is tested at runtime to determine whether it conforms to its functional requirements. Requirements that state how the application will respond when a specific event occurs are referred to as positive requirements. Typically, a positive requirement is mapped to a specific software artifact meant to implement that requirement. This provides traceability from requirements to implementation and informs the tester of which code artifact to test to validate the expected functionality. An example of a positive requirement is "the application should lock the user account after three failed login attempts." A tester can validate the expected functionality (the lockout) by attempting to log in to the application three times with the same username and incorrect passwords. This type of test can be easily automated with a functional testing tool suite, such as the open source Canoo WebTest, available at `http://webtest.canoo.com`.

Functional testing also includes negative requirements which state the things that software should not do as opposed to what they should do. An example of a negative requirement is "the application should not allow for the stored data to be disclosed." This requirement is more difficult to test because the expected behavior is not implemented in a specific software artifact. Testing this requirement properly would require the tester to anticipate every anomalous input, condition, cause, and effect. Instead, the testing should be driven by risk analysis and threat modeling. This would allow the negative requirement to be documented as a threat scenario and the functionality of the countermeasure as a factor to mitigate a threat. The following example is a summary of this approach from the Open Web Application Security Project (OWASP) Testing Guide (`www.owasp.org/index.php/Category:OWASP_Testing_Project`).

First, the security requirements are documented from a threats and countermeasure perspective:

- Encrypt authentication data in storage and transit to mitigate risk of information disclosure and authentication protocol attacks

[2]Sun, X., Feng, C., Shen, Y., and Lombardi, F., *Protocol Conformance Testing Using Unique Input/Output Sequences* (Hackensack, NJ: World Scientific Publishing Co., 1997).

- Encrypt passwords using nonreversible encryption such as a hashing algorithm and a salt to prevent dictionary attacks
- Lock out accounts after reaching a login failure threshold and enforce password complexity to mitigate risk of brute force password attacks
- Display generic error messages upon validation of credentials to mitigate risk of account harvesting/enumeration
- Mutually authenticate client and server to prevent nonrepudiation and man-in-the-middle (MITM) attacks

Artifacts produced in the threat modeling process, such as threat trees and attack libraries, can then be used to derive negative test scenarios.

A threat tree will assume a root attack (e.g., attack might be able to read other users' messages) and identify different exploits of security controls (e.g., data validation fails because of a SQL injection vulnerability) and necessary countermeasures (e.g., implement data validation and parameterized queries) that could be tested to be effective in mitigating such attacks.

Typically, functional testing is used to test the functionality of implemented features or after the software is feature complete. However, code coverage is limited by the number of available use cases. If a test is not created for a specific use case, a number of execution paths in the software will go untested. Therefore, even if the functionality is validated for all available use cases, that is not a guarantee that the software is free of defects.

Logic Testing

Logic testing is a type of functional testing that involves ensuring that business logic is predicated on the correct assumptions. Business logic is the code that satisfies the business purpose of the software and typically models and automates a "real-life" or "paper" business process such as loan processing, e-commerce, or inventory management. Business logic is comprised of both business rules and workflows:

- Business rules that express business policy (such as channels, location, logistics, prices, and products)
- Workflows based on the ordered tasks of passing document or data from one participant (a person or a software system) to another

Business logic flaws are typically specific to the application being tested and difficult to detect. Automated tools do a poor job of discovering logic flaws because they do not understand the context of the decisions. Therefore, discovering logic flaws is typically a manual process performed by a human tester.

When looking for business logic flaws, the tester begins by considering the rules for the business function being provided by the application. Next, the tester searches for any limits or restrictions on people's behavior. Then the application can be tested to validate that it enforces those rules. A classic example of a business logic flaw is the modification of prices allowed by e-commerce applications on the early Web-based Internet.

Setting the price of a product on an e-commerce site as a negative number could result in funds being credited to an attacker. A countermeasure to this vulnerability is to implement positive validation of the price so that the application allows only positive numbers in a specific numerical range. Of course, the application should never accept and process any data from the client that did not require user input in the first place.

Another example of a logic flaw is the bypass of "multistage login," that is, multiple layers of authentication, in an application such as an online banking application. Some banks use multiple stages of authentication to enhance the security of the online banking application. The concept behind this mechanism is to require the user to prove his identity by presenting multiple pieces of information that only he knows. This prevents the situation where the theft of a single set of credentials, typically username and password, could be used to compromise the bank account.

When an authorized user initially configures the bank account online, he answers a series of questions to set "secrets" that only he knows. After logging in to the banking application with the primary credentials of username and password, the application brings the user to subsequent screens where he is prompted for his secrets, such as "pet's name" or "street you grew up on." A screen may even show a picture to help the user recall the corresponding secret. The authentication mechanism is designed with the intention that the user performs each stage of authentication in order. However, a tester may first map out all the stages and corresponding code related to the authentication mechanism and then attempt to bypass one or more stages. This could result in an access denial or internal server error but may also result in the access failing open.

Performance Testing

In an online report, NIST (`http://vote.nist.gov/vvsg-report.htm`) states that "what distinguishes performance testing from functional testing is the form of the experimental result. A functional test yields a yes or no verdict, while a performance test yields a quantity." Performance testing measures how well the software system executes according to its required response times, throughput, CPU, usage, and other quantified features in operation. The quantity resulting from a test may subsequently be reduced to a yes or no verdict by comparison with a benchmark.

Performance testing is also commonly known by other names and/or associated with other testing activities, such as stress testing, capacity testing, load testing, volume testing, and benchmark testing. These various performance testing activities all have approximately the same goal: "measuring the software product under a real or simulated load."[3]

Typically, performance testing is conducted late in the software life cycle when the software is fully developed. In order to obtain accurate measurements, the software is deployed and tested in an environment that simulates the operational environment. This can be achieved by creating a "staging" environment, essentially a mirror copy of the production infrastructure, and simulating typical operating conditions.

A major benefit of performance testing is that it is typically designed specifically for pushing system limits over a long period of time. This form of testing has

[3]Tassey, G., "The Economic Impacts of Inadequate Infrastructure for Software Testing."

commonly been used to uncover unique failures not discovered during conformance or interoperability tests. In addition, benchmarking is typically used to provide competitive baseline performance comparisons. For instance, these tests are used to characterize performance prior to manufacturing as well as to compare performance characteristics of other software products prior to purchase.

Performance testing procedures provide steps for determining the ability of software to function properly, particularly when near or beyond the boundaries of its specified capabilities or requirements. These boundaries are usually stated in terms of the volume of information used. The specified metrics are usually stated in terms of time to complete an operation. Ideally, performance testing is conducted by running a software element against standard datasets or scenarios, known as reference data.

Performance measures and requirements are quantitative, which means they consist of numbers that can be measured and confirmed by rational experiments. A performance specification consists of a set of specified numbers that can be reduced to measured numbers, often in the form of a probability distribution. The numbers measured for the software product are either less than, more than, or equal to the specified values. If less than, the software product fails; if more than or equal to, the software product passes the tests. Every performance specification is a variation of these simple ideas. Common metrics used in performance testing include:

- **Throughput**—The rate at which the system processes transactions, commonly measured in bytes per second
- **Processing delay**—The time it takes to process those transactions, measured in seconds
- **Load**—The rate at which transactions are submitted to a software product, measured in arriving transactions per second

Stress Testing

Stress testing is a kind of performance testing that involves increasing the load on a software system beyond normal operating capacity and observing the results. Stress testing can be used to ensure that the software remains stable and reliable, and can continue to provide a specific quality of service, although the software is often tested to the point of failure. Extreme operating conditions, such as those associated with resource exhaustion—out of memory or hardware failures—are simulated.

Stress testing can also be used to test the security properties of software because it can induce anomalous behavior. For example, extreme operating conditions may cause an error that is poorly handled by the application causing it to fail insecurely. In a real-world scenario, a DoS attack targeted against a Web application could slow down the execution of the application such that it exposes a race condition, which could subsequently be exploited as a security vulnerability.[4]

[4]Du, W., and Mathur, A. P., "Testing for Software Vulnerability Using Environment Perturbation," Proceedings of the International Conference on Dependable Systems and Networks (DSN 2000), Workshop on Dependability versus Malicious Faults, New York, NY, June 25–28, 2000 (Los Alamitos, CA: IEEE Computer Society Press, 2000), pp. 603–612.

NOTE The Microsoft *Web Application Stress Tool* (`www.microsoft.com`) is a freely available tool that simulates multiple browsers requesting pages from a Web site. It can be used to gather performance and stability information about a Web application. It simulates a large number of requests with a relatively small number of client machines. The goal is to create an environment that is as close to production as possible so that problems can be discovered and eliminated in a Web application prior to deployment.

Security Testing

Security testing should assess the security properties and behaviors of software as it interacts with external entities (human users, environment, other software) and as its own components interact with each other. Security testing should verify that software exhibits the following properties and behaviors, summarized from the "Software Security Assurance State-of-the-Art Report (SOAR)"[5]:

- Its behavior is predictable and secure.
- It exposes no vulnerabilities or weaknesses.
- Its error and exception handling routines enable it to maintain a secure state when confronted by attack patterns or intentional faults.
- It satisfies all of its specified and implicit nonfunctional security requirements.
- It does not violate any specified security constraints.
- As much of its runtime-interpretable source code and byte code as possible has been obscured or obfuscated to deter reverse engineering.

A security test plan should be included in the overall test plan and should define all testing activities, including the following:

- Security test cases or scenarios (based on abuse cases)
- Test data, including attack patterns
- Test oracle (if one is to be used)
- Test tools (white box, black box, static, and dynamic)
- Analyses to be performed to interpret, correlate, and synthesize the results from the various tests and outputs from the various tools

Software security testing techniques can be categorized as white box, gray box, or black box:

- **White box**—Testing from an internal perspective, i.e., with full knowledge of the software internals; the source code, architecture and design documents, and configuration files are available for analysis

[5]Information Assurance Technology Analysis Center (IATAC)/Data and Analysis Center for Software (DACS), "Software Security Assurance State-of-the-Art Report (SOAR)," July 31, 2007.

- **Gray box**—Analyzing the source code for the purpose of designing the test cases, but using black box testing techniques; both the source code and the executable binary are available for analysis
- **Black box**—Testing the software from an external perspective, i.e., with no prior knowledge of the software; only the binary executable or intermediate byte code is available for analysis

An example of a white box testing technique is the static analysis of source code that should be performed iteratively as the software is being written. Chapter 4 discussed the use of source code analysis in the code review process.

Table 5-2 lists other common security testing techniques and how they are typically categorized.

Table 5-2: Common Security Testing Techniques

TESTING TECHNIQUE	CATEGORY
Source code analysis	White box
Property-based	White box
Source code fault injection	White box, Gray box
Dynamic code analysis	Gray box
Binary fault injection	Gray box, Black box
Fuzz testing	Black box
Binary code analysis	Black box
Byte code analysis	Black box
Black box debugging	Black box
Vulnerability scanning	Black box
Penetration testing	Black box

Fault Injection

Fault injection is a technique used to improve code coverage by testing all code paths, especially error handling code paths that may not be exercised during functional testing. In fault injection testing, errors are injected into the software to simulate unintentional user errors and intentional attacks on the software through its environment, and attacks on the environment itself.

Source Code Fault Injection

In source code fault injection, the tester decides when environment faults should be triggered. The tester then "instruments" the source code by non-intrusively inserting changes into the program that reflect the changed environment data that would result from those faults.[6] The instrumented source code is then compiled and executed, and the tester observes the ways in which the executing software's state changes when the instrumented portions of code are executed. This allows the tester to observe the secure and nonsecure state changes in the software resulting from changes in its environment.

The tester can also analyze the ways in which the software's state changes resulting from a fault propagating through the source code. This type of analysis is typically referred to as fault propagation analysis, and involves two techniques of source code fault injection: extended propagation analysis and interface propagation analysis.

To prepare for fault propagation analysis, the tester must generate a fault tree from the software's source code. To perform an extended propagation analysis, the tester injects faults into the fault tree, then traces how each injected fault propagates through the tree. This shows the impact a particular fault will have on the overall behavior of the software.

Interface propagation analysis is focused on the ways in which faults are propagated through the interfaces between the component/module and other application-level and environment-level components. In interface propagation analysis, the tester injects a fault into the data inputs between components, views how the resulting faults propagate, and observes whether any new anomalies result. This type of analysis enables the tester to determine how the failure of one component can affect the failure of a neighboring component, particularly important if a neighboring component is of high consequence.

Source code fault injection is particularly useful in detecting:

- Incorrect use of pointers and arrays
- Use of dangerous calls
- Race conditions

Source code fault injection should be performed iteratively as the software is being written. When new threats (attack types and intrusion techniques) are discovered, the source code can be re-instrumented with faults representative of those new threat types.

Binary Fault Injection

Binary fault injection is a runtime analysis technique whereby an executing application is monitored as faults are injected. By monitoring system call traces, a tester can identify the names of system calls, the parameters to each call, and the call's return code. This allows the tester to discover the names and types of resources being accessed by the calling software, how the resources are being used, and the success or failure of each access attempt. In binary fault analysis, faults are injected into the environment

[6]Goertzel, K. M., Winograd, T., et al., "Enhancing the Development Life Cycle to Produce Secure Software," Version 2.0., Rome, New York: United States Department of Defense Data and Analysis Center for Software, October 2008.

resources that surround the application. Environmental faults provide the tester with a number of benefits:

- They simulate real-world attack scenarios and can be easily automated.
- They simulate environment anomalies without requiring an understanding of how those anomalies actually occur in the real world. This enables fault injection by testers who do not have prior knowledge of the environment whose faults are being simulated.
- The tester can choose when to trigger a particular environmental fault. This avoids the problem of a full environment emulation in which the environment state when the application interacts with it may not be what is expected, or may not have the expected effect on the software's behavior.

It is difficult to predict the complex inputs the software will actually receive in its target environment. Therefore, fault injection scenarios should be designed to give the tester the most complete understanding possible of the security of the behaviors, states, and properties of the software system under all possible operating conditions. Once the application has been deployed to production, the tester can employ penetration testing and vulnerability scanning to provide an additional measure of the application's security posture.

Binary fault injection tools include binary fault injectors and brute force testers. These tools should support the common functionality found in the application. For example, the commercial fault injection tool Holodeck (`www.securityinnovation.com/holodeck/`) is often used to simulate faults in Microsoft operating system applications. Holodeck injects faults for common functionality found in a typical Windows environment such as the following:

- **Network**—Cable disconnected, network not installed, wrong Winsock version, Winsock task limit reached, no ports available, network is down
- **Disk**—Insufficient disk space, cyclic redundancy check (CRC) errors, too many files open, disk is write-protected, no disk in drive
- **Memory**—Insufficient memory, failure to allocate, locked memory

Holodeck also supports the monitoring of an application to watch its interactions with the environment.

Dynamic Code Analysis

Dynamic code analysis examines the code as it executes in a running application, with the tester tracing the external interfaces in the source code to the corresponding interactions in the executing code, so that any vulnerabilities or anomalies that arise in the executing interfaces are simultaneously located in the source code, where they can then be fixed.

Unlike static analysis, dynamic analysis enables the tester to exercise the software in ways that expose vulnerabilities introduced by interactions with users and changes in the configuration or behavior of environment components. Because the software isn't fully linked and deployed in its actual target environment, these interactions and their associated inputs and environment conditions are essentially simulated by the testing tool.

An example of a dynamic code analysis toolset is the open source Valgrind (`www.valgrind.org`). The Valgrind suite includes a memory error detector, two thread error detectors, a cache and branch-prediction profiler, a call-graph generating cache profiler, and a heap profiler.

Property-Based Testing

Property-based testing is a formal analysis technique developed by the University of California at Davis.[7] Property-based testing validates that the software's implemented functionality satisfies its specifications. It does this by examining security-relevant properties revealed by the source code, such as the absence of insecure state changes. Then these security-relevant properties in the code are compared against the software's specification to determine if the security assumptions have been met.

Like direct code analysis, property-based testing requires the full concentration of the tester and is a detail-oriented process. Because it requires the tester to dedicate a significant amount of time to the code, it is often used only to analyze the code that implements high-consequence functions.

Black Box Debugging

Debuggers for low-level programming languages such as C or ASM are software tools that enable the tester to monitor the execution of a program, start and stop a program, set breakpoints, and modify values. Debuggers are typically used to debug an application when the source code or the compiler symbols are available. The source code and compiler symbols allow information—the values of internal variables—to be tracked to discover some aspect of internal program behavior. However, sometimes only the binary is available and the binary was compiled from code with no compiler symbols or debug flags set. This is typical in commercial software, legacy software, and software that implements protective measures, such as code obfuscation, to prevent reverse engineering. In this case, traditional debugging is not possible.

However, if the focus of the debugging effort is on the software's interaction with an external component, then the binary may be all that is needed. Complex relationships are created when functionality comes from an external component, and an application inherits the problems of the external components upon which it has dependencies. If a bug exists in an external component or the documentation describing the components API, it can be difficult to isolate the bug. The tendency may be to think that the bug exists in the application's code when it really exists in the external component. Another problem exists in expecting a discrete set of values to be returned from an external function call. Often, these calls are expected to succeed and the return value is not checked. Observing the data passed between the external component and the application can help track down that problem.

[7]Fink, G., and Bishop, M., "Property-Based Testing: A New Approach to Testing for Assurance," *SIGSOFT Software Engineering Notes* 22, 4 (July 1997): 74–80.

Black box debugging[8] is a technique to monitor behaviors external to the binary component or system while it is executing, and thereby observes the data that passes between that component/system and external entities.

Additionally, by observing how data passes across the software's boundary, the analyst can also determine ways in which externally sourced data might be manipulated to force the software down certain execution paths, or to cause the software to fail. This can reveal errors and failures that originate not in the software itself, but are forced by the external entities with which it interacts, or by an incorrectly implemented API.

Environment

Software should first be tested in a staging (test) environment, separate from development, which duplicates the production (target) environment. Testing in an environment similar to production will help detect any integration or interoperability problems that could arise between the software and integrated components, or between the software and external components/applications.

Integration Testing

Integration testing evaluates the functionality, performance, and reliability of a group of software components or modules. The goal of integration testing is to ensure that the components interact properly. This type of testing is typically performed after each software component has been individually unit tested. Typically, integration testing simulates usage of shared data areas, interprocess communication, and error conditions by passing parameters to the components through their respective or combined interfaces. Common types of integration testing include:

- **Top-down**—Testing begins at the top of the software hierarchy and branches to the next lowest level of components until all components have been tested.
- **Bottom-up**—The base level of components are integrated and then tested followed by the next highest level of components up until the top-level components of the software hierarchy have been exercised.

Security weaknesses and vulnerabilities are also introduced during component assembly and integration. Testing for the causes of weakness and vulnerability can help ensure a more secure environment. The following list summarizes security objectives for integration testing from the paper "Enhancing the Development Life Cycle to Produce Secure Software"[9]:

- Verify that all programmatic interfaces and procedure calls are secure or that security mechanisms (countermeasures) are added to secure them.
- Ensure that external access to high-consequence and known-vulnerable components is minimized.

[8]Whittaker, J. A., and Thompson, H. H., "Black Box Debugging," *Queue* 1, 9 (December/January 2003–2004).

[9]Goertzel, K. M., Winograd, T., et al.

- Verify that trust relationships among components or between components and human users are based on correct assumptions.
- Verify the correct or effective use of environment-level and other extra-component security protections and services.
- Ensure that integrated OSS or COTS components do not contain known security vulnerabilities or embedded malicious logic.

Interoperability Testing

Interoperability testing evaluates whether an application can exchange data (interoperate) with other components or applications. Interoperability testing activities determine the capability of applications to exchange data via a common set of exchange formats, to read and write the same file formats, and to communicate using the same protocols. A major goal of interoperability testing is to detect interoperability problems between software applications before these applications are put into operation. Interoperability testing requires the majority of the application to be completed before testing can occur.

Interoperability testing typically takes one of three approaches:

- **Test all pairs**—This is often conducted by a third-party independent group of testers who possesses the knowledge of the interoperability characteristics across software products and between software vendors.
- **Test some of the combinations**—Testing only part of the combinations and assuming the untested combinations will also interoperate.
- **Test against a reference implementation**—Establish a reference implementation, e.g., using the accepted standard, and test all products against the reference. In a paper on metrology in information technology, researchers in the NIST Information Technology Laboratory state that a typical procedure used to conduct interoperability testing includes "developing a representative set of test transactions in one software product for passage to another software product for processing verification."[10]

One challenge in software component integration is how to build a secure composite system from components which may or may not be individually secure. In a paper by Verizon Communications and the University of Texas,[11] researchers describe a systematic approach for determining interoperability of components from a security perspective and unifying the security features, policies, and implementation mechanisms of components. This is a goal-oriented and model-driven approach to analyzing the security features of components to determine interoperability. Along with this

[10]National Institute of Standards and Technology (NIST), 1997, "Metrology for Information Technology (IT)," `www.nist.gov/itl/lab/nistirs/ir6025.htm`.

[11]Oladimeji, E. A., and Chung, L., "Analyzing Security Interoperability during Component Integration," in *Proceedings of the 5th IEEE/ACIS International Conference on Computer and Information Science and 1st IEEE/ACIS International Workshop on Component-Based Software Engineering, Software Architecture and Reuse* (July 10–12, 2006). ICIS-COMSAR, IEEE Computer Society, Washington, DC, pp. 121–129.

approach, the researchers provide a guideline for integrating the components to fulfill the security goals of the composite system. Following the proposed analysis procedure could lead to discovery of some classes of security interoperability conflicts that help to determine whether or not the components should be used together.

Bug Tracking

A software bug is an error, defect, mistake, vulnerability, failure, or fault in a computer system. Bugs are typically discovered in the source code or the design of the software and often prevent the software from operating as intended. Bug tracking refers to the process of reporting and tracking a software bug during the software life cycle. Bugs are typically submitted to a bug tracking system, which is a software application that is designed to help developers and other stakeholders keep track of the software bugs until they are fixed.

Common bug tracking system functionality includes:

- **Reporting**—The developers, QA team, security analysts and other stakeholders can submit bugs through a graphical front end.
- **Prioritization**—Bugs can be prioritized from low priority to high priority.
- **Assignment**—Bugs can be assigned to the project lead, individual developers, or other stakeholders.
- **Tracking**—Tracking provides the status of a bug from the time it is reported until it is closed.
- **Database**—Bug information is typically stored in a backend database.

Bug tracking functionality can also be part of a generic issue tracking system. These systems typically provide basic bug tracking functionality but are customizable to support software assurance goals and can integrate better with the organization's infrastructure. An example of this type of product is JIRA (`www.atlassian.com/software/jira/`). JIRA ships with a number of predefined issue types, including base task, new feature, improvement, and bug, and allows new types of issues to be defined, such as security vulnerability. It also supports other features such as simple authentication integration with LDAP, role-based access control, an IDE connector (to manage bugs directly within an IDE such as Eclipse), a plug-in library (created by the developer community and third parties), and an open API for further customization.

Regardless of the type of system, issues should be reported centrally using a single process. The report should include the following criteria:

- A unique number within the project to identify the issue
- Description of the issue
- Type of issue if known
- The date submitted
- The due date if known
- The version or release of the software

- The component or tier of the application
- The personnel assigned
- A recommendation to fix the problem if known

The project lead or other stakeholder should have the responsibility of reviewing all submitted issues, determining whether the issue has been identified correctly or is a duplicate of an existing issue, and assigning it to the correct individual.

Progress on each issue should be reported periodically and the issue status should be updated to reflect the progress. Bugs should be prioritized using a risk-based approach. For example, security vulnerabilities that pose a high risk should also be a high priority. If the security vulnerability is in a deployed product, the fix should be coordinated with the security response personnel so that a patch can be made available to the customer when ready.

The type and number of bugs is often used as a gauge of the quality of the software. For example, a high number of high priority bugs can delay the acceptance of the software—that is, the release of the software to the customer.

When a bug is fixed, the solution should be added to a best practices document and shared with all stakeholders, particularly members of the development team. The best practices document can increase the awareness of common problems and solutions specific to the software application, and help prevent future coding mistakes.

Attack Surface Validation

It is not possible to test all code in an application considering the normal constraints of time and resources. However, at a minimum, testing should cover the entry points and exit points of an application that may be accessible to an attacker, commonly referred to as the application's attack surface. Accessibility increases the attack surface. For example, code that is restricted to local access by an administrator has a smaller attack surface than code exposed to remote access by an anonymous user.

The attack surface should be fully tested by exercising all the code paths in an application that are part of the attack surface. The elements of the attack surface can be identified with the use of scanning tools, such as port scanning tools for open ports, and code analysis tools to locate the portions of the code that receive input and send output. It may even be necessary to develop custom tools, for example, to locate entry points and exit points specific to a custom application.

The minimum attack surface is typically defined early in the software life cycle and measured again through the later phases. It is often helpful to formally define and measure the attack surface before testing.

The paper "An Approach to Measuring a System's Attack Surface"[12] formalizes the notion of a system's attack surface and proposes a method to measure the attack surface systematically. The following information is summarized from the paper.

Not all resources are part of a system's attack surface. The attack surface is the subset of the system's resources that an attacker can use to cause damage to the system.

[12]Pratyusa, K. M., Tan, K. M. C., Maxion, R. A., and Wing, J. M., "An Approach to Measuring a System's Attack Surface," *CMU Technical Report*, CMU-CS-07-146, August 2007.

And not all resources contribute equally to the measure of a system's attack surface. A resource's contribution to the attack surface reflects the likelihood of the resource being used in attacks. For example, a method running with root privilege is more likely to be used in attacks than methods running with non-root privileges.

A system's attack surface measurement does not represent code quality. A large attack surface measurement does not imply that a system has many vulnerabilities and few vulnerabilities does not imply a small measurement. Instead, a larger attack surface measurement indicates that an attacker is likely to exploit the vulnerabilities present in the system with less effort and cause more damage to the system. Since a system's code is likely to contain vulnerabilities, it is prudent to choose a system with a smaller attacker surface measurement in order to mitigate security risk.

The measurement of a software system's attack surface can be characterized in terms of three kinds of resources used in attacks on the system: methods, channels, and data.

- **Methods**—The methods of a system that receive data items from the system's environment are the system's entry points. The methods of a system that send data items to the system's environment are the system's exit points.
- **Channels**—An attacker uses the system's channels to connect to the system and attack the system. In this way, a system's channels act as another basis for attacks. For example, the channel of a POP server is the TCP socket opened by the POP server.
- **Data**—The data is the collection of persistent and transient data items. The data items that are visible to both a system and the user across different executions are the persistent data items, e.g., cookies, files, database records, registry entries.

Therefore, the set of entry points and exit points, the set of channels, and the set of untrusted data items are the resources that the attacker can use to send data into the system or receive data from the system and hence attack the system.

It is not possible to measure a system's attack surface by counting the number of resources that contribute to the attack surface, since all resources do not contribute equally to the attack surface. Instead, an estimation of a resource's contribution to a system's attack surface is the *damage potential-effort ratio*, where *damage potential* is the level of harm the attacker can cause to the system in using the resource in an attack and *effort* is the amount of work done by the attacker to acquire the necessary access rights in order to be able to use the resource in an attack. The higher the damage potential, the higher the contribution; the higher the effort, the lower the contribution.

It is assumed that a method of a system can receive data items from the system's environment by invoking specific C library methods. Therefore, a method is a direct entry point if the method contains a call to one of the specific C library methods. For example, a method is a direct entry point if it contains a call to the *read* method defined in *unistd.h*.

Monitoring the runtime behavior of the system makes possible the identification of the channels open by the system and the determination of the protocol and access rights level of each channel. Runtime monitoring is also used to identify the untrusted data items and to determine the data type and access rights levels of each untrusted data item.

The attack surface measure method then estimates the total contribution of the methods, the total contribution of the channels, and the total contribution of the data items to the attack surface.

Test Types

A tester who is assigned or hired to evaluate the security of an organization's software system from the perspective of an attacker is known as an *ethical hacker*. In attempting to break into a computer resource and its associated networks, the ethical hacker will emulate the steps taken by a malicious hacker. An ethical hacker explores all the available avenues of gaining access to an organization's network and information systems. For example, an ethical hacker will dial into an organization's telephone exchange and try to locate an open modem that will provide access. Another approach is to attempt to access an organization's network directly through a local area connection used by employees. A third method is to gain access remotely through the Internet. An additional valuable resource for an ethical hacker would be to obtain an employee's laptop and use it to enter an organization's network and access computer resources. The laptop can be used to log in to an organization's internal Web applications and intranet portals, bypassing the normal authentication mechanisms.

Wireless networks in organizations provide opportunities for creative ethical hackers to get into an organization's computer systems. Social engineering also provides the ethical hacker with an opportunity to gain information from unsuspecting employees. Finally, as a complement to all these methods, an ethical hacker can physically access computer hardware and software resources.

In summary, the methods of ethical hacking are:

- Dial-up network connection
- Insider local network connection
- Remote outsider network connection
- Stolen equipment connection
- Wireless network connection
- Social engineering–enabled connection
- Physical entry attack

Testing Concepts

It is important to understand the following categories of software testing that are widely used, even though they do not primarily address security issues:

- **Unit testing**—The tester, usually a programmer, performs a detailed evaluation of code modules and code functions. This type of testing requires knowledge of the program algorithm and implementation.

- **Incremental integration testing**—As new functionality is added to code, additional testing of the application is performed.
- **Integration testing**—This test integrates applications and individual code modules to determine if they work properly together.
- **Load or stress testing**—Testing conducted to determine if the system can operate under heavy loads or demands and what effect the loads have on the system response time.
- **Certification testing**—Testing is part of a certification process.
- **Usability testing**—This type of test is conducted to determine whether the system meets the customer's user-friendliness expectations.
- **Functional testing**—Testers conduct black box tests to ensure that the functional requirements of an application are satisfied.
- **Alpha testing**—This test evaluates an application when the development is nearing completion and minor changes are anticipated.
- **Beta testing**—Beta testing is conducted when development and testing are completed and final problems are found before software release.
- **System testing**—The system test is another black box test that evaluates satisfaction of the overall system requirements.
- **Recovery testing**—Tests conducted to evaluate how the system recovers from crashes and failures.
- **Regression testing**—The testers perform retesting after changes or upgrades to the software or its operating environment.
- **Acceptance testing**—This test is conducted on project completion to determine if the customer specifications have been met over a specified period of time.

The Institute for Security and Open Methodologies (`www.isecom.org`) has developed an Open Source Security Testing Methodology Manual (OSSTMM) (`http://isecom.securenetltd.com/osstmm.en.2.1.pdf`) that provides guidance and metrics for conducting security tests. It has test cases that "are divided into five channels (sections) which collectively test information and data controls, personnel security awareness levels, fraud and social engineering control levels, computer and telecommunications networks, wireless devices, mobile devices, physical security access controls, security processes, and physical locations such as buildings, perimeters, and military bases." The manual is applicable to ethical hacking, penetration tests, vulnerability, and other types of security assessments. The following areas, taken from the OSSTMM, indicate the tests that should be part of a security testing paradigm.

I. Information Security Testing

1. Posture Assessment
2. Information Integrity Review
3. Intelligence Survey

4. Internet Document Grinding
5. Human Resources Review
6. Competitive Intelligence Scouting
7. Privacy Controls Review
8. Information Controls Review

II. Process Security Testing
1. Posture Review
2. Request Testing
3. Reverse Request Testing
4. Guided Suggestion Testing
5. Trusted Persons Testing

III. Internet Technology Security Testing
1. Logistics and Controls
2. Posture Review
3. Intrusion Detection Review
4. Network Surveying
5. System Services Identification
6. Competitive Intelligence Scouting
7. Privacy Review
8. Document Grinding
9. Internet Application Testing
10. Exploit Research and Verification
11. Routing
12. Trusted Systems Testing
13. Access Control Testing
14. Password Cracking
15. Containment Measures Testing
16. Survivability Review
17. Denial of Service Testing
18. Security Policy Review
19. Alert and Log Review

IV. Communications Security Testing
1. Posture Review
2. PBX Review
3. Voicemail Testing

4. FAX Testing
5. Modem Survey
6. Remote Access Control Testing
7. Voice over IP Testing
8. X.25 Packet Switched Networks Testing

V. Wireless Security Testing
1. Posture Review
2. Electromagnetic Radiation (EMR) Testing
3. 802.11 Wireless Networks Testing
4. Bluetooth Networks Testing
5. Wireless Input Device Testing
6. Wireless Handheld Testing
7. Cordless Communications Testing
8. Wireless Surveillance Device Testing
9. Wireless Transaction Device Testing
10. RFID Testing
11. Infrared Testing
12. Privacy Review

VI. Physical Security Testing
1. Posture Review
2. Access Controls Testing
3. Perimeter Review
4. Monitoring Review
5. Alarm Response Review
6. Location Review
7. Environment Review

Additional information is provided on the OSSTMM later in this chapter in the "Standards for Software Quality Assurance" section.

In the following sections, the security-related testing topics of penetration testing, fuzzing, scanning, simulation testing, testing for failure, and cryptographic validation will be presented.

Penetration Testing

A penetration test is a security testing methodology that gives the tester insight into the strength of the target's network security by simulating an attack from a malicious source. The process involves an active analysis of the system for any potential vulnerabilities that may result from poor or improper system configuration, known and/or unknown hardware or software flaws, or operational weaknesses in process or technical countermeasures. This analysis is carried out from the position of a potential attacker, and can involve active exploitation of security vulnerabilities. Any security issues that are found will be presented to the system owner together with an assessment of their impact and often with a proposal for mitigation or a technical solution. The intent of a penetration test is to determine feasibility of an attack and the amount of business impact of a successful exploit, if discovered. It is a component of a full security audit, which includes:

- **A Level I, high-level assessment**—A top-down look at the organization's policies, procedures, standards, and guidelines. A Level I assessment is not usually hands-on, in that the system's security is not actually tested.
- **A Level II, network evaluation**—More hands-on than a Level I assessment, a Level II assessment has some of the Level I activities with more information gathering and scanning.
- **A Level III, penetration test**—A penetration test is not usually concerned with policies. It is more about taking the adversarial view of a hacker, by seeing what can be accomplished, and with what difficulty.

Several factors have converged in the IT environment to make penetration testing a necessity. The evolution of information technology has focused on ease of use at the operational end, while exponentially increasing the complexity of the computer. Unfortunately, the administration and management requirements of these systems have increased because:

- The skill level required to execute a hacker exploit has steadily decreased.
- The size and complexity of the network environment has mushroomed.
- The number of network and Web-based applications has increased.
- The detrimental impact of a security breach on corporate assets and goodwill is greater than ever.

Penetration testing is most commonly carried out within a "black box," that is, with no prior knowledge of the infrastructure to be tested. At its simplest level, the penetration test involves three phases:

1. **Preparation phase**—A formal contract is executed containing nondisclosure of the client's data and legal protection for the tester. At a minimum, it also lists the IP addresses to be tested and the time to test.
2. **Execution phase**—In this phase the penetration test is executed, with the tester looking for potential vulnerabilities.
3. **Delivery phase**—The results of the evaluation are communicated to the tester's contact in the organization, and corrective action is advised.

Whether the penetration test is a full knowledge (white box) test, a partial knowledge (gray box) test, or a zero knowledge (black box) test, after the report and results are obtained, mitigation techniques have to be applied to reduce the risk of compromise to an acceptable, tolerable level. The test should address vulnerabilities and corresponding risks to such areas as applications, remote access systems, Voice over Internet Protocol (VoIP), wireless networks, and so on.

Legal and Ethical Implications

Because an ethical hacker works for an organization to assist in evaluating its network security, this individual must adhere to a high standard of conduct. In fact, there is a Certified Ethical Hacker (CEH) certification sponsored by the International Council of E-Commerce Consultants (EC-Council) at `www.eccouncil.org` that attests to the ethical hacker's knowledge and subscription to ethical principles. The EC-Council also provides the Licensed Penetration Tester (LPT) certification, which, to quote their Web site, provides the following benefits:

- Standardizes the knowledge base for penetration testing professionals by incorporating best practices followed by experienced experts in the field
- Ensures that each professional licensed by EC-Council follows a strict code of ethics
- Is exposed to the best practices in the domain of penetration testing
- Is aware of all the compliance requirements required by the industry
- Trains security professionals to analyze the security posture of a network exhaustively and recommend corrective measures.

When an ethical hacker or licensed penetration tester agrees to conduct penetration tests for an organization and to probe the weaknesses of their information systems, he or she can be open to dismissal and prosecution unless contract terms are included to protect the individuals conducting the test. It is vitally important that the organization and ethical hacking team have an identical understanding of what the team is authorized to do and what happens if the team inadvertently causes some damage.

Attacking a network from the outside carries ethical and legal risk to the tester, and remedies and protections must be spelled out in detail before the test begins. For example, the Cyber Security Enhancement Act of 2002 indicates life sentences for hackers who "recklessly" endanger the lives of others, and several other U.S. statutes address cyber crime. Statute 1030, "Fraud and Related Activity in Connection with Computers," specifically states that whoever intentionally accesses a protected computer without authorization, and as a result of such conduct, recklessly causes damage or impairs medical treatment, can receive a fine or imprisonment of five to twenty years. It is vital that the tester receive specific written permission to conduct the test from the most senior executive possible. A tester should be specifically indemnified against prosecution for the task of testing.

For his or her protection, the ethical hacking tester should keep the following items in mind:

- **Protect information uncovered during the penetration test**—In the course of gaining access to an organization's networks and computing resources, the ethical hacker will find that he or she has access to sensitive information that would be valuable to the organization's competitors or enemies. Therefore, this information should be protected to the highest degree possible and not divulged to anyone, either purposely or inadvertently.

- **Conduct business in an ethical manner**—Ethics is a relative term and is a function of a number of variables, including background, religion, ethnicity, upbringing, and so on. However, the ethical hacker should conduct his or her activities in an ethical fashion and in the best interest of the organization that commissioned the penetration testing. Similarly, the organization should treat the ethical hacker with the same respect and ethical conduct.
- **Limitation of liability**—As discussed earlier in this section, during a penetration test, the ethical hacking team will most likely have access to sensitive files and information. The ethical hacker is trained to not cause any harm, such as modifying files, deleting information, and so on, in the course of his or her activities. But since errors do occur, the organization and ethical hacker should have terms in the contract between the two that address the situation where harm is done inadvertently. There should be a limitation to the liability of the ethical hacker if this scenario occurs. Another option that is commonly used by consultants is to obtain an insurance policy that will cover the consultant's activities in his or her chosen profession.
- **Remain within the scope of the assignment**—The scope of the penetration testing should be delineated beforehand and agreed upon by all parties involved. With that accomplished, the testing team should conduct the testing strictly within those bounds. For example, only the networks and computing resources specified should come under penetration testing as well as the methods and extent of trying to break in to the information system.
- **Develop a testing plan**—As with any endeavor, the ethical hacking team should develop a test plan in advance of the testing and have it approved by the hiring organization. The plan should include the scope of the test, resources to be tested, support provided by the hiring organization, times for the testing, location of the testing, the type of testing (white box, gray box, or black box), extent of the penetration, individuals to contact in the event of problems, and deliverables.
- **Comply with relevant laws and regulations**—Business organizations are required to comply with a variety of laws and regulations, including the Health Insurance Portability and Accountability Act (HIPAA), Sarbanes-Oxley, and the Gramm-Leach-Bliley Act (GLBA). These acts are one of the reasons why companies hire ethical hackers and demonstrate that they are acting to protect their information resources.

The Open-Source Security Testing Methodology Manual, OSS OSSTMM 2.2, (`http://isecom.securenetltd.com/osstmm.en.2.2.pdf`), also provides rules of engagement for ethical practices in a number of areas, including penetration testing. The following list summarizes some of the pertinent rules from the OSSTMM 2.2:

- Testing of very insecure systems and installations is not to be performed until appropriate remediation measures have been taken.

- The auditor is required to ensure nondisclosure of client proprietary information.
- Contracts should limit the liability of the auditor.
- The engagement contract should provide permissions for the specific types of tests to be performed.
- The scope of the testing effort should be clearly defined.
- The auditor must operate legally.
- In reporting test results, the auditor must respect the privacy of all concerned.

The Three Pre-test Phases

Penetration testing is usually initiated with *reconnaissance*, which comprises three pre-test phases: footprinting, scanning, and enumerating. These pre-test phases are very important and can make the difference between a successful penetration test that provides a complete picture of the target's network and an unsuccessful test that does not.

The reconnaissance process seeks to gather as much information about the target network as possible, following these seven steps during the footprinting, scanning, and enumerating activities:

1. Gather initial information
2. Determine the network range
3. Identify active machines
4. Discover open ports and access points (APs)
5. Fingerprint the operating system
6. Uncover services on ports
7. Map the network

Footprinting

Footprinting is obtaining information concerning the security profile of an organization. It involves gathering data to create a blueprint of the organization's networks and systems. It is an important way for an attacker to gain information about an organization without the organization's knowledge.

Footprinting employs the first two steps of reconnaissance, gathering the initial target information and determining the network range of the target. It may also require manual research, such as studying the company's Web page for useful information, such as:

- Company contact names, phone numbers and email addresses
- Company locations and branches
- Other companies with which the target company partners or deals
- News, such as mergers or acquisitions
- Links to other company-related sites

- Company privacy policies, which may help identify the types of security mechanisms in place

Other resources that may have information about the target company are:

- The U.S. Securities and Exchange Commission (SEC) EDGAR database, if the company is publicly traded
- Job boards, either internal to the company or external sites
- Disgruntled employee blogs
- The target organization's Web site and other related Web sites
- Business social networking Web sites such as LinkedIn
- Personal/business Web sites such as Facebook
- Trade press

Scanning

The next four steps of gathering information (identifying active machines, discovering open ports and access points, fingerprinting the operating system, and uncovering services on ports) are considered part of the scanning phase. The goal in this step is to discover open ports and applications by performing external or internal network scanning, pinging machines, determining network ranges, and scanning the ports of individual systems. (Scanning will be discussed in more detail later in this chapter.)

Enumerating

The last step in reconnaissance, mapping the network, is the result of the scanning phase and leads to the enumerating phase. As the final pre-test phase, the goal of enumeration is to paint a fairly complete picture of the target.

To enumerate a target, a tester tries to identify valid user accounts or poorly protected resource elements by using directed queries and active connections to and from the target. The type of information sought by testers during the enumeration phase can be names of users and groups, network resources and shares, and applications.

The techniques used for enumerating include:

- Obtaining Active Directory information and identifying vulnerable user accounts
- Discovering NetBIOS name with Nbtscan
- Using the SNMPutil command-line utility for Simple Network Management Protocol (SNMP)
- Employing Windows DNS queries
- Establishing null sessions and connections

Penetration Testing Tools and Techniques

There are a variety of tools and techniques, including some used by malicious hackers, which can be valuable in conducting penetration tests. Some tools, such as Whois and Nslookup, are public software that can help gather information about the target network. Whois is usually the first stop in reconnaissance. With it, you can find information like the domain's registrant, its administrative and technical contacts, and a listing of their domain servers. Nslookup allows you to query Internet domain name servers. It displays information that can be used to diagnose Domain Name System (DNS) infrastructure and find additional IP addresses. It can also use the MX record to reveal the IP of the mail server.

Another information source is American Registry of Internet Numbers (ARIN). ARIN allows you to search the Whois database for a network's autonomous system numbers (ASNs), network-related handles, and other related point-of-contact information. ARIN's Whois function enables you to query the IP address to find information on the target's use of subnet addressing.

The common traceroute utility is also useful. Traceroute works by exploiting a feature of the Internet Protocol called time-to-live (TTL). It reveals the path IP packets travel between two systems by sending out consecutive User Datagram Protocol (UDP) packets with ever-increasing TTLs. As each router processes an IP packet, it decrements the TTL. When the TTL reaches zero, the router sends back a "TTL exceeded" Internet Control Message Protocol (ICMP) message to the origin. Thus, routers with DNS entries reveal their names, network affiliations, and geographic locations. Traceroute will be discussed in more detail in the scanning portion of this chapter.

A utility called Visual Trace by McAfee displays the traceroute output visually in map view, node view, or IP view. Additional useful Windows-based tools for gathering information include:

- **VisualRoute**—VisualRoute by VisualWare includes integrated traceroute, ping tests, and reverse DNS and Whois lookups. It also displays the actual route of connections and IP address locations on a global map.
- **SmartWhois**—Like Whois, SmartWhois by TamoSoft obtains comprehensive info about the target: IP address, hostname or domain, including country, state or province, city, name of the network provider, administrator and technical support contact information. Unlike Whois utilities, SmartWhois can find the information about a computer located in any part of the world, intelligently querying the right database and delivering all the related records within a few seconds.
- **Sam Spade**—Sam Spade, a freeware tool primarily used to track down spammers, can also be used to provide information about a target. It comes with a host of useful network tools including ping, nslookup, Whois, IP block Whois, dig, traceroute, finger, SMTP, VRFY, Web browser, keep-alive, DNS zone transfer, SMTP relay check, and more.

Port Scanners

Port scanning is one of the most common reconnaissance techniques used by testers to discover the vulnerabilities in the services listening to well known ports. Once you've identified the IP address of a target through footprinting, you can begin the process of port scanning: looking for holes in the system through which you—or a malicious intruder—can gain access. A typical system has $2^{16}-1$ port numbers, each with its own

Transmission Control Protocol (TCP) and UDP port that can be used to gain access, if unprotected.

NMap, the most popular port scanner for Linux, is also available for Windows. NMap can scan a system in a variety of stealth modes, depending upon how undetectable you want to be. NMap can determine a wealth of information about a target, like what hosts are available, what services are offered, and what OS is running.

Other port scanning tools for Linux systems include SATAN, NSAT, VeteScan, SARA, PortScanner, Network Superscanner, CGI Port Scanner, and CGI Sonar.

Port scanning is also covered later in this chapter in additional detail.

Vulnerability Scanners

Nessus, a popular open source tool, is an extremely powerful network scanner that can be configured to run a variety of scans. While a Windows graphical front end is available, the core Nessus product requires Linux to run.

Microsoft's Baseline Security Analyzer (MBSA) is a free Windows vulnerability scanner. MBSA can be used to detect security configuration errors on local computers or on computers across a network. It does have some issues with Windows Update, however, and can't always tell if a patch has been installed.

Popular commercial vulnerability scanners include Retina Network Security Scanner, which runs on Windows, and SAINT, which runs on several Unix/Linux variants, including Mac OS X.

Password Crackers

Password cracking doesn't have to involve fancy tools, but it is a fairly tedious process. If the target doesn't lock you out after a specific number of tries, you can spend an infinite amount of time trying every combination of alphanumeric characters. It's just a question of time and bandwidth before you break into the system.

The most common passwords found are password, root, administrator, admin, operator, demo, test, webmaster, backup, guest, trial, member, private, beta, [company_name], or [known_username].

There are three basic types of password cracking tests that can be automated with tools:

- **Dictionary**—A file of words is run against user accounts. If the password is a simple word, it can be found fairly quickly.
- **Hybrid**—A hybrid attack works like a dictionary attack, but adds simple numbers or symbols to the file of words. This attack exploits a weakness of many passwords: they are common words with numbers or symbols tacked to the ends.
- **Brute force**—The most time-consuming, but comprehensive way to crack a password. Every combination of character is tried until the password is broken.

Some common Web password cracking tools are:

- **Brutus**—Brutus is a password cracking tool that can perform both dictionary attacks and brute force attacks where passwords are randomly generated from a given character. It can crack the multiple authentication types, HTTP (basic authentication, HTML form/CGI), POP3, FTP, SMB, and Telnet.

- **WebCracker**—WebCracker is a simple tool that takes text lists of usernames and passwords, and uses them as dictionaries to implement basic password guessing.
- **ObiWan**—ObiWan is a Web password cracking tool that can work through a proxy. It uses wordlists and alternates numeric or alphanumeric characters with roman characters to generate possible passwords.
- **Burp Intruder**—Burp Intruder is a Web application security tool that can be used to configure and automate attacks. It can be used to test for Web application vulnerabilities to such attacks as buffer overflow, SQL injection, path traversal, and cross-site scripting.
- **Burp Repeater**—Burp Repeater is a manual tool that can be used to attack Web applications. It operates by supporting the reissuing of HTTP requests from the same window. It also provides a graphical environment to support the manual Web application testing procedures and complements other tools such as Burp Intruder.

Trojan Horses

A Trojan horse is a program that performs unknown and unwanted functions. It could take one or more of the following forms:

- An unauthorized program contained within a legitimate program
- A legitimate program that has been altered by the placement of unauthorized code within it
- Any program that appears to perform a desirable and necessary function but does something unintended

Trojan horses can be transmitted to the computer in several ways—through email attachments, freeware, physical installation, ICQ/IRC chat, phony programs, or infected Web sites. When the user signs on and goes online, the Trojan horse is activated and the attacker gains access to the system.

Unlike a worm, a Trojan horse doesn't typically self-replicate. The exact type of attack depends on the type of Trojan horse.

Trojans horses can be:

- Remote access Trojan horses
- Keystroke loggers or password-sending Trojan horses
- Software detection killers
- Purely destructive or denial-of-service Trojan horses

The list of Trojan horses in the wild is expanding quickly, but a few of the earliest have remained relevant since the beginning, and many of these serve as platforms for the development of more lethal variations.

Back Orifice 2000, known as BO2K, is the grandfather of Trojan horses and has spawned a considerable number of imitators. Once installed on a target PC or server machine, BO2K gives the attacker complete control of the victim.

BO2K has stealth capabilities, will not show up on the task list and runs completely in hidden mode. Back Orifice and its variants have been credited with the highest number of infestations of Windows systems.

Another Trojan horse that has been around for a considerable time is SubSeven, although it is becoming less and less of a problem. SubSeven is a back door program that enables others to gain full access to Windows systems through the network.

Other common Trojans and spyware currently in the wild include Rovbin, Canary, Remacc.RCPro Jgidol, IRC.mimic, and NetBus. The SANS Internet Storm Center (`http://isc.sans.org/`) is a good source of information on the latest malware exploits and attack activity.

Buffer Overflows

A buffer overflow (or overrun) occurs when a program allocates a specific block length of memory for something, but then attempts to store more data than the block was intended to hold. This overflowing data can overwrite memory areas and interfere with information crucial to the normal execution of the program. While buffer overflows may be a side effect of poorly written code, they can also be triggered intentionally to create an attack.

A buffer overflow can allow an intruder to load a remote shell or execute a command, allowing the attacker to gain unauthorized access or escalate user privileges. To generate the overflow, the attacker must create a specific data feed to induce the error, as random data will rarely produce the desired effect.

For a buffer overflow attack to work, the target system must fail to test the data or stack boundaries and must also be able to execute code that resides in the data or stack segment. Once the stack is smashed, the attacker can deploy his payload and take control of the attacked system.

Three common ways to test for a buffer overflow vulnerability are as follows:

- Look for strings declared as local variables in functions or methods, and verify the presence of boundary checks in the source code.
- Check for improper use of input/output or string functions.
- Feed the application large amounts of data and check for abnormal behavior.

Products like Immunix's Stackguard and ProPolice employ stack-smashing protection to detect buffer overflows on stack-allocated variables. Also, vulnerability scanners like Proventia can help protect against buffer overflow.

Buffer overflow vulnerabilities can be detected by manual auditing of the code as well as by boundary testing. Other countermeasures include updating C and C++ software compilers and C libraries to more secure versions, and disabling stack execution in the program.

SQL Injection Attack

SQL injection is an example of a class of injection exploits that occur when one scripting language is embedded inside another scripting language.

The injection targets the data residing in a database through the firewall in order to alter the SQL statements and retrieve data from the database or execute commands. It accomplishes this by modifying the parameters of a Web-based application.

Preventing SQL injection vulnerability involves enforcing better coding practices and database administration procedures. Here are some specific steps to take:

- Disable verbose error messages that give information to the attacker.
- Protect the system account `sa`. It's very common for the `sa` password to be `blank`.
- Enforce the concept of least privilege at the database connection.
- Secure the application by auditing the source code to restrict length of input.

Cross Site Scripting (XSS)

Web application attacks are often successful because the attack is not noticed immediately. One such attack exploits the cross-site scripting (XSS) vulnerability. An XSS vulnerability is created by the failure of a Web-based application to validate user-supplied input before returning it to the client system.

Attackers can exploit XSS by crafting malicious URLs and tricking users into clicking on them. These links enable the attacker's client-side scripting language, such as JavaScript or VBScript, to execute on the victim's browser.

If the application accepts only expected input, then the XSS vulnerability can be significantly reduced. Many Web application vulnerabilities can be minimized by adhering to proper design specifications and coding practices, and implementing security early in the application's development life cycle.

Another piece of advice: don't rely on client-side data for critical processes during the application development process, and use an encrypted session, such as SSL, without hidden fields.

Social Engineering

Social engineering describes the acquisition of sensitive information or inappropriate access privileges by an outsider, by manipulating people. It exploits the human side of computing, tricking people into providing valuable information or allowing access to that information.

Social engineering is the hardest form of attack to defend against because it cannot be prevented with hardware or software alone. A company may have rock-solid authentication processes, VPNs, and firewalls, but still be vulnerable to attacks that exploit the human element.

Social engineering can be divided into two types: human-based, person-to-person interaction, and computer-based interaction using software that automates the attempt to engineer information.

Common techniques used by an intruder to gain either physical access or system access are:

- Asserting authority or pulling rank
- Professing to have the authority, perhaps supported with altered identification, to enter a facility or system

- Attempting to intimidate an individual into providing information
- Praising, flattering, or sympathizing
- Using positive reinforcement to coerce a subject into providing access or information for system access

Some examples of successful social engineering attacks are:

- Emails to employees from a tester requesting their passwords to validate the organizational database after a network intrusion has occurred
- Emails to employees from a tester requesting their passwords because work has to be done over the weekend on the system
- An email or phone call from a tester impersonating an official who is conducting an investigation for the organization and requires passwords for the investigation
- An improper release of medical information to individuals posing as medical personnel and requesting data from patients' records
- A computer repair technician who convinces a user that the hard disk on his or her PC is damaged and irreparable, and installs a new hard disk for the user, then takes the hard disk, extracts the information, and sells the information to a competitor or foreign government

The only real defense against social engineering attacks is an information security policy that addresses such attacks and educates the users about these types of attacks.

Intrusion Detection System (IDS)

An intrusion detection system (IDS) monitors packets on the network wire and endeavors to discover if a tester is attempting to break into a system. The two common types of IDSs monitor a little differently from each other. Signature recognition systems are like virus scanners; a pattern recognition is coded for every tester technique. Anomaly detection systems employ a baseline of statistics such as CPU utilization, disk activity, user logins, file activity, and so on, then network activity is matched against this baseline. Anomaly detection systems can detect attacks without specific coded patterns.

After capturing packets, a good IDS uses several techniques to identify information in the packets indicative of an attack, such as protocol stack verification and application protocol verification.

Protocol stack verification looks for intrusions, such as "ping-of-death" and TCP stealth scanning, that use violations of the IP protocols to attack. The verification system can flag invalid packets, which can include valid, but suspicious, behavior such as frequent fragmented IP packets.

Application protocol verification looks for intrusions that use invalid protocol behavior, such as WinNuke. WinNuke uses the NetBIOS protocol.

Since many IDSs simply rely on matching the patterns of well-known attack scripts, they can easily be evaded by simply changing the script and altering the appearance of the attack. For example, some POP3 servers are vulnerable to a buffer overflow when a long password is entered. This may be easy to evade by simply changing the password script.

Another way to avoid IDS detection is to send a TCP FIN packet that the IDS sees, but the victim host does not see. This causes the IDS to believe the connection is closed when in fact it is not. Depending upon the router configuration, a tester can first flood the link with high priority IP packets, and then send a TCP FIN as a low priority packet. This may result in the router's queue dropping the packet.

Wireless Network Penetration Testing

The rapid popularity of wireless networking technologies has introduced a host of new security issues. This popularity is being driven by two major factors: ease of implementation and cost effectiveness. The convenience of constant access to networks and data, regardless of location, is very reasonably priced for most companies.

The most common wireless LAN (WLAN) standards are the IEEE 802.11 standards as defined by the IEEE 802.11 working group. This family of standards specifies wireless connectivity and defines aspects of frequency hopping and direct-sequence spread spectrum (DSSS) systems for use in the 2.4 MHz ISM (industrial, scientific, medical) band. This family of standards includes 802.11b and 802.11g. Newer standards include 802.11n and 802.11e. Most hardware today is 802.11b and 802.11g compatible. For example, the 802.11g standard for wireless networking supports a maximum bandwidth of 54 megabits per second (Mbps) and 802.11n operates at approximately 160 Mbps, depending on conditions.

War driving is a term used to describe the process of a hacker who, armed with a laptop and a wireless adapter card and traveling by car, bus, subway train, or other form of mechanized transport, goes around sniffing for WLANs. *War walking* refers to the same process, commonly in public areas like malls, hotels, or city streets, but using shoe leather instead of motorized transportation methods.

The concept of war driving is simple. Using a device capable of receiving an 802.11b or 802.11g signal, a device capable of locating itself on a map, and software that will log data from the moment that a network signal is detected, the hacker moves from place to place, letting these devices do their jobs. Over time, the hacker builds up a database containing the network name, signal strength, location, and IP/namespace in use for all of the discovered wireless hotspots.

With SNMP, the hacker may even log packet samples and probe the access points for available data. The hacker may also mark the locations of the vulnerable wireless networks with chalk on the sidewalk or building itself. This is called *war chalking* and alerts other intruders that an exposed WLAN is nearby.

Common war driving exploits find many wireless networks with WEP disabled, and using only the service set identifier (SSID) for access control. The SSID for wireless networks can be found quickly, because it is usually broadcast. This vulnerability makes these networks susceptible to what's called the *parking lot attack*, where, at a safe distance from the building's perimeter, an attacker gains access to the target network.

WLAN Vulnerabilities

Wireless LANs are susceptible to the same protocol-based attacks that plague a wired LAN, but also have their own set of unique vulnerabilities. Since wireless access points may proliferate in the organization, unsecured wireless access points can be a danger to organizations because they offer the attacker a route around the company's firewall and into the network.

SSID Issues The service set identifier (SSID) is an identification value programmed in the access point or group of access points to identify the local wireless subnet. This segmentation of the wireless network into multiple networks is a form of an authentication check; the SSID acts as a simple password, providing a measure of security. When a client computer is connected to the access point, the network tries to confirm the SSID with the computer. If the wireless station does not know the value of the SSID, access is denied to the associated access point.

The wireless access point is configured to broadcast its SSID. When enabled, any client without an SSID is able to receive it and have access to the access point. Users are also able to configure their own client systems with the appropriate SSID because they are widely known and easily shared.

Many access points use default SSIDs provided by the manufacturers, and a list of those default SSIDs is available for download on the Internet. This means that it's very easy for a hacker to determine an access point's SSID and gain access to it via software tools.

Also, a nonsecure access WLAN mode exists, which allows clients to connect to the access point using the configured SSID, a blank SSID, or an SSID configured as ''any.''

Wired Equivalent Privacy Issues Wired Equivalent Privacy (WEP) is a component of the IEEE 802.11 wireless local area network WLAN standard. Its primary purpose is to provide confidentiality of data on wireless networks at a level equivalent to that of wired LANs.

IEEE chose to employ encryption at the Data Link layer to prevent unauthorized eavesdropping on a network. This is accomplished by encrypting data with the RC4 encryption algorithm.

Nevertheless, WEP is vulnerable because of relatively short keys that remain static. Most WEP products implement a 64-bit shared key, using 40 bits of this for the secret key and 24 bits for the initialization vector. The key is installed at the wired network AP and must be entered into each client as well.

WEP was not designed to withstand a directed cryptographic attack. WEP has well-known flaws in the encryption algorithms used to secure wireless transmissions. Two programs capable of exploiting the RC4 vulnerability, AirSnort and WEPCrack, both run under Linux, and both require a relatively small amount of captured data.

WPA2 (Wi-Fi Protected Access 2), based on the IEEE 802.11i standard, should be used instead of WEP. It employs the Rijndael block cipher-based NIST Advanced Encryption Standard (AES). AES employs a variable block length and supports key sizes of 128, 192, and 256 bits. WPA2 comes in enterprise and personal versions. Wireless networks are vulnerable to DoS attacks as well, due to the nature of the wireless transmission medium. WLANs send information via radio waves on public frequencies, thus they are susceptible to interference from traffic using the same radio band, whether the interference is deliberate or accidental.

If an attacker makes use of a powerful transmitter, enough interference can be generated to prevent wireless devices from communicating with one another. DoS attack devices do not have to be right next to the devices being attacked; they need only be within range of the wireless transmissions.

Examples of techniques used to deny service to a wireless device are:

- Request for authentication at such a frequency as to disrupt legitimate traffic.
- Request deauthentication of legitimate users. These requests may not be refused according to the current 802.11 standard.
- Mimic the behavior of an access point to convince unsuspecting clients to communicate with it.
- Repeatedly transmit Request to Send/Clear to Send (RTS/CTS) frames to silence the network. These frames are used by the 802.11 wireless networking protocol to reduce frame collisions.

MAC Address Spoofing A Media Access Control (MAC) address is a unique identifier assigned to network adapters or network interface cards (NICs) by the card manufacturer. The MAC address is associated with the Media Access Control sublayer of the OSI model Data Link layer and controls a network node's transmission and reception of data.

MAC addresses are easily sniffed by an attacker since they must appear in the clear even when WEP is enabled. An attacker can masquerade as a valid MAC address by programming the wireless card to enter the wireless network.

Wireless Scanning Tools

A number of wireless scanning tools have become available, including the following:

- **NetStumbler**—NetStumbler displays wireless access points, SSIDs, channels, whether WEP encryption is enabled and signal strength. NetStumbler can connect with GPS technology to log the precise location of access points.
- **MiniStumbler**—This is a smaller version of NetStumbler designed to work on PocketPC platforms. It provides support for ARM, MIPS, and SH3 central processing unit types.
- **AirSnort**—AirSnort is a WLAN tool that cracks WEP encryption keys. AirSnort passively monitors wireless transmissions and automatically computes the encryption key when enough packets have been gathered.
- **Kismet**—Kismet is an 802.11 wireless network detector, sniffer, and intrusion detection system. Kismet identifies networks by passively collecting packets and detecting standard named networks, detecting (and given time, decloaking) hidden networks, and inferring the presence of nonbeaconing networks via data traffic.
- **SSID Sniff**—A tool to use when looking to discover access points and save captured traffic. Comes with a configured script and supports Cisco Aironet and random prism2-based cards.
- **WifiScanner**—WifiScanner analyzes traffic and detects 802.11b stations and access points. It can listen alternatively on all 14 channels, write packet information

in real time, and search access points and associated client stations. All network traffic may be saved in the libpcap format for analysis.

Wireless packet analyzers, or sniffers, basically work the same way as wired network packet analyzers: they capture packets from the data stream and allow the user to open them up and look at, or decode, them. Some wireless sniffers don't employ full decoding tools but show existing WLANs and SSIDs. A few of the wireless sniffers available are:

- **AirMagnet**—AirMagnet is a wireless tool originally developed for WLAN inventory, but it has become a useful wireless security assessment utility.
- **AiroPeek**—WildPackets's AiroPeek is a packet analyzer for IEEE 802.11b and 802.11g wireless LANs, supporting all higher-level network protocols such as TCP/IP, AppleTalk, NetBEUI, and IPX. AiroPeek is used to isolate security problems by decoding 802.11b and 802.11g WLAN protocols and by analyzing wireless network performance with an identification of signal strength, channel, and data rates.
- **Sniffer Wireless**—McAfee Sniffer Wireless is a packet analyzer for managing network applications and deployments on wireless LAN 802.11a, 802.11b, and 802.11g networks. It has the ability to decrypt Wired Equivalent Privacy–based traffic (WEP).

Wireless offers the possibility of always-on, instant mobile communications; however, the vulnerabilities inherent to wireless computing present daunting hurdles. It is vulnerable to eavesdropping, session hijacking, data alteration and manipulation, in conjunction with an overall lack of privacy. These weaknesses are major challenges posed by wireless technologies.

Fortunately, steps can be taken to lessen the impact of these threats. Securing wireless networks includes adopting a suitable strategy such as MAC address filtering, firewalls, or a combination of protocol-based measures. A few specific steps are:

- Change the access point's default admin password
- Change the access point's default SSID
- Disable the "Broadcast SSID" function on the AP
- Employ Wi-Fi Protected Access 2 (WPA2), which is based on the IEEE 802.11i standard and uses the AES encryption algorithm
- Employ MAC address filtering
- Implement an authentication server to provide strong authentication
- Physically locate the AP in an area that limits its radio emanations
- Logically put the AP in a DMZ with the firewall between the DMZ and the internal network
- Implement VPN tunnels
- Disable DHCP and assign static IP addresses
- Test penetration vulnerability regularly

- Research migrating to newer 802.11 technologies and new WEP encryption workarounds

Additional Penetration Testing Considerations

Because there is normally no revenue generation associated with IT and information security functions, it is important to frame penetration testing and related initiatives in terms of risk reduction, employee productivity, income generated per employee, and transaction processing time.

Penetration testing is a component of risk management; therefore penetration testing is associated with the protection of an organization's high-value assets. This relationship is directly linked to the actual and perceived value of the business.

Decisions concerning penetration testing must be based on sound business rationale. These decisions include the type of testing, expected results, remediation approaches, reporting format, and financial considerations.

As with other business decisions, the penetration test must demonstrate benefit and a return on investment through mitigation of risk, correcting design flaws, and correcting vulnerabilities. These returns have to be quantified in terms of benefits to the organization such as increased productivity and financial gains. One means of achieving this quantification is by making the penetration test a recognized and critical component of an income-generating initiative in the business organization. In fact, a successful outcome of a penetration test for the project should be one of the requirements for successful project completion.

Penetration testing is also addressed in NIST SP 800-115, *Technical Guide to Information Security Testing and Assessment*, September 2008.

Many organizations will decide to engage an outside organization with specialized expertise to conduct their penetration testing. Therefore, choosing and contracting a penetration testing partner for an engagement becomes a critical business decision. The selection should be made based on obtaining the greatest return on the investment and minimizing risks associated with the effort.

Some specific factors to be considered are:

- Determine which security areas to be addressed.
- Ensure that the penetration testing organization has the appropriate experience and expertise to perform the required tasks.
- Investigate to be certain that the testing organization provides the specific set of services that your organization desires.
- Obtain references from current and past customers of the potential provider.
- Have the penetration testing organization sign an agreement to include liability for any harm that occurs during the test, including accidents and negligence. The testing organization should have appropriate insurance to cover any damage caused during the test process.
- Make sure that the company you are considering does not employ former malicious hackers.

- Costs of the penetration test should be validated by obtaining cost estimates and quotes from a number of qualified suppliers.
- Determine the types of tools that will be used by the supplier in the penetration test. Will the tools be custom developed by the testing organization, commercially developed, or open source tools? Has the testing organization checked the tools to make sure they have not been infected and could be a source of compromise to the information systems that will be under test? Are the signatures in the tools up to date? How will the testing organization detect recently discovered vulnerabilities in the tested system?
- Confirm that the testing organization has a solid plan for conducting the test.
- Ensure that the testing organization uses formal methodologies that meet or exceed industry standard approaches, such as developed in the Open Source Security Testing Methodology Manual (OSSTMM) and the CESG IT Health Check (CHECK) method.
- Determine the format, clarity, completeness, and accuracy of deliverable penetration test reports and results briefing.
- Obtain guarantees that the experienced professionals promised by the testing organization are the actual personnel performing the testing and are not replaced by inexperienced individuals.
- Ensure that the personnel performing the penetration testing are experienced and competent, and hold relevant certifications.
- Investigate to guarantee that the testing organization will keep confidential all items and information relating to the penetration test.

Fuzzing

Fuzzing is a technique that is used to detect faults and security-related bugs in software by providing random inputs (fuzz) to a program. According to OWASP, "Fuzz testing or fuzzing is a black box software testing technique, which basically consists of finding implementation bugs using malformed/semi-malformed data injection in an automated fashion." Another definition of fuzzing by Oehlert is "A highly automated testing technique that covers numerous boundary cases using invalid data (from files, network protocols, API calls, and other targets) as application input to better ensure the absence of exploitable vulnerabilities. The name comes from modem applications' tendency to fail due to random input caused by line noise on 'fuzzy' telephone lines."[13]

As opposed to *static analysis*, where source code is reviewed line by line for bugs, fuzzing conducts *dynamic analysis* by generating a variety of valid and invalid inputs to a program and monitoring the results. In some instances, the result might be the program crashing.

[13]Oehlert, P., "Violating Assumptions with Fuzzing," *IEEE Security & Privacy* (March/April 2005): 58–62.

The person credited with the concept of fuzzing is Barton Miller of the University of Wisconsin-Madison.[14]

In general, fuzzing is not as difficult to set up and is less time-consuming than static analysis, but does require planning in developing the test inputs. By its nature, fuzzing also lends itself to automated testing by using computer-generated data as inputs to the software system. Data can be provided by pseudo-random generators, known invalid inputs, and other processes such as genetic algorithms. Detection of software faults is usually accomplished using debugging tools.

Some of the types of inputs fed to the target software to determine its robustness include:

- Integers, such as large negative and positive numbers, zero, signed and unsigned numbers
- Positive and negative floating point numbers
- Random binary strings
- Characters such as instructions, escape characters, command line statements

Fuzzing inputs can also be generated from different perspectives, as in the following examples:

- A mutation approach by taking known, valid inputs and modifying them, for example, by randomly changing bits or field lengths and observing the results. The modifications to the valid data may be heuristic or random.
- A generation-based approach that uses a specification, such as that for a network protocol or file format, and develops test inputs from these specifications. The test cases are modifications of the specification formats.
- A conformance approach by applying the known, mandatory constraints such as file formats and field sizes to inputs and monitoring the results.
- A protocol testing approach that sends malformed and false packets to the software.
- A replacement approach in which part of a request to a system is made by replacing it with a set value or fuzz vector.
- An event-driven test in which the input to the software system is a queue of data structures with random values.
- An application-based approach that generates and inserts a variety of command-lines and text input sequences.
- A file format method that produces files with an improper format, such as a malformed header, and causes software crashes.
- A recursive approach in which part of a request to a system is made by iterating through all the possible combinations of a set alphabet.

[14]Barton P., Miller, B., Fredriksen, L., and So, B., "An Empirical Study of the Reliability of Unix Utilities," *Communications of the ACM* 33 (12), December 1990: 32–44.

OWASP provides some fuzzing tools, including WSFuzzer (`www.owasp.org/index.php/WSFuzzer`), JBroFuzz (`www.owasp.org/index.php/JBroFuzz`), and WebScarab (`www.owasp.org/index.php/Fuzzing_with_WebScarab`).

CODE COVERAGE

When conducting fuzzing, it is useful to know which lines of application code have not been tested. With this information, the untested code can be reviewed by static analysis or tested with new fuzzing inputs. Code coverage methods can assist in determining if all options in branch statements have been executed, if functions have been exercised, if all paths through the code have been executed, if a line of code has been executed, and if conditional statements have been run.

In order to implement code coverage, the software under test usually can be set up to execute in an environment that provides coverage options or can call libraries and debugging software for tracking coverage. Regression testing is often used to evaluate the results of code coverage information.

Scanning

The goal of scanning is to discover open ports and applications by pinging machines, determining network ranges, and port scanning individual systems. The primary scanning steps are: identify active machines, discover open ports and available services, fingerprint the operating system, and map the network.

In scanning, the tester begins to get a more detailed picture of the target by:

- Detecting "live" machines on the target network
- Discovering services running on targeted servers
- Identifying which TCP and UDP services are running
- Identifying the operating system
- Using active and passive fingerprinting

Identifying Active Machines

It is important to detect active machines on the target network for the following reasons:

- It provides information to fill in accurate details of the network map.
- It identifies the perimeter and outer boundary of the target system.
- It helps create an inventory of the networked systems accessible on the target.

The utilities *traceroute* and *ping* are useful tools for identifying active systems, mapping their location, and learning more about their location. Traceroute and ping will be discussed in the following sections.

Traceroute

Traceroute can be used to determine what path the packet takes to get to the target computer. The traceroute utility is available in Linux and in Windows, where it is labeled as *tracert*. In Windows, tracert uses the ICMP protocol while the Linux version uses UDP.

Traceroute uses an IP header field called *Time to Live* (TTL) and shows the path packets travel between two hosts by sending out consecutive packets with ever-increasing TTLs. TTL is a counter that keeps track of each router hop as the packet travels to the target. The TTL field is set by the sender of the datagram, and each router that a packet passes through on the route to its destination reduces the TTL field by one.

The TTL is limited to 16 hops, which means that after 16 tries, the packet is discarded as undeliverable. If the TTL reaches 0, the packet is discarded and an Internet Control Message Protocol (ICMP) message is sent to the originating computer.

The TTL process proceeds as follows:

1. A computer sends out a packet with a TTL of 1.
2. If the first router is not the correct one, it subtracts 1 from the TTL, effectively resetting it to 0, sends a "time exceeded in transit" error message to the origination (with its IP address), and the packet expires.
3. The originating computer increments the TTL by one (TTL + 1) and sends the packet back out, with the TTL now 2.
4. The first incorrect router subtracts 1 from the TTL again, but since it's now not 0 (it's 1), it forwards the datagram to the next router.
5. The second router either delivers the packet if it's destined for its network, or if not, resets the TTL to 0, sends an error message to the origination, and drops the packet.
6. This process continues until the packet is either delivered or the TTL exceeds 16, at which time the packet is dropped permanently.

Figure 5-1 illustrates the routing hops.

TTL PURPOSE

When each router receives an IP packet, it subtracts 1 from the TTL field in the packet's header. When the TTL reaches zero, it's not forwarded any more, but is sent back to the originating computer with a "time exceeded in transit" ICMP message. TTL is needed to keep the Internet from being swamped with undeliverable packets, as without TTL, these packets would travel the Internet forever.

Traceroute is useful not only for showing the path the packet takes to the target, but also what routers are used along the way, through the ICMP messages generated. Traceroute can reveal the name of routers, DNS entries, network affiliation, and geographic location of routers.

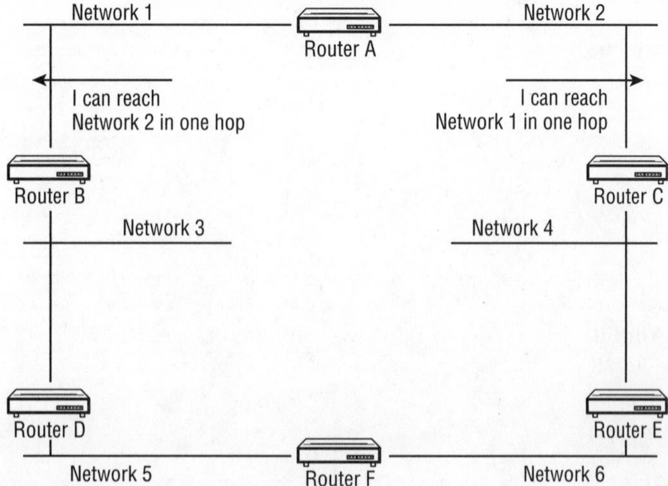

Figure 5-1: Routing hops

It is quite common for firewalls to be configured to block ICMP or UDP, and thereby preventing traceroute from returning useable information. One program designed to get around this issue is Michael Toren's TCPTraceroute (`http://michael.toren.net/code/tcptraceroute/`). TCPTraceroute uses TCP SYN packets instead of ICMP, and is able to bypass many firewall filters.

GUI Traceroute Utilities Some traceroute utilities provide a graphical user interface to better view the traceroute information. For example, NeoTrace (`www.neotrace.com`) displays the route between the attacker and the target, including all intermediate nodes and their registrant information, all in a graphical map. Figure 5-2 shows Neo mapping a traceroute to Google.

Foundstone's Trout (`www.snapfiles.com/get/trout.html`) performs parallel pinging by sending multiple TTL packets at once, making it one of the fastest traceroute programs available. Figure 5-3 shows sample output from Trout.

VisualRoute by VisualWare (`www.visualroute.com`) includes integrated traceroute, ping tests, reverse DNS and Whois lookups, and displays the actual route of connections and IP address locations on a global map, as shown in Figure 5-4. VisualWare also has several other graphics route and bandwidth utilities.

Other useful traceroute programs include:

- **PingPlotter** (`www.pingplotter.com`)—A GUI with many features
- **3d Trace Route** (`www.d3tr.de`)—A simple-to-use traceroute from Germany, with many graphic choices
- **AnalogX HyperTrace** (`www.analogx.com`)—Displays each hop, machine name, machine response time, and the route TTL

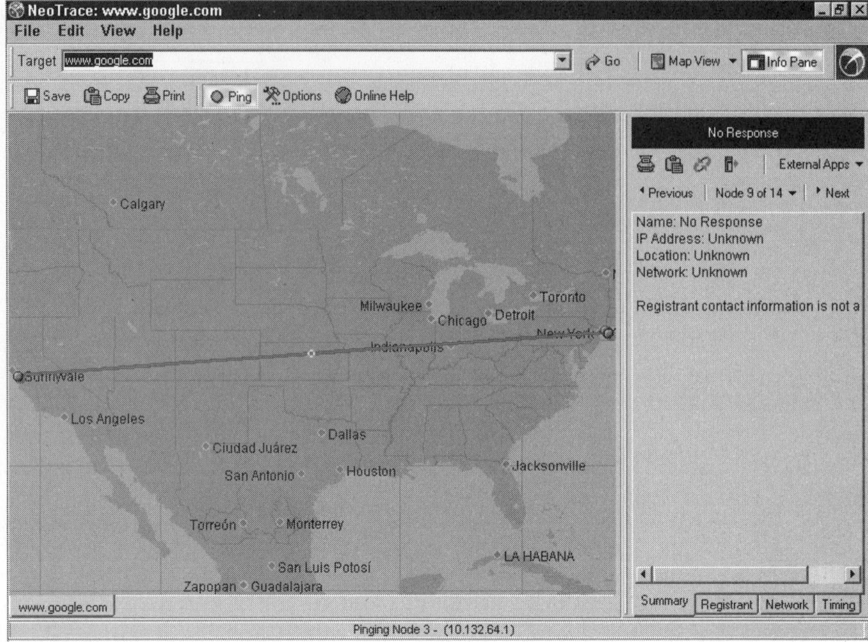

Figure 5-2: Google NeoTrace

Trout 2.00 - www.google.com (216.239.37.104)

File Edit View Trace Options Help

www.google.com

Hop	IP Address	Host Name	Sent	Recv	RTT	Av RTT	Min RTT	Max RTT	%
1	10.132.64.1	[Unknown]	1	2	10 ms	20 ms	10 ms	10 ms	-100.
2	10.132.64.1	[Unknown]	1	1	20 ms	20 ms	20 ms	20 ms	0.0
3	67.83.224.34	dstswr2-vlan2.rh.whplny.cv.net	1	1	20 ms	20 ms	20 ms	20 ms	0.0
4	67.83.224.5	r2-ge10-2.mhe.whplny.cv.net	1	1	20 ms	20 ms	20 ms	20 ms	0.0
5	65.19.120.17	r1-srp1-0.cr.whplny.cv.net	1	1	20 ms	20 ms	20 ms	20 ms	0.0
6	---	[No response]	---	---	---	---	---	---	
7	64.15.0.41	[Unknown]	1	1	20 ms	20 ms	20 ms	20 ms	0.0
8	---	[No response]	---	---	---	---	---	---	
9	66.249.94.235	[Unknown]	1	1	30 ms	30 ms	30 ms	30 ms	0.0
10	66.249.95.127	[Unknown]	1	1	30 ms	30 ms	30 ms	30 ms	0.0
11	216.239.48.94	[Unknown]	1	1	30 ms	30 ms	30 ms	30 ms	0.0
12	216.239.48.110	[Unknown]	1	1	30 ms	30 ms	30 ms	30 ms	0.0
13	216.239.37.104	va-in-f104.google.com	1	1	30 ms	30 ms	30 ms	30 ms	0.0

Ready

Figure 5-3: Google Trout Traceroute

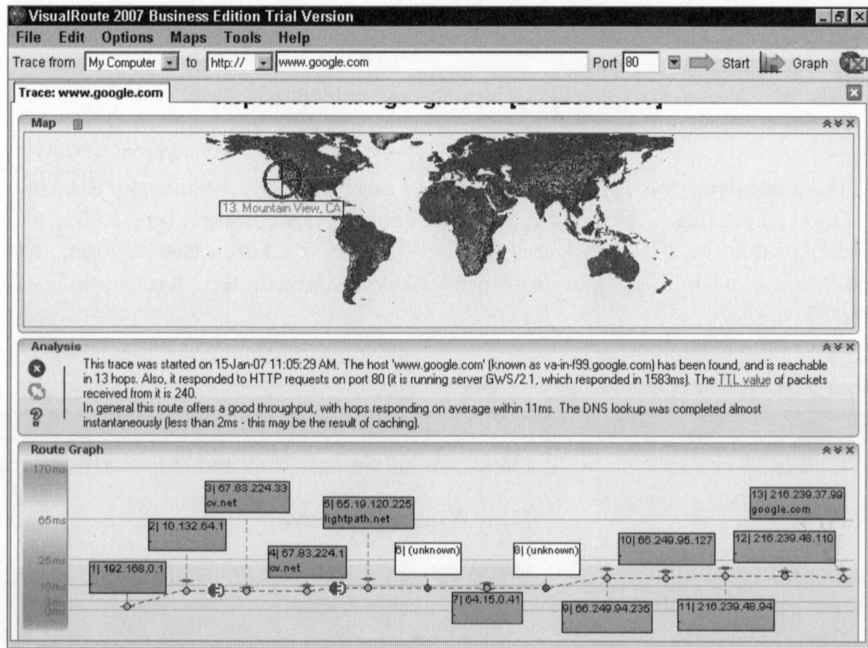

Figure 5-4: Google VisualRoute Traceroute

Ping

Before initiating the scanning phase, it is important to identify active machines. The ping utility can provide this information. Ping is a useful ICMP utility to measure the speed at which packets are moved across the network, and get some basic details about the target, like time-to-live (TTL) details. Ping also helps in assessing network traffic by time stamping each packet, and can also be used for resolving hostnames.

Ping sends out an ICMP Echo Request packet and awaits an ICMP Echo Reply message from an active machine, as follows:

```
Pinging 192.168.0.1 with 32 bytes of data:
Reply from 192.168.0.1: bytes=32 time=2ms TTL=127Reply from
 192.168.0.1: bytes=32 time=1ms TTL=127Reply from 192.168.0.1:
bytes=32 time=2ms TTL=127Reply from 192.168.0.1: bytes=32 time=2ms
 TTL=127
Ping statistics for 192.168.0.1: Packets: Sent = 4, Received =
4, Lost = 0 (0% loss),Approximate round trip times in milli-
seconds: Minimum = 1ms, Maximum = 2ms, Average = 1ms
```

If the target isn't up and running, however, it returns a "Request timed out" message:

```
Pinging 10.1.1.1 with 32 bytes of data:
Request timed out.
Request timed out.
```

```
Request timed out.
Request timed out.
Ping statistics for 10.1.1.1: Packets: Sent = 4, Received = 0,
 Lost = 4 (100% loss),Approximate round trip times in milli-
seconds: Minimum = 0ms, Maximum = 0ms, Average = 0ms
```

TTL is useful not only for determining that a machine is live, but also for determining the target's operating system type. Table 5-3 shows some common time-to-live values. Remember that the TTL will decrement each time the packet passes through a router. This means that the TTL of a router 6 hops away (as determined by traceroute) will be 249 (255 – 6).

Table 5-3: Typical Time-to-Live (TTL) Values

TIME TO LIVE	OPERATING SYSTEM OR DEVICE TYPE
255	Many network devices, Unix and Macintosh systems
128	Many Windows systems
60	Hewlett-Packard Jet Direct printers

TCP/UDP PING

Unfortunately the usefulness of ping for reconnaissance is somewhat limited, due to ISPs blocking ICMP Echo Requests at the network perimeter. Since ICMP is quite often blocked, modern ping utilities were developed that can send TCP/UDP packets. A good list of UDP Ping tools is located at www.freedownloadscenter.com/Best/ping-udp-tools.html.

Since it is often time-consuming and tedious to ping every possible address individually, a technique known as a *ping sweep* can be performed, which will ping a batch of devices and help the attacker determine which ones are active or not. Ping sweeps aid in network mapping by polling network blocks and/or IP address ranges, rather than individual hosts. Pinged hosts will often reply with an ICMP Echo Reply indicating they are alive, whereas no response may mean the target is down or nonexistent or the ICMP protocol is disabled.

In addition to the ping utility included with the operating system, several vendors offer ping tools that provide various levels of functionality and extra features, such as ping sweep ability:

- WS_PingProPack (www.ipswitch.com)
- NetScan Tools (www.nwpsw.com)
- Hping (www.hping.org/download.html)
- icmpenum (www.nmrc.org/files/sunix/icmpenum-1.1.1.tgz)
- NMap (www.insecure.org/NMap/), which is also a port scanner

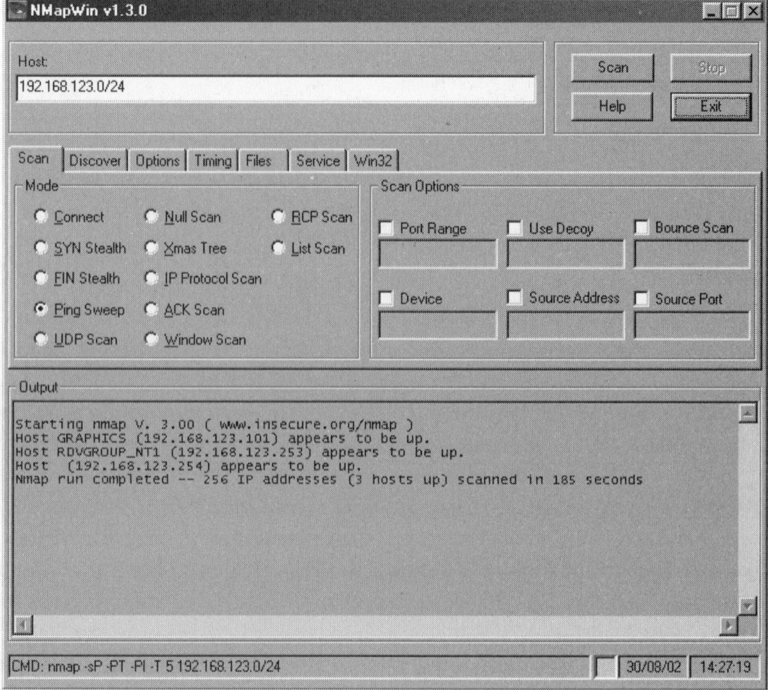

Figure 5-5: Ping sweep with NMap

Some of these tools can also return more information than just the TTL, as shown by the result of an NMap ping sweep in Figure 5-5

Tools that can be used to detect ping sweeps of a network are very useful. Some of these ping sweep detection utilities include:

- Network-based IDS (`www.snort.org`)
- Genius (`www.indiesoft.com`)
- BlackICE (`www.networkice.com`)
- Scanlogd (`www.openwall.com/scanlogd/`)

Discover Open Ports and Available Services

Now that the network range has been determined and a list of active computers has been developed, the next step is to locate any open ports on those machines and identify which services are running. If the available services are running on the target computer, the following information can be obtained:

- Live hosts in the event ICMP is blocked
- Potential ports for creating attack vectors
- Operating system information
- Specific applications

This data can then provide a path into the computer system. Techniques to locate the open ports and discover services include:

- Port scanning
- Banner grabbing
- War dialing
- War walking

Port Scanning

Basically, scanning is a method adopted by administrators and attackers alike to discover more about a network. Port scanning is the process of connecting to TCP and UDP ports for the purpose of finding what services and applications are running on the target device. This helps the attacker decide the best way to attack the system.

The target computer runs many services that listen at well-known ports. Port scanning is one of the most common reconnaissance techniques used by testers to discover the vulnerabilities in these services. Port scanning is functionally the process of sending a data packet to a port to gather information about the state of the port.

A scan may first be implemented using the ping utility. Then, after determining which hosts and associated ports are active, the attacker can initiate different types of probes on the active ports.

Recall that a typical system has $2^{16}-1$ port numbers (65,535), each with its own TCP and UDP port that can be used to gain access, if unprotected.

TCP and UDP must use port numbers to communicate with the upper layers. Port numbers are used to keep track of the different conversations that are simultaneously crossing the network. Originating source port numbers dynamically assigned by the source host are usually some number greater than 1,023.

Port scanning makes it possible to find what TCP and UDP ports are in use. For example, if ports 25, 80, and 110 are open, the device is running the SMTP, HTTP, and POP3 services.

An attacker can use port scanning software to determine which hosts are active and which are inactive (down) in order to avoid wasting time on inactive hosts. A port scan can gather data about a single host or hosts within a subnet (256 adjacent network addresses).

Types of information gathered from scanning include:

- Details about the target's Domain Name System (DNS)
- What network services are available and running, such as email, FTP, or remote login on the target hosts
- The type and release version of the operating system running on the target hosts

Ports have three states: they are either open, closed, or filtered.

- An open port is accepting communications with the target device on that port.
- A closed port is not accepting connectivity on that port.
- A filtered port has some type of network device, like a firewall, preventing the port from being probed to discover whether it's open or closed.

The NMap utility has the ability to determine which of the three states a port is in.

TCP/UDP Scanning Types Many types of TCP/UDP scanning techniques exist. Some are simple and easily detectable by firewalls and intrusion detection systems, whereas some are more complicated and harder to detect. The use of the particular scan types, such as SYN, FIN, connect, ACK, RPC, inverse mapping, FTP bounce, idle host, and so on, depends on the objective of the attack and the platform of the target.

Most scans are intended to be "stealth" or "spoofed" scans. Reduced visibility of the scanner is the goal. Several scans, such as the TCP SYN or TCP FIN scan, are excellent stealth scans. NMap has a mature "stealth" setting that allows the scanner to execute a scan over an extended period of time, to lessen the chance of detection by IDS. The NMap stealth mode scan is shown in Figure 5-6.

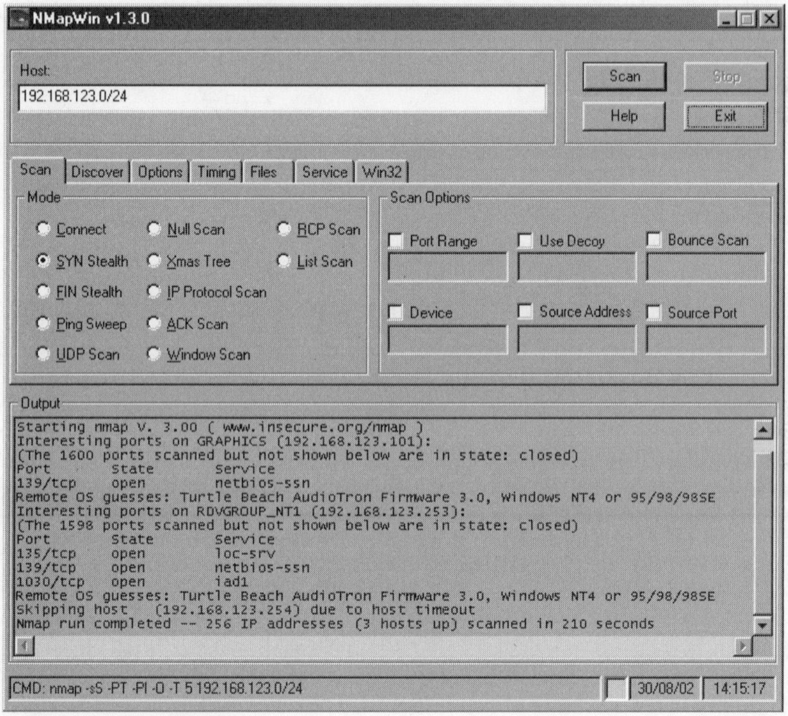

Figure 5-6: NMap stealth scan

Often a stealth scan is implemented by fragmenting the IP datagram within the TCP header. This will bypass some packet-filtering firewalls because they don't get a complete TCP header to match the filter rules.

Spoofing allows an attacker to probe the target's ports without revealing the attacker's own IP address. The FTP proxy bounce attack is an example of a spoofed scan that compromises a third-party FTP server.

The HPing network analysis tool, described later, hides the source of its scans by using another host through which to probe the target site. Also, NMap provides spoofing capability by allowing the operator to enter an optional "source" address for the scanning packet.

TCP vs. UDP TCP provides a full-duplex, connection-oriented, reliable connection. Incoming TCP packets are sequenced to match the original transmission sequence numbers. Because any lost or damaged packets are retransmitted, TCP is very costly in terms of network overhead and is slower than UDP. Reliable data transport is addressed by TCP to ensure that the following goals are achieved:

- An acknowledgment is sent back to the sender upon receipt of delivered segments.
- Any unacknowledged segments are retransmitted.
- Segments are sequenced back in their proper order upon arrival at their destination.
- A manageable data flow is maintained in order to avoid congestion, overloading, and data loss.

UDP is similar to TCP but gives only a "best effort" delivery, which means it offers no error correction, does not sequence the packet segments, and does not care in which order the packet segments arrive at their destination. Consequently, it's referred to as an unreliable protocol.

UDP does not create a virtual circuit and does not contact the destination before delivering the data. Thus, it is also considered a connectionless protocol. UDP imposes much less overhead, however, which makes it faster than TCP for applications that can afford to lose a packet now and then, such as streaming video or audio. Table 5-4 illustrates the differences between the TCP and UDP protocols.

Table 5-4: Differences Between TCP and UDP Protocols

TCP	UDP
Sequenced	Unsequenced
Connection-oriented	Connectionless
Reliable	Unreliable
High overhead	Low overhead
Slower	Faster

UDP is almost useless for obtaining scanning information as opposed to TCP. Since UDP uses "best effort" and is focused on speed (which is why it's better than TCP for streaming audio and video), the hacker can't manipulate a response to generate error messages or avoid detection by an IDS like TCP. The UDP scan might generate an ICMP "unreachable message" code, but since ICMP is likely to be blocked, you'll most often get no response at all.

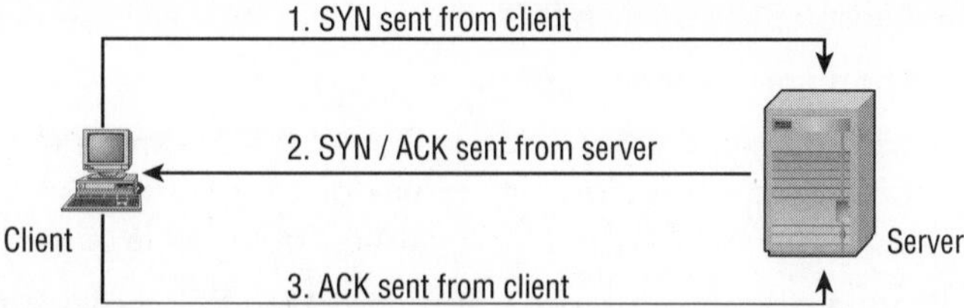

Figure 5-7: TCP three-way handshake

Manipulation of TCP's three-way handshake is the basis for most TCP-based scanning. As shown in Figure 5-7 in its basic form, the steps in the TCP three-way handshake are:

1. SYN sent from client
2. SYN/ACK sent from server
3. ACK sent from client

The following are examples of TCP-based scanning techniques:

- **TCP connect()**—`connect()` is the most basic and fastest scanning technique. `connect()` is able to scan ports quickly simply by attempting to connect to each port in succession. The biggest disadvantage for attackers is that it is the easiest to detect and can be stopped at the firewall.
- **TCP SYN (half open) scanning**—TCP SYN scanning is often referred to as *half-open* scanning because, unlike TCP `connect()`, a full TCP connection is never opened. The scan works by:
  1. Scanner sends a SYN packet to a target port.
  2. If a SYN/ACK is received, this indicates the port is listening.
  3. The scanner then breaks the connection by sending an RST (reset) packet.
  4. If an RST is received, this indicates the port is closed.

  This is harder to trace because fewer sites log incomplete TCP connections, but some packet-filtering firewalls look for SYNs to restricted ports.
- **TCP SYN/ACK scanning**—TCP SYN/ACK is another way to determine if ports are open or closed. The TCP SYN/ACK scan works by:
  1. Scanner initially sends a SYN/ACK.
  2. If the port is closed, it assumes the SYN/ACK packet was a mistake and sends an RST.
  3. If the port was open, the SYN/ACK packet will be ignored and dropped.

  This is considered a stealth scan since it isn't likely to be logged by the host being scanned, but many intrusion detection systems may catch it.
- **TCP FIN scanning**—TCP FIN is a stealth scan that works like the TCP SYN/ACK scan:
  1. Scanner sends a FIN packet to a port.

2. A closed port replies with an RST.
3. An open port ignores the FIN packet.

One issue with this type of scanning is that TCP FIN can be used only to find listening ports on non-Windows machines or to identify Windows machines because Windows ports send an RST regardless of the state of the port.

- **TCP FTP proxy (bounce attack) scanning**—TCP FTP proxy (bounce attack) scanning is a very stealthy scanning technique. It takes advantage of a weakness in proxy FTP connections. It works like this:
  1. The scanner connects to an FTP server and requests that the server initiate a data transfer process to a third system.
  2. The scanner uses the PORT FTP command to declare that the data transfer process is listening on the target box at a certain port number.
  3. It then uses the LIST FTP command to try to list the current directory. The result is sent over the server data transfer process channel.
  4. If the transfer is successful, the target host is listening on the specified port.
  5. If the transfer is unsuccessful, a ''425 Can't build data connection: Connection refused'' message is sent.

  Some FTP servers disable the proxy feature to prevent TCP FTP proxy scanning.
- **IP fragments**—Fragmenting IP packets is a variation on the other TCP scanning techniques. Instead of sending a single probe packet, the packet is broken into two or more packets and reassembled at the destination, thus bypassing the packet filters.

Other TCP scan types include:

- **RPC scan**—A remote program call (RPC) scan is used to locate and identify RPC applications. After open ports are identified with another scan type, the RPC scan sends each open port an RPC null to provoke a response from any RPC application that might be running.
- **IDLE scan**—Considered the only totally stealth scan, an IDLE scan is a way of scanning a remote device to gather port information using another station on the network. It will appear that the scanning process is initiated from this third-party IP address instead of the source host.
- **Xmas tree scan**—The Xmas tree scan sends a TCP frame to a remote device with the URG, PUSH, and FIN flags set.

Determining the OS Type Determining the type of OS is also an objective of scanning, as this will determine the type of attack to be launched.

Sometimes a target's operating system details can be found very simply by examining its Telnet banners or its File Transfer Protocol (FTP) servers, after connecting to these services.

TCP/IP stack fingerprinting is another technique to identify the particular version of an operating system. Since OS and device vendors implement TCP/IP differently, these differences can help in determining the OS. We describe fingerprinting in more detail later in this chapter.

Another type of OS identification technique is *TCP initial sequence number sampling*. After responding to a connection request, information about the operating system can be inferred from the pattern of the sequence numbers.

Scanning Tools While many of these tools are used by attackers and intruders, they also help the security administrator detect and stop malicious scans. Used with intrusion detection systems, these tools can provide some level of protection by identifying vulnerable systems, and they can provide data about the level of activity directed against a machine or network. Since scanning is a continuous activity (that is, all networked systems are being scanned all the time), it's very important that the security professional know what can be compromised. Some common scanning tools are:

- **HPing**—A network analysis tool that sends packets with nontraditional IP stack parameters. It allows the scanner to gather information from the response packets generated.
- **Legion**—Scans for and identifies shared folders on scanned systems, allowing the scanner to map drives directly. Older software.
- **Nessus**—A free security-auditing tool for Linux, BSD, and a few other platforms. It requires a back-end server that has to run on a Unix-like platform.
- **NMap**—A very common port scanning package. More information on NMap follows this section.
- **Security Administrator's Integrated Network Tool (SAINT)**—Examines network services, such as finger, NFS, NIS, ftp and tftp, rexd, statd, and others, to report on potential security flaws.
- **System Administrator Tool for Analyzing Networks (SATAN)**—One of the oldest network security analyzers. SATAN scans network systems for well known and often exploited vulnerabilities.
- **Tcpview**—Allows identification of what application opened which port on Windows platforms.
- **Snort**—A utility used for network sniffing. Network sniffing is the process of gathering traffic from a network by capturing the data as it passes and storing it to analyze later.
- **SuperScan**—A TCP/UDP port scanner, pinger, and hostname revolver. It can perform ping scans and port scans using a range of IP addresses, or it can scan a single host. It also has the capability to resolve or reverselookup IP addresses.
- **THCAmap**—A scanning and banner grabbing utility that probes ports to find out what is really running there, helping to find services that might have been redirected from their standard ports.
- **Scanrand**—A very fast scanning tool. It scans multiple TCP ports at once by implementing stateless parallel scanning.

Other scanning and cracking tools include Network Security Analysis Tool (NSAT), VeteScan, Security Auditor's Research Assistant (SARA), PortScanner, Network Superscanner, CGI Port Scanner, and CGI Sonar.

NMap The most popular port scanner for Linux, NMap (`http://nmap.org`), is also available for the Windows platform. Considered a required tool for all ethical hackers, NMap can scan a system in variety of stealth modes, depending upon how undetectable you want to be. NMap can determine a lot of information about a target, such as what hosts are available, what services are offered, and what OS is running.

NMap scans for most ports from 1 through 1,024 and a number of others in the registered and undefined ranges. This scanning helps identify software like PCAnywhere, SubSeven, and Back Orifice. Now that a Windows interface has been written, it no longer has to be run only on a Unix system.

NMap allows scanning of both TCP and UDP ports, with root privilege required for UDP. While NMap doesn't have signature or password cracking capabilities, like L0pht Crack, it will estimate how hard it will be to hijack an open session.

Vulnerable Ports There are a total of 65,535 TCP and 65,535 UDP port numbers systems use to identify a specific process that is communicating to other processes. Because the complete listing of well-known and registered ports is extensive, some ports are attacked more often than others. In fact, most attackers will focus on the first 1,024 ports, called the well-known ports, because most standard services and applications run in this area.

A good list of well-known ports can be found at `www.iana.org/assignments/port-numbers/`.

In Table 5-5, we've listed the ports that are most commonly used and likely to be scanned.

Port Scanning Issues Some precautions need to be taken when the security administrator begins a program of vulnerability scanning on his or her own network. Some of these issues could cause a system crash or create unreliable scan data:

- **False positives**—Some legitimate software uses port numbers registered to other software, which can cause false alarms when port scanning. This can lead to blocking legitimate programs that appear to be intrusions.
- **Heavy traffic**—Port scanning can have an adverse effect on WAN links and even effectively disable slow links. Because heavy port scanning generates a lot of traffic, it is usually preferable to perform the scanning outside normal business hours.
- **False negatives**—Port scanning can sometimes exhaust resources on the scanning machine, creating false negatives and not properly identifying vulnerabilities.
- **System crash**—Port scanning has been known to render needed services inoperable or actually crash systems. This may happen when systems have not been currently patched or the scanning process exhausts the targeted system's resources.

Table 5-5: Commonly Used Ports

PORT #	SERVICE NAME	SERVICE DESCRIPTION
21	ftp	File Transfer Protocol
22	ssh	Secure Shell
23	telnet	Telnet virtual terminal
25,109,110 143	smtp pop3 imap	Simple Mail Protocol, POP2, POP3 and IMAP Messaging
53	dns	Domain Name Services
80, 8000, 8080	http	Hypertext Transfer Protocol and HTTP proxy servers
118	sqlserv	SQL database service
119	nntp	Network News Transfer Protocol
161	snmp	Simple Network Management Protocol
194	irc	Internet Relay Chat
389,636	ldap	Lightweight Directory Access Protocol
443, 8443	https	Hypertext Transfer Protocol over Secure Socket Layer
2049	nfs	Networking File Systems
3389	rdp	Remote Desktop Protocol/Terminal Services
5631	PCAnywhere	PCAnywhere remote control

- **Unregistered port numbers**—Many port numbers in use are not registered, which complicates the act of identifying what software is using them.

Banner Grabbing

One of the easiest ways to discover what services are running on the open ports is by banner grabbing. Banner grabbing also provides important information about what type and version of software are running. Although most port scanners can perform banner grabbing, banner grabbing can be performed with just native Telnet or FTP.

If the Web server is not properly patched, Telnet can be used to grab HTTP, FTP, and SMTP server information, using the command syntax:

```
Telnet (IP Address) (Port #)
```

For example, executing a Telnet banner grab against a MicrosoftIIS/5.0 server creates the following result:

```
C:\>telnet 192.168.0.100 80
HTTP/1.1 400 Bad Request
Server: Microsoft-IIS/5.0
Date: Mon, 05 Feb Oct 2007 16:04:52 GMT
Content-Type: text/html
```

Another way to grab banners is to use the free utility Netcat (`http://netcat.sourceforge.net/`) distributed freely under the GNU General Public License (GPL). Netcat has many uses, including banner grabbing. To grab a banner, execute Netcat from the command line with the syntax:

```
nc -v -n IP-Address Port
```

Some of Netcat's features include:

- Can create outbound and inbound connections, TCP or UDP, to or from any ports
- Has a tunneling mode which allows also special tunneling such as UDP to TCP, with the possibility of specifying all network parameters (source port/interface, listening port/interface, and the remote host allowed to connect to the tunnel
- Can randomize port scanning
- Can parse RFC854 telnet codes

UrlScan Microsoft's UrlScan security tool is designed to help restrict the types of HTTP requests that Internet Information Services (IIS) will process. By blocking specific HTTP requests, the UrlScan security tool helps prevent potentially harmful requests from reaching the server.

Although UrlScan 2.5 is available on Web servers running IIS 4.0 or later, it's not included with IIS 6.0 because Microsoft feels IIS 6.0 has built-in features that provide security functionality that is equal to or better than most of the features of UrlScan 2.5.

But organizations running IIS 6.0 sometimes choose to install UrlScan because they feel that it provides an added level of security above and beyond IIS 6.0, and some organizations have integrated UrlScan features into their server management practices for IIS and for other Microsoft servers.

Also, UrlScan has several features that help lessen IIS's vulnerability to banner grabbing reconnaissance, in addition to other hacking vulnerabilities, such as:

- **DenyExtensions**—Limits the attack surface of the server by preventing, based on filename extensions, specific requests from running ISAPI or CGI code on the server
- **RemoveServerHeader**—Removes or alters the identity of the server from the "Server" response header

- **DenyVerbs**—Limits the attack surface of the server by preventing requests that would invoke WebDAV
- **DenyHeaders**—Limits the attack surface of the server by preventing requests that would invoke WebDAV
- **RequestLimits**—Enforces limits on the size, in bytes, of separate parts of requests reaching the server
- **DenyUrlSequences**—Allows UrlScan to detect sequences that are used in URL-based attacks on a Web server

War Dialing and War Walking

These concepts were covered earlier in this chapter in the section entitled "Wireless Network Penetration Testing."

Fingerprinting

At this point the attacker has gathered a lot of information, but needs to know more about the operating system of the target. Fingerprinting is a process to determine the operating system on the target computer. One advantage of fingerprinting over some of the more robust scanning techniques is that it allows the attacker to leave smaller footprint—that is, it's less detectable. Any time the reconnaissance is less noticeable, it is more likely to succeed.

Fingerprinting exploits the fact that various operating system vendors implement the TCP stack differently. Uniquely built packets are sent to the target host, and the response is logged. This response is compared with a database to aid in determining the target's operating system.

There are two ways an attacker can implement fingerprinting, passive and active.

Passive Fingerprinting

Passive fingerprinting is less accurate than active fingerprinting, but is less detectable by intrusion detection systems. Like active fingerprinting, passive fingerprinting is also based on the different ways the TCP stack is implemented by different operating systems and by comparing those differences. However, instead of relying on scanning the target host, passive fingerprinting captures packets from the target host (sniffing), which are then examined for specific operating system identifiers.

Many different identifiers can be used to fingerprint the OS, but the four TCP stack elements that are most commonly examined are:

- **Time to Live (TTL)**—Various operating systems set the Time to Live value differently.
- **Initial TCP Window Size**—Different operating systems use different values for the initial window size.
- **Don't Fragment (DF) bit**—Not all operating systems handle fragmentation in the same way.
- **Type of Service (TOS)**—This three-bit field controls the priority of specific packets.

Active Fingerprinting

Active fingerprinting is more accurate than passive fingerprinting, but it's not as stealthy. It's similar to passive fingerprinting, in that active fingerprinting also looks for variations in the implementation of the TCP/IP stack. However, since it involves actually sending altered packets, rather than just passively sniffing packets, it is more powerful and accurate, and more detectable.

Some of the scanning methods employed in active fingerprinting, such as the FIN probe, TCP initial window size, TOS, fragmented packet handling, and initial sequence number sampling, have been mentioned above in the passive fingerprinting and port scanning discussions. Other methods include examining the ACK value, sampling the IPID value, or sending a bogus flag probe.

Several tools exist that support active fingerprinting, including the ubiquitous NMap, Xprobe (`http://xprobe.sourceforge.net/`), and Winfingerprint (`http://winfingerprint.com/`).

Mapping the Network

After the attacker has compiled extensive information about the target, he can create a map of the target's organizational and network structure.

This is primarily a manual process, although some automated tools exist for this, like NLog (`www.nlog-project.org`), which can help compile NMap output, or Cheops (`www.marko.net/cheops/`), a popular Linux network utility.

Depending upon how much work the attacker put into the footprinting, scanning, and fingerprinting phases, the organizational map could have the following information:

- **Network info**—Public domain name information, DNS servers, IP addressing scheme and IPs in use, types of operating systems in use, running machines and services, open ports, WLAN access points, and modem and fax lines open
- **Company info**—Company and branch locations, public phone numbers and email addresses, merger and acquisition information, public financial records, and some individual employee information

Simulation Testing

As a complement to static and dynamic testing methods, simulation incorporating software system models is also used to evaluate assurance and compliance with relevant information system security policies. This approach is effective in identifying threats realized, which can result in harm to the computing environment, as well as possible physical damage.

Simulation can assist in testing possible attack scenarios as follows:

- Simulation of a virus attack
- Simulation of a disaster striking servers and other network resources
- Simulation of acquiring critical information from employees using social engineering methods

- Simulation of a Trojan horse attack that results in critical data being sent to an external source and corruption of system resources
- Simulation of possible attacks on specific test networks that allow for detailed data acquisition and analysis; this test environment should be analogous to the actual operating environment

Simulation and the Computing Environment

A software system must operate and interact correctly and securely with its environment, which can include hardware, other software systems, users, interfaces, and so on. The inability of a software system to communicate with its environment is a major cause of software failures. Thus, a testing simulation of the interaction of software with other resources and modeling of parameters such as bandwidth constraints, memory requirements, user GUI processing, and database accesses can provide invaluable insight into possible software failure modes.

Also, variables provided by the environmental elements to the software system under test are critical in evaluating the security of the software, particularly if the variables are malformed and manipulated to stress the software.

Simulation and Data

Valid simulation testing scenarios depend on the validity of the input data and data at various points in the software system. In most test instances, there will be an interface between data that has not been validated and trusted data. Therefore, it is an important part of security testing to examine the validity of the data that enters the system from sources such as file systems, networks, and Web sites.

Simulation tests should also incorporate malformed and mutated data in the form that attackers can use to access and take control of a computer resource.

Simulation in Load and Stress Tests

Simulations are useful in load and stress tests and can provide the following capabilities:

- Apply different protocols in the middle of load-recording session
- Support testing on a variety of hardware and software configurations
- Model various types of browsers
- Schedule load runs and groups of users within load runs to run at different times
- Automatically generate summary load testing analysis reports
- Model resource, workload, and performance modeling
- Simulate IP addresses for virtual users
- Model different modem connection speeds
- Model different access methods
- Perform process-based and thread-based virtual user simulation
- Perform automated attack simulations

Quality Assurance Simulation Acceptance Testing

Simulation testing also has a role in quality assurance (QA) acceptance testing. QA testing is useful in uncovering the following:

- Failure to implement a critical security requirement
- General implementation errors
- Incorrect implementation of security requirements
- Errors in the test plan

Black box testing using automated simulations of attack vectors can also play an important role in conducting QA acceptance testing.

Testing for Failure

Another mode of testing is to apply failure assessment techniques to software security evaluation. According to the IEEE, a *failure* is "the inability of a system or component to perform its required functions within specified performance requirements."[15]

A *fault*, which is sometimes confused with a failure, is defined as "A manifestation of an error in software. A fault, if encountered, may cause a failure."[16]

Software testing for failure is orthogonal to most individual's inclinations to create items that function correctly and not fail. In order to be successful at software testing, the goal is to make the software fail—that is, to find bugs. Because it is difficult to prove definitively that bugs do not exist in all parts of the software system, testing for failure should focus on areas of the software that are most at risk.

Testing for failure attempts to discover the following:

- The system failure modes
- The consequences of a failure
- The number of failures that might occur

Two effective methods for testing for failure in secure software systems are software failure modes and effects analysis (SFMEA) and software failure modes, effects and criticality analysis (SFMECA). These approaches are based on the failure modes and effects analysis (FMEA) paradigm. Another useful related technique is bi-directional safety analysis (BDSA).

FMEA is a static analysis method that operates from the bottom up and normally considers one failure at a time. FMEA evaluates failure modes on a lower level element of a software system and then applies these modes to the next higher level elements.

[15]*IEEE Standard Glossary of Software Engineering Terminology* (IEEE Std 610.12-1990) (Los Alamitos, CA: IEEE Computer Society Press, 1990).

[16]RTCA, Inc., DO-178B, "Software Considerations in Airborne Systems and Equipment Certification," issued in the U.S. by RTCA, Inc. (document RTCA SC167/DO-178B) and in Europe by the European Organization for Civil Aviation Electronics (EUROCAE document ED-12B), December 1992.

FMEA takes a design description of a system element as an input and then develops the failure modes of each element. These failure modes can be generated by the analyst or obtained from extant failure mode libraries of the respective components. The consequences of these failure modes and the system environment are then developed.

Software Failure Modes and Effects Analysis (SFMEA)

SFMEA is a bottom-up analysis method that evaluates the consequences of an assumed failure mode that proliferates through a software system. Thus, SFMEA is also called a forward analysis test in that it develops the consequences of a failure mode as it propagates through the software. The effects of this failure mode on the software system and the software environment during development are important outputs of this approach.

SFMEA is implemented using tables illustrating the failure modes and the effects of the failure modes on the elements and global environment. These tables are generated by processing inputs through the standard failure modes of the specific components. To thoroughly exercise the SFMEA test, the inputs should include malformed data and unexpected events. Because SFMEA is based on FMEA, the method is not able to accommodate multiple failures in all instances.

When the criticality of the impact of the failure modes is also included in the assessment, the modified technique is known as Software Failure Modes, Effects, and Criticality Analysis (SFMECA). In this method, a rating of low, medium, or high is given to each failure mode as a function of the degree of the impact and likelihood of occurrence.

Bi-Directional Safety Analysis (BDSA)

BDSA is a method that incorporates the forward analysis of SFMEA with a backward search to conduct a more robust static analysis of the software design. Generally, the forward search is applied initially to determine failures that generate high-risk impacts and then the backward search is used to identify the causes of these failures. Through its application of these forward and backward search paradigms, BDSA provides the following capabilities:

- Determines if the software design is free of critical flaws
- Identifies the events that contribute to the possible occurrence of a particular failure mode
- Determines the effects of each failure mode as it propagates through the software system and its environment
- Identifies the failure modes of each software element

The BDSA process can be used to evaluate the software design and identify which malformed input values and abnormal environmental events can result in insecure software system operation.

Security Stress Testing

A related failure testing method is stress testing, which subjects the software to extreme conditions such as inadequate memory capacity, insufficient communication bandwidth, denial-of-service attacks, and hardware malfunctions. During these stressful conditions, the security performance of the software must be sustained, even if the software performs at reduced capability. Therefore, testing must determine if the reduced program execution might provide openings that could be exploited by attackers.

Cryptographic Validation

Simulations, cryptographic algorithms, and cryptographic keys require reliable sources of random numbers for their implementation. In addition, random numbers are critical in generating digital signatures or providing challenges in authentication protocols. The associated numbers have to be random or pseudo-random to the extent that an attacker cannot discern a pattern in them that would allow the prediction of future values.

One aspect of software security testing is to test for weak random number generation and evaluate if the numbers show a predictable pattern. In simulations and key generation, weak random numbers can benefit an attacker by biasing a simulation and producing weak keys, respectively. NIST has developed Special Publication 800-22, "A Statistical Test Suite for Random and Pseudorandom Number Generators for Cryptographic Applications," which presents methods for testing and evaluation of random and pseudorandom number generators. The following paragraphs taken from NIST SP 800-22 provide the logic employed in testing a generator for randomness.

> *A statistical test is formulated to test a specific* null hypothesis *(H_0). For the purpose of this document, the null hypothesis under test is that the sequence being tested is* random. *Associated with this null hypothesis is the alternative hypothesis (H_a), which, for this document, is that the sequence is not random. For each applied test, a decision or conclusion is derived that accepts or rejects the null hypothesis, i.e., whether the generator is (or is not) producing random values, based on the sequence that was produced.*
>
> *During a test, a test statistic value is computed on the data (the sequence being tested). This test statistic value is compared to a critical value. If the test statistic value exceeds the critical value, the null hypothesis for randomness is rejected. Otherwise, the null hypothesis (the randomness hypothesis) is* not *rejected (i.e., the hypothesis is accepted). In practice, the reason that statistical hypothesis testing works is that the reference distribution and the critical value are dependent on and generated under a tentative assumption of randomness.*
>
> *Statistical hypothesis testing is a conclusion-generation procedure that has two possible outcomes, either accept H_0 (the data is random) or accept Ha (the data is non-random)*
>
> *If the data is, in truth, random, then a conclusion to reject the null hypothesis (i.e., conclude that the data is non-random) will occur a small percentage of the time. This conclusion is called a Type I error. If the data is, in truth, non-random, then a conclusion to accept the null hypothesis (i.e., conclude that the data is actually random) is called a Type II error.*

The conclusions to accept H_0 when the data is really random, and to reject H_0 when the data is non-random, are correct.

Table 5-6 illustrates the test procedure conclusion process.

Table 5-6: Test Procedure Decision Process

TRUE SITUATION ACCEPT H_0	CONCLUSION ACCEPT H_A (REJECT H_0)	
Data is random (H0 is true)	No error	Type I error
Data is not random (Ha is true)	Type II error	No error

The NIST tests specified in SP 800-22 can be found at `http://csrc.nist.gov/publications/nistpubs/800-22-rev1/SP800-22rev1.pdf`. Additional batteries of tests, such as the Diehard battery and ent battery, have also been developed to test the strength of random number generators. The Diehard battery of tests can be found at `http://stat.fsu.edu/pub/diehard/` and ent can be located at `www.fourmilab.ch/random/`. However, even if a random number generator passes these tests, it still might not be secure enough for some cryptographic applications.

NIST Cryptographic Module Validation Program (CMVP)

The CMVP program is a joint effort of the U.S. National Institute of Standards and Technology (NIST) and the Communications Security Establishment (CSE) of Canada. The program was established in July 1995 to validate cryptographic modules. These modules are components that contain a cryptographic algorithm. The standards for validation were first published as Federal Information Processing Standard (FIPS) PUB 140-1, "Security Requirements for Cryptographic Modules." FIPS 140-1 was superseded in May 2001 by FIPS PUB 140-2, "Security Requirements for Cryptographic Modules." As of this writing, FIPS PUB 140-3 is in draft form and will supersede FIPS PUB 140-2.

Cryptographic modules developed by vendors will be tested to the requirements of FIPS PUB 140-2 by accredited, independent cryptographic module testing (CMT) laboratories. To qualify, a cryptographic module must implement at least one approved security function. The module testing process is summarized in Figure 5-8.

FIPS 140-3 (draft) defines the following four levels of security:

- **Level 1**—The lowest level of assurance. Basic security requirements are specified for a cryptographic module (e.g., at least one approved security function must be used). No specific physical security mechanisms are required in a Security Level 1 cryptographic module beyond the basic requirement for production-grade components.
- **Level 2**—Enhances the physical security mechanisms of a Security Level 1 cryptographic module by adding the requirement for tamper-evidence, which includes the use of tamper-evident coatings or seals, or for pick-resistant locks on removable covers or doors of the module.

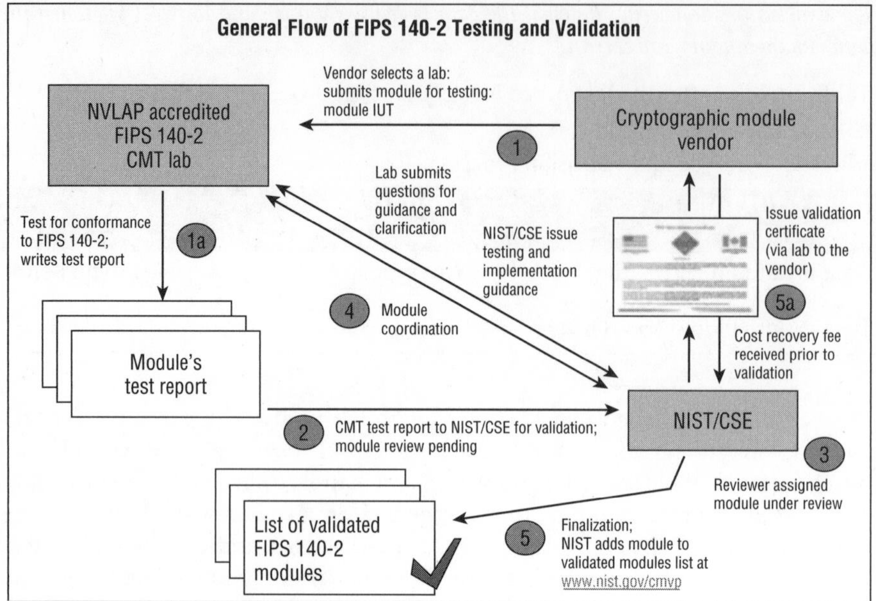

Figure 5-8: The cryptographic module testing process

(From NIST Special Publication, "Frequently Asked Questions for the Cryptographic Module Validation Program," initial release: April 25, 2003, last update, December 04, 2007)

- **Level 3**—In addition to the tamper-evident physical security mechanisms required at Security Level 2, Security Level 3 attempts to prevent the unauthorized access to critical security parameters (CSPs) held within the cryptographic module. Physical security mechanisms required at Security Level 3 are intended to have a high probability of detecting and responding to attempts that provide direct physical access, and use of or modification of the cryptographic module.
- **Level 4**—The physical security mechanisms provide a complete envelope of protection around the cryptographic module with the intent of detecting and responding to all unauthorized attempts at physical access. Penetration of the cryptographic module enclosure from any direction has a high probability of being detected, resulting in the immediate zeroization of all plaintext CSPs.

Additional information on the CMVP along with listings of validated cryptographic modules can be viewed at `www.nist.gov/cmvp/`.

Impact Assessment and Corrective Action

Testing for secure software adds value if it can be shown that successful functioning of the organization, including revenue and profit generation, can depend on the results of the test. The important assets of the organization have to be defined and the cost to the organization of their compromise has to be determined. This activity is formalized under the risk analysis process to determine the impact on the organization's computer resources and a mitigation strategy.

Risk Analysis Summary

Risk analysis entails identifying critical assets, the corresponding threats to these assets, the estimated frequency of occurrence of the threats, and the impact of the threats realized. The following definitions associated with the risk analysis process are reviewed:

- **Asset**—An entity in the organization that is designated to be protected. The value of the asset has to be estimated.
- **Risk**—The potential for harm or loss to an information system.
- **Threat**—An event that has the potential to cause harm.
- **Vulnerability**—A weakness or lack of a safeguard that can be exploited by a threat and cause harm.
- **Safeguard**—A safeguard is a control employed to reduce the risk associated with a specific threat or group of threats.
- **Residual risk**—The risk that remains after the implementation of controls. There is always a residual risk because risk can never be completely eliminated.

Annualized Loss Expectancy

One analysis that is useful is to calculate the annualized loss expectancy (ALE) if a critical asset is disabled or compromised by a malicious attack on an organization's software system. The ALE is defined as follows:

$$\text{ALE} = \text{single loss expectancy (SLE)} \times \text{annualized rate of occurrence (ARO)}$$

ALE is the expected annual loss to an organization from a threat inflicting harm to an asset, SLE is the dollar figure that represents an organization's loss from a single threat realized, and ARO is the estimated annual frequency of the single threat occurring.

For example, assume that an asset with a value of \$700,000 is subject to a successful malicious attack threat twice a year; the ALE is calculated as:

$$\text{ALE} = \text{SLE} \times \text{ARO} = \$700,000 \times 2 = \$1,400,000$$

If the asset has some protection and will not be totally taken out by the threat, the SLE can be modified by an exposure factor (EF) that takes into account that the asset is not completely eliminated by the threat. Formally, EF is the percentage of loss that a realized threat event would have on a specific asset. Therefore,

$$\text{SLE} = \text{asset value (\$)} \times \text{exposure factor (EF)}$$

Thus, in the previous example, if the \$700,000 asset has an exposure of 40 percent to the threat, the SLE is \$700,000 × 0.40 = \$280,000 and the ALE is:

$$\text{ALE} = \text{SLE} \times \text{ARO} = \$280,000 \times 2 = \$560,000$$

In summary, a risk analysis is performed by:

1. Determining the value of assets in order to estimate potential loss amounts
2. Determining potential realistic threats to the assets
3. Calculating the annualized loss expectancy (ALE)

This type of analysis brings home the consequences of an organization losing a critical asset and supports conducting penetration tests and other software security tests to ensure the continuing operations and revenue generation of the organization.

Typical Threats and Attacks

Some typical potential threats that should be considered when calculating the ALE include the following:

- Flaws in security software that provide opportunities for malicious code exploitation of information systems
- Communication systems failures
- Covert channels, which can be used to transfer information in unauthorized ways
- Data aggregation that can be used to obtain information that is not authorized
- Failures in utility services
- Information warfare for military or economic espionage
- Malicious software such as viruses or Trojan horses that can be used to compromise information systems
- Natural disasters such as floods, hurricanes, and winds
- Personnel-related attacks in which information is obtained through unauthorized means or malicious compromises of information systems by disgruntled employees
- Physical destruction or theft of assets or information
- Software and hardware failures in information systems

Malicious individuals attacking software systems are one of the most serious threats to information systems. Attacks mounted by these individuals are of different types and origin and are a critical subset of harmful incursions that penetration tests and other secure software tests are designed to prevent. The Information Assurance Technical Framework (IATF) Document 3.1 (`www.niap-ccevs.org/cc-scheme/sitemap`), which provides a technical process for developing systems with inherent information assurance, categorizes five different classes of attacks as shown in Table 5-7.

Criteria for determining asset value include:

- The sensitivity of the information held in the asset
- The legal liability incurred by loss of information from the asset
- The amount of sensitive information held in the asset

Table 5-7: Classes of Attack

ATTACK	DESCRIPTION
Passive	Passive attacks include traffic analysis, monitoring of unprotected communications, decrypting weakly encrypted traffic, and capture of authentication information (such as passwords). Passive intercept of network operations can give adversaries indications and warnings of impending actions. Passive attacks can result in disclosure of information or data files to an attacker without the consent or knowledge of the user. Examples include the disclosure of personal information such as credit card numbers and medical files.
Active	Active attacks include attempts to circumvent or break protection features, introduce malicious code, or steal or modify information. These attacks may be mounted against a network backbone, exploit information in transit, electronically penetrate an enclave, or attack an authorized remote user during an attempt to connect to an enclave. Active attacks can result in the disclosure or dissemination of data files, denial of service, or modification of data.
Close-in	Close-in attack consists of individuals attaining close physical proximity to networks, systems, or facilities for the purpose of modifying, gathering, or denying access to information. Close physical proximity is achieved through surreptitious entry, open access, or both.
Insider	Insider attacks can be malicious or nonmalicious. Malicious insiders intentionally eavesdrop, steal, or damage information; use information in a fraudulent manner; or deny access to other authorized users. Nonmalicious attacks typically result from carelessness, lack of knowledge, or intentional circumvention of security for such reasons as "getting the job done."
Distribution	Distribution attacks focus on the malicious modification of hardware or software at the factory or during distribution. These attacks can introduce malicious code into a product, such as a back door to gain unauthorized access to information or a system function at a later date.

- The loss of public confidence in the organization caused by compromise of information held by the asset
- The dependencies among the assets
- The cost to protect the asset
- The revenue generated by the asset

These criteria form an additional basis for justifying software security testing in that ensuring the security of critical organizational assets is an important consideration for the organization's customers. From a customer's or potential customer's point of view, demonstrating that a variety of sound information security-related measures are consistently practiced is an important factor that is considered in doing business with an organization. Thus, software security testing can be viewed as a component of marketing, operations, income generation, and establishing customer loyalty. Typical customer concerns in doing business with an organization include:

- Is my proprietary intellectual property information being protected?
- Is my financial information being protected?
- Are my transaction records being protected?
- Is billing and delivery information being protected?
- Is information concerning any problems associated with the transaction and deliverables being protected?
- Is it easy to conduct business by means of a secure intranet, including perusing available products and services, placing and tracking orders, reviewing billing data, checking on shipping dates, and so on?

Impact Determination

As with other metrics in evaluating the performance of an organization, business management requires a measure of the impact of a threat realized on the organization's network and information system. One popular and useful approach to impact characteristics is provided by the National Institute of Standards and Technology (NIST) Federal Information Processing Publication (FIPS) 199, "Standards for Security Categorization of Federal Information and Information Systems."

FIPS 199 defines three levels of potential impact of a threat realized on the security objectives of confidentiality, integrity, and availability. Table 5-8 provides these impact definitions from the FIPS 199 document.

FIPS 199 also defines the term *security category* (SC) as a function of the potential impact on information or information systems should a threat successfully exploit vulnerability in the system. A security category can apply to information types and information systems.

The general formula developed in FIPS 199 for defining a security category of an *information type* is:

$$SC_{\text{information type}} = \{(\text{confidentiality}, \textit{impact}), (\text{integrity}, \textit{impact}), (\text{availability}, \textit{impact})\}$$

where the acceptable values for potential *impact* are LOW, MODERATE, HIGH, or NOT APPLICABLE.

For example, if the payroll department of an organization determines that there is a high potential impact from a loss of confidentiality, a high potential impact from a loss of integrity, and a moderate potential impact from a loss of availability, the security category, SC, of this information type would be:

$$SC_{\text{payroll information}} = \{(\text{confidentiality, HIGH}), (\text{integrity, HIGH}), (\text{availability, MODERATE})\}$$

For information systems, the corresponding formula is:

$$SC_{\text{information system}} = \{(\text{confidentiality}, \textit{impact}), (\text{integrity}, \textit{impact}), (\text{availability}, \textit{impact})\}$$

Table 5-8: Impact Definitions for Security Objectives

SECURITY OBJECTIVE	POTENTIAL LOW	IMPACT MODERATE	HIGH
Confidentiality			
Preserving authorized restrictions on information access and disclosure, including means for protecting personal privacy and proprietary information.	The unauthorized disclosure of information could be expected to have a limited adverse effect on organizational operations, organizational assets, or individuals.	The unauthorized disclosure of information could be expected to have a serious adverse effect on organizational operations, organizational assets, or individuals.	The unauthorized disclosure of information could be expected to have a severe or catastrophic adverse effect on organizational operations, organizational assets, or individuals.
Integrity			
Guarding against improper information modification or destruction, including ensuring information nonrepudiation and authenticity.	The unauthorized modification or destruction of information could be expected to have a limited adverse effect on organizational operations, organizational assets, or individuals.	The unauthorized modification or destruction of information could be expected to have a serious adverse effect on organizational operations, organizational assets, or individuals.	The unauthorized modification or destruction of information could be expected to have a severe or catastrophic adverse effect on organizational operations, organizational assets, or individuals.
Availability			
Ensuring timely and reliable access to and use of information.	The disruption of access to or use of information or an information system could be expected to have a limited adverse effect on organizational operations, organizational assets, or individuals.	The disruption of access to or use of information or an information system could be expected to have a serious adverse effect on organizational operations, organizational assets, or individuals	The disruption of access to or use of information or an information system could be expected to have a severe or catastrophic adverse effect on organizational operations, organizational assets, or individuals

NIST Federal Information Processing Publication (FIPS) 199, " Standards for Security Categorization of Federal Information and Information Systems."

where the acceptable values for potential impact are LOW, MODERATE, or HIGH. A value of NOT APPLICABLE cannot be applied to an impact level of an information system. To develop a category for an information system, the potential impact values assigned to the security objectives of confidentiality, integrity, and availability must be the maximum (worst case) values assigned among the security categories that have been assigned to the different types of information residing on the system.

For example, suppose a health care provider has billing information for patients, including their treatment type and personal information, residing on a billing information system. The CIO determines that for these records, the potential impact from a loss of confidentiality is high, the potential impact from a loss of integrity is high, and the potential impact from a loss of availability is moderate.

The corresponding security category, SC, would be expressed as:

$$SC_{\text{billing information}} = \{(\text{confidentiality, HIGH}), (\text{integrity, HIGH}), (\text{availability, MODERATE})\}$$

Now, assume that the same billing information system also supports some of the health care organization's administrative functions and has the following SC for the administrative information:

$$SC_{\text{administrative information}} = \{(\text{confidentiality, LOW}), (\text{integrity, HIGH}), (\text{availability, LOW})\}$$

The security category of the acquisition information system would be comprised of the highest values of the two information categories resident on the system. Thus, the SC would be:

$$SC_{\text{billing information system}} = \{(\text{confidentiality, HIGH}), (\text{integrity, HIGH}), (\text{availability, MODERATE})\}$$

Management Responsibilities in Risk Analysis Relating to Software Security Testing

Management in an organization has to make decisions regarding software security testing. These decisions and subsequent actions take place before, during, and after software security testing. Table 5-9 summarizes these management roles and actions.

Note that just because software successfully passes all of its security tests, this does not mean that novel attack patterns and anomalies will never arise in deployment to compromise the software. For this reason, iterative testing throughout the software's lifetime is imperative to ensure that its security posture does not degrade over time.

Corrective Action and Mitigation

There are three choices available to management regarding risk. One option is to use software security tests as a component of a risk management program that uses controls and safeguards to reduce risk and, correspondingly, impact. The second choice is to transfer the risk to another organization such as an insurance company. The third approach is to accept the status quo risk and accept the losses that might occur.

Obviously, the latter is a problematic choice. The other two are reasonable options, but the risk reduction approach is the most prudent of the three and demonstrates due care taken by corporate management.

Table 5-9: Management Roles and Activities

ROLES	ACTIVITIES
Senior organization officers	Meet requirements of reasonable care for legal liability and provide supporting resources
Chief information officer	Incorporate risk analysis in IT planning and meeting operational requirements
Business unit managers	Integrate information system security into business functions and operations
Information and data owners	Provide confidentiality, integrity, and availability protections
Information system security officer	Determine risks and implement controls to reduce risks to information systems
Security awareness training personnel	Include risk analysis concepts and practices in training programs

NIST SP 800-30, *Risk Management Guide for Information Technology Systems*, provides a risk mitigation strategy as shown in Figure 5-9.

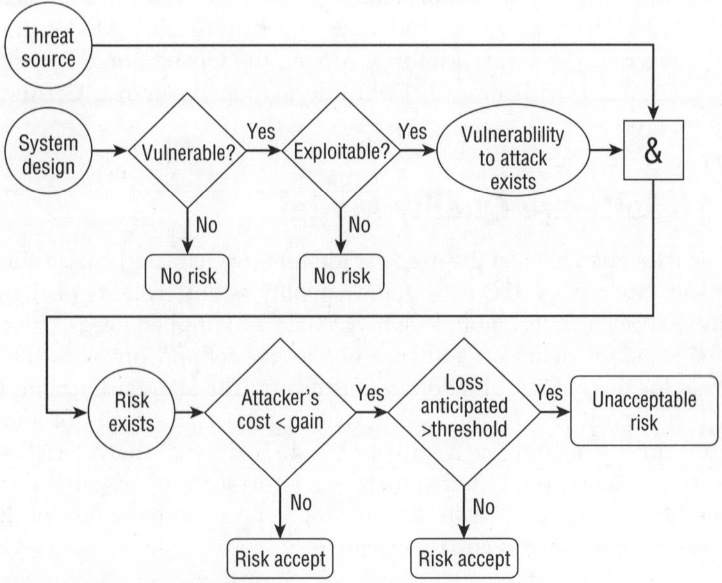

Figure 5-9: Risk mitigation strategy

Implementing the strategy after analyzing the results of a software security test and other evaluations includes using appropriate controls. Controls can be technical, managerial, operational, or a combination of those.

To address software security specifically, the following actions should be taken after testing:

1. Enter test results and the corresponding version of the software module under test into configuration management
2. Ascertain security requirements that were not included in the original specification and implementation
3. Assess risk posed to the software system from failure to incorporate security requirements that were not included in the original specification
4. Determine risk to the software system from failure to modify the software to address security requirements that were not included in the original specification
5. Determine the amount of rework necessary to address the new requirements

Most importantly, the cumulative test results should provide an indication of whether the software is able to defend against attacks or recover from attacks so that risk is kept at an acceptable level.

Standards for Software Quality Assurance

There are a number of standards and guidelines for software quality assurance that provide valuable insight into developing secure software. In this section, some prominent models are presented.: ISO 9126 Software Quality Model, the Systems Security Engineering Capability Maturity Model, the Open Source Security Testing Methodology Manual, and the U.S. DoD Information Assurance Certification and Accreditation Process.

ISO 9126 Software Quality Model

ISO 9126 was designed to meet the need for identifying characteristics in software that constitute software quality. ISO 8204 defines quality as the "Totality of characteristics of an entity that bears on its ability to satisfy stated and implied needs."[17]

Thus, the standard defines a software quality model and provides the means to project goals for the quality of a software product. The standard accomplishes this objective in two parts: modeling the internal and external quality of software and modeling the quality in applying a software product. Internal characteristics are those that refer to static measures. External metrics refer to software execution. ISO 9126 is not designed to evaluate a software product for a specific use because of the varying requirements of different software products.

[17]DIN EN ISO 8402, *Qualitätsmanagement Begriffe*, 1995.

The ISO 9126 international standard covers the following areas:

- Software quality model
- External metrics
- Internal metrics
- Quality in use metrics

The standard focuses on human issues that affect software quality and develops methods of understanding software project objectives. Part I of the standard, ISO 9126-1, defines the Software Quality Model and will be the main topic of this section.

ISO 9126-1 discusses the following six primary quality characteristics:

- **Functionality**—The set of required functions of a product or service and their respective properties
- **Reliability**—The capability of the software system to maintain its performance level under defined conditions for specific periods of time
- **Usability**—The ease of use and assessment of the effort required to perform a given function
- **Efficiency**—The amount of system resources used when providing a specified level of performance under defined conditions
- **Maintainability**—The effort required to implement a specified set of modifications to a software system
- **Portability**—The ability of a software system to adapt to changes in its environment and support porting to a different environment

In the ISO 9126-1 standard, these quality characteristics are further divided into the subcharacteristics shown in Table 5-10

Even though the standard provides a mechanism to define a quality model for a software product, an organization has to specifically define its own specific model and the effective incorporation of quality characteristics.

SSE-CMM

The Systems Security Engineering Capability Maturity Model (SSE-CMM), version 3.0, 2003, `www.issea.org`, is another standard applicable to software quality assurance that describes those characteristics of security engineering processes essential to ensure good security engineering. It addresses the following areas of security:

- Operations security
- Information security
- Network security
- Physical security
- Personnel security
- Administrative security

Table 5-10: ISO/IEC 9126 Model for Internal and External Quality

FUNCTIONALITY	RELIABILITY	USABILIITY	EFFICIENCY	MAINTAINABILITY	PORTABILITY
Suitability	Maturity	Understandability	Time behavior	Analyzability	Adaptability Installability
Accuracy	Fault tolerance	Learnability	Resource utilization	Changeability	Co-existence
Interoperability	Recoverability	Operability	Efficiency compliance	Stability	
Security	Reliability compliance	Attractiveness		Testability	Replaceability
Functionality compliance		Usability compliance		Maintainability compliance	Portability compliance

- Communications security
- Emanations security
- Computer security

The SSE-CMM is covered in detail in Chapter 1 of this text.

OSSTMM

The Open Source Security Testing Methodology Manual (OSSTMM) 3.0 defines an approach to security testing at an operational level. It also addresses legislative, regulatory, and policy compliance.

OSSTMM was created by Peter Herzog and developed and maintained by the Institute for Security and Open Methodologies (ISECOM). ISECOM (`www.isecom.org`) is an open community that is registered in Spain and in the United States as a nonprofit organization and which encourages and supports peer review. Because the OSSTMM is open source, this allows for free dissemination of its information and intellectual property.

The following excerpt defines the scope of the OSSTMM:

The primary purpose of this manual is to provide a scientific methodology for the accurate characterization of security through examination and correlation of test results in a consistent and reliable way. A secondary purpose is to provide guidelines which, when followed correctly, will allow the auditor to perform a certified OSSTMM audit. These guidelines exist to assure the following:

1. *The test was conducted thoroughly.*
2. *The test included all necessary channels.*
3. *The posture for the test complied with the law.*
4. *The results are measurable in a quantifiable way.*
5. *The results are consistent and repeatable.*
6. *The results contain only facts as derived from the tests themselves.*

Toward this end, the OSSTMM Version 3 covers the following areas:

- Risk assessment values for the quantification of security
- The rules of engagement for driving a proper test
- Channel tests (wireless, physical, telecommunications, human, and data networks)
- Error types
- A detailed testing process

Figure 5-10 illustrates the position of the OSSTMM relative to standards, regulations, policies, and procedures.

The OSSTMM defines test types as shown in Table 5-11.

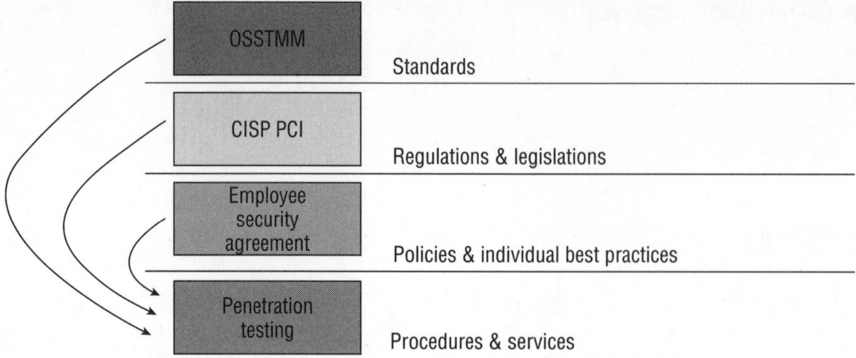

Figure 5-10: OSSTMM positioning

(From OSSTMM 3.0 LITE, "Introduction and Sample to the Open Source Security Testing Methodology Manual," created by Peter Herzog and developed by ISECOM)

The manual defines the scope of an audit as "the total possible operating security environment for any interaction with any asset, which may include the physical components of security measures as well." Specifically, the OSSTMM defines the scope as encompassing the following three channels and corresponding subchannels as shown:

- COMSEC (communications security)
  - **Data networks**—Comprises all electronic systems and data networks where interaction takes place over established cable and wired network lines.
  - **Telecommunications**—Comprises all telecommunication networks, digital or analog, where interaction takes place over established telephone or telephone-like network.
- PHYSSEC (physical security)
  - **Human**—Comprises the human element of communication where interaction is either physical or psychological.
  - **Physical**—Physical security testing where the channel is both physical and nonelectronic in nature. Comprises the tangible element of security where interaction requires physical effort or an energy transmitter to manipulate.
- SPECSEC (spectrum security)
  - **Wireless communications**—Comprises all electronic communications, signals, and emanations which take place over the known EM spectrum. This includes ELSEC as electronic communications, SIGSEC as signals, and EMSEC, which are emanations untethered by cables.

The OSSTMM test module operation is initiated with an estimation of the posture of the test software. The OSSTMM has 17 modules that are applicable to all five channel categories. A module takes as input the information used in performing tasks and produces output such as processed data that might be used as an input to another module.

Table 5-11: OSSTMM Test Types

Blind	The auditor engages the target with no prior knowledge of its defenses, assets, or channels. The target is prepared for the audit, knowing in advance all the details of the audit. A blind audit primarily tests the skills of the auditor. The breadth and depth of a blind audit can only be as vast as the auditor's applicable knowledge and efficiency allows. In COMSEC and SPECSEC, this is often referred to as ethical hacking. In other PHYSSEC and HUMSEC channels, this is generally scripted as war gaming or role playing.
Double blind	The auditor engages the target with no prior knowledge of its defenses, assets, or channels. The target is not notified in advance of the scope of the audit, the channels tested, or the test vectors. A double blind audit tests the skills of the auditor and the preparedness of the target to unknown variables of agitation. The breadth and depth of a blind audit can only be as vast as the auditor's applicable knowledge and efficiency allows. This is also known as a black box audit or penetration test.
Gray box	The auditor engages the target with limited knowledge of its defenses and assets and full knowledge of channels. The target is prepared for the audit, knowing in advance all the details of the audit. A gray box audit tests the skills of the auditor and the preparedness of the target to unknown variables of agitation. The nature of the test is efficiency. The breadth and depth depends upon the quality of the information provided to the auditor before the test as well as the auditor's applicable knowledge. This type of test is often referred to as a vulnerability test and is most often initiated by the target as a self assessment.
Double gray box	The auditor engages the target with limited knowledge of its defenses and assets and full knowledge of channels. The target is notified in advance of the scope and time frame of the audit but not the channels tested or the test vectors. A double gray box audit tests the skills of the auditor and the target's preparedness to unknown variables of agitation. The nature of the test is efficiency. The breadth and depth depends upon the quality of the information provided to the auditor and the target before the test as well as the auditor's applicable knowledge. This is also known as a white box audit.
Tandem	The auditor and the target are prepared for the audit, both knowing in advance all the details of the audit. A tandem audit tests the protection and controls of the target. However, it cannot test the preparedness of the target to unknown variables of agitation. The true nature of the test is thoroughness as the auditor does have full view of all tests and their responses. The breadth and depth depends upon the quality of the information provided to the auditor before the test (transparency) as well as the auditor's applicable knowledge. This is often known as an in-house audit or a crystal box audit, and the auditor is often part of the security process.

Continued

Table 5-11: *(continued)*

Reversal	The auditor engages the target with full knowledge of its processes and operational security, but the target knows nothing of what, how, or when the auditor will be testing. The true nature of this test is to audit the preparedness of the target to unknown variables and vectors of agitation. The breadth and depth depends upon the quality of the information provided to the auditor and the auditor's applicable knowledge and creativity. This is also often called a red team exercise.

From OSSTMM 3.0 LITE, "Introduction and Sample to the Open Source Security Testing Methodology Manual," created by Peter Herzog and developed by ISECOM.

The methodology flow is shown in Figure 5-11.

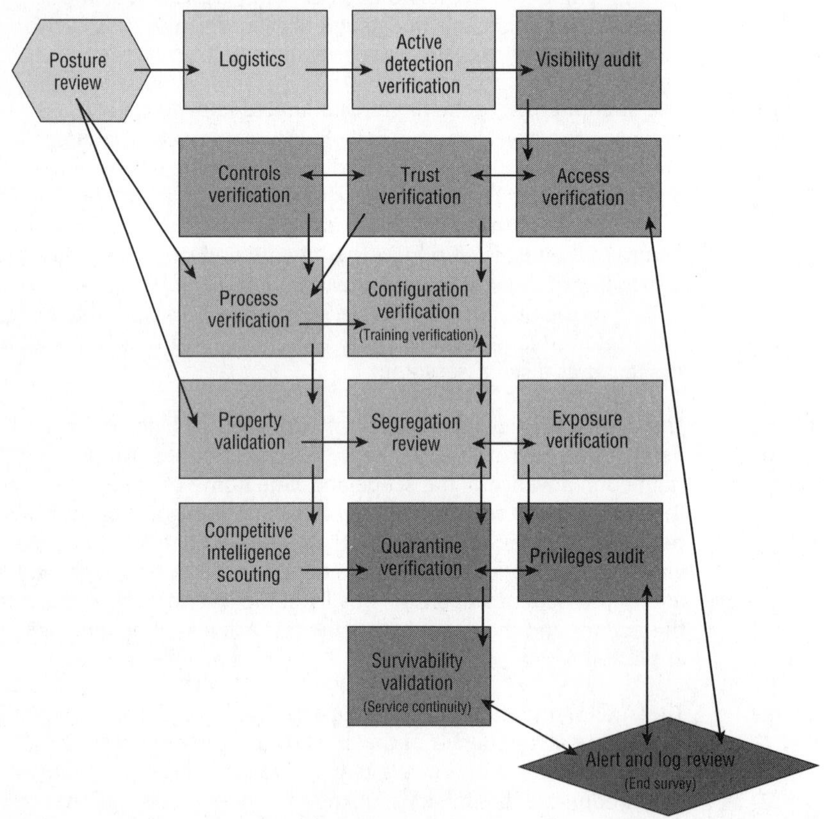

Figure 5-11: OSSTMM methodology channel flow

(From OSSTMM 3.0 LITE, "Introduction and Sample to the Open Source Security Testing Methodology Manual," created by Peter Herzog and developed by ISECOM)

The OSSTMM methodology is executed in four phases. These four phases and their relation to the 17 modules are described in Figure 5-12.

Module		Description	Explanation
A. Regulatory Phase			
Every trip begins with a direction. In the regulatory phase, the auditor begins the audit with an understanding of the audit requirements, the scope, and the constraints to the auditing of this scope. Often, the test type is best determined after this phase.			
A.1	Posture Review	The review of the culture, rules, norms, regulations, legislation, and policies applicable to the target.	Know the scope and what tests must be done. Required if Phase C is to be properly conducted.
A.2	Logistics	The measurement of interaction constraints such as distance, speed, and fallibility to determine margins of accuracy within the results.	Know the limitations of the audit itself. This will minimize error and improve efficiency.
A.3	Active Detection Verification	The verification of the practice and breadth of interaction detection, response, and response predictability.	Know the restrictions imposed on interactive tests. This is required to properly conduct Phases B and D.
B. Definitions Phase			
The core of the basic security test requires knowing the scope in relation to interactions with the targets conveyed to interactions with assets. This phase will define the scope.			
B.4	Visibility Audit	The determination of the applicable targets to be tested within the scope. Visibility is regarded as "presence" and not limited to human sight.	Know what targets exist and how they interact with the scope, if at all. A dead or missing target is also an unresponsive target. However, an unresponsive target is not necessarily a missing target.
B.5	Access Verification	The measurement of the breadth and depth of interactive access points within the target and required authentication.	The access point is the main point of any asset interaction. Verifying an access point exists is one part of determining its purpose. Full verification requires knowing all there is to know about the access point.
B.6	Trust Verification	The determination of trust relationships from and between the targets. A trust relationship exists wherever the target accepts interaction freely and without credentials.	Trusts for new processes are after very limited where older processes have a seemingly chaotic evolution to the outsider. Knowing trust relationships between targets will show the age or value of the interaction.
B.7	Controls Verification	The measurement of the use and effectiveness of the process-based (Class B) loss controls: non-repudiation, confidentiality, privacy, and integrity. The control of alarm is verified at the end of the methodology.	Most processes are defined in response to a necessary interaction and some remain long after that interaction stops or has changed. Knowing what process controls are in place is a type of security archeology.
C. Information Phase			
Much of security auditing is about the information that the auditor uncovers. In this phase, the various types of value and detriment of misplaced and mismanaged information as an asset are brought to light.			
C.8	Process Verification	The determination of the existence and effectiveness of the record and maintenance of existing actual security levels and/or diligence defined by the posture review and indemnification controls.	Know the controllers and their routines for the controls. Most processes will have a defined set of rules, however actual operations reflect any efficiency, laziness, or paranoia which may redefine the rules. So it's not just that the process is there but also how it works.
C.9	Configuration Verification Training Verification (HUMSEC)	The research of the steady state (normal operation) of the targets as they have been designed to operate under normal conditions to determine underlying problems outside of the application of security stress tests.	This module explores the default conditions under which the targets operate regularly to understand the intent, business justification, and reasoning for the targets. Additionally, many regulations require information regarding how something is planned to work and this is not always evident in the execution of that work.

Figure 5-12: OSSTMM method overview

(From OSSTMM 3.0 LITE, "Introduction and Sample to the Open Source Security Testing Methodology Manual," created by Peter Herzog and developed by ISECOM)

C.10	Property Validation	The measurement of the breadth and depth in the use of illegal and/or unlicensed intellectual property or applications within the target.	Know the status of property ownership rights.
C.11	Segregation Review	A determination of the levels of personally identifiable information defined by the posture review.	Know which privacy rights apply and to what extent the uncovered personally identifiable information can be classified based on these requirements.
C.12	Exposure Verification	The search for freely available information which describes indirect visibility of targets or assets within the chosen channel of the scope.	The word on the street has value. Uncover information on targets and assets from public sources including that from the targets themselves.
C.13	Competitive intelligence Scouting	The search for freely available information, directly or indirectly, which could harm or adversely affect the target owner through external, competitive means.	There may be more value in the information from processes and targets than the assets which they are protecting. Uncover information that by itself or in aggregate can influence competitive business decisions.
D. Interactive Controls Test Phase			
These tests are focused on penetration and disruption. This is often the final phase of a security test to assure disruptions do not affect responses of less invasive tests and because the information for making these tests may not be known untill other phases have been carried through. The final module, D17, of Alert and Log Review, is required to verify that prior test assumptions are true. Most security tests that do not include this phase may still need to run an end review from the vector of the targets and assets to clarify disruptions that did not respond during standard echo tests.			
D.14	Quarantine Verification	The determination and measurement of effective use of quarantine for all access to and within the target.	Determine the effectiveness of authentication and subjugation controls in terms of black and white list quarantines.
D.15	Privileges Audit	The mapping and measurement of the impact of misuse of subjugation controls, credentials and privileges or the unauthorized escalation of privilege to a higher level privilege.	Determine the effectiveness of authorization on authentication, indemnification, and subjugation controls in terms of depth and roles.
D.16	Survivability Validation Service Continuity (HUMSEC)	The determination and measurement of the resistance of the target to excessive or adverse changes where continuity and resilience controls would be impacted.	Determine the effectiveness of continuity and resistance controls through the verification of denial of service and denial of interactivity.
D.17	Alert and Log Review End Survey (HUMSEC)	A review of audit activities performed with the true depth of those activities as recorded by the target or from a third-party as in the control of alarm.	Know what parts of the audit left a usable and reliable trail.

Figure 5-12: *(continued)*

An OSSTMM audit identifies vulnerabilities and provides a measurement of security, but does not necessarily present solutions. The requirement to provide solutions is not inherent in the OSSTMM and is a function of the agreement between the audited organization and the audit provider.

ISECOM is an independent, nonprofit security research organization and the certification authority for OSSTMM. Certification in OSSTMM audits provides the assurance that security tests are valid and conducted according to the OSSTMM standards and guidelines.

DIACAP

The U.S. Department of Defense has established the DoD Information Assurance Certification and Accreditation Process (DIACAP) for authorizing the operation of DoD Information Systems. DoD Instruction 8510.01, signed on November 28, 2007, is the official governing document for the DIACAP process.

The DIACAP applies to the "acquisition, operation and sustainment of all DoD-owned or controlled information systems that receive, process, store, display, or transmit DoD information, regardless of classification or sensitivity of the information or information system. This includes Enclaves, AIS Applications (e.g., Core Enterprise Services), Outsourced Information Technology (IT)-Based Processes, and Platform IT Interconnections."

The DIACAP was developed to reduce the burden of documentation requirements over previous methods. A typical DIACAP package will contain a minimal set of documentation, such as:

- System Identification Profile
- DIACAP Strategy
- IA Implementation Plan
- DIACAP Scorecard
- Certification Determination
- DIACAP Plan of Actions and Milestones
- Accreditation Decision
- Artifacts and Evidence of Compliance

The DIACAP Scorecard is the "report card" of how the system compared against mandatory information assurance controls.

Regression Testing

As software evolves, new features are added and existing features are modified. Sometimes, these new features and modifications "break" existing functionality—that is, cause accidental damage to existing software components. According to the IEEE Software Engineering Body of Knowledge (IEEE610.12-90), regression testing is the "selective retesting of a system or component to verify that modifications have not caused unintended effects." Regression testing can show that software that previously passed the tests no longer does. The problem code can then be identified and fixed to restore the lost functionality. However, as software evolves, a fault that was previously fixed sometimes "reemerges." This kind of reemergence of faults is common and occurs for a number of reasons including:

- **Poor revision control practices**—The fix was not documented properly or the change was accidentally reversed.
- **Software brittleness**—The fix for the initial fault was too narrow in scope. As the software ages and the code base grows larger (becoming "legacy" software), new problems emerge relating to the initial fault, but are more difficult to fix without negatively affecting other areas of the software.
- **Repetition of mistakes**—Problematic code is sometimes copied from one area of the software to another, or when some feature is redesigned, the same mistakes

will be made in the redesign that were made in the original implementation of the feature.

Increasing the code execution coverage of regression testing can help prevent the reemergence of software faults. For example, regression tests could be varied—such as by introducing new sample data or combining tests—to catch problems that were missed with the existing tests. In this way, regression testing would not only verify that previous tests still work, but would also mitigate the risk of unintended side effects of change.

For greater assurance, regression testing should also be more extensive for code surrounding vulnerability fixes, code that may contain the same class of vulnerability, and other high-consequence areas of the software. A regression security test plan should be developed containing misuse/abuse cases and attack scenarios (based in part on relevant attack patterns). Earlier test cases can be augmented by any new abuse/misuse cases and attack scenarios suggested by real-world attacks that have emerged since the software was last tested.

Regression testing is often performed by different stakeholders in the software life cycle. During the coding phase, programmers run unit tests to verify that individual units of source code are working properly. The unit is the smallest testable part of the software, often a function or method and its encapsulated data. Unit testing as part of a software development methodology, such as extreme programming, typically relies upon an automated unit testing framework, such as JUnit (`www.junit.org`). The automated unit testing framework integrates with an IDE and allows the developer to generate a stub for a unit test that can then be completed with sample data and additional business logic. In test-driven development, unit code should be created for every software unit. When a programmer follows this discipline, it can result in more confident coding, and can allow a programmer to verify that a fault has been fixed earlier in the life cycle (reducing overall development costs).

At the system level, regression testing is a form of functional testing the software quality assurance team performs by using an automated testing suite. Typically, if a software fault is discovered in the process of testing, it is submitted to the bug tracking system and assigned to a programmer for remediation. Once the bug is fixed, the software will need to be run through all the regression test cases once again. Consequently, fixing a bug at the quality assurance stage is more expensive than during coding.

Summary

According to the IEEE Computer Society, testing is defined as "an activity performed for evaluating product quality, and for improving it, by identifying defects and problems. Software testing consists of the dynamic verification of the behavior of a program on a finite set of test cases, suitably selected from the usually infinite executions domain, against the expected behavior."[18]

[18] Abran, A., Moore J., (executive editors), Bourque, P., Dupuis, R., and Tripp, L. (editors), "Guide to the Software Engineering Body of Knowledge," IEEE Computer Society, 2004.

Secure software testing involves testing for quality assurance through functional, white box and black box, environment, and defect testing. Penetration tests, fuzzing, and simulation tests complemented by conducting Web scans provide additional secure software test tools.

Analyses of test results form the basis for assessing impacts of possible threats realized and means of remediation. Standards such as ISO 9126, the SSE-CMM, and the OSSTMM provide additional guidance for secure software evaluation and mitigation. Regression testing of secure software that has been modified to mitigate risks provides assurance that the original software system functionality and security characteristics are not negatively affected by the respective changes.

Assessment Questions

1. Assessing whether a software product meets the requirements of a particular specification or standard is known as which one of the following?

   A. Logic testing

   B. Stress testing

   C. Conformance testing

   D. Unit testing

2. Increasing the load on a software system beyond normal operating capacity describes which of the following?

   A. Logic testing

   B. Stress testing

   C. Conformance testing

   D. Unit testing

3. Code written by a developer to test an individual method best describes which of the following?

   A. Logic testing

   B. Stress testing

   C. Conformance testing

   D. Unit testing

4. Analysis of the context of a business decision best describes which of the following?

   A. Logic testing

   B. Stress testing

   C. Conformance testing

   D. Unit testing

5. Which of the following involves validating the positive and negative requirements of the software?

   A. Functional testing

B. Performance testing
C. Environment testing
D. Fault injection

6. Throughput, processing delay, and load are metrics used in which kind of testing?
   A. Functional testing
   B. Performance testing
   C. Environment testing
   D. Fault injection
7. Which of the following techniques involves examining the source code for the absence of security characteristics?
   A. Source code analysis
   B. Property-based testing
   C. Black box debugging
   D. Dynamic code analysis
8. Which of the following techniques is used to monitor behaviors external to the binary component?
   A. Source code analysis
   B. Property-based testing
   C. Black box debugging
   D. Dynamic code analysis
9. Which of the following techniques is used to trace system calls as the software is executing?
   A. Source code analysis
   B. Property-based testing
   C. Black box debugging
   D. Dynamic code analysis
10. Which of the following techniques is particularly useful for finding incorrect use of pointers and arrays?
    A. Binary fault injection
    B. Property-based testing
    C. Source code fault injection
    D. Black box debugging
11. Which of the following uses environmental data to simulate and automate real-world attack scenarios?
    A. Binary fault injection
    B. Property-based testing
    C. Source code fault injection
    D. Black box debugging

12. Which of the following evaluates the functionality, reliability, and performance of a group of components?
    A. Regression testing
    B. Interoperability testing
    C. Functional testing
    D. Integration testing
13. Which of the following evaluates whether an application can exchange data with other components?
    A. Regression testing
    B. Interoperability testing
    C. Functional testing
    D. Integration testing
14. Which of the following involves testing against a reference implementation of the software?
    A. Regression testing
    B. Interoperability testing
    C. Functional testing
    D. Integration testing
15. Bug-tracking systems commonly allow reporting, assignment, tracking, and which other necessary feature?
    A. Functionality
    B. Determination
    C. Prioritization
    D. Visualization
16. Which of the following has the largest attack surface?
    A. Code that is restricted to remote access by an anonymous user
    B. Code that is restricted to local access by an administrative user
    C. Code that is restricted to remote access by an authorized user
    D. Code that is restricted to local access by an authorized user
17. The testing of a system to verify that modifications have not caused unintended effects is:
    A. Regression testing
    B. Interoperability testing
    C. Functional testing
    D. Integration testing
18. The reemergence of software faults could be caused by which of the following?
    A. Regression testing
    B. Software brittleness

C. Functional testing

D. Software rigidness

19. A tester who is assigned or hired to evaluate the security of an organization's software system from the perspective of an attacker is known as which one of the following?

A. An ethical hacker

B. A cracker

C. A phreaker

D. A system administrator

20. Which one of the following best describes a white box test conducted by a testing team?

A. The testing team has knowledge that might be relevant to a specific type of attack by a person internal to the organization.

B. The testing team is provided with no information and begins the testing by gathering information on its own initiative.

C. The team has as much knowledge as possible about the network and computing resources to be evaluated.

D. The team is restricted in the type of results that can be reported.

21. Which one of the following test types evaluates an application when the development is nearing completion and minor changes are anticipated?

A. Acceptance

B. Unit

C. Beta

D. Alpha

22. Which one of the following is a security testing methodology that gives the tester insight into the strength of the target's network security by simulating an attack from a malicious source?

A. Integration test

B. Load test

C. Regression test

D. Penetration test

23. Which one of the following provides guidance and metrics for conducting security tests and has test cases that are divided into five channels (sections)?

A. Open Source Security Testing Methodology Manual (OSSTMM)

B. System Security Engineering Capability Maturity Model

C. ISO 9126

D. DoD Information Assurance Process (DIAP)

24. In general, a penetration test involves which one of the following three stages?

A. Specification, execution, and delivery

B. Preparation, execution, and delivery

C. Preparation, operation, and review

D. Review, execution, and delivery

25. Which one of the following is true regarding an individual or team that is hired by an organization to perform a penetration test?

A. The test carries no legal and ethical risks to the tester.

B. The tester is not subject to any possibility of prosecution if damage is caused.

C. The legal implications of conducting the test are implied and do not have to be agreed upon with the employer.

D. The test carries legal and ethical risks to the tester.

26. Penetration testing is usually initiated with reconnaissance, which comprises which of the following pre-test phases?

A. Footprinting, injecting, and enumerating

B. Footprinting, scanning, and hiding tracks

C. Monitoring, scanning, and enumerating

D. Footprinting, scanning, and enumerating

27. Which one of the following is "obtaining information concerning the security profile of an organization and involves gathering data to create a blueprint of the organization's networks and systems"?

A. Enumerating

B. Scanning

C. Footprinting

D. Monitoring

28. Which utility works by exploiting a feature of the Internet Protocol called time-to-live (TTL) and reveals the path IP packets travel between two systems?

A. Whois

B. Nslookup

C. Traceroute

D. NRoute

29. Which one of the following is a popular port scanner for Linux and Windows and can scan a system in a variety of stealth modes?

A. Nmap

B. LinMap

C. WinMap

D. NRoute

30. Which one of the following is a popular open source, powerful network vulnerability scanner that can be configured to run a variety of scans?

A. Nvul

B. Nessus

C. Nscan

D. NRoute

31. Which one of the following are the three basic types of password cracking tests?

A. Dictionary, hybrid, and brute force

B. Encyclopedia, hybrid, and brute force

C. Dictionary, true, and brute force

D. Dictionary, hybrid, and statistical

32. Which one of the following is a program that performs unknown and unwanted functions and is an unauthorized program contained in a legitimate program?

A. Stealth

B. Trojan horse

C. Proxy

D. Hybrid

33. Which one of the following is considered the grandfather of Trojan horses and has spawned a considerable number of imitators?

A. BackOrifice 2000 (BO2K)

B. NetCat

C. FrontOrifice 2000 (FO2K)

D. Hybrid

34. Which one of the following attacks occurs when a program allocates a specific block length of memory for storage, but then attempts to store more data than the block was intended to hold?

A. Denial of service

B. Capacity overrun

C. SQL injection

D. Buffer overflow

35. Which one of the following are the two basic types of intrusion detection systems (IDSs)?

A. Signature recognition and anomaly detection

B. Anomaly recognition and anomaly detection

C. Signature recognition and signature detection

D. File recognition and anomaly detection

36. Which one of the following refers to the LAN (WLAN) family of standards that specifies wireless connectivity and defines aspects of frequency hopping and direct-sequence spread spectrum (DSSS) systems for use in the 2.4 MHz ISM (industrial, scientific, medical) band?

A. IEEE 804.12

B. IEEE 802.11

C. IEEE 802.16

D. IEEE 803.11

37. Which one of the following is a term used to describe the process of a hacker who, armed with a laptop and a wireless adapter card and traveling by car, bus, subway train, or other form of mechanized transport, goes around sniffing for WLANs?

A. War scanning

B. WLAN scanning

C. WLAN driving

D. War driving

38. Which one of the following refers to a black box software testing technique that basically consists of finding implementation bugs using malformed/semi-malformed data injection in an automated fashion?

A. Fuzzing

B. Impersonating

C. Simulation

D. Scuzzing

39. Which one of the following is a testing method based on inputs derived from mutation, generation, and conformance approaches?

A. Fuzzing

B. Regression

C. Simulation

D. Scanning

40. Which testing method comprises the steps of identifying active machines, discovering open ports and available services, fingerprinting the operating system, and mapping the network?

A. Fuzzing

B. Regression

C. Enumeration

D. Scanning

41. Which one of the following refers to an IP header field that is an ever-increasing counter that keeps track of each router hop as the packet travels to a target?

A. Time-to-Travel (TTT)

B. Round Trip Time (RTT)

C. Time-for-Loop (TFL)

D. Time-to-Live (TTL)

42. The ping utility is useful in identifying active machines. To accomplish this identification, ping sends which one of the following packets?

A. ICMP Echo Request

B. TCP Echo Request
C. ICMP Echo Reply
D. TCP Echo Reply

43. Which one of the following is the response to a ping if the target is not live?
A. An ICMP Echo Reply message
B. A ''Request timed out'' message
C. A TCP Echo Reply packet
D. An ICMP Echo Request message

44. How many total TCP and UDP port numbers are there?
A. 1,024
B. 8,984
C. 16,664
D. 65,535

45. Which range of ports is called the ''well-known ports''?
A. 1 to 1,024
B. 1 to 10,240
C. 1,024 to 8,984
D. 1 to 8,984

46. Which one of the following is the best description of active vs. passive fingerprinting?
A. Active fingerprinting is less accurate.
B. Active fingerprinting is less detectable.
C. Passive fingerprinting is more detectable.
D. Passive fingerprinting is less detectable.

Answer: D

The correct option is D.

47. Which scanning method is often referred to as half-open scanning because, unlike TCP connect(), a full TCP connection is never opened?
A. TCP SYN
B. TCP SYN/ACK
C. TCP FIN
D. TCP FTP proxy

48. Which one of the following is a technique used to ping a batch of devices and help the attacker determine which are active and which are not?
A. Ping all
B. Ping SYN
C. Ping footprint
D. Ping sweep

49. Ports can have which one of the following sets of three states?
    A. Open, closed, or filtered
    B. Open, listening, or filtered
    C. Set, closed, or filtered
    D. Open, closed, or engaged
50. Which one of the following best describes one of the characteristics of the User Datagram Protocol (UDP) relative to the Transmission Control Protocol (TCP)?
    A. Full-duplex
    B. Best-effort delivery
    C. Connection-oriented
    D. Reliable
51. Which one of the following methods can be used to discover what services are running on the open ports and also provides important information about what type and version of software is running?
    A. IP grabbing
    B. Banner grabbing
    C. Connection scanning
    D. Data capturing
52. Which type of black box simulation testing is useful in detecting a failure to implement a critical security requirement, discovering general implementation errors, and finding errors in the test plan?
    A. Data enumeration unit testing
    B. Requirements simulation testing
    C. Quality assurance (QA) acceptance testing
    D. System valuation testing
53. Which one of the following terms is best described by "the inability of a system or component to perform its required functions within specified performance requirements"?
    A. Fault
    B. Error
    C. Tested element
    D. Failure
54. Which one of the following is an effective method for testing for failure in secure software systems?
    A. Software failure modes and effects analysis (SFMEA)
    B. Software failure modes and regression analysis (SFMRA)
    C. Software testing modes and results analysis (STMRA)
    D. Software effects and modes analysis (SEMA)

55. Which one of the following types of testing subjects the software to extreme conditions such as inadequate memory capacity, insufficient communication bandwidth, denial-of-service attacks, and hardware malfunctions?
    A. Software failure modes and effects analysis (SFMEA)
    B. Software failure modes and regression analysis (SFMRA)
    C. Stress testing
    D. Constraint testing
56. The tests in NIST Special Publication 800-22, the diehard tests, and the "ent" tests are useful in determining which one of the following characteristics?
    A. Strength of cryptographic algorithms
    B. Strength of cryptographic keys
    C. Strength of random number generators
    D. Strength of secure software
57. Which one of the following programs is a joint effort of the U.S. National Institute of Standards and Technology (NIST) and the Communications Security Establishment (CSE) of Canada to validate cryptographic modules?
    A. Cryptographic Module Validation Program (CMVP)
    B. Cryptographic Module Verification Program (CMVP)
    C. Cryptographic Module Assurance Program (CMAP)
    D. Cryptographic Module Certification Program (CMCP)
58. Which one of the following NIST publications is entitled "Security Requirements for Cryptographic Modules" and is designed for cryptographic modules to be tested against by vendors of these modules?
    A. SP 800-22
    B. FIPS PUB 140-3
    C. FIPS PUB 140-7
    D. SP 800-26
59. The NIST publication "Security Requirements for Cryptographic Modules" specifies a security level that "attempts to prevent the unauthorized access to Critical Security Parameters (CSPs) held within the cryptographic module." This security level is labeled as which one of the following?
    A. Level 1
    B. Level 2
    C. Level 3
    D. Level 4
60. The annualized loss expectancy (ALE) if a critical asset is disabled or compromised by a malicious attack on a organization's software system is calculated as follows:
    A. ALE = SLE x ARO
    B. ALE = SLA x ARO

C. ALE = SLE x AYO

D. ALE = SLE x ARR

61. The Information Assurance Technical Framework (IATF) Document 3.1 defines which one of the following attacks as traffic analysis, monitoring of unprotected communications, decrypting weakly encrypted traffic, and capture of authentication information (such as passwords)?

A. Close-in

B. Insider

C. Active

D. Passive

62. Which one of the following refers to the NIST publication "Standards for Security Categorization of Federal Information and Information Systems," which address characterization of impacts of threats realized?

A. SP 800-22

B. SP 800-30

C. FIPS 205

D. FIPS 199

63. When should the following actions be performed? Enter test results and the corresponding version of the software module under test into configuration management; ascertain security requirements that were not included in the original specification and implementation; assess risk posed to the software system from failure to incorporate security requirements that were not included in the original specification; and determine risk to the software system from failure to modify the software to address security requirements that were not included in the original specification.

A. Before testing

B. Following testing

C. During testing

D. During installation

64. Which one of the following is defined as the "totality of characteristics of an entity that bears on its ability to satisfy stated and implied needs"?

A. Quality

B. Assurance

C. Reliability

D. Security

65. Standard ISO 9126-1 defines which one of the following models?

A. Software assurance model

B. Software quality model

C. Software capability maturity model

D. System security engineering capability maturity model

66. Which one of the following sets names characteristics of ISO Standard 9126-1?

A. Functionality, reliability, usability, and efficiency

B. Operability, reliability, usability, and efficiency

C. Functionality, quality, usability, and efficiency

D. Functionality, reliability, usability, and assessibility

67. The Open Source Security Testing Methodology Manual (OSSTMM) 3.0 defines an approach to security testing at an operational level. Specifically, the OSSTMM defines the scope of an audit as encompassing which one the following three sets of channels?

A. Communications Security, Physical Security, Operational Security

B. Encryption Security, Physical Security, Spectrum Security

C. Communications Security, Disaster Recovery, Spectrum Security

D. Communications Security, Physical Security, Spectrum Security

68. The Open Source Security Testing Methodology Manual (OSSTMM) 3.0 is executed in which one of the following sets of four phases?

A. Specification, Definitions, Information, Interactive Controls

B. Regulatory, Operational, Information, Interactive Controls

C. Regulatory, Definitions, Information, Interactive Controls

D. Regulatory, Definitions, Evaluation, Interactive Controls

69. The U.S. Department of Defense has established which one of the following processes for authorizing the operation of DoD information systems?

A. DoD Information Assurance Certification and Accreditation Process (DIACAP)

B. DoD Information System Certification Process (DISCP)

C. DoD Computer System Assurance Process (DCSAP)

D. National Information Assurance Accreditation Process (NIAAP)

70. Implementing a risk mitigation strategy following secure software testing includes applying appropriate controls. These controls are which one of the following types?

A. Administrative, management, operational, or a combination of these

B. Technical, maintenance, operational, or a combination of these

C. Technical, management, predictive, or a combination of these

D. Technical, management, operational, or a combination of these

CHAPTER

6

Software Acceptance

During the secure software development cycle, it is critical that secure software issues be addressed prior to deployment. Specifying and including secure software principles as an integral part of the development life cycle rather than attempting to correct vulnerabilities after delivery of the software system will result in lower costs. Costs to repair software defects are much lower in the pre-deployment phase than in the post-deployment phase.

If used during the system software test phase prior to deployment, black box security tests can be an effective means to uncover and address software security issues and reduce risk.

If software vulnerabilities or security failures emerge during the post-deployment phase of the secure software system development life cycle, they are usually the result of design or development errors that were not detected due to inadequate testing paradigms.

In this chapter, pre-release and pre-deployment software system completion criteria, risk acceptance, and disaster recovery/business continuity planning will be addressed along with post-release testing, validation, and verification.

Pre-release or Pre-deployment Activities

During the delivery and completion phases of the software supply process, final reports of the test management system are provided to the acquirer as part of the project completion documentation. A set of test data should be created that verifies that all specified quality control test points have been covered according to previously agreed upon terms. All the prescribed tests should have been executed and accepted.

Completion Criteria

In completion delivery, the secure software system must be evaluated and tested against previously specified quantitative test completion criteria. The completion goals should be based on the type of software system to be delivered and the types of defects that might be inherent in the software. The completion criteria specify when these goals should be reached. These test criteria should have the following characteristics:

- Provide code coverage capability
- Produce quantifiable results
- Provide previously demonstrated ability to detect defects
- Allow for functional variation coverage

Documentation associated with the completion criteria must be provided that demonstrates the following:

- The degree of achievement of the completion criteria
- Mitigating issues in instances where the completion criteria were not achieved
- The case for not including specific code units in completion testing
- The software system performance under test
- Correlation of inputs and outputs and coverage of all interfaces to the software system
- Problems in conducting the tests for completion
- Determining of areas in the software requiring rewrite and repair

Software Disaster Recovery Plan

An organization should develop a software disaster recovery plan that includes a policy for handling an event that results in harm to or loss of the organization's software systems. The plan should address the continuity of business operations and revenue generation that depend on software systems. Disaster recovery and business continuity planning will be covered in more detail later in this chapter.

Risk Acceptance

United Kingdom Ministry of Defense Standard 00-56, Issue 4, June 2007, defines risk acceptance as the final step in risk management and as "the systematic process by which relevant stakeholders agree that risk may be accepted." Prior to risk acceptance, management must evaluate the level of each individual risk and system aggregated risk. Risk is usually accepted when the level of risk has been reduced to a level that is tolerable and practical to achieve.

An appropriate authority is responsible for accepting the residual risk in a software system based on a thorough evaluation of risks and mitigation options. In reality, there might be risks in a software system that cannot be accepted, requiring a reiteration of risk management and risk reduction processes.

Documentation has to be generated that provides adequate proof that risk reduction and residual risk tolerance levels have been met.

In summary, an effective risk acceptance methodology should incorporate the following elements:

- The risk acceptance process should be a part of the initial software system specifications.
- The risk acceptance process should specify how the evidence for a residual risk tolerance level is to be developed and presented.
- Risk acceptance should be treated as a continuing process that takes into account new threats and mitigation activities.
- Procedures should be established to ensure that upgrades and modifications to the software system do not nullify earlier risk reduction and acceptance actions. Configuration management is an important component of this process.
- Risk acceptance criteria should not be based on restrictions in funding.
- Risk acceptance procedures should be based on proven, successful methods that have yielded reliable results in the past.

Configuration Management

Configuration management is the process of tracking and approving changes to a system. It involves identifying, controlling, and auditing all changes made to the system. It can address hardware and software changes, networking changes, or any other change affecting security. Configuration management can also be used to protect a trusted system while it is being designed and developed.

The primary security goal of configuration management is to ensure that changes to the system do not unintentionally diminish security. For example, configuration management might prevent an older version of a system from being activated as the production system. Configuration management also makes it possible to accurately roll back to a previous version of a system in case a new system is found to be faulty. Another goal of configuration management is to ensure that system changes are reflected in current documentation to help mitigate the impact that a change might have on the security of other systems, while in either the production or planning stages.

Configuration management is a discipline applying technical and administrative direction to do the following:

- Identify and document the functional and physical characteristics of each configuration item for the system
- Manage all changes to these characteristics
- Record and report the status of change processing and implementation

Configuration management involves process monitoring, version control, information capture, quality control, bookkeeping, and an organizational framework to support these activities. The configuration being managed is the verification system plus all tools and documentation related to the configuration process. In application development, change control involves the analysis and understanding of the existing code and the design of changes, and corresponding test procedures.

Primary Functions of Configuration Management

The primary functions of configuration management or change control are as follows:

- To ensure that the change is implemented in an orderly manner through formalized testing
- To ensure that the user base is informed of the impending change
- To analyze the effect of the change on the system after implementation
- To reduce the negative impact that the change might have had on the computing services and resources

Five generally accepted procedures exist to implement and support the change control process:

1. Applying to introduce a change
2. Cataloging the intended change
3. Scheduling the change
4. Implementing the change
5. Reporting the change to the appropriate parties

Definitions and Procedures

The five major components of configuration management and their functions are as follows:

- Configuration identification
- Configuration control
- Configuration status accounting
- Configuration auditing
- Documentation change control

These components are explained in the following sections.

Configuration Identification Configuration management entails decomposing the verification system into identifiable, understandable, manageable, trackable units known as *configuration items* (CIs). The decomposition process of a verification system into configuration items is called *configuration identification*. A CI is a uniquely identifiable subset of the system that represents the smallest portion that is subject to independent configuration control procedures.

CIs can vary widely in size, type, and complexity. Although there are no hard-and-fast rules for decomposition, the granularity of CIs can have great practical importance. A favorable strategy is to designate relatively large CIs for elements that are not expected to change over the life of the system, and small CIs for elements likely to change more frequently.

Configuration Control *Configuration control* is a means of ensuring that system changes are approved before being implemented, only the proposed and approved changes are implemented, and the implementation is complete and accurate. This activity involves strict procedures for proposing, monitoring, and approving system changes and their implementation. Configuration control entails central direction of the change process by personnel who coordinate analytical tasks, approve system changes, review the implementation of changes, and supervise other tasks such as documentation.

All analytical and design tasks are conducted under the direction of a corporate entity called the *configuration control board* (CCB). The CCB is headed by a chairperson who is responsible for ensuring that changes made do not jeopardize the soundness of the verification system and are approved, tested, documented, and implemented correctly.

The members of the CCB should interact periodically, either through formal meetings or other available means, to discuss configuration management topics, such as proposed changes, configuration status accounting reports, and other topics that may be of interest to the different areas of the system development. These interactions should be held to keep the entire system team updated on all advancements to or alterations in the verification system.

Configuration Status Accounting *Configuration accounting* documents the status of configuration control activities and, in general, provides the information needed to manage a configuration effectively. It allows managers to trace system changes and establish the history of any developmental problems and associated fixes. Configuration accounting also tracks the status of current changes as they move through the configuration control process. Configuration accounting establishes the granularity of recorded information and thus shapes the accuracy and usefulness of the audit function. The configuration accounting reports are reviewed by the CCB.

Configuration Auditing *Configuration auditing* is the quality assurance component of configuration management. It involves periodic checks to determine the consistency and completeness of accounting information and to verify that all configuration management policies are being followed. A vendor's configuration management program must be able to sustain a complete configuration audit by a review team.

Documentation Change Control It's important to update all relevant documentation when system changes occur. Such changes could include the following:

- Changes to the system infrastructure
- Changes to security policies or procedures
- Changes to the disaster recovery or business continuity plans

- Changes to the facility environment, such as office moves or HVAC and electrical changes

Documentation control is a cornerstone of configuration management. Configuration management specifies strict adherence to documenting system changes, and the process of the documentation itself.

Business Continuity Planning and Disaster Recovery Planning

Business continuity planning (BCP) addresses the preservation of the business in the face of major disruptions to normal operations. Business continuity includes the preparation, testing, and updating of the actions required to protect critical business processes from the effects of major system and network failures.

A disruptive event is any intentional or unintentional occurrence that suspends normal operations. The aim of BCP is to minimize the effects of a disruptive event on a company. The primary purpose of business continuity plans is to reduce the risk of financial loss and enhance a company's capability to recover from a disruptive event promptly. The business continuity plan should also help minimize the cost associated with the disruptive event and mitigate the risk associated with it.

Disaster recovery planning is concerned with restoring the operation of the business's information systems following a harmful event.

The following definitions clarify some of the relevant terminology:

- **Contingency plan (CP)**—The documented, organized plan for emergency response, backup operations, and recovery maintained by an organization as part of its security program that will ensure the availability of critical resources and facilitate the continuity of operations in an emergency situation.
- **Disaster recovery plan (DRP)**—The plan and procedures developed to recover from a disaster that has interfered with the network and other information system operations.
- **Continuity of operations plan (COOP)**—The plans and procedures documented to ensure continued critical operations during any period where normal operations are impossible.
- **Business continuity plan (BCP)**—The plan and procedures developed that identify and prioritize the critical business functions that must be preserved and the associated procedures for continued operations of those critical business functions.

Business Continuity Planning

Business continuity plans should evaluate all critical information processing areas of the organization, such as workstations and laptops, networks, servers, application software, storage media, and personnel procedures.

A wide variety of events can affect the operations of a business and the information systems used by that business. These events can be natural or manmade. Examples of such events include the following:

- Sabotage
- Arson
- Strikes
- Bombings
- Earthquakes
- Fire
- Floods
- Fluctuations in or loss of electrical power
- Storms
- Communication system failures
- Unavailability of key employees

Goals and the BCP Process

There are four major elements of the BCP process:

- **Scope and plan initiation**—Creating the scope and the other elements needed to define the parameters of the plan
- **Business impact assessment (BIA)**—A process to help business units understand the impact of a disruptive event
- **Business continuity plan development**—A process that includes the areas of plan implementation, plan testing, and ongoing plan maintenance
- **Plan approval and implementation**—Final senior management signoff, enterprise-wide awareness of the plan, and implementing a maintenance procedure for updating the plan as needed

These elements are discussed in more detail in the following sections.

Scope and Plan Initiation

The scope and plan initiation phase is the first step in creating a business continuity plan. It entails creating the scope for the plan and the other elements needed to define the parameters of the plan. This phase embodies an examination of the company's operations and support services. Scope activities could include creating a detailed account of the work required, listing the resources to be used, and defining the management practices to be employed.

Business Impact Assessment

A business impact assessment is a process used to help business units understand the impact of a disruptive event. This phase includes the execution of a vulnerability assessment. A BIA is performed as one step during the creation of the BCP. It is similar to a risk assessment.

The purpose of a BIA is to create a document to help understand what impact a disruptive event would have on the business. The impact might be financial (quantitative) or operational (qualitative), such as the inability to respond to customer complaints.

A BIA has three primary goals:

- **Prioritization of critical systems**—Every critical business unit process must be identified and prioritized, and the impact of a disruptive event must be evaluated.
- **Estimation of downtime**—The BIA is used to help estimate the maximum tolerable downtime (MTD) that the business can tolerate and still remain a viable company; that is, what is the longest period of time a critical process can remain interrupted before the company can never recover. It is often found during the BIA process that this time period is much shorter than expected.
- **Identification of resource requirements**—The resource requirements for the critical processes are identified at this time, with the most time-sensitive processes receiving the most resource allocation.

A BIA is usually conducted in the following manner:

1. **Gather appropriate assessment materials**—The BIA process begins with identifying the critical business units and their interrelationships. Additional documents might also be collected in order to define the functional interrelationships of the organization.

   As the materials are collected and the functional operations of the business are identified, the BIA will examine these business function interdependencies with an eye toward several factors, such as the business success factors involved, establishing a set of priorities between the units, and what alternate processing procedures can be utilized.

2. **Perform the vulnerability assessment**—The vulnerability assessment usually comprises quantitative (financial) and qualitative (operational) sections. The vulnerability assessment is smaller than a full risk assessment and is focused on providing information that is used solely for the business continuity plan or disaster recovery plan. A key function of a vulnerability assessment is to conduct a loss impact analysis. Quantitative loss criteria include:

   - Incurring financial losses from loss of revenue, capital expenditure, or personal liability resolution
   - The additional operational expenses incurred due to the disruptive event
   - Incurring financial loss from resolution of violation of contract agreements
   - Incurring financial loss from resolution of violation of regulatory or compliance requirements

   Typical qualitative loss criteria comprise:

   - The loss of competitive advantage or market share
   - The loss of public confidence or credibility, or incurring public embarrassment

The vulnerability assessment should address critical support functions such as the physical infrastructure, accounting, payroll, and telecommunications systems.

3. **Analyze the compiled information**—Analyzing the information as part of the BIA includes:
   - Identifying interdependencies
   - Documenting required processes
   - Determining acceptable interruption periods
4. **Document the results; present recommendations**—All processes, procedures, analyses, and results should be documented and presented to management, including associated recommendations.

The report will contain the previously gathered material, list the identified critical support areas, summarize the quantitative and qualitative impact statements, and provide the recommended recovery priorities generated from the analysis.

Business Continuity Plan Development

The *business continuity plan* (BCP) is developed by using the information collected in the BIA to create the recovery strategy plan to support the critical business functions. This process includes the areas of plan implementation, plan testing, and ongoing plan maintenance.

Plan Approval and Implementation

The object of this activity is to obtain the final senior management signoff, create enterprise-wide awareness of the plan, and implement a maintenance procedure for updating the plan as needed.

- **Senior management approval**—Because senior management is ultimately responsible for all phases of the BCP, they must have final approval. When a disaster strikes, senior management must be able to make informed decisions quickly during the recovery effort.
- **Plan awareness**—Enterprise-wide awareness of the plan is important and emphasizes the organization's commitment to its employees. Specific training may be required for certain personnel to carry out their tasks, and quality training is perceived as a benefit that increases the interest and the commitment of personnel in the BCP process.
- **Plan maintenance**—Because of events such as reorganization, employee turnover, relocation, or upgrading of critical resources, a BCP might become outdated. Whatever the reason, plan maintenance techniques must be employed from the outset to ensure that the plan remains fresh and usable. It's important to build maintenance procedures into the organization by using job descriptions that centralize responsibility for updates. Also, audit procedures that can report regularly on the state of the plan should be put in place.

Roles and Responsibilities

The BCP process involves many personnel from various parts of the enterprise. Creation of a BCP committee represents the first enterprise-wide involvement of the major critical functional business units. All other business units will be involved in some way later, especially during the implementation and awareness phases.

- **BCP committee**—A BCP committee should be formed and given the responsibility to create, implement, and test the plan. The committee is made up of representatives from senior management, all functional business units, information systems, and security administration. The committee initially defines the scope of the plan, which should deal with how to recover promptly from a disruptive event and mitigate the financial and resource losses due to a disruptive event.
- **Senior management**—Senior management has the ultimate responsibility for all phases of the plan, which includes not only initiation of the plan process but also monitoring and managing the plan during testing and supervision and execution of the plan during a disruptive event. This support is essential, and without management being willing to commit adequate tangible and intangible resources, the plan will not be successful. Because of the concept of due diligence, stockholders might hold senior managers as well as the board of directors personally responsible if a disruptive event causes losses that adherence to base industry standards of due care could have prevented. For this reason and others, it is in the senior manager's best interest to be fully involved in the BCP process.

Disaster Recovery Planning

Disaster recovery planning is concerned with the protection of critical business processes from the effects of major information system and network failures, by quickly recovering from an emergency with a minimum impact to the organization.

A disaster recovery plan (DRP) is a comprehensive statement of consistent actions to be taken before, during, and after a disruptive event that causes a significant loss of information systems resources.

Disaster recovery plans are the procedures for responding to an emergency, providing extended backup operations during the interruption, and managing recovery and salvage processes afterwards, should an organization experience a substantial loss of processing capability. Another objective of a properly executed DRP is to provide the capability to implement critical processes at an alternate site and return to the primary site and normal processing within a time frame that minimizes the loss to the organization.

The disaster recovery planning process involves developing the DRP, testing the DRP, and executing the DRP in the event of an emergency.

Developing the DRP

This first step involves developing the recovery plan and defining the necessary steps required to protect the business in the event of a disaster.

Table 6-1: Rating Class and Recovery Times

RATING CLASS	RECOVERY TIME FRAMES
AAA	Immediate
AA	Full functional recovery within 4 hours
A	Same business day
B	Up to 24 hours downtime permitted
C	24 to 72 hours downtime acceptable
D	Greater than 72 hours downtime acceptable

Automated tools are available to assist in the development of the DRP. These tools can improve productivity by providing formatted templates customized to the particular organization's needs.

Determining Recovery Time Objectives

Early in the DRP process, all business functions and critical systems must be examined to determine their recovery time requirements. Recovery time objectives are assigned to each function or system in order to guide the selection of alternate processing procedures. Table 6-1 summarizes the rating classes and associated recovery time frame objectives.

Establishing Backup Sites

An important component of DRP is maintaining a backup site that provides some degree of duplication of computing resources located away from the primary site. The types of backup sites are differentiated primarily by the extent to which the primary computing resources are replicated.

Hot sites, warm sites, and *cold sites* are the most common types of remote off-site backup processing facilities. They are differentiated by how much preparation is devoted to the site, and, therefore, how quickly the site can be used as an alternate processing site. The characteristics of each of these sites are as follows:

- **Cold site**—A designated computer operations room with HVAC that has no computing systems installed and, therefore, would require a substantial effort to install the hardware and software required to begin alternate processing. This type of site is rarely useful in an actual emergency.
- **Warm site**—An alternative processing facility with most supporting peripheral equipment, but without the principal computing platforms.
- **Hot site**—A site with all required computer hardware, software, and peripherals installed to begin alternative processing either immediately or within an acceptably short time frame. This site would be a duplicate of the original site and might require an upgrade of only the most current data to duplicate operations.

Additional options for providing backup capabilities include the following:

- **Mutual aid agreements**—An arrangement with another company that might have similar computing needs. Both parties agree to support each other in the case of a disruptive event by providing alternative processing resources to the other party. While appealing, this is not a good choice if the emergency affects both parties. Also, capacity at either facility might not be available when needed.
- **Rolling or mobile backup**—Contracting with a vendor to provide mobile power and HVAC facilities sufficient to stage the alternate processing.
- **Multiple centers**—In a multiple-center concept, the processing is spread over several operations centers, creating a distributed approach to redundancy and sharing of available resources. These multiple centers could be owned and managed by the same organization (in-house sites) or used in conjunction with a reciprocal agreement.
- **Service bureaus**—An organization might contract with a service bureau to provide alternate backup-processing services. The advantages of this type of arrangement are the quick response and availability of the service bureau, the possibility of testing without disrupting normal operations, and additional support functions provided by the service bureau. The disadvantages of this type of setup are the expense and resource contention during a large emergency.

Plan Testing

The DRP must be tested and evaluated at regular intervals. Testing is required to verify the accuracy of the recovery procedures, verify the processing capability of the alternate backup site, train personnel, and identify deficiencies. The most common types of testing modes, by increasing level of thoroughness, are as follows:

- **Checklist review**—The DRP is distributed and reviewed by business units for its thoroughness and effectiveness.
- **Tabletop exercise or structured walk-through test**—Members of the emergency management group meet in a conference room setting to discuss their responsibilities and how they would react to emergency scenarios by stepping through the plan.
- **Walk-through drill or simulation test**—The emergency management group and response teams perform their emergency response functions by walking through the test, without actually initiating recovery procedures. This approach is more thorough than the table-top exercise.
- **Functional drill**—This approach tests specific functions, such as medical response, emergency notifications, warning and communications procedures and equipment, although not necessarily all at once. It also includes evacuation drills, where personnel walk the evacuation route to a designated area where procedures for accounting for the personnel are tested.
- **Parallel test or full-scale exercise**—A real-life emergency situation is simulated as closely as possible. It involves all of the participants that would be responding

to the real emergency, including community and external organizations. The test may involve ceasing some real production processing.

- **Full-interruption test**—Normal production is shut down and the disaster recovery processes are fully executed. This type of test is dangerous and, if not properly executed, can cause a disaster situation.

Implementing the Plan

If an actual disaster occurs, there are three options for recovery:

- Recover at the primary operating site
- Recover to an alternate site for critical functions
- Restore full system after a catastrophic loss

Two teams should be organized to execute the recovery, the *recovery* and *salvage* teams. The functions of these teams are as follows:

- **Recovery team**—Restore operations of the organization's critical business functions at the alternate backup processing site. The recovery team is concerned with rebuilding production processing.
- **Salvage team**—Repair, clean, salvage, and determine the viability of the primary processing infrastructure immediately after the disaster.

The DRP should also address other concerns such as paying employees during a disaster, preventing fraud, media relations, and liaison with local emergency services.

Post-release Activities

Software acceptance activities conducted post-release include verification and validation, security testing, certification for software system security, and accreditation of an operational system. These activities are typically performed in-house by the organization or by a third-party depending on compliance requirements. Certification and accreditation are often mandated for software systems that operate on government networks and in highly regulated industries such as the financial industry. Requirements for these activities are typically informed by regulations, laws, and standards.

Verification and Validation

Verification is a process to evaluate whether software conforms to the specifications, regulations, or other conditions imposed on it while it was being developed.

Validation is a process to evaluate whether software will satisfy its particular requirements (functional and nonfunctional) for its specific intended purpose.

The term V&V typically refers to all of the verification and validation activities undertaken to ensure that software will function according to its specification.

Certification and Accreditation

Certification and accreditation (C&A) is a process to ensure that information and software systems adhere to formal and established security requirements. Typically, systems are developed according to both functional and nonfunctional (security) requirements and the resulting configuration is well documented (certification). Then the security controls of the system are evaluated against recommended standards and practices (testing). Finally, the system is authorized to operate if it presents an acceptable level of risk to the operating organization (accreditation).

A number of C&A processes exist for the formal evaluation of networked information systems, such as DIACAP and FISMA. These C&A processes have traditionally focused on the software components of the systems from a network and platform security perspective (a holistic approach), which includes the people, process, and technology (inclusive of the environment) as opposed to delving deeply into the actual software security. In other words, the focus in these processes is on configuration of technology that meets baseline security requirements along with people and process aspects rather than a detailed review of the security of the code. Consequently, the emphasis is on activities performed later in the software life cycle such as secure software deployment, operations, and maintenance, as opposed to secure software design, coding, and testing. Since the C&A process does not verify that these earlier secure software development activities were performed, there is a resulting lack of certainty that these components are free of security vulnerabilities before they go into production. To provide for a greater level of software assurance or software security, software assurance criteria should be part of a formal evaluation process for software or part of an existing evaluation process for information systems. The Software Assurance State-of-the-Art Report (SOAR) describes some benefits that could result from adopting a general set of criteria[1]:

- Promote the establishment of defined steps and processes
- Facilitate management oversight for secure programming practices
- Promote the recognition of design patterns for vulnerabilities
- Provide for security verification that security mechanisms have been implemented
- Provide a testing process so the removal of vulnerabilities can be demonstrated
- Support the certification, formal review, and acceptance of software by a designated manager such as a Designated Approving Authority (DAA) International Organization for Standardization (ISO) Certification

International Organization for Standardization Certification

ISO/IEC 27002:2005 is entitled "Information Technology —Security Techniques — Code of Practice for Information Security Management." It specifies best practices for initiating, implementing, or maintaining information security management systems (ISMS). The ISO 27002 standard is composed of 12 security clauses:

- Risk assessment and treatment
- Security policy

[1]Information Assurance Technology Analysis Center, (IATAC), Data & Analysis Center for Software (DACS), State-of-the-Art Report (SOAR), July, 2007.

- Organization of information security
- Asset management
- Human resources security
- Physical and environmental security
- Communications and operations management
- Access control
- Information systems acquisition, development, and maintenance
- Information security incident management
- Business continuity management
- Compliance

BITS Certification

The Financial Services Round Table BITS certification program tests technology products used to deliver financial services. The BITS security criteria are drafted as security requirement packages and use the schema and language of the Common Criteria certification program. The BITS process focuses on the security functionality of the product. Source code reviews are not performed nor are on-site reviews of the development process.

ICSA Labs Antivirus Product Certification

The ICSA Labs antivirus certification criteria are intended for products and services that detect computer viruses prior to causing an infection. The criteria do not contain specific requirements for products or product components that eliminate other nonreplicating, malicious software, such as spyware, adware, back doors, Trojan horses, and so on. The criteria consist of:

- **Primary modules**—Correspond to a particular type of antivirus product or service: desktop/server, gateway, groupware, managed application services, managed email services, enterprise content management (ECM), inline security, and online services
- **Secondary modules**—Additional criteria targeted at antivirus product and service offerings that have already met one of the primary detection modules; this criteria defines secondary capabilities, such as cleaning a virus from infected files and sectors
- **Addendum**—Matrix of criteria referred to by the primary modules
- **Glossary**—Contains definitions for terms appearing in the primary and secondary criteria modules as well as the addendum

A candidate for certification must satisfy all requirements in one of the primary modules. Testing against one of the secondary modules, such as antivirus cleaning, is optional.

Election Assistance Commission Certification

The U.S. Election Assistance Commission (EAC) was established by the Help America Vote Act (HAVA) of 2002. EAC is an independent, bipartisan commission charged with developing guidance to meet HAVA requirements, adopting voluntary voting system guidelines, and serving as a national clearinghouse of information about election administration. EAC also accredits testing laboratories and certifies voting systems.

To assist the Election Assistance Commission with the development of voluntary voting system guidelines, HAVA established the Technical Guidelines Development Committee (TGDC) and directs the National Institute of Standards and Technology (NIST) to chair the TGDC. NIST research activities include:

- Securing computers, computer networks, and computer data storage used in voting systems
- Implementing methods to detect and prevent fraud
- Protecting voter privacy
- Designing the voting system applications to account for the role of human needs, including assistive technologies for individuals with disabilities (including blindness) and varying levels of literacy
- Recommending testing laboratories to the EAC

Defense Information Assurance Certification and Accreditation Process

The Defense Information Assurance Certification and Accreditation Process (DIACAP) applies to the "acquisition, operation, and sustainment of all U.S. Department of Defense (DoD)-owned or controlled information systems that receive, process, store, display or transmit DoD information, regardless of classification or sensitivity of the information or information system. This includes Enclaves, AIS Applications (e.g., Core Enterprise Services), Outsourced Information Technology (IT)-Based Processes, and Platform IT Interconnections."

The DIACAP specifies four information system categories:

- Enclave
- AIS application or service
- Outsourced IT-based process
- Platform IT interconnection

A typical DIACAP package will contain a minimal amount of documentation, which could include:

- System Identification Profile
- DIACAP Strategy
- IA Implementation Plan

- DIACAP Scorecard
- Certification Determination
- DIACAP Plan of Actions and Milestones
- Accreditation Decision
- Artifacts and Evidence of Compliance

The DIACAP Scorecard is the "report card" of how the system compared against mandatory IA controls.

Intelligence Community Directive 503

Intelligence Community (IC) Directive 503 establishes U.S. intelligence community (such as the Central Intelligence Agency [CIA]) policy for information technology systems, security risk management, certification, and accreditation. IC Directive 503, September 2008, rescinds and replaces the Director of Central Intelligence Directive (DCID) 6/3 Policy, "Protecting Sensitive Compartmented Information within Information Systems," and the associated DCID 6/3 Manual of the same title.

The stated focus of ICD 503 is a "more holistic and strategic process for the risk management of information technology systems, and on processes and procedures designed to develop trust across the intelligence community information technology enterprise through the use of common standards and reciprocally accepted certification and accreditation decisions."

Federal Information Security Management Act

To increase the security of U.S. civil agency federal information systems, the Federal Information Security Management Act (FISMA), which is Title III of the E-Government Act of December 2002 (Public Law 107-347), was passed. FISMA was enacted to:

- Provide a comprehensive framework for ensuring the effectiveness of information security controls over information resources that support federal operations and assets
- Recognize the highly networked nature of the current federal computing environment and provide effective government-wide management and oversight of the related information security risks, including coordination of information security efforts throughout the civilian, national security, and law enforcement communities
- Provide for development and maintenance of minimum controls required to protect federal information and information systems
- Provide a mechanism for improved oversight of federal agency information security programs

FISMA, the Paperwork Reduction Act (PRA) of 1980, as amended by the Paperwork Reduction Act of 1995 (44 U.S.C. Chapter 35), and the Clinger-Cohen Act, also known as the "Information Technology Management Reform Act of 1996" (Pub. L. 104-106,

Division E.), promote a risk-based policy for cost effective security. The Clinger-Cohen Act supplements the information resources management policies contained in the PRA by establishing a comprehensive approach for executive agencies to improve the acquisition and management of their information resources. FISMA also specifies that national security classified information should be handled in accordance with the appropriate national security directives as provided by DoD and NSA.

FISMA charges the director of the Office of Management and Budget (OMB) with the responsibility of overseeing the security policies and practices of all agencies of the executive branch of the federal government, including "coordinating the development of standards and guidelines between NIST and the NSA and other agencies with responsibility for national security systems." Agencies of the executive branch of the U.S. government are defined as:

- An executive department specified in 5 U.S.C., Section 101
- Within the Executive Office of the President, only OMB and the Office of Administration
- A military department specified in 5 U.S.C., Section 102
- An independent establishment as defined in 5 U.S.C., Section 104(1)
- A wholly owned government corporation fully subject to the provisions of 31 U.S.C., Chapter 91

OMB Circular A-130, Appendix III, "Security of Federal Automated Information Resources," specifies that federal government agencies perform the following functions:

- Plan for security
- Ensure that appropriate officials are assigned security responsibility
- Review the security controls in their information systems
- Authorize system processing prior to operations and periodically thereafter

OMB Circular A-130, Appendix III, also requires that each agency perform security accreditation, which is considered "a form of quality control and challenges managers and technical staffs at all levels to implement the most effective security controls possible in an information system, given mission requirements, technical constraints, operational constraints, and cost/schedule constraints. By accrediting an information system, an agency official accepts responsibility for the security of the system and is fully accountable for any adverse impacts to the agency if a breach of security occurs."

The actions that FISMA requires each government agency to perform in developing and implementing an agency-wide information security program are specified in NIST Special Publication 800-37, *Guide for the Security Certification and Accreditation of Federal Information Systems*, Revision 1 IPD, August 2008. FISMA specifies that the program must include:

- Periodic assessments of risk, including the magnitude of harm that could result from the unauthorized access, use, disclosure, disruption, modification, or destruction of information and information systems that support the operations and assets of the agency

- Policies and procedures that are based on risk assessments, cost-effectively reduce information security risks to an acceptable level, and ensure that information security is addressed throughout the life cycle of each agency information system
- Subordinate plans for providing adequate information security for networks, facilities, information systems, or groups of information systems, as appropriate
- Security awareness training to inform personnel (including contractors and other users of information systems that support the operations and assets of the agency) of the information security risks associated with their activities and their responsibilities in complying with agency policies and procedures designed to reduce these risks
- Periodic testing and evaluation of the effectiveness of information security policies, procedures, practices, and security controls to be performed with a frequency depending on risk, but no less than annually
- A process for planning, implementing, evaluating, and documenting remedial action to address any deficiencies in the information security policies, procedures, and practices of the agency
- Procedures for detecting, reporting, and responding to security incidents
- Plans and procedures to ensure continuity of operations for information systems that support the operations and assets of the agency

Another purpose of FISMA is to ensure that federal agencies take the necessary precautions to secure agency IT systems to protect personally identifiable information (PII) and mitigate the risk of a breach to PII. The OMB defines PII as "any information about an individual maintained by an agency, including, but not limited to, education, financial transactions, medical history, and criminal or employment history and information which can be used to distinguish or trace an individual's identity, such as their name, Social Security number, date and place of birth, mother's maiden name, biometric records, etc., including any other personal information which is linked or linkable to an individual."

The OMB has issued several memos directing agencies to implement privacy and security requirements, such as reducing the unnecessary collection of Social Security numbers and other PII and implementing data breach notification response teams. Agencies are also directed to conduct privacy impact assessments (PIA) on new and revised systems that collect PII and to assure privacy and security of the data.

In addition to determining how well PII is safeguarded, the OMB also directs the agency to examine other aspects of privacy, such as how persistent tracking technology is implemented. For example, persistent tracking technologies, such as persistent cookies in Web applications, can record and maintain information about Web site visitors after the user leaves the Web site. If persistent tracking technologies are used, the agency must describe the usage in the PIA and determine if it is in compliance with the agency security policy.

To assist agencies with how to properly manage PII, NIST created Special Publication 800-122, *Guide to Protecting the Confidentiality of Personally Identifiable Information (PII) (Draft)*, published in January 2009. The NIST guidance states that to effectively protect PII, organizations should implement the following recommendations:

- Organizations should identify all PII residing in their environment.
- Organizations should categorize their PII by the confidentiality impact level.
- Organizations should apply the appropriate safeguards for PII based on the PII confidentiality impact level.
- Organizations should minimize the collection and retention of PII to what is strictly necessary to accomplish their business purpose and mission.
- Organizations should develop an incident response plan to handle breaches of PII.
- Organizations should encourage close coordination among their privacy officers, chief information officers, information security officers, and legal counsel when addressing issues related to PII.

FIPS 199

FISMA assigned to NIST the responsibility for developing the following information system-related standards and guidelines:

- Standards to be used by all federal agencies to categorize all information and information systems collected or maintained by or on behalf of each agency based on the objectives of providing appropriate levels of information security according to a range of risk levels
- Guidelines recommending the types of information and information systems to be included in each category
- Minimum information security requirements (i.e., management, operational, and technical controls)

To satisfy the first item above, NIST developed FIPS Publication 199, ''Standards for Security Categorization of Federal Information and Information Systems.'' FIPS 199 and the FIPS 200 standard, entitled ''Minimum Security Requirements for Federal Information and Federal Information Systems,'' are two mandatory standards specified in the FISMA legislation.

FIPS 199 is used to identify and categorize information and information systems and, as cited in the standard, should be used ''To provide a common framework and understanding for expressing security that, for the Federal government, promotes: (i) effective management and oversight of information security programs, including the coordination of information security efforts throughout the civilian, national security, emergency preparedness, homeland security, and law enforcement communities; and (ii) consistent reporting to the Office of Management and Budget (OMB) and Congress on the adequacy and effectiveness of information security policies, procedures, and practices.''

The FIPS PUB 199 standard is applicable to:

- All information within the federal government other than that information that has been determined pursuant to Executive Order 12958, as amended by Executive Order 13292, or any predecessor order, or by the Atomic Energy Act of 1954, as amended, to require protection against unauthorized disclosure and is marked to indicate its classified status.
- All federal information systems other than those information systems designated as national security systems as defined in 44 United States Code Section 3542(b)(2). National security systems are information systems operated by the U.S. government, its contractors, or agents that contain classified information or that[2]:
    - Involve intelligence activities
    - Involve cryptographic activities related to national security
    - Involve command and control of military forces
    - Involve equipment that is an integral part of a weapon or weapons systems
    - Are critical to the direct fulfillment of military or intelligence missions, not including routine administrative and business applications
    - Agency officials shall use the security categorizations described in FIPS 199 whenever there is a federal requirement to provide such a categorization of information or information systems

Section 508 Compliance

Like FISMA, Section 508 has a profound impact for U.S. federal agencies on the way security features and requirements are addressed in software security.

Section 508 of the U.S. Rehabilitation Act Amendments of 1998 (`www.section508.gov`) requires federal agencies to make their electronic and information technology accessible to people with disabilities. Section 508 was enacted to eliminate barriers in information technology, to make available new opportunities for people with disabilities, and to encourage development of technologies that will help achieve these goals. The law applies to all federal agencies when they develop, procure, maintain, or use electronic and information technology. Under Section 508 (29 U.S.C. 794d), agencies must give disabled employees and members of the public access to information that is comparable to the access available to others.

[2]National Institute of Standards and Technology, Federal Information Processing Standards Publication 199, "Standards for Security Categorization of Federal Information and Information Systems" February 2004.]

The Section 508 standard defines the types of technologies covered and includes provisions for meeting the minimum standards for accessibility. The technologies include:

- Software applications and operating systems
- Web-based information or applications
- Telecommunications products
- Video and multimedia products
- Self-contained, closed products (e.g., information kiosks, calculators, and fax machines)
- Desktop and portable computers

Technical specifications and performance-based requirements are provided for the functional capabilities of the covered technologies. For example, the standard states the following specifications for Web-based intranet and Internet information and applications:

> *The criteria for web-based technology and information are based on access guidelines developed by the Web Accessibility Initiative of the World Wide Web Consortium at (`www.w3.org/WAI/`). Many of these provisions ensure access for people with vision impairments who rely on various assistive products to access computer-based information, such as screen readers, which translate what's on a computer screen into automated audible output, and refreshable Braille displays. Certain conventions, such as verbal tags or identification of graphics and format devices, like frames, are necessary so that these devices can "read" them for the user in a sensible way. The standards do not prohibit the use of web site graphics or animation. Instead, the standards aim to ensure that such information is also available in an accessible format. Generally, this means use of text labels or descriptors for graphics and certain format elements. (HTML code already provides an "Alt Text" tag for graphics which can serve as a verbal descriptor for graphics). This section also addresses the usability of multimedia presentations, image maps, style sheets, scripting languages, applets and plug-ins, and electronic forms.*
>
> *The standards apply to Federal web sites but not to private sector web sites (unless a site is provided under contract to a Federal agency, in which case only that web site or portion covered by the contract would have to comply). Accessible sites offer significant advantages that go beyond access. For example, those with "text-only" options provide a faster downloading alternative and can facilitate transmission of web-based data to cell phones and personal digital assistants.*

FIPS 140 Certification

As discussed in Chapter 5, NIST has established the Cryptographic Module Validation Program (CMVP) to validate cryptographic modules (including software) to standards set by Federal Information Processing Standard (FIPS) 140-1 and 140-2. In the future, FIPS 140-3, which is in draft form, will replace FIPS 140-2. The CMVP is a joint effort between NIST and the Communications Security Establishment Canada (CSEC).

Vendors of cryptographic modules use independent, accredited cryptographic module testing (CMT) laboratories to test their modules. The CMT laboratories use the Derived Test Requirements (DTR), Implementation Guidance (IG), and applicable CMVP programmatic guidance to test cryptographic modules against the applicable standards. NIST's Computer Security Division (CSD) and CSEC jointly serve as the validation authorities for the program, validating the test results and issuing certificates.

FIPS 140-2 defines four levels of security, from Level 1 (the lowest) to Level 4 (the highest). It does not specify in detail what level of security is required by a particular application.

Relating to the Common Criteria, if the operational environment can be modified, the operating system requirements of the Common Criteria are applicable at Level 2 and above.

FIPS 140-1 required evaluated operating systems that referenced the Trusted Computer System Evaluation Criteria (TCSEC) classes C2, B1, and B2. However, TCSEC is no longer in use and has been replaced by the Common Criteria. Consequently, FIPS 140-2 now references the Common Criteria for Information Technology Security Evaluation (CC), ISO/IEC 15408:1999.

The Common Criteria (CC) and FIPS 140-2 are different in the abstractness and focus of tests. FIPS 140-2 testing is against a defined cryptographic module and provides a suite of conformance tests to four security levels. FIPS 140-2 describes the requirements for cryptographic modules and includes such areas as physical security, key management, self tests, roles and services, and so on. The standard was initially developed in 1994, prior to the development of the CC. The CC is an evaluation against a created protection profile (PP) or security target (ST). Typically, a PP covers a broad range of products.

A CC evaluation does not supersede or replace a validation to either FIPS 140-1 or FIPS 140-2. The four security levels in FIPS 140-1 and FIPS 140-2 do not map directly to specific CC EALs or to CC functional requirements. A CC certificate cannot be a substitute for a FIPS 140-1 or FIPS 140-2 certificate.

Certification and Accreditation (C&A) Transformation Initiative

NIST is working with the Office of the Director of National Intelligence (DNI), the Department of Defense (DOD), and the Committee on National Security Systems (CNSS) to establish a common foundation for information security across the U.S. federal government. The common foundation for information security will apply to the intelligence, defense, and civil sectors of the federal government and their support contractors. It will provide more uniform and consistent ways to manage the risk to organizational operations, organizational assets, individuals, other organizations, and the nation.

The goals of the effort are:

- Define a common set of impact levels and adopt and apply them across the DoD and intelligence community (IC)
- Adopt reciprocity as the norm, enabling organizations to accept the approvals by others without retesting or reviewing

- Define, document, and adopt common security controls, using NIST SP 800-53 as a baseline
- Adopt a common lexicon, using CNSSI 4009 as a baseline, thereby providing both the DoD and IC a common language and common understanding
- Institute a senior risk executive function, which bases decisions on an enterprise view of risk considering all factors, including mission, IT, budget, and security
- Incorporate information assurance (IA) into enterprise architectures and deliver IA as common enterprise services across the DoD and IC
- Enable a common adaptable process that incorporates security within the life cycle processes and eliminates security-specific processes

Many of the underlying transformational concepts are already being implemented in the DoD through the DIACAP and in the IC through IC Directive 503.

Other principal documents of the transformation include:

- **CNSSP 22**—Establishes a national risk management policy for national security systems.
- **CNSSI 1199**—Establishes the way the national security community categorizes information and information systems with regard to confidentiality, integrity, and availability.
- **CNSSI 1253**—Consolidates DCID 6/3, DOD Instruction 8500.2, NIST SP 800-53, and other security sources into a single cohesive repository of security controls.
- **CNSSI 1253A**—Provides methodology for assessing adequacy of each security control, e.g., testing.
- **CNSSI 1260**—Provides guidance to organizations with the characterization of their information and information systems.
- **NIST 800-37, Revision 1**—Defines the C&A process. This revision to 800-37 is a joint effort of DNI, DoD, and NIST.

Independent Testing

Independent testing activities include independent verification and validation, independent security testing, certification of the software system, and accreditation of an operational system.

Independent Verification and Validation

The Software Security Assurance State-of-the-Art Report (SOAR) describes independent V&V as "a process whereby the products of the software development life cycle are reviewed, verified, and validated by an entity that is neither the developer nor the acquirer of the software, which is technically, managerially, and financially independent of the developer and acquirer, and which has no stake in the success or failure of the software."[3]

Independent Security Testing

Third-party organizations are often contracted to conduct the Security Test and Evaluation (ST&E) of Federal Information Systems to satisfy U.S. government Federal Information Security Management Act (FISMA) compliance requirements. The testing typically follows standards such as the NIST SP 800-53A *Guide for Assessing the Security Controls in Federal Information Systems* and is governed by agency information security policy. Typically the ST&E determines if the system satisfies information system security requirements as a whole. The extent to which software security properties are evaluated often depends on the criticality of the system, how software security is addressed in the agency information security policy, and the mandate of system stakeholders. Once the system has been assessed, the agency determines whether the risk is low enough to authorize the system to operate.

Independent security testing is also a useful activity to facilitate software acceptance when a formal certification and accreditation process is not required, or to meet specific security requirements. For example, a department in a large organization contracts with an offshore software development shop to build an internal high-consequence Web application. The software development shop builds the Web application according to software security best practices, but the organization's board of directors want additional assurance—for example, ensuring that the code contains no back doors and that the workflow (business logic) cannot be bypassed—before they deploy the software. To convince the board of directors that the software is secure, the department hires a well-regarded independent security tester (an ethical hacker), who performs a targeted source code review and security testing of the Web application with the goals of locating any possible back doors (or other critical security issues) and subverting the business logic. Once the application has been vetted for these issues, the acquiring organization gives the stamp of approval to deploy the application in production.

Summary

The costs to correct software defects are much lower in the pre-deployment phase than in the post-deployment phase.

Black box security tests can be effective means to uncover and address software security issues and reduce risk if used during the system software test phase prior to deployment.

In the post-deployment phase of the security software system development life cycle, if software vulnerabilities or security failures emerge, they are usually the result

[3]Information Assurance Technology Analysis Center (IATAC)/Data and Analysis Center for Software (DACS), "Software Security Assurance State-of-the-Art Report (SOAR)," July 31, 2007.

of design or development errors that were not detected due to inadequate testing paradigms.

This chapter addressed pre-release and pre-deployment software system completion criteria, risk acceptance, and disaster recovery/business continuity planning along with post-release testing, validation, and verification.

Assessment Questions

1. In the secure software development cycle, which one of the following statements is false?
   A. Secure software issues should be addressed prior to deployment.
   B. Costs to repair software defects are much lower in the pre-deployment phase than in the post-deployment phase.
   C. Black box security tests can be effective means to uncover and address software security issues if used during the system software test phase prior to deployment.
   D. Costs to repair software defects are much higher in the pre-deployment phase than in the post-deployment phase.
2. In what part of the software supply process are final reports of the test management system provided to the acquirer along with a set of test data to verify that all specified quality control test points have been covered according to previously agreed-upon terms?
   A. During the specification phase
   B. During the delivery and completion phases
   C. During the implementation and testing phases
   D. During the operations and maintenance phases
3. In completion delivery, what elements should be based on the type of software system to be delivered and anticipated types of defects which might be inherent in the software?
   A. Completion goals
   B. System specifications
   C. System requirements
   D. System validation items
4. The degree of achievement of the completion criteria, mitigating issues in instances where the completion criteria were not achieved, the case for not including specific code units in completion testing, and the performance of the software system are components of which of the following items?
   A. Test cases
   B. Documentation associated with the completion criteria
   C. Verification of the system against the specifications
   D. Validation of the system against the real-world requirements

5. According to the United Kingdom Ministry of Defense Standard 00-56, Issue 4, June 2007, what is defined as the final step in risk management?
   A. Risk acceptance
   B. Risk assessment
   C. Risk analysis
   D. Disposal
6. In the event there are risks in a software system that cannot be accepted, which one of the following is the best practice to follow?
   A. Transfer the risk to an outside party
   B. Accept the risk anyway
   C. Conduct more research
   D. Reiterate the risk management and risk reduction processes.
7. Which one of the following elements is *not* a part of an effective risk acceptance methodology?
   A. The risk acceptance process should be a part of the initial software system specifications.
   B. The risk acceptance process should specify how the evidence for a residual risk tolerance level is to be developed and presented.
   C. Risk acceptance criteria should be based on available funding.
   D. Risk acceptance should be treated as a continuing process that takes into account new threats and mitigation activities.
8. The process of tracking and approving changes to a software system is known as which one of the following?
   A. Configuration management
   B. Requirements specification
   C. Patching
   D. Rework
9. Which one of the following is *not* a primary function of configuration management or change control?
   A. To ensure that the change is implemented in an orderly manner through formalized testing
   B. To analyze the effect of the change on the system after implementation
   C. To insulate the user base from knowledge of the impending change
   D. To reduce the negative impact that the change might have had on the computing services and resources
10. Which one of the following are the five generally accepted procedures to implement and support the change control process?
   A. Evaluating, cataloging, scheduling, implementing, and reporting the change
   B. Applying for, cataloging, scheduling, implementing, and reporting the change
   C. Applying for, cataloging, scheduling, implementing, and evaluating the change

D. Applying for, reviewing, scheduling, implementing, and reporting the change

11. Which one of the following regarding configuration management entails decomposing the verification system into identifiable, understandable, manageable, trackable units known as configuration items (CIs)?

    A. Configuration control

    B. Configuration auditing

    C. Configuration status accounting

    D. Configuration identification

12. What are the four major elements of the BCP process?

    A. Requirements development, business impact assessment, business continuity plan development, plan approval and implementation

    B. Scope and plan initiation, business impact assessment, business continuity plan development, plan approval and implementation

    C. Scope and plan initiation, business impact assessment, disaster recovery plan development, plan approval and implementation

    D. Scope and plan initiation, business impact assessment, business continuity plan development, plan maintenance

13. What activity addresses the preservation of the business in the face of major disruptions to normal operations?

    A. Business continuity planning (BCP)

    B. Disaster recovery planning (DRP)

    C. Business recovery planning (BRP)

    D. Intrusion detection and prevention (IDP)

14. The documented, organized plan for emergency response, backup operations, and recovery maintained by an organization as part of its security program that will ensure the availability of critical resources and facilitate the continuity of operations in an emergency situation is known as which one of the following?

    A. Disaster recovery plan

    B. Continuity of operations plan

    C. Contingency plan

    D. Business continuity plan

15. What are the three primary goals of a business impact assessment?

    A. Prioritization of critical systems, estimation of downtime, identification of resource requirements

    B. Prioritization of critical systems, estimation of downtime, estimation of impact costs

    C. Prioritization of critical systems, identification of alternate courses of action, identification of resource requirements

D. Development of off-site resources, estimation of downtime, identification of alternate processing methods

16. In disaster recover planning, a critical system with a rating class of AA has which one of the following recovery time frames?

    A. Immediate

    B. Same business day

    C. Full functional recovery within 4 hours

    D. 24 to 72 hours downtime acceptable

17. An alternate processing facility with most supporting peripheral equipment, but without the principal computing platforms is known as which one of the following?

    A. A hot site

    B. A cold site

    C. A warm site

    D. A neutral site

18. In implementing a disaster recovery plan, two teams should be organized to execute the recovery. These teams are known as which one of the following?

    A. Recovery and salvage teams

    B. Investigation and recovery teams

    C. Recovery and reconstructing teams

    D. Estimation and salvage teams

19. Which of the following evaluates whether or not software conforms to the specifications, regulations, or other conditions imposed on it while it was being developed?

    A. Verification

    B. Validation

    C. Security testing

    D. Accreditation

20. Which of the following evaluates whether or not software will satisfy its particular requirements (functional and nonfunctional) for its specific intended purpose?

    A. Verification

    B. Validation

    C. Security testing

    D. Accreditation

21. Which of the following is an attestation that a system has the authority to operate?

    A. Verification

    B. Validation

    C. Security testing

    D. Accreditation

22. Which of the following is the element of the Common Criteria that defines an implementation-independent specification of the security requirements and protections of a product that could be built?
    A. Protection profile
    B. Target of evaluation
    C. Security target
    D. Trusted computing base
23. Which of the following is the element of the Common Criteria that defines a listing of the security claims for a particular IT security product?
    A. Protection profile
    B. Target of evaluation
    C. Security target
    D. Trusted computing base
24. Which of the following is the element of the Common Criteria that refers to the product to be tested?
    A. Protection profile
    B. Target of evaluation
    C. Security target
    D. Trusted computing base
25. Which of the following involves testing against a defined cryptographic module and provides a suite of conformance tests to four security levels?
    A. BITS
    B. Common Criteria
    C. Federal Information Processing Standard (FIPS)
    D. ICSA Labs
26. Which of the following defines criteria intended for products and services that detect computer viruses prior to causing an infection?
    A. BITS
    B. Common Criteria
    C. Federal Information Processing Standard (FIPS)
    D. ICSA Labs
27. Which of the following is used to test technology products used to deliver financial services?
    A. BITS
    B. Common Criteria
    C. Federal Information Processing Standard (FIPS)
    D. ICSA Labs

28. Which of the following refers to information systems used to receive, process, store, display or transmit DoD information?
    A. Defense Information Assurance Certification and Accreditation Process (DIACAP)
    B. Federal Information Security Management Act (FISMA)
    C. Election Assistance Commission (EAC)
    D. Office of Management and Budget (OMB)
29. Which of the following assigned to NIST the responsibility for developing the following information system–related standards and guidelines?
    A. Defense Information Assurance Certification and Accreditation Process (DIACAP)
    B. Federal Information Security Management Act (FISMA)
    C. Election Assistance Commission (EAC)
    D. Office of Management and Budget (OMB)
30. Which of the following activities is conducted by a party that has no stake in the success or failure of the software?
    A. Certification and accreditation
    B. Verification and validation
    C. Validation
    D. Independent security testing

CHAPTER

7

Software Deployment, Operations, and Maintenance

All secure software life cycle activities are driven by the risk management process according to the criticality and sensitivity of information assets.

This chapter stresses the importance of maintaining information assurance during installation, deployment, operation, maintenance, and disposal of secure software systems.

After an organization conducts the activities recommended in this chapter, it should document the specific procedures, practices, and lessons learned in a knowledge base called the Standard Operating Procedures (SOP). This is used by operations and maintenance staff and tiered help desks to ensure a common approach and service level commensurate with the criticality of the system and sensitivity of the data.

Installation and Deployment

All software, including software that is retrieved by download, should first be installed in a staging (test) environment, separate from development, which duplicates the production (target) environment.

The installation should follow documented procedures that describe how to secure the software against threats, such as attacks and exploits, that could be encountered in the production environment. For example, the installation instructions should describe the purpose and identify the location of all software configuration files and provide instructions to modify configuration parameters so they are as restrictive as possible.

Ideally, the software should be preconfigured by the vendor or software development team with secure defaults. Even so, the installation procedures should recommend, or the setup utility should enforce, the reconfiguration of the default parameters upon installation so that secure configuration parameters can be set; this includes establishing and setting access control parameter values for accounts, roles, groups, files, and directories.

The installation instructions should also specify security constraints required for the software to securely interoperate with COTS, GOTS, OSS, or legacy components, such as mail transfer agents or mainframe connectors, in the production environment.

The configuration parameters that are operating environment specific, including Internet Protocol (IP) addresses, machine names, or database login credentials, should be separated (for example in configuration files) for each specific environment, such as staging or production.

After configuration of the software in the staging environment has been completed, testing should be performed. The testing should indicate how well the software would behave under hostile conditions in the real-world production environment. The testing should also inform a formal risk assessment of the software.

The risk assessment is typically a product of the overall risk management process. If deficiencies are discovered during testing, they are typically ranked in the risk assessment from highest risk to lowest risk. The software stakeholders should evaluate the risk and formally approve the software for operation before the software is deployed to production.

When it comes time to deploy the software to production, instructions should be carefully followed to ensure that all operating parameters are correctly configured.

Bootstrapping

The general process for the startup of a computer is typically referred to as either bootstrapping, booting, or initial program load (IPL).

In most IBM PC–compatible computers, when the computer first powers on, a program called the basic input/output system (BIOS) is loaded into memory from firmware (software embedded in hardware).

The BIOS then initiates a pre-boot sequence called the power-on self-test (POST). The principal duties of the BIOS during POST are as follows:

- Verify the integrity of the BIOS code itself
- Discover, size, and verify system memory
- Discover, initialize, and catalog system hardware, including peripheral devices
- Delegate control to other BIOS, e.g., to initialize video and SCSI, if necessary
- Present a user interface for system configuration
- Identify, organize, and select boot devices
- Execute the bootstrap program

After POST, the BIOS loads a secondary program, called the bootstrap or bootloader, which resides in the Master Boot Record (MBR) on the selected boot device. Examples of second-stage bootloader programs are the GRand Unified Bootloader (GRUB) in Linux and the NT Loader (NTLDR) in Windows.

In the last few years, the Unified Extensible Firmware Interface (UEFI) has begun to replace the BIOS. The UEFI was originally a technology devised by Intel as an improvement over the legacy BIOS and is now an open source standard maintained by the Unified EFI Forum (www.uefi.org).

The UEFI preserves some of the recent improvements to the legacy BIOS such as Advanced Configuration and Power Interface (ACPI) and System Management BIOS (SMBIOS), but is not constrained by the BIOS 16-bit limitation. The UEFI is also expandable, as implied by its name. For example, since the UEFI contains a full network stack, it enables add-ons such as a messenger application and a Web browser. A full network stack also enables the update of the UEFI firmware over the network.

The UEFI provides a graphical boot manager with full mouse and keyboard support, removing the need for a dedicated second-stage bootloader. An example of a UEFI implementation is Boot Camp on the Apple Intel-based Macintosh computers. Boot Camp produces a Windows drivers disk and a nondestructive partitioning tool to allow the installation and boot of legacy BIOS operating systems such as Windows XP.

A number of operating systems also support boot from UEFI (called UEFI-aware OSes) including Mac OS X v10.5, Windows Server 2008, and Windows Vista Service Pack 1.

Since the BIOS and UEFI are high-consequence components, they are an attractive vector for attack. One notable malware attack against the BIOS was the CIH (Chernobyl) virus that first appeared in 1998. The CIH virus filled the first 1024 KB of the host's boot drive with zeros and then attacked certain types of BIOS. Both of these payloads rendered the host computer inoperable, although it was possible to replace the BIOS chip in order to recover the system. The advent of write-protected BIOS was partly a response to this attack.[1]

A recent BIOS-level exploit, termed the "Persistent BIOS Infection" was demonstrated by Core Security Technologies researchers at the CanSecWest security conference in March 2009. This attack takes advantage of the fact that the BIOS can be upgraded to a new version, and the upgrade can be performed through several operating systems and technologies, including DOS, Windows, and ActiveX.

Since the BIOS contains several checksums, any modification could lead to an unbootable system. To circumvent this safeguard, the researchers used the following technique to patch the BIOS:

1. Dump the BIOS using `flashrom` (a utility to read/write the BIOS)
2. Patch and compensate the 8-bit checksum
3. Re-flash the BIOS

Once the BIOS is controlled by the exploit, it is possible to access the hard drive, memory manager, network, modem and other hardware. In the Core demonstration, hard disk content was modified, including the shadow file on Unix, and code was injected into Windows binaries. The researchers also demonstrated the exploit of a virtual machine BIOS in a popular platform virtualization software.[2]

For this attack to be successful, it requires that the BIOS first be switched to write-allow mode. The attacker must also have either physical access to the system

[1]http://en.wikipedia.org/wiki/CIH_virus

[2]www.coresecurity.com/files/attachments/Persistent_BIOS_Infection_CanSecWest09.pdf

or remote root-level access. If an attacker is able to gain root-level access or physical access to the machine, then the host operating system or operating environment is already insecure, and the attacker may lack sufficient additional motivation to exploit the BIOS. However, since a BIOS exploit can remain invisible and survive reboots and reloads, the attacker could use the exploit to establish a semi-permanent foothold in the operating environment.

Although it is impossible to prevent this attack if an attacker has physical access to the machine, safeguards can be put in place to deter an attacker. For example, an administrative password should be set on the BIOS configuration GUI to restrict access and all BIOS options should be set as restrictive as possible, such as limiting the boot selection to a single boot device. The BIOS upgrade feature should also be turned off or the BIOS should be write-protected after upgrading the BIOS to the latest version and setting the configuration parameters for the system hardware.

Security is also a concern in environments that implement UEFI. For example, since UEFI implements a full network stack and is expandable, attack vectors include a vulnerable add-on component running in the UEFI such as a Web browser or messenger application. The network component itself could be infected with malware, or an administrator could unknowingly install a malicious add-on. The UEFI environment is also prone to the same risks as the BIOS—a malicious version of the UEFI firmware could be installed if an attacker could control the firmware upgrade process. Since the UEFI can be upgraded over the network, an attack might be conducted by poisoning the DNS cache used by the UEFI firmware to look up the address of the server where it searches and downloads an update to the installed firmware. Instead of downloading a good version of the firmware from a trusted source, it might download an exploited version from an attacker-controlled site.

Offline Environment

When a computer system is offline—powered off or in a mode such as suspend or hibernate—it is vulnerable to attack.

Trusted Platform Module

One way to provide a degree of tamper resistance to a computer system while it is offline is through the use of a trusted platform module (TPM). The TPM is an implementation of a secure cryptoprocessor, a dedicated microprocessor for performing cryptographic operations. It facilitates the secure generation of cryptographic keys through the use of a hardware pseudo-random number generator, stores the keys, and limits access to the keys. The TPM also includes capabilities such as attestation and sealed storage.

Attestation involves the creation and secure storage of a hash key summary or unique "fingerprint" of the boot environment using measurements of the hardware and software configuration. Local applications and remote systems (remote attestation) can use the attestation process to prove that the platform is trustworthy and has not been breached. For example, the fingerprint should not change unless the boot environment is modified. When the system first boots up, the TPM generates a fingerprint of the boot environment and compares it to the stored fingerprint. If the fingerprints do not match, that could indicate a breach, and the TPM should block access until the changes have been verified (if a policy has been set up that requires such action).

Sealing is the process of encrypting data and allowing the data to be decrypted only if the TPM releases the associated decryption key, which it does only for software that can provide the same password that was supplied when software ownership of the TPM was initially established. *Binding* encrypts data using the TPM endorsement key, a unique RSA key burned into the chip during its production, or another trusted key descended from it.[3]

An example of a security feature that uses a TPM is the BitLocker encryption system from Microsoft. BitLocker uses a TPM to protect user data and to ensure that a computer running Windows Vista has not been tampered with while the system was offline. A goal of BitLocker is to provide more data protection to mobile workers when their systems are lost or stolen.

The TPM specification is OS-agnostic, and software stacks exist for several operating systems.

Cold Boot Attacks

One type of side-channel attack against offline computer systems is an enhanced memory imaging attack known as a cold boot attack. To conduct a cold boot attack, an adversary must gain physical access to the computer system.

In the research paper "Lest We Remember: Cold Boot Attacks on Encryption Keys,"[4] researchers took advantage of an unexpected property of dynamic random access memory (DRAM). Ordinary DRAM loses its contents gradually over a period of seconds. This is an effect known as DRAM remanence. Even at standard operating temperatures, and even if the chips are removed from the motherboard, the data will persist for minutes or even hours if the chips are kept at low temperatures.

Cold boot attacks enhance and exploit the DRAM remanence effect to recover cryptographic keys held in memory. To increase the remanence times, a simple technique can be used such as spraying an inverted can of "canned air" on the DRAM, cooling it to around −50 degrees Celsius. Then the machine can be power cycled, and upon powering back up, it can boot a malicious operating system—for example, from a thumb drive—that copies the contents of memory. The attacker can then use algorithms for finding cryptographic keys in memory images as well as algorithms to correct for errors caused by bit decay. Once the cryptographic keys are found, they can be used to decrypt hard drive contents.

Cold boot attacks pose a particular threat to laptop users who rely on disk encryption products. For example, if an adversary steals a laptop while an encrypted disk is mounted, a cold boot attack could be used to access the contents, even if the laptop is screen-locked or suspended.

According to the researchers, successful attacks have been conducted against popular disk encryption products such as BitLocker, TrueCrypt, dm-crypt, and FileVault. These

[3]`http://en.wikipedia.org/wiki/Trusted_Platform_Module`

[4]Halderman, J. A., Schoen, S. D., Heninger, N., Clarkson, W., Paul, W., Calandrino, J. A., Feldman, A. J., Appelbaum, J., and Felten, E. W., "Lest We Remember: Cold Boot Attacks on Encryption Keys," Center for Information Technology Policy, Princeton University, 2008.

products no longer have a safe place to store cryptographic keys. Even the BitLocker encryption system was defeated despite its use of a TPM to store the encryption keys.

Although there are some countermeasures to defend against memory imaging attacks, there is no way to eliminate them. Since cryptographic keys in active use need to be stored somewhere, they are an available and attractive target for attack. Most countermeasures focus on discarding or obscuring encryption keys before an adversary might gain physical access, preventing memory-dumping software from being executed on the machine, physically protecting DRAM chips, and making the contents of memory decay at a faster rate.

Chapter 4 discussed these countermeasures and their limitations in detail.

Configuration Management

Configuration management consists of activities that are performed throughout the entire software life cycle. For example, Chapter 4 discussed how secure version control is used to control changes to software during coding/implementation, and Chapter 6 described how configuration management activities are a component of risk acceptance. Configuration management also involves activities such as maintaining software documentation, securing the operating environment before deployment, and managing the configuration of the operating environment post-deployment.

The operating environment is the execution environment of the software and contains not just the software itself, but other components on which the software is dependent. These components contribute to the security posture and could be used as attack vectors to compromise the software system. Operating environment components include desktops, servers, network appliances, and their respective operating systems. For example, the client portion of a client/server software application depends on the security of the desktop computer and operating system, the security of the server computers and operating systems, and of course, the networks in between.

Hardening

Securing the operating environment involves activities that reduce the attack surface and thereby improve the overall security posture. These activities typically involve modifying services or settings that are not necessary for the software application to function. The process of disabling and removing unnecessary services and settings on an operating system is commonly known as *hardening*. Hardening also involves modifying the operating system so that the access controls are as restrictive as possible, while still allowing the software to function properly.

The Center for Internet Security (CIS) (`www.cisecurity.org`) purports to be the "only distributor of consensus best practice standards for security configuration." The benchmarks, as they are known, are widely accepted by U.S. government agencies for FISMA compliance and by auditors for compliance with the ISO standard as well as other regulations, including GLB, SOX, and HIPAA. The consensus technical specifications represent a prudent level of due care and best-practice security configurations for computers connected to the Internet.

The CIS benchmarks enumerate security configuration settings and actions that "harden" the system. CIS also distributes automated scoring tools that can be run on a system to compare the system configuration against the CIS benchmarks, and result in scores for each configuration item and explanations of deficiencies.

The CIS benchmarks were designed in such a way that the benchmark can be applied during the hardening process, and the system can be subsequently audited for compliance with the benchmark using a scoring tool or a commercial CIS-certified tool. This makes it convenient for organizations to mandate compliance with the CIS benchmarks in the information security policy and later audit compliance to ensure that all devices, applications, and systems meet a standard minimum security baseline. For example, each recommendation in the CIS benchmark is annotated with a security level, from the minimum measure of security to prudent security beyond the minimum. An organization's security policy can mandate compliance with the minimum level of security, Security Level 1, in order to achieve a minimum security baseline. The security policy can also specify that high-risk systems and systems that must meet specific regulatory requirements should be hardened to an even more secure state, and should therefore be in compliance with the CIS benchmark Security Level 2. Examples of high-risk systems include systems that contain personally identifiable information such as human resources applications, systems that process financial information such as a payroll application, and servers that are exposed to the Internet on the perimeter of the network, known as *bastion hosts*. The following is an explanation of the CIS security levels from the CIS Mac OS X 10.5 Benchmark v1.0:

- Level 1:
  - Can be understood and performed by system administrators with any level of security knowledge and experience
  - Are unlikely to cause an interruption of service to the operating system or the applications that run on it
  - Can be automatically monitored either by CIS scoring tools or by CIS-certified tools available from security software vendors
- Level 2:
  - Prudent security beyond the minimum level
  - May affect operating system function and are therefore of greatest value to system administrators who have sufficient security knowledge to apply them with consideration to OS functions and software applications running in their particular environments

CIS benchmarks are available for the following 40 operating systems, network devices, applications (including middleware), and mobile devices at the time of writing:

- Operating systems
  - Windows XP Professional SP1/SP2
  - Windows Server 2003
  - Windows 2000 Professional

- Windows 2000 Server
- Windows 2000
- Windows NT
- Mac OS X 10.5 (Leopard)
- Mac OS X 10.4 (Tiger)
- FreeBSD
- Solaris 10
- Solaris 10 11/06 and 8/07
- Solaris 2.5.1 - 9.0
- HP-UX
- AIX
- Red Hat Linux 5 (RHEL5)
- Red Hat Linux 4 (for RHEL 2.1, 3.0, 4.0 and Fedora Core 1-5)
- SUSE Linux
- Slackware Linux
- Debian Linux
- Novell OES:NetWare

- Network devices
  - Wireless networks
  - Cisco IOS Router
  - Cisco ASA, FWSM, and PIX
  - Check Point Firewall
- Applications
  - Exchange Server 2003
  - Exchange Server 2007
  - Oracle Database 8i
  - Oracle Database 9/10g
  - Oracle Database 11g
  - Apache Web Server
  - MySQL
  - Microsoft SQL Server 2005
  - Microsoft SQL Server 2000
  - BIND
  - Novell eDirectory
  - IIS

  - OpenLDAP
  - FreeRADIUS
  - Virtual Machine
  - Xen Server
  - VMWare ESX Server
- Mobile devices
  - Apple iPhone 2.2.1

It is typically necessary for a user to possess administrative privileges in order to implement the CIS benchmark recommendations. The CIS benchmarks also provide scripts that can be modified and run in an automated fashion in addition to the recommended manual configuration steps.

Although the CIS benchmarks contain a large number of good recommendations, it is often necessary to secure the configuration further based on the unique threats faced by the software application in its operating environment. Additional security best practices can be consulted to assist with this process. For example, Karen Goertzel, Theodore Winograd, and their contributors in "Enhancing the Development Life Cycle to Produce Secure Software"[5] from the United States Department of Defense Data and Analysis Center for Software (DACS) recommend the following best practices for securing the operating environment:

- **Configure restrictive file system access controls for initialization files and target directories**—The software should be installed with the most restrictive access control policy possible on all files and directories that it touches. All non-production user accounts, files, and directories should be removed, e.g., temporary user accounts, sample files, test configurations, and test data should be removed from the execution environment. If the software reads initialization files to allow the default settings to be configured, the initialization files should be protected. For example, an attacker should not be able to change which initialization file is used, nor create nor modify the initialization file, and the file should be stored in a directory other than the current directory, i.e., outside the execution path of the application.
- **Validate install-time security assumptions**—When installing the software, the system administrator should verify that all security assumptions made by the software are valid for the execution environment. For example, the source code and all library routines used by the software should be adequately protected by the access controls in the execution environment. The system administrator should also verify that the software is being installed in the anticipated execution environment before making assumptions about the environment's security mechanisms and posture.

[5]Goertzel, K., Winograd, T., et al., "Enhancing the Development Life Cycle to Produce Secure Software," Version 2.0, Rome, New York: United States Department of Defense Data and Analysis Center for Software, October 2008.

- **Remove all unused and unreferenced files**—All unnecessary files should be removed from the execution environment, including:
  - Commercial and open source executables known to contain exploitable faults
  - Hidden or unreferenced files and programs, i.e., demo programs, sample code, installation files
  - Temporary files and backup files stored on the same server as the files they duplicate
  - Dynamic link libraries, extensions, and any other executable that is not explicitly required for application functionality
- **Change passwords and account names on default accounts**—Typically COTS software comes preconfigured with default accounts such as a default user and password. Common account names and passwords include "administrator," "test," "guest," and "nobody." Sometimes the password is blank or is set as the same value as the account name. These accounts are well-known by attackers and are often the target of password-guessing attacks. Ideally, the software should be preconfigured by the vendor or software development team with secure defaults. Even so, the installation procedures should recommend or the setup utility should enforce the reconfiguration of the default parameters upon installation so that secure configuration parameters can be set. For example, the Oracle Installer automatically locks and expires most accounts and/or forces password resets on newer Oracle products, while the Oracle Default Password Scanner can be run against legacy Oracle installations to locate unchanged default account names and passwords, e.g., a common default account name and password in legacy Oracle products was "Scott/Tiger."
- **Delete unused default accounts**—Web and database vulnerability scanners can be run to detect any commonly used default passwords and default accounts that may have been overlooked. For example, a well-known account such as "Administrator" on Windows systems can be renamed to a less obvious name.
- **Lock down the execution environment**—Some COTS software ships with a tool to assist with the configuration of the software—referred to as a setup configuration tool, or wizard—which provides the installer with configuration choices and verbose explanations so they can choose the most secure settings for the software. For example, Microsoft offers a tool called the Security Configuration Wizard (SCW), introduced with Microsoft Windows Server 2003 Service Pack 1, that can be used to minimize the attack surface for servers by disabling Windows functionality that is not required. If the software does not ship with a lockdown tool and no guidelines or procedures exist elsewhere for locking down the operating environment, the software's installation instructions may need to include environment lockdown procedures. Specific lockdown considerations include:
  - Configure the required security protections and services and their interfaces for protection and interaction with the software
  - Disable all nonessential services

- Configure the available file system directory access controls, virtual machine monitor, TPM, or other environment compartmentalization mechanisms to isolate the trusted components of the software from the untrusted components and from other high-risk entities on the same host, and to constrain the execution of untrusted components of the software
- Set access privileges on the directory in which the software executables will be stored to ensure that the software is execute-only accessible to all individuals except the administrator
- Disable any non-secure protocols or utilities, e.g., "r" utilities like `rsh`, `rlogin`, and `rcp`
- Move production data if necessary to separate it from the application's control or management data
- Install all current security patches for environment components
- Establish and test all environment recovery procedures
- Configure all intrusion detection/prevention, anomaly detection, firewall, honeypot/honeynet/honeytoken, insider threat/security monitoring, and event/incident reporting capabilities

NIST Special Publication 800-123, "Guide to General Server Security" (`http://csrc.nist.gov/publications/PubsSPs.html`) is a comprehensive general resource for securing servers. For securing servers that process national security information, additional guidance can be found in the Security Technical Implementation Guides (STIG) (`http://iase.disa.mil/stigs/stig/index.html`) published by the U.S. Defense Information Systems Agency (DISA), including guides published by the National Security Agency (NSA).

Elevated Privileges

In a software system, each component or process should only have the privileges required to perform a specific task, and should not be granted a general set of privileges for all tasks performed. Each component or process may also temporarily elevate privileges to perform a specific task, but must immediately relinquish privileges when the task is completed. The level of privilege should be enforced at the lowest level in the software stack and at the finest granularity.

In practice, this means the most restrictive set of operating system permissions or access control list (ACL) entries should be applied to all application files, including executables and configuration files. The application should also run as a low-privilege user account, with the smallest amount of privileges necessary to accomplish the application tasks. If the application is compromised, it should not have access to the resources of the entire operating environment.

This same principle applies to individuals who must perform tasks in the operating environment. Normal users should be granted only the privileges necessary to use the basic functionality of the software system. They should be prevented from making administrative changes to the environment, such as modifying configuration files or registry entries; installation or removal of programs; and viewing or modifying security or audit logs. A user whose role in the organization is to perform administrative tasks can elevate his privileges to perform those tasks using facilities that are designed for that purpose. For example, the administrative user may need administrative rights to apply patches to the operating system and to install and secure a user application. The administrative user could log on as a normal, unprivileged user and then elevate his privileges to accomplish these tasks. Facilities for temporarily elevating privileges include the Run As command in Windows XP, which is used for running programs as a different user than the currently logged-on user. The Run As command typically requires the user to know the valid administrator password to run a command as administrator. Some *nix systems provide the `sudo` facility to allow a user to run an executable that requires administrative or root user privileges. The `sudo` facility can be configured to require the user to enter the valid root password or may not even require the password, the latter case being less secure.

As soon as the administrative user performs the required tasks, he should be required to drop the administrative privileges. If possible, the relinquishing of privileges should be automatically enforced. For example, in the Windows Vista operating system, users are normal, unprivileged users even if they are a member of the local administrators group. This restriction is enforced by a built-in feature called User Account Control (UAC). When the user requests to perform an administrative action that requires elevated privileges (such as double-clicking an executable to install software), the operating system prompts him for authorization before performing the action.

Platform Change

All changes to the deployed software and operating environment must be controlled, documented, tested, and approved. The change control process is typically part of the overall configuration management process employed by an organization.

All changes to the components of the operating environment should be documented; ideally the hardware and software configurations should be documented and tracked in an automated information system that facilitates this task and is dedicated to this purpose. For example, the Information Technology Infrastructure Library (ITIL) framework's configuration management process advises the use of a configuration management database (CMDB). The CMDB represents the authorized configuration of the components of the operating environment. A key goal of the CMDB is to help an organization understand the relationships between these components and track their configuration. CMDB implementations often involve integration with other automated information systems, such as asset management systems.[6]

Organizations have also started to use virtual infrastructure throughout the entire software life cycle, for example, in development, test, and production environments. In platform-based virtualization, the guest operating systems (virtual machines) can be easily moved, copied, modified, and backed up to support the changing capacity needs of the environment. To manage this type of infrastructure, virtualization vendors such as VMWare are creating full software life cycle solutions that enable virtual machine libraries, virtual lab automation, configuration capture and management, and

[6]http://en.wikipedia.org/wiki/CMDB

policy-based self -service access to virtual machines.[7] One proven practice created by VMWare for virtualization configuration management involves mapping virtualization configuration items (CIs) such as virtual machines and the owners of services that purchased them, in order to represent a complete virtualization solution. The goal of this practice is to enable the easy input of all the virtualization objects into the CMDB. It facilitates this task by providing mappings for all of the CIs typically found in a virtual infrastructure. Each CI has a CI ID, a CI type field, and a CI status field as recommended by the ITIL configuration management process.[8]

Patching is an activity that should be properly managed by the change control process. For example, a COTS operating system vendor may release patches that are deemed important to secure an operating system that is deployed in the production environment. The patches should first be applied to an operating system in an environment that ideally mirrors the production environment for purposes of testing. After applying the patches, the test environment should be fully exercised, typically with the support of automated tools, to ensure that the changes do not break any functionality or adversely impact the security posture of the environment. For example, patches sometimes replace existing files with new files containing less restrictive permissions on systems that have been previously hardened, and may also enable services that were previously disabled. A CIS scoring tool or vulnerability scanner can be run on the operating system after the patches have been applied to detect any unintended changes that the patch may have introduced. Automated tools can also generate a report that can demonstrate to the approving authority that the operating system is still compliant with the minimum security baseline, and thus facilitate the approval of the patch for deployment in the production environment.

Upgrades and changes to software components should also follow a similar controlled process. All changes to the software should be applied as part of a release tagged in the secure version control system. The software should first be upgraded in the test environment. Software upgrades typically require more rigorous testing, including testing for quality assurance, security testing, and regression testing, before the upgrade is approved by the software stakeholders for deployment to production.

The Security Content Automation Protocol (SCAP) (`http://scap.nist.gov`), pronounced "S-Cap," is a method for using specific standards to enable automated vulnerability management, measurement, and policy compliance evaluation (e.g., FISMA compliance). More specifically, SCAP is a suite of selected open standards that enumerate software flaws, security-related configuration issues, and product names; measure systems to determine the presence of vulnerabilities; and provide mechanisms to rank (score) the results of these measurements in order to evaluate the impact of the discovered security issues. SCAP defines how these standards are combined. The National Vulnerability Database provides a repository and data feeds of content that utilize the SCAP.

NIST defines and maintains the protocol and the data feeds of content in the SCAP standards. Thus, NIST defines how to use the open standards within the SCAP context and defines the mappings between the SCAP enumeration standards. However, NIST

[7]www.vmware.com

[8]http://viops.vmware.com/home/docs/DOC-1022

does not control the underlying standards that are used within the protocol. SCAP is comprised of the following standards:

- Common Vulnerabilities and Exposures (CVE®)
- Common Configuration Enumeration (CCE™)
- Common Platform Enumeration (CPE™)
- Common Vulnerability Scoring System (CVSS)
- Extensible Configuration Checklist Description Format (XCCDF)
- Open Vulnerability and Assessment Language (OVAL™)

These open standards were created and are maintained by a number of different institutions, including the MITRE Corporation, the NSA, and a special interest group within the Forum of Incident Response and Security Teams (FIRST). NIST recommends the use of SCAP for security automation and policy compliance activities.

Operations and Maintenance

Operations involve the software and hardware in a computing facility, the data media used in a facility, the operators using these resources, and the work products of the information systems. Because desktop and distributed computing resources also contain sensitive information, similar issues apply to those systems.

In this section, the operations topics of controls, monitoring, auditing, incident management, problem management, maintenance, and patching will be addressed. Operations hardware and software security refer to the act of understanding the threats and vulnerabilities associated with computer operations and the implementation of security controls for critical activities. Some typical threats include internal intruders, external attackers, malicious and incompetent users, and other threats in the operating environment. Operations controls should address the protection of resources and privileged-entity controls.

Resource Protection

Resource protection is designed to help reduce the possibility of damage that can result from the unauthorized disclosure and/or alteration of data by limiting the opportunities for its misuse. Some typical operational hardware resources include routers, firewalls, storage media, file servers, Web servers, and printers. Operational software resources are operating systems, utilities, program libraries, and applications.

Privileged Entity Protection

Privileged entity access, which is also known as privileged operations functions, is defined as an extended or special access to computing resources given to operators, system administrators and some distributed computing users that have administrator privileges on their machines. Privileged operators have access to system commands and the system control program. A system control program restricts the execution of certain computing functions and permits them only when a processor is in a particular functional state, known as privileged or supervisor state. Applications can run in different states, during which different commands are permitted. To be authorized to execute privileged instructions, a program should be running in a restrictive state.

Categories of Operations Controls

Operations controls fall into the following categories:

- **Preventive controls**—Preventive controls are designed to lower the amount and impact of unintentional errors and to prevent unauthorized intruders from internally or externally accessing the system.
- **Detective controls**—Detective controls detect errors that have occurred and operate after the fact.
- **Corrective (or recovery) controls**—Corrective controls mitigate the impact of a loss event through data recovery procedures.
- **Deterrent controls**—Deterrent controls are used to encourage compliance with external controls, such as regulatory compliance.
- **Application controls**—Application controls are designed into a software application to minimize and detect the software's operational irregularities.

Some specific operational software controls include:

- **Antivirus management**—If personnel can load or execute any software on a system, the system is more vulnerable to viruses, unexpected software interactions, and the subversion of security controls.
- **Software testing**—A rigid and formal software testing process is required to determine compatibility with custom applications or to identify other unforeseen interactions. This procedure should also apply to software upgrades.
- **Software utilities**—Powerful systems utilities can compromise the integrity of operations systems and logical access controls. Their use must be controlled by security policy.
- **Safe software storage**—A combination of logical and physical access controls should be implemented to ensure that the software and copies of backups have not been modified without proper authorization.
- **Backup controls**—Not only do support and operations personnel back up software and data, but in a distributed environment users may also back up their own data. It is very important to routinely test the restore accuracy of a backup system. A backup should also be stored securely to protect it from theft, damage, or environmental problems.

Monitoring and Auditing

Operational software assurance requires the process of reviewing an operational system to see that security controls, both automated and manual, are functioning correctly and effectively. Operational assurance addresses whether the system's technical features are being bypassed or have vulnerabilities and whether required procedures are being followed. To maintain operational assurance, organizations use two basic methods: monitoring and system audits. *Monitoring* refers to an ongoing activity that examines either the system or the users; a system audit is a one-time or periodic event to evaluate security. Problem identification and problem resolution are the primary goals of monitoring, and monitoring is integral to maintaining secure software.

Monitoring

Monitoring consists of the mechanisms, tools, and techniques that permit the identification of security events that could affect the operation of a computer facility. It also includes actions to identify the important elements of an event and to report that information appropriately.

The concept of monitoring includes monitoring for illegal software installation, monitoring the hardware for faults and error states, and monitoring operational events for anomalies. To perform monitoring for software security, the following methods can be applied:

- Cyber-threat analysis
- Intrusion detection
- Penetration testing
- Violation analysis

Cyber-Threat Analysis

Cyber-threat analysis involves threat identification, threat reporting, and advanced analysis that includes reverse engineering and data forensics methods to discover and respond to intrusions. This method was developed by NASA and is outlined in the November 10, 2008, report of the National Aeronautics and Space Administration Office of the Inspector General, entitled "NASA's Most Serious Management and Performance Challenges." The report states that that the Cyber-Threat Analysis Program will "proactively discover and handle sensitive intrusions into NASA's cyber assets."

Cyber-threat analysis employs intelligence-gathering methods such as intelligent agents to monitor Web sites and IRC channels for indications of a pending attack or attack in progress. With this knowledge, a response can be generated to handle the attack. For example, one type of attack involves an adversary harvesting email addresses from a public-facing Web site. The adversary then crafts malware and credible email messages and sends them to the email recipients. This is a targeted attack known as *spear phishing*. The attackers know who they are attacking and want information possessed by the victims. The attack may be detected using an intrusion detection system, log analysis, egress analysis (malware infected machines communicating back to a server), or malware detected on the perimeter by appliances scanning incoming email. All this information has to be correlated by a human analyst. The analyst can then coordinate resources to respond to the attack by blocking attacking IP addresses, sending out warnings to affected users, and so on. Any required operational and configuration changes are subsequently incorporated into the organization's operations and maintenance procedures.

Cyber-threat analysis also leverages open source intelligence and proprietary threat feeds. For example, the all-volunteer Shadowserver Foundation (`www.shadowserver.org`) is a "watchdog group of security professionals that gather, track, and report on malware, botnet activity, and electronic fraud." Its mission is "to improve the security of the Internet by raising awareness of the presence of compromised servers, malicious attackers, and the spread of malware." Shadowserver works alongside other security groups to develop strategies against the threats and to form action plans to help mitigate the threats as they develop. Shadowserver is actively involved in:

- Capturing and receiving malicious software or information related to compromised devices
- Disassembling, sandboxing, and analyzing viruses and Trojan horses
- Monitoring and reporting on malicious attackers
- Tracking and reporting on botnet activities
- Disseminating cyber-threat information
- Coordinating incident response

In addition to open source intelligence, cyber-threat intelligence can be obtained from proprietary threat feeds. For example, the global security intelligence service, iDefense Labs (`http://labs.idefense.com`) sells an iAlert security intelligence service that provides timely warnings and detailed threat data that can be used by an organization to proactively defend against cyber-threats, including viruses and worms, technical vulnerabilities, and attacks.

The cyber-threat analysis approach also relies on collaboration among many different entities to determine if unknown malware that is discovered poses a threat. This activity involves cooperation among security organizations and security researchers, software vendors, government entities such as US-CERT, as well as gleaning information from the hacking underground.

The United States Computer Emergency Readiness Team (US-CERT) (`www.us-cert.gov`) is charged with providing response support and defense against cyber-attacks for the Federal Civil Executive Branch (.gov) and information sharing and collaboration with state and local government, industry, and international partners. US-CERT interacts with federal agencies, industry, the research community, state and local governments, and others to disseminate reasoned and actionable cyber-security information to the public. US-CERT also provides a way for citizens, businesses, and other institutions to communicate and coordinate directly with the United States government about cyber-security.

Intrusion Detection

An intrusion detection system (IDS) is a system that monitors network traffic and/or monitors host audit logs in order to determine whether any violations of an organization's security policy have taken place. An IDS can detect intrusions that have circumvented or passed through a firewall or that are occurring within the local area network behind the firewall.

A networked system's security policy should require that designated system and network administrators and response team members are trained in the use of intrusion response tools and environments. Also, the policy should require that the inventory of all applications software, operating systems, supporting tools, and hardware be kept up to date, and require quick access to backups in an emergency, even if they are stored at a remote site. This may include defining procedures that give specific managers the responsibility to authorize such access.

Intrusion detection (ID) processes must be planned and implemented to help organizations detect and respond to incidents before they occur. It's important to respond to incidents in an efficient and effective manner. For example, the information system security officer (ISSO) must determine how the organization is going to monitor the intrusion detection system, who will monitor it, how alerts will be processed, and how the incident is remediated and with what level of response. The critical issues involved are:

- Protecting assets that could be compromised
- Protecting resources that could be utilized more profitably if an incident did not require their services
- Complying with (government or other) regulations
- Preventing the use of your systems in attacks against other systems (which could cause you to incur legal liability)
- Minimizing the potential for negative exposure

The most common approaches to ID are statistical anomaly detection (also known as behavior-based) and pattern-matching (also known as knowledge-based or signature-based) detection. ID systems that operate on a specific host and detect malicious activity on that host only are called host-based ID systems. ID systems that operate on network segments and analyze that segment's traffic are called network-based ID systems. Since there are pros and cons for each, an effective IDS should use a combination of both network- and host-based intrusion detection systems. A truly effective IDS will detect common attacks as they occur, which includes distributed attacks.

Network-Based ID

Network-based ID systems commonly reside on a discrete network segment and monitor the traffic on that network segment. They usually consist of a network appliance with a network interface card (NIC) that is operating in promiscuous mode and is intercepting and analyzing the network packets in real time.

Network-based ID involves looking at the packets on the network as they pass by some sensor. The sensor can see only the packets that happen to be carried on its particular network segment. Network traffic on other segments cannot be monitored properly by a network-based IDS.

Packets are identified to be of interest if they match a signature. Three primary types of signatures are:

- **String signatures**—String signatures look for a text string that indicates a possible attack.
- **Port signatures**—Port signatures watch for connection attempts to well-known, frequently attacked ports.
- **Header condition signatures**—Header signatures watch for dangerous or illogical combinations in packet headers.

A network-based IDS usually provides reliable, real-time information without consuming network or host resources because it is passive when acquiring data. Because a network-based IDS reviews packets and headers, it can also detect denial-of-service (DoS) attacks. Furthermore, because this IDS is monitoring an attack in real time, it can also respond to an attack in progress to limit damage.

A problem with a network-based IDS system is that it will not detect attacks against a host made by an intruder who is logged in at the host's terminal. If a network IDS along with some additional support mechanism determines that an attack is being mounted against a host, it is usually not capable of determining the type or effectiveness of the attack being launched.

Host-Based ID

Host-based ID systems use small programs (intelligent agents), which reside on a host computer. They monitor the operating system detecting inappropriate activity, writing to log files, and triggering alarms. Host-based systems look for activity only on the host computer; they do not monitor the entire network segment.

A host-based IDS can review the system and event logs to detect an attack on the host and to determine whether the attack was successful. (It is also easier to respond to an attack from the host.) Detection capabilities of host-based ID systems are limited by the incompleteness of most host audit log capabilities.

In summary, host-based ID systems have the following characteristics:

- Monitor accesses and changes to critical system files and changes in user privileges
- Detect trusted-insider attacks better than network-based IDS
- Are relatively effective for detecting attacks from the outside
- Can be configured to look at all network packets, connection attempts, or login attempts to the monitored machine, including dial-in attempts or other non-network-related communication ports

An IDS detects an attack through one of two conceptual approaches: a signature-based ID or a statistical anomaly-based ID. These two mechanisms are also referred to as knowledge-based and behavior-based IDS.

Signature-Based ID

In a signature-based ID or knowledge-based ID system, signatures or attributes that characterize an attack are stored for reference. When data about events are acquired from host audit logs or from network packet monitoring, this data is compared with the attack signature database. If there is a match, a response is initiated.

These systems use a database of previous attacks and known system vulnerabilities to look for current attempts to exploit their vulnerabilities, and trigger an alarm if an attempt is found. These systems are more common than behavior-based ID systems. The advantages of signature-based ID systems are:

- The system is characterized by low false alarm rates (or positives).
- The alarms are standardized and are clearly understandable by security personnel.

A weakness of a signature-based ID or knowledge-based approach is the failure to characterize slow attacks that extend over a long time period. To identify these types of attacks, large amounts of information must be held for extended time periods. Another issue with signature-based IDs is that only attack signatures that are stored in their database are detected. The disadvantages of signature-based ID systems are:

- The system is resource-intensive. The knowledge database continually needs maintenance and updating with new vulnerabilities and environments to remain accurate.
- Since knowledge about attacks is very focused (dependent on the operating system, version, platform, and application), new, unique, or original attacks often go unnoticed.

Statistical Anomaly-Based ID

Statistical anomaly- or behavior-based ID systems dynamically detect deviations from the learned patterns of user behavior and trigger an alarm when an intrusive (outside of normal system use) activity occurs. Behavior-based ID systems are less common than knowledge-based ID systems. Behavior-based ID systems learn normal or expected behavior of the system or the users and assume that an intrusion can be detected by observing deviations from this norm.

With this method, an IDS acquires data and defines a normal usage profile for the network or host that is being monitored. This characterization is accomplished by taking statistical samples of the system over a period of normal use. Typical characterization information used to establish a normal profile includes memory usage, CPU utilization, and network packet types. With this approach, new attacks can be detected because they produce abnormal system statistics. The advantages of behavior-based ID systems are:

- The system can dynamically adapt to new, unique, or original vulnerabilities.
- A behavior-based ID system is not as dependent upon specific operating systems as a knowledge-based ID system.
- They help detect abuse of privileges types of attacks that do not actually involve exploiting any security vulnerability.

Some disadvantages of a statistical anomaly-based ID are that it will not detect an attack that does not significantly change the system operating characteristics, or it might falsely detect a non-attack event that had caused a momentary anomaly in the system. The disadvantages of behavior-based ID systems are:

- They are characterized by high false alarm rates. High positives are the most common failure of behavior-based ID systems and can create data noise that can make the system unusable or difficult to use.
- Activity and behavior of the users while in the networked system might not be static enough to effectively implement a behavior-based ID system.
- The network may experience an attack at the same time the intrusion detection system is learning the behavior.

IDS Issues

Many issues confront the effective use of IDS. Some of these include:

- Increases in the types of intruder goals, intruder abilities, tool sophistication, and diversity, as well as the use of more complex, subtle, and new attack scenarios
- The use of encrypted messages to transport malicious information
- The need to interoperate and correlate data across infrastructure environments with diverse technologies and policies
- Ever-increasing network traffic
- The lack of widely accepted ID terminology and conceptual structures
- Volatility in the ID marketplace that makes the purchase and maintenance of ID systems difficult
- Risks inherent in taking inappropriate automated response actions
- Attacks on the ID systems themselves
- Unacceptably high levels of false positives and false negatives, making it difficult to determine true positives
- The lack of objective ID system evaluation and test information
- The fact that most computing infrastructures are not designed to operate securely
- Limited network traffic visibility resulting from switched local area networks; faster networks preclude effective real-time analysis of all traffic on large pipes

An issue with the implementation of intrusion detection systems is the performance of the IDS when the network bandwidth begins to reach saturation levels. Obviously, there is a limit to the number of packets a network intrusion detection sensor can accurately analyze in any given time period. The higher the network traffic level and the more complex the analysis, the more the IDS may experience high error rates, such as the premature discard of copied network packets.

Another issue with IDS is the proper implementation of IDS sensors in a switched environment. This issue arises from the basic differences between standard hubs and switches. Hubs exclude only the port the packet came in on and echo every packet to every port on the hub. Therefore, in networks employing only hubs, IDS sensors can be placed almost anywhere in the infrastructure.

However, when a packet comes into a switch, a temporary connection in the switch is first made to the destination port and then the packets are forwarded. This means more care must be exerted when placing IDS sensors in a switched environment to assure the sensor is able to see all of the network traffic.

Some switches permit spanning port configuration, which configures the switch to behave like a hub only for a specific port. The switch can be configured to span the data from a specific port to the IDS port. Unfortunately, some switches cannot be guaranteed to pass all the traffic to the spanned port, and most switches allow only one port to be spanned at a time.

Another partial solution is to place a hub between the monitored connections, say between two switches, a router and switch, or a server and switch. This allows traffic to flow between the switch and the target but with traffic copied off to the IDS. This solution, however, spells the beginning of the end for the switched network, and removes the benefits of a switched solution.

Penetration Testing

Penetration testing is the process of testing a network's defenses by attempting to access the system from the outside, using the same techniques that an external intruder (for example, a cracker) would use. This testing gives a security professional a better snapshot of the organization's security posture. Penetration testing is addressed in depth in Chapter 5.

Violation Analysis

One of the most-used techniques to track anomalies in user activity is violation analysis. To make violation analysis effective, clipping levels must be established. A *clipping level* is a baseline of user activity that is considered a routine level of user errors. A clipping level enables a system to ignore normal user errors. When the clipping level is exceeded, a violation record is then produced. Clipping levels are also used for variance detection.

Using clipping levels and profile-based anomaly detection, the following types of violations should be tracked, processed, and analyzed:

- Repetitive mistakes that exceed the clipping level number
- Individuals who exceed their authority
- Too many people with unrestricted access
- Patterns indicating serious intrusion attempts

Profile-based anomaly detection uses profiles to look for abnormalities in user behavior. A profile is a pattern that characterizes the behavior of users. Patterns of usage are established according to the various types of activities the users engage in, such as processing exceptions, resource utilization, and patterns in actions performed, for example. The ways in which the various types of activity are recorded in the profile are referred to as *profile metrics*.

Because most IDS devices do not analyze Layer 7 (Application layer) traffic, they have difficulty in detecting attacks on Web applications. To handle this deficiency, application firewalls and Layer 7–aware proxies can be used to monitor and protect applications. Another approach is to employ real-time analysis.

One excellent tool called Real-Time Analyzer (RTA) has been developed by Fortify. According to Fortify, "RTA monitors deployed applications in real-time to detect attacks at the instant they occur. In addition to identifying the nature, origin and timing of attacks, RTA can actively defend vulnerable applications until appropriate remediation steps are developed."

RTA is able to monitor security-critical functions and the application programming interfaces (APIs) inside the Web application. It makes use of the business logic semantics of the application, thereby eliminating the need for a learning process required by external Web application firewall products. Also, unlike external Web application firewalls, RTA adds very little overhead because monitoring and protection are only invoked for security-critical functions, not the entire feature set of the application.

Auditing

The implementation of regular system audits is the foundation of operational software security controls monitoring. In addition to enabling internal and external compliance checking, regular auditing of audit (transaction) trails and logs can assist the monitoring function by helping to recognize patterns of abnormal user behavior.

It is necessary to regularly review user accounts on a system. Such reviews may examine the levels of access each individual has, conformity with the concept of least privilege, whether all accounts are still active, whether management authorizations are up to date, or whether required training has been completed, for example. These reviews can be conducted on at least two levels: on an application-by-application basis or on a system-wide basis. Both kinds of reviews can be conducted by, among others, in-house systems personnel (a self-audit), the organization's internal audit staff, or external auditors

According to NCSC-TG-001, "A Guide to Understanding Audit in Trusted Systems,"[9] the audit mechanism of a computer system has the following five important security goals:

- Allow the review of patterns of access to individual objects, access histories of specific processes and individuals, and the use of the various protection mechanisms supported by the system and their effectiveness.
- Allow discovery of both users' and outsiders' repeated attempts to bypass the protection mechanisms.
- Allow discovery of any use of privileges that may occur when a user assumes a functionality with privileges greater than his or her own, i.e., programmer

[9]Gligor, V., NCSC-TG-001, "A Guide to Understanding Audit in Trusted Systems [Tan Book]; Guidelines for Trusted Facility Management and Audit," University of Maryland, 1985.

to administrator. In this case, there may be no bypass of security controls, but nevertheless, a violation is made possible.

- Act as a deterrent against perpetrators' habitual attempts to bypass the system protection mechanisms. However, [for the mechanism] to act as a deterrent, the perpetrator must be aware of the audit mechanism's existence and its active use to detect any attempts to bypass system protection mechanisms.
- Supply an additional form of user assurance that attempts to bypass the protection mechanisms that are recorded and discovered. Even if the attempt to bypass the protection mechanism is successful, the audit trail will still provide assurance by its ability to aid in assessing the damage done by the violation, thus improving the system's ability to control the damage.

Other important security issues regarding the use of audit logs include:

- Retention and protection of the audit media and reports when their storage is offsite
- Protection against the alteration of audit or transaction logs
- Protection against the unavailability of an audit media during an event

Auditing of the controls relating to physical access is also an important part of operations security. The following lists provide examples of some of the elements of the operations resources that need physical access control:

- Hardware
  - Control of communications and the computing equipment
  - Control of the storage media
  - Control of the printed logs and reports
- Software
  - Control of the backup files
  - Control of the system logs
  - Control of the production applications
  - Control of the sensitive/critical data

Additional aspects of security auditing are also presented in Chapter 1.

INCIDENT MANAGEMENT

An incident management and response capability has two primary components:

- Creation and maintenance of intrusion detection systems (IDS) and processes for host and network monitoring and event notification
- Creation of a computer security incident response team (CSIRT) for:
  - Analysis of an event notification
  - Response to an incident if the analysis warrants it

- Escalation path procedures
- Resolution, post-incident follow-up, and reporting to the appropriate parties

NIST Special Publication 800-61, "Computer Security Incident Handling Guide, Recommendations of the National Institute of Standards and Technology," January 2004, defines the incident response life cycle as:

1. Preparation
2. Detection and analysis
3. Containment, eradication, and recovery
4. Post-incident activity

Preparation

The preparation phase involves establishing an incident response capability as well as securing computing resources to prevent intrusions. A useful tool for reducing the number of incidents is to conduct risk assessments to determine the risks posed by threats and vulnerabilities. NIST SP 800-61 recommends implementing patch management, host security, network security, malicious code prevention, and user awareness training to secure networks and minimize risks.

Detection and Analysis

NIST SP 800-61 also defines the following incident categories:

- **Denial of service**—An attack that prevents or impairs the authorized use of networks, systems, or applications by exhausting resources
- **Malicious code**—A virus, worm, Trojan horse, or other code-based malicious entity that infects a host
- **Unauthorized access**—A person gains logical or physical access without permission to a network, system, application, data, or other resource
- **Inappropriate usage**—A person violates acceptable computing use policies
- **Multiple component**—A single incident that encompasses two or more incidents

In many instances, identifying a true incident is difficult. Some of the methods used to provide incident validation include the profiling of expected system activity in order to detect anomalous conditions, understanding normal system behavior, creating logs of activities, recording and analyzing system traffic, and correlating times of event occurrences.

If an incident has occurred or is suspected of being in progress, all the relevant information should be documented and preserved. If multiple incidents have occurred, the responses should be prioritized to address the most critical system resources. Table 7-1 provides examples of typical response times as a function of the predicted negative impact of a threat realized.

Table 7-1: Incident Response Times

CURRENT IMPACT OR LIKELY FUTURE IMPACT OF THE INCIDENT	CRITICALITY OF RESOURCES CURRENTLY IMPACTED OR LIKELY TO BE IMPACTED BY THE INCIDENT		
	HIGH (e.g., INTERNET CONNECTIVITY, PUBLIC WEB SERVERS, FIREWALLS, CUSTOMER DATA)	MEDIUM (e.g., SYSTEM ADMINISTRATOR WORKSTATIONS, FILE AND PRINT SERVERS, XYZ APPLICATION DATA)	LOW (e.g., USER WORK-STATIONS)
Root-level access	15 minutes	30 minutes	1 hour
Unauthorized data modification	15 minutes	30 minutes	2 hours
Unauthorized access to sensitive data	15 minutes	1 hour	1 hour
Unauthorized user-level access	30 minutes	2 hours	4 hours
Services unavailable	30 minutes	2 hours	4 hours
Annoyance	30 minutes	Local IT staff	Local IT staff

NIST SP 800-61 "Computer Security Incident Handling Guide, Recommendations of the National Institute of Standards and Technology," January 2004.

After an incident is detected and prioritized, it should be reported to the appropriate authorities in the organization. Typically, the incident should be reported to the chief security officer, the chief information officer, the system owner, the legal department, and, possibly, the public affairs department.

Containment, Eradication, and Recovery

It is important to contain an attack to prevent damage to the system and to keep an incident from spreading to other parts of the organization's computing resources. However, in some instances, containment can be postponed to allow the attacker to proceed into the system in order to track his or her activities for later use as evidence. Information about the attacker should be obtained only if it does not detract from containing and eradicating the incident. Information such as the attacker's true IP address, email address, or Internet relay chat (IRC) name will provide leads to determine the attacker's identity and the source of the incident.

Following containment, the next step is to eradicate the components of the incident, such as removing viruses, and determining which user accounts have been compromised and disabling access to those accounts. In addition, files that are suspected of being breached or modified should be replaced from backup storage, new passwords should be issued, and appropriate patches should be installed.

Post-Incident Activity

An important component of incident response and management is to analyze the actions taken in the preparation, detection and analysis, and containment, eradication, and recovery phases and learn from those activities. Some typical questions to be asked, taken from NIST SP 800-61 include:

- Exactly what happened, and at what times?
- How well did staff and management perform in dealing with the incident? Were the documented procedures followed? Were they adequate?
- What information was needed sooner?
- Were any steps or actions taken that might have inhibited the recovery?
- What would the staff and management do differently the next time a similar incident occurs?
- What corrective actions can prevent similar incidents in the future?
- What additional tools or resources are needed to detect, analyze, and mitigate future incidents?

NIST Incident-Handling Summary

Table 7-2, from NIST 800-61, summarizes the important steps in incident handling.

Internet Engineering Task Force Incident-Handling Guidelines

Additional guidance on incident handling is provided by the Internet Engineering Task Force (IETF) RFC 2196, Site Security Handbook. The following approach, taken from the handbook, is recommended for the handling of incidents:

1. **Preparing and planning**—What are the goals and objectives in handling an incident?
2. **Notification**—Who should be contacted in the case of an incident?
   - Local managers and personnel
   - Law enforcement and investigative agencies
   - Computer security incident handling teams
   - Affected and involved sites

Table 7-2: Incident Handling Summary

DETECTION AND ANALYSIS
Prioritize handling the incident based on the business impact
Identify which resources have been affected and forecast which resources will be affected
Estimate the current and potential technical effect of the incident
Find the appropriate cell(s) in the prioritization matrix, based on the technical effect and affected resources
Report the incident to the appropriate internal personnel and external organizations
CONTAINMENT, ERADICATION, AND RECOVERY
Acquire, preserve, secure, and document evidence
Contain the incident
Eradicate the incident
Identify and mitigate all vulnerabilities that were exploited
Remove malicious code, inappropriate materials, and other components
Recover from the incident
Return affected systems to an operationally ready state
Confirm that the affected systems are functioning normally
If necessary, implement additional monitoring to look for future related activity
POST-INCIDENT ACTIVITY
Create a follow-up report
Hold a lessons-learned meeting

NIST SP 800-61 "Computer Security Incident Handling Guide, Recommendations of the National Institute of Standards and Technology," January 2004.

- Internal communications
- Public relations and press releases

3. **Identifying an incident**—Is it an incident and how serious is it?
4. **Handling**—What should be done when an incident occurs?
   - **Notification**—Who should be notified about the incident?
   - **Protecting evidence and activity logs**—What records should be kept from before, during, and after the incident?

- **Containment**—How can the damage be limited?
- **Eradication**—How [do we] eliminate the reasons for the incident?
- **Recovery**—How [do we] reestablish service and systems?
- **Follow Up**—What actions should be taken after the incident?

5. **Aftermath**—What are the implications of past incidents?

Layered Security and IDS

Computer security is most effective when multiple layers of security controls are used within an organization, and IDS are best utilized when implemented using a *layered security* approach. This means that multiple steps are taken to secure the data, thereby increasing the workload and time required for an intruder to penetrate the network. Although a firewall is an excellent perimeter security device, it is just one element of an effective security strategy. The more elements, or layers, of security that can be added to protect the data, the more secure the infrastructure will remain.

Elements of an effective layered security approach include:

- Security policies, procedures, standards and guidelines, including high-level security policy
- Perimeter security, such as routers, firewalls, and other edge devices
- Hardware and/or software host security products
- Auditing, monitoring, intrusion detection and response

Each of these layers may be implemented independently of the others, yet are interdependent when functioning. An IDS that alerts to unauthorized access attempts or port scanning is useless without a response plan to react to the problem. Since each layer provides elements of protection, the defeat of any one layer should not lead to a failure of protection.

Computer Security and Incident Response Teams

As part of a structured program of intrusion detection and response, a computer security incident response team (CSIRT) may be created. The prime directive of every CSIRT is incident response management, which manages an organization's response to events that pose a risk to its computing environment. This management often consists of the following:

- Coordinating the notification and distribution of information pertaining to the incident to the appropriate parties (those with a need to know) through a predefined escalation path
- Mitigating risk to the enterprise by minimizing the disruptions to normal business activities and the costs associated with remediating the incident (including public relations)

- Assembling teams of technical personnel to investigate the potential vulnerabilities and to resolve specific intrusions

Additional examples of CSIRT activities are:

- Management of the network logs, including collection, retention, review, and analysis of data
- Management of the resolution of an incident, management of the remediation of a vulnerability, and post-event reporting to the appropriate parties

Numerous CSIRTs have formed to address the issue of coordination and communication in response to security incidents. These response teams provide a coordinated and organized method of data sharing in their sphere of influence. This coordination may include the detection, prevention, and handling of security incidents; understanding the current state of security; and identifying trends in activity within their constituency. Because the Internet is a cooperative network, there is no single entity with the authority or responsibility for its security. Instead, authority is scattered across logical domains.

CERT/CC

The CERT Coordination Center (CERT/CC) is a unit of the Carnegie Mellon University Software Engineering Institute (SEI). SEI is a federally funded research and development center. CERT's mission is to alert the Internet community to vulnerabilities and attacks and to conduct research and training in the areas of computer security, including incident response.

FedCIRC

The Federal Computer Incident Response Center is an organization that "establishes a collaborative partnership of computer incident response, security and law enforcement professionals who work together to handle computer security incidents and to provide both proactive and reactive security services for the U.S. Federal government." The FedCIRC charter states: "FedCIRC provides assistance and guidance in incident response and provides a centralized approach to incident handling across agency boundaries." The mission of FedCIRC is to:

- Provide civil agencies with technical information, tools, methods, assistance, and guidance
- Be proactive and provide liaison activities and analytical support
- Encourage the development of quality products and services through collaborative relationships with federal civil agencies, Department of Defense, academia, and private industry
- Promote the highest security profile for government information technology (IT) resources
- Promote incident response and handling procedural awareness with the federal government

Forum of Incident Response and Security Teams

The Forum of Incident Response and Security Teams (FIRST) brings together a variety of computer security incident response teams from government, commercial, and academic organizations. FIRST aims to foster cooperation and coordination in incident prevention, to prompt rapid reaction to incidents, and to promote information sharing among members and the community at large.

The goals of FIRST are:

- To foster cooperation among information technology constituents in the effective prevention and detection of and recovery from computer security incidents
- To provide a means for the communication of alert and advisory information on potential threats and emerging incident situations
- To facilitate the actions and activities of the FIRST members, including research and operational activities
- To facilitate the sharing of security-related information, tools, and techniques

Security Incident Notification Process

All potential, suspected, or known information security incidents should be reported to a computer security and incident response team. The CSIRT then assigns personnel who will assemble all needed resources to handle the reported incident. The incident coordinator makes decisions as to the interpretation of policy, standards, and procedures when applied to the incident.

Law enforcement and investigative agencies are notified, as needed and required, by the CSIRT. In the event of an incident that has legal consequences, it is important to establish contact with investigative agencies such as the FBI as soon as possible. Local law enforcement should also be informed as appropriate. Legal counsel should be notified of an incident as soon as it is reported. At a minimum, legal counsel should be involved in protecting the legal and financial interests of an organization.

The security incident notification process should provide some escalation mechanisms. To define such a mechanism, the CSIRT should create an internal classification scheme for incidents. The appropriate procedures are associated with each level of incident. The following list is an example of various levels of incidents.

Priority One—Protect human life and people's safety; human life always has precedence over all other considerations.

Priority Two—Protect restricted and/or internal data. Prevent exploitation of restricted systems, networks, or sites. Inform affected restricted sensitive systems, networks, or sites about already occurred penetrations while abiding by any applicable government regulations.

Priority Three—Protect other data, including managerial, because loss of data is costly in terms of resources. Prevent exploitations of other systems, networks, or sites, and inform already affected systems, networks, or sites about successful penetrations.

Priority Four—Prevent damage to systems (e.g., loss or alteration of system files, damage to disk drives, etc.). Damage to systems can result in costly downtime and recovery.

Priority Five—Minimize disruption of computing resources (including processes). It is better in many cases to shut a system down or disconnect from a network than to risk damage to data or systems. Each data and system owner must evaluate the trade-off between shutting down and disconnecting, and staying up. This decision must be made prior to an incident occurring. There may be service agreements in place that may require keeping the systems up even in light of further damage occurring. However, the damage and scope of an incident may be so extensive that service agreements may have to be overridden.

Automated Notice and Recovery Mechanisms

Automated notice and recovery mechanisms can provide capabilities in one or more of the following areas: intruder prevention, intruder detection, and damage assessment. A number of automated intruder responses have been implemented as part of intrusion detection systems. Some responses may be active, such as terminating processes, closing connections, and disabling accounts. Other responses are passive, such as sending an email to the system administrator.

Damage assessment is normally performed after an attack. A number of vulnerability scanning tools, such as Tiger, may be used to perform damage assessment. Other tools, such as Tripwire, were specifically developed to aid in damage assessment. At Texas A&M, a prototype tool called the Automated Incident Response System (AIRS) was developed to perform damage control and damage assessment on individual hosts in a network.

The electronic quarantine concept requires the use of host-based intrusion detection systems, which perform real-time activity monitoring and maintain a suspicion level for each user as well as an overall suspicion level of the monitored host. Although not absolutely required, host-based intrusion detection systems have the important ability to cooperate and share information in order to track users as they connect to other monitored hosts.

Automated notice and recovery are appealing. Because they do not require continuous human oversight, they can act more rapidly than humans and can be tailored to, and will consistently follow, specified policies. Common automated response capabilities include session logging, session termination, posting events on the event console, and alerting personnel through email, paging, and other means. The architecture to collect incident information consists of four crucial components: sensor, collector, backing store, and analysis engine.

However, most often an IDS requires a human operator to be in the loop. Given the current maturity of IDS technology, the dangers of automated response are significant and outweigh the above advantages. With the frequency of false positives that exists in the current generation of ID systems, the potential for inappropriate response to misdiagnosis is too high. In addition, automated response could be exploited by a perpetrator whose aim is to induce denial of service by spoofing an attack from a legitimate user. Also, many intrusion detection tools provide some form of automated intruder response, but few security tools perform any automated recovery.

CIDDS, the Common Intrusion Detection Director System (also known as CID Director), is a dedicated hardware/software/operating system platform supporting the Air Force Information Warfare Center's (AFIWC) Intrusion Detection Tools (IDT) program. AFIWC is the U.S. Air Force Office of Primary Responsibility for the IDT program. Within AFIWC, the Air Force Computer Emergency Response Team (AFCERT) is charged with the responsibility for day-to-day administration and network security operations involving the IDT program.

CIDDS receives near-real-time connections data and associated transcripts from Automated Security Incident Measurement (ASIM) Sensor host machines and selected other intrusion detection tools. It stores this data on a local database and allows for detailed (local, regional, or theater-wide) correlation and analysis by human analysts and automated tools.

PROBLEM MANAGEMENT

A critically important aspect of the software development environment is the handling and resolving of problems and conflicts in an IT and information security environment. Problem management can be defined as a set of policies, procedures, and tools to manage and resolve problems. Problems in the information security arena can be categorized as unusual or unexpected events; compromise of confidentiality, integrity, and availability; divergence from best practices or standards; and any abnormal situations.

Good problem management identifies, tracks, and resolves problems using a variety of methods and tools. The objectives of problem management are to prevent problems from occurring in the first place, reducing the occurrence of problems that cannot be prevented, and minimizing the effect of problems on information systems. Effective problem management requires the participation of all levels of management as well as team leaders and team members.

Tools

A project management effort can be aided significantly by the use of automated tools that support the identification and remediation of problems. Some of the functions provided by such tools are the following:

- Incorporating standards, policies, and procedures
- Tracking problems
- Providing mechanisms for reporting problems, including information on the initiator of the problem report and the initiator's comments
- Identifying the individual responsible for handling the problem report
- Identifying the other individuals involved
- Displaying the status of the problem
- Recording the time required to resolve the problem

- Prioritizing problem resolution assignments
- Supporting the determination of the impact of the problem on the organization or project

In managing problems involving individuals, the problems are usually the result of an argument, competition, or conflict. An argument can be viewed as either a positive or negative situation, whereas competition can be seen as a positive activity. Conflict, on the other hand, usually is a negative occurrence. Competition can be used to motivate personnel positively, distinguish among different levels of performance, and promote higher standards in the conduct of the project. To use argument in a positive fashion, the problem manager has to get to the root of the problem and identify the fundamental differences or lack of information that caused the argument. Conflict has to be turned into competition or argument to have a chance of resolution.

Problem Management in Auditing

Problem management can also be incorporated as a component of auditing that is useful in identifying problems and effecting their solutions. In the context of this chapter, it can be applied to resolving problems associated with secure software development. Problem management can be applied to reduce software failure occurrences, eliminate or mitigate the impact of the failures, and ensure that the failures do not recur. In IT systems, some typical problem areas include:

- Unavailability of software or hardware resources
- Failures in software functionality
- Failures in software security
- Malfunctions in the processing chain
- Potential harm to personnel
- Vulnerabilities in the networking infrastructure

Another useful tool in identifying problems in the software and hardware development life cycles is root cause analysis.

Root Cause Analysis

In software development, hardware implementation, and any other areas where it is critical to identify the causes of undesired outcomes or events, root cause analysis (RCA) is a technique that can be of value. RCA is a process that can be applied to determine the root causes of events that can have negative consequences on health, quality, safety, reliability, and production. In general terms, root cause analysis can assist in determining what event happened, as well as how and why it happened, with the goal of preventing a recurrence.

The U.S. National Aeronautics and Space Administration (NASA)[10] has developed the following formal definitions associated with root cause analysis:

- **Proximate cause(s)**—The event(s) that occurred, including any condition(s) that existed immediately before the undesired outcome, directly resulted in its occurrence and, if eliminated or modified, would have prevented the undesired outcome. Examples of undesired outcomes are failure, anomaly, schedule delay, broken equipment, product defect, problem, close call, mishap, etc.
- **Root cause(s)**—One of multiple factors (events, conditions or organizational factors) that contributed to or created the proximate cause and subsequent undesired outcome and, if eliminated, or modified would have prevented the undesired outcome. Typically multiple root causes contribute to an undesired outcome.
- **Organizational factors**—Any operational or management structural entity that exerts control over the system at any stage in its life cycle, including but not limited to the system's concept development, design, fabrication, test, maintenance, operation, and disposal.
- **Root cause analysis (RCA)**—A structured evaluation method that identifies the root causes for an undesired outcome and the actions adequate to prevent recurrence. Root cause analysis should continue until organizational factors have been identified, or until data are exhausted.

In principle, RCA is an iterative, continuous improvement process that attempts to address problems by finding and correcting the root causes instead of treating symptoms of the problems. The basic steps in RCA are shown in Figure 7-1.

Root cause analysis is sometimes broken into the following categories:

- **Systems-based**—Incorporates methods from risk and systems analysis
- **Safety-based**—Includes ideas from the health and safety arenas
- **Process-based**—Incorporates business process procedures
- **Failure-based**—Addresses failure analysis processes
- **Production-based**—Integrates quality control paradigms

Maintenance

The IEEE Standard 1219[11] defines software maintenance as "the modification of a software product after delivery to correct faults, to improve performance or other attributes, or to adapt the product to a modified environment."

[10] "Root Cause Analysis Overview," NASA Office of Safety and Mission Assurance, Chief Engineer's Office, July 2003.

[11] IEEE Std 1219-1998, IEEE Standard for Software Maintenance, 1998.

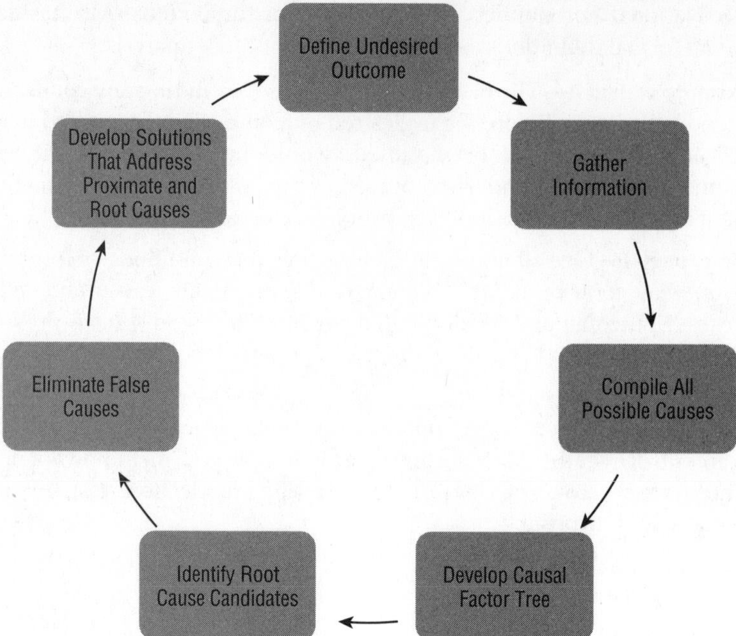

Figure 7-1: RCA basic steps

Software maintenance takes place through the operational life cycle and comprises logging of changes, determining the impact of pending changes, testing new code, and releasing new versions. IEEE/EIA Standard 12207[12] states that software maintenance comprises the following activities:

1. Process implementation
2. Problem and modification analysis
3. Modification implementation
4. Maintenance review/acceptance
5. Migration
6. Retirement

Software maintenance can be broken into the following four categories:

- **Corrective**—Changing the software to fix problems uncovered after delivery
- **Adaptive**—Upgrading software so that it can perform as required in a different operating environment
- **Perfective**—Incorporating changes into software to improve its performance, security, or maintainability

[12]IEEE/EIA 12207.0-1996//ISO/IEC12207:1995, Industry Implementation of Int. Std. ISO/IEC 12207:95, ''Standard for Information Technology- Software Life Cycle Processes,'' IEEE, 1996.

- **Preventive**—Adaptation of software to discover hidden or latent faults and then effect required changes

In order to track changes throughout the maintenance process, configuration management has to be employed, as discussed earlier in this chapter and in Chapter 6.

During the operational life cycle, software maintenance is conducted in a cyclical fashion. Modifications to the software can be requested, and these requests have to be recorded and followed. Then the effects of the proposed modifications have to be evaluated. Following these stages, the software changes are made and testing is conducted. Finally, the new version of the software is released and training is provided.

Figure 7-2 summarizes the actions involved as software transitions from program development to maintenance.

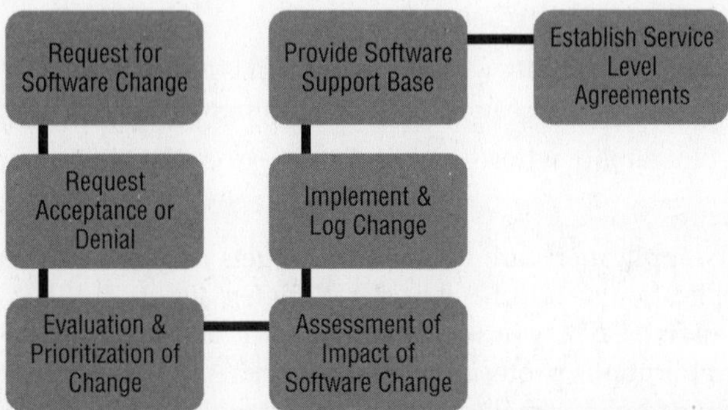

Figure 7-2: Actions in software transfer from development to maintenance

Software maintenance can be performed for a number of reasons, ranging from incorporating improvements to repairing faults. Some typical additional reasons to modify software include:

- Porting the software to different platforms
- Modifying the design to react to changing requirements
- Providing interfaces to additional software and hardware systems
- Preparing the software for retirement and disposal

Patching

If a vulnerability exists in software, an attacker can apply scripts to exploit that particular vulnerability. With the advent of patches and upgrades for a particular application, the attacker's mode of operation changes somewhat. The attacker can search for systems that have not been patched or upgraded. Determining if a system has been patched or upgraded is generally simpler than attempting a full exploit. Therefore, the ready availability of patches and upgrades for applications in an organization may in the end make the information systems in that organization more vulnerable if the appropriate patches and upgrades have not been applied.

Patch management, then, is the process of controlling the deployment and maintenance of interim software releases into operational environments.

When software is rushed to meet deadlines without adequate and rigorous security testing, it is often left for users to find problems and report them. This situation leads to an environment in which patches and upgrades are more frequent and more important to the network administrator.

Microsoft security bulletins include a rating system to indicate the severity of the problem addressed by the security updates. The Microsoft ratings are as follows:

- **Critical**—A vulnerability whose exploitation can allow the propagation of an Internet worm without user action
- **Important**—A vulnerability whose exploitation can result in compromise of the confidentiality, integrity, or availability of users' data or of the integrity or availability of processing resources
- **Moderate**—A vulnerability whose exploitation is mitigated to a significant degree by factors such as default configuration, auditing, or difficulty of exploitation
- **Low**—A vulnerability whose exploitation is extremely difficult or whose impact is minimal

High-visibility applications are well-known targets of hackers in search of vulnerabilities. An application should be considered high-visibility if it has a large market share or large user base. There is a constant back and forth battle to keep these high-visibility applications protected against attack. As hackers discover vulnerabilities, the developers quickly make patches to secure the application. This leads to a series of patches and upgrades for most high-visibility software.

It is certainly easy to develop a policy that states, ''All applications will be kept current with patches and upgrades.'' In practice, however, this activity is very resource intensive. Accurate inventories need to be maintained, and application and system baselines have to be identified and verified. Backups should be done before every patch and upgrade. Patches and upgrades should be loaded on a test platform to verify the stability of the resulting application and system. These unanticipated testing and backup requirements can tax an already overworked IT department.

Patch Management Phases

The primary phases of patch management are:

1. **Appraisal and inventory**—In this phase, the software elements of the operational environment are identified and documented. In addition, the associated vulnerabilities and threats are classified.
2. **Patch categorization**—This phase determines if new patches have been issued, if they are applicable to an organization's information systems, and if the patches are rated critical or normal.
3. **Assessment and planning**—In this step, the decision is made on which patches to deploy and plans are made to implement the deployment into the operational environment.

4. **Testing**—The testing phase involves running and monitoring the patch software in a environment similar to the operating environment in order to ensure that it is safe to deploy.
5. **Deployment**—The deployment phase implements the software changes in the operational environment.

The curriculum guide to the Common Body of Knowledge[13] states that "configuration management of patches (patch management) must extend to security patches, to ensure that they are applied in a timely manner (both to the commercial and open source software in the software system itself and to its execution environment), and that interim risk analyses are performed to determine the impact the patch will have and to identify any conflicts that may be caused by applying the patch, particularly those impacts/conflicts with security implications, to mitigate those effects to the extent possible (which, in some cases, may mean not installing the patch because its impact/conflicts may put the software at greater risk than the vulnerability the patch is meant to address)."

The curriculum guide also stresses that software should be developed and tested in a manner that patches and upgrades will be minimized or no longer required. To quote the guide, "Collaborative efforts seek to shift the paradigm away from patch management to achieving a broader ability to routinely develop and deploy software products known to be trustworthy. These efforts focus on contributing to the production of higher quality, more secure software that contributes to operations that are more resilient."

END-O-LIFE POLICIES

Policies and procedures addressing the end of life and disposal of hardware and software have to be developed, implemented, rehearsed, and reviewed. NIST SP 800-30, "Risk Management Guide for Information Technology Systems," July 2002, states that "risk management activities are performed for system components that will be disposed of or replaced to ensure that the hardware and software are properly disposed of, that residual data is appropriately handled, and that system migration is conducted in a secure and systematic manner."

A critical aspect of end-of-life procedures is the control and secure disposal of storage media.

Media Security Controls

Media security controls should be designed to prevent the loss of sensitive information when the media are stored outside the system. Some relevant definitions are:

- **Logging**—Logging the use of data media provides accountability. Logging also assists in physical inventory control by preventing media from "walking away" and by facilitating their recovery process.

[13]Redwine, S. T., Jr. (Editor), *Software Assurance: A Guide to the Common Body of Knowledge to Produce, Acquire, and Sustain Secure Software*, Version 1.1., U.S. Department of Homeland Security, September 2006.

- **Access control**—Physical access control to the media is used to prevent unauthorized personnel from accessing the media. This procedure is also a part of physical inventory control.
- **Proper disposal**—Proper disposal of the media after use is required to prevent data remanence. The process of removing information from used data media is called *sanitization*. Three techniques are commonly used for sanitization: overwriting, degaussing, and destruction.

Overwriting

Simply recopying new data to the media is not recommended because the application may not completely overwrite the old data properly, and strict configuration controls must be in place on both the operating system and the software itself. Also, bad sectors on the media may not permit the software to overwrite old data properly.

To purge the media, the DoD requires overwriting with a pattern, then its complement, and finally with another pattern; for example, overwriting first with 0011 0101, followed by 1100 1010, then 1001 0111. To satisfy the DoD clearing requirement, a character must be written to all data locations in the disk. The number of times an overwrite must be accomplished depends on the storage media, sometimes on its sensitivity, and sometimes on differing DoD component requirements, but seven times is most commonly recommended.

Degaussing

Degaussing is often recommended as the best method for purging most magnetic media. Degaussing is a process whereby the magnetic media are erased, that is, returned to the initial virgin state. Erasure via degaussing may be accomplished in two ways:

- In AC erasure, the media is degaussed by applying an alternating field that is reduced in amplitude over time from an initial high value (i.e., AC-powered)
- In DC erasure, the media is saturated by applying a unidirectional field (i.e., DC-powered or by employing a permanent magnet)

Degaussed magnetic hard drives will generally require restoration of factory-installed timing tracks, so data purging is recommended.

Destruction

Paper reports and diskettes need to be physically destroyed before disposal. Also, physical destruction of optical media (CD-ROM or WORM disks) is necessary.

Destruction techniques can include shredding or burning documentation, physically breaking CD-ROMS and diskettes, and destroying with acid. Paper reports should be shredded by personnel with the proper level of security clearance. Some shredders cut in straight lines or strips; others cross-cut or disintegrate the material into pulp. Care must be taken to limit access to the reports prior to disposal and those stored for long periods. Reports should never be disposed of without shredding—for example, they should never be placed in a dumpster intact. Burning is also sometimes used to destroy paper reports, especially in the DoD.

In some cases, acid is used to destroy disk pack surfaces. Applying a concentration of hydriodic acid (55 to 58 percent solution) to the gamma ferric oxide disk surface is a rarely used method of media destruction, and acid solutions should be used in a well-ventilated area only by qualified personnel.

Record Retention

Record retention refers to how long transactions and other types of records (legal, audit trails, email, and so forth) should be retained according to management, legal, audit, or tax compliance requirements. The retention of data media (tapes, diskettes, and backup media) can be based on one or more criteria, such as the number of days elapsed, number of days since creation, hold time, or other factors. An example of record retention issues could be the mandated retention periods for trial documentation or financial records.

In the United States, organizations must also comply with e-discovery requirements established by the amended Federal Rules of Civil Procedure and various state court rules. *E-discovery* refers to the process in which electronic data is sought, located, secured, and searched with the intent of using it as evidence in the prosecution of a civil or criminal legal case.

Data Remanence

Data remanence refers to the data left on the media after the media has been erased. After erasure, there might be some physical traces left, which could allow data that might contain sensitive material to be reconstructed. Object reuse mechanisms ensure that system resources are allocated and reassigned among authorized users in a way that prevents the leak of sensitive information, and they ensure that the authorized user of the system does not obtain residual information from system resources.

Object reuse is defined as "The reassignment to some subject of a storage medium (e.g., page frame, disk sector, magnetic tape) that contained one or more objects. To be securely reassigned, no residual data can be available to the new subject through standard system mechanisms."[14]

Systems administrators and security administrators should be informed of the risks involving the issues of object reuse, declassification, destruction, and disposition of storage media.

Due Care and Due Diligence

The concepts of due care and due diligence require that an organization engage in good business practices relative to the organization's industry. Training employees in

[14]NCSC-TG-018, "A Guide to Understanding Object Reuse in Trusted Systems [Light Blue Book]", Publisher: [Ft. George G. Meade, MD] : National Computer Security Center, [1992], ISBN: 0160362547.

security awareness could be an example of due care, unlike simply creating a policy with no implementation plan or follow-up. Mandating statements from employees that they have read and understood appropriate computer behavior is another example of due care.

Due diligence might be mandated by various legal requirements in the organization's industry or through compliance with governmental regulatory standards.

Due care and due diligence are becoming serious issues in computer operations today. In fact, the legal system has begun to hold major partners liable for the lack of due care in the event of a major security breach. Violations of security and privacy are hot-button issues confronting the Internet community, and standards covering best practices of due care are necessary for an organization's protection.

Documentation Control

A security system needs documentation control. Documentation can include several things: security plans, contingency plans, risk analyses, and security policies and procedures. Most of this documentation must be protected from unauthorized disclosure; for example, printer output must be in a secure location. Disaster recovery documentation must also be readily available in the event of a disaster.

Summary

This chapter stresses the importance of maintaining information assurance during installation, deployment, operation, maintenance, and disposal of secure software systems. Modifications and upgrades to software and hardware must proceed in an orderly fashion to avoid causing failures and disrupting users' activities. Any changes must be evaluated, approved, tracked, and fielded under controlled processes in order to ensure that the modified software performs as required and does not compromise the organization's computer resources.

Retirement and disposal of hardware and software systems must also be conducted according to secure procedures so that critical and sensitive data are not compromised and made available to unauthorized entities.

Assessment Questions

1. An extended or special access to computing resources given to operators, system administrators, and some distributed computing users who have administrator privileges on their machines is known as which one of the following?

   A. Privileged entity access

   B. Resource access

   C. System entity access

   D. Managed user

2. Which type of operational control is designed to lower the amount and impact of unintentional errors and to prevent unauthorized intruders from internally or externally accessing the system?

   A. Detective

   B. Preventive

   C. Corrective

   D. Application

3. Which one of the following is used to maintain operational assurance by conducting an ongoing activity that examines either the system or the users?

   A. Testing

   B. Evaluating

   C. Auditing

   D. Monitoring

4. Intrusion detection, penetration testing, and violation analysis are tools used to perform which one of the following?

   A. Evaluation

   B. Modification

   C. Auditing

   D. Monitoring

5. Which type of intrusion detection system (IDS) operates on network segments and analyzes that segment's traffic?

   A. Network-based

   B. Segment-based

   C. Web-based

   D. Host-based

6. What type of intrusion detection system consists of a network appliance with a network interface card (NIC) that is operating in promiscuous mode and is intercepting and analyzing packets in real time?

   A. Packet-based

   B. Network-based

   C. Segment-based

   D. Interface-based

7. Which one of the following best describes the types of packet signatures analyzed by a type of intrusion detection system?

   A. String signatures, port signatures, and attack signatures

   B. Sync signatures, port signatures, and header condition signatures

   C. String signatures, IP signatures, and header condition signatures

   D. String signatures, port signatures, and header condition signatures

8. Which type of intrusion detection system monitors a host operating system in order to detect inappropriate activity, writes to log files, and triggers alarms?
   A. Host-based
   B. Log-based
   C. Segment-based
   D. Platform-based
9. An IDS can detect an attack through which of the following conceptual approaches?
   A. Character-based or statistical anomaly-based
   B. Signature-based or knowledge-based
   C. Signature-based or statistical anomaly-based
   D. Behavior-based or statistical anomaly-based
10. Which type of intrusion detection system is characterized by relatively lower false alarm rates (or positives) and provides alarms that are standardized and are clearly understandable by security personnel?
    A. Segment-based
    B. Statistical anomaly-based
    C. Signature-based
    D. Platform-based
11. What is defined as "a baseline of user activity that is considered a routine level of user errors"?
    A. Clipping level
    B. Error level
    C. Threshold level
    D. Trigger level
12. Which operational mechanism supports the discovery of both users' and outsiders' repeated attempts to bypass a system's protection mechanisms and allows for discovery of any use of privileges that may occur when a user assumes a functionality with privileges greater than his or her own?
    A. Profiling
    B. Audit
    C. Scanning
    D. Testing
13. Which one of the following has these two primary components? (1) Creation and maintenance of intrusion detection systems (IDS) and processes for host and network monitoring and event notification, and (2) creation of a computer security incident response team (CSIRT)?
    A. Incident management and response
    B. Intrusion detection system
    C. System audit
    D. System monitoring

14. NIST Special Publication 800-61, "Computer Security Incident Handling Guide, Recommendations of the National Institute of Standards and Technology," January 2004, defines the incident response life cycle as which one of the following?
    A. Evaluation; detection and analysis; containment, eradication, and recovery; and post-incident activity
    B. Preparation; detection and analysis; containment, eradication, and recovery; and post-incident activity
    C. Preparation; testing; containment, eradication, and recovery; and post-incident activity
    D. Preparation; detection and analysis; containment, eradication, and recovery; and disposal
15. Which one of the following are steps in the incident handling guidelines of the Internet Engineering Task Force (IETF) RFC 2196, Site Security Handbook?
    A. Preparing and planning, notification, identification, handling, and aftermath
    B. Evaluation, notification, identification, handling, and aftermath
    C. Preparing and planning, notification, confirmation, handling, and aftermath
    D. Preparing and planning, notification, identification, handling, and recovery
16. As part of a structured program of intrusion detection and response, what is the commonly used, general name for a type of response group that may be created in an organization?
    A. Computer security technical response team (CSTRT)
    B. Computer incident response handling team (CIRHT)
    C. Enterprise security incident response team (ESIRT)
    D. Computer security incident response team (CSIRT)
17. In responding to an incident, what is the *first* and *primary* responsibility of the responding team?
    A. Protect human life and people's safety
    B. Protect restricted and/or internal data
    C. Prevent damage to systems
    D. Minimize disruption of computing resources
18. One of multiple factors (events, conditions, or organizational factors) that contributed to or created the proximate cause and subsequent undesired outcome and if eliminated or modified would have prevented the undesired outcome is the definition of which one of the following?
    A. Principal cause
    B. Root cause
    C. Primary cause
    D. Fault cause

19. Which one of the following defines a process that can be applied to determine the true causes of events that can have negative consequences on health, quality, safety, reliability, and production?

    A. Primary cause analysis

    B. Principal cause analysis

    C. True cause analysis

    D. Root cause analysis

20. Process implementation, problem and modification analysis, modification implementation, migration, and retirement are components of which one of the following?

    A. Software maintenance

    B. Software testing

    C. Software evaluation

    D. Software development

21. Incorporating changes into software maintenance to improve its performance, security, or maintainability is known as which one of the following?

    A. Perfective

    B. Adaptive

    C. Corrective

    D. Preventive

22. The process of controlling the deployment and maintenance of interim software releases into operational environments is known as which one of the following?

    A. Static analysis

    B. Policy management

    C. Debugging

    D. Patch management

23. "A vulnerability whose exploitation can result in compromise of the confidentiality, integrity, or availability of users' data or of the integrity or availability of processing resources" describes which one of the following Microsoft severity levels for security upgrades?

    A. Important

    B. Critical

    C. Moderate

    D. Low

24. Which one of the following best describes the primary phases in patch management?

    A. Appraisal and inventory, patch categorization, assessment and planning, testing, and deployment

B. Scheduling, patch categorization, assessment and planning, testing, and deployment

C. Appraisal and inventory, patch categorization, assessment and planning, testing, and evaluation

D. Appraisal and inventory, validation, assessment and planning, testing, and deployment

25. Three techniques commonly used for sanitization of data media are:

A. Overwriting, degaussing, and cleansing

B. Overwriting, degaussing, and destruction

C. Saturation, degaussing, and destruction

D. Overwriting, frosting, and destruction

26. The condition that refers to the data left on the media after the media has been erased is known as which one of the following?

A. Degaussed state

B. Residuals

C. Object reuse

D. Data remanence

27. Configuring software with the most secure settings possible prior to deployment of the software is known as what?

A. Security through obscurity

B. Secure by design

C. Security design principles

D. Secure by default

28. Why should software be tested in an environment that is similar to production instead of the actual production environment?

A. The untested software could expose the test environment to threats.

B. The production environment is isolated from real-world hostile conditions.

C. The untested software could expose the production environment to threats.

D. The production environment prevents all testing activities including attacks and exploits.

29. Which of the following is one of the principal duties of the BIOS during POST?

A. Verify the integrity of the BIOS code itself

B. Discover, size, and verify the UEFI checksum

C. Interrupt the execution of all other running programs

D. Protect the computer from pre-boot attacks

30. A successful Chernobyl exploit against a computer's BIOS would cause which of the following actions to occur?

A. The BIOS would be forced to boot an alternate operating system.

B. The host computer would be rendered inoperable.

C. The read-write head of the primary boot device would be "parked."

D. This attack has never been successfully executed.

31. Security measures that should be taken to prevent the corruption of the BIOS include which of the following?

    A. The BIOS chip should be replaced every three months.

    B. The BIOS should be write-protected.

    C. The BIOS chip should be rebooted every three months.

    D. The CMOS battery should be discharged on a regular basis.

32. Computers that implement UEFI could face different threats than BIOS-based computers for which of the following reasons?

    A. UEFI is a tamper-resistant hardware device.

    B. UEFI is write-protected by default.

    C. UEFI implements a full network stack.

    D. UEFI is write-allow by default.

33. A trusted platform module (TPM) is used to protect sensitive information because a TPM:

    A. Is a tamper-resistant hardware device

    B. Has a feature known as open storage

    C. Has a feature known as remote assertion

    D. Is a tamper-evident hardware device

34. Which of the following describes sealing in a TPM?

    A. The process of proving that the platform is trustworthy and has not been breached

    B. The process of encrypting data and only allowing the data to be decrypted if the TPM releases the associated decryption key

    C. The process of encrypting data using the TPM endorsement key, a unique RSA key burned into the chip during its production

    D. The process of generating cryptographic keys through the use of a hardware pseudo-random number generator

35. Which of the following describes binding in a TPM?

    A. The process of proving that the platform is trustworthy and has not been breached

    B. The process of encrypting data and only allowing the data to be decrypted if the TPM releases the associated decryption key

    C. The process of encrypting data using the TPM endorsement key, a unique RSA key burned into the chip during its production

    D. The process of generating cryptographic keys through the use of a hardware pseudo-random number generator

36. Which of the following describes attestation in a TPM?
    A. The process of proving that the platform is trustworthy and has not been breached
    B. The process of encrypting data and only allowing the data to be decrypted if the TPM releases the associated decryption key
    C. The process of encrypting data using the TPM endorsement key, a unique RSA key burned into the chip during its production
    D. The process of generating cryptographic keys through the use of a hardware pseudo-random number generator
37. Cold boot attacks are made possible by what property of dynamic random access memory (DRAM)?
    A. Ordinary DRAM loses its contents gradually over a period of seconds.
    B. Ordinary DRAM loses its contents rapidly over a period of seconds.
    C. Ordinary DRAM loses its contents gradually over a period of minutes.
    D. Ordinary DRAM loses its contents rapidly over a period of minutes.
38. The process of disabling and removing unnecessary services and settings on an operating system is commonly known as:
    A. Tightening
    B. Hardening
    C. Shredding
    D. Hacking
39. CIS benchmarks enumerate security configuration settings and actions that increase the security of the system and also come with which type of tools to verify the security measures?
    A. Scoring
    B. Counting
    C. Enumerating
    D. Evaluating
40. All unnecessary files should be removed from the production execution environment, including which of the following?
    A. Safe open source executables
    B. Production link libraries
    C. Vulnerable open source executables
    D. Production executables
41. The Run As command in Windows XP is a facility that is intended to allow a user to do which of the following?
    A. Run commands with the security privileges of another user
    B. Impersonate another user to perform unauthorized actions

C. Impersonate another user to bypass nonrepudiation

D. Run commands with the security privileges of the logged-on user

42. Which of the following is used to control, document, test, and approve all the changes to the operating environment?

A. Configuration management database (CMDB)

B. Information technology infrastructure library (ITIL)

C. Configuration management

D. Secure version control

43. The condition that refers to the data left on the media after the media has been erased is known as which of the following?

A. Degaussed state

B. Residuals

C. Object reuse

D. Data remanence

APPENDIX

A

Answers to Assessment Questions

Chapter 1

1. The level of confidence that software functions as intended and is free of vulnerabilities, either intentionally or unintentionally designed or inserted as part of the software, is the definition of:

   A. Software risk

   B. Software impact

   C. Software assurance

   D. Software accountability

   Answer: C

   Option C is the definition of assurance from the U.S. Department of Defense (DoD) Software Assurance Initiative. Options A, B, and D are made-up distracters.

2. Seven complementary elements that support information assurance are confidentiality, integrity, availability, authentication, authorization, accountability, and:

   A. Repudiation

   B. Auditing

C. Operations

D. Acquisition

Answer: B

Options A, C, and D are not directly involved with the support of assurance.

3. A form of confidentiality breach that is accomplished by studying the volume, rate, source, and destination of transmitted messages is:

   A. Inference analysis

   B. Covert channel analysis

   C. Messaging analysis

   D. Traffic analysis

   Answer: D

   Option D is correct by the definition of traffic analysis. Options A and C are made-up distracters, and option B refers to hidden data transfer paths.

4. An unauthorized and unintended communication path that provides for exchange of information is a:

   A. Secret link

   B. Covert channel

   C. Covert encryption

   D. Communication pipe

   Answer: B

   The correct option is B.

5. The ability of an entity to use and correlate information protected at one level of security to uncover information that is protected at a higher security level is called:

   A. Inference

   B. Knowledge acquisition

   C. Covert channeling

   D. Cryptanalysis

   Answer: A

   The correct option is A.

6. Confidentiality, integrity, and availability are the principal components of information system security. The reverse of these concepts is:

   A. Disclosure, authentication, and destruction

   B. Disclosure, alteration, and destruction

   C. Encryption, alteration, and destruction

   D. Disclosure, alteration, and disposal

   Answer: B

   Option B describes the reverse of confidentiality, integrity, and availability. The other groups include made-up distracters.

7. The testing or reconciliation of evidence of a user's identity is:

   A. Authorization

   B. Accountability

   C. Auditing

   D. Authentication

   Answer: D

   Authentication verifies a user's identity. Authorization takes place after authentication to determine the resources accessible to the user. Accountability is the ability to hold a user responsible for his or her actions, and auditing is evaluating data after the fact.

8. An ongoing activity that examines either the system or the users, such as intrusion detection, is:

   A. Auditing

   B. Monitoring

   C. Accounting

   D. Eavesdropping

   Answer: B

   Option B, monitoring, involves real-time or near real-time analysis of data; option A, auditing, involves review of information after the fact, such as analyzing logs; option C, accounting, is concerning with financial issues; option D, eavesdropping, is listening in on another's communications.

9. A set of records that collectively provides documentary evidence of processing used to aid in tracing from original transactions forward to related records and reports, and/or backward from records and reports to their component source transactions, is called:

   A. Data library

   B. Data dictionary

   C. Audit trail

   D. Monitor data

   Answer: C

   Option C is correct by the definition of an audit trail.

10. The ability to determine the actions and behaviors of a single individual within a system and to identify that particular individual is:

    A. Authentication

    B. Accountability

    C. Authorization

    D. Nonrepudiation

    Answer: B

    The correct option is B.

11. Economy of mechanism, separation of duties, fail-safe, open design, and psychological acceptability are 5 of the 11:

    A. Security design principles

    B. Security bible principles

    C. Defense-in-depth principles

    D. Security trade-off principles

    Answer: A

    Option A is the nomenclature given to 11 security design principles put forth by Saltzer and Schroeder.

12. What principle maintains that an individual, process, or other type of entity should be given the minimum privileges and resources for the minimum period of time required to complete a task?

    A. Separation of duties

    B. Complete mediation

    C. Least privilege

    D. Limited access

    Answer: C

    Option C corresponds to the definition of least privilege. Option A, separation of duties, requires that completion of a specified sensitive activity or access to sensitive objects is dependent on the satisfaction of multiple conditions. Option B, complete mediation, refers to one of the security design principles where every request by a subject to access an object in a computer system must undergo a valid and effective authorization procedure. Option D, limited access, is a made-up distracter.

13. The principle that requires that completion of a specified sensitive activity or access to sensitive objects is dependent on the satisfaction of multiple conditions is:

    A. Defense-in-depth

    B. Fail-safe

    C. Economy of mechanism

    D. Separation of duties

    Answer: D

    The correct option is D.

14. The application of multiple layers of protection wherein a subsequent layer will provide protection if a previous layer is breached is:

    A. Defense-in-depth

    B. Weakest link

    C. Fail-safe

    D. Control analysis

    Answer: A

    The correct option is A.

15. The condition that every request by a subject to access an object in a computer system must undergo a valid and effective authorization procedure, and must not be suspended or become capable of being bypassed, is known as:
    A. Fail-safe
    B. Complete mediation
    C. Economy of mechanism
    D. Accountability

    Answer: B

    The correct option is B.

16. According to the National Institute for Standards and Technology (NIST) Special Publication (SP) 800-30, the three major components of risk management are:
    A. Risk assessment, risk analysis, and evaluation
    B. Risk assessment, risk mitigation, and risk reduction
    C. Risk assessment, risk determination, and evaluation
    D. Risk assessment, risk mitigation, and evaluation

    Answer: D

    The correct option is D.

17. Which of the following steps are components of the NIST SP 800-30 risk assessment process?
    A. System characterization, threat elimination, vulnerability identification, and control analysis
    B. System characterization, threat identification, vulnerability identification, and control implementation
    C. System characterization, threat identification, vulnerability identification, and control analysis
    D. System characterization, threat identification, vulnerability reduction, and control analysis

    Answer: C

    The correct option is C.

18. In the NIST SP 800-30 risk assessment process, which one of the following is the likelihood rating in which a highly motivated and capable threat-source will exploit an existing vulnerability? In addition, there are also ineffective controls to prevent exploitation of the associated vulnerability.
    A. Medium
    B. High
    C. Low
    D. Intermediate

    Answer: B

    The correct option is B, high, based on the definition in NIST SP 800-30.

19. In the NIST SP 800-30 risk assessment process, the type of analysis that is more easily accomplished and provides identifiable areas for immediate improvement, but does not provide specific magnitudes of measures, is called:

    A. Qualitative analysis

    B. Measurable analysis

    C. Quantitative analysis

    D. Qualified analysis

    Answer: A

    Option A is correct by the definition of qualitative analysis. Options B and D are made-up distracters. Option C, quantitative analysis, is difficult to accomplish and requires solid numerical data that is not easy to obtain or may not be obtainable at all.

20. NIST SP 800-30 risk mitigation options include which one of the following groups?

    A. Risk assumption, risk avoidance, risk planning, and research and development

    B. Risk assumption, risk avoidance, risk planning, and risk elimination

    C. Risk assumption, risk avoidance, risk deterrence, and research and development

    D. Risk calculation, risk avoidance, risk planning, and research and development

    Answer: A

    The correct option is A.

21. The categories of controls to mitigate risks are:

    A. Administrative, management, operational, and a combination of these

    B. Technical, logical, operational, and a combination of these

    C. Technical, management, qualitative, and a combination of these

    D. Technical, management, operational, and a combination of these

    Answer: D

    The correct option is D, technical, management, operational controls, and a combination of these as defined in NIST SP 800-30. Options A, B, and C include made-up distracters.

22. The Microsoft Security Risk Management Discipline (SRMD) comprises which one of the following groups of steps?

    A. Aggregation, development and implementation, operating

    B. Assessment, development and implementation, operating

    C. Assessment, evaluation, operating

    D. Assessment, development and implementation, maintenance

    Answer: B

    The correct option is B.

23. The LeGrand Vulnerability-Oriented Risk Management method includes which one of the following groups of steps?

    A. Risk mitigation, vulnerability management, adherence to security standards and policies

    B. Risk assessment, vulnerability management, adherence to operational standards and policies

    C. Risk assessment, vulnerability elimination, adherence to security standards and policies

    D. Risk assessment, vulnerability management, adherence to security standards and policies

    Answer: D

    The correct option is D.

24. The Morana Risk Management Activities include which one of the following groups of steps that map onto the software development life cycle?

    A. Requirements, architecture and design, development, and testing

    B. Assessment, architecture and design, development, and testing

    C. Requirements, vulnerability management, development, and testing

    D. Requirements, architecture and design, vulnerability management, and testing

    Answer: A

    The correct option is A.

25. In black box testing of information systems:

    A. The testing team is provided full knowledge of the resources to be tested.

    B. The testing team is provided partial knowledge of the resources to be tested and has to acquire some information on its own.

    C. The testing team is provided no knowledge of the resources to be tested and has to acquire information on its own.

    D. The testing team is not permitted direct access to the resources to be tested.

    Answer: C

    Option C is the correct answer. Option A refers to "white box" testing, and option B is known as "gray box" testing. Option D is a made-up distracter.

26. The Information Assurance Technical Framework (IATF) document 3.1 defines the five phases of the system development life cycle (SDLC) as:

    A. Initiation, development/acquisition, implementation, operation/maintenance, upgrade

    B. Initiation, evaluation, implementation, operation/maintenance, disposal

    C. Initiation, development/acquisition, assessment, operation/maintenance, disposal

D. Initiation, development/acquisition, implementation, operation/maintenance, disposal

Answer: D

The correct option is D.

27. The IATF document 3.1 stresses the importance of which one of the following groups to provide information assurance?

A. People, operations, and technology

B. Assessment, operations, and technology

C. People, security, and technology

D. People, operations, and management

Answer: A

The correct option is A. Options B, C, and D are made-up distracters.

28. In NIST SP 800-64, the process for determining the need for property or services and ending with contract completion and closeout is defined as:

A. Initiation

B. Acquisition

C. Subcontracting

D. Development

Answer: B

The correct option is B by the definition of acquisition from NIST SP 800-64.

29. The U.S. federal act that was passed to "provide a comprehensive framework for ensuring the effectiveness of information security controls over information resources that support Federal operations and assets" and "to provide for development and maintenance of minimum controls required to protect Federal information and information systems" is known as the:

A. Gramm-Leach-Bliley Act (GLB Act)

B. Sarbanes-Oxley (SOX) Act

C. Federal Information Security Management Act (FISMA)

D. Health Insurance Portability and Accountability Act (HIPAA)

Answer: C

The correct option is C.

30. Which one of the following specifies that U.S. federal government agencies plan for security, ensure that appropriate officials are assigned security responsibility, review the security controls in their information systems, and authorize system processing prior to operations and periodically thereafter?

A. Sarbanes-Oxley (SOX)

B. U.S. Office of Management and Budget (OMB) Circular A-130

C. Health Insurance Portability and Accountability Act (HIPAA) Final Security Rule

D. Gramm-Leach-Bliley

Answer: B

The correct option is B, OMB Circular A-130. Option A, Sarbanes-Oxley, was enacted to regulate corporate financial practices and reporting. Option C, HIPAA, addresses health care security and privacy issues, and option D, Gramm-Leach-Bliley, the Financial Services Modernization Act, applies to banks, security firms, and insurance companies.

31. Which NIST publication is used to identify and categorize U.S. federal information and information systems?

A. Federal Information Processing Standard (FIPS) 200

B. Federal Information Processing Standard (FIPS) 300

C. Federal Information Processing Standard (FIPS) 199

D. Federal Information Processing Standard (FIPS) 198

Answer: C

The correct option is C.

32. The right of an individual to protection from unauthorized disclosure of personally identifiable information (PII) is the definition of:

A. Security

B. Confidentiality

C. Authorization

D. Privacy

Answer: D

Option D, privacy, is correct. Option A, security, is formally defined as comprising confidentiality, integrity, and availability. Option B, confidentiality, refers to protecting information from unauthorized disclosure, and option C addresses resources that can be accessed by an authenticated user.

33. Notice, choice, access, security, and enforcement are fundamental principles of:

A. Privacy

B. Assurance

C. Access

D. Authorization

Answer: A

The correct option is A.

34. The U.S. act that was passed to regulate corporate financial practices and reporting is:

A. Sarbanes-Oxley (SOX)

B. U.S. Office of Management and Budget (OMB) Circular A-130
C. Health Insurance Portability and Accountability Act (HIPAA)
D. Gramm-Leach-Bliley

Answer: A

The correct option is A.

35. The U.S. Financial Services Modernization Act, Public Law 106-102, is also known as:

A. Sarbanes-Oxley (SOX)
B. U.S. Office of Management and Budget (OMB) Circular A-130
C. FISMA
D. Gramm-Leach-Bliley

Answer: D

The correct option is D.

36. Which U.S. health care–related law addresses protection for transmitted data, protection for data at rest, physical protection, and administrative procedures?

A. Health Insurance Portability and Accountability Act (HIPAA) Final Privacy Rule
B. Health Insurance Portability and Accountability Act (HIPAA) Final Security Rule
C. Health Insurance Portability and Accountability Act (HIPAA) Transactions and Code Sets Rule
D. Health Insurance Portability and Accountability Act (HIPAA) Final Authorization Rule

Answer: B

The correct option is B.

37. Which standard addresses credit card and cardholder authentication and is organized as 12 requirements under 6 logically consistent control objectives?

A. Payment Card Industry (PCI) Data Privacy Standard (DPS)
B. Payment Card Industry (PCI) Data Confidentiality Standard (DCS)
C. Payment Card Industry (PCI) Data Security Standard (DSS)
D. Payment Card Industry (PCI) Data Authorization Standard (DAS)

Answer: C

The correct option is C. Options A, B, and D are made-up distracters.

38. A high-level design structure comprising abstract-level components of the required software system functionality and descriptions of their interactions is the definition of:

A. Software specification
B. Software assurance

C. Software requirements

D. Software architecture

Answer: D

Option D is correct by the definition of software architecture.

39. A software architecture can be considered a composition system comprising the following elements:

A. Components, connectors, operators

B. Components, requirements, operators

C. Specifications, connectors, operators

D. Components, connectors, links

Answer: A

The correct option is A. Options B, C, and D are made-up distracters.

40. Software architecture systems can also be represented by a component model that includes the following concepts:

A. Binding point, operators, glue code, separation of application and communication

B. Binding point, connector, glue code, separation of application and communication

C. Binding point, connector, authorization, separation of application and communication

D. Binding point, connector, glue code, requirements

Answer: B

The correct option is B. Options A, C, and D are made-up distracters. An additional component model element is a composition language such as an Architecture Description Language (ADL).

41. Some typical software architecture styles include:

A. Pipes and filters, layered, P-level, heterogeneous

B. Matrix, layered, N-tiered, homogeneous

C. Pipes and filters, layered, N-tiered, heterogeneous

D. Matrix, layered, N-tiered, heterogeneous

Answer: C

The correct option is C. Options A, B, and D are made-up distracters.

42. The document that lists a number of important architectural design assurance objectives—including: the architecture should provide predictable execution behavior; the architectural design should ease traceability, verification, validation, and evaluation; and the architecture should eliminate possibilities for violations—is entitled:

A. The Software Assurance Common Body of Knowledge (CBK), developed by the U.S. Department of Homeland Security Software

B. The Microsoft Trustworthy Security Development Life Cycle Paradigm

C. The Microsoft Software Development Baseline Process

D. The Comprehensive, Lightweight Application Security Process (CLASP)

Answer: A

The correct option is A.

43. Which type of software development life cycle process employs extensive reviews, evidence, and formal methods?

A. Lightweight

B. Agile

C. Spiral

D. Heavyweight

Answer: D

The correct option is D, heavyweight. Option A, a lightweight process, is less restrictive than a heavyweight process and builds on elements of an extant software development process. Option B, agile, refers to a process characterized by early and frequent delivery of workable and usable software, customer involvement in the development process, iterative development, and acceptance of late requirements changes. Option C, spiral, depicts the software development process as a set of phases and decision points in a circular representation.

44. Which software development process is characterized by early and frequent delivery of workable and usable software, customer involvement in the development process, iterative development, acceptance of late requirements changes, employment of self-managing teams with appropriate expertise, and delivery of multiple releases?

A. Agile

B. Evolutionary

C. Waterfall

D. Unified

Answer: A

The correct option is A.

45. Which software development process operates by first developing prototypes that are tested and evaluated and then going back to continue the development process and incorporating feedback obtained during the prototyping phase?

A. Waterfall

B. Spiral

C. Evolutionary

D. Concurrent release

Answer: C

The correct option is C.

46. The basic Microsoft Software Development Baseline Process is a spiral approach in that the software requirements and design are reviewed and updated, if necessary, during the implementation phase. The phases of this process are:

    A. Requirements, review, implementation, verification, release, support and servicing

    B. Requirements, design, implementation, verification, release, support and servicing

    C. Evaluation, design, implementation, verification, release, support and servicing

    D. Requirements, design, implementation, verification, release, disposal

    Answer: B

    The correct option is B. Options A, C, and D are made-up distracters.

47. The Microsoft Security Development Life Cycle (SDL) is based on which one of the following sets of principles?

    A. Secure in requirements, secure by default, secure in deployment, communications

    B. Secure by design, secure by evaluation, secure in deployment, communications

    C. Secure by design, secure by default, secure in deployment, verification

    D. Secure by design, secure by default, secure in deployment, communications

    Answer: D

    The correct option is D.

48. The Microsoft Security Development Life Cycle (SDL) set of principles is known as:

    A. SD^3+C

    B. SD^3+V

    C. SD^2+E+C

    D. SD^2+R+C

    Answer: A

    The correct option is A and stands for secure by design, secure by default, secure in deployment, and communications. Options B, C, and D are made-up distracters.

49. Which security process includes 7 key best practices for application security and 30 security activities?

    A. Microsoft Security Development Life Cycle (SDL)

    B. The Comprehensive, Lightweight Application Security Process (CLASP)

    C. Touchpoints for Software Security

    D. Team Software Process (TSP)-Secure

    Answer: B

    The correct option is B.

50. What mechanism in the Comprehensive, Lightweight Application Security Process (CLASP) provides a classification structure that enables development teams to find vulnerability information acquired from different historical views and sources of data?

    A. Vulnerability View

    B. Vulnerability Resource

    C. Vulnerability Module

    D. Vulnerability Lexicon

    Answer: D

    The correct option is D. Options A, B, and C are made-up distracters

51. To provide guidelines for employing information assurance processes into the security development life cycle (SDL), CLASP is structured into:

    A. Views, resources, and vulnerability use cases

    B. Views, principles, and vulnerability use cases

    C. Views, resources, and security use cases

    D. Views, activities, and vulnerability use cases

    Answer: A

    The correct option is A. Options B, C, and D are made-up distracters

52. The five CLASP views are:

    A. Concepts view, resource-based view, activity-assessment view, activity-implementation view, vulnerability view

    B. Concepts view, role-based view, resource-assessment view, activity-implementation view, vulnerability view

    C. Concepts view, role-based view, activity-assessment view, activity-implementation view, vulnerability view

    D. Requirements view, role-based view, activity-assessment view, activity-implementation view, vulnerability view

    Answer: C

    The correct option is C. Options A, B, and D are made-up distracters

53. When a system is under attack, one of the following includes these activities: Employ static analysis of source code; conduct risk analysis of architecture and design; perform penetration testing; and categorize abuse cases by analyzing system behavior. Which one?

    A. Comprehensive, Lightweight Application Security Process (CLASP)

    B. Microsoft Security Development Life Cycle

    C. Team Software Process (TSP)-Secure

    D. Seven Touchpoints for Software Security

    Answer: D

    The correct option is D.

54. The Carnegie Mellon University Software Engineering Institute (SEI) and CERT Coordination Center (CERT/CC) have developed a method designed to estimate the probability of vulnerabilities in production software and to minimize or eliminate software vulnerabilities. This method is called:

    A. Team Software Process (TSP)-Secure

    B. Digital Design Process

    C. Design Capability Maturity Model (CMM)

    D. Seven Touchpoints for Software Security

    Answer: A

    The correct option is A.

55. Which one of the following provides the owner with a legally enforceable right to exclude others from practicing a covered invention for a specified period of time?

    A. Copyright

    B. Patent

    C. Warranty

    D. Trade Secret

    Answer: B

    The correct option is B, patent. Option, A, copyright, protects original works of authorship; option C, warranty, is a contract that commits an organization to stand behind its product. Option D, trade secret, secures and maintains the confidentiality of proprietary technical or business-related information that is adequately protected from disclosure by the owner.

56. In the U.S., patent law protects which one of the following groups of items?

    A. Original works of authorship, ornamental designs, and new varieties of plants

    B. Inventions and processes; words, names, or symbols; and new varieties of plants

    C. Inventions and processes, ornamental designs, and words, names, or symbols

    D. Inventions and processes, ornamental designs, and new varieties of plants

    Answer: D

    The correct option is D.

57. Which one of the following ''secures and maintains the confidentiality of proprietary technical or business-related information that is adequately protected from disclosure by the owner''?

    A. Trade secret

    B. Trademark

    C. Warranty

    D. Patent

    Answer: A

    The correct option is A.

58. The International Organization for Standardization (ISO) series 27000 (2700X) standards are dedicated to the field of information system security. Which one of the ISO 27000 series is designed to "provide a model for establishing, implementing, operating, monitoring, reviewing, maintaining, and improving an Information Security Management System (ISMS)"?

    A. 27002

    B. 27004

    C. 27001

    D. 27006

    Answer: C

    The correct option is C, 27001.

59. The ISO 27000 series emphasizes the PDCA cycle. PDCA stands for:

    A. Plan-Do-Check-Act

    B. Prepare-Do-Check-Act

    C. Plan-Develop-Check-Act

    D. Plan-Do-Certify-Act

    Answer: A

    The correct option is A.

60. The Code of Practice for Information Security Management is a repackaged version of (ISO) 17779:2005. It is designed to serve as a single source for best practices in the field of information security and presents a range of controls applicable to most situations. It is:

    A. ISO 27001

    B. ISO 27002

    C. ISO 27003

    D. ISO 27006

    Answer: B

    The correct option is B.

61. What provides a minimum standard for Web application security and summarizes the primary Web application security vulnerabilities based on input from a variety of information system security experts?

    A. The British Standards Institute (BSI) 7799

    B. ISO 27002

    C. The Open Web Application Security Project (OWASP) Top Ten Project

    D. TSP-Secure

    Answer: C

    The correct option is C.

62. In an access matrix, an active entity that is seeking rights to a resource is called:

    A. Object

    B. Subject

C. Capability

D. Grantor

Answer: B

The correct option is B. Option A, object, is usually a passive entity that is accessed by the subject. Option C, capability, refers to the rows of the access control matrix, and option D is a made-up distracter.

63. The columns of the access matrix are called:

A. Access control lists (ACLs)

B. Capability lists

C. Triples

D. Properties

Answer: A

The correct option is A.

64. What model uses a directed graph to specify the rights that a subject can transfer to an object or that a subject can acquire from another subject?

A. Access matrix

B. Information flow

C. Take-Grant

D. Bell-LaPadula

Answer: C

The correct option is C.

65. What model was developed to formalize the U.S. Department of Defense (DoD) multi-level security policy?

A. Biba

B. Take-Grant

C. Clark-Wilson

D. Bell-LaPadula

Answer: D

The correct answer, by definition, is D. The Bell-LaPadula model addresses confidentiality only.

66. What model was developed to address the first integrity goal of protecting data from modification by unauthorized users?

A. Bell-LaPadula

B. Biba

C. Clark-Wilson

D. Information flow

Answer: B

The correct option is B.

67. What model is built on the state machine concept and addresses only the confidentiality of classified material?

    A. Bell-LaPadula

    B. Biba

    C. Clark-Wilson

    D. Information flow

    Answer: A

    The correct option is A.

68. The * (star) property of which one of the following models states that writing of information by a subject at a higher level of sensitivity to an object at a lower level of sensitivity is not permitted (no write-down)?

    A. Take-Grant

    B. Biba

    C. Clark-Wilson

    D. Bell-LaPadula

    Answer: D

    The correct option is D.

69. Which one of the following is the * (star) integrity axiom of the Biba model?

    A. A subject at one level of integrity is not permitted to observe (read) an object of a lower integrity (no read-down).

    B. An object at one level of integrity is not permitted to modify (write to) an object of a higher level of integrity (no write-up).

    C. A subject at one level of integrity is prohibited from invoking a subject at a higher level of integrity.

    D. Integrity labels are required to verify the integrity of an object.

    Answer: B

    The correct option is B.

70. In the Clark-Wilson model, an activity that confirms that all constrained data items are in valid states of integrity is:

    A. Invocation procedure

    B. Unconstrained data item procedure

    C. Transformation procedure

    D. Integrity verification procedure

    Answer: D

    The correct option is D.

71. What model describes those characteristics of security engineering processes essential to ensure good security engineering?

    A. Systems Security Engineering Capability Maturity Model (SSE-CMM)

    B. Capability Maturity Model Integration (CMMi)

C. Bell-LaPadula model

D. Systems Engineering Capability Maturity Model (SE-CMM)

Answer: A

The correct option is A, SSE-CMM, which addresses system security engineering. Option B, CMMI, as defined by the Carnegie Mellon Software Engineering Institute (`www.sei.cmu.edu/cmmi/general/`), "consists of best practices that address the development and maintenance of products and services covering the product life cycle from conception through delivery and maintenance." CMMI integrates the best practices and knowledge from the disciplines of software engineering, acquisition, and systems engineering. Option C, the Bell-LaPadula model, formalizes the U.S. Department of Defense (DoD) multi-level security policy. Option D, SE-CMM, develops system engineering best practices.

72. The Trusted Platform Module (TPM), the Software Stack (TSS), and the Trusted Network Connect (TNC) specifications are key elements of the:

A. Trusted Computing Base (TCB)

B. Trusted Computing Group (TCG)

C. Security Boundary

D. Security Perimeter

Answer: B

The correct option is B.

73. The total combination of protection mechanisms within a computer system, which includes the hardware, software, and firmware that are trusted to enforce a security policy, defines the:

A. Trusted platform module (TPM)

B. Security perimeter

C. Trusted path

D. Trusted computing base (TCB)

Answer: D

The correct option is D by the definition of the TCB.

74. According to the U.S. Department of Defense (DoD) and Department of Homeland Security (DHS) Acquisition and Outsourcing Working Group, the major phases of the software assurance acquisition project are:

A. Planning, contracting, monitoring and acceptance, and follow-on

B. Requirements, contracting, monitoring and acceptance, and follow-on

C. Planning, contracting, implementation, and follow-on

D. Planning, contracting, monitoring and acceptance, and auditing

Answer: A

The correct option is A. Options B, C, and D are made-up distracters.

75. According to NIST Special Publication 800-64, "Security Considerations in the System Development Life Cycle," "all stages of the process of acquiring property

or services, beginning with the process for determining the need for the property or services and ending with contract completion and closeout'' is the definition of:

A. Contracting

B. Acquisition

C. Planning

D. Purchasing

Answer: B

The correct option is B by the definition of acquisition.

Chapter 2

1. Risk assessment, abuse/misuse cases, threat analysis, and models are additional elements that can be used to augment traditional software requirements engineering in order to accomplish which one of the following?

   A. Increase software security

   B. Develop a use case diagram

   C. Develop an abuse/case diagram

   D. Support requirements traceability

   Answer: A

   The correct option is A.

2. In goal-oriented software requirements engineering, active components such as humans, devices, and legacy software that play some role toward goal satisfaction are called:

   A. Actors

   B. Agents

   C. Users

   D. Objects

   Answer: B

   The correct option is B. Actors, option A, are found in use and abuse cases and are external entities that interact with a system. Options C and D are distracters and are not in the formal definition of goal-oriented software requirements.

3. One implementation of goal-oriented requirements engineering that provides a basis for determining if a goal has been satisfied through meeting lower-level goals such as reliability, performance, security, and reliability is known as:

   A. Noncritical requirements (NFR) framework

   B. Noninterference requirements (NFR) framework

   C. Misuse case

   D. Nonfunctional requirements (NFR) framework

Answer: D

Option D is correct by the definition of a nonfunctional requirements (NFR) framework.

4. One goal-oriented requirements engineering approach uses generic specification patterns that map to the information system's properties of confidentiality, integrity, availability, privacy, authentication, authorization, and nonrepudiation. The security patterns are then transformed into goals that are used to develop a correlated "anti-model." This approach is known as the:

   A. Nonfunctional requirements (NFR) framework

   B. MILOS security model

   C. Noninterference requirements (NFR) framework

   D. MODE security model

   Answer: B

   The correct option is B. Option A, NFR, uses security patterns and develops an anti-model. Options C and D are made-up distracters.

5. The phases of the SDLC according to NIST SP 800-14 are:

   A. Initiation, development/acquisition, implementation, operation/maintenance, disposal

   B. Initiation, design, implementation, operation/maintenance, disposal

   C. Initiation, development/acquisition, implementation, operation/maintenance, re-initiation

   D. Initiation, development/acquisition, implementation, testing, disposal

   Answer: A

   The correct option is A.

6. One approach to defining elements of an information security policy is to correlate the system engineering process and the secure software engineering process. This correlation can be accomplished through which one of the following models?

   A. Secure model

   B. Zee model

   C. Verify model

   D. Vee model

   Answer: D

   The correct option is D. Options A, B, and C are made-up distracters.

7. The left side of the model that correlates the system engineering process and the secure software engineering process and contains the major technical phases involved in transforming systems requirements into an operational software system is known as the:

   A. Integration and verification sequence

   B. Decomposition and verification sequence

   C. Decomposition and definition sequence

D. Integration and definition sequence

Answer: C

Option C is correct by the definition of the ''Vee'' model. Option A is the definition of the right side of the ''Vee'' model and options B and D are made-up distracters.

8. The right side of the model that correlates the system engineering process and the secure software engineering process and contains the major technical phases involved in transforming systems requirements into an operational software system is known as the:

   A. Integration and verification sequence

   B. Decomposition and verification sequence

   C. Decomposition and definition sequence

   D. Integration and definition

   Answer: A

   The correct option is A. Option C is the definition of the left side of the ''Vee'' model, and options B and D are made-up distracters

9. Which NIST Special Publication presents 33 security principles that start at the design phase of the information system or application and continue until the system's retirement and secure disposal?

   A. NIST Special Publication 800-64

   B. NIST Special Publication 800-30

   C. NIST Special Publication 800-27

   D. NIST Special Publication 800-20

   Answer: C

   The correct option is C.

10. The NIST FIPS Publication ''Minimum Security Requirements for Federal Information and Information Systems'' specifies items that can be used to provide inputs to secure software policies. This NIST publication is:

    A. FIPS 300

    B. FIPS 200

    C. FIPS 220

    D. FIPS 210

    Answer: B

    The correct option is B.

11. NIST categorizes computer system security policies into which one of the following three basic types?

    A. Project, issue-specific, system-specific

    B. Program, issue-specific, implementation-specific

    C. Program, security-specific, system-specific

    D. Program, issue-specific, system-specific

Answer: D

Option D is correct. The other options are made-up distracters.

12. Which one of the following is a nontechnical policy addressing a single or specific item of concern to an organization?

    A. System specific

    B. Issue specific

    C. Security specific

    D. Project specific

    Answer: B

    The correct option is B.

13. Which policy is technically focused and addresses only one computer system or device type and includes security objectives and operational security rules?

    A. Security specific

    B. Program specific

    C. Issue specific

    D. System specific

    Answer: D

    The correct option is D.

14. Security policies that an organization must implement due to compliance or other legal requirements are called:

    A. Guidelines

    B. Advisory policies

    C. Regulatory policies

    D. Organizational policies

    Answer: C

    The correct option is C. Options A, B, and D are not driven by regulations or laws.

15. Which one of the following specifies the use of particular technologies in a uniform way and is usually compulsory?

    A. Standards

    B. Guidelines

    C. Procedures

    D. Baselines

    Answer: A

    The correct option is A by definition of a standard. Option B, guidelines, are not mandatory; option C, procedures, are step-by-step descriptions of implementing a policy. Option D, baselines, are implemented based on good organizational practices.

16. Which one of the following refers to the methodologies of securing systems, but are recommended actions only and are not compulsory.

A. Standards

B. Guidelines

C. Procedures

D. Baselines

Answer: B

Option B is correct. Options A, C, and D are all compulsory.

17. Which one of the following embodies the detailed steps that are followed to perform a specific task?

    A. Standards

    B. Guidelines

    C. Procedures

    D. Baselines

    Answer: C

    The correct option is C.

18. Who is assigned the overall responsibility for the security of information?

    A. Senior-level management

    B. Data owners

    C. Users

    D. Information systems auditors

    Answer: A

    The correct option is A. Senior management is always ultimately responsible for an organization's information system security.

19. Which one of the following refers to rights and privileges granted to an individual or process that enable access to computer resources and information assets?

    A. Authentication

    B. Authorization

    C. Auditing

    D. Identification

    Answer: B

    The correct option is B, by definition. Option A is the verification of an identity. Option C involves reviewing procedures, policies, and logs to ensure proper security practices are being followed. Option D is claiming to be an entity.

20. According to the Data and Analysis Center for Software (DACS), which one of the following "is concerned, in large part, with defining the set of rules by which system subjects are allowed to change the states of data objects in the system"?

    A. Risk analysis

    B. Regulatory policy

C. Guidelines

D. Information security policy

Answer: D

Option D is correct, by definition.

21. Which one of the following policy requirements is concerned with denying illegitimate access to computing resources and prevention of external attacks such as denial-of-service attacks?

A. Confidentiality

B. Availability

C. Integrity

D. Authentication

Answer: B

The correct option is B.

22. The information system security policy should decompose the audit requirements to risk-based elements that consider which one of the following three types of audit-related risks?

A. Aggregation risk, development risk, implementation risk

B. Inherent risk, detection risk, control risk

C. Assessment risk, evaluation risk, operating risk

D. Inherent risk, development risk, control risk

Answer: B

Option B is correct. Options A, C, and D are made-up distracters.

23. Which one of the following is an accounting statement of position that defines how information technology software development or acquisition costs are to be expended or capitalized?

A. SOP 90-1

B. SOP 98-1

C. SOP 98-3

D. SOP 95-1

Answer: B

The correct option is B.

24. Which one of the following tests is defined as "the level of diligence that a prudent and competent person would exercise under a given set of circumstances"?

A. Due care

B. Separation of duties

C. Exigent circumstances

D. Authorization

Answer: A

The correct option is A.

25. The confidentiality and integrity of audit information must be protected at which one of the following levels of security?

    A. Moderate

    B. Lowest

    C. Highest

    D. Not at all

    Answer: C

    The correct option is C. Because audit information provides insight into past events and forensic evidence of malpractice, it must be protected at the highest level of security.

26. Which one of the following is a valuable audit planning and execution tool that was introduced by the Information Systems Audit and Control Association (ISACA)?

    A. CobiT

    B. SATAN

    C. AuditSecure

    D. ATEST

    Answer: A

    The correct option is A.

27. Which one of the following represents the two of types of secure software requirements analysis that should be performed pursuant to an information system security policy?

    A. Internal and external

    B. Detailed and specific

    C. Qualitative and quantitative

    D. Development and operational

    Answer: A

    Option A is correct, by definition. Options B, C, and D are made-up distracters

28. Which one of the following groups of states describes the best complete set of states in which data can exist for the purposes of software assurance?

    A. In storage or "at rest," being created, in motion from one location to another, being modified or overwritten

    B. In storage or "at rest," being created, in motion from one location to another

    C. In storage or "at rest," in motion from one location to another, being modified or overwritten

D. Being created, in motion from one location to another, being modified or overwritten

Answer: A

The correct option is A.

29. Data can be categorized according to its value or its frequency of access. Important and frequently accessed data should be stored on the fastest storage media. This data can be classified as which one of the following?

A. Input data, output data, external data, security-critical data, hidden data

B. Input data, output data, internal data, security-critical data, hidden data

C. Input data, output data, internal data, security-critical data, visible data

D. Input data, output data, internal data, pseudo- data, hidden data

Answer: B

The correct option is B.

30. In software engineering and systems engineering, what is a description of a system's behavior as it responds to a request that originates from outside of that system?

A. Misuse case

B. Use case

C. Abuse case

D. External case

Answer: B

Option B is correct. Options A and C are types of cases involving malicious actors. Option D is a made-up distracter.

31. What is a specification of a type of complete interaction between a system and one or more actors, where the results of the interaction are harmful?

A. Abuse case

B. Use case

C. Internal case

D. Malicious case

Answer: A

Option A is correct. Option B does not involve malicious actors. Options C and D are made-up distracters.

32. Use cases can be represented graphically by a use case diagram through the application of which one of the following?

A. Uniform Method Language (UML)

B. Unified Case Language (UCL)

C. Unified Simulation Language (USL)

D. Unified Modeling Language (UML)

Answer: D

Option D is correct. Options A, B and C are made-up distracters.

33. In a use case diagram, associations between actors and use cases are depicted by which one of the following?

A. Solid lines

B. Dotted lines

C. Oval shapes

D. Flags

Answer: A

The correct option is A.

34. In a use case, an internal, external, or time-based occurrence that initiates the use case is called a:

A. Threshold

B. Boundary

C. Trigger

D. Starter

Answer: C

The correct option is C. Options A, B, and D are made-up distracters.

35. A use case that is presented at a high level with minimal technical language and represents processes that provide services to the actor is known as which one of the following?

A. System use case

B. Real use case

C. Implementation use case

D. Business use case

Answer: D

The correct option is D, by definition.

36. Actors in an abuse case usually have which one of the following characteristics?

A. Do not intend harm to the system

B. Are not normally malicious

C. Are authorized users

D. Are malicious and labeled as such

Answer: D

The correct option is D.

37. In an abuse case, an actor is usually defined by its:
   A. Type, skills, and resources
   B. Objectives, persistence, and resources
   C. Objectives, skills, and resources
   D. Type, persistence, and resilience

   Answer: C

   The correct option is C. Options A, B, and D are made-up distracters.

38. In most situations, an abuse case describes which one of the following?
   A. A family of possible harmful interactions
   B. A single interaction
   C. An interaction as conducted in a use case
   D. A benign interaction

   Answer: A

   The correct option is A.

39. Advantages such as simplicity, ease of understanding, illustrating what can and cannot be protected, and prioritizing of threats refer to which one of the following?
   A. Using abuse cases in requirements specification
   B. Using use cases in requirements specification
   C. Using component cases in requirements specification
   D. Using trade-off cases in requirements specification

   Answer: A

   The correct option is A. Options C and D are made-up distracters. In Option B, use cases do not involve threats.

Chapter 3

1. Entry points in a software application include interfaces, protocols, code and:
   A. Error messages
   B. Services
   C. Packaging
   D. Response codes

   Answer: B

   The correct option is B.

2. Using a custom build process to enable specific features in the Apache Web server is an example of what design principle?
   A. Least privilege
   B. Leveraging existing components

C. Economy of mechanism

D. Fail safe

Answer: C

The correct option is C.

3. Applying the most restrictive set of operating system permissions to all application files is an example of what design principle?

A. Least common mechanism

B. Least privilege

C. Separation of duties

D. Weakest link

Answer: B

The correct option is B.

4. Mitigating the risk of one security control being compromised by providing multiple layers of security controls is an example of what specific security strategy?

A. Secure-by-default

B. Secure-by-design

C. Defense-in-depth

D. Defense-by-design

Answer: C

The correct option is C.

5. Which of the following is a security advantage of managed code over unmanaged code?

A. Size of the attack surface

B. Number of roles

C. Number of lines of code

D. Size of the chroot jail

Answer: A

The correct option is A.

6. UDP has a larger attack surface than TCP because:

A. It allows the spread of worms.

B. It is a connection-oriented protocol.

C. It is a "fire and forget" protocol.

D. The IP address is easily spoofed.

Answer: D

The correct option is D.

7. Which of the following is a process for assessing and documenting the weaknesses or security risks associated with an application?

A. Control identification

B. Threat modeling

C. Control prioritization

D. Attack surface evaluation

Answer: B

The correct option is B.

8. Which of the following is attempting to gain access to a system by using a false identity?

A. Repudiation

B. Eavesdropping

C. Spoofing

D. Hijacking

Answer: C

The correct option is C.

9. Which of the following is the ability of users to deny that they performed specific actions or transactions?

A. Repudiation

B. Eavesdropping

C. Spoofing

D. Hijacking

Answer: A

The correct option is A.

10. An advantage of using a threat modeling tool over a manual process is:

A. It is faster for analyzing small software projects.

B. It can provide useful visualizations.

C. It defines the application context for you.

D. It can only be used by a security expert.

Answer: B

The correct option is B.

11. A risk calculation methodology created by Microsoft is known as:

A. STRIDE

B. DREAD

C. Monte Carlo

D. MSRCM

Answer: B

The correct option is B.

12. What is the best method for prioritizing a threat and its related countermeasures?
    A. Measuring the relative attack surface
    B. Quantifying the level of risk
    C. Enumerating the entry points and exit points
    D. Identifying the type of accessibility required

    Answer: B

    The correct option is B.

13. What type of aid provides low-level detail and thus greater understanding of specific use cases, especially security relevant use cases?
    A. Subject object matrix
    B. Component access control matrix
    C. Data flow diagram
    D. Attack surface

    Answer: C

    The correct option is C.

14. Which mitigation technique is the best match for the elevation of privilege threat type?
    A. Authentication
    B. Authorization
    C. Auditing
    D. Confidentiality

    Answer: B

    The correct option is B.

15. Which mitigation technique is the best match for the tampering threat type?
    A. Integrity
    B. Availability
    C. Auditing
    D. Confidentiality

    Answer: A

    The correct option is A.

16. Why should a host-based firewall not be relied upon solely to mitigate a risk?
    A. It does not block incoming traffic.
    B. It does not block outgoing traffic.
    C. It can be turned off.
    D. It can't be turned off.

    Answer: C

    The correct option is C.

17. The choice of mitigation technologies should:

    A. Follow security best practices

    B. Depend on the number of sources researched

    C. Not depend on the technology of the application

    D. Address as few threat types as possible

    Answer: A

    The correct option is A.

18. A normal user assuming the identity of an administrator is what kind of attack?

    A. Elevation of privilege

    B. Denial of service

    C. Spoofing

    D. Repudiation

    Answer: A

    The correct option is A.

19. A hardened operating system (OS):

    A. Has a smaller attack surface than an unhardened OS

    B. Implements mandatory access control

    C. Is less secure than an unhardened OS

    D. Has more entry and exit points than an unhardened OS system

    Answer: A

    The correct option is A.

20. It is important to create detailed security configuration instructions for end users because:

    A. All configuration information should be documented.

    B. The end users are not normally a part of the process.

    C. Configuration decisions have security implications.

    D. Documentation should be placed under secure version control.

    Answer: C

    The correct option is C.

21. Ranking risks based on the type of application and the characteristics of threats is:

    A. More objective than using numeric ratings

    B. The DREAD method

    C. More subjective than using numeric ratings

    D. The STRIDE method

    Answer: A

    The correct option is A.

22. Which of the following is a reverse engineering countermeasure?
    A. Encrypted password
    B. Code obfuscation technology
    C. Embed a salt in the code
    D. Secure random number generator

    Answer: B

    The correct option is B.

23. Which of the following is used to preserve confidentiality in software?
    A. Encryption
    B. Hashing
    C. Recovery
    D. Redundancy

    Answer: A

    The correct option is A.

24. Which of the following is used to preserve integrity in software?
    A. Encryption
    B. Hashing
    C. Recovery
    D. Redundancy

    Answer: B

    The correct option is B.

25. Which of the following is used to ensure availability in software?
    A. Encryption
    B. Hashing
    C. Recovery
    D. Redundancy

    Answer: C

    The correct option is C.

26. Which of the following is a property of an ideal hash function?
    A. Likely that two different messages will have the same hash
    B. Easy to compute the hash for any given data
    C. Easy to construct a text that has a given hash
    D. Easy to modify a given text without changing its hash

    Answer: B

    The correct option is B.

27. Which of the following is a property of fault-tolerant software?
    A. A single point of failure
    B. A single point of repair

C. Fault propagation to the failing component

D. Availability of "fallback" or reversion modes

Answer: D

The correct option is D.

28. How does software exhibit graceful degradation in response to a denial-of-service (DoS) attack?

A. Fail-over to a higher-availability service

B. Vary its response times to subsequent requests

C. Disconnect the affected connectivity point

D. Fail-over to a hot standby

Answer: B

The correct option is B.

29. Which of the following provides redundancy in a software system?

A. The use of redundant arrays of inexpensive disks (RAID)

B. Deploying the software to a single location

C. A variable backup schedule

D. An uninterruptible power supply

Answer: A

The correct option is A.

30. What is the basis of NIST SP 800-63-1 Electronic Authentication Guideline assurance levels?

A. Single-factor remote network authentication

B. Cryptographic authentication of all parties

C. The likely consequences of an authentication error

D. The verification of identifying materials and information

Answer: C

Option C is a risk-based approach to determining the required level of assurance. The other options are properties of each of the assurance levels.

31. Which of the following is an authentication design defect?

A. Using authentication based on trustworthy attributes

B. Unifying authentication and authorization

C. Using authentication when it is required

D. Propagating authentication across a multi-tier platform

Answer: B

The correct option is B.

32. Checking privileges before granting access to a restricted service is known as:

A. Authentication

B. Authorization

C. Auditing

D. Accountability

Answer: B

The correct option is B.

33. What distinguishes auditing from standard event logging?

A. The type of information captured in the audit record

B. The level of confidentiality applied to the audit records

C. The addition of debug information to the audit record

D. The level of availability applied to the audit records

Answer: A

The correct option is A.

34. Which security design principle espouses the practice "Security should not depend on security-through-obscurity"?

A. Defense-in-depth

B. Open design

C. Complete mediation

D. Analyzability

Answer: B

The correct option is B.

35. Which principle can be categorized under "Minimize the number of high-consequence targets"?

A. Design for controllability

B. Traceability from requirements to design

C. Segregate trusted entities from untrusted entities

D. Least privilege

Answer: D

The correct option is D.

36. Which principle can be categorized under "Don't expose vulnerable or high-consequence components"?

A. Design for controllability

B. Traceability from requirements to design

C. Segregate trusted entities from untrusted entities

D. Least privilege

Answer: C

The correct option is C.

37. Which principle can be categorized under "Deny attackers the means to compromise"?

    A. Design for controllability

    B. Traceability from requirements to design

    C. Segregate trusted entities from untrusted entities

    D. Least privilege

    Answer: A

    The correct option is A.

38. What does it mean to "Hold all actors accountable, not just human actors"?

    A. Attacker actions are observed and recorded.

    B. Keep the design as simple as possible.

    C. Components are neither dependable nor trustworthy.

    D. Software execution ends in a secure state.

    Answer: A

    The correct option is A.

39. What software feature follows the principle "Design for controllability"?

    A. Ability to enter a secure state

    B. State changes should always be deliberate

    C. Ability to self-monitor and limit resource usage

    D. Ability to choose most appropriate secure state

    Answer: C

    The correct option is C. The other options refer to the principle, "Make secure states easy to enter and vulnerable states difficult to enter."

40. Implementing a watchdog timer is part of what secure design principle?

    A. Design for survivability

    B. Design for secure failure

    C. Design for controllability

    D. Design for redundancy

    Answer: B

    The correct option is B.

41. Taking advantage of rapid recovery features at the system level is part of what secure design principle?

    A. Design for survivability

    B. Design for secure failure

C. Design for controllability

D. Design for redundancy

Answer: A

The correct option is A.

42. Security design patterns:

A. Uphold secure design principles

B. Define poorly understood design features

C. Are not reusable

D. Are not applicable to software assurance

Answer: A

The correct option is A.

43. Flow, sharing, and timing dependencies refer to what aspect of software?

A. Reusability

B. Survivability

C. Interconnectivity

D. Availability

Answer: C

The correct option is C.

44. Which of the following provides control over the trust features in a software application?

A. Security management interfaces

B. Secure configuration management

C. Application container

D. Security manager

Answer: A

The correct option is A.

45. Identity management provides for the following:

A. Integrity

B. Deniability

C. Confidentiality

D. Nonrepudiation

Answer: D

The correct option is D.

46. What describes software processes running simultaneously on multiple processors on the same computer?

A. Distributed computing
B. Parallel computing
C. Pervasive computing
D. Ubiquitous computing

Answer: B

The correct option is B.

47. What is a technique for dealing with processes that use old data in distributed systems?

A. Propagate security state changes
B. Implement network links of varying latencies
C. Include additional processes that run simultaneously
D. Run the data in a heterogeneous environment

Answer: A

The correct option is A. Option B refers to one of the problems of distributed systems; option C is a distracter; option D refers to one of the problems of distributed systems.

48. What is a technique for dealing with conflicting resource updates?

A. Propagate security state changes
B. Locking to prevent inconsistent updates
C. Running a clock synchronization protocol
D. Recovery from failures must be addressed by systems design

Answer: B

The correct option is B. Option A refers to processes using old data; option C refers to inconsistent or inaccurate time across the system; option D refers to non-convergence in transaction-oriented systems.

49. Identifying and removing the root cause of the defect is known as:

A. Error detection
B. Damage confinement
C. Error recovery
D. Fault treatment

Answer: D

The correct option is D.

50. Which type of redundancy allows software to be run simultaneously on multiple geographically distributed locations?

A. Hardware
B. Process

C. Data

D. Application

Answer: B

The correct option is B.

51. What does Web Services (WS)-Security accomplish?

A. Supports message integrity and confidentiality

B. Enables the authorization of the information published

C. Provides mechanisms for authentication and authorization

D. Enables the selective signing of XML data

Answer: A

The correct option is A.

52. What is the best mechanism to address nonrepudiation in Web services?

A. Performance techniques

B. Threat modeling

C. Logging

D. Data replication

Answer: C

The correct option is C.

53. One of the key security protections of rich Internet applications is:

A. Offline operation

B. Loose coupling with the Web browser

C. Ability to store data locally

D. Same origin policy

Answer: D

The correct option is D. The other options are characteristics of rich Internet applications. Sandbox is the other key security protection.

54. Which type of computing involves a high degree of communication among devices?

A. Distributed computing

B. Parallel computing

C. Pervasive computing

D. Standard computing

Answer: C

The correct option is C.

55. Which kind of trust management scheme tracks the behavior of nodes?

A. Bayesian trust framework

B. Reputation-based trust system

C. Trust analysis methodology

D. Trust analysis grid

Answer: B

The correct option is B.

56. A type of system where the end user does not own the software is:

A. Ubiquitous computing

B. Software-as-a-service

C. Hosted software

D. Subscription-based software

Answer: B

The correct option is B. Options C and D are characteristics of SaaS.

57. Something you know and something you have are authentication:

A. Passwords

B. Factors

C. Credentials

D. Identities

Answer: B

The correct option is B.

58. Biometrics are an example of:

A. Something you know

B. Something you have

C. Something you are

D. Something you need

Answer: C

The correct option is C. All are authentication factors except for option D.

59. A centralized repository of user data is characteristic of what type of identity management system?

A. Directory services

B. Federated identity management

C. User provisioning system

D. Directory provisioning system

Answer: A

The correct option is A. Option D is a distracter.

60. Which of the following has properties such as revocation and expiration?

A. Transaction signing

B. Secure Remote Password (SRP) protocol

C. X.509 digital certificate

D. Two-factor authentication

Answer: C

The correct option is C.

61. Problems exhibited by user provisioning systems include:

A. Slow execution of workflow processes

B. Lack of a single source of coherent information

C. Need for a local user database

D. Some services need to keep state

Answer: A

The correct option is A. Options B, C, and D are problems in directory services.

62. Reducing password fatigue from different username and password combinations is a characteristic of:

A. Two-factor authentication

B. Transaction signing

C. X.509 digital certificate

D. Single sign-on (SSO)

Answer: D

The correct option is D.

63. A Web application firewall may actively defend a Web application by:

A. Invalidating the application session

B. Intercepting data flowing to and from a Web application

C. Running in a separate process and memory space

D. Learning about the application behavior

Answer: A

The correct option is A. Options B, C, and D are operational and deployment characteristics of Web application firewalls.

64. Drawbacks of Web application firewall technology include:

A. Detection of some attacks

B. Configuration and performance

C. Flexible policy enforcement

D. Specialized security knowledge

Answer: B

The correct option is B. Options A, C, and D are benefits of Web application firewalls.

65. Which logging technology provides agent-oriented and agent-less operation?

A. Syslog protocol

B. Web application firewall

C. Security information and event management (SIEM)

D. Simple Network Management Protocol (SNMP)

Answer: C

The correct option is C. Options B and D are not logging technologies.

66. Reliable log delivery is an enhancement to which logging technology?

A. Syslog protocol

B. Web application firewall

C. Security information and event management (SIEM)

D. Simple Network Management Protocol (SNMP)

Answer: A

The correct option is A. Options B and D are not logging technologies.

67. Security information and event management (SIEM) products include which of the following features?

A. Security knowledge base

B. Rate limiting

C. Limited log format support

D. Transmission over User Datagram Protocol (UDP)

Answer: A

The correct option is A. Option B is a feature of enhanced Syslog. Options C and D are drawbacks of Syslog.

68. Data loss prevention (DLP) technology may take the following action when it detects a policy violation:

A. Hash the data

B. Encrypt the data

C. Reconstruct the session

D. Analyze the content

Answer: B

The correct option is B. Option A is a distracter. Options C and D are how data analysis is performed on data in motion.

69. Dynamic allocated resources are a security concern of which programming language?

A. C

B. Java

C. .NET

D. Managed Code

Answer: A

The correct option is A. Options C (.NET) and D (Managed Code) are not programming languages.

70. Authentication and session management are security concerns of which programming language?

    A. C

    B. Java

    C. .NET

    D. Managed Code

    Answer: B

    The correct option is B. Options C and D are not programming languages.

71. Potential security disadvantages of virtualization include:

    A. VM layer configuration is security relevant

    B. More intrusive intrusion detection via introspection

    C. An extra layer for defense-in-depth

    D. More flexible discovery/eviction of kernel root kits

    Answer: A

    The correct option is A. Options B, C, and D are potential advantages of virtualization.

72. Which of the following defines minimum techniques to secure each asset in digital rights management (DRM)?

    A. Compliance rules

    B. Licensing

    C. Robustness rules

    D. Requirements

    Answer: C

    The correct option is C.

73. Which of the following specifies the required behaviors in digital rights management (DRM)?

    A. Compliance rules

    B. Licensing

    C. Robustness rules

    D. Requirements

    Answer: A

    The correct option is A.

74. Specialized, professional, and what other type of tool is used to attack digital rights management (DRM):

    A. Power

    B. Hand

    C. Widely available

    D. Software

Answer: C

The correct option is C. Options A, B, and D are distracters.

75. At the highest level of robustness in digital rights management (DRM), security functions should be:

    A. Immune to professional tools

    B. Resistant to professional tools

    C. Resistant to specialized tools

    D. Immune to all tools

    Answer: B

    The correct option is B.

76. An example of over-the-air (OTA) provisioning in digital rights management (DRM) is:

    A. Use of software and hardware to achieve deployment goals

    B. Use of concealment to evade tampering attacks

    C. Use of device properties for unique identification

    D. Use of shared secrets to initiate or reestablish trust

    Answer: D

    The correct option is D. Option A is a distracter; options B and C are security challenges in DRM.

77. A means of validating the origin and integrity of software is:

    A. Code signing

    B. Digital rights management

    C. Robustness rules

    D. Compliance rules

    Answer: A

    The correct option is A. Options B, C, and D are distracters.

Chapter 4

1. Programmatic security controls access by:

    A. Calling functions to determine authorizations

    B. Delegating security decisions to the Web application container

    C. Defining the security constraints in the deployment descriptor

    D. D. Reading parameters defined in an external configuration file

    Answer: A

    The correct option is A.

2. Which of the following serves as a common language for describing software security weaknesses in architecture, design, or code?

   A. OWASP Top 10

   B. CWE/SANS Top 25

   C. OWASP

   D. CWE

   Answer: D

   The correct option is D.

3. Which of the following is a list that educates programmers on how to eliminate the most common mistakes in all types of software?

   A. OWASP Top 10

   B. CWE/SANS Top 25

   C. OWASP

   D. CWE

   Answer: B

   The correct option is B.

4. Which of the following is a list of the most common Web application security vulnerabilities?

   A. OWASP Top 10

   B. CWE/SANS Top 25

   C. OWASP

   D. CWE

   Answer: A

   The correct option is A.

5. Which of the following is an organization that promotes Web application security?

   A. OWASP Top 10

   B. CWE/SANS Top 25

   C. OWASP

   D. CWE

   Answer: C

   The correct option is C.

6. Which kind of vulnerability may result when data originates from a user and is sent to an interpreter as part of a command or query?

   A. Malicious file execution

   B. Injection flaw

   C. Insecure direct object reference

   D. Cross-site request forgery

   Answer: B

   The correct option is B.

7. Which kind of vulnerability occurs when an attacker forces a logged-on victim's browser to send a request to a vulnerable Web application?

   A. Malicious file execution

   B. Injection flaw

   C. Insecure direct object reference

   D. Cross-site request forgery

   Answer: D

   The correct option is D.

8. Which kind of vulnerability occurs when an application directly uses or concatenates potentially hostile input with file or stream functions?

   A. Malicious file execution

   B. Injection flaw

   C. Insecure direct object reference

   D. Cross-site request forgery

   Answer: A

   The correct option is A.

9. Which kind of vulnerability may occur when a developer refers to an internal implementation construct?

   A. Malicious file execution

   B. Injection flaw

   C. Insecure direct object reference

   D. Cross-site request forgery

   Answer: C

   The correct option is C.

10. Which kind of vulnerability may occur when an application takes data that originated from a user and sends it to a Web browser without first validating that content?

    A. Cross-site scripting

    B. Information leakage

    C. Failure to restrict URL access

    D. Insecure cryptographic storage

    Answer: A

    The correct option is A.

11. Which kind of vulnerability occurs when applications fail to encrypt sensitive data?

    A. Cross-site scripting

    B. Information leakage

    C. Failure to restrict URL access

    D. Insecure cryptographic storage

    Answer: D

    The correct option is D.

12. Which kind of vulnerability may occur when an application only protects sensitive functionality by preventing the display of links to unauthorized users?

    A. Cross-site scripting

    B. Information leakage

    C. Failure to restrict URL access

    D. Insecure cryptographic storage

    Answer: C

    The correct option is C.

13. Which kind of vulnerability occurs if an application unintentionally discloses information about its configuration?

    A. Cross-site scripting

    B. Information leakage

    C. Failure to restrict URL access

    D. Insecure cryptographic storage

    Answer: B

    The correct option is B.

14. Which type of attack involves taking over control of the virtual machine monitor (VMM) in order to take over the host computer?

    A. Virtualization

    B. Hyperjacking

    C. Hijacking

    D. Man-in-the-middle

    Answer: B

    The correct option is B. Option A, virtualization, is not a type of attack. Options C and D are distracters, but real types of attacks.

15. Which type of attack exploits CPU virtualization extensions?

    A. Memory injection

    B. Blue Pill

    C. Red Pill

    D. SubVirt

    Answer: B

    The correct option is B.

16. Which of the following detects software-based hypervisors?

    A. Memory injection

    B. Blue Pill

    C. Red Pill

    D. SubVirt

Answer: C

The correct option is C.

17. Which of the following is an attack that exploits known security flaws to install a hypervisor in Windows or Linux?

A. Memory injection

B. Blue Pill

C. Red Pill

D. SubVirt

Answer: D

The correct option is D.

18. Which type of attack involves monitoring the physical interaction between a system and its environment?

A. Passive

B. Active

C. Side-channel

D. Cryptanalysis

Answer: C

The correct option is C.

19. Which type of side-channel attack exerts behavior on a system such that an observer would notice a difference in the operation?

A. Passive

B. Active

C. Side-channel

D. Cryptanalysis

Answer: B

The correct option is B.

20. In which type of side-channel attack is information gained about the system without interfering with its operation?

A. Passive

B. Active

C. Side-channel

D. Cryptanalysis

Answer: A

The correct option is A.

21. Invasive attack of a cryptographic security module involves:

A. Decompiling to understand the implementation

B. De-packaging to get access to the internal components

C. Access to the device but no damage to the passivation layer

D. Close observation or manipulation of the device's operation

Answer: B

The correct option is B.

22. Non-invasive attack of a cryptographic security module involves:

A. Decompiling to understand the implementation

B. De-packaging to get access to the internal components

C. Access to the device but no damage to the passivation layer

D. Close observation or manipulation of the device's operation

Answer: D

The correct option is D.

23. Semi-invasive attack of a cryptographic security module involves:

A. Decompiling to understand the implementation

B. De-packaging to get access to the internal components

C. Access to the device but no damage to the passivation layer

D. Close observation or manipulation of the device's operation

Answer: C

The correct option is C.

24. A countermeasure to a timing attack involves:

A. Carefully measuring the time it takes to carry out cryptographic operations

B. Making the operational parameters independent of the input data

C. Protecting public-key algorithms by using checksums and execution randomizations

D. Using an internal power source and randomized register renaming

Answer: B

The correct option is B. Option A describes the timing attack itself.

25. A countermeasure to a fault attack involves:

A. Carefully measuring the time it takes to carry out cryptographic operations

B. Making the operational parameters independent of the input data

C. Protecting public-key algorithms by using checksums and execution randomizations

D. Using an internal power source and randomized register renaming

Answer: C

The correct option is C.

26. A countermeasure to a power analysis attack involves:

A. Carefully measuring the time it takes to carry out cryptographic operations

B. Making the operational parameters independent of the input data

C. Protecting public-key algorithms by using checksums and execution randomizations

D. Using an internal power source and randomized register renaming

Answer: D

The correct option is D.

27. A countermeasure to an electromagnetic attack involves:

A. Reducing signal strength and signal information

B. Shielding the CRT to protect against leakage

C. Using application-specific algorithm masking

D. Physically protecting the memory

Answer: A

The correct option is A.

28. A countermeasure to a visible light attack involves:

A. Reducing signal strength and signal information

B. Shielding the CRT to protect against leakage

C. Using application-specific algorithm masking

D. Physically protecting the memory

Answer: B

The correct option is B.

29. A countermeasure to a cache-based attack involves:

A. Reducing signal strength and signal information

B. Shielding the CRT to protect against leakage

C. Using application-specific algorithm masking

D. Physically protecting the memory

Answer: C

The correct option is C.

30. A countermeasure to a cold boot attack involves:

A. Reducing signal strength and signal information

B. Shielding the CRT to protect against leakage

C. Using application-specific algorithm masking

D. Physically protecting the memory

Answer: D

The correct option is D.

31. A countermeasure to protect an embedded system is:

A. Reducing signal strength and signal information

B. Shielding the CRT to protect against leakage

C. Using application-specific algorithm masking

D. Strengthening the physical packaging

Answer: D

The correct option is D.

32. Software that avoids ambiguities and hidden assumptions relates best to what secure design principle?

A. Keep code simple and small

B. Use a consistent coding style

C. Use encapsulation cautiously

D. Allocate memory and other resources carefully

Answer: A

The correct option is A.

33. Proper indentation and spacing contribute to what secure design principle?

A. Keep code simple and small

B. Use a consistent coding style

C. Use encapsulation cautiously

D. Allocate memory and other resources carefully

Answer: B

The correct option is B.

34. Preventing the leakage of security information contributes to what secure design principle?

A. Keep code simple and small

B. Use a consistent coding style

C. Use encapsulation cautiously

D. Allocate memory and other resources carefully

Answer: C

The correct option is C.

35. The type of mechanism that manages events that interrupt the normal flow of software is:

A. Flow control

B. Event handling

C. Interrupt handling

D. Exception handling

Answer: D

Option D is the correct answer. Options A, B, and C are distracters.

36. The best or highest level of exception-safe software is:
    A. Basic exception safety
    B. Strong exception safety
    C. Failure transparency
    D. No-leak guarantee

    Answer: C

    The correct option is C.
37. The worst or lowest level of exception-safe software is:
    A. No guarantee
    B. Strong exception safety
    C. Failure transparency
    D. No-leak guarantee

    Answer: A

    The correct option is A.
38. An effective exception handling practice for detecting abnormal behavior is:
    A. Event monitors
    B. Anomaly awareness
    C. Core dump prevention
    D. Security error and failure handling

    Answer: B

    The correct option is B.
39. Which of the following does ''secure'' configuration management provide?
    A. Strong authentication of SDLC participants
    B. Version control for SDLC artifacts
    C. Change management for SDLC artifacts
    D. Capability to roll back changes

    Answer: A

    The correct option is A.
40. Which of the following categories of tools addresses taint analysis?
    A. Compiler security checking and enforcement
    B. Safe software libraries
    C. Runtime error checking and safety enforcement
    D. Code obfuscation

    Answer: A

    The correct option is A.

41. Which of the following categories of tools addresses security wrappers?
    A. Compiler security checking and enforcement
    B. Safe software libraries
    C. Runtime error checking and safety enforcement
    D. Code obfuscation

    Answer: C

    The correct option is C.

42. Which of the following categories of tools addresses functions that bound the buffer?
    A. Compiler security checking and enforcement
    B. Safe software libraries
    C. Runtime error checking and safety enforcement
    D. Code obfuscation

    Answer: B

    The correct option is B.

43. Which of the following categories of tools addresses changes to the control flow?
    A. Compiler security checking and enforcement
    B. Safe software libraries
    C. Runtime error checking and safety enforcement
    D. Code obfuscation

    Answer: D

    The correct option is D.

44. Which type of code is highest priority in a code review?
    A. Code written in managed programming languages
    B. Code written in unmanaged programming languages
    C. Old code
    D. Code that increases the attack surface

    Answer: D

    The correct option is D.

45. A wholly manual code review can produce good results if:
    A. The code base is small and simple.
    B. The code base is large and complex.
    C. The code does not contain high-consequence functions.
    D. The code does not handle sensitive data.

    Answer: A

    The correct option is A.

46. An automated code review is more efficient if:

    A. The code base is small.

    B. The code base is large.

    C. The code contains high-consequence functions.

    D. The code handles sensitive data.

    Answer: B

    The correct option is B.

47. The degree to which the source code of the program has been inspected is:

    A. Code definition

    B. Code specification

    C. Code complexity

    D. Code coverage

    Answer: D

    Option D is the correct answer. Options A, B, and C are distracters.

48. Software flaws can be considered vulnerabilities if they can be exploited in a way that can prevent the software's reliable information and:

    A. They are outside the control of an attacker.

    B. They are externally accessible to an attacker.

    C. They are extensible by an attacker.

    D. They are part of the attack surface.

    Answer: B

    Option B is the correct answer. A, C and D are distracters.

49. No security vulnerability is possible if:

    A. The data is outside the control of an attacker.

    B. The data is externally accessible to an attacker.

    C. The data is extensible by an attacker.

    D. The data is part of the attack surface.

    Answer: A

    Option A is the correct answer. Options B, C and D are distracters.

50. An off-by-one error is caused by:

    A. An increase in bug density

    B. Improper error handling

    C. Improper data validation

    D. Misuse of bounded functions

    Answer: D

    Option D is the correct answer. Options A, B, and C are distracters.

51. Examining software code without executing it is:
    A. Tracing
    B. Static analysis
    C. Dynamic analysis
    D. Profiling

    Answer: B

    The correct option is B. Options A and D are types of dynamic analysis.

52. Examining software code as it executes in a running application is:
    A. Tracing
    B. Static analysis
    C. Dynamic analysis
    D. Profiling

    Answer: C

    The correct option is C. Options A and D are types of dynamic analysis.

53. A type of static analysis performed on intermediate code is:
    A. Binary analysis
    B. Byte code scanning
    C. Source code analysis
    D. Manual code review

    Answer: B

    The correct option is B.

54. A type of static analysis performed on compiled C code is:
    A. Binary analysis
    B. Byte code scanning
    C. Source code analysis
    D. Manual code review

    Answer: A

    The correct option is A.

55. A false positive in code analysis refers to a:
    A. False alarm
    B. Vulnerability missed
    C. Code flaw
    D. Software weakness

    Answer: A

    The correct option is A.

56. A false negative in code analysis refers to a:
    A. False alarm
    B. Vulnerability missed

C. Code flaw

D. Software weakness

Answer: B

The correct option is B.

57. What can increase the difficulty of finding the real security vulnerabilities in the software?

A. A large number of false positives

B. A large number of false negatives

C. A small number of false positives

D. A small number of false negatives

Answer: A

The correct option is A.

58. The primary advantage of a byte code scanner over a source code security analyzer for a managed code programming language is:

A. It has a lower false positive rate.

B. It does not require the source code.

C. It has a lower false negative rate.

D. It analyzes the software in its execution environment.

Answer: B

The correct option is B.

59. A dynamic program analysis tool:

A. Has a lower false positive rate than a static analysis tool

B. Analyzes the source code of the program

C. Has a lower false negative rate than a static analysis tool

D. Analyzes the software in its execution environment

Answer: D

Option D is the correct answer. Options A, B, and C are distracters.

60. Attack path tracing:

A. Is a static code analysis technique

B. Is used to transparently observe an application during testing

C. Has a lower false negative rate than a static analysis tool

D. Analyzes the source code of the software

Answer: B

Option B is the correct answer. Options A, C, and D are distracters.

61. Code analysis tools are used in the development phase of the software life cycle (SDL) to:

A. Performance test the application

B. Transparently observe an application during testing

C. Quality assurance test the application

D. Analyze the source code of the software

Answer: D

Option D is the correct answer. Options A, B, and C discuss activities that are typically conducted in the quality assurance phase of the SDL.

62. Preventing unauthorized modification of software is known as:

A. Anti-corruption

B. Anti-tampering

C. Anti-modification

D. Un-deletion

Answer: B

The correct option is B.

63. The most common hardware-based anti-tampering protection is:

A. Hardware dongles

B. Trusted processors

C. Trusted platform modules (TPMs)

D. Key fobs

Answer: B

The correct option is B. Options A and C are not the most common hardware-based anti-tampering protections. Option D, a key fob, can take on a variety of meanings, including security token, keychain, or USB flash drive, and is not the best available answer.

64. Which type of anti-tampering device checks and verifies every piece of hardware and software that requests to be run on a computer during the boot-up process?

A. Hardware dongles

B. Trusted processors

C. Trusted platform modules (TPMs)

D. Key fobs

Answer: B

The correct option is B.

65. Which type of anti-tampering device dynamically encrypts and decrypts critical portions (or all) of the software code at runtime?

A. Encryption wrappers

B. Code obfuscation

C. Software watermarking and fingerprinting

D. Guarding

Answer: A

The correct option is A.

66. Which type of anti-tampering devices embeds information into software?

    A. Encryption wrappers

    B. Code obfuscation

    C. Software watermarking and fingerprinting

    D. Guarding

    Answer: C

    The correct option is C.

67. Which type of anti-tampering transforms code so it is more difficult to reverse engineer?

    A. Encryption wrappers

    B. Code obfuscation

    C. Software watermarking and fingerprinting

    D. Guarding

    Answer: B

    The correct option is B.

68. Which type of anti-tampering technique injects cooperating protection components into code?

    A. Encryption wrappers

    B. Code obfuscation

    C. Software watermarking and fingerprinting

    D. Guarding

    Answer: D

    The correct option is D.

69. A device designed to show that tampering occurred is:

    A. Tamper evident

    B. Tamper resistant

    C. Tamper proof

    D. Steganography

    Answer: A

    The correct option is A. Option C is a distracter. Option D, steganography, is hidden writing.

70. A device designed to be resilient to tampering is:

    A. Tamper evident

    B. Tamper resistant

    C. Tamper proof

    D. Steganography

    Answer: B

    The correct option is B. Option C is a distracter. Option D, steganography, is hidden writing.

71. Preventing direct communication between components is a characteristic of:

 A. Interfaces

 B. Guards

 C. Watermarking

 D. Encryption wrappers

 Answer: A

 Option A is the correct answer. Options B, C, and D are types of anti-tampering techniques.

Chapter 5

1. Assessing whether a software product meets the requirements of a particular specification or standard is known as which one of the following?

 A. Logic testing

 B. Stress testing

 C. Conformance testing

 D. Unit testing

 Answer: C

 The correct option is C.

2. Increasing the load on a software system beyond normal operating capacity describes which of the following?

 A. Logic testing

 B. Stress testing

 C. Conformance testing

 D. Unit testing

 Answer: B

 The correct option is B.

3. Code written by a developer to test an individual method best describes which of the following?

 A. Logic testing

 B. Stress testing

 C. Conformance testing

 D. Unit testing

 Answer: D

 The correct option is D.

4. Analysis of the context of a business decision best describes which of the following?

A. Logic testing
B. Stress testing
C. Conformance testing
D. Unit testing

Answer: A

The correct option is A.

5. Which of the following involves validating the positive and negative requirements of the software?

A. Functional testing
B. Performance testing
C. Environment testing
D. Fault injection

Answer: A

The correct option is A.

6. Throughput, processing delay, and load are metrics used in which kind of testing?

A. Functional testing
B. Performance testing
C. Environment testing
D. Fault injection

Answer: B

The correct option is B.

7. Which of the following techniques involves examining the source code for the absence of security characteristics?

A. Source code analysis
B. Property-based testing
C. Black box debugging
D. Dynamic code analysis

Answer: B

The correct option is B.

8. Which of the following techniques is used to monitor behaviors external to the binary component?

A. Source code analysis
B. Property-based testing
C. Black box debugging
D. Dynamic code analysis

Answer: C

The correct option is C.

9. Which of the following techniques is used to trace system calls as the software is executing?

   A. Source code analysis

   B. Property-based testing

   C. Black box debugging

   D. Dynamic code analysis

   Answer: D

   The correct option is D.

10. Which of the following techniques is particularly useful for finding incorrect use of pointers and arrays?

    A. Binary fault injection

    B. Property-based testing

    C. Source code fault injection

    D. Black box debugging

    Answer: C

    The correct option is C.

11. Which of the following uses environmental data to simulate and automate real-world attack scenarios?

    A. Binary fault injection

    B. Property-based testing

    C. Source code fault injection

    D. Black box debugging

    Answer: A

    The correct option is A.

12. Which of the following evaluates the functionality, reliability, and performance of a group of components?

    A. Regression testing

    B. Interoperability testing

    C. Functional testing

    D. Integration testing

    Answer: D

    The correct option is D.

13. Which of the following evaluates whether an application can exchange data with other components?

    A. Regression testing

    B. Interoperability testing

C. Functional testing

D. Integration testing

Answer: B

The correct option is B.

14. Which of the following involves testing against a reference implementation of the software?

A. Regression testing

B. Interoperability testing

C. Functional testing

D. Integration testing

Answer: B

The correct option is B.

15. Bug-tracking systems commonly allow reporting, assignment, tracking, and which other necessary feature?

A. Functionality

B. Determination

C. Prioritization

D. Visualization

Answer: C

Option C is the correct answer. Options A and B are distracters. Option D is a good feature, but not necessary.

16. Which of the following has the largest attack surface?

A. Code that is restricted to remote access by an anonymous user

B. Code that is restricted to local access by an administrative user

C. Code that is restricted to remote access by an authorized user

D. Code that is restricted to local access by an authorized user

Answer: A

The correct option is A.

17. The testing of a system to verify that modifications have not caused unintended effects is:

A. Regression testing

B. Interoperability testing

C. Functional testing

D. Integration testing

Answer: A

The correct option is A.

18. The reemergence of software faults could be caused by which of the following?

    A. Regression testing

    B. Software brittleness

    C. Functional testing

    D. Software rigidness

    Answer: B

    The correct option is B. Option A is used to ensure that faults have not reemerged. Options C and D are distracters.

19. A tester who is assigned or hired to evaluate the security of an organization's software system from the perspective of an attacker is known as which one of the following?

    A. An ethical hacker

    B. A cracker

    C. A phreaker

    D. A system administrator

    Answer: A

    The correct option is A. Option B refers to a malicious hacker; option C is a hacker of telecommunication systems such as the public telephone network; and option D, a system administrator, is an individual responsible for an organization's computer system operation and maintenance.

20. Which one of the following best describes a white box test conducted by a testing team?

    A. The testing team has knowledge that might be relevant to a specific type of attack by a person internal to the organization.

    B. The testing team is provided with no information and begins the testing by gathering information on its own initiative.

    C. The team has as much knowledge as possible about the network and computing resources to be evaluated.

    D. The team is restricted in the type of results that can be reported.

    Answer: C

    The correct option is C. Option A refers to a gray box test; option B describes a black box test; and option D is a made-up distracter.

21. Which one of the following test types evaluates an application when the development is nearing completion and minor changes are anticipated?

    A. Acceptance

    B. Unit

    C. Beta

    D. Alpha

    Answer: D

The correct option is D. Option A refers to a test that is conducted on project completion to determine if the customer specifications have been met over a specified period of time; option B is a test in which a programmer performs a detailed evaluation of code modules and code functions; and option C is conducted when development and testing are completed and final problems are found before software release.

22. Which one of the following is a security testing methodology that gives the tester insight into the strength of the target's network security by simulating an attack from a malicious source?

A. Integration test

B. Load test

C. Regression test

D. Penetration test

Answer: D

The correct option is D. Option A refers to a test that integrates applications and individual code modules to determine if they work properly together; option B is a test conducted to determine if the system can operate under heavy loads or demands and what effect the loads have on the system response time; and option C is conducted to perform re-testing after changes or upgrades to the software or its operating environment.

23. Which one of the following provides guidance and metrics for conducting security tests and has test cases that are divided into five channels (sections)?

A. Open Source Security Testing Methodology Manual (OSSTMM)

B. System Security Engineering Capability Maturity Model

C. ISO 9126

D. DoD Information Assurance Process (DIAP)

Answer: A

The correct option is A. Option B refers to the method that describes those characteristics of security engineering processes essential to ensure good security engineering. Option C defines a software quality model and provides the means to project goals for the quality of a software product, and option D is a made-up distracter.

24. In general, a penetration test involves which one of the following three stages?

A. Specification, execution, and delivery

B. Preparation, execution, and delivery

C. Preparation, operation, and review

D. Review, execution, and delivery

Answer: B

The correct option is B. The other options are made-up distracters.

25. Which one of the following is true regarding an individual or team that is hired by an organization to perform a penetration test?
    A. The test carries no legal and ethical risks to the tester.
    B. The tester is not subject to any possibility of prosecution if damage is caused.
    C. The legal implications of conducting the test are implied and do not have to be agreed upon with the employer.
    D. The test carries legal and ethical risks to the tester.

    Answer: D

    The correct option is D. Penetration testing does pose risks to the tester and testing team, and written agreements should be in place to ensure that the testers are not responsible for inadvertent damage to data or systems. The employer and tester should mutually agree upon all aspects of the test.

26. Penetration testing is usually initiated with reconnaissance, which comprises which of the following pre-test phases?
    A. Footprinting, injecting, and enumerating
    B. Footprinting, scanning, and hiding tracks
    C. Monitoring, scanning, and enumerating
    D. Footprinting, scanning, and enumerating

    Answer: D

    The correct option is D. The other options are made-up distracters.

27. Which one of the following is ''obtaining information concerning the security profile of an organization and involves gathering data to create a blueprint of the organization's networks and systems''?
    A. Enumerating
    B. Scanning
    C. Footprinting
    D. Monitoring

    Answer: C

    The correct option is C. Option A refers to enumeration, which tries to paint a fairly complete picture of the target and identify valid user accounts or poorly protected resource elements; option B is the discovery of open ports and applications; and option D is a made-up distracter.

28. Which utility works by exploiting a feature of the Internet Protocol called time-to-live (TTL) and reveals the path IP packets travel between two systems?
    A. Whois
    B. Nslookup
    C. Traceroute
    D. NRoute

    Answer: C

The correct option is C. Option A acquires information such as the domain's registrant, its administrative and technical contacts, and a listing of their domain servers; option B queries Internet domain name servers and displays information that can be used to diagnose Domain Name System (DNS) infrastructure and find additional IP addresses; and option D is a made-up distracter.

29. Which one of the following is a popular port scanner for Linux and Windows and can scan a system in a variety of stealth modes?

    A. Nmap

    B. LinMap

    C. WinMap

    D. NRoute

    Answer: A

    The correct option is A. The other options are made-up distracters.

30. Which one of the following is a popular open source, powerful network vulnerability scanner that can be configured to run a variety of scans?

    A. Nvul

    B. Nessus

    C. Nscan

    D. NRoute

    Answer: B

    The correct option is B. Options A, C, and D are made-up distracters.

31. Which one of the following are the three basic types of password cracking tests?

    A. Dictionary, hybrid, and brute force

    B. Encyclopedia, hybrid, and brute force

    C. Dictionary, true, and brute force

    D. Dictionary, hybrid, and statistical

    Answer: A

    The correct option is A. Options B, C, and D are made-up distracters.

32. Which one of the following is a program that performs unknown and unwanted functions and is an unauthorized program contained in a legitimate program?

    A. Stealth

    B. Trojan horse

    C. Proxy

    D. Hybrid

    Answer: B

    The correct option is B. Options A, C, and D are made-up distracters.

33. Which one of the following is considered the grandfather of Trojan horses and has spawned a considerable number of imitators?

A. BackOrifice 2000 (BO2K)

B. NetCat

C. FrontOrifice 2000 (FO2K)

D. Hybrid

Answer: A

The correct option is A.

34. Which one of the following attacks occurs when a program allocates a specific block length of memory for storage, but then attempts to store more data than the block was intended to hold?

A. Denial of service

B. Capacity overrun

C. SQL injection

D. Buffer overflow

Answer: D

The correct option is D. Option A refers to an attack that overloads the capacity of a computing resource and causes it to degrade or crash; option B is a made-up distracter; and option C describes a class of injection exploits that occur when one scripting language is embedded inside another scripting language.

35. Which one of the following are the two basic types of intrusion detection systems (IDSs)?

A. Signature recognition and anomaly detection

B. Anomaly recognition and anomaly detection

C. Signature recognition and signature detection

D. File recognition and anomaly detection

Answer: A

The correct option is A. Options B, C, and D are made-up distracters.

36. Which one of the following refers to the LAN (WLAN) family of standards that specifies wireless connectivity and defines aspects of frequency hopping and direct-sequence spread spectrum (DSSS) systems for use in the 2.4 MHz ISM (industrial, scientific, medical) band?

A. IEEE 804.12

B. IEEE 802.11

C. IEEE 802.16

D. IEEE 803.11

Answer: B

The correct option is B. Options A, C, and D are made-up distracters.

37. Which one of the following is a term used to describe the process of a hacker who, armed with a laptop and a wireless adapter card and traveling by car, bus, subway train, or other form of mechanized transport, goes around sniffing for WLANs?

    A. War scanning

    B. WLAN scanning

    C. WLAN driving

    D. War driving

    Answer: D

    The correct option is D. Options A, B, and C are made-up distracters.

38. Which one of the following refers to a black box software testing technique that basically consists of finding implementation bugs using malformed/semi-malformed data injection in an automated fashion?

    A. Fuzzing

    B. Impersonating

    C. Simulation

    D. Scuzzing

    Answer: A

    The correct option is A. Options B, C, and D are made-up distracters.

39. Which one of the following is a testing method based on inputs derived from mutation, generation, and conformance approaches?

    A. Fuzzing

    B. Regression

    C. Simulation

    D. Scanning

    Answer: A

    The correct option is A.

40. Which testing method comprises the steps of identifying active machines, discovering open ports and available services, fingerprinting the operating system, and mapping the network?

    A. Fuzzing

    B. Regression

    C. Enumeration

    D. Scanning

    Answer: D

    The correct option is D. Option A uses malformed data as inputs; option B is involved with re-testing; and option C, enumeration, attempts to compile a complete picture of the target by incorporating all obtained information.

41. Which one of the following refers to an IP header field that is an ever-increasing counter that keeps track of each router hop as the packet travels to a target?

    A. Time-to-Travel (TTT)

    B. Round Trip Time (RTT)

    C. Time-for-Loop (TFL)

    D. Time-to-Live (TTL)

    Answer: D

    The correct option is D. Options A, B, and C are made-up distracters.

42. The ping utility is useful in identifying active machines. To accomplish this identification, ping sends which one of the following packets?

    A. ICMP Echo Request

    B. TCP Echo Request

    C. ICMP Echo Reply

    D. TCP Echo Reply

    Answer: A

    The correct option is A. Options B, C, and D are made-up distracters.

43. Which one of the following is the response to a ping if the target is not live?

    A. An ICMP Echo Reply message

    B. A "Request timed out" message

    C. A TCP Echo Reply packet

    D. An ICMP Echo Request message

    Answer: B

    The correct option is B. Options A, C, and D are made-up distracters.

44. How many total TCP and UDP port numbers are there?

    A. 1,024

    B. 8,984

    C. 16,664

    D. 65,535

    Answer: D

    The correct option is D.

45. Which range of ports is called the "well-known ports"?

    A. 1 to 1,024

    B. 1 to 10,240

    C. 1,024 to 8,984

    D. 1 to 8,984

    Answer: A

    The correct option is A.

46. Which one of the following is the best description of active vs. passive fingerprinting?

    A. Active fingerprinting is less accurate.

    B. Active fingerprinting is less detectable.

    C. Passive fingerprinting is more detectable.

    D. Passive fingerprinting is less detectable.

    Answer: D

    The correct option is D.

47. Which scanning method is often referred to as half-open scanning because, unlike TCP connect(), a full TCP connection is never opened?

    A. TCP SYN

    B. TCP SYN/ACK

    C. TCP FIN

    D. TCP FTP proxy

    Answer: A

    The correct option is A. Option B, SYN/ACK is used to determine if a port is open or closed; option C, TCP FIN, works similarly to a SYN/ACK scan; and option D, TCP FTP proxy, is a bounce attack that uses a proxy machine.

48. Which one of the following is a technique used to ping a batch of devices and help the attacker determine which are active and which are not?

    A. Ping all

    B. Ping SYN

    C. Ping footprint

    D. Ping sweep

    Answer: D

    The correct option is D. Options A, B, and C are made-up distracters.

49. Ports can have which one of the following sets of three states?

    A. Open, closed, or filtered

    B. Open, listening, or filtered

    C. Set, closed, or filtered

    D. Open, closed, or engaged

    Answer: A

    The correct option is A. Options B, C, and D are made-up distracters.

50. Which one of the following best describes one of the characteristics of the User Datagram Protocol (UDP) relative to the Transmission Control Protocol (TCP)?

    A. Full-duplex

    B. Best-effort delivery

C. Connection-oriented

D. Reliable

Answer: B

The correct option is B. Options A, C, and D are characteristics of TCP.

51. Which one of the following methods can be used to discover what services are running on the open ports and also provides important information about what type and version of software is running?

A. IP grabbing

B. Banner grabbing

C. Connection scanning

D. Data capturing

Answer: B

The correct option is B. Options A, C, and D are made-up distracters.

52. Which type of black box simulation testing is useful in detecting a failure to implement a critical security requirement, discovering general implementation errors, and finding errors in the test plan?

A. Data enumeration unit testing

B. Requirements simulation testing

C. Quality assurance (QA) acceptance testing

D. System valuation testing

Answer: C

The correct option is C. Options A, B, and D are made-up distracters.

53. Which one of the following terms is best described by ''the inability of a system or component to perform its required functions within specified performance requirements''?

A. Fault

B. Error

C. Tested element

D. Failure

Answer: D

The correct option is D. Option A, fault, is ''a manifestation of an error in software. A fault, if encountered, may cause a failure.'' Option B, error, can result in a fault, and option C is a made-up distracter.

54. Which one of the following is an effective method for testing for failure in secure software systems?

A. Software failure modes and effects analysis (SFMEA)

B. Software failure modes and regression analysis (SFMRA)

C. Software testing modes and results analysis (STMRA)

D. Software effects and modes analysis (SEMA)

Answer: A

The correct option is A. Options B, C, and D are made-up distracters.

55. Which one of the following types of testing subjects the software to extreme conditions such as inadequate memory capacity, insufficient communication bandwidth, denial-of-service attacks, and hardware malfunctions?

A. Software failure modes and effects analysis (SFMEA)

B. Software failure modes and regression analysis (SFMRA)

C. Stress testing

D. Constraint testing

Answer: C

The correct option is C. Option A is testing for failure; options B and D are made-up distracters.

56. The tests in NIST Special Publication 800-22, the diehard tests, and the ''ent'' tests are useful in determining which one of the following characteristics?

A. Strength of cryptographic algorithms

B. Strength of cryptographic keys

C. Strength of random number generators

D. Strength of secure software

Answer: C

The correct option is C. Options A, B, and D are made-up distracters.

57. Which one of the following programs is a joint effort of the U.S. National Institute of Standards and Technology (NIST) and the Communications Security Establishment (CSE) of Canada to validate cryptographic modules?

A. Cryptographic Module Validation Program (CMVP)

B. Cryptographic Module Verification Program (CMVP)

C. Cryptographic Module Assurance Program (CMAP)

D. Cryptographic Module Certification Program (CMCP)

Answer: A

The correct option is A. Options B, C, and D are made-up distracters.

58. Which one of the following NIST publications is entitled ''Security Requirements for Cryptographic Modules'' and is designed for cryptographic modules to be tested against by vendors of these modules?

A. SP 800-22

B. FIPS PUB 140-3

C. FIPS PUB 140-7

D. SP 800-26

Answer: B

The correct option is B. Options A, C, and D are made-up distracters.

59. The NIST publication "Security Requirements for Cryptographic Modules" specifies a security level that "attempts to prevent the unauthorized access to Critical Security Parameters (CSPs) held within the cryptographic module." This security level is labeled as which one of the following?

A. Level 1

B. Level 2

C. Level 3

D. Level 4

Answer: C

The correct option is C by the definition of Level 3.

60. The annualized loss expectancy (ALE) if a critical asset is disabled or compromised by a malicious attack on a organization's software system is calculated as follows:

A. ALE = SLE x ARO

B. ALE = SLA x ARO

C. ALE = SLE x AYO

D. ALE = SLE x ARR

Answer: A

The correct option is A by the definition of ALE. Options B, C, and D are made-up distracters.

61. The Information Assurance Technical Framework (IATF) Document 3.1 defines which one of the following attacks as traffic analysis, monitoring of unprotected communications, decrypting weakly encrypted traffic, and capture of authentication information (such as passwords)?

A. Close-in

B. Insider

C. Active

D. Passive

Answer: D

The correct option is D. Option A, close-in, refers to an attack where individuals attain close physical proximity to networks and systems; option B, insider, refers to insiders intentionally eavesdropping, stealing, or damaging information. Option C, active, is an attack that includes attempts to circumvent or break protection features, introduce malicious code, or steal or modify information.

62. Which one of the following refers to the NIST publication "Standards for Security Categorization of Federal Information and Information Systems," which address characterization of impacts of threats realized?

    A. SP 800-22

    B. SP 800-30

    C. FIPS 205

    D. FIPS 199

    Answer: D

    The correct option is D.

63. When should the following actions be performed? Enter test results and the corresponding version of the software module under test into configuration management; ascertain security requirements that were not included in the original specification and implementation; assess risk posed to the software system from failure to incorporate security requirements that were not included in the original specification; and determine risk to the software system from failure to modify the software to address security requirements that were not included in the original specification.

    A. Before testing

    B. Following testing

    C. During testing

    D. During installation

    Answer: B

    The correct option is B. Options A, C, and D are made-up distracters.

64. Which one of the following is defined as the "totality of characteristics of an entity that bears on its ability to satisfy stated and implied needs"?

    A. Quality

    B. Assurance

    C. Reliability

    D. Security

    Answer: A

    The correct option is A, by definition.

65. Standard ISO 9126-1 defines which one of the following models?

    A. Software assurance model

    B. Software quality model

    C. Software capability maturity model

    D. System security engineering capability maturity model

    Answer: B

    The correct option is B, by definition.

66. Which one of the following sets names characteristics of ISO Standard 9126-1?

    A. Functionality, reliability, usability, and efficiency

    B. Operability, reliability, usability, and efficiency

    C. Functionality, quality, usability, and efficiency

    D. Functionality, reliability, usability, and assessibility

    Answer: A

    The correct option is A. Options B, C, and D are made-up distracters.

67. The Open Source Security Testing Methodology Manual (OSSTMM) 3.0 defines an approach to security testing at an operational level. Specifically, the OSSTMM defines the scope of an audit as encompassing which one the following three sets of channels?

    A. Communications Security, Physical Security, Operational Security

    B. Encryption Security, Physical Security, Spectrum Security

    C. Communications Security, Disaster Recovery, Spectrum Security

    D. Communications Security, Physical Security, Spectrum Security

    Answer: D

    The correct option is D. Options A, B, and C are made-up distracters.

68. The Open Source Security Testing Methodology Manual (OSSTMM) 3.0 is executed in which one of the following sets of four phases?

    A. Specification, Definitions, Information, Interactive Controls

    B. Regulatory, Operational, Information, Interactive Controls

    C. Regulatory, Definitions, Information, Interactive Controls

    D. Regulatory, Definitions, Evaluation, Interactive Controls

    Answer: C

    The correct option is C. Options A, B, and D are made-up distracters.

69. The U.S. Department of Defense has established which one of the following processes for authorizing the operation of DoD information systems?

    A. DoD Information Assurance Certification and Accreditation Process (DIACAP)

    B. DoD Information System Certification Process (DISCP)

    C. DoD Computer System Assurance Process (DCSAP)

    D. National Information Assurance Accreditation Process (NIAAP)

    Answer: A

    The correct option is A. Options B, C, and D are made-up distracters.

70. Implementing a risk mitigation strategy following secure software testing includes applying appropriate controls. These controls are which one of the following types?

    A. Administrative, management, operational, or a combination of these

    B. Technical, maintenance, operational, or a combination of these

C. Technical, management, predictive, or a combination of these

D. Technical, management, operational, or a combination of these

Answer: D

The correct option is D. Options A, B, and C are made-up distracters.

Chapter 6

1. In the secure software development cycle, which one of the following statements is false?

   A. Secure software issues should be addressed prior to deployment.

   B. Costs to repair software defects are much lower in the pre-deployment phase than in the post-deployment phase.

   C. Black box security tests can be effective means to uncover and address software security issues if used during the system software test phase prior to deployment.

   D. Costs to repair software defects are much higher in the pre-deployment phase than in the post-deployment phase.

   Answer: D

   The correct option is D. It is a general fact that costs to repair defects are less the earlier in the development life cycle they are addressed.

2. In what part of the software supply process are final reports of the test management system provided to the acquirer along with a set of test data to verify that all specified quality control test points have been covered according to previously agreed-upon terms?

   A. During the specification phase

   B. During the delivery and completion phases

   C. During the implementation and testing phases

   D. During the operations and maintenance phases

   Answer: B

   The correct option is B. The items listed are part of the deliverables in the completion phase of a software project.

3. In completion delivery, what elements should be based on the type of software system to be delivered and anticipated types of defects which might be inherent in the software?

   A. Completion goals

   B. System specifications

   C. System requirements

   D. System validation items

   Answer: A

The correct option is A. The secure software system must be evaluated and tested against previously specified quantitative test completion criteria, and these completion criteria specify when the completion goals have been reached.

4. The degree of achievement of the completion criteria, mitigating issues in instances where the completion criteria were not achieved, the case for not including specific code units in completion testing, and the performance of the software system are components of which of the following items?

   A. Test cases

   B. Documentation associated with the completion criteria

   C. Verification of the system against the specifications

   D. Validation of the system against the real-world requirements

   Answer: B

   The correct option is B. Documentation has to be provided to the acquiring organization showing that the completion criteria have been met. The other options are distracters.

5. According to the United Kingdom Ministry of Defense Standard 00-56, Issue 4, June 2007, what is defined as the final step in risk management?

   A. Risk acceptance

   B. Risk assessment

   C. Risk analysis

   D. Disposal

   Answer: A

   The correct option is A. Risk is usually accepted when the level of risk has been reduced to a level that is tolerable and practical to achieve.

6. In the event there are risks in a software system that cannot be accepted, which one of the following is the best practice to follow?

   A. Transfer the risk to an outside party

   B. Accept the risk anyway

   C. Conduct more research

   D. Reiterate the risk management and risk reduction processes.

   Answer: D

   The correct option is D. Option A, risk transference, is usually an option where some level of risk mitigation as been applied and the residual risk is transferred to an outside party such as an insurance company. Option B, accept the risk, should not be done because it has already been stated the risk is unacceptable. Option C is a distracter.

7. Which one of the following elements is *not* a part of an effective risk acceptance methodology?

   A. The risk acceptance process should be a part of the initial software system specifications.

B. The risk acceptance process should specify how the evidence for a residual risk tolerance level is to be developed and presented.

C. Risk acceptance criteria should be based on available funding.

D. Risk acceptance should be treated as a continuing process that takes into account new threats and mitigation activities.

Answer: C

Option C should not be part of a risk acceptance methodology because accepting risk should not be influenced by budget conditions.

8. The process of tracking and approving changes to a software system is known as which one of the following?

A. Configuration management

B. Requirements specification

C. Patching

D. Rework

Answer: A

Option A is the definition of configuration management. The other options are made-up distracters.

9. Which one of the following is *not* a primary function of configuration management or change control?

A. To ensure that the change is implemented in an orderly manner through formalized testing

B. To analyze the effect of the change on the system after implementation

C. To insulate the user base from knowledge of the impending change

D. To reduce the negative impact that the change might have had on the computing services and resources

Answer: C

The correct option is C. One of the main functions of configuration management is to ensure that the user base is informed of the impending change.

10. Which one of the following are the five generally accepted procedures to implement and support the change control process?

A. Evaluating, cataloging, scheduling, implementing, and reporting the change

B. Applying for, cataloging, scheduling, implementing, and reporting the change

C. Applying for, cataloging, scheduling, implementing, and evaluating the change

D. Applying for, reviewing, scheduling, implementing, and reporting the change

Answer: B

The correct option is B. Options A, C, and D are made-up distracters.

11. Which one of the following regarding configuration management entails decomposing the verification system into identifiable, understandable, manageable, trackable units known as configuration items (CIs)?

A. Configuration control
B. Configuration auditing
C. Configuration status accounting
D. Configuration identification

Answer: D

The correct option is D. Option A, configuration control, is a means of ensuring that system changes are approved before being implemented. Option B, configuration auditing, is the quality assurance component of configuration management. Option C, configuration status accounting, documents the status of configuration control activities and, in general, provides the information needed to manage a configuration effectively.

12. What are the four major elements of the BCP process?

    A. Requirements development, business impact assessment, business continuity plan development, plan approval and implementation
    B. Scope and plan initiation, business impact assessment, business continuity plan development, plan approval and implementation
    C. Scope and plan initiation, business impact assessment, disaster recovery plan development, plan approval and implementation
    D. Scope and plan initiation, business impact assessment, business continuity plan development, plan maintenance

    Answer: B

    The correct option is B. Options A, C, and D are made-up distracters.

13. What activity addresses the preservation of the business in the face of major disruptions to normal operations?

    A. Business continuity planning (BCP)
    B. Disaster recovery planning (DRP)
    C. Business recovery planning (BRP)
    D. Intrusion detection and prevention (IDP)

    Answer: A

    The correct option is A. Option B, DRP, is concerned with restoring the operation of the business's information systems following a harmful event. Options C and D are distracters.

14. The documented, organized plan for emergency response, backup operations, and recovery maintained by an organization as part of its security program that will ensure the availability of critical resources and facilitate the continuity of operations in an emergency situation is known as which one of the following?

    A. Disaster recovery plan
    B. Continuity of operations plan

C. Contingency plan

D. Business continuity plan

Answer: C

The correct option is C, by definition. See previous question for definitions of BCP and DRP. Option B, continuity of operations plan, contains the procedures documented to ensure continued critical operations during any period where normal operations are impossible.

15. What are the three primary goals of a business impact assessment?

    A. Prioritization of critical systems, estimation of downtime, identification of resource requirements

    B. Prioritization of critical systems, estimation of downtime, estimation of impact costs

    C. Prioritization of critical systems, identification of alternate courses of action, identification of resource requirements

    D. Development of off-site resources, estimation of downtime, identification of alternate processing methods

    Answer: A

    The correct option is A. Options B, C, and D are made-up distracters.

16. In disaster recover planning, a critical system with a rating class of AA has which one of the following recovery time frames?

    A. Immediate

    B. Same business day

    C. Full functional recovery within 4 hours

    D. 24 to 72 hours downtime acceptable

    Answer: C

    The correct option is C. Option A corresponds to a AAA rating class, option B is in an A rating class, and option D refers to a rating class of C.

17. An alternate processing facility with most supporting peripheral equipment, but without the principal computing platforms is known as which one of the following?

    A. A hot site

    B. A cold site

    C. A warm site

    D. A neutral site

    Answer: C

    The correct option is C. Option A, hot site, is a site with all required computer hardware, software, and peripherals installed to begin alternate processing either immediately or within an acceptably short time frame. Option B, cold site, is a designated computer operations room with HVAC that has no computing systems installed and, therefore, would require a substantial effort to install the hardware and software required to begin alternate processing. Option D is a made-up distracter.

18. In implementing a disaster recovery plan, two teams should be organized to execute the recovery. These teams are known as which one of the following?

    A. Recovery and salvage teams

    B. Investigation and recovery teams

    C. Recovery and reconstructing teams

    D. Estimation and salvage teams

    Answer: A

    The correct option is A. Options B, C, and D are made-up distracters.

19. Which of the following evaluates whether or not software conforms to the specifications, regulations, or other conditions imposed on it while it was being developed?

    A. Verification

    B. Validation

    C. Security testing

    D. Accreditation

    Answer: A

    The correct option is A.

20. Which of the following evaluates whether or not software will satisfy its particular requirements (functional and nonfunctional) for its specific intended purpose?

    A. Verification

    B. Validation

    C. Security testing

    D. Accreditation

    Answer: B

    The correct option is B.

21. Which of the following is an attestation that a system has the authority to operate?

    A. Verification

    B. Validation

    C. Security testing

    D. Accreditation

    Answer: D

    The correct option is D.

22. Which of the following is the element of the Common Criteria that defines an implementation-independent specification of the security requirements and protections of a product that could be built?

    A. Protection profile

    B. Target of evaluation

    C. Security target

    D. Trusted computing base

    Answer: A

    The correct option is A.

23. Which of the following is the element of the Common Criteria that defines a listing of the security claims for a particular IT security product?

    A. Protection profile

    B. Target of evaluation

    C. Security target

    D. Trusted computing base

    Answer: C

    The correct option is C.

24. Which of the following is the element of the Common Criteria that refers to the product to be tested?

    A. Protection profile

    B. Target of evaluation

    C. Security target

    D. Trusted computing base

    Answer: B

    The correct option is B.

25. Which of the following involves testing against a defined cryptographic module and provides a suite of conformance tests to four security levels?

    A. BITS

    B. Common Criteria

    C. Federal Information Processing Standard (FIPS)

    D. ICSA Labs

    Answer: C

    The correct option is C.

26. Which of the following defines criteria intended for products and services that detect computer viruses prior to causing an infection?

    A. BITS

    B. Common Criteria

C. Federal Information Processing Standard (FIPS)

D. ICSA Labs

Answer: D

The correct option is D.

27. Which of the following is used to test technology products used to deliver financial services?

A. BITS

B. Common Criteria

C. Federal Information Processing Standard (FIPS)

D. ICSA Labs

Answer: A

The correct option is A.

28. Which of the following refers to information systems used to receive, process, store, display or transmit DoD information?

A. Defense Information Assurance Certification and Accreditation Process (DIACAP)

B. Federal Information Security Management Act (FISMA)

C. Election Assistance Commission (EAC)

D. Office of Management and Budget (OMB)

Answer: A

The correct option is A.

29. Which of the following assigned to NIST the responsibility for developing the following information system–related standards and guidelines?

A. Defense Information Assurance Certification and Accreditation Process (DIACAP)

B. Federal Information Security Management Act (FISMA)

C. Election Assistance Commission (EAC)

D. Office of Management and Budget (OMB)

Answer: B

The correct option is B.

30. Which of the following activities is conducted by a party that has no stake in the success or failure of the software?

A. Certification and accreditation

B. Verification and validation

C. Validation

D. Independent security testing

Answer: D

The correct option is D.

Chapter 7

1. An extended or special access to computing resources given to operators, system administrators, and some distributed computing users who have administrator privileges on their machines is known as which one of the following?

   A. Privileged entity access

   B. Resource access

   C. System entity access

   D. Managed user

   Answer: A

   The correct option is A. Options B, C, and D are made-up distracters.

2. Which type of operational control is designed to lower the amount and impact of unintentional errors and to prevent unauthorized intruders from internally or externally accessing the system?

   A. Detective

   B. Preventive

   C. Corrective

   D. Application

   Answer: B

   The correct option is B. Option A, detective controls, are used to detect errors that have occurred and operate after the fact. Option C, corrective controls, are used to mitigate the impact of a loss event through data recovery procedures. Option D, application controls, are designed into a software application to minimize and detect the software's operational irregularities.

3. Which one of the following is used to maintain operational assurance by conducting an ongoing activity that examines either the system or the users?

   A. Testing

   B. Evaluating

   C. Auditing

   D. Monitoring

   Answer: D

   The correct option is D. Options A and B are made-up distracters. Option C, auditing, is a one-time or periodic event to evaluate security.

4. Intrusion detection, penetration testing, and violation analysis are tools used to perform which one of the following?

   A. Evaluation

   B. Modification

C. Auditing

D. Monitoring

Answer: D

The correct option is D. Options A and B are made-up distracters. Option C, auditing, makes use of logs and audit trails.

5. Which type of intrusion detection system (IDS) operates on network segments and analyzes that segment's traffic?

A. Network-based

B. Segment-based

C. Web-based

D. Host-based

Answer: A

The correct option is A. Options B and C are made-up distracters. Option D refers to an IDS that operates on a specific host and detects malicious activity on that host only.

6. What type of intrusion detection system consists of a network appliance with a network interface card (NIC) that is operating in promiscuous mode and is intercepting and analyzing packets in real time?

A. Packet-based

B. Network-based

C. Segment-based

D. Interface-based

Answer: B

The correct option is B. The other options are made-up distracters.

7. Which one of the following best describes the types of packet signatures analyzed by a type of intrusion detection system?

A. String signatures, port signatures, and attack signatures

B. Sync signatures, port signatures, and header condition signatures

C. String signatures, IP signatures, and header condition signatures

D. String signatures, port signatures, and header condition signatures

Answer: D

The correct option is D. String signatures look for a text string that indicates a possible attack; port signatures watch for connection attempts to well-known, frequently attacked ports, and header condition signatures watch for dangerous or illogical combinations in packet headers. Options A, B, and C are made-up distracters.

8. Which type of intrusion detection system monitors a host operating system in order to detect inappropriate activity, writes to log files, and triggers alarms?

A. Host-based

B. Log-based

C. Segment-based

D. Platform-based

Answer: A

The correct option is A. The other options are made-up distracters.

9. An IDS can detect an attack through which of the following conceptual approaches?

   A. Character-based or statistical anomaly-based

   B. Signature-based or knowledge-based

   C. Signature-based or statistical anomaly-based

   D. Behavior-based or statistical anomaly-based

   Answer: C

   The correct option is C. Option A is a made-up distracter. In option B, signature-based and knowledge-based refer to the same type of ID. In Option D, behavior-based and statistical anomaly-based also refer to the same type of ID.

10. Which type of intrusion detection system is characterized by relatively lower false alarm rates (or positives) and provides alarms that are standardized and are clearly understandable by security personnel?

    A. Segment-based

    B. Statistical anomaly-based

    C. Signature-based

    D. Platform-based

    Answer: C

    The correct option is C. Options A and D are made-up distracters. Option B, statistical anomaly-based, has relatively higher false alarm rates than signature-based ID systems.

11. What is defined as "a baseline of user activity that is considered a routine level of user errors"?

    A. Clipping level

    B. Error level

    C. Threshold level

    D. Trigger level

    Answer: A

    The correct option is A. The other options are made-up distracters.

12. Which operational mechanism supports the discovery of both users' and outsiders' repeated attempts to bypass a system's protection mechanisms and allows for

discovery of any use of privileges that may occur when a user assumes a functionality with privileges greater than his or her own?

A. Profiling

B. Audit

C. Scanning

D. Testing

Answer: B

The correct option is B. Options A, C, and D are made-up distracters.

13. Which one of the following has these two primary components? (1) Creation and maintenance of intrusion detection systems (IDS) and processes for host and network monitoring and event notification, and (2) creation of a computer security incident response team (CSIRT)?

A. Incident management and response

B. Intrusion detection system

C. System audit

D. System monitoring

Answer: A

The correct option is A, by definition. Options B, C, and D are made-up distracters.

14. NIST Special Publication 800-61, "Computer Security Incident Handling Guide, Recommendations of the National Institute of Standards and Technology," January 2004, defines the incident response life cycle as which one of the following?

A. Evaluation; detection and analysis; containment, eradication, and recovery; and post-incident activity

B. Preparation; detection and analysis; containment, eradication, and recovery; and post-incident activity

C. Preparation; testing; containment, eradication, and recovery; and post-incident activity

D. Preparation; detection and analysis; containment, eradication, and recovery; and disposal

Answer: B

The correct option is B. Options A, C, and D are made-up distracters.

15. Which one of the following are steps in the incident handling guidelines of the Internet Engineering Task Force (IETF) RFC 2196, Site Security Handbook?

A. Preparing and planning, notification, identification, handling, and aftermath

B. Evaluation, notification, identification, handling, and aftermath

C. Preparing and planning, notification, confirmation, handling, and aftermath

D. Preparing and planning, notification, identification, handling, and recovery

Answer: A

The correct option is A. Options B, C, and D are made-up distracters.

16. As part of a structured program of intrusion detection and response, what is the commonly used, general name for a type of response group that may be created in an organization?

    A. Computer security technical response team (CSTRT)

    B. Computer incident response handling team (CIRHT)

    C. Enterprise security incident response team (ESIRT)

    D. Computer security incident response team (CSIRT)

    Answer: D

    The correct option is D. Options A, B, and C are made-up distracters.

17. In responding to an incident, what is the *first* and *primary* responsibility of the responding team?

    A. Protect human life and people's safety

    B. Protect restricted and/or internal data

    C. Prevent damage to systems

    D. Minimize disruption of computing resources

    Answer: A

    The correct option is A. Protecting human life is *always* the first priority in the event of an emergency or disaster.

18. One of multiple factors (events, conditions, or organizational factors) that contributed to or created the proximate cause and subsequent undesired outcome and if eliminated or modified would have prevented the undesired outcome is the definition of which one of the following?

    A. Principal cause

    B. Root cause

    C. Primary cause

    D. Fault cause

    Answer: B

    The correct option is B. Options A, C, and D are made-up distracters.

19. Which one of the following defines a process that can be applied to determine the true causes of events that can have negative consequences on health, quality, safety, reliability, and production?

    A. Primary cause analysis

    B. Principal cause analysis

    C. True cause analysis

    D. Root cause analysis

    Answer: D

    The correct option is D. Root cause analysis is also defined as "a structured evaluation method that identifies the root causes for an undesired outcome and the actions adequate to prevent recurrence. Root cause analysis should continue until organizational factors have been identified, or until data are exhausted." Options A, B, and C are made-up distracters.

20. Process implementation, problem and modification analysis, modification implementation, migration, and retirement are components of which one of the following?

    A. Software maintenance

    B. Software testing

    C. Software evaluation

    D. Software development

    Answer: A

    The correct option is A. Options B, C, and D are made-up distracters.

21. Incorporating changes into software maintenance to improve its performance, security, or maintainability is known as which one of the following?

    A. Perfective

    B. Adaptive

    C. Corrective

    D. Preventive

    Answer: A

    The correct option is A. Option B, adaptive, is upgrading software so that it can perform as required in a different operating environment; option C, corrective, is changing the software to fix problems uncovered after delivery. Option D, preventive, is the adaptation of software to discover hidden or latent faults and then effect required changes.

22. The process of controlling the deployment and maintenance of interim software releases into operational environments is known as which one of the following?

    A. Static analysis

    B. Policy management

    C. Debugging

    D. Patch management

    Answer: D

    The correct option is D. Options A, B, and C are made-up distracters.

23. "A vulnerability whose exploitation can result in compromise of the confidentiality, integrity, or availability of users' data or of the integrity or availability of processing resources" describes which one of the following Microsoft severity levels for security upgrades?

    A. Important

    B. Critical

    C. Moderate

    D. Low

    Answer: A

The correct option is A. Option B, critical, refers to a vulnerability whose exploitation can allow the propagation of an Internet worm without user action. Option C, moderate, refers to a vulnerability whose exploitation is mitigated to a significant degree by factors such as default configuration, auditing, or difficulty of exploitation. Option D, low, describes a vulnerability whose exploitation is extremely difficult or whose impact is minimal.

24. Which one of the following best describes the primary phases in patch management?

    A. Appraisal and inventory, patch categorization, assessment and planning, testing, and deployment

    B. Scheduling, patch categorization, assessment and planning, testing, and deployment

    C. Appraisal and inventory, patch categorization, assessment and planning, testing, and evaluation

    D. Appraisal and inventory, validation, assessment and planning, testing, and deployment

    Answer: A

    The correct option is A. Options B, C, and D are made-up distracters.

25. Three techniques commonly used for sanitization of data media are:

    A. Overwriting, degaussing, and cleansing

    B. Overwriting, degaussing, and destruction

    C. Saturation, degaussing, and destruction

    D. Overwriting, frosting, and destruction

    Answer: B

    The correct option is B. Options A, C, and D are made-up distracters.

26. The condition that refers to the data left on the media after the media has been erased is known as which one of the following?

    A. Degaussed state

    B. Residuals

    C. Object reuse

    D. Data remanence

    Answer: D

    The correct option is D, by definition. Options A and B are made-up distracters. Option C, object reuse, refers to reassignment to some subject of a storage medium (e.g., page frame, disk sector, magnetic tape) that contained one or more objects.

27. Configuring software with the most secure settings possible prior to deployment of the software is known as what?

    A. Security through obscurity

    B. Secure by design

C. Security design principles

D. Secure by default

Answer: D

The correct option is D. Options A, B, and C are distracters.

28. Why should software be tested in an environment that is similar to production instead of the actual production environment?

A. The untested software could expose the test environment to threats.

B. The production environment is isolated from real-world hostile conditions.

C. The untested software could expose the production environment to threats.

D. The production environment prevents all testing activities including attacks and exploits.

Answer: C

The correct option is C. Options A, B, and D are made-up distracters.

29. Which of the following is one of the principal duties of the BIOS during POST?

A. Verify the integrity of the BIOS code itself

B. Discover, size, and verify the UEFI checksum

C. Interrupt the execution of all other running programs

D. Protect the computer from pre-boot attacks

Answer: A

The correct option is A. Options B, C, and D are made-up distracters.

30. A successful Chernobyl exploit against a computer's BIOS would cause which of the following actions to occur?

A. The BIOS would be forced to boot an alternate operating system.

B. The host computer would be rendered inoperable.

C. The read-write head of the primary boot device would be "parked."

D. This attack has never been successfully executed.

Answer: B

The correct option is B. Options A, C, and D are made-up distracters.

31. Security measures that should be taken to prevent the corruption of the BIOS include which of the following?

A. The BIOS chip should be replaced every three months.

B. The BIOS should be write-protected.

C. The BIOS chip should be rebooted every three months.

D. The CMOS battery should be discharged on a regular basis.

Answer: B

The correct option is B. Options A, C, and D are made-up distracters.

32. Computers that implement UEFI could face different threats than BIOS-based computers for which of the following reasons?

    A. UEFI is a tamper-resistant hardware device.

    B. UEFI is write-protected by default.

    C. UEFI implements a full network stack.

    D. UEFI is write-allow by default.

    Answer: C

    The correct option is C. Options A, B, and D are made-up distracters.

33. A trusted platform module (TPM) is used to protect sensitive information because a TPM:

    A. Is a tamper-resistant hardware device

    B. Has a feature known as open storage

    C. Has a feature known as remote assertion

    D. Is a tamper-evident hardware device

    Answer: A

    The correct option is A. Options B, C, and D are made-up distracters.

34. Which of the following describes sealing in a TPM?

    A. The process of proving that the platform is trustworthy and has not been breached

    B. The process of encrypting data and only allowing the data to be decrypted if the TPM releases the associated decryption key

    C. The process of encrypting data using the TPM endorsement key, a unique RSA key burned into the chip during its production

    D. The process of generating cryptographic keys through the use of a hardware pseudo-random number generator

    Answer: B

    The correct option is B. Options A and C are other attributes of a TPM. Option D is how the TPM generates cryptographic keys.

35. Which of the following describes binding in a TPM?

    A. The process of proving that the platform is trustworthy and has not been breached

    B. The process of encrypting data and only allowing the data to be decrypted if the TPM releases the associated decryption key

    C. The process of encrypting data using the TPM endorsement key, a unique RSA key burned into the chip during its production

    D. The process of generating cryptographic keys through the use of a hardware pseudo-random number generator

    Answer: C

The correct option is C. Options A and B are other attributes of a TPM. Option D is how the TPM generates cryptographic keys.

36. Which of the following describes attestation in a TPM?
    A. The process of proving that the platform is trustworthy and has not been breached
    B. The process of encrypting data and only allowing the data to be decrypted if the TPM releases the associated decryption key
    C. The process of encrypting data using the TPM endorsement key, a unique RSA key burned into the chip during its production
    D. The process of generating cryptographic keys through the use of a hardware pseudo-random number generator

    Answer: A

    The correct option is A. Options B and C are other attributes of a TPM. Option D is how the TPM generates cryptographic keys.

37. Cold boot attacks are made possible by what property of dynamic random access memory (DRAM)?
    A. Ordinary DRAM loses its contents gradually over a period of seconds.
    B. Ordinary DRAM loses its contents rapidly over a period of seconds.
    C. Ordinary DRAM loses its contents gradually over a period of minutes.
    D. Ordinary DRAM loses its contents rapidly over a period of minutes.

    Answer: A

    The correct option is A. Options B, C, and D are made-up distracters.

38. The process of disabling and removing unnecessary services and settings on an operating system is commonly known as:
    A. Tightening
    B. Hardening
    C. Shredding
    D. Hacking

    Answer: B

    The correct option is B. Options A, C, and D are made-up distracters.

39. CIS benchmarks enumerate security configuration settings and actions that increase the security of the system and also come with which type of tools to verify the security measures?
    A. Scoring
    B. Counting
    C. Enumerating
    D. Evaluating

    Answer: A

    The correct option is A. Options B, C, and D are made-up distracters.

40. All unnecessary files should be removed from the production execution environment, including which of the following?

    A. Safe open source executables

    B. Production link libraries

    C. Vulnerable open source executables

    D. Production executables

    Answer: C

    The correct option is C. Options A, B, and D are made-up distracters.

41. The Run As command in Windows XP is a facility that is intended to allow a user to do which of the following?

    A. Run commands with the security privileges of another user

    B. Impersonate another user to perform unauthorized actions

    C. Impersonate another user to bypass nonrepudiation

    D. Run commands with the security privileges of the logged-on user

    Answer: A

    The correct option is A. Options B, C, and D are made-up distracters.

42. Which of the following is used to control, document, test, and approve all the changes to the operating environment?

    A. Configuration management database (CMDB)

    B. Information technology infrastructure library (ITIL)

    C. Configuration management

    D. Secure version control

    Answer: C

    The correct option is C. Options A, B, and D are related to configuration management.

43. The condition that refers to the data left on the media after the media has been erased is known as which of the following?

    A. Degaussed state

    B. Residuals

    C. Object reuse

    D. Data remanence

    Answer: D

    The correct answer is D, by definition. Answers A and B are made-up distracters. Answer C refers to reassignment to some other object of a storage media (such as page frame, disc sector, magnetic tape) that contained one or more objects.

APPENDIX

B

Glossary of Terms and Acronyms

The following is a Glossary of Terms and Acronyms used throughout the book compiled here for your quick reference and convenience.

802.11—IEEE standard that specifies 1 Mbps and 2 Mbps wireless connectivity. Defines aspects of frequency hopping and direct-sequence spread spectrum (DSSS) systems for use in the 2.4 MHz ISM (industrial, scientific, medical) band. Also refers to the IEEE committee responsible for setting wireless LAN standards.

802.11a—Specifies high-speed wireless connectivity in the 5GHz band using orthogonal frequency division multiplexing (OFDM) with data rates up to 54 Mbps.

802.11b—Specifies high-speed wireless connectivity in the 2.4GHz ISM band up to 11 Mbps.

abuse—Malicious misuse, with the objective of intentional denial, alteration, or destruction.

acceptance testing—A type of testing used to determine whether the software is acceptable to the actual users.

access—A specific type of interaction between a subject and an object that results in the flow of information from one to the other.

access control mechanism—Hardware or software features, operating procedures, management procedures, and various combinations thereof that are designed to detect and prevent unauthorized access and to permit authorized access in an automated system.

access control—The process of limiting access to system or software resources only to authorized programs, processes, or other systems (on a network). This term is synonymous with *controlled access* and *limited access*.

access list—A list of users, programs, and/or processes and the specifications of access categories to which each is assigned; a list denoting which users have what privileges to a particular resource.

access point (AP)—A wireless LAN transceiver interface between the wireless network and a wired network. Access points forward frames between wireless devices and hosts on the LAN.

access type—The nature of an access right to a particular device, program, or file (for example, read, write, execute, append, modify, delete, or create).

accountability—Property that allows auditing of IT system activities to be traced to persons or processes that may then be held responsible for their actions. Accountability includes *authenticity* and *nonrepudiation*.

accreditation—A formal declaration by the designated approving authority (DAA) that the AIS is approved to operate in a particular security mode by using a prescribed set of safeguards. Accreditation is the official management authorization for operation of an AIS and is based on the certification process as well as other management considerations. The accreditation statement affixes security responsibility with the DAA and shows that due care has been taken for security.

accreditation authority—Synonymous with *designated approving authority*.

acquisition—The act of procurement or purchase of a product or service under license, subscription, or contract.

Advanced Encryption Standard (AES) (Rijndael)—A symmetric block cipher with a block size of 128 bits in which the key can be 128, 192, or 256 bits. The Advanced Encryption Standard replaces the Data Encryption Standard (DES) and was announced on November 26, 2001, as Federal Information Processing Standard Publication (FIPS PUB 197).

AIS—Automated information system.

API—Application programming interface.

Application layer—The top layer of the OSI model, which is concerned with application programs. It provides services such as file transfer and email to the network's end users.

application process—An entity, either human or software, that uses the services offered by the Application layer of the OSI reference model.

application programming interface (API)—An interface to a library of software functions. An API is designed for software developers to call functions from the library, to make requests of an operating system or another software component.

application software—Software that accomplishes functions such as database access, electronic mail, and menu prompts.

architecture—When referring to a computer system, an architecture describes the type of components, interfaces, and protocols the system uses and how they fit together. The configuration of any equipment or interconnected system or subsystems of equipment that is used in the automatic acquisition, storage, manipulation, management, movement, control, display, switching, interchange, transmission, or reception of data or information; includes computers, ancillary equipment, and services, including support services and related resources.

asset—An object of value.

assurance—A measure of confidence that the security features and architecture of an AIS accurately mediate and enforce the security policy. Grounds for confidence that an IT product or system meets its security objectives.

asymmetric (public) key encryption—Cryptographic system that employs two keys, a public key and a private key. The public key is made available to anyone wishing to send an encrypted message to an individual holding the corresponding private key of the public-private key pair. Any message encrypted with one of these keys can be decrypted with the other. The private key is always kept private. It should not be possible to derive the private key from the public key.

attack—The act of trying to bypass security controls on a system. An attack can be active, resulting in data modification, or passive, resulting in the release of data. Note: The fact that an attack is made does not necessarily mean that it will succeed. The degree of success depends on the vulnerability of the system or activity and the effectiveness of existing countermeasures.

audit trail—A chronological record of system activities that is sufficient to enable the reconstruction, reviewing, and examination of the sequence of environments and activities surrounding or leading to an operation, a procedure, or an event in a transaction from its inception to its final result.

authenticate—(1) To verify the identity of a user, device, or other entity in a computer system, often as a prerequisite to allowing access to system resources. (2) To verify the integrity of data that have been stored, transmitted, or otherwise exposed to possible unauthorized modification.

authentication—Generically, the process of verifying "who" is at the other end of a transmission.

authentication device—A device whose identity has been verified during the lifetime of the current link based on the authentication procedure.

authenticity—The property that allows the ability to validate the claimed identity of a system entity.

authorization—The granting of access rights to a user, program, or process.

automated information system (AIS)—An assembly of computer hardware, software, and/or firmware that is configured to collect, create, communicate, compute, disseminate, process, store, and/or control data or information.

automated information system security—Measures and controls that protect an AIS against denial of service (DoS) and unauthorized (accidental or intentional) disclosure, modification, or destruction of AISs and data. AIS security includes consideration of all hardware and/or software functions, characteristics, and/or features; operational procedures, accountability procedures, and access controls at the central computer facility, remote computers and terminal facilities; management constraints; physical structures and devices; and personnel and communication controls that are needed to provide an acceptable level of risk for the AIS and for the data and information contained in the AIS. It includes the totality of security safeguards needed to provide an acceptable protection level for an AIS and for data handled by an AIS.

automated security monitoring—The use of automated procedures to ensure that security controls are not circumvented.

availability—Timely, reliable access to data and information services for authorized users.

availability of data—The condition in which data is in the place needed by the user, at the time the user needs it, and in the form needed by the user.

backbone network—A network that interconnects other networks.

back door—Synonymous with *trapdoor*.

backup plan—Synonymous with *contingency plan*.

bandwidth—Specifies the amount of the frequency spectrum that is usable for data transfer. In other words, bandwidth identifies the maximum data rate a signal can attain on the medium without encountering significant attenuation (loss of power). Also, the amount of information one can send through a connection.

Bell-LaPadula model—A formal state transition model of computer security policy that describes a set of access control rules. In this formal model, the entities in a computer system are divided into abstract sets of subjects and objects. The notion of a secure state is defined, and each state transition preserves security by moving from secure state to secure state, thereby inductively proving that the system is secure. A system state is defined to be secure only if the permitted access modes of subjects to objects are in accordance with a specific security policy. In order to determine whether a specific access mode is allowed, the clearance of a subject is compared to the classification of the object, and a determination is made as to whether the subject is authorized for the specific access mode. See * property (or star property) and simple security property.

between-the-lines entry—Unauthorized access obtained by tapping the temporarily inactive terminal of a legitimate user. See *piggyback*.

binary digit—See *bit*.

biometrics—Access control method in which an individual's physiological or behavioral characteristics are used to determine that individual's access to a particular resource.

BIOS—Basic input/output system. The BIOS is the first program to run when the computer is turned on. BIOS initializes and tests the computer hardware, loads and runs the operating system, and manages setup for making changes in the computer.

bit—Short for *binary digit*. A single digit number in binary (0 or 1).

bit decay—The gradual loss of information stored in bits on storage media over time.

bit splitting—Splitting bits into groups of bits and processing the groups such that after they are recombined the correct result is obtained. A countermeasure to a differential power analysis attack that does not expose the target bits internally to the processor, so the power trace is not affected.

black box test—A test in which an ethical hacking team has no knowledge of the target network.

black hat hacker—A hacker who conducts unethical and illegal attacks against information systems to gain unauthorized access to sensitive information.

block cipher—A symmetric key algorithm that operates on a fixed-length block of plaintext and transforms it into a fixed-length block of ciphertext. A block cipher is obtained by segregating plaintext into blocks of *n* characters or bits and applying the same encryption algorithm and key to each block.

browsing—The act of searching through storage to locate or acquire information without necessarily knowing the existence or the format of the information being sought.

BSI ISO/IEC 17799:2000,BS 7799-I: 2000, "Information Technology—Code of Practice for Information Security Management," British Standards Institution, London, UK—A standard intended to "provide a comprehensive set of controls comprising best practices in information security." ISO refers to the International Organization for Standardization, and IEC is the International Electrotechnical Commission.

buffer overflow—A condition in which more input is placed into a buffer or data holding area than the allowed or allocated capacity, overwriting other information. Such a condition is exploited by attackers to crash or gain control of a system.

bug—An error, defect, mistake, vulnerability, failure, or fault in a computer system.

byte—A set of bits, usually eight, that represent a single character.

C&A—Certification and accreditation.

CA—Certificate authority/agent. See *certificate authority.*

calls—The operations performed by an application to perform a task.

call graph—A visual representation of the sequence of calls.

capability—A protected identifier that identifies an object and specifies the access rights allowed to the accessor who possesses the capability. In a capability-based system, access to protected objects (such as files) is granted if the would-be accessor possesses a capability for the object.

category—A restrictive label that has been applied to classified or unclassified data as a means of increasing the protection of the data and further restricting its access.

CBC—See *cipher block chaining.*

CC—See *Common Criteria.*

central processing unit (CPU)—The microprocessor unit or units responsible for interpreting and executing instructions in a computer system.

CERT Coordination Center (CERT/CC)—A unit of the Carnegie Mellon University Software Engineering Institute (SEI). SEI is a federally funded R&D center. CERT's mission is to alert the Internet community to vulnerabilities and attacks and to conduct research and training in the areas of computer security, including incident response.

certification—The comprehensive evaluation of the technical and nontechnical security features of an AIS and other safeguards, made in support of the accreditation process, that establishes the extent to which a particular design and implementation meets a specified set of security requirements.

certificate authority (CA)—The official responsible for performing the comprehensive evaluation of the technical and nontechnical security features of an IT system and other safeguards, made in support of the accreditation process, to establish the extent that a particular design and implementation meet a set of specified security requirements.

certificate revocation list—A list of certificates that have been revoked or are no longer valid and should not be relied upon.

cipher-block chaining (CBC)—Cipher block chaining is an encryption mode of the Data Encryption Standard (DES) that operates on plaintext blocks 64 bits in length. Each block of plaintext is XORed with the previous ciphertext block before being encrypted.

cipher—A cryptographic transformation that operates on characters or bits.

ciphertext or cryptogram—An unintelligible encrypted message.

client—A computer that accesses a server's resources.

client/server architecture—A network system design in which a processor or computer designated as a file server or database server provides services to other client processors or computers. Applications are distributed between a host server and a remote client.

cluster—A group of computers linked together over a fast local area network or other means. Clustered computers work closely together such that they act and appear like a single large computer. Clusters are typically created to improve the availability, performance, or redundancy beyond that provided by a single computer.

collision—When simultaneous transmissions on a communications medium interfere with one another or "collide."

Component Object Model (COM)—A Microsoft technology that enables software components to communicate.

Common Criteria—A standard for specifying and evaluating the features of computer products and systems.

Common Object Request Broker Architecture (CORBA)—A standard that uses the Object Request Broker (ORB) to implement exchanges among objects in a heterogeneous, distributed environment.

communications security (COMSEC)—Measures and controls taken to deny unauthorized persons information derived from telecommunications and to ensure the authenticity of such telecommunications. Communications security includes cryptosecurity, transmission security, emission security, and physical security of COMSEC material and information.

component—A software component is a functional component that is part of a larger system.

compromise—A violation of a system's security policy such that unauthorized disclosure of sensitive information might have occurred.

compromising emanations—Unintentional data-related or intelligence-bearing signals that, when intercepted and analyzed, disclose the information transmission that is received, handled, or otherwise processed by any information processing equipment. See *TEMPEST*.

computer abuse—The misuse, alteration, disruption, or destruction of data-processing resources. The key is that computer abuse is intentional and improper.

computer cryptography—The use of a crypto-algorithm in a computer, microprocessor, or microcomputer to perform encryption or decryption in order to protect information or to authenticate users, sources, or information.

computer facility—The physical structure housing data processing operations.

computer forensics—Information collection from and about computer systems that is admissible in a court of law.

computer fraud—Computer-related crimes involving deliberate misrepresentation, alteration, or disclosure of data in order to obtain something of value (usually for monetary gain). A computer system must have been involved in the perpetration or cover-up of the act or series of acts. A computer system might have been involved through improper manipulation of input data, output or results, application programs, data files, computer operations, communications, computer hardware, systems software, or firmware.

computer security (COMPUSEC)—Synonymous with *automated information system security.*

computing environment—The total environment in which an automated information system, network, or a component operates. The environment includes physical, administrative, and personnel procedures as well as communication and networking relationships with other information systems.

COMSEC—See *communications security.*

concealment—Keeping a secret attribute of a program hidden to prevent it from being discovered by an attacker.

confidentiality—Assurance that information is not disclosed to unauthorized persons, processes, or devices. The concept of holding sensitive data in confidence, limited to an appropriate set of individuals or organizations.

configuration control—The process of controlling modifications to the system's hardware, firmware, software, and documentation that provides sufficient assurance that the system is protected against the introduction of improper modifications prior to, during, and after system implementation. Compare with *configuration management.*

configuration management—The management of security features and assurances through control of changes made to a system's hardware, software, firmware, documentation, test, test fixtures, and test documentation throughout the development and operational life of the system. Compare with *configuration control.*

confinement—The prevention of the leaking of sensitive data from a program.

confinement property—Synonymous with *star property* (* property).

conformance—Planned activities such as testing to ensure that software processes and products conform to applicable requirements, standards, and procedures.

connection-oriented service—Service that establishes a logical connection that provides flow control and error control between two stations that need to exchange data.

connectivity—A path through which communications signals can flow.

containment—Preventing a successful attack on a software system from spreading to other parts of an organization's computing resources.

contamination—The intermixing of data at different sensitivity and need-to-know levels. The lower-level data is said to be contaminated by the higher-level data; thus, the contaminating (higher-level) data might not receive the required level of protection.

contingency management—Establishing actions to be taken before, during, and after a threatening incident.

contingency plan—A plan for emergency response, backup operations, and post-disaster recovery maintained by an activity as a part of its security program; this plan ensures the availability of critical resources and facilitates the continuity of operations in an emergency situation.

correctness—If software performs all of its intended functions as specified, it is said to be correct, and exhibits the property of correctness.

continuity of operations—Maintenance of essential IP services after a major outage.

controlled sharing—The condition that exists when access control is applied to all users and components of a system.

Copper Data Distributed Interface (CDDI)—A version of FDDI specifying the use of unshielded twisted pair wiring.

cost-risk analysis—The assessment of the cost of providing data protection for a system versus the cost of losing or compromising the data.

COTS—Commercial off-the-shelf.

countermeasure—Any action, device, procedure, technique, or other reactive measure that reduces the vulnerability of or threat to a system.

covert channel—A communications channel that enables two cooperating processes to transfer information in a manner that violates the system's security policy.

covert storage channel—A covert channel that involves the direct or indirect writing of a storage location by one process and the direct or indirect reading of the storage location by another process. Covert storage channels typically involve a finite resource (for example, sectors on a disk) shared by two subjects at different security levels.

covert timing channel—A covert channel in which one process signals information to another by modulating its own use of system resources (for example, CPU time) in such a way that this manipulation affects the real response time observed by the second process.

CPU—See *central processing unit*.

criteria—See *DoD Trusted Computer System Evaluation Criteria*.

CRL—See *certificate revocation list.*

cryptanalysis—Refers to the ability to ''break'' the cipher so that the encrypted message can be read. Cryptanalysis can be accomplished by exploiting weaknesses in the cipher or in some fashion determining the key.

crypto-algorithm—A well-defined procedure, sequence of rules, or steps used to produce a key stream or ciphertext from plaintext, and vice versa. A step-by-step procedure that is used to encipher plaintext and decipher ciphertext. Also called a *cryptographic algorithm.*

cryptographic algorithm—See *crypto-algorithm.*

cryptographic application programming interface (CAPI)—An interface to a library of software functions that provide security and cryptography services. CAPI is designed for software developers to call functions from the library, which makes it easier to implement security services.

cryptography—The principles, means, and methods for rendering information unintelligible and for restoring encrypted information to intelligible form. The word *cryptography* comes from the Greek *kryptos,* meaning ''hidden,'' and *graphein,* ''to write.''

cryptosystem—A set of transformations from a message space to a ciphertext space. This system includes all cryptovariables (keys), plaintexts, and ciphertexts associated with the transformation algorithm.

cryptovariable—See *key.*

cyclic redundancy check (CRC)—A common error-detection process. A mathematical operation is applied to the data when transmitted. The result is appended to the core packet. Upon receipt, the same mathematical operation is performed and checked against the CRC. A mismatch indicates a very high probability that an error has occurred during transmission.

DAA—See *designated approving authority.*

damage potential—The level of harm the attacker can cause to the system in using the resource in an attack.

damage potential-effort ratio—The amount of work done by the attacker to acquire the necessary access rights in order to be able to use the resource in an attack.

DAC—See *discretionary access control.*

data dictionary—A database that comprises tools to support the analysis, design, and development of software and to support good software engineering practices.

Data Encryption Standard (DES)—A cryptographic algorithm for the protection of unclassified data, published in Federal Information Processing Standard (FIPS) 46. The DES, which was approved by the National Institute of Standards and Technology (NIST), is intended for public and government use.

data flow control—See *information flow control.*

data integrity—The attribute of data that is related to the preservation of its meaning and completeness, the consistency of its representation(s), and its correspondence to what it represents. When data meets a prior expectation of quality.

Data Link layer—The OSI level that performs the assembly and transmission of data packets, including error control.

data security—The protection of data from unauthorized (accidental or intentional) modification, destruction, or disclosure.

database—A persistent collection of data items that form relations among each other.

datagram service—A connectionless form of packet switching whereby the source does not need to establish a connection with the destination before sending data packets.

decipher—To unscramble the encipherment process in order to make the message human readable.

declassification of AIS storage media—An administrative decision or procedure to remove or reduce the security classification of the subject media.

DeCSS—A program that bypasses the Content Scrambling System (CSS) software used to prevent the viewing of DVD movie disks on unlicensed platforms.

default—A value or option that is automatically chosen when no other value is specified.

DoD Information Technology Security Certification and Accreditation Process (DITSCAP)—Establishes for Department of Defense entities a standard process, set of activities, general task descriptions, and management structure to certify and accredit IT systems that will maintain the required security posture. The process is designed to certify that the IT system meets the accreditation requirements and that the system will maintain the accredited security posture throughout the system life cycle. The four phases of the DITSCAP are Definition, Verification, Validation, and Post-Accreditation.

degauss—To degauss a magnetic storage medium is to remove all the data stored on it by demagnetization. A *degausser* is a device used for this purpose.

Degausser Products List (DPL)—A list of commercially produced degaussers that meet National Security Agency specifications. This list is included in the NSA *Information Systems Security Products and Services Catalogue* and is available through the Government Printing Office.

denial of service (DoS)—Any action (or series of actions) that prevents any part of a system from functioning in accordance with its intended purpose. This action includes any action that causes unauthorized destruction, modification, or delay of service. Synonymous with *interdiction*.

dependability—A property of software that can be attained with justifiable confidence when the software functions only as intended.

DES—See *Data Encryption Standard.*

designated approving authority—The official who has the authority to decide whether to accept the security safeguards prescribed for an AIS, or the official who might be responsible for issuing an accreditation statement that records the decision to accept those safeguards.

developer—The organization or individual that develops the information system.

dial-up—The service whereby a computer terminal can use the telephone to initiate and effect communication with a computer.

diffusion—A method of obscuring redundancy in plaintext by spreading the effect of the transformation over the ciphertext.

Digital Millennium Copyright Act (DMCA) of 1998—In addition to addressing licensing and ownership information, the DMCA prohibits trading, manufacturing, or selling in any way that is intended to bypass copyright protection mechanisms.

direct-sequence spread spectrum (DSSS)—A method used in 802.11b to split the frequency into 14 channels, each with a frequency range, by combining a data signal with a chipping sequence. Data rates of 1, 2, 5.5, and 11 Mbps are obtainable. DSSS spreads its signal continuously over this wide-frequency band.

disaster—A sudden, unplanned, calamitous event that produces great damage or loss; any event that creates an inability on the organization's part to provide critical business functions for some undetermined period of time.

disaster plan—Synonymous with *contingency plan.*

disaster recovery plan—Procedure for emergency response, extended backup operations, and post-disaster recovery when an organization suffers a loss of computer resources and physical facilities.

discretionary access control—A means of restricting access to objects based on the identity and need-to-know of the user, process, and/or groups to which they belong. The controls are discretionary in the sense that a subject that has certain access permissions is capable of passing that permission (perhaps indirectly) on to any other subject. Compare with *mandatory access control.*

disk image backup—Conducting a bit-level copy of a disk, sector by sector, which provides the capability to examine slack space, undeleted clusters, and possibly, deleted files.

Distributed Component Object Model (DCOM)—A distributed object model that is similar to the Common Object Request Broker Architecture (CORBA). DCOM is the distributed version of COM that supports remote objects as if the objects reside in the client's address space. A COM client can access a COM object through the use of a pointer to one of the object's interfaces and then invoke methods through that pointer.

DITSCAP—See *DoD Information Technology Security Certification and Accreditation Process.*

DNS enumeration—Gathering information on DNS servers.

DoD—U.S. Department of Defense.

DoD Trusted Computer System Evaluation Criteria (TCSEC)—A document published by the National Computer Security Center containing a uniform set of basic requirements and evaluation classes for assessing degrees of assurance in the effectiveness of hardware and software security controls built into systems. These criteria are intended for use in the design and evaluation of systems that process and/or store sensitive or classified data. This document is Government Standard DoD 5200.28-STD and is frequently referred to as "the Criteria" or "the Orange Book."

domain—The unique context (for example, access control parameters) in which a program is operating; in effect, the set of objects that a subject has the ability to access. See *process* and *subject*.

DoS attack—Denial-of-service attack.

DPL—Degausser Products List.

due care—The care which an ordinary prudent person would have exercised under the same or similar circumstances. The terms *due care* and *reasonable care* are used interchangeably.

Dynamic Host Configuration Protocol (DHCP)—A protocol that issues IP addresses automatically within a specified range to devices such as PCs when they are first powered on. The device retains the use of the IP address for a specific license period that the system administrator can define.

Electronics Industry Association (EIA)—A U.S. standards organization that represents a large number of electronics firms.

emanations—See *compromising emanations*.

embedded software—Software that is an element of a larger system and performs some of the requirements of that system, such as controlling, measuring, or monitoring the actions of the system's physical components.

embedded system—A system that performs or controls a function, either in whole or in part, as an integral element of a larger system or subsystem.

emergency plan—Synonymous with *contingency plan.*

emission(s) security (EMSEC)—The protection resulting from all measures taken to deny unauthorized persons information of value derived from the intercept and analysis of compromising emanations from crypto-equipment or an IT system.

EMSEC—See *emissions security.*

encipher—To make the message unintelligible to all but the intended recipients.

end-to-end encryption—Encrypted information sent from the point of origin to the final destination. In symmetric key encryption, this process requires the sender and the receiver to have the identical key for the session.

enumeration—Gathering detailed information about a target information system.

environment—The aggregate of external procedures, conditions, and objects that affect the development, operation, and maintenance of a system.

erasure—A process by which a signal recorded on magnetic media is removed. Erasure is accomplished in two ways: 1) by alternating current erasure, by which the information is destroyed when an alternating high and low magnetic field is applied to the media; 2) by direct current erasure, in which the media is saturated by applying a unidirectional magnetic field.

error—An error occurs 1) if an individual interacts with a software system and creates an error, e.g., a coding error, or an operational failure; 2) when a discrepancy in the value actually produced by the software is different than the correct value; 3) when one of the software's state changes from correct to incorrect.

Ethernet switch—More intelligent than a hub, with the capability to connect the sending station directly to the receiving station.

ethical hacker—Trusted individual who performs penetration tests without malicious intent.

evaluation—Assessment of an IT product or system against defined security functional and assurance criteria performed by a combination of testing and analytic techniques.

event—Something that occurs such as a specific situation or an activity. Within a software system, an event handler is a subroutine that handles input received from the software.

execution environment—The entities in software's operational environment such as servers, middleware, and network devices that support, affect or influence its execution.

exploit—To exploit means to take advantage of a security weakness in software in order to compromise the software, e.g., to gain control of a system. An exploit also refers to the portion of code, data, or sequence of commands used to conduct the attack.

Evaluation Assurance Level (EAL)—In the Common Criteria, the degree of examination of the product to be tested. EALs range from EA1 (functional testing) to EA7 (detailed testing and formal design verification). Each numbered package represents a point on the CC's predefined assurance scale. An EAL can be considered a level of confidence in the security functions of an IT product or system.

executive state—One of several states in which a system can operate and the only one in which certain privileged instructions can be executed. Such instructions cannot be executed when the system is operating in other (for example, user) states. Synonymous with *supervisor state*.

exploitable channel—Any information channel that is usable or detectable by subjects that are external to the trusted computing base, whose purpose is to violate the security policy of the system. See *covert channel*.

exposure—An instance of being exposed to losses from a threat.

external dependencies—The network and architectural components that the network interacts with but does not control.

fail-over—Operations automatically switching over to a backup system when one system/application fails.

fail safe—A term that refers to the automatic protection of programs and/or processing systems to maintain safety when a hardware or software failure is detected in a system.

fail secure—A term that refers to a system that preserves a secure state during and after identified failures occur.

failure—When software is unable to perform its intended functions within the operational parameters specified for those functions.

false negative—When a security tool does not report a weakness where one is present.

false positive—When a security tool reports a weakness where no weakness is present.

false positive rate—The number of false positives divided by the sum of the number of false positives and the number of true positives.

fault—A condition that causes a device or system component to fail to perform in a required manner.

fault-resilient systems—Systems designed without redundancy; in the event of failure, they result in a slightly longer downtime.

FCC—Federal Communications Commission.

FDMA—Frequency division multiple access. A spectrum-sharing technique whereby the available spectrum is divided into a number of individual radio channels.

FDX—Full-duplex.

Federal Intelligence Surveillance Act (FISA) of 1978—An act that limited wiretapping for national security purposes as a result of the Nixon administration's history of using illegal wiretaps.

fetch protection—A system-provided restriction to prevent a program from accessing data in another user's segment of storage.

Fiber-Distributed Data Interface (FDDI)—An ANSI standard for token-passing networks. FDDI uses optical fiber and operates at 100 Mbps in dual, counter-rotating rings.

Fiestel cipher—An iterated block cipher that encrypts by breaking a plaintext block into two halves and, with a subkey, applying a ''round'' transformation to one of the halves. The output of this transformation is then XOR'd with the remaining half. The round is completed by swapping the two halves.

FIFO—First in, first out.

file server—A computer that provides network stations with controlled access to sharable resources. The network operating system (NOS) is loaded on the file server, and most sharable devices, including disk subsystems and printers, are attached to it.

file protection—The aggregate of all processes and procedures in a system designed to inhibit unauthorized access, contamination, or elimination of a file.

file security—The means by which access to computer files is limited to authorized users only.

File Transfer Protocol (FTP)—A TCP/IP protocol for file transfer.

FIPS—Federal Information Processing Standard.

firewall—A network device that shields the trusted network from unauthorized users in the untrusted network by blocking certain specific types of traffic. Many types of firewalls exist, including packet filtering and stateful inspection.

firmware—Executable programs stored in nonvolatile memory.

flaw—A shortcoming in software's requirements, architecture, or design specification that results in a weak design or errors in the implementation. A flaw may or may not be a vulnerability.

flow-sensitive analysis—Analysis of a computer program that takes into account the flow of control.

flow control—See *information flow control*.

footprinting—Gathering information in both active and passive modes.

formal method—A technique to verify through use of mathematical proofs that software is consistent with its specified requirements, architecture, design, or security policy.

formal proof—A complete and convincing mathematical argument presenting the full logical justification for each proof step for the truth of a theorem or set of theorems.

formal security policy model—A mathematically precise statement of a security policy. To be adequately precise, such a model must represent the initial state of a system, the way in which the system progresses from one state to another, and a definition of a secure state of the system. To be acceptable as a basis for a TCB, the model must be supported by a formal proof that if the initial state of the system satisfies the definition of a secure state and if all assumptions required by the model hold, then all future states of the system will be secure. Some formal modeling techniques include state transition models, denotational semantics models, and algebraic specification models. See *Bell-LaPadula model.*

formal verification—The process of using formal proofs to demonstrate the consistency between a formal specification of a system and a formal security policy model (design verification) or between the formal specification and its high-level program implementation (implementation verification).

functional testing—The segment of security testing in which the advertised security mechanisms of the system are tested, under operational conditions, for correct operation.

gateway—A network component that provides interconnectivity at higher network layers.

gigabyte (GB, Gbyte)—A unit of measure for memory or disk storage capacity; usually 1,073,741,824 bytes.

gigahertz (GHz)—A measure of frequency; one billion hertz.

GOTS—Government off-the-shelf software.

Gramm-Leach-Bliley (GLB) Act of November 1999—An act that removes Depression-era restrictions on banks that limited certain business activities, mergers, and affiliations. It repeals the restrictions on banks affiliating with securities firms contained in sections 20 and 32 of the Glass-Steagall Act. GLB became effective on November 13, 2001. GLB also requires health plans and insurers to protect member and subscriber data in electronic and other formats. These health plans and insurers will fall under new state laws and regulations that are being passed to implement GLB because GLB explicitly assigns enforcement of the health plan and insurer regulations to state insurance authorities (15 U.S.C. §6805). Some of the privacy and security requirements of Gramm-Leach-Bliley are similar to those of HIPAA.

granularity—An expression of the relative size of a data object; for example, protection at the file level is considered coarse granularity, whereas protection at the field level is considered to be of a finer granularity.

gray box test—A test in which the ethical hacking team has partial knowledge of the target information system.

gray hat hacker—A hacker who normally performs ethical hacking but sometimes reverts to malicious, black hat hacking.

guard—A processor that provides a filter between two disparate systems operating at different security levels or between a user terminal and a database in order to filter out data that the user is not authorized to access.

Hamming weight—The Hamming weight of a string is the number of symbols that are different from the zero-symbol of the alphabet used.

handshaking procedure—A dialogue between two entities (for example, a user and a computer, a computer and another computer, or a program and another program) for the purpose of identifying and authenticating the entities to one another.

hertz (Hz)—A unit of frequency measurement; one cycle of a periodic event per second. Used to measure frequency.

HIPAA—See *Kennedy-Kassebaum Act of 1996*.

host—A time-sharing computer accessed via terminals or terminal emulation; a computer to which an expansion device attaches.

HTTP—Hypertext Transfer Protocol.

Hypertext Markup Language (HTML)—A standard used on the Internet for defining hypertext links between documents.

I&A—Identification and authentication.

IA—Information assurance.

IAC—Inquiry access code; used in inquiry procedures. The IAC can be one of two types: a dedicated IAC for specific devices or a generic IAC for all devices.

ICV—Integrity check value. In WEP encryption, the frame is run through an integrity algorithm, and the generated ICV is placed at the end of the encrypted data in the frame. Then the receiving station runs the data through its integrity algorithm and compares it to the ICV received in the frame. If it matches, the unencrypted frame is passed to the higher layers. If it does not match, the frame is discarded.

ID—Common abbreviation for "identifier" or "identity."

identification—The process that enables a system to recognize an entity, generally by the use of unique machine-readable usernames.

identities—The type of service provided by a software component, e.g., NETWORK_SERVICE.

IDS—Intrusion detection system.

IETF—Internet Engineering Task Force.

IKE—Internet key exchange.

impersonating—Synonymous with *spoofing*.

implementation—Refers to the phase in the software life cycle when the software is coded from specifications and/or integrated from components.

incomplete parameter checking—A system design flaw that results when all parameters have not been fully examined for accuracy and consistency, thus making the system vulnerable to penetration.

individual accountability—The ability to positively associate the identity of a user with the time, method, and degree of access to a system.

industrial, scientific, and medicine (ISM) bands—Radio frequency bands authorized by the Federal Communications Commission (FCC) for wireless LANs. The ISM bands are located at 902MHz, 2.400GHz, and 5.7GHz. The transmitted power is commonly less than 600mw, but no FCC license is required.

information flow control—A procedure undertaken to ensure that information transfers within a system are not made from a higher security level object to an object of a lower security level. See *covert channel*, *simple security property*, and *star property (* property)*. Synonymous with *data flow control* and *flow control*.

information security policy—The aggregate of public law, directives, regulations, and rules that regulate how an organization manages, protects, and distributes information. For example, the information security policy for financial data processed on DoD systems may be in USC, EO, DoD directives, and local regulations. The information security policy lists all the security requirements applicable to specific information.

information system (IS)—Any telecommunications or computer-related equipment or interconnected systems or subsystems of equipment used in the acquisition, storage, manipulation, management, movement, control, display, switching, interchange, transmission, or reception of voice and/or data; includes software, firmware, and hardware.

information system security officer (ISSO)—The person who is responsible to the designated approving authority (DAA) for ensuring that security is provided for and implemented throughout the life cycle of an AIS, from the beginning of the concept development plan through its design, development, operation, maintenance, and secure disposal. In C&A, the person responsible to the DAA for ensuring the security of an IT system is approved, operated, and maintained throughout its life cycle in accordance with the SSAA.

information technology (IT)—The hardware, firmware, and software used as part of the information system to perform information functions. This definition includes computers, telecommunications, automated information systems, and automatic data processing equipment. IT includes any assembly of computer hardware, software, and/or firmware configured to collect, create, communicate, compute, disseminate, process, store, and/or control data or information.

information technology security (ITSEC)—Protection of information technology against unauthorized access to or modification of information, whether in storage, processing, or transit, and against the denial of service to authorized users, including those measures necessary to detect, document, and counter such threats. Protection and maintenance of confidentiality, integrity, availability, and accountability.

infrared (IR) light—Light waves that range in length from about 0.75 to 1,000 microns; this is a lower frequency than the spectral colors but a higher frequency than radio waves.

inheritance (in object-oriented programming)—When all the methods of one class, called a *superclass*, are inherited by a subclass. Thus, all messages understood by the superclass are understood by the subclass.

input validation—Checking the data that is input to a software application for acceptable parameters such as data type, length, and range.

Institute of Electrical and Electronic Engineers (IEEE)—A U.S.–based standards organization participating in the development of standards for data transmission systems. The IEEE has made significant progress in the establishment of standards for LANs, namely the IEEE 802 series.

integration testing—A testing process used to verify the interface among network components as the components are installed. The installation crew should integrate components into the network one by one and perform integration testing when necessary to ensure proper gradual integration of components.

integrator—An organization or individual that unites, combines, or otherwise incorporates information system components with another system(s).

integrity—(1) A term that refers to a sound, unimpaired, or perfect condition. (2) Quality of an IT system reflecting the logical correctness and reliability of the operating system, the logical completeness of the hardware and software implementing the protection mechanisms, and the consistency of the data structures and occurrence of the stored data. It is composed of data integrity and system integrity.

interdiction—See *denial of service.*

inter-file analysis—Analysis of code resulting in different files that have procedural, data, or other interdependencies.

inter-procedural analysis—Analysis between calling and called procedures within a computer program.

internal security controls—Hardware, firmware, and software features within a system that restrict access to resources (hardware, software, and data) to authorized subjects only (persons, programs, or devices).

International Standards Organization (ISO)—A non-treaty standards organization active in the development of international standards, such as the Open System Interconnection (OSI) network architecture.

International Telecommunications Union (ITU)—An intergovernmental agency of the United States responsible for making recommendations and standards regarding telephone and data communications systems for public and private telecommunication organizations and for providing coordination for the development of international standards.

Internet—The largest network in the world. The successor to ARPANET, the Internet includes other large internetworks. The Internet uses the TCP/IP protocol suite and connects universities, government agencies, and individuals around the world.

Internet Protocol (IP)—The Internet standard protocol that defines the Internet datagram as the information unit passed across the Internet. IP provides the basis of a best-effort packet delivery service. The Internet Protocol suite is often referred to as TCP/IP because IP is one of the two fundamental protocols, the other being the Transfer Control Protocol.

Internetwork Packet Exchange (IPX)—NetWare protocol for the exchange of message packets on an internetwork. IPX passes application requests for network services to the network drives and then to other workstations, servers, or devices on the internetwork.

ionization—To convert an atom or molecule into an ion by adding or removing charged particles such as electrons or other ions.

ionize—The act of converting an atom or molecule into an ion by adding or removing charged particles such as electrons or other ions.

IS—See *information system.*

isolation—The containment of subjects and objects in a system in such a way that they are separated from one another as well as from the protection controls of the operating system.

ISP—Internet service provider.

ISSE—Information systems security engineering/engineer.

ISSO—See *information system security officer.*

IT—See *information technology.*

ITSEC—See *information technology security.*

IV—Initialization vector; for WEP encryption.

justifiable confidence—A high level of certainty achieved with actions, arguments, and evidence.

Kennedy-Kassebaum Health Insurance Portability and Accountability Act (HIPAA) of 1996—A set of regulations that mandates the use of standards in health care record keeping and electronic transactions. The act requires that health care plans, providers, insurers, and clearinghouses do the following:

- Provide for restricted access by the patient to personal health care information

- Implement administrative simplification standards
- Enable the portability of health insurance
- Establish strong penalties for health care fraud

key—Information or sequence that controls the enciphering and deciphering of messages. Also known as a *cryptovariable*. Used with a particular algorithm to encipher or decipher the plaintext message.

kilobyte (KB, Kbyte)—A unit of measurement of memory or disk storage capacity; a data unit of 2^{10}(1,024) bytes.

kilohertz (kHz)—A unit of frequency measurement equivalent to 1,000 hertz.

knowledge base—Refers to the rules and facts of the particular problem domain in an expert system.

least privilege—The principle that requires each subject to be granted the most restrictive set of privileges needed for the performance of authorized tasks. The application of this principle limits the damage that can result from accident, error, or unauthorized use.

light-emitting diode (LED)—Used in conjunction with optical fiber, an LED emits incoherent light when current is passed through it. Its advantages include low cost and long lifetime, and it is capable of operating in the Mbps range.

limited access—Synonymous with *access control.*

local area network (LAN)—A network that interconnects devices in the same office, floor, building, or close buildings.

MAC—See *mandatory access control* if used in the context of a type of access control. MAC also refers to the *media access control* address assigned to a network interface card on an Ethernet network.

magnetic remanence—A measure of the magnetic flux density that remains after removal of the applied magnetic force. Refers to any data remaining on magnetic storage media after removal of the power.

mail gateway—A type of gateway that interconnects dissimilar email systems.

maintainer—The organization or individual that maintains the information system.

maintenance organization—The organization that keeps an IT system operating in accordance with prescribed laws, policies, procedures, and regulations. In the case of a contractor-maintained system, the maintenance organization is the government organization responsible for, or sponsoring the operation of, the IT system.

malicious code—Hardware, software, or firmware that is intentionally included in a system for an unauthorized purpose (for example, a Trojan horse).

malicious logic—Synonymous with *malicious code.*

malware—Malware is a conjunction of the words *malicious* and *software*. Malware is inserted into a system, usually covertly, with the intention of compromising the confidentiality, availability, or integrity of the system's data, applications, and operating system. It may come to the attention of a user by inhibiting the operational abilities of the system. Often referred to as *malicious code*.

mandatory access control (MAC)—A means of restricting access to objects based on the sensitivity (as represented by a label) of the information contained in the objects and the formal authorization (in other words, clearance) of subjects to access information of such sensitivity. Compare *discretionary access control*.

masquerading—See *spoofing*.

media access control (MAC)—An IEEE 802 standards sublayer used to control access to a network medium, such as a wireless LAN. Also deals with collision detection. Each computer has its own unique MAC address.

megabits per second (Mbps)—One million bits per second.

megabyte (MB, Mbyte)—A unit of measurement for memory or disk storage capacity; usually 1,048,576 bytes.

megahertz (MHz)—A measure of frequency equivalent to one million cycles per second.

middleware—An intermediate software component located on the wired network between the wireless appliance and the application or data residing on the wired network. Middleware provides appropriate interfaces between the appliance and the host application or server database.

mission—The assigned duties to be performed by a resource.

misuse—Usage of software that deviates from what is expected based on the software's specifications. If the misuse is malicious in nature, it is typically referred to as *abuse*.

mobile code—Software obtained from remote computer systems across a network, and downloaded and executed on a local computer system without explicit installation or execution by the recipient. Examples include JavaScript, Java applets, ActiveX controls, Flash animations, and so on.

modes of operation—A description of the conditions under which an AIS functions, based on the sensitivity of data processed and the clearance levels and authorizations of the users. Four modes of operation are authorized:

1. *Dedicated mode*—An AIS is operating in the dedicated mode when each user who has direct or indirect individual access to the AIS, its peripherals, remote terminals, or remote hosts has all of the following:

   a. A valid personnel clearance for all information on the system

   b. Formal access approval; furthermore, the user has signed nondisclosure agreements for all the information stored and/or processed (including all compartments, subcompartments, and/or special access programs)

   c. A valid need-to-know for all information contained within the system

2. *System-high mode*—An AIS is operating in the system-high mode when each user who has direct or indirect access to the AIS, its peripherals, remote terminals, or remote hosts has all of the following:
   a. A valid personnel clearance for all information on the AIS
   b. Formal access approval, and signed nondisclosure agreements, for all the information stored and/or processed (including all compartments, subcompartments, and/or special access programs)
   c. A valid need-to-know for some of the information contained within the AIS
3. *Compartmented mode*—An AIS is operating in the compartmented mode when each user who has direct or indirect access to the AIS, its peripherals, remote terminals, or remote hosts has all of the following:
   a. A valid personnel clearance for the most restricted information processed in the AIS
   b. Formal access approval, and signed nondisclosure agreements, for that information which he or she will be able to access
   c. A valid need-to-know for that information which he or she will be able to access
4. *Multilevel mode*—An AIS is operating in the multilevel mode when all of the following statements are satisfied concerning the users who have direct or indirect access to the AIS, its peripherals, remote terminals, or remote hosts:
   a. Some do not have a valid personnel clearance for all the information processed in the AIS.
   b. All have the proper clearance and the appropriate formal access approval for that information to which they are to have access.
   c. All have a valid need-to-know for that information to which they are to have access.

multilevel device—A device that is used in a manner that permits it to simultaneously process data of two or more security levels without risk of compromise. To accomplish this, sensitivity labels are normally stored on the same physical medium and in the same form (for example, machine-readable or human-readable) as the data being processed.

multilevel secure—A class of system containing information with different sensitivities that simultaneously permits access by users with different security clearances and needs-to-know but that prevents users from obtaining access to information for which they lack authorization.

multilevel security mode—See *modes of operation*.

multiple inheritance—In object-oriented programming, a situation where a subclass inherits the behavior of multiple superclasses.

multiuser mode of operation—A mode of operation designed for systems that process sensitive, unclassified information in which users might not have a need-to-know for all information processed in the system. This mode is also used for microcomputers processing sensitive unclassified information that cannot meet the requirements of the standalone mode of operation.

mutually suspicious—A state that exists between interacting processes (subsystems or programs) in which neither process can expect the other process to function securely with respect to some property.

National Computer Security Center (NCSC)—Originally named the DoD Computer Security Center, the NCSC is responsible for encouraging the widespread availability of trusted computer systems throughout the federal government. It is a branch of the National Security Agency (NSA) that also initiates research and develops and publishes standards and criteria for trusted information systems.

National Information Assurance Certification and Accreditation Process (NIACAP)—Provides a standard set of activities, general tasks, and a management structure to certify and accredit systems that will maintain the information assurance and security posture of a system or site. The NIACAP is designed to certify that the information system meets documented accreditation requirements and continues to maintain the accredited security posture throughout the system life cycle.

NCSC—See *National Computer Security Center.*

need-to-know—The necessity for access to, knowledge of, or possession of specific information that is required to carry out official duties.

Network Basic Input/Output System (NetBIOS)—A standard interface between networks and PCs that enables applications on different computers to communicate within a LAN. NetBIOS was created by IBM for its early PC network, was adopted by Microsoft, and has since become a de facto industry standard. It is not routable across a WAN.

network interface card (NIC)—A network adapter inserted into a computer that enables the computer to be connected to a network.

network monitoring—A form of operational support enabling network management to view the network's inner workings. Most network-monitoring equipment is nonobtrusive and can be used to determine the network's utilization and to locate faults.

NIACAP—See *National Information Assurance Certification and Accreditation Process.*

NIAP—National Information Assurance Partnership.

NIST—National Institute of Standards and Technology.

node—Any network-addressable device on the network, such as a router or network interface card. Any network station.

nonrepudiation—Measures such as digital signatures that are intended to prevent a software actor (human or computer) from later denying responsibility for taking a specific action.

NSA—National Security Agency.

object—A passive entity that contains or receives information. Access to an object potentially implies access to the information that it contains. Examples of objects include records, blocks, pages, segments, files, directories, directory trees, and programs, as well as bits, bytes, words, fields, processors, video displays, keyboards, clocks, printers, and network nodes.

object request broker (ORB)—The fundamental building block of the object request architecture (ORA), which manages the communications among the ORA entities. The purpose of the ORB is to support the interaction of objects in heterogeneous, distributed environments. The objects may be on different types of computing platforms.

object reuse—The reassignment and reuse of a storage medium (for example, page frame, disk sector, and magnetic tape) that once contained one or more objects. To be securely reused and assigned to a new subject, storage media must contain no residual data (data remanence) from the object(s) that were previously contained in the media.

object services—Services that support the ORB in creating and tracking objects as well as performing access control functions.

OMB—Office of Management and Budget.

open security environment—An environment that includes those systems in which at least one of the following conditions holds true: l) application developers (including maintainers) do not have sufficient clearance or authorization to provide an acceptable presumption that they have not introduced malicious logic, and 2) configuration control does not provide sufficient assurance that applications are protected against the introduction of malicious logic prior to and during the operation of system applications.

open source software (OSS)—Software that is publicly available and provided under a license that is less restrictive than a typical commercial license. A typical license may permit users to change the software and redistribute the software in modified or unmodified form.

Open System Interconnection (OSI)—An ISO standard specifying an open system capable of enabling communications between diverse systems. OSI has the following seven layers of distinction: Physical, Data Link, Network, Transport, Session, Presentation, and Application. These layers provide the functions that enable standardized communications between two application processes.

operations security—Controls over hardware, media, and operators who have access; protects against asset threats, baseline, or selective mechanisms.

operator—An individual who supports system operations from the operator's console, monitors execution of the system, controls the flow of jobs, and mounts input/output volumes (be alert for shoulder surfing).

Orange Book—Alternate name for the DoD Trusted Computer System Evaluation Criteria.

original equipment manufacturer (OEM)—A manufacturer of products for integration in other products or systems.

OS—Commonly used abbreviation for *operating system.*

overt channel—A path within a computer system or network that is designed for the authorized transfer of data. Compare with *covert channel.*

overwrite procedure—A stimulation to change the state of a bit followed by a known pattern. See *magnetic remanence.*

packet—A basic message unit for communication across a network. A packet usually includes routing information, data, and (sometimes) error-detection information.

packet-switched—(1) A network that routes data packets based on an address contained in the data packet is said to be a *packet-switched network.* Multiple data packets can share the same network resources. (2) A communications network that uses shared facilities to route data packets from and to different users. Unlike a circuit-switched network, a packet-switched network does not set up dedicated circuits for each session.

passivation layer—A protective layer that covers an integrated circuit.

password—A protected/private character string that is used to authenticate an identity.

penetration—The successful act of bypassing a system's security mechanisms.

penetration testing—The portion of security testing in which the evaluators attempt to circumvent the security features of a system. The evaluators might be assumed to use all system design and implementation documentation, which can include listings of system source code, manuals, and circuit diagrams. The evaluators work under the same constraints that are applied to ordinary users.

performance modeling—The use of simulation software to predict network behavior, allowing developers to perform capacity planning. Simulation makes it possible to model the network and impose varying levels of utilization to observe the effects.

permissions—A description of the type of authorized interactions that a subject can have with an object. Examples of permission types include read, write, execute, add, modify, and delete.

personnel security—(1) The procedures that are established to ensure that all personnel who have access to sensitive information possess the required authority as well as appropriate clearances. (2) Procedures to ensure a person's background; provides assurance of necessary trustworthiness.

physical security—The application of physical barriers and control procedures as preventive measures or countermeasures against threats to resources and sensitive information.

piggyback—Gaining unauthorized access to a system via another user's legitimate connection. See *between-the-lines entry*.

PKI—Public key infrastructure.

plaintext—Message text in clear, human-readable form.

Platform for Privacy Preferences (P3P)—Proposed standards developed by the World Wide Web Consortium (W3C) to implement privacy practices on Web sites.

portability—Defines network connectivity that can be easily established, used, and then dismantled.

port scanning—Connecting to UDP and TCP ports in order to determine the services and applications running on the target host.

Presentation layer—The layer of the OSI model that negotiates data transfer syntax for the Application layer and performs translations between different data types, if necessary.

private key encryption—See *symmetric (private) key encryption*.

privileged instructions—A set of instructions (for example, interrupt handling or special computer instructions) to control features such as storage protection features that are generally executable only when the automated system is operating in the executive state.

PRNG—Pseudorandom number generator.

procedural language—Implies sequential execution of instructions based on the von Neumann architecture of a CPU, memory, and input/output device. Variables are part of the sets of instructions used to solve a particular problem, and therefore, the data is not separate from the statements.

process—A program in execution. See *domain* and *subject*.

program—An executable software entity.

program manager—The person ultimately responsible for the overall procurement, development, integration, modification, operation, and maintenance of the IT system.

Protected Health Information (PHI)—Individually identifiable health information that is:

- Transmitted by electronic media
- Maintained in any medium described in the definition of electronic media (under HIPAA)
- Transmitted or maintained in any other form or medium

Protection Profile (PP)—In the Common Criteria, an implementation-independent specification of the security requirements and protections of a product that could be built.

protection-critical portions of the TCB—Those portions of the TCB whose normal function is to deal with access control between subjects and objects. Their correct operation is essential to the protection of the data on the system.

protocols—A set of rules and formats—semantic and syntactic—that permits entities to exchange information.

prototyping—A method of determining or verifying requirements and design specifications. The prototype normally consists of network hardware and software that support a proposed solution. The approach to prototyping is typically a trial-and-error experimental process.

public key cryptography—See *asymmetric key encryption*.

public key infrastructure (PKI)—A PKI binds public keys to entities, enables other entities to verify public key bindings, and provides the services needed for ongoing management of keys in a distributed system. The goal of the PKI security architecture is to protect and distribute information that is needed in a widely distributed environment, where the users, resources and stakeholders, are in different places at different times. PKI allows business to be conducted with the justifiable confidence that:

- The person or process sending the transaction is the actual originator.
- The person or process receiving the transaction is the intended recipient.
- Data integrity has not been compromised.

purge—The removal of sensitive data from an AIS, AIS storage device, or peripheral device with storage capacity at the end of a processing period. This action is performed in such a way that there is assurance proportional to the sensitivity of the data that the data cannot be reconstructed. An AIS must be disconnected from any external network before a purge. After a purge, the medium can be declassified by observing the review procedures of the respective agency.

quality—The degree to which software meets its specifications and satisfies its intended purpose.

RADIUS—Remote Authentication Dial-In User Service.

RC4—RSA cipher algorithm 4.

read—A fundamental operation that results only in the flow of information from an object to a subject.

read access—Permission to read information.

recovery planning—The advance planning and preparations that are necessary to minimize loss and to ensure the availability of the critical information systems of an organization.

recovery procedures—The actions that are necessary to restore a system's computational capability and data files after a system failure or outage/disruption.

reference-monitor concept—An access-control concept that refers to an abstract machine that mediates all accesses to objects by subjects.

reference-validation mechanism—An implementation of the reference monitor concept. A security kernel is a type of reference-validation mechanism.

regression testing—Testing process used to ensure that existing software functions of the product have not been accidentally damaged as an unintended by-product of adding raw software features.

relevancies—Attributes of a software component that are applicable to its attack surface.

reliability—The probability of a given system performing its mission adequately for a specified period of time under expected operating conditions.

requirement—A description of a functional or nonfunctional (security) behavior that software must satisfy.

residual risk—The portion of risk that remains after security measures have been applied.

resilience—If software is compromised, damage to the software will be minimized and it will recover quickly to an acceptable level of service.

RFC—Request for comment.

RFP—Request for proposal.

risk—(1) A combination of the likelihood that a threat will occur, the likelihood that a threat occurrence will result in an adverse impact, and the severity of the resulting impact. (2) The probability that a particular threat will exploit a particular vulnerability of the system.

risk analysis—The process of identifying security risks, determining their magnitude, and identifying areas needing safeguards. Risk analysis is a part of risk management. Synonymous with *risk assessment*.

risk assessment—Process of analyzing threats to an IT system, vulnerabilities of a system, and the potential impact that the loss of information or capabilities of a system would have on security. The resulting analysis is used as a basis for identifying appropriate and effective measures.

risk management—The total process of identifying, controlling, eliminating, or minimizing uncertain events that might affect system resources. It includes risk analysis, cost-benefit analysis, selection, implementation, tests, a security evaluation of safeguards, and an overall security review.

robustness—The degree to which a software component or system can function correctly in the presence of invalid or unexpected inputs and unexpected or stressful environmental conditions, including input and conditions that are intentional and malicious.

role—In role-based access control, a role is a set of rights granted to a user to perform specific functions within a software application.

ROM—Read-only memory.

router—A network component that provides internetworking at the Network layer of a network's architecture by allowing individual networks to become part of a WAN. A router works by using logical and physical addresses to connect two or more separate networks. It determines the best path by which to send a packet of information.

Routing Information Protocol (RIP)—A common type of routing protocol. RIP bases its routing path on the distance (number of hops) to the destination. RIP maintains optimum routing paths by sending out routing update messages if the network topology changes.

safeguards—See *security safeguards*.

safety—Software that is part of a system that is life-critical should exhibit the property of safety, i.e., it should behave as necessary even if components of the system fail.

sandbox—An access control-based protection mechanism. It is commonly applied to restrict the access rights of mobile code that is downloaded from a Web site as an applet. The code is set up to run in a "sandbox" that blocks its access to the local workstation's hard disk, thus preventing the code from malicious activity. The sandbox is usually interpreted by a virtual machine such as the Java Virtual Machine (JVM).

scalar—A computer language variable or field that can hold only one value at a time.

scanning—Actively connecting to a system to obtain a response.

SDLC—Software development life cycle.

secure coding—The use of software programming practices that reduce or eliminate software defects or programming errors so that software can be built with a higher level of security and quality assurance.

secure configuration management—The set of procedures that are appropriate for controlling changes to a system's hardware and software structure for the purpose of ensuring that changes will not lead to violations of the system's security policy.

secure state—A condition in which no subject can access any object in an unauthorized manner.

security—Measures and controls that ensure the confidentiality, integrity, availability, and accountability of the information processed and stored by a computer.

security evaluation—An evaluation that is performed to assess the degree of trust that can be placed in systems for the secure handling of sensitive information. One type, a product evaluation, is an evaluation performed on the hardware and software features and assurances of a computer product from a perspective that excludes the application environment. The other type, a system evaluation, is made for the purpose of assessing a system's security safeguards with respect to a specific operational mission; it is a major step in the certification and accreditation process.

security failure—An event that is a violation of a particular system's explicit or implicit security policy.

security fault analysis—A security analysis, usually performed on hardware at the gate level, to determine the security properties of a device when a hardware fault is encountered.

security features—The security-relevant functions, mechanisms, and characteristics of system hardware and software. Security features are a subset of system security safeguards.

security flaw—An error of commission or omission in a system that might enable protection mechanisms to be bypassed.

security flow analysis—A security analysis performed on a formal system specification that locates the potential flows of information within the system.

security functional requirements—Requirements, preferably from the Common Criteria, Part 2, that when taken together specify the security behavior of an IT product or system.

security kernel—The hardware, firmware, and software elements of a trusted computing base (TCB) that implement the reference monitor concept. The security kernel must mediate all accesses, must be protected from modification, and must be verifiable as correct.

security level—The combination of a hierarchical classification and a set of nonhierarchical categories that represents the sensitivity of information.

security measures—Elements of software, firmware, hardware, or procedures that are included in a system for the satisfaction of security specifications.

security objective—A statement of intent to counter specified threats and/or satisfy specified organizational security policies and assumptions.

security perimeter—The boundary where security controls are in effect to protect assets.

security policy—The set of laws, rules, and practices that regulates how an organization manages, protects, and distributes sensitive information.

security policy model—A formal presentation of the security policy enforced by the system. It must identify the set of rules and practices that regulate how a system manages, protects, and distributes sensitive information. See *Bell-LaPadula model* and *formal security policy model*.

security process—The series of activities that monitor, evaluate, test, certify, accredit, and maintain the system accreditation throughout the system life cycle.

security requirements—The types and levels of protection that are necessary for equipment, data, information, applications, and facilities to meet the security policy.

security requirements baseline—A description of minimum requirements necessary for a system to maintain an acceptable level of security.

security safeguards—The proactive protective measures and controls that are prescribed to meet the security requirements specified for a system. Those safeguards can include (but are not necessarily limited to) the following: hardware and software security features, operating procedures, accountability procedures, access and distribution controls, management constraints, personnel security, and physical structures, areas, and devices. Also called *safeguards*.

security specifications—A detailed description of the safeguards required to protect a system.

Security Target (ST)—(1) In the Common Criteria, a listing of the security claims for a particular IT security product. (2) A set of security functional and assurance requirements and specifications to be used as the basis for evaluating an identified product or system.

Security Test and Evaluation (ST&E)—Examination and analysis of the safeguards required to protect an IT system, as they have been applied in an operational environment, to determine the security posture of that system.

security testing—A process that is used to determine that the security features of a system are implemented as designed. This process includes hands-on functional testing, penetration testing, and verification.

security vulnerability—A property of system requirements, design, implementation, or operation that could be accidentally triggered or intentionally exploited and result in a security failure.

sensitive information—Information that, if lost, misused, modified, or accessed by unauthorized individuals, could affect the national interest or the conduct of federal programs or the privacy to which individuals are entitled under Section 552a of Title 5, U.S. Code, but that has not been specifically authorized under criteria established by an executive order or an act of Congress to be kept classified in the interest of national defense or foreign policy. The concept of sensitive information can apply to private-sector entities as well.

sensitivity label—A piece of information that represents the security level of an object. Sensitivity labels are used by the TCB as the basis for mandatory access control decisions.

service roles—The context in which a software component operates consisting of type of service, authentication mechanism, and identities.

Session layer—One of the seven OSI model layers. Establishes, manages, and terminates sessions between applications.

shared key authentication—A type of authentication that assumes each station has received a secret shared key through a secure channel, independent from an 802.11 network. Stations authenticate through shared knowledge of the secret key. Use of shared key authentication requires implementation of the 802.11 Wired Equivalent Privacy (WEP) algorithm.

Simple Mail Transfer Protocol (SMTP)—The Internet email protocol.

Simple Network Management Protocol (SNMP)—The network management protocol of choice for TCP/IP-based Internets. Widely implemented with 10BASE-T Ethernet, this network management protocol defines information transfer among management information bases (MIBs).

simple security condition—See *simple security property*.

simple security property—A Bell-LaPadula security model rule enabling a subject read access to an object only if the security level of the subject dominates the security level of the object. Synonymous with *simple security condition*.

SLC—Software life cycle.

social engineering—Attacks targeting an organization's employees through the use of social skills to obtain sensitive information.

software assurance—The level of confidence that software is free from vulnerabilities, either intentionally designed into the software or accidentally inserted at any time during its life cycle, and that the software functions in the intended manner.

software development life cycle process—The process using a model to translate user needs into a software product.

software engineering—The science and art of specifying, designing, implementing, and evolving programs, documentation, and operating procedures whereby computers can be made useful to humans.

software process—A set of activities, methods, and practices that are used to develop and maintain software and associated products.

software process capability—Describes the range of expected results that can be achieved by following a software process.

software process maturity—The extent to which a software process is defined, managed, measured, controlled, and effective.

software process performance—The result achieved by following a software process.

software security—General-purpose executive, utility, or software development tools and applications programs or routines that protect data that are handled by a system.

software system test and evaluation process—A process that plans, develops, and documents the quantitative demonstration of the fulfillment of all baseline functional performance and operational and interface requirements.

software weakness—A portion of code that may lead to a vulnerability.

software-intensive system—A system in which the majority of components and functionalities are implemented in software.

source code—A series of statements written in a human-readable computer programming language.

spoofing—An attempt to gain access to a system by posing as an authorized user. Synonymous with *impersonating, masquerading,* or *mimicking*.

SQL injection—The process of an attacker inserting SQL statements into a query by exploiting vulnerability for the purpose of sending commands to a Web server database.

SSL—Secure Sockets Layer.

SSO—System security officer.

ST&E—See *Security Test and Evaluation*.

standalone (shared system)—A system that is physically and electrically isolated from all other systems and intended to be used by more than one person, either simultaneously (for example, a system that has multiple terminals) or serially, with data belonging to one user remaining available to the system while another user uses the system (for example, a personal computer that has nonremovable storage media, such as a hard disk).

standalone (single-user system)—A system that is physically and electrically isolated from all other systems and is intended to be used by one person at a time, with no data belonging to other users remaining in the system (for example, a personal computer that has removable storage media, such as a floppy disk).

star property (* property)—A Bell-LaPadula security model rule giving a subject write access to an object only if the security level of the object dominates the security level of the subject. Also called the *confinement property*.

state variable—A variable that represents either the state of the system or the state of some system resource.

Structured Query Language (SQL)—An international standard for defining and accessing relational databases.

subject—An active entity, generally in the form of a person, process, or device, that causes information to flow among objects or that changes the system state. Technically, a process/domain pair.

subversion—An intentional violation of software's integrity or security controls in order to compromise the software or system.

supervisor state—See *executive state.*

survivability—The capability of software is to fulfill its objectives in the presence of attacks, failures, or accidents.

symmetric (private) key encryption—Cryptographic system in which the sender and receiver both know a secret key that is used to encrypt and decrypt a message.

synchronous optical networking (SONET)—A fiber-optic transmission system for high-speed digital traffic. SONET is part of the B-ISDN standard.

synchronous transmission—A type of communications data synchronization whereby frames are sent within defined time periods. It uses a clock to control the timing of bits being sent. See *asynchronous transmission.*

system—A set of interrelated components consisting of mission, environment, and architecture as a whole. Also, a data processing facility.

system development methodologies—Methodologies developed through software engineering to manage the complexity of system development. Development methodologies include software engineering aids and high-level design analysis tools.

system entity—A system subject (user or process) or object.

system integrity—A characteristic of a system when it performs its intended function in an unimpaired manner, free from deliberate or inadvertent unauthorized manipulation of the system.

security mode—The lowest security level supported by a system at a particular time or in a particular environment.

system testing—A type of testing that verifies the installation of the entire network. Testers normally complete system testing in a simulated production environment, simulating actual users in order to ensure the network meets all stated requirements.

tainted input—Input data that has not been examined or sanitized prior to use by an application.

tampering—An unauthorized modification that alters the proper functioning of an equipment or system in a manner that degrades the security or functionality that it provides.

Target of Evaluation (TOE)—In the Common Criteria, TOE refers to the product to be tested.

TCB—See *trusted computing base.*

technical attack—An attack that can be perpetrated by circumventing or nullifying hardware and software protection mechanisms, rather than by subverting system personnel or other users.

technical vulnerability—A hardware, firmware, communication, or software flaw that leaves a computer processing system open for potential exploitation, either externally or internally—thereby resulting in a risk to the owner, user, or manager of the system.

TELNET—A virtual terminal protocol used in the Internet, enabling users to log in to a remote host. TELNET is defined as part of the TCP/IP protocol suite.

TEMPEST— Transient ElectroMagnetic Pulse Emanations Standard, the U.S. Government standard for control of spurious compromising emanations emitted by electrical equipment; also used to refer to the investigation, study, and control of such emanations.

test case—An executable test with a specific set of input values and a corresponding expected result.

threat agent—A method that is used to exploit a vulnerability in a system, operation, or facility.

threat analysis—The examination of all actions and events that might adversely affect a system or operation.

threat—Any circumstance or event with the potential to cause harm to an IT system in the form of destruction, disclosure, adverse modification of data, and/or denial of service.

threat factor—A characterization of the threat based on a violation of confidentiality, integrity, or availability (CIA); the asset being targeted; the role of the user; and type of accessibility. Helps refine the application context to aid in the process of analyzing the threats.

threat monitoring—The analysis, assessment, and review of audit trails and other data that are collected for the purpose of searching for system events that might constitute violations or attempted violations of system security.

TLS—Transport Layer Security.

top-level specification—A nonprocedural description of system behavior at the most abstract level; typically, a functional specification that omits all implementation details.

topology—A description of the network's geographical layout of nodes and links.

traceroute—Software utility used to determine the path to a target computer.

Transmission Control Protocol (TCP)—A commonly used protocol for establishing and maintaining communications between applications on different computers. TCP provides full-duplex, acknowledged, and flow-controlled service to upper-layer protocols and applications.

Transmission Control Protocol/ Internet Protocol (TCP/IP)—A de facto industry-standard protocol for interconnecting disparate networks. TCP/IP are standard protocols that define both the reliable full-duplex transport level and the connectionless, best-effort unit of information passed across an internetwork.

Transport layer—OSI model layer that provides mechanisms for the establishment, maintenance, and orderly termination of virtual circuits while shielding the higher layers from the network implementation details.

trap door—A hidden software or hardware mechanism that can be triggered to permit system protection mechanisms to be circumvented. It is activated in a manner that appears innocent—for example, a special "random" key sequence at a terminal. Software developers often introduce trap doors in their code to enable them to re-enter the system and perform certain functions. Synonymous with *back door*.

Trojan horse—A computer program that has an apparently or actually useful function but contains additional (hidden) functions that surreptitiously exploit the legitimate authorizations of the invoking process to the detriment of security or integrity.

true positive—When a security tool reports a weakness that is actually present.

trust—In a relationship between entities, the confidence that each entity will behave as expected.

trusted computer system—A system that employs sufficient hardware and software assurance measures to enable its use for simultaneous processing of a range of sensitive or classified information.

trusted computing base (TCB)—The totality of protection mechanisms within a computer system, including hardware, firmware, and software, the combination of which is responsible for enforcing a security policy. A TCB consists of one or more components that together enforce a unified security policy over a product or system. The ability of a TCB to correctly enforce a unified security policy depends solely on the mechanisms within the TCB and on the correct input of parameters by system administrative personnel (for example, a user's clearance level) related to the security policy

trusted distribution—A trusted method for distributing the TCB hardware, software, and firmware components, both originals and updates, that provides methods for protecting the TCB from modification during distribution and for the detection of any changes to the TCB that might occur.

trusted path—A mechanism by which a person at a terminal can communicate directly with the TCB. This mechanism can be activated only by the person or by the TCB and cannot be imitated by untrusted software.

trusted process—A process whose incorrect or malicious execution is capable of violating system security policy.

trusted software—The software portion of the TCB.

trustworthiness—The property of software that can be attained with justifiable confidence that the software does not contain any exploitable vulnerabilities or malicious logic.

untrusted process—A process that has not been evaluated or examined for adherence to the security policy. It might include incorrect or malicious code that attempts to circumvent the security mechanisms.

user—(1) A person or process that is accessing an AIS either by direct connections (for example, via terminals) or by indirect connections (in other words, preparing input data or receiving output that is not reviewed for content or classification by a responsible individual). (2) Person or process authorized to access an IT system.

User Datagram Protocol—UDP uses the underlying Internet Protocol (IP) to transport a message. This is an unreliable, connectionless delivery scheme. It does not use acknowledgments to ensure that messages arrive and does not provide feedback to control the rate of information flow. UDP messages can be lost, duplicated, or arrive out of order.

user ID—A unique symbol or character string that is used by a system to identify a specific user.

validation—Validation is a process to evaluate whether software will satisfy its particular requirements (functional and nonfunctional) for its specific intended purpose.

verification—Verification is a process to evaluate whether software conforms to the specifications, regulations, or other conditions imposed on it while it was being developed.

verification and validation (V&V)—The term V&V typically refers to all of the verification and validation activities that are undertaken to ensure that software will function according to its specification.

virus—A self-propagating Trojan horse composed of a mission component, a trigger component, and a self-propagating component.

vulnerability—A weakness in system security procedures, system design, implementation, internal controls, and so on that could be exploited to violate system security policy.

vulnerability analysis—A measurement of vulnerability that includes the susceptibility of a particular system to a specific attack and the opportunities that are available to a threat agent to mount that attack.

vulnerability assessment—Systematic examination of an information system or product to determine the adequacy of security measures, identify security deficiencies, provide data from which to predict the effectiveness of proposed security measures, and confirm the adequacy of such measures after implementation.

weakness—A bug found in software that has the potential of being exploited as a vulnerability when the software is operational.

weakness suppression system—A feature that permits the user to flag a line of code not to be reported by the tool in subsequent scans.

white box test—A test in which the ethical hacking team has full knowledge of the target information system.

white hat hacker—An individual who conducts ethical hacking to help secure and protect and organization's information systems.

wide area network (WAN)—A network that interconnects users over a wide area, usually encompassing different metropolitan areas.

Wired Equivalency Privacy (WEP)—The algorithm of the 802.11 wireless LAN standard that is used to protect transmitted information from disclosure. WEP is designed to prevent the violation of the confidentiality of data transmitted over the wireless LAN. WEP generates secret shared encryption keys that both source and destination stations use to alter frame bits to avoid disclosure to eavesdroppers.

wireless—Describes any computing device that can access a network without a wired connection.

WLAN—Wireless local area network.

work factor—An estimate of the effort or time needed by a potential intruder who has specified expertise and resources to overcome a protective measure.

work function (factor)—The difficulty in recovering plaintext from ciphertext, as measured by cost and/or time. The security of the system is directly proportional to the value of the work function. The work function need only be large enough to suffice for the intended application. If the message to be protected loses its value after a short period of time, the work function need only be large enough to ensure that the decryption would be highly infeasible in that period of time.

write—A fundamental operation that results only in the flow of information from a subject to an object.

write access—Permission to write to an object.

zeroize—The act of erasing sensitive parameters from a cryptographic module.

zeroization—The practice of erasing sensitive parameters (especially keys) from a cryptographic module to prevent their disclosure. The keys are typically zeroized (erased) in response to an attempt to tamper with the module.

Index

Index

B

D

E

F

G

H

J

K

L

M

N

O

P

Q

R

S

T

X

Z

Wiley Publishing, Inc. End-User License Agreement

READ THIS. You should carefully read these terms and conditions before opening the software packet(s) included with this book "Book". This is a license agreement "Agreement" between you and Wiley Publishing, Inc. "WPI". By opening the accompanying software packet(s), you acknowledge that you have read and accept the following terms and conditions. If you do not agree and do not want to be bound by such terms and conditions, promptly return the Book and the unopened software packet(s) to the place you obtained them for a full refund.

1. **License Grant.** WPI grants to you (either an individual or entity) a nonexclusive license to use one copy of the enclosed software program(s) (collectively, the "Software," solely for your own personal or business purposes on a single computer (whether a standard computer or a workstation component of a multi-user network). The Software is in use on a computer when it is loaded into temporary memory (RAM) or installed into permanent memory (hard disk, CD-ROM, or other storage device). WPI reserves all rights not expressly granted herein.

2. **Ownership.** WPI is the owner of all right, title, and interest, including copyright, in and to the compilation of the Software recorded on the physical packet included with this Book "Software Media". Copyright to the individual programs recorded on the Software Media is owned by the author or other authorized copyright owner of each program. Ownership of the Software and all proprietary rights relating thereto remain with WPI and its licensers.

3. **Restrictions On Use and Transfer.**

   (a) You may only (i) make one copy of the Software for backup or archival purposes, or (ii) transfer the Software to a single hard disk, provided that you keep the original for backup or archival purposes. You may not (i) rent or lease the Software, (ii) copy or reproduce the Software through a LAN or other network system or through any computer subscriber system or bulletin-board system, or (iii) modify, adapt, or create derivative works based on the Software.

   (b) You may not reverse engineer, decompile, or disassemble the Software. You may transfer the Software and user documentation on a permanent basis, provided that the transferee agrees to accept the terms and conditions of this Agreement and you retain no copies. If the Software is an update or has been updated, any transfer must include the most recent update and all prior versions.

4. **Restrictions on Use of Individual Programs.** You must follow the individual requirements and restrictions detailed for each individual program in the About the CD-ROM appendix of this Book or on the Software Media. These limitations are also contained in the individual license agreements recorded on the Software Media. These limitations may include a requirement that after using the program for a specified period of time, the user must pay a registration fee or discontinue use. By opening the Software packet(s), you will be agreeing to abide by the licenses and restrictions for these individual programs that are detailed in the About the CD-ROM appendix and/or on the Software Media. None of the material on this Software Media or listed in this Book may ever be redistributed, in original or modified form, for commercial purposes.

5. **Limited Warranty.**

   (a) WPI warrants that the Software and Software Media are free from defects in materials and workmanship under normal use for a period of sixty (60) days from the date of purchase of this Book. If WPI receives notification within the warranty period of defects in materials or workmanship, WPI will replace the defective Software Media.

   (b) WPI AND THE AUTHOR(S) OF THE BOOK DISCLAIM ALL OTHER WARRANTIES, EXPRESS OR IMPLIED, INCLUDING WITHOUT LIMITATION IMPLIED WARRANTIES OF MERCHANTABILITY AND FITNESS FOR A PARTICULAR PURPOSE, WITH RESPECT TO THE SOFTWARE, THE PROGRAMS, THE SOURCE CODE CONTAINED THEREIN, AND/OR THE TECHNIQUES DESCRIBED IN THIS BOOK. WPI DOES NOT WARRANT THAT THE FUNCTIONS CONTAINED IN THE SOFTWARE WILL MEET YOUR REQUIREMENTS OR THAT THE OPERATION OF THE SOFTWARE WILL BE ERROR FREE.

   (c) This limited warranty gives you specific legal rights, and you may have other rights that vary from jurisdiction to jurisdiction.

6. **Remedies.**

   (a) WPI's entire liability and your exclusive remedy for defects in materials and workmanship shall be limited to replacement of the Software Media, which may be returned to WPI with a copy of your receipt at the following address: Software Media Fulfillment Department, Attn: CSSLP Prep Guide: Mastering the Certified Secure Software Lifecycle Professional, Wiley Publishing, Inc., 10475 Crosspoint Blvd., Indianapolis, IN 46256, or call 1-800-762-2974. Please allow four to six weeks for delivery. This Limited Warranty is void if failure of the Software Media has resulted from accident, abuse, or misapplication. Any replacement Software Media will be warranted for the remainder of the original warranty period or thirty (30) days, whichever is longer.

   (b) In no event shall WPI or the author be liable for any damages whatsoever (including without limitation damages for loss of business profits, business interruption, loss of business information, or any other pecuniary loss) arising from the use of or inability to use the Book or the Software, even if WPI has been advised of the possibility of such damages.

   (c) Because some jurisdictions do not allow the exclusion or limitation of liability for consequential or incidental damages, the above limitation or exclusion may not apply to you.

7. **U.S. Government Restricted Rights.** Use, duplication, or disclosure of the Software for or on behalf of the United States of America, its agencies and/or instrumentalities "U.S. Government" is subject to restrictions as stated in paragraph (c)(1)(ii) of the Rights in Technical Data and Computer Software clause of DFARS 252.227-7013, or subparagraphs (c) (1) and (2) of the Commercial Computer Software - Restricted Rights clause at FAR 52.227-19, and in similar clauses in the NASA FAR supplement, as applicable.

8. **General.** This Agreement constitutes the entire understanding of the parties and revokes and supersedes all prior agreements, oral or written, between them and may not be modified or amended except in a writing signed by both parties hereto that specifically refers to this Agreement. This Agreement shall take precedence over any other documents that may be in conflict herewith. If any one or more provisions contained in this Agreement are held by any court or tribunal to be invalid, illegal, or otherwise unenforceable, each and every other provision shall remain in full force and effect.